T0336770

Applied Cryptography for Cyber Security and Defense:

Information Encryption and Cyphering

Hamid R. Nemati
University of North Carolina at Greensboro, USA

Li Yang
University of Tennessee, USA

INFORMATION SCIENCE REFERENCE

Hershey · New York

Director of Editorial Content:	Kristin Klinger
Director of Book Publications:	Julia Mosemann
Acquisitions Editor:	Lindsay Johnston
Development Editor:	Christine Bufton
Publishing Assistant:	Milan Vracarich Jr.
Typesetter:	Casey Conapitski
Production Editor:	Jamie Snavely
Cover Design:	Lisa Tosheff

Published in the United States of America by
Information Science Reference (an imprint of IGI Global)
701 E. Chocolate Avenue
Hershey PA 17033
Tel: 717-533-8845
Fax: 717-533-8661
E-mail: cust@igi-global.com
Web site: http://www.igi-global.com

Library of Congress Cataloging-in-Publication Data

Applied cryptography for cyber security and defense : information encryption and cyphering / Hamid R. Nemati and Li Yang, editors.
     p. cm.
  Includes bibliographical references and index.
  Summary: "This book is written for professionals who want to improve their understanding about how to bridge the gap between cryptographic theory and real-world cryptographic applications and how to adapt cryptography solutions to emerging areas that have special requirements"--Provided by publisher.
  ISBN 978-1-61520-783-1 (hardcover) -- ISBN 978-1-61520-784-8 (ebook) 1. Telecommunication--Security measures. 2. Data encryption (Computer science) 3. Cryptography. I. Nemati, Hamid R., 1958- II. Yang, Li, 1974 Oct. 29- TK5102.94. A67 2010
  005.8'2--dc22

British Cataloguing in Publication Data
A Cataloguing in Publication record for this book is available from the British Library.

All work contributed to this book is new, previously-unpublished material. The views expressed in this book are those of the authors, but not necessarily of the publisher.

Dedication

This book is dedicated to my wonderful son Daniel as he is about to embark on a new and exciting chapter of his life and to the love of my life, my beautiful wife Mary for being there to celebrate it with me.

Hamid R. Nemati

I dedicate this book to my dearest mother Xiuqing, father Wenjun, my husband Hong, and my precious daughter Helen-Tianyang who always support me in every endeavor. They are the reason I'm here at all, and made me who I am today.

Li Yang

List of Reviewers

Moses Acquaah, *The University of North Carolina at Greensboro, USA*
Xinliang Zheng, *Frostburg State University, USA*
B. Dawn Medlin, *Appalachian State University, USA*
Alessandro Acquisti, *Carnegie Mellon University, USA*
Pierre Balthazard, *Arizona State University, USA*
Christopher Barko, *Laboratory Corporation of America, USA*
Dieter Bartmann, *University of Regensburg, Germany*
Joseph Cazier, *Appalachian State University, USA*
Elizabeth Chang, *Curtin University of Technology, Australia*
John Eatman, *The University of North Carolina at Greensboro, USA*
Simone Fischer-Hübner, *Karlstad University, Sweden*
Keith Frikken, *Purdue University, USA*
Philippe Golle, *Palo Alto Research Center, USA*
Rüdiger Grimm, *University Koblenz-Landau, Germany*
Harry Hochheiser, *Towson University, USA*
Earp Julie, *North Carolina State University, USA*
Chang Koh, *University of North Texas, USA*
Mary Jane Lenard, *Meredith College, USA*
Gregorio Martinez, *University of Murcia, Spain*
Dawn Medlin, *Appalachian State University, USA*
Mihir Parikh, *University of Central Florida, USA*
Norman Pendegraft, *The University of Idaho, USA*
Carol Pollard, *Appalachian State University, USA*
Ellen Rose, *Massey University, New Zealand*
Alain Mohsen Sadeghi, *eTechSecurity Pro, USA*
Kathy Schwaig, *Kennesaw State University, USA*
Victoria Skoularidou, *Athens University of Economics and Business, USA*
William Tullar, *The University of North Carolina at Greensboro, USA*
Sameer Verma, *San Francisco State University, USA*
Liisa von Hellens, *Griffith University, Australia*

Table of Contents

Detailed Table of Contents

Section 1
Cryptography in Networking and Cyber Space

Three pillars of security—confidentiality, integrity, and availability—are examined in the context of networks. Each is explained with known practical attacks and possible defenses against them, demonstrating that strong mathematical techniques are necessary but not sufficient to build practical systems that are secure. This chapter illustrates how adversaries commonly side-step cryptographic protections. In addition, we contend that effective key management techniques, along with privacy concerns must be taken into account during the design of any secure online system. This chapter concludes with a discussion of open problems for which fundamentally new methods are needed.

Entity authentication is a fundamental building block for system security and has been widely used to protect cyber systems. Nonetheless, the role of cryptography in entity authentication is not very clear, although cryptography is known for providing confidentiality, integrity, and non-repudiation. This chapter studies the roles of cryptography in three entity authentication categories: knowledge-based authentication, token-based authentication, and biometric authentication. For these three authentication categories, we discuss (1) the roles of cryptography in the generation of password verification data, in password-based challenge/response authentication protocol, and in password-authenticated key exchange protocols; (2) the roles of cryptography in both symmetric key-based and private key-based token authentications; (3) cryptographic fuzzy extractors, which can be used to enhance the security and privacy of biometric authentication. This systematic study of the roles of cryptography in entity authentication will deepen our understanding of both cryptography and entity authentication and can help us better protect cyber systems.

Section 2
Cryptography in E-Mail and Web Services

Chapter 3

Wasim A. Al-Hamdani, Kentucky State University, USA

Cryptography is the study and practice of protecting information and has been used since ancient times in many different shapes and forms to protect messages from being intercepted. However, since 1976, when data encryption was selected as an official Federal Information Processing Standard (FIPS) for the United States, cryptography has gained large attention and a great amount of application and use. Furthermore, cryptography started to be part of protected public communication when e-mail became commonly used by the public. There are many electronic services. Some are based on web interaction and others are used as independent servers, called e-mail hosting services, which is an Internet hosting service that runs e-mail servers. Encrypting e-mail messages as they traverse the Internet is not the only reason to understand or use various cryptographic methods. Every time one checks his/her e-mail, the password is being sent over the wire. Many Internet service providers or corporate environments use no encryption on their mail servers and the passwords used to check mail are submitted to the network in clear text (with no encryption). When a password is put into clear text on a wire, it can easily be intercepted. Encrypting email will keep all but the most dedicated hackers from intercepting and reading a private communications. Using a personal email certificate one can digitally sign an email so that recipients can verify that it's really from the sender as well as encrypt the messages so that only the intended recipients can view it. Web service is defined as "a software system designed to support interoperable machine-to-machine interaction over a network" and e-mail is "communicate electronically on the computer". This chapter focus on introduce three topics: E-mail structure and organization, web service types, their organization and cryptography algorithms which integrated in the E-mail and web services to provide high level of security. The main issue in this chapter is to build the general foundation through Definitions, history, cryptography algorithms symmetric and asymmetric, hash algorithms, digital signature, suite B and general principle to introduce the use of cryptography in the E-mail and web service.

Chapter 4

Wasim A. Al-Hamdani, Kentucky State University, USA

Cryptography has been used since ancient times in many different shapes and forms to protect messages from being intercepted. However, since 1976, cryptography started to be part of protected public communication when e-mail became commonly used by the public. Webmail (or Web-based e-mail) is an e-mail service intended to be primarily accessed via a web browser, as opposed to through an e-mail client, such as Microsoft Outlook, Mozilla's Thunderbird Mail. Very popular webmail providers include Gmail, Yahoo! Mail, Hotmail and AOL. Web based email has its advantages, especially for people who travel. Email can be collected by simply visiting a website, negating the need for an email client, or to logon from home. Wherever a public terminal with Internet access exists one can check, sends and receive email quickly and easily. Another advantage of web based email is that it provides an alternate address allowing user to reserve his/her ISP address for personal use. If someone would like to subscribe to a newsletter, enter a drawing, register at a website, participate in chats, or send feedback to a site, a web based email address is the perfect answer. It will keep non-personal mail on a server for you to check when you wish, rather than filling up your private email box Web service is defined as "a software system designed to support interoperable machine-to-machine interaction over a network". Web services are frequently just Internet application programming interfaces (API) that can be accessed over a network, such as the Internet, and executed on a remote system hosting the requested services. Other approaches with nearly the same functionality as web services are Object Management Group's (OMG) Common Object Request Broker Architecture (CORBA), Microsoft's Distributed Component Object Model (DCOM) or SUN's Java/Remote Method Invocation (RMI). Integrating Encryption with web service could be performing in many ways such as: XML Encryption and XML Signature. In this chapter we present client and Web-based E-mail, next generation E-mail and secure E-mail, followed by cryptography in web service and the last part is the future of web service security. The chapter start with the integration of cryptography with E-mail client and web base then the integration of cryptography and web service is presented. At the end of the major two sections: e-mail service and web service there is a general prospect vision of encryption future for e-mail service and web service. This section presents our view for the cryptography integration with the second generation of e-mail and web service.

Chapter 5

E-mail services are the method of sending and receiving electronic messages over communication networks. Web services on the other hand provide a channel of accessing interlinked hypermeida via the World Wide Web. As these two methods of network communications turn into the most popular services over the Internet, applied cryptography and secure authentication protocols become indispensable in securing confidential data over public networks. In this chapter, we first review a number of cryptographic ciphers widely used in secure communication protocols. We then discuss and compare the popular trust system Web of Trust, the certificate standard X.509, and the standard for public key systems Public Key Infrastructure (PKI). Two secure e-mail standards, OpenPGP and S/MIME, are examined and compared. The de facto standard cryptographic protocol for e-commerce, Secure Socket Layer (SSL) / Transport Layer Security (TLS), and XML Security Standards for secure web services are also discussed.

Section 3
Cryptography in Wireless Communication

Chapter 6
Dulal C. Kar, Texas A&M University-Corpus Christi, USA
Hung Ngo, Texas A&M University-Corpus Christi, USA
Clifton J. Mulkey, Texas A&M University-Corpus Christi, USA

It is challenging to secure a wireless sensor network (WSN) because of its use of inexpensive sensor nodes of very limited processing capability, memory capacity, and battery life that preclude using traditional security solutions. Due to perceived excessive computational and architectural overhead, public key algorithms are altogether avoided for WSNs. Currently security in WSNs is provided using only symmetric key cryptography, but it requires keys to be embedded in sensor nodes before deployment and the entire network has to go through a key establishment phase after deployment. Accordingly, in this chapter, we summarize, discuss, and evaluate recent results reported in literature on sensor network security protocols such as for key establishment, random key pre-distribution, data confidentiality, and broadcast authentication. In addition, we discuss promising research results in public key cryptography for WSNs, particularly related to elliptic curve cryptography and its application for identity based encryption.

Chapter 7
Lei Zhang, Frostburg State University, USA
Chih-Cheng Chang, Rutgers University, USA
Danfeng Yao, Rutgers University, USA

This chapter presents the technical challenges and solutions in securing wireless networks, in particular infrastructure-less wireless networks such as mobile ad hoc networks and wireless sensor networks. Communications in infrastructure-less wireless networks are challenging, as there are no trusted base stations to coordinate the activities of mobile hosts. Applied cryptographic tools, in particular threshold cryptography, play an important role in the trust establishment, message security, and key management in such networks. We describe several technical approaches that integrate applied cryptography techniques into mobile ad hoc networks and wireless sensor networks. We also outline several research directions in these areas.

Section 4
Cryptography in Electronic Commerce

Chapter 8
Sławomir Grzonkowski, National University of Ireland, Ireland
Brian D. Ensor, National University of Ireland, Ireland
Bill McDaniel, National University of Ireland, Ireland

Electronic commerce has grown into a vital segment of the economy of many nations. It is a global phenomenon providing markets and commercialization opportunities world-wide with a significantly reduced barrier to entry as compared to global marketing in the 20th century. Providing protocols to secure such commerce is critical and continues to be an area for both scientific and engineering study. Falsification, fraud, identity theft, and disinformation campaigns or other attacks could damage the credibility and value of electronic commerce if left unchecked. Consequently, cryptographic methods have emerged to combat any such efforts, be they the occasional random attempt at theft or highly organized criminal or political activities. This chapter covers the use of cryptographic methods and emerging standards in this area to provide the necessary protection. That protection, as is common for web-based protocols, evolves over time to deal with more and more sophisticated attacks. At the same time, the provision of security in a manner convenient enough to not deter electronic commerce has driven research efforts to find easier to use and simpler protocols to implement even as the strength of the cryptographic methods has increased. This chapter covers current standards, looking at several facets of the secure commercialization problem from authentication to intrusion detection and identity and reputation management. Vulnerabilities are discussed as well as capabilities.

Chapter 9

Harkeerat Bedi, University of Tennessee at Chattanooga, USA
Li Yang, University of Tennessee at Chattanooga, USA
Joseph M. Kizza, University of Tennessee at Chattanooga, USA

Fair exchange between two parties can be defined as an instance of exchange such that either both parties obtain what they expected or neither one does. Protocols that facilitate such transactions are known as "fair exchange protocols". We analyze one such protocol by Micali that demonstrates fair contract signing, where two parties exchange their commitments over an already negotiated contract. In this chapter we show that Micali's protocol is not completely fair and demonstrate the possibilities for one party cheating by obtaining the other party's commitment and not offer theirs. A revised version of this protocol by Bao provides superior fairness by handling the above mentioned weakness but fails to handle the possibility of a replay attack. Our proposed protocol improves upon Bao's protocol by addressing the weakness that leads to a replay attack and makes the overall transmission smaller by removing excess information from signatures. We also demonstrate a software implementation of our system which provides fair contract signing along with properties like user authentication achieved through the use of a fingerprint based authentication system and features like confidentiality, data-integrity and non-repudiation through implementation of hybrid cryptography and digital signatures algorithms based on Elliptic Curve Cryptography.

Section 5
Cryptography in Emerging Areas

Chapter 10

Feng Zhu, University of Alabama in Huntsville, USA
Wei Zhu, Intergraph Co, USA

With the convergence of embedded computers and wireless communication, pervasive computing has become the inevitable future of computing. Every year, billions of computing devices are built. They are ubiquitously deployed and are gracefully integrated with people and their environments. Service discovery is an essential step for the devices to properly discover, configure, and communicate with each other. Authentication for pervasive service discovery is difficult. In this chapter, we introduce a user-centric service discovery model, called PrudentExposure, which automates authentication processes. It encodes hundreds of authentication messages in a novel code word form. Perhaps the most serious challenge for pervasive service discovery is the integration of computing devices with people. A critical privacy challenge can be expressed as a "chicken-and-egg problem": both users and service providers want the other parties to expose sensitive information first. We discuss how a progressive and probabilistic model can protect both users' and service providers' privacy.

     Ming Yang, Jacksonville State University, USA
     Monica Trifas, Jacksonville State University, USA
     Nikolaos Bourbakis, Wright State University, USA
     Lei Chen, Sam Houston State University, USA

Information security has traditionally been ensured with data encryption techniques. Different generic data encryption standards, such as DES, RSA, AES, have been developed. These encryption standards provide high level of security to the encrypted data. However, they are not very efficient in the encryption of multimedia contents due to the large volume of digital image/video data. In order to address this issue, different image/video encryption methodologies have been developed. These methodologies encrypt only the key parameters of image/video data instead of encrypting it as a bitstream. Joint compression-encryption is a very promising direction for image/video encryption. Nowadays, researchers start to utilize information hiding techniques to enhance the security level of data encryption methodologies. Information hiding conceals not only the content of the secret message, but also its very existence. In terms of the amount of data to be embedded, information hiding methodologies can be classified into low bitrate and high bitrate algorithms. In terms of the domain for embedding, they can be classified into spatial domain and transform domain algorithms. In this chapter, we have reviewed various data encryption standards, image/video encryption algorithms, and joint compression-encryption methodologies. Besides, we have also presented different categories of information hiding methodologies as well as data embedding strategies for digital image/video contents.

     Xunhua Wang, James Madison University, USA
     Ralph Grove, James Madison University, USA
     M. Hossain Heydari, James Madison University, USA

In recent years, computer and network-based voting technologies have been gradually adopted for various elections. However, due to the fragile nature of electronic ballots and voting software, computer voting has posed serious security challenges. This chapter studies the security of computer voting and focuses on a cryptographic solution based on mix-nets. Like traditional voting systems, mix-net-based computer voting provides voter privacy and prevents vote selling/buying and vote coercion. Unlike traditional voting systems, mix-net-based computer voting has several additional advantages: (1) it offers vote verifiability, allowing individual voters to directly verify whether their votes have been counted and counted correctly; (2) it allows voters to check the behavior of potentially malicious computer voting machines and thus does not require voters to blindly trust computer voting machines. In this chapter, we give the full details of the building blocks for the mix-net-based computer voting scheme, including semantically secure encryption, threshold decryption, mix-net, and robust mix-net. Future research directions on secure electronic voting are also discussed.

Chapter 13

Kunal Sharma, DOEACC Centre, India
A.J. Singh, H.P. University, India

The rising number of networked computers and the evolution of the WWW have witnessed the emergence of an E-World where the users are often referred to as e-people. In the new e-world, the evolution of WWW and Internet applications has become a focal point to the question of sustainable competitive advantage (Brennan & Johnson,2001).The increase in information access terminals along with the growing use of information sensitive applications such as e-commerce, e-learning, e-banking and e-healthcare have generated a real requirement of reliable, easy to use, and generally acceptable control methods for confidential and vital information. On the other hand, the necessity for privacy must be balanced with security requirements for the advantage of the general public. Current global events have shown the significance to provide the police, airport area, and other exposed area, new reliable component security tools such as biometrics. Access to systems that need security from unauthorized access is generally restricted by requesting the user to confirm her identity and to authenticate. Payment systems are undergoing radical changes stirred largely by technical advancement such as distributed network technology, real-time processing and online consumers' inclination to use e-banking interfaces making the study of biometrics even more important in this new E-World.

Preface

Cryptography is the art and science of concealment of information. Without the ability to conceal information, the current networked computing environment would not be possible. In the most fundamental way, cryptography provides a logical barrier to secure information from unauthorized prying eyes. To understand cryptography, we need to answer four simple yet interrelated questions: What information do we need to conceal? Why do we need to conceal it and from whom? How can we optimally conceal it without diminishing its usefulness? And finally, how do we reveal that which was concealed? The answers to these questions characterize the essence of information and what it represents.

We view the age we live in as the "*information age*" and our societies as "*information societies*". What mostly characterizes this information age is the pervasiveness of information technologies in our daily lives. Almost everything we do in the course of our lives creates an electronic footprint resulting in an explosion in the amount of data that we generate.

Data experts estimate that in 2002 the world generated 5 exabytes of data. This amount of data is more than all the words ever spoken by human beings. The rate of growth is just as staggering – the amount of data produced in 2002 was up 68% from just two years earlier (Stuhler, 2010). The size of the typical business database has grown a hundred-fold during the past five years as a result of internet commerce, ever-expanding computer systems and mandated recordkeeping by government regulations. The rate of growth in data has not slowed. International Data Corporation (IDC) estimates that the amount of data generated in 2009 was 1.2 million Petabytes (IDC, 2010). (A Petabyte is a million gigabytes.) (IDC, 2010). For example, it is estimated that in 2007, the size of world internet's hard drive was 161 Billion gigabytes and the volume skyrocketed to 487 Billion gigabytes in 2009 (IDC, 2010). The research comes from technology consultancy IDC, and their prediction is that the current size of the internet's hard drive will double in the next 18 months as more and more net users get interactive. According to Julian Stuhler (Stuhler, 2010), worldwide data volumes are currently doubling every two years. Although this seems to be an astonishingly large amount of data, it is paled in compression to what IDC estimates that amount to be in 2020. IDC estimates that the amount of data generated in 2010 will be 44 times as much as this year to an incomprehensible amount of 35 Zettabytes, where a Zettabyte is 1 trillion gigabytes (Stuhler, 2010). IDC reports that by 2020, we will generate 35 trillion gigabytes of data, enough data to fill a stack of DVDs reaching from the Earth to the moon. To better grasp how much data this is, consider the following: if one byte of data is the equivalent of this dot (•), the amount of data produced globally in 2002 would equal the diameter of 4,000 suns. Moreover, that amount probably doubles every two years (Hardy, 2004). One of the reasons for this astonishingly large growth, according to a survey by US Department of Commerce, is that an increasing number of Americans are going online and engaging in several online activities, including online purchases, conducting banking online, engaging in commerce, and interacting socially. The growth in Internet usage and e-commerce has offered businesses and governmental agencies the opportunity to collect and analyze information in ways never previously imagined. "Enormous amounts of consumer data have long been available through offline sources such as credit card transactions, phone orders, warranty cards, applications and a host of other traditional methods. What the digital revolution has done is increase the efficiency and effectiveness with which such information can be collected and put to use" (Adkinson, Eisenach, & Lenard, 2002). This digital footprint including our digital shadow represents us, as humans, it represents who we are, and how we conduct our lives. It needs to be secured, protected, and managed appropriately. This information presented in the digital form and spread over the world is now very large, and this information requires protection against malicious intrusion, eavesdrops, substitution, falsification, and so on. In addition, information is a critical asset that supports the mission of any organization and protecting this asset is critical to survivability and longevity of the organization. Maintaining and improving information security is critical to the operations, reputation, and ultimately the success and longevity of any organization. Information and the systems that support it are vulnerable to many threats that can inflict serious damage to organizations resulting in significant losses.

Whether we are using credit cards, surfing the Internet or viewing a YouTube video, we are generating data. John Gantz senior vice president of International Data Corporation, states: "About half of your digital footprint is related to your individual actions—taking pictures, sending e-mails, or making digital voice calls. The other half is what we call the 'digital shadow'—information about you—names in financial records, names on mailing lists, web surfing histories or images taken of you by security cameras in airports or urban centers. For the first time your digital shadow is larger than the digital information you actively create about yourself." (IDS, 2010) Our digital shadow, the sum of all the digital information generated about us on a daily basis, now exceeds the amount of digital information we actively create ourselves (IDC, 2010). In essence, this digital shadow defines who we are, what we like and what we do. It needs to be protected and secured. Concerns over information security risks can originate from a number of different security threats. They can come from hacking and unauthorized attempts to access private information, fraud, sabotage, theft and other malicious acts or they can originate from more innocuous sources, but no less harmful, such as natural disasters or even user errors. Cryptography provides the most efficient services for defending against these threats and holds great promise as the technology to provide security in cyberspace, especially when security becomes one of top concerns for business worldwide.

Cryptography studies methods of information encryption that prevent an opponent from extracting information contained in the intercepted messages. In this approach the message communicated through the insecure channel is not the original message, but the result of its transformation using a cipher. The opponent must break the cipher, which may prove to be a challenging problem. Cracking of a cipher is the process of extracting relevant information from an encrypted text without knowing the cipher. Besides cracking, the adversary may try to obtain desired information in a number of other ways. The adversary can eavesdrop or monitor transmission of the information by release of message contents or traffic analysis. Another threat that an adversary can create is to try to destroy or modify the information that is being transmitted. This threat requires specific security methods including masquerade and modification of message. A masquerade takes place when one entity pretends to be a different entity. Modification of message simply means that some portion of a legitimate message is altered, or that message is delayed or reordered, to produce an unauthorized effect. Therefore, on the way from one authorized user to another, information must be protected using different tools against different threats.

These tools form an information protecting chain, consisting of links of different kinds, and the adversary, of course, will search for the weakest link in this chain in order to obtain least possible cost. This means that when developing a security strategy, the authorized users must also take into account that it makes no sense to establish a strong link if there are much weaker ones.

Cryptography provides a set of security services to ensure adequate security of the systems or of data transfer to counter the above threats. The services include authentication, data confidentiality, data integrity and non-repudiation (Stallings, 2006, p17). Entity authentication provides confidence in the identity of the entities connected. Data origin authentication provides assurance that the source of data is as claimed in an insecure transmission. Data integrity assures that data received are exactly as sent by an authorized entity. Non-repudiation provides protection against denial by one of the entities involved in a communication. Security services can be mapped to one of security mechanisms whose implementation relies on cryptography: enciphering, digital signature, data integrity, authentication exchange, and notarization. Enciphering is the use mathematical algorithms to transform data into a form that is not readily intelligible. The transformation and subsequent recovery of the data depend on an algorithm and zero or more encryption keys. Digital signature is to append data or to cryptographically transform data, which allows a recipient of the data unit to prove the source and integrity of the data unit and protect against forgery. Data integrity is to ensure that a data unit or stream is not modified by unauthorized adversaries. Notarization is to use a trusted third party to assure certain properties of a data exchange.

Nowadays cryptographic algorithms have already been applied to some cryptographic means like encrypting electronic mails or smart bank cards, and so on. Naturally, the main question that the user asks is whether a given cryptographic tool provides sufficient defense. Whom are we protecting from? What are the capabilities of our opponents? What goals do they pursue? How to measure the level of security? The list of these questions can be extended. The reality is that cryptography has done no more than creating an illusion of a secure system for the users. The security of a system is decided by the weakest link and the real-world constraints make the cryptography much less effective than they are in pure mathematical world. The cryptography in real-world networks and systems has been less effective than cryptography as a mathematical science because of engineering discipline that converts the mathematical promise of cryptographic security into a reality of security. Building real-world cryptographic systems is different from the abstract theories of cryptography with only pure mathematics. Designers and implementers face real-world constraints which are experienced by most cryptographic systems. In order to achieve real-world security goals, cryptographic techniques should be applied in a real-world setting in order to build and engineer a secure cryptographic system. Applied cryptography bridges the gap between cryptographic theory and real-world cryptographic applications. Applied cryptography gives concrete advice about how to design, implement and evaluate cryptographic system within real-world settings.

This book gives guidelines to cryptographic systems with consideration of real-world constraints and opponents. Different systems have different constraints and opponents such as computation constraints, especially those in emerging areas. The constraints and opponents are analyzed first during requirements analysis, and then the cryptographic algorithms and services are selected to achieve the objective of cryptographic system. The system is evaluated against the requirements, constraints and possible threats from opponents. The book discusses applied cryptography as an engineering discipline to meet specific requirements in real-world applications. This book strives to bridge the gap between cryptographic theory and real-world cryptographic applications. This book also delves into the specific security requirements and opponents in various emerging application areas and discusses the procedure about engineering cryptography into system design and implementation. For example, wireless sensor networks have energy and computation as cryptographic constraints, entity authentication requires zero knowledge, electronic commence requires fair electronic exchange besides confidentiality, authentication, and integrity. Our main goal is to engineer cryptography into a real-world secure system and to bridge cryptographic algorithms and techniques with real-world constraints of a specific area. This book introduces how to build a secure system in real settings, which is the essence of applied cryptography in information security and privacy.

SECTION 1: CRYPTOGRAPHY IN NETWORKING AND CYBER SPACE

When communication and transaction take place in a digital form, the security of transaction in cyber space have become of critical importance. Cryptography is one of the traditional and effective to fight off massive invasion of individual privacy and privacy and security, guarantee data integrity and confidentiality, and to bring trust in computer networking and cyber space. Cryptography has become the main tool for providing the needed digital security in the modern digital communication medium that far exceeds the kind of security that was offered by any medium before. It ensures confidentiality, integrity, authentication, authorization, and non-repudiation in all data exchanges in cyber space.

The first chapter in *Section 1* focuses on cryptography in network security. "*Network Security*" is authored by Ramakrishna Thurimella and Leemon C. Baird III. The authors examine three pillars of security—confidentiality, integrity, and availability—in the context of networks. Each is explained with known practical attacks and possible defenses against them, demonstrating that strong mathematical techniques are necessary but not sufficient to build practical systems that are secure. They illustrate how adversaries commonly side-step cryptographic protections. In addition, they contend that effective key management techniques, along with privacy concerns must be taken into account during the design of any secure online system. The chapter is concluded with a discussion of open problems for which fundamentally new methods are needed.

The focus of the second chapter in this section, "*Cryptography-Based Authentication for Protecting Cyber Systems*" authored by Xunhua Wang and Hua Lin, discusses authentication technology in protecting cyber systems. Entity authentication is a fundamental building block for system security and has been widely used to protect cyber systems. This chapter studies the roles of cryptography in three entity authentication categories: knowledge-based authentication, token-based authentication, and biometric authentication. The roles of cryptography in the following areas are covered: the generation of password verification data, in password-based challenge/response authentication protocol, and in password-authenticated key exchange protocols; both symmetric key-based and private key-based token authentications; and cryptographic fuzzy extractors, which can be used to enhance the security and privacy of biometric authentication. This systematic study of the roles of cryptography in entity authentication will deepen understanding of both cryptography and entity authentication and can help us better protect cyber systems.

SECTION 2: CRYPTOGRAPHY IN E-MAIL AND WEB SERVICES

E-mail and Web services are two major techniques for people to exchange and share information remotely over the Internet. E-mail services are the method of sending and receiving electronic messages over communication networks. Web services on the other hand provide a channel of accessing interlinked hypermedia via the World Wide Web. As these two methods of network communications turn into the most popular services over the Internet, applied cryptography and secure authentication protocols become indispensable in securing confidential data over public networks.

The first chapter in *Section 2* is titled "*E-Mail, Web Service and Cryptography*", and is authored by Professor Wasim A Al-Hamdani. This chapter introduces E-mail structure and organization, web service types, their organization and cryptography algorithms which integrated in the E-mail and web services to provide high level of security. The main issue in this chapter is to build the general foundation through definitions, history, cryptography algorithms symmetric and asymmetric, hash algorithms, digital signature, suite B and general principle to introduce the use of cryptography in the E-mail and web service.

The second chapter in *Section 2* is titled "*Cryptography in E-Mail and Web Services*", and is authored by Professor Wasim A Al-Hamdani. This chapter presents client and Web-based e-mail, next generation e-mail and secure e-mail, followed by cryptography in web service and the last part is the future of web service security. The chapter starts with the integration of cryptography with e-mail client and web base then the integration of cryptography and web service is presented. At the end of the chapter, they present their view for the cryptography integration with the second generation of e-mail and web service.

The third chapter in *Section 2* is titled, "*Applied Cryptography in E-Mail Services and Web Services*" is coauthored by Professors Lei Chen, Wen-Chen Hu, Ming Yang, and Lei Zhang. This chapter first reviews a number of cryptographic ciphers widely used in secure communication protocols. We then discuss and compare the popular trust system Web of Trust, the certificate standard X.509, and the standard for public key systems Public Key Infrastructure (PKI). Two secure e-mail standards, OpenPGP and S/MIME, are examined and compared. The de facto standard cryptographic protocol for e-commerce, Secure Socket Layer (SSL) / Transport Layer Security (TLS), and XML Security Standards for secure web services are also discussed.

SECTION 3: CRYPTOGRAPHY IN WIRELESS COMMUNICATION

The first research chapter in *Section 3* deals with a very timely issue of how to secure a wireless sensor network (WSN), which employs a large number of wireless sensors to collectively monitor and disseminate information about an area of interest and is independent from fixed infrastructure. The WSN finds its application in military surveillance, habitat and weather monitoring, and emergency rescue operations. The network is usually deployed in a hostile unattended environment which is vulnerable to various attacks. Challenges faced by enforcing security in WSN lies in energy constraints in tiny sensors and how to implement security in two major techniques in WSN: data aggregation and passive participation. This chapter, titled "*Applied Cryptography in Wireless Sensor Networks*" is authored by Dulal C. Kar and Hung Ngo. This chapter summarizes, discusses, and evaluates recent symmetric key based results reported in literature on sensor network security protocols such as for key establishment, random key pre-distribution, data confidentiality, data integrity, and broadcast authentication as well as expose limitations and issues related to those solutions for WSNs. They also present significant advancement in public key cryptography for WSNs with promising results from elliptic curve cryptography and identity based encryption as well as their limitations for WSNs.

The second chapter in this section is on "*Applied Cryptography in Infrastructure-Free Wireless Networks*" authored by Lei Zhang, Danfeng Yao, and Chih-Cheng Chang. This chapter presents the technical challenges and solutions in securing wireless networks, in particular infrastructure-less wireless networks such as mobile ad hoc networks and wireless sensor networks. Communications in infrastructure-less wireless networks are challenging, as there are no trusted base stations to coordinate the activities of mobile hosts. Applied cryptographic tools, in particular threshold cryptography, play an important role in the trust establishment, message security, and key management in such networks. This chapter also describes several technical approaches that integrate applied cryptography techniques into mobile ad hoc networks and wireless sensor networks.

SECTION 4: CRYPTOGRAPHY IN ELECTRONIC COMMERCE

Electronic commerce has grown into a vital segment of the economy of many nations. It is a global phenomenon providing markets and commercialization opportunities world-wide with a significantly reduced barrier to entry as compared to global marketing in the 20th century. Providing protocols to secure such commerce is critical and continues to be an area for both scientific and engineering study. Falsification, fraud, identity theft, and disinformation campaigns or other attacks could damage the credibility and value of electronic commerce if left unchecked. Consequently, cryptographic methods have emerged to combat any such efforts, be they the occasional random attempt at theft or highly organized criminal or political activities.

The first chapter in *Section 4*, "*Applied Cryptography in Electronic Commerce*" is authored by Sławomir Grzonkowski, Brian D. Ensor, and Bill McDaniel. This chapter covers the use of cryptographic methods and emerging standards in this area to provide the necessary protection. That protection, as is common for web-based protocols, evolves over time to deal with more and more sophisticated attacks. At the same time, the provision of security in a manner convenient enough to not deter electronic commerce has driven research efforts to find easier to use and simpler protocols to implement even as the strength of the cryptographic methods has increased. This chapter also introduces current standards, looking at several facets of the secure commercialization problem from authentication to intrusion detection and identity and reputation management. Vulnerabilities are discussed as well as capabilities.

Exchanging in a fair manner is important in electronic commerce. This means both parties obtain what they expect or they obtain nothing at all. The second chapter, "*An Electronic Contract Signing Protocol Using Fingerprint Biometrics*" by Harkeerat Bedi, Li Yang, and Joseph Kizza investigates vulnerabilities and attacks in existing fair electronic exchange protocols and provide a solution for dispute resolution and countering replay attacks. Involvement of fingerprint biometrics makes authentication stronger and password management easier. The chapter demonstrates how to use cryptography and biometrics to realize confidentiality, integrity, non-repudiation and fairness in electronic commerce.

SECTION 5: CRYPTOGRAPHY IN EMERGING AREAS

We live in a pervasive computing environment formed by devices such as computers, printers, iPods, smartcards, RFID tags, etc. Pervasive computing faces two challenges: dynamic computing environment and unattended devices. Service discovery can help to solve above challenges and simplify communication among various electronic devices. In the meanwhile, service discovery introduces new security and privacy challenges. The first chapter in *Section 5*, *"Secure and Private Service Discovery in Pervasive Computing Environments"* by Feng Zhu and Wei Zhu, discusses how to use a progressive and probabilistic model to protect privacy of both users and service providers. A novel exposure negotiation is proposed to facilitate the communication when two parties expect the other one to expose information first. Users and service providers expose identity, service request and service information progressively in multiple rounds. In each round few bits of information are exchanged. If there is a mismatch at any point, the user or service provider can quit the service discovery process. Because both parties only exchange partial information in multiple rounds, privacy exposure is minimized.

Multimedia data need to be transmitted in a secure manner under certain scenario. However, data encryption standard such as DES, RAS, are not efficient in the encryption of multimedia content due to large volume. The second chapter in this section, *"Multimedia Information Security: Cryptography and Steganography"*, by Ming Yang, Monica Trifas, Nikolaos Bourbakis, and Lei Chen, attempts to address this issue. The chapter discusses how to encrypt image/video by encrypting only the key parameters in stead of the whole image/video as a bit stream. The chapter also covers how to utilize information hiding to enhance security level of data encryption methodologies, which conceals not only the content of the secret message but also existence of the message. A joint cryptograph-steganography methodology, which combines both encryption and information hiding techniques to ensure information security and privacy in medical images, is also presented.

This third chapter in this section, *"Secure Electronic Voting with Cryptography"* authored by Xunhua Wang, Ralph Grove, and M. Hossain Heydari discusses computer and network-based voting technologies which have been gradually adopted for various elections. This chapter especially concerns serious security challenges face by computer voting due to the fragile nature of electronic ballots and voting software. This chapter studies the security of computer voting and focuses on a cryptographic solution based on mix-nets. Like traditional voting systems, mix-net-based computer voting provides voter privacy and prevents vote selling/buying and vote coercion. Unlike traditional voting systems, mix-net-based computer voting has several additional advantages: 1) it offers vote verifiability, allowing individual voters to directly verify whether their votes have been counted and counted correctly; 2) it allows voters to check the behavior of potentially malicious computer voting machines and thus does not require voters to blindly trust computer voting machines. Building blocks for the mix-net-based computer voting scheme, including semantically secure encryption, threshold decryption, mix-net, and robust mix-net are given in this chapter.

The fourth chapter *"Biometric Security in the E-World"* authored by Mayank Vatsa and Kunal Sharma, and A.J. Singh discusses biometrics as a novel authentication and access control supplement to cryptography.

Hamid R. Nemati, PhD.
The University of North Carolina at Greensboro

Li Yang, PhD.
University of Tennessee at Chattanooga

REFERENCES

Adkinson, W., Eisenach, J., & Lenard, T. (2002). *Privacy Online: A Report on the Information Practices and Policies of Commercial Web Sites*. Retrieved August, 2010, from http://www.pff.org/publications/privacyonlinefinalael.pdf

Hardy, Q. (2004, May 10). *Data of Reckoning*. Forbes, 173, 151-154.

IDC Report (2010). The Digital Universe Decade: Are You Ready?" Retrieved May 2010, from http://www.emc.com/collateral/demos/microsites/idc-digital-universe/iview.htm

Stuhler, J. (2010). Managing the data explosion. Retrieved May 2010, from http://www.it-director.com/technology/data_mgmt/content.php?cid=11025

Section 1
Cryptography in Networking and Cyber Space

Chapter 1
Network Security

Ramakrishna Thurimella
University of Denver, USA

Leemon C. Baird III
United States Air Force Academy, USA

ABSTRACT

Three pillars of security—confidentiality, integrity, and availability—are examined in the context of networks. Each is explained with known practical attacks and possible defenses against them, demonstrating that strong mathematical techniques are necessary but not sufficient to build practical systems that are secure. We illustrate how adversaries commonly side-step cryptographic protections. In addition, we contend that effective key management techniques, along with privacy concerns must be taken into account during the design of any secure online system. We conclude with a discussion of open problems for which fundamentally new methods are needed.

INTRODUCTION

Confidentiality, integrity and availability, often abbreviated CIA, are key security requirements in any risk analysis. In short, confidentiality is the privacy of an object, integrity is the trustworthiness and dependability (accuracy and consistency of information), and availability refers to the fact that a resource can reliably be used when desired. Stamp (2006) contains more detailed definitions of these concepts.

The most common use of cryptography online is to provide confidential and authenticated communication between two parties, either in the context of web transactions or for remote access. In order to accomplish this, one needs an effective key management scheme. As a way of demonstrating that many security concepts are intertwined, we present keyless jam resistance, a method that can broadcast messages using radio frequency communication without any prior secret shared between the sender and receiver.

Possibly the most difficult to achieve form of confidentiality is privacy of the identity of an individual performing some action, more com-

DOI: 10.4018/978-1-61520-783-1.ch001

monly referred to as anonymity. While a common security goal is non-repudiation—the assurance that an individual can not retract his responsibility for an action—it's dual, the ability to disclaim responsibility for an action can be equally desirable. Modern mechanisms for generating anonymity combine the use of large groups of operators with a public-key infrastructure and data encryption to decouple an individual's action from their identity.

The remainder of this chapter is organized as follows. The following section presents the necessary background material for this chapter. Next we discuss confidentiality and integrity. After that, a key aspect of privacy, online anonymity, is discussed. Availability is described throughout the chapter and discussed briefly in a separate section. Key Management section presents a comprehensive list of methods to distribute secret keys. Wireless Availability section shows how to eliminate the need for keys by presenting a novel algorithm to do jam resistance communication. We conclude with a discussion of open problems in the last section.

BACKGROUND

In this section, we begin with the basics of cryptography, pointing out the difference between symmetric and asymmetric encryption, followed by a description of the Diffie-Hellman key exchange protocol. Next, we present an abstract description of the man-in-the-middle attack. After that, we give some networking details that are necessary to understand a concrete man-in-the-middle attack on modern local-area networks.

Cryptography

We first begin with a general discussion on cryptography. Figure 1 shows the process of encryption followed by a description. First, the plaintext is transformed into cipher text by applying a key K_e. Applying another key K_d, possibly different from K_e, retrieves the original.

In symbols, this process is shown as $P = D(K_d, E(K_e, P))$.

The encryption and decryption methods, when combined, are known as a *cipher*. When the decryption key is the same as the encryption key, or efficiently derivable from it, the process is known as *symmetric* encryption; otherwise, it is called *asymmetric* encryption. Two popular symmetric encryption methods are Advanced Encryption Standard (AES) (Daemen & Rijmen, 2002) and Triple Data Encryption Standard (3DES) ("Data Encryption Standard," (2009)). The main difficulty with symmetric encryption is *key distribution*—getting the communicating parties to agree upon a common key. This problem is discussed at length later in the Chapter.

In public key cryptography, each communicating entity maintains one private key and one public key, K_{priv} and K_{pub} respectively. Extending the previous notation, asymmetric encryption can be shown as $P = D(K_{priv}, E(K_{pub}, P))$.

As the names imply, the public key is made available freely to anyone who wishes to use it, but the private key is kept secret. So, if Alice wishes to communicate with Bob, she encrypts the message with Bob's public key (which is openly available) and sends the encrypted message to Bob. Anyone eavesdropping on this communication cannot de-

Figure 1. Process of encryption and decryption

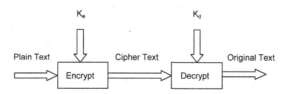

crypt the message unless they have Bob's secret key. Since anyone who wants to communicate with Bob can easily get access to his public key, public key cryptography does not suffer from the key distribution problem. However, public key cryptography does have a different drawback. It entails performing modular arithmetic over large integers (few hundred digits long) which is computationally expensive. In practice, a hybrid method is used: public key cryptography is used initially to exchange a random symmetric key, and this random key is used for the remainder of the session. Two popular public key methods are RSA (Rivest et al., 1978) and ElGamal (1985).

Public key cryptography has another very desirable property. The public and private keys can be applied in the reverse order: $P = D(K_{pub}, E(K_{priv}, P))$.

If Bob sends Alice $E(K_{priv}, P)$, then Alice can be assured that the message P came from Bob as only Bob has access to K_{priv}. In this case, P is said to be *digitally signed* by Bob.

Diffie-Hellman Key Exchange Protocol

The Diffie-Hellman (DH) protocol allows two parties that have no prior knowledge of each other to jointly establish a shared secret key over an insecure communication channel (Diffie & Hellman, 1976). This protocol is also known as Diffie-Hellman-Merkle ("Diffie-Hellman," 2009). In short, DH is based on the fact that

$$(g^a \bmod p)^b \bmod p = (g^b \bmod p)^a \bmod p$$

where all computations are performed over a group of integers modulo p for some large prime p. Its cryptographic strength comes from the fact that it is easy to compute powers modulo a prime but hard to reverse the process when large integers are involved. This intractable problem is known as the *discrete log* problem. For example, if p were a prime of at least 300 digits, and a and b were at least 100 digits long, then even the best algorithms known today could not find a given only g, p, and

$g^a \bmod p$, even using all of mankind's computing power ("Diffie-Hellman," 2009). In practice is g usually either 2 or 5.

Alice and Bob can agree on a shared secret by perform the following steps (all arithmetic is modulo p):

1. Alice and Bob agree on a large prime p and a generator g.
2. Alice picks a random number a, $0 < a < p$, sends g^a to Bob, and keeps a secret.
3. Bob picks a random number b, $0 < b < p$, sends g^b to Alice, and keeps b secret.
4. Alice computes $(g^b)^a$.
5. Bob computes $(g^a)^b$.

Both Alice and Bob are now in possession of the group element g^{ab}, which can serve as the shared secret key. The values of $(g^b)^a$ and $(g^a)^b$ are the same because multiplication in groups is associative. Only a, b and $g^{ab} = g^{ba} \bmod p$ are kept secret. All the other values—p, g, $g^a \bmod p$, and $g^b \bmod p$—are sent in the clear.

Trust, Certificates, and Man-in-the-Middle (MITM) Attack

Say Alice wishes to communicate with Bob using public-key cryptography. In this attack, Mallory, the attacker can participate actively or passively. In the latter role, she faithfully proxies the communication between Alice and Bob, while eavesdropping on their conversation—a breach of confidentiality. In the active mode, Mallory can choose to edit, delete, or inject packets.

If Alice requests Bob's public key and Mallory is able to intercept it, then Mallory can mount a man-in-the-middle attack. Mallory responds back to Alice with her public key K_m. Alice is under the impression that she is talking to Bob and encrypts all her messages with K_m which Mallory can decrypt.

Meanwhile, Mallory, pretending to be Alice, sends K_m to Bob, telling him that it is Alice's public key and requests his public key. Bob, like Alice, encrypts all his messages with K_m which Mallory can decrypt.

Both Bob and Alice are under the impression that they are talking to each other, but all communication passes through Mallory and is completely controlled by Mallory. The attack mounted by Mallory is known as the *man-in-the-middle attack*.

This problem arose because the public keys are sent directly by their owners. The solution is to exchange public keys through a trusted third party. This is accomplished by using *digital certificates* that contain the public key for an entity and an assurance from a trusted third party that the public key belongs to that entity. The trusted third party that issues digital certificates is called a *Certification Authority* (CA). As these certificates are digitally signed by CAs, the certificates provide protection against impersonation. Authenticity of certificates is easily verified since a CA's public key is "universally" available (e.g. embedded in browsers). When a certificate is for an individual

entity (resp. Certification Authority), the certificate is a *personal (resp. root) certificate*.

Digital certificates contain at least the following information about the entity being certified:

- The public key of the certificate holder
- The common name of the certificate holder
- The common name of the CA that is issuing the certificate
- The date certificate was issued on
- The expiration date of the certificate
- The serial number of the certificate

For obvious reasons, digital certificates do not contain the private key of the owner because it must be kept secret by the owner. See an example certificate in Figure 2.

A *Public-Key Infrastructure* (PKI) is a system of facilities, policies, and services that support the use of public-key cryptography for authenticating the parties involved in a transaction ("Public Key Infrastructure", 2009). There is no single standard that defines the components of a PKI, but it typically comprises of CAs and Registration Authorities (RAs) that provide the following services:

- Issuing digital certificates
- Validating digital certificates
- Revoking digital certificates
- Distributing public keys

The X.509 is an International Telecommunication Union standard for a Public Key Infrastructure (Cooper, 2008). RAs verify the information provided at the time when digital certificates are requested. If the information is verified successfully by the RA, the CA can issue a digital certificate to the requester.

Networking Basics

The Transmission Control Protocol (TCP) and the Internet Protocol (IP) together are at the heart of

Figure 2. Digital certificate received from PayPal web server as viewed from a browser

communication protocols used for the Internet. These protocols resulted from years of research funded by Defense Advanced Research Projects Agency (DARPA). The TCP/IP suite defines a set of rules that enable computers to communicate over a network. The rules specify data formatting, addressing, shipping, routing and delivery to the correct destination.

The TCP/IP stack is an abstraction of four layers as shown in Figure 3. Conceptually similar functions are aggregated into a layer and the resulting layers are stratified based on the services provided. For example, in the 4-layer model, TCP at level 3 provides reliable packet delivery. Building on this, the application layer at level 4 can offer a stateful telnet session to the end user without having to worry about dropping the connection.

In contrast, the Open Systems Interconnection Reference Model (OSI Reference Model or OSI Model) is a more detailed 7-layer model (Zimmermann, 1980). From top to bottom these are the Application, Presentation, Session, Transport, Network, Data-Link, and Physical Layers.

It is useful to understand the role played by various networking components and map their functionality to the services provided in the 4-layer model.

Computers that are in close proximity and connected into the same LAN communicate with each other using Ethernet. This protocol operates at Layer 2 in the OSI model and at the Link Layer in the 4-layer model. In this protocol, frames are sent to a destination Media Access Control (MAC) address, a 48-bit address that is unique to each Network Interface Card (NIC) on the network. The nodes on a LAN are connected using a hub or a switch. The only difference between them is that a hub is less intelligent and cheaper than a switch. It simply broadcasts every packet it receives to every computer on the LAN. For many years, hubs were very common and posed serious security problems for system administrators, as anyone on the LAN can connect to the LAN, put their NIC into "promiscuous" mode and eavesdrop on all data transferred on the LAN. Switches, on the other hand, direct Ethernet frames to where they need to go instead of broadcasting. In addition to improved security, switches also increase the rate at which data can be transferred.

To connect a LAN to the Internet, one needs a more intelligent device that can route packets to the Internet. This device is called a *router*. This is a Layer 3 device in the OSI model. It is smarter than a switch in the sense that it is programmable and usually includes an interface by which it can be configured. Routers have the ability to communicate with other routers and determine the best way to route network traffic from one point to another on the Internet. For simplicity, let us assume that there is only one router on any given LAN. Then, since all traffic from the LAN must enter and exit through the router, it provides a

Figure 3. Seven-layer versus the four-layer networking model

OSI 7-layer model	TCP/IP 4-layer model
7. Application	4. Application (Telnet,SMTP, HTTP,FTP,…)
6. Presentation	
5. Session	3. Transport (TCP,UDP)
4. Transport	
3. Network	2. Internet (IP)
2. Data Link	
1. Physical	1. Link (Ethernet,Token Ring)

Figure 4. Local area network (LAN) connected to the Internet via a router. A router is seen by the switch as another host on the LAN

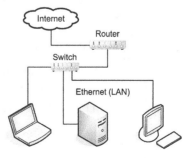

useful *choke point*. The computers on the LAN can be protected from outside attackers by running a firewall along with an intrusion detection system at this choke point.

A *default gateway* is the node on the LAN that is chosen by the switch when it encounters an IP address that does not belong to any node on the LAN. A router usually assumes the role of a default gateway. In home networks, the functionality of a switch, router, and wireless access point are often combined into one physical unit.

SSL/TLS

Transport Layer Security (TLS) is a security protocol from the Internet Engineering Task Force (IETF) that is based on the Secure Sockets Layer (SSL) 3.0 protocol developed by Netscape. TLS is the successor to SSL. Both protocols include cryptographic frameworks which are intended to provide secure communications on the Internet. SSL is not an industry standard as it was developed by Netscape. TLS is the widely recognized standard issued by the IETF for securing transmitted data. The current version of TLS is 1.1 and is described in RFC 4346 (Dierks & Allen, 1999). It is now supported on most commercial browsers, web and email servers. For the most part, SSL and TLS are interchangeable.

The SSL protocol runs above TCP/IP and below higher-level protocols such as HTTP or SMTP. It uses TCP/IP on behalf of the higher-level protocols, and facilitates the establishment of an encrypted connection between the client and server. See Figure 5.

Figure 5 SSL/TLS run above TCP/IP and below the Application Layer that consists of protocols used for accessing the Internet HTTP, send and receive email using SMTP etc.

Both SSL and TLS follow a standard handshake process to establish communication. The handshake prior to an HTTPS session is as follows:

1. The client contacts a server that hosts a secured URL.
2. The server responds to the client's request and sends the server's digital certificate to the browser.
3. The client now verifies that the received certificate is valid. Certificates are issued by well-known authorities (e.g. Thawte or Verisign).
4. The server could *optionally* choose to confirm a user's identity. Using the same techniques as those used for server authentication, SSL-enabled server software can check that the client's certificate is valid and has been issued by a certificate authority (CA) listed in the server's list of trusted CAs. This confirmation might be important if the server is a bank sending confidential financial information to a customer and wants to check the recipient's identity. (See the benefits of performing this optional step in Possible Defenses against MITM.)
5. Once the certificate is validated, the client generates a random one-time session key, which will be used to encrypt all communication with the server.
6. The client now encrypts the session key with the server's public key, which was transmitted with the digital certificate. Encrypting using the server's public key ensures that others cannot eavesdrop on this sensitive exchange.

At this point, a secure session is established because the client and server both know the ses-

Figure 5.

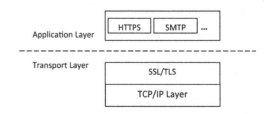

sion key. Now, both parties can communicate via a secure channel. See Figure 6.

MITM Attack on a Switched LAN using ARP Spoofing

How does Mallory eavesdrop on the exchange between Alice and Bob on modern computer networks? Aren't they built on secure technology? The answer is no, unfortunately. The problem is that Ethernet, upon which virtually all modern LANs are based, was designed without *any* sort of authentication mechanism. An attack known as *ARP spoofing* takes advantage of this weakness and can intercept communications on a LAN running the Ethernet protocol (Wagner, 2001). This attack works against most networks that are in use at the time of this writing.

The attack works as follows. Recall our discussion from the Networking Basics section on how two computers communicate on a LAN us-

ing Ethernet frames. To connect to a LAN, each host must be equipped with a Network Interface Card (NIC). Each NIC is assigned a unique Media Access Control (MAC) address by the manufacturer. Communication on Ethernet takes place by sending frames to destination MAC addresses. If a MAC address is unknown, the source node broadcasts an ARP request. This request specifies an IP address and asks the host with this IP address to reply back with its physical address. In other words, *Address Resolution Protocol* (ARP) finds MAC address given an IP address.

Every node on the LAN receives every ARP request, but only the host with the matching IP address replies back with its physical address; the rest simply ignore it. The response is sent back using an ARP Reply that contains the requested IP number and the corresponding MAC address. When the source node receives this information, it stores it in a table of IP and MAC address pairs. This table is known as the *ARP cache* and the mappings are considered valid for a fixed amount time, after which they expire and are removed. Every node on the LAN maintains such a cache. Note that the source node enters the IP-MAC address pair contained in the ARP Reply into its cache without any validation or further checks. Put differently, there is *total trust* between the nodes on a LAN. To make the matters worse ARP is a *stateless protocol*, i.e. an ARP Reply is not matched to see if there are outstanding ARP Requests. Therefore, any malicious node can takeover

Figure 6. SSL/TLS protocol handshake and session key establishment. (Adapted from The SSL Handshake (2009).)

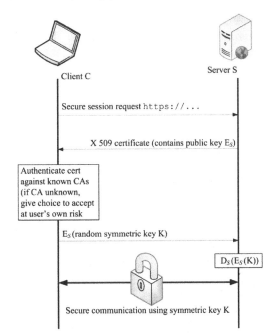

Figure 7. ARP request broadcast and response. Here host A is requesting a MAC (physical) address that corresponds to IP# 192.168.0.73 (host C)

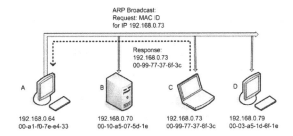

a LAN and route all traffic through itself by sending unsolicited ARP Reply messages to various hosts—the only requirement that needs to be met is that the malicious node is a host on that LAN. One easy way is to accomplish this is by connecting to an insecure wireless access point. Many corporations, hospitals, and retail outlets still use easily breakable WEP encryption (Tews et al., 2007). This weakness exists within the TCP/IP stack. Hence, it is a multi-platform vulnerability.

By injecting merely two ARP Reply packets into a LAN, any malicious node M can control all traffic going back and forth between any two nodes on that LAN, e.g. between an unsuspecting victim node A and the default gateway G. First, M sends G a spoofed ARP Reply $<IP_A, MAC_M>$ claiming that it was assigned IP_A (which really belongs to A) but gives its own MAC address MAC_M. The gateway would blindly replace its current correct entry with the spoofed one. At the same time M would send a similar spoofed ARP Reply $<IP_G, MAC_M>$ to A, replacing the correct ARP cache entry for the gateway computer at A with the spoofed one. From this point on, any traffic from A bound for the default gateway would instead go to the attacking computer M.

Similarly, all traffic from G destined to A is routed instead to M. Neither A nor G would be aware of the intermediary that is relaying the traffic in the middle. See Figure 8.

On a LAN with *n* nodes, that consists of (*n*-2) nodes, 1 router, and 1 attacker, by inserting 2(*n*-2) spoofed ARP Replies, the attacker can take full control of the traffic destined to the Internet from that LAN. This process of inserting false entries into an ARP cache is also referred to *ARP poisoning*. It is worth noting that cache entries are purged after a timeout period. Therefore, to keep control of the network, the attacker must periodically poison each host for the duration of the hijacked session.

In addition to compromising the confidentiality and the integrity of the data as it passes through the local network (as described in detail in the next section), MITM attacks can also adversely affect availability by simply slowing down or completely dropping the network communication by associating a nonexistent MAC address to the IP address of the victim's default gateway. Refer to the Availability section on other ways of affecting availability.

Figure 8. ARP cache values before and after poisoning by node C to insert itself between B and the Default Gateway (Router). The second column shows after ARP poisoning. The two spoofed entries are shown in bold

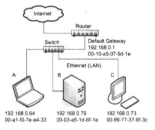

After C inserts itself between B and the Default Gateway

At the Default Gateway	
192.168.0.1	00-10-a5-07-5d-1e
192.168.0.64	00-a1-f0-7e-e4-33
192.168.0.73	00-99-77-37-6f-3c
192.168.0.79	***00-99-77-37-6f-3c***

ARP Cache (at every node)	
192.168.0.1	00-10-a5-07-5d-1e
192.168.0.64	00-a1-f0-7e-e4-33
192.168.0.73	00-99-77-37-6f-3c
192.168.0.79	00-03-a5-1d-6f-1e

At B	
192.168.0.1	***00-99-77-37-6f-3c***
192.168.0.64	00-a1-f0-7e-e4-33
192.168.0.73	00-99-77-37-6f-3c
192.168.0.79	00-03-a5-1d-6f-1e

CONFIDENTIALITY AND INTEGRITY

Other than insider attacks, a man-in-the-middle (MITM) attack is probably the easiest and most common attack on network connections secured with SSL. This section presents one such attack. During this attack, in a 24-hour period, the author of the attack, Marlinspike, managed to collect a few hundred user ID/passwords of accounts at popular web email servers, financial institutions, social networking sites, etc.

Futile Defenses against MITM

It has become fashionable at many financial institutions in the United States to present the online user with a set of "secret" questions, in addition to their login credentials. After a successful login, the session might proceed along the following lines:

```
To protect the security of your ac-
count, please answer the following
questions:
Note: Your answers are NOT case sen-
sitive.
What is the name of the school where
you went to kindergarten?
```

Or questions such as

```
What is the last name of your favor-
ite actor?
What is your favorite color?
```

Sometimes this "extra" security comes in the form of storing your favorite picture which is transmitted during the beginning of an encrypted session.

The purpose of this section is to demonstrate that these so called additional security measures are *totally ineffective* against MITM attacks. The attack described here is due to Marlinspike (2009).

MITM Attack on SSL Using Bogus Certificates

The *certificate chain* is a list of certificates used to authenticate an entity. Certificate chaining is a process by which *root* certificate authorities delegate the certificate issuing authority to intermediate CAs for efficiency and scalability reasons. This mechanism is part of the trusted computing paradigm. When certificate chains are involved in verification, to check authenticity of a certificate for an entity, the certificate chain is used to reach the *root CA* certificate. The root CA certificate is self-signed. However, the signatures of the intermediate CAs must be verified.

Chains can be longer than three. Most browsers verify certificate chains as follows:

1. Verify that the name on the certificate matches the name of the entity the client wishes to connect.
2. Check the certificate's expiration date.
3. Check the signature. If the signing certificate is in the list of root CAs in the client, stop, otherwise, move up the chain one link and repeat.

Figure 9. Certificate chain verification process by a client program. (Adapted from Figure 1 of Certificate Chain Verification (2009).)

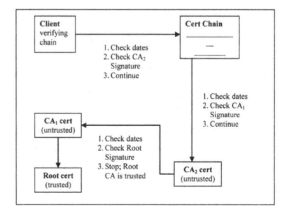

Assume an attacker is in possession of the domain attacker.com and a certificate is issued to it by CA_2. Consider the following certificate chain:

```
              Root
CA→CA₁→CA₂→attacker.com→victim.com
```

Anyone connecting to victim.com, first checks its name and expiration, and then verifies its signature by applying the public key of attacker.com. Assuming that this is successful, the process is repeated with attacker.com, CA_2, and CA_1, until Root CA is reached. In this example, all signatures and dates pass the validity test, and the Root CA would be reached successfully. Since the Root CA is always trusted, the whole chain is considered to be intact. Unfortunately there is a problem; attacker.com should not have the authority to issue certificates to other domains. This restriction is imposed in the Basic Constraints Extension of the X.509 specification (Cooper et al., 2008). It identifies whether the subject of the certificate is a CA and length of a certificate chain, including itself. The intent in the Standard is to prevent non-CAs from issuing certificates. For non-CAs, this field should be CA:FALSE indicating that the entity to which this certificate was issued is not a CA. Unfortunately many CAs did not explicitly set this field and most browsers simply ignored it. The implication of this careless practice is that any entity with a valid certificate could create a certificate for any domain.

In 2002, Marlinspike released a software tool, *sslsniff* that took advantage of this weakness. This tool has the capability to dynamically generate certificates for domains that are being accessed on the fly. The new certificate becomes part of a certificate chain that is signed by any certificate provided to sslsniff.

Using sslsniff, one can perform MITM attack on an HTTPS session as follows. First, an HTTPS request from victimClient trying to connect to victimServer is intercepted using standard techniques such as ARP poisoning. The attacker then sends a bogus certificate in the name of victimServer.

Unsuspecting, victimClient authenticates the certificate chain and sends a symmetric key, encrypted using the public key supplied by the attacker. The attacker decrypts the symmetric key, which is used as a session key. Simultaneously, the attacker opens an HTTPS session with victimServer and proxies the traffic between victimClient and victimServer, relaying the set "secret" questions and answers back and forth. All the data that is in transmitted between the client and the server is available to the attacker *in the clear* including sensitive information such as credit card numbers.

This weakness in the Basic Constraints field of X.509 has since been addressed by the CAs and the newer generation of popular browsers are no longer susceptible to this attack.

MITM Attack Using Other Means

Even though one may not be able to carry out MITM attacks using bogus certificates against newer web technology without raising too many red flags, there are a variety of other techniques that one can employ to launch an MITM attack and breach the confidentiality of secure web transactions. The techniques presented here are browser independent and are effective against web sites of some leading financial institutions.

Since it now appears as if HTTPS has been secured, what is the best way to hijack a web session? Marlinspike (2009) provides an answer to this question by asking the following questions related to human-computer interaction (HCI):

1. How do people start an HTTPS session?
2. How are people assured that they are using a secured session?
3. How are people warned that there maybe a problem with the security of the session?

Most often, the answer to question 1 is either

1. User clicking on a button that posts to HTTPS, or

Figure 10. MITM attack on secure web sessions using bogus certificates

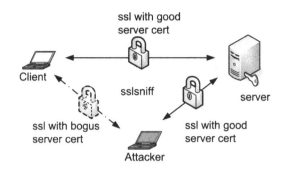

2. Through rerouting from the web server (HTTP response code 302).When the user types victimServer.com, the browser resolves it to http://www.victimServer.com. For example, the exchange might look like

```
GET /index.html HTTP/1.1
Host: www.victimServer.com
When victimServer receives the above
request, it reroutes the client as
HTTP/1.1 302 Found
Location: https://www.victimServer.
com/index.html
```

That is, no one really types https:// before starting an online transaction. In other words, *access to HTTPS is via HTTP*. The strategy of the attacker becomes, attack HTTP if HTTPS is secure.

Questions 2 and 3 can be best understood by studying how browsers have evolved over the years. Seven years ago, when sslsniff was released, excessive positive feedback was given by the browser that a user was using a secure connection. There were many lock icons, the address bar or uniform resource locator (URL) bar changed color, and a number of other indicators were deployed to give a "warm-and-fuzzy" feeling to the user that the page was secure. A *favicon*, short for favorites icon, is a 16x16 pixel square icon associated with a particular website that is displayed in URL bar. A popular favicon in the older browsers during secure sessions was a small padlock (see Figure 11).

Another example of positive feedback is as follows. When a bogus certificate is detected by the browser, a dialog similar to the one shown in Figure 12 is presented to the user. Notice that by default, the certificate chain would be accepted for the session. According to Marlinspike (2009), users typically click through these warning dialogs as they don't completely understand the meaning of the warning.

The trend in the newer browsers is to scale back the positive feedback while emphasizing the negative. For instance, instead of encouraging the user to simply click through the dialog as shown in Figure 12, more ominous looking dialogs like the ones shown in Figure 13 are generated when an invalid certificate is found in the certificate chain. In addition, newer browsers control the proliferation of lock icons, use plain colors for the URL bar, and employ normal favicons.

This shift in HCI with respect to online security has been referred by Marlinspike as going from giving the user *positive feedback* to *negative feedback*. His recent attack is based on the observation that any attack that triggers negative feedback is bound to fail, but the absence positive feedback during the attack is not so bad.

The attack proceeds as follows:

Figure 11.

Figure 12. Warning dialogs that are routinely ignored by most online users

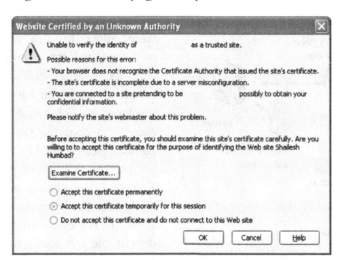

1. Intercept all web (HTTP) traffic and replace
   a. <a href=https://...> by <a href=http://...>
   b. Location: href=https://...> by Location: href=http://...

   And keep a map of all replacements.

2. If there is an HTTP request from the client for a resource for which there was replacement in the previous step, issue an HTTPS connection to the server for the same resource, and
3. Relay the response from the server to the client using HTTP.

The key difference between this MITM attack and the attack using bogus certificates is that in the previous attack, the attacker uses HTTPS to connect to both the client and the server. By comparison, in this new MITM attack, the attacker only communicates with the server in encrypted mode. From the point of view of the server, this would appear like a normal secure online transaction. Compare Figures 10 and 14.

On the client side, there are no tell-tale signs of a breach since the attack suppresses nasty dialogs from popping up. This accomplishes the goal of not triggering any negative feedback. To complete the attack, Marlinspike adds some positive feedback. This is done by adding a lock favicon in the URL bar. That is, whenever a favicon request is noticed for a URL that is in the map, a lock favicon is returned. The only difference a security savvy user would notice is the absence of a lock icon in the status bar and http instead of https in the address bar.

The results from this experiment are remarkable. The security of over a hundred email accounts, a few credit card numbers, and a few hundred secure logins was breached in a matter of a single *24-hour period*. Another surprising aspect of this test was that *not a single user* attempting to initiate a secure transaction aborted it because the user became suspicious.

Marlinspike also showed how to extend the *homograph* attack (attack that attempts to deceive remote users about what server they are communicating with, by taking advantage of the fact that many different characters have nearly indistinguishable glyphs) to mount MITM against SSL. We omit the details of this attack and the technical problems posed by cached pages. The interested reader is referred to Marlinspike (2009).

Figure 13. Negative Feedback

Figure 14. Hijacking secure online transactions

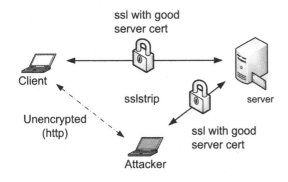

Possible Defenses against MITM

We conclude this section by presenting some effective measures an online user can take to defend against MITM attacks. First and foremost is to educate oneself to look for signs of a breach. It is also important to understand the meaning of different warning dialogs presented by the browser.

If a web server offers its services only over HTTPS (on TCP port 443) and routinely redirects all HTTP (port 80) requests to the secure port 443, then sessions can still be hijacked. As long as HTTPS depends on HTTP, it is vulnerable because HTTP is not secure. Why not just turn off port 80? Unfortunately this would cause many Server Not Found errors for the users and it would not be good for business. One work around is to have the user type in https://... in the address bar. Alternately, the user could bookmark the secure site and issue an HTTPS request by selecting the bookmark. It is tempting to think that if browsers always try to connect over port 443 first, and ers always try to connect over port 443 first, and only connect only to port 80 as a last resort, we can avoid the MITM attacks mentioned here. Unfortunately, the attacker can simply drop the requests to connect to port 443 and make the browsers think that the web server does not offer HTTPS. While this defense might not help in all cases, by including into browsers a select set of sites for which service over HTTPS is known to exist, one can reduce the risk of MITM attacks. The only long term solution is to secure everything, i.e. run only HTTPS.

Another measure that could improve security, that is not currently popular, is the verification of client certificates. By having servers verify the identity of the client, one can achieve better security. But, this requires significant changes to the existing PKI and is not immediately applicable.

ONLINE ANONYMITY

The notion of privacy and anonymity are closely related. When an element from a well-defined set is not identifiable within that set, then that element is said to be *anonymous*. This element could be a human being, a computer, or an email. One way to remain private is to stay anonymous. While encryption guarantees confidentiality, it provides no privacy; an attacker can observe communication patterns and deanonymize the users. For example, if the attacker notices that there are packets flowing between your home computer and a particular bank's web server, then he can reasonably conclude that you have an account at this institution and you are performing a transaction. Since public networks do not hide routing information, this is a real concern. This way of identifying information is known as *traffic analysis*. On the Internet, the main goal of anonymity is to make the communicating parties *unlinkable* by building defenses against traffic analysis. Chaum (1981) is widely credited for introducing and making a case for anonymous communication. He was the first to propose the *mix* as an essential unit for anonymity.

Why is online anonymity important? Who and what needs to be protected? These questions can be answered by considering the following scenarios:

1. **Censorship resistant publishing** The following paragraph from the Publius (2009) homepage, an online censorship resistant publishing system, motivates the importance of such a system: The publication of written words has long been a tool for spreading new (and sometimes controversial) ideas, often with the goal of bringing about social change. Thus the printing press, and more recently, the World Wide Web, are powerful revolutionary tools. But those who seek to suppress revolutions possess powerful tools of their own. These tools give them the ability to stop publication, destroy published materials, or prevent the distribution of publications. And even if they cannot successfully censor the publication, they may intimidate and physically or financially harm the author or publisher in order to send a message to other would-be-revolutionaries that they would be well advised to consider an alternative occupation. Even without a threat of personal harm, authors may wish to publish their works anonymously or pseudonymously because they believe they will be more readily accepted if not associated with a person of their gender, race, ethnic background, or other characteristics.

2. **Socially sensitive communication** The fact that a person visits certain websites related to a disease with the goal of educating himself, and frequents online support groups for a disorder should be kept private. Otherwise, this person could be denied insurance coverage or be subjected to workplace discrimination.

3. **Law enforcement** In many crime reporting situations, witnesses will not come forward unless they are assured of anonymity. Also when police conduct surveillance, including sting operations, they must remain unidentifiable.

4. **Whistleblower protection** *Whistleblowers* are insiders who reveal questionable practices at their workplace to the public. They need to be protected from retaliation by the management.

5. **Personal information** The websites an individual visits, the set of people she communicates with, the doctors she sees, or the medicines she takes, are all examples of personal information that should remain private.

There are many other cases including open-source intelligence gathering (the Secret Service might want to visit news websites of rogue nations anonymously), elections and voting where anonymity is indispensable.

Anonymizing networks are not without their detractors. The main criticism leveled against these networks is that online criminals can hide behind them and carry out their nefarious activities. Law enforcement would have a hard time convicting these criminals as their illegal acts cannot be easily linked back to them. As with any technology, the pros and cons of online anonymity must be carefully weighed before judging its merit. Most people in the security community are of the opinion that the benefits of anonymizing networks far outweigh the risks.

Onion Routing

Goldschlag et al. (1999) introduced the idea of Onion Routing to provide unlinkable communication. It is based on *mix cascades* (or *mixes* for short) (Chaum, 1981): messages travel from source to destination via a sequence of proxies randomly chosen by the sender. To prevent the adversary from eavesdropping on the message content, it is encrypted between routers.

To keep the discussion at the conceptual level, we omit many important practical considerations and introduce Onion Routing with an example.

Say Alice wants to send a message M to Bob. If anonymity is not a concern, she can simply establish a session key K_B as in SSL, use it to encrypt M and send the encrypted message. But, anyone watching the packet flow can link Alice and Bob.

To make the path taken by the encrypted message unidentifiable, Alice first picks a random path to Bob. Assume that the path goes through Carol and David. Next, she establishes symmetric keys with every Onion Router on the path, in this case with Carol, David and Bob, denoted K_c, K_d, and K_b respectively. The process of establishing these keys must be done in a manner so that it does not give away the path. This is described in the next subsection.

The communication between Alice and Bob starts with Alice finding O_3 and sending it to Carol where

```
O₃ = K_c (nexthop=David, K_d
(nexthop=Bob, K_b(M)))
```

Carol decrypts O_3, discovers the next hop (David in this case), retrieves O_2 passes it to David where

```
O₂ = K_d (nexthop=Bob, K_b (M))
```

David in turn "peels" another layer and sends O_1 to Bob where

```
O₁ =K_b (M)
```

Bob decrypts O_1 with K_b and retrieves M (see Figure 15).

Unless Carol and David collude, Carol (resp. David) does not know David's successor (resp. Carol's predecessor). Equivalently, Carol cannot link O_2 to O_1 without the secret key David shares with Alice K_d. Similarly, David cannot link O_2 to O_3 without Carol's secret key K_c. The only person who knows the entire path is the person who chose the path—the sender, Alice; not even the receiver knows the path. Furthermore, the receiver cannot infer the sender's identity from the header information unless the message somehow identifies the sender.

Notice that as the data moves from the source to destination, it gets smaller in size because it has fewer and fewer routing instructions. As an attacker could infer routing information from

Figure 15. Onion routing. Intermediate onion routers are only aware of the predecessor and successor nodes, but unaware of the contents of the data or the path the data follows

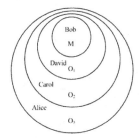

Kₓ: X's secret symmetric key with Alice
Alice sends message M to Bob as follows:
- Alice constructs & sends O₃ to Carol where
  O₃ = K_c (nexthop = David, O₂)
- Carol decrypts O₃, retrieves & sends O₂ to David where O₂ = K_d (nexthop = Bob, O₁)
- David decrypts O₂, retrieves & sends O₁ to Bob where O₁ = K_b (M)
- Bob decrypts O₁ & retrieves M

this monotonically decreasing packet size, the intermediate Onion Routers pad the data with random bits (equal to the number of bits peeled off at that router) so that the size of data remains constant between hops.

Once the path chosen by the sender is established, it remains active for some period of time, i.e. a session. This path is suitable for two-way communication as Bob can reply back to Alice along the same path, i.e. every node on the path would simply do the opposite: encrypt with its session key and the send the data upstream, one step closer to the sender. In our example, when Alice finally receives the response she decrypts it using K_c first, K_d next, and K_b last. Routing information is not included for the reverse path and for all subsequent two-way communication between Alice and Bob as each intermediate node is aware of its two neighbors on the path.

Note that Onion Routing does not provide complete anonymity. A local eavesdropper can observe that Alice is sending and receiving messages, but he cannot infer that the receiver of the messages is Bob.

The Onion Router

The remainder of our discussion on Onion Routing is specific to the way it is implemented in *The onion router (Tor)*, a widely used anonymizing network. Tor is a free software product distributed under GNU General Public License (GPL). Its low latency, high-bandwidth, stream-level anonymous communication ability makes it suitable for common TCP-based applications such as web browsing and instant messaging (Dingledine et al., 2004). Tor's popularity can be attributed to its ease of use and *forward security* (protection of past network activity in the event the current secret key is exposed).

Two potential risks exist for a client who is directly interacting with Tor: 1) Domain Name Service requests (translation service that is needed to resolve URLs to IP numbers) can give away

the sites that a client wishes to visit, and 2) web servers typically leave cookies that invade the privacy of the client. To prevent problems of this kind Tor is commonly used with a web proxy such as *Privoxy*, another free program released under GPL. See Figure 16.

The Tor network is a distributed overlay network that is comprised of a set of nodes that act as relays. Anyone who meets certain bandwidth requirements can volunteer to be a relay and Tor server software runs in user space, i.e. no need to have root/administrator privileges. It is the responsibility of each relay to ensure that the correspondence between the incoming streams and outgoing streams is hidden from the attacker.

The *threat model* of Tor assumes that the adversary is not global, i.e. she can observe and control only part of the network, but not the entire network. This is a common assumption in all practical low-latency systems. The threat model of Tor does allow for an adversary who can observe and control (add, delete, delay packets) some fraction of the Tor nodes, and operate their own Tor nodes.

There are many similarities between the way Tor routes its traffic and circuit switched networks from telecommunications. In fact, the random path chosen by the sender is referred to as the

Figure 16. Different components involved when routing through the Tor network. (Adapted from Tor: Overview (2009).)

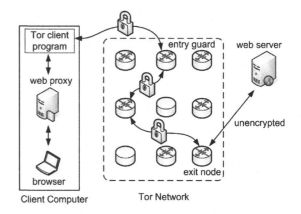

circuit. The discussion on path construction so far glossed over one important detail—establishment of secret keys with the Onion Routers along the path without compromising anonymity. The next subsection discusses the manner in which Tor preserves anonymity when creating circuits.

Circuit Creation and Destruction

Circuits are constructed incrementally, one relay at a time. Symmetric keys with each Onion Router (OR) on the circuit are negotiated using the Diffie-Hellman key exchange protocol. Returning to our example from Figure 15, we show the step-by-step process Alice follows to create a circuit between her and Bob.

Alice starts out by sending the Create Cell message which contains the first step of the Diffie-Hellman (DH) handshake g^i encrypted with Carol's public key. Carol responds with the second step of DH by sending g^j, along with a hash of the negotiated key $K_c = g^{ij}$. This key K_c is used for all subsequent communication with Carol for this session, and computationally expensive public encryption is not used for the remainder of the session with Carol. This completes the construction of the first segment of the circuit. Alice and Carol refer to this segment of the circuit as C_{ac}.

Next, Alice sends an Extend Cell message to Carol. This message contains the address of the next OR (David in this example) and g^k encrypted with David's public key. Carol creates a new Circuit ID C_{cd} and associates C_{ac} with it. The association is known only to Carol; neither Alice nor David is aware of it. David completes the DH handshake initiated by Alice by responding with g^l, along with a hash of the negotiated key $K_d = g^{kl}$ and sends it to Carol who relays the response back to Alice with the Extended Cell message containing this information. With this, building of the second segment is done. Alice and David now share the symmetric key $K_d = g^{kl}$.

This process continues with Alice sending David an Extend Cell request, resulting in Alice establishing a symmetric key K_b with Bob.

Once the entire circuit is established two-way communication takes place between the end nodes as described in the Onion Routing section.

There are two points about this construction that are noteworthy: 1) though Alice knows that she is handshaking with David and Bob, they have no idea that it is Alice on the other end, and 2) according to protocol analysis performed by Dingledine et al. (2004) this method of constructing circuits is secure and achieves perfect forward secrecy under the Dolev & Yao (1981) model.

Circuits are torn down at the request of the initiator with the Destroy message. Each OR in the circuit that receives a Destroy message

- closes all streams on that circuit and
- forwards the Destroy message.

There is another mechanism to take down a circuit—the Relay Truncate message that is directed at a single OR on a circuit. When an OR receives Relay Truncate message from the initiator, it

- sends out a Destroy message forward
- responds back with the Relay Truncated message to the initiator
- the initiator then sends the Extend Cell message to form a modified circuit.

This is also useful when one of the ORs goes down—the neighboring OR can send the Relay Truncated message to the initiator.

Attacks on Tor

Tor, and Onion Routing networks in general, are vulnerable to several attacks. In this section, we consider some that are theoretical in nature and some that are very practical.

There is a broad category of attacks called *path selection attacks*. It is important in Tor that the initiator pick the nodes on the circuit so that that the end nodes cannot collude. If they do, the whole circuit can be inferred as the default circuit length is three. The default circuit length value is chosen so that the latency is kept to a minimum. It appears that an immediate fix for this problem is to choose a longer path length. That may not always work; if an adversary-controlled OR cooperates to extend the circuit *only* to other adversary-controlled ORs while refusing to extend the path to any other ORs, then even a longer path does not help. A related attack involves overloading the legitimate ORs to a point where they cannot respond to requests for new circuit construction, introducing a new set of adversary-controlled ORs into the mix, and steering new circuits to choose a path through them.

Next consider *intersection* attacks. These attacks are based on the assumption that ORs that are not continuously present on the network could not have been part of any circuits. Hence the attacker can eliminate them from consideration and narrow the set of ORs that might have participated.

The Tor exit nodes pose a threat to confidentiality. Since anyone can volunteer to run a Tor node, an attacker would have total access to the data that is being routed if the attacker happens to run the exit node of a circuit. Zetter (2007) reports how Dan Egerstad, a security researcher, collected several hundred email account passwords by sniffing on an exit node. He reportedly collected thousands of private e-mail messages sent by foreign embassies and human rights groups around the world. The exit nodes can also carry out an MITM attack by sending back a bogus certificate for the website the initiator wishes to connect. In fact the attack described in the MITM Attack Using Other Means section that netted Marlinspike several hundred email account credentials was mounted from Tor exit nodes.

The most powerful attacks on Tor, and onion routing in general, are statistical attacks based on time measurements and correlations in traffic patterns. These are usually carried out using *congestion* attacks. In these attacks, the adversary monitors the connection between two nodes, creates a path through the network and clogs it to see if that affects the speed of the connection. If one of the nodes is on the path being monitored, the speed should change. In the next subsection, we demonstrate one such practical attack.

Concrete Attack

This section presents a powerful attack that is due to Murdoch & Danezis (2005). It takes advantage of Tor's overly simplistic round-robin policy of relaying cells from the input queues to the output buffer at ORs. The implication of this policy is that a higher load, even due to one extra connection, on a Tor node will result in higher latency of all other connections routed through it. Their attack is particularly powerful because it proves that adversaries with even with modest capabilities can deanonymize Tor users. Our presentation here follows a slight modification to the original attack proposed recently by Evans et al. (2009). The modified attack is effective against the current Tor system with hundreds of ORs. Even though the attack works only for HTTP connections, it is conceptually simple to describe.

In order to describe the attack, we must include a brief description of the scheduling policy each relay implements to forward data from the input queues to the output queue. Tor data is packaged into fixed-size cells (512 bytes), which upon arrival at a relay are buffered before forwarding. Cells from each circuit are queued separately. Each relay simply iterates over all input queues, removes the first cell from every nonempty queue and places it in the output buffer. While this simple round-robin forwarding scheme is fair, it makes the flow pattern through the relay very predictable. As a result, relays become susceptible to congestion attacks.

Three design features of Tor are necessary for this attack to work: 1) the round robin policy at every OR without any addition of random delays,

2) free availability of the addresses of all Tor routers, and 3) no restriction on users from creating paths of arbitrary length.

The attack begins by the attacker running an exit node and attempting to deanonymize the Tor users accessing HTTP servers through the node. For each path that he attempts to deanonymize, he already knows the middle node—he only needs to find out the entry node.

For every Tor node X that he suspects to be the entry node of the path between victim A connecting to web site B, he runs the following test. He creates a long circuit that goes through X multiple times and places X under load by clogging the circuit with fake traffic. At the same time, he modifies the HTML response back from the web server B to the client A by inserting a small amount JavaScript code so that the client browser issues a periodic HTTP request to the server. The requests issued by JavaScript are tiny in size, and their sole purpose is to create a steady stream of probe traffic from the client to the attacker under light load conditions. The attacker sends empty responses to these requests which are thrown away by the browser.

With this setup in place, the attacker can determine whether or not X is the entry node of the path in question: if X is not present on the path, the probe traffic should arrive at periodic intervals under a congestion attack through X. But how does the normal traffic interfere with the arrival times of the probe traffic? After all, it is not reason-able to assume that the network is lightly loaded while the attack is taking place. The solution is to establish a baseline for normal traffic load on the circuit before and after the congestion attack.

Newer versions of Tor implement a fix to this attack. The fix involves keeping track of the path lengths and limiting each circuit to at most eight hops long. Unfortunately this is not a satisfactory solution as the attacker can easily defeat this measure by exiting and reentering the network.

Defenses

To defend against the attacks described in the previous section, one could disable cookies, JavaScript, Java, and all plug-ins in the browser. But, these measures result in unacceptable degradation in browsing experience of the end user. Another solution is to use HTTPS. This will prevent sniffing and MITM attacks at the exit node. Also, the JavaScript injection attack fails when HTTPS is used.

The other options include increasing the default path length in Tor at the expense of increasing the latency. This defense has an adverse effect on the responsiveness of the system in general because it creates more traffic on Tor. Simply increasing the default path length from three to four would increase the traffic by 33%. Another solution is to introduce random delays at ORs in place of the simple round robin policy that is currently used. This again increases the latency of the network.

Figure 17. Traffic analysis attack on Tor

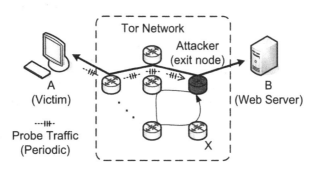

AVAILABILITY

An attack that makes a computer or network resource unavailable is called a *Denial-of-Service* (DoS) attack. When it is a concerted attack by multiple attackers against a single resource, it is termed *Distributed Denial-of-Service (DDoS)* attack. These are generally carried out against high profile targets such as large corporations and financial institutions with intent to disrupt the service provided by them.

A classic DoS example from network security is SYN flooding (Eddy, 2007). To understand this attack, we need to describe the three-way handshake that every client and server must engage in before establishing a TCP connection. In a nutshell, it involves the client initiating a TCP connection request with SYN (synchronize) message. The server acknowledges with SYN-ACK message, which the client acknowledges back with ACK message, completing the handshake.

If the server allocates resources to deal with a new connection request right after receiving a SYN message from the client, then the attacker can exhaust the network resources at the server by flooding the server with SYN requests. Of course, the attacker has no intention of completing any of the initiated handshakes; his only goal is to exhaust server's resource with SYN requests. Once this happens, the server is not in a position to accept any legitimate SYN requests. The attacker has met the objective of disabling the server from establishing any TCP connections with normal clients.

Consider the examples given in the previous sections. During MITM attack, the attacker could simply drop all in-bound and out-bound packets, thus isolating the LAN from the Internet and causing loss of connectivity to all the hosts on the LAN.

Similarly, the adversary can volunteer to run Tor nodes, accept packets, but not relay them. Congestion attacks described in Attacks on Tor section are another form of DoS attack.

As these examples show, it is very easy for an adversary to mount DoS attacks.

KEY MANAGEMENT

The cryptographic techniques discussed in this chapter depend on secure generation, distribution, and management of keys. A number of different approaches have been used for key management, including:

1. Physical key distribution (e.g. couriers)
2. Symmetric key distribution (e.g. Kerberos)
3. Asymmetric key distribution (e.g. PKI certificates)
4. Key agreement protocols (e.g. Diffie-Hellman)
5. Quantum key distribution (also know as. "quantum cryptography")
6. Key elimination (e.g. BBC encoding for jam resistance)

Each of these six approaches has different strengths and weaknesses, so each is typically used in different situation.

Physical Key Distribution

The oldest and simplest method for key distribution is to physically transport the key. This can be slow and cumbersome, but there are several situations where it can be a reasonable way to manage keys.

For example, suppose a small number of banks want to transfer money electronically among them. Security is important, because the ability to modify such messages is equivalent to the ability to counterfeit arbitrarily-large amounts of money. Therefore, the banks might choose to be conservative, using the most thoroughly analyzed cipher available.

By that reasoning, the most conservative cipher would be a symmetric cipher, the Data Encryption Standard (DES). This cipher was approved by the US government three decades ago, and has received more public scrutiny than any other cipher in history. There are no known ways to break it that are significantly faster than a brute force attack of trying all possible keys. The key size of DES is only 56 bits, which allows brute force attacks using modern computers. However, this can problem can be overcome by encrypting the message three times, using two or three different keys. This Triple DES (3DES) gives an effective key size of 112 bits, which cannot be broken by brute force with publically-known algorithms using current technology in a reasonable number of years. Even if someone discovered how to build a large quantum computer, it is not clear that this would allow 3DES to be broken, since the best known algorithm for this, Grover's algorithm, would still require the quantum computer to run for on the order of 2^{56} steps.

Banks commonly use armored courier vehicles to transport cash and other valuables, so it is natural to also use them to distribute 3DES keys. If there are only a handful of major banks in a country that need to communicate this way, then it is possible to establish a separate key for every pair of banks, and distribute these keys by courier. This would be more difficult if new institutions were joining or leaving the network frequently, but banks tend to be stable and new ones are created infrequently.

A system like this can be strengthened by splitting the keys. A bank can protect a key K by generating several random strings of bits $K_1, K_2, \ldots, K_n$, each of which is the same size as K. Then the true key K can be encrypted by XORing it with all of the random keys. The encrypted key and all the random keys are sent by separate armored cars. If all of the cars arrive safely, then the receiver XORs all $n+1$ keys to obtain K. If any cars are lost, then a new key can be generated, and the process repeated. An attacker can only obtain the key K by stealing the keys from all $n+1$ armored

cars, without the thefts being detected; clearly a difficult task.

Another example is distributing keys to diplomats and spies. In that case, the sender and receiver can meet and physically hand over the key. In this case, the key may be used for only a few short messages, and so it may actually be practical to use a perfect, unbreakable cipher: the *One Time Pad* (OTP).

In the OTP, a message is encrypted by XORing it with the key. The resulting cipher text is decrypted by XORing it with the same key. The sender and receiver both destroy the key after use, so the pad of key material is only used one time. The sender and receiver must both have a large set of key material, at least as long as the combination of all the messages that will ever be sent. The OTP is theoretically unbreakable, if the key is perfectly random, used only once, and kept secret.

The Soviet Union started using this system in the 1930 for diplomats and spies, and continued to use it for decades. Kahn (1996) describes how the keys were printed in small books of many pages which were the size of a postage stamp, or were rolled up into pads the size of a cigarette. One of these tiny books could hold hundreds of characters of key, which would be enough to send a number of short messages. The pads were printed on highly flammable sheets, and the spies carried chemicals that could ignite them quickly, destroying the key and all evidence of its existence.

Although physical key distribution for symmetric keys is sometimes used, it is clearly impractical for most networks. A network of n nodes would require on the order of n^2 separate keys to be transferred securely. Also, it is not clear how the system would work when strangers want to communicate. That is why physical key distribution is much less commonly used than the methods described in the next few sections.

Symmetric Key Distribution

A more efficient way to distribute symmetric keys is by sending them through the network itself, using a trusted third party. This can be done using systems such as Kerberos. Typically, such systems are used for communication between people in a single organization, such as a single company or university.

For example, suppose Alice and Bob are on a network and want to communicate, but have not pre-arranged any shared key between them. If they both know and trust Trent, then they can communicate in the following way.

First, Alice will send a message to Trent using a symmetric key that she and Trent share. This key may have been physically transferred earlier. She will tell Trent that she would like to communicate with Bob. Trent then generates a random key, called a session key, and sends it back to her. Alice's message to Trent and his reply including the new key will both be encrypted with the key Alice and Trent share.

Trent then sends a message to Bob, telling him that Alice would like to communicate with him, and sending him the same session key. This message is encrypted with a key shared by Trent and Bob. After that, Alice and Bob can communicate using the new key, and no further communication with Trent is needed.

With this system, every user has only a single key to manage in the long term: the one shared with Trent. Trent must maintain a list of keys for all users, and must be able to generate new random keys quickly. The simple system described here can be extended by adding various acknowledgement messages, stronger forms of authentication (e.g. message authentication codes), time stamps to avoid replay attacks, and other refinements.

There are several drawbacks to such a system. No two people can ever communicate until they first communicate with Trent. This wastes bandwidth, and also paralyzes the entire system if the Trent server ever goes down or becomes inaccessible. The security of Trent is critical, since an attacker that compromises that one server will be able to eavesdrop on all conversations between all users. Furthermore, there is still the problem of establishing the initial keys shared by Trent and each user. In a company or university, that key can be physically handed to each person when a new employee or student arrives, or physically installed on their computer by a trusted employee. But if this were scaled up to cover all users of the Internet, that could become difficult.

Asymmetric Key Distribution

The last two methods were appropriate for any key, especially symmetric keys. In the case of asymmetric keys, other methods become possible. These methods are typically much easier to scale to large networks, including the entire Internet.

The Background section on cryptography described asymmetric algorithms such as RSA which have a public and private key. This makes key distribution far easier, because the private key doesn't need to be distributed (it is known by only one person), and the public key doesn't need to be kept secret (it's known by everyone).

Suppose Alice wants to be able to receive encrypted messages and send signed messages. To do so, she can generate a public/private key pair. She will keep the private key secret. She could publicize the public key, perhaps by posting it on her website or emailing to other people.

If Bob then wants to communicate with Alice, he would need her public key in order to encrypt his message. But even if he receives her public key from her website or email, he has a problem. How does he know that key truly belongs to Alice? If the key actually belonged to the eavesdropper Eve, and if Bob used that key to encrypt his message to Alice, then Eve could easily decrypt and read the message, re-encrypt it with Alice's true public key, and send it on to Alice. This would allow Eve to perform an MITM attack, as described in the Trust, Certificates, Man-In-The-Middle Attack section.

So for asymmetric keys, the problem is not key distribution, but key authentication. This is usually done by certificates, as mentioned before. There are a number of ways that certificates can be handled.

Programs like Pretty Good Privacy (PGP) work on the principle of a "web of trust". Alice might have several friends sign certificates for her public key. If any of her friends are also friends of Bob, then he might trust them, and accept the key as genuine. Or he might be more cautious, and require at least *n* signatures by people he trusts before he will believe a key is real. Or he might be less cautious and accept Carol's signature on Alice's certificate, because even though he doesn't know Carol personally, he does see that Carol's key is signed by someone he does know. Hence the "web" of trust.

This approach raises an interesting question. Is trust actually transitive? If Bob trusts his friends, does that mean he should trust strangers who have simply had their identity verified by his friends? It also raises the question of what trust means. If Bob trusts his friends to be honest, does that also mean he trusts them to be experts in recognizing fake drivers' licenses? Does it mean he trusts that their computers will never become infected with malware that will sign certificates in their name?

For these reasons, Certificate Authorities (CAs) have become a much more common way of authenticating public keys. If a trusted company signs Alice's certificate, then presumably Bob can trust that the public key truly belongs to Alice.

However, there are still a number of questions that are raised. A modern computer typically comes with a number of different CAs pre-installed as trusted. If even one of them is compromised, then Eve will be able to use it to create false certificates in Alice's name, and launch MITM attacks on her.

Even if the CA is trustworthy, there are still questions about what the certificate means. Some certificates merely say that a given public key is associated with whoever controls a given email account. Some might be more thorough, verifying that the person's claimed name ("Alice Smith") actually appeared on something that looked like a driver's license or birth certificate. Theoretically, certificates could even include verified DNA measurements to prove identity, but that hasn't been done much in practice.

Key Agreement Protocols

Certificates are a powerful mechanism, but they are not always convenient. Most Internet users do not currently have a certificate. Key agreement protocols can be used to achieve some of the same benefits, with less work on the user's part. A common example of this is the Diffie-Hellman key exchange protocol described in the Background section.

Suppose Alice and Bob want to communicate securely over the Internet, but have never met, have no certificates, and have no trusted friends in common. Clearly, no matter what they do, they will not be able to protect themselves from an active attack by Eve, who cuts their communication wires, and inserts herself in between. She will be able to launch MITM attacks without detection.

However, this can actually be difficult for Eve in some situations. She must be able to not only read the traffic flowing between Alice and Bob, but actively intercept those messages and prevent them from getting through. If the network is the Internet, then Eve can't just passively eavesdrop; she must actively control servers or routers to stop or modify certain packets.

Therefore, Alice and Bob may decide that there is some benefit to having a protocol that protects them from passive eavesdropping, even if it doesn't protect them from active MITM attacks. Fortunately, Diffie-Hellman key exchange can do that. It generates a session key that will securely encrypt all messages during the session. As long as Eve is only a passive eavesdropper, she will not get the session key.

Protocols like Diffie-Hellman can be further strengthened if the messages are signed. This is implemented in SSL. Suppose Alice has no certificate and is a customer, and Bob is an online store and has a certificate signed by a CA that Alice trusts. Then theoretically, Alice should be able to perform Diffie-Hellman with Bob (who digitally signs each message), and be secure even from active attacks by Eve. The MITM Attack on SSL Using Bogus Certificates section gives an example of how this has failed in practice because of flaws in how the system is designed and implemented.

Even when such flaws are fixed, there can still be problems. On current browsers, if Alice goes to a website with an invalid certificate, there will typically be a popup dialog asking her if that is OK. Most users have been trained by long experience to automatically click OK on all such popup boxes. So security can be compromised, even when the cryptography and protocols are flawless.

Quantum Key Distribution

The perfect security of a One Time Pad is very appealing. The only problem is key distribution. There is a form of key distribution based on quantum mechanics that is also perfectly secure. This is called *Quantum Key Distribution* (QKD) and is also known by the name of *quantum cryptography*.

If Alice are in separate buildings that have good security, and if they correctly implement QKD systems, then they can run a fiber optic cable between their buildings and communicate in a way that is perfectly secure. Eve can cut the fiber and manipulate it any way she wants, she will never be able to read or modify any messages, assuming the QKD was implemented perfectly.

The system takes advantage of an interesting property of quantum mechanics. It is possible to force a photon of light to be polarized in one of two orthogonal directions (vertically or horizontally) or in one of two diagonal directions (tilted left 45 degrees or tilted right). A person receiving that photon can measure it in one of two ways: orthogonally or diagonally.

If the photon was polarized vertically or horizontally, then an orthogonal measurement will determine which way it was polarized. If the photon was polarized diagonally to the left or right, then a diagonal measurement will determine which. However, if the photon was polarized orthogonally (vertically or horizontally) and is measured diagonally, the result will be random: there is an equal chance of getting the result "tilted left" or "tilted right". Similarly, if it was polarized with a tilt of left or right, and it's measured orthogonally, then the result is random ("vertical" or "horizontal"). Finally, a measurement of either type will destroy the photon's polarization. So the receiver gets only one chance to measure the photon before all information is lost.

The core idea in QKD is simple. Alice will send Bob a sequence of photons. Alice will randomly choose one of the 4 polarizations for each one. Bob will randomly choose one of two measurements for each photon: orthogonal or diagonal. After many photons have been sent and measured, Alice and Bob will communicate on an ordinary channel, such as through the Internet.

On that ordinary channel, Alice will tell Bob whether each photon she sent was orthogonal or diagonal. Bob will tell Alice which measurement he performed on each photon. For about half the

Figure 18. Quantum key distribution

photons, Alice's choice will be different from his measurement, so the two of them will ignore those. For the rest, each photon will have transmitted one random bit. If Alice and Bob both happened to chose orthogonal for a given photon, then Bob's measurement will reveal a result that is identical to what Alice chose, either vertical or horizontal. This generates a bit, say 0 for horizontal and 1 for vertical, that becomes a shared secret between Alice and Bob. Given a large number of such bits, Alice and Bob can use them as a One Time Pad to encrypt other messages.

If Eve simply eavesdrops, she'll learn nothing useful. She'll know which photons they agreed on, and which were orthogonal and which were diagonal. But she won't know whether they were vertical/horizontal/tilted left/tilted right. So she won't know any bits of the pad.

If Eve cuts the fiber, she can intercept all the photons, measure them, and then send them on. But if there is a photon that Alice and Bob happen to measure the same way, but which Eve happens to measure differently, Eve will learn nothing about that bit, and the bit received by Bob will be random, so Alice and Bob can erroneously end up with a different bit in that position in the shared pad that is created.

The description above is simplified. There are a number of details involved in condensing the pad to deal with small errors introduced by Eve, and verifying that the open communication about measurements is not corrupted by Eve. But the description above has the essential elements of quantum key distribution.

This approach has the advantage that it is theoretically perfect. Even an infinite number of computers could not break the resulting cipher in infinite time. There are several drawbacks to it. By its very nature, it requires a direct connection from Alice to Bob. It can't be done over the existing Internet. Alice and Bob must lay fiber between them, or have a direct line of sight. Fortunately, it has been demonstrated over fairly long distances (hundreds of kilometers). In fact, it should be

possible to perform such communication from a ground station to a satellite, and then have the satellite perform the reverse back to the ground. The sender and receiver hardware must be very sensitive to make it work. One might ask whether any given implementation is perfect, or whether some small flaw leaks information that could be useful to an attacker. There is no simple way to test whether the implementation is perfect. So although it is perfect in theory, it is an open question how secure it would be in practice.

Key Elimination

The best way to manage keys is to eliminate the need for them in the first place. This is especially important in areas where there are no asymmetric algorithms, and only symmetric algorithms exist. Perhaps the best example of this is in the assurance of availability for wireless networks.

When combating DoS attacks on wireless networks, one important factor is jam resistance. It should be difficult for an attacker to jam the communication by broadcasting radio frequency noise or other wireless signals. Jam resistant methods have been known for many decades. All of them are based on the use of a symmetric key. There is no equivalent of asymmetric keys for jam resistance.

For this reason, key management can be a problem in large wireless networks that are intended to be resistant to jamming. The problem is even worse for Mobile Ad Hoc Networks (MANETs), which involve many radios that are in motion, and that constantly form new connections to create a constantly-changing network. In that case, the secret key would have to be loaded into every node that might ever connect to the network. For very large MANETs, this can pose a serious problem. If an attacker captures even one of the radios and extracts the key from it, that key could be used to jam the entire network. Therefore the key should be changed frequently. But that can be a challenge when there is a large, distributed network of radios.

This key management problem was solved for the first time in 2007 with the development of concurrent codes and the BBC algorithm (Baird et. al., 2007; Bahn et. al., 2008). With these new techniques, it was finally possible to have jam resistance without any key or secret at all. That eliminated the need for keys for jam resistance, and so eliminated the need to manage the symmetric keys. Messages traversing such a network might still have encryption and digital signatures, to ensure confidentiality and authenticity, but those could be achieved with symmetric keys. As seen in the previous sections, key management tends to be much easier for symmetric keys than for asymmetric.

The next section describes this new algorithm in more detail.

WIRELESS AVAILABILITY— JAM RESISTANCE

Availability is one of the three goals of network security as mentioned in the Introduction. For a wireless network, this includes resistance to jamming. An attacker can launch a DoS attack by broadcasting radio frequency noise, with a large amount of power. This can overwhelm the legitimate signal, and prevent wireless messages from being received. In many cases, the attacker can accomplish the same thing without using much power at all, by crafting special signals designed to disrupt the particular form of wireless communication being used.

The attacker would usually prefer a low-power attack. If an attack requires megawatts of energy, that prevents the attacker from using small, battery-powered devices. It is also much easier for the authorities to track down the attacker (or the attacking device) and shut it down. The attacker would prefer to use cheap, low-power devices

to do the jamming. These low-power attacks are foiled by jam resistant systems.

In traditional jam resistance, some form of spread spectrum radio communication is used. In order to be jam resistant, it must create a communication channel that is a function of a secret key, shared by the sender and receiver.

For example, in a frequency hopping system, the sender broadcasts a signal at a particular frequency. Then, it jumps to a new frequency. These jumps occur many times per second. The key is used to choose the sequence of frequencies. The legitimate receiver knows the secret key, and so is able to listen to the correct frequencies in the correct sequence, in order to receive the message. If the attacker does not know the key, then the attacker cannot guess which frequency sequence will be used. So the attacker must jam all of the frequencies (or a large fraction of them), which requires a large amount of power. However, if the attacker discovers the key, then the jammer can jam just the frequency in use at each moment, jumping in synchrony with the sender and receiver, and can accomplish this jamming with very little power.

Another approach is pulse-based systems. The following is a simplified version of it. If a message is to be sent during a one-second period, the sender divides that period into many small time slices. The key is used to select a small number of time slices, perhaps one out of every thousand. For the nth chosen time slice, if the nth bit of the message is a 0, then the sender is silent. If it is a 1, then the sender broadcasts a short, powerful burst of radio frequency noise that spans a very broad part of the spectrum. A receiver who knows the secret key will be able to calculate which time slices to observe, and will easily recover the message. An attacker who knows the secret key will be able to broadcast pulses in all of the chosen time slices, which the receiver will interpret as the message "111111…", and so the jammer is successful with very little power consumption. Conversely, if the attacker does not know the key, then the attacker must fill every time slice with a pulse (or a large fraction of them). That requires 1000 times as much power, in this example.

With the development of concurrent codes and the BBC algorithm (Baird et. al., 2007), it is now possible to send jam-resistant messages without any secret key at all. The algorithms to encode and decode BBC are given in Figures 19 and 21.

Figure 20 gives an example of BBC encoding the message "1011" without using a key. The encoding is simple. First, several zeros are appended to the message to act as checksum bits. In this example, two zeros are appended, yielding

the string "101100". Next, all possible prefixes of that string are found. These are shown in the table in the first column, under the "S". The period of time used for the message is divided up into time slices. In this example, the period is divided up into 25 slices, which are numbered from 1 to 25. Finally, a hash function is used to convert each prefix string into a number from 1 to 25. A hash function is simply a function that scrambles its inputs in a random-looking way. A standard hash function such as SHA-1 or MD5 could be used. It doesn't have to be secret. It is assumed that the sender, receiver, and attacker all

Figure 19. Algorithm for BBC encoding

```
Algorithm: BBCencode(M)
This function broadcasts an m-bit message M[1 . . .m], adding k checksum bits
to the end of the message. H is a hash function. The definition of H and the
values of m and k are public (not secret).

Append k zero bits to the end of M
for  i ← 1 ... m + k do
          Send a pulse at the time given by H(M[1 . . . i])
end for
```

Figure 20. BBC encoding of the message "1011"

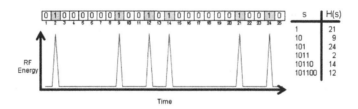

s	H(s)
1	21
10	9
101	24
1011	2
10110	14
101100	12

Figure 21. Algorithm for BBC decoding

```
Algorithm: BBCdecode(n)
This recursive function can be used to decode all the messages found in a given packet by calling
BBCdecode(1). There must be a global M[1 . . .m + k] which is a string of m + k bits. The number
of bits in a message is m, and the number of checksum zeros appended to the message is k. H is
a hash function. The definition of H and values of m and k are public (not secret).

if n = m + k + 1
          output "One of the messages is:" M[1 . . .m]
else
          if n > m
                    limit←0
          else
                    limit←1
          end if
          for  i ← 0 ... limit do
                    M[n] ←i
                    if there was a pulse at time H(M[1 . . . n])
                              BBCdecode(n + 1)
                    end if
          end for
end if
```

know the hash function. In this example the hash function is given in the table. Each of the strings in the "S" column maps to the number in the "H(S)" column. Finally, the sender broadcasts a strong pulse of radio noise in each time slot chosen by the hash function.

This is a simple algorithm. Any message can be quickly converted to a sequence of pulses. There are no secrets involved. An attacker cannot jam this by broadcasting just a few pulses. If an attacker can broadcast a pulse in every single time slot, then of course it would be jammed, but that would require far more energy. This system has been mathematically proven to be secure, in the sense that no attacker can jam it without using far more energy than the legitimate sender (Baird et. al., 2008).

Figure 22 shows the decoding of two messages sent at the same time. The receiver observes the bitwise OR of the two packets. The timing of pulses observed by the receiver is labeled "Both simultaneously", with a 1 for each pulse detected, and a 0 for radio silence. The receiver must decode those 25 bits to recover the two messages that were sent: "1000" and "1011".

The packet is decoded by following a tree of possible prefixes. The receiver knows that whatever messages were sent, each one must have started with either a 0 or 1. If a message started with 0, then the shortest prefix would have been

simply "0", and there would have been a pulse at time H(0). Similarly, if any messages started with 1, there would be a pulse at time H(1). In this example, H(0) = 4 and H(1) = 21. Note that there is a pulse at time 21, but not at time 4. That tells the receiver that at least one message was sent that started with 1, but none were sent that started with 0. In the tree, the box labeled "0" is white, indicating that there was no pulse at time H(0), and the box for "1" is gray, indicating that there was a pulse at time H(1).

At this point, the first bit of the message has been decoded. It is a 1. The receiver knows that whatever messages were sent that started with 1, the second bit must be 0 or 1. Therefore the first two bits together must be 10 or 11. The receiver therefore checks at time H(10) = 9 and H(11) = 21 and notices a pulse in both locations. Therefore, the receiver concludes there are actually two messages being received, and continues exploring the tree down both of those branches.

When the receiver finishes the fourth bit, the complete messages are now obtained. In this example, the receiver obtained the messages 1000, 1011, and 1110. That last message is actually spurious: it only appeared to exist because each of its prefixes happened to hash to the same location as some prefix of one of the legitimate messages. However, the receiver doesn't stop there. There were several checksum zeros appended to the end

Figure 22. BBC decoding of two messages sent simultaneously

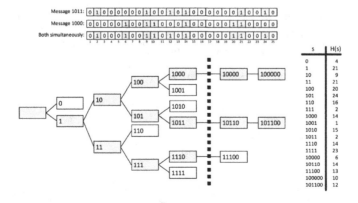

of the message (2 of them, in this example). The receiver adds on each of those zeros, and checks to ensure there are pulses at those locations as well. The spurious message is caught this way, and only the two legitimate messages survive.

Of course, an attacker can always read the messages and send additional messages. If this is undesirable, the sender would encrypt and sign messages before doing the BBC encoding. And the receiver would check the signature and decrypt them after doing the BBC decoding. The encryption and signatures can be done with asymmetric keys. The BBC encoding eliminates the symmetric keys required by traditional jam resistance. This greatly simplifies the key distribution and management problem, as discussed in the previous section.

OPEN PROBLEMS

We conclude this chapter with some open problems in network security. Defending anonymizing networks like Tor against the attacks described in this chapter, while minimizing latency and keeping the system usable is a challenging open problem. Unless the system is responsive and useable, not enough users would use it. If there are not enough users on the system, it is not possible to achieve a high degree of anonymity.

Network security is a broad area with issues ranging from identity theft, network intrusions, to session hijacking. The case studies presented here show that without strong mathematical techniques, it is impossible to build practical systems that are secure. The attacks we presented show adversaries commonly side-step cryptographic protections, thus proving that mathematical foundations are necessary but not sufficient. One area that is in need of formal methods is network intrusion detection. The goal is to build a system that can automatically identify attempts by an intruder to compromise the confidentiality, integrity or availability of a resource over the network. The current

systems fall significantly short of achieving this goal. The alarm volume from sensors deployed at different client sites can be in the millions at managed security service centers, out of which over 99% are false alarms (Treinen & Thurimella, 2006). Finding true alarms from false ones in this environment is a great challenge. Past attempts using statistical modeling, analysis of traffic patterns, and enumeration of possible attack paths have all met with limited success. We believe fundamentally new techniques based on solid mathematical foundations are required.

ACKNOWLEDGMENT

The authors are grateful to the referee, Christian Grothoff, Will Mitchell, and James Treinen for their helpful comments. Their feedback helped improve the presentation significantly. Dr. Thurimella would also like to gratefully acknowledge the partial support he received from the NSF under Grants No. DUE – 0416969 and DUE – 0911991. Dr. Baird would also like to gratefully acknowledge support that he received from the Air Force Information Operations Center (AFIOC), Lackland AFB, TX, for work performed at the Academy Center for Cyberspace Research (ACCR) at the United States Air Force Academy. Any opinions, findings and conclusions or recommendations expressed in this material are those of the author and do not necessarily reflect those of the NSF or AFIOC.

REFERENCES

Bahn, W. L., Baird, L. C., III, & Collins, M. D. (2008). Jam resistant communications without shared secrets. In *Proceedings of the 3rd International Conference on Information Warfare and Security*, 37-44, Omaha, Nebraska, 2008.

Baird III, L. C., & Bahn, W. L. (2008). *Security Analysis of BBC Coding* (Technical Report). U. S. Air Force Academy, Academy Center for Cyberspace Research, USAFA-TR-2008-ACCR-01, Dec 8

Baird III, L. C., Bahn, W. L., & Collins, M. D. (2007). *Jam-Resistant Communication Without Shared Secrets Through the Use of Concurrent Codes* (Technical Report). U. S. Air Force Academy, USAFA-TR-2007-01, Feb 14.

CCV. (2009). *Certificate chain verification.* Retrieved March 15, 2009, from http://publib. boulder.ibm.com/infocenter/tpfhelp/current/index.jsp?topic=/com.ibm.ztpf-ztpfdf.doc_put.cur/gtps5/s5vctch.html

Chaum, D. (1981). Untraceable electronic mail, return addresses, and digital pseudonyms. *Communications of the ACM, 24*(2), 84–88. doi:10.1145/358549.358563

Cooper, D., Santesson, S., Farrell, S., Boeyen, S., Housley, R., & Polk, W. (2008). *Internet X.509 Public Key Infrastructure Certificate and Certificate Revocation List (CRL) Profile,* RFC 5280, at http://tools.ietf.org/html/rfc5280

Daemen, J., & Rijmen, V. (2002). *The Design of Rijndael: AES-The Advanced Encryption Standard.* Berlin-Heidelberg, Germany: Springer-Verlag.

Data Encryption Standard (DES). (1999). *Federal Information Processing Standards Publication.* Retrieved May 29, 2009, from http://csrc.nist.gov/publications/fips/fips46-3/fips46-3.pdf

Dierks, T., & Allen, C. (1999). *The TLS Protocol.* RFC 2246, at http://www.ietf.org/rfc/rfc2246.txt

Diffie, W., & Hellman, M. E. (1976). New Directions in Cryptography. *IEEE Transactions on Information Theory, IT-22*(6), 644–654. doi:10.1109/TIT.1976.1055638

Diffie, W., & Hellman, M. E. (2009). *Diffie-Hellman key exchange.* Retrieved March 15, 2009, from http://en.wikipedia.org/wiki/Diffie-Hellman

Dingledine, R., Mathewson, N., & Syverson, P. (2004). Tor: The second-generation onion router. In *Proceedings of the 13th USENIX Security Symposium,* 303–320.

Dolev, D., & Yao, A. C. (1981). On the security of public key protocols. In *Proceedings of the IEEE 22nd Annual Symposium on Foundations of Computer Science,* 350-357.

Eddy, W. (2007). *TCP SYN Flooding Attacks and Common Mitigations,* RFC 4987, at http://www.ietf.org/rfc/rfc4987.txt

ElGamal, T. (1985). A Public-Key Cryptosystem and a Signature Scheme Based on Discrete Logarithms. *IEEE Transactions on Information Theory, IT-31*(4), 469–472. doi:10.1109/TIT.1985.1057074

Evans, N. S., Dingledine, R., & Grothoff, C. (2009). *A Practical Congestion Attack on Tor Using Long Paths.* To be presented at the 18th USENIX Security Symposium, Montreal, Canada.

Goldschlag, D. M., Reed, M. G., & Syverson, P. F. (1999). Onion routing. *Communications of the ACM, 42*(2), 39–41. doi:10.1145/293411.293443

Kahn, D. (1996). *The Code-Breakers: The Comprehensive History of Secret Communication from Ancient Times to the Internet.* New York: Scribner.

Marlinspike, M. (2009). *New Techniques for Defeating SSL/TLS.* Presented at Black Hat DC Briefings 2009, Crystal City, USA, Feb 16-19, 2009. Slides are at http://www.blackhat.com/presentations/bh-dc-09/Marlinspike/BlackHat-DC-09-Marlinspike-Defeating-SSL.pdf

Murdoch, S. J., & Danezis, G. (2005). Low-Cost Traffic Analysis of Tor. In *Proceedings of the 2005 IEEE Symposium on Security and Privacy*, 183-195, Washington DC.

PCRPS. (n.d.). *Publius Censorship Resistant Publishing System*, Retrieved March 16, 2009, from http://cs.nyu.edu/~waldman/publius/

PKI. (n.d.). *Public Key Infrastructure*. Retrieved March 15, 2009, from http://en.wikipedia.org/wiki/Public_key_infrastructure

Rivest, R., Shamir, A., & Adleman, L. (1978). A Method for Obtaining Digital Signatures and Public-Key Cryptosystems. *Communications of the ACM, 21*(2), 120–126. doi:10.1145/359340.359342

SSL. (n.d.). *The SSL Handshake*, Retrieved March 15, 2009, from http://publib.boulder.ibm.com/infocenter/tivihelp/v2r1/index.jsp?topic=/com.ibm.itame2.doc_5.1/ss7aumst18.htm

Stamp, M. (2006). *Information Security: Principles and Practice*. Hoboken, NJ: John Wiley & Sons.

Syverson, P., Goldschlag, D., & Reed, M. (1997). Anonymous Connections and Onion Routing. In *Proceedings of the IEEE Symposium on Security and Privacy*, 44-54.

Tews, E., Weinmann, R. P., & Pyshkin, A. (2007). *Breaking 104 bit WEP in less than 60 seconds.* Cryptology ePrint Archive, no. 2007/120. Retrieved from http://eprint.iacr.org

Tor (n.d.). *Tor: Overview*. Retrieved March 16, 2009, from http://www.torproject.org/overview.html.en

Treinen, J. J., & Thurimella, R. (2006). A Framework for the Application of Association Rule Mining in Large Intrusion Detection Infrastructures. In *Proceedings of Recent Advances in Intrusion Detection* (pp. 1–18). RAID. doi:10.1007/11856214_1

Wagner, R. (2001). *Address Resolution Protocol Spoofing and Man-in-the-Middle Attacks*. Retrieved from http://www.sans.org/rr/whitepapers/threats/474.php

Zetter, K. (n.d.). *Rogue Nodes Turn Tor Anonymizer into Eavesdropper's Paradise*, http://www.wired.com/politics/security/news/2007/09/embassy_hacks

Zimmermann, H. (1980). OSI Reference Model—The ISO Model of Architecture for Open Systems Interconnection. *IEEE Transactions on Communications, 28*(4), 425–432. doi:10.1109/TCOM.1980.1094702

Chapter 2
Cryptography–Based Authentication for Protecting Cyber Systems

Xunhua Wang
James Madison University, USA

Hua Lin
University of Virginia, USA

ABSTRACT

Entity authentication is a fundamental building block for system security and has been widely used to protect cyber systems. Nonetheless, the role of cryptography in entity authentication is not very clear, although cryptography is known for providing confidentiality, integrity, and non-repudiation. This chapter studies the roles of cryptography in three entity authentication categories: knowledge-based authentication, token-based authentication, and biometric authentication. For these three authentication categories, we discuss (1) the roles of cryptography in the generation of password verification data, in password-based challenge/response authentication protocol, and in password-authenticated key exchange protocols; (2) the roles of cryptography in both symmetric key-based and private key-based token authentications; (3) cryptographic fuzzy extractors, which can be used to enhance the security and privacy of biometric authentication. This systematic study of the roles of cryptography in entity authentication will deepen our understanding of both cryptography and entity authentication and can help us better protect cyber systems.

INTRODUCTION

Entity authentication studies how to verify the identity of an entity (either a human being or a computer) and it is a fundamental issue in protecting cyber systems, including web services and web applications.

DOI: 10.4018/978-1-61520-783-1.ch002

Four factors can be used to authenticate an entity, namely, *what you know*, *what you have*, *who you are*, and *where you are*. A what-you-know authentication verifies an entity through the proof of memorable knowledge, such as a password, a PIN number, or the answer to a specific question. Password authentication is the most commonly seen *knowledge-based authentication*. A what-you-have authentication verifies an entity through the proof of possession of a hardware *token*, which stores a strong secret that most human beings have difficulty to remember. Example hardware tokens include a USB token, a smartcard, and a Radio Frequency Identification (RFID). A who-you-are authentication verifies a *human being user* through his/her biological or behavioral characteristics and hence is also called *biometric authentication*. Example biological characteristics include fingerprints, voices, faces, iris and DNA; example behavioral characteristics include handwritten signature and keystrokes. A where-you-are authentication verifies an entity through its geographical location, for example, through the global positioning system (GPS).

What roles does cryptography play in these entity authentication categories? This question turns out to be surprisingly elusive. This is in sharp contrast to the fact that cryptography is widely known for providing *data confidentiality* through encryption (including symmetric-key encryption and public-key encryption), *data integrity* through message authentication code (MAC, such as cipher-based MAC and hash-based MAC), and *non-repudiation* through digital signatures.

This book chapter is to fill this gap and provide a comprehensive view on the important roles of cryptography in the first three authentication factors for protecting cyber systems. First, in the what-you-know authentication category, we will focus on three significant roles of cryptography in password authentication: (1) the application of cryptographic hash functions in the generation of password verification data (PVD) to protect against malicious server administrator and server compromise-based network attacks; (2) the use of cryptographic algorithms in the password-based challenge/response protocol, which has been used by Microsoft Windows authentication and HTTP digest authentication; (3) the marriage of password authentication with cryptographic key exchange protocols, resulting in password-authenticated key exchange (PAKE) protocols that offer password-based *mutual* authentication.

Second, in the token-based what-you-have authentication category, we will study the cases where a token stores either a symmetric key or the private key of a public/private key pair. For symmetric key-based authentication, we focus on the symmetric key-based challenge/response authentication paradigm and its applications. For private key-based authentication, we shall focus on the authenticated key exchange paradigm, which has been used in IP Security (IPsec) Internet Key Exchange (IKE), Secure Socket Layer (SSL), and Secure Shell (SSH).

Third, in the biometric-based who-you-are authentication category, we will study *fuzzy extractor*, a new cryptographic primitive that can be used to enhance the security and privacy of biometric authentication through protecting biometric reference templates.

This chapter is organized around cryptography's roles in these authentication categories. Before going into these details, we shall first review some basic authentication concepts in next section.

BACKGROUND

Network-Based Entity Authentication

Some network applications are designed to serve certain users, not the public. Example applications of this type include online banking, web email, and online payment services. To access such a service, an entity has to authenticate itself first. In this authentication scenario, the entity to be authenticated is called *the client* and the service provider is called *the server*. The authentication of the client to the server is called *client-side authentication*; the authentication of the server to the client is called *server-side authentication*. When used alone, client-side authentication is a *one-way authentication*; so is server-side authentication. When the client and the server are authenticated together, the authentication is *mutual*.

In a *local authentication*, the authenticate data between the client and the server travel in a *trusted* local environment. In this environment, the server is often trusted and only the client is needed to be authenticated.

In contrast, in a *remote authentication*, the authentication data are transported over an *insecure* public network such as the Internet, where the authentication data may be eavesdropped, modified, replayed, and forged. In this malicious environment, the server may also be spoofed and thus mutual authentication is often required.

Attacks against Network-Based Entity Authentication

An authentication mechanism is considered *broken* if an imposter can impersonate the client or the server with a non-negligible probability.

For a what-you-know authentication, having the knowledge (such as a reusable password or a PIN number) will allow the attacker to impersonate the user until the knowledge is obsolete. For a what-you-have authentication, having the token will allow the attacker to impersonate that user until the token is revoked. In both cases, the system can recover through revoking the authentication credential.

In a biometric authentication, however, it is not as easy to recover from a compromise, since people's biometrics, especially those biological biometrics, do not change much over time. Consequently, a compromised biometric characteristic will allow an attacker to impersonate that user until the authentication method is changed or that user is disabled permanently.

CRYPTOGRAPHY IN KNOWLEDGE-BASED AUTHENTICATION

The most common knowledge-based authentication is password authentication. As a result, our discussion of the roles of cryptography in knowledge-based authentication focuses on the application of cryptography in password authentication.

Password Authentication

In a typical password-based authentication scenario, a user (i.e., the client) remembers a reusable password and the server stores the corresponding *password verification data* (PVD), which is a piece of data derived from the password. The client authenticates itself by demonstrating the knowledge of the password, which the server verifies with the stored PVD. (Passwords are typically used for client-side authentication but as we shall see shortly, passwords can also be used for mutual authentication.)

The simplest way to demonstrate the knowledge of an appropriate password is to give the password to the server. However, as we will see below, the client does *not* need to send the password to demonstrate the knowledge of it.

Dictionary Attacks against Password Authentication

Suppose the length of a password is eight characters. How many different password combinations can we have?

If the password characters are alphanumeric and case sensitive, the number of all possible password combinations is $62^8 = 218340105584896$, which is about 2^{48}. If we allow other printable characters such as \verb=`!@#$%^&*()~';,./:"<>?|{} []=, the total number of combinations may get close to 127^8, which is about 2^{56} (this is the size of DES's key space).

With the fastest computer at the world, it is easy to brute-force the space of 2^{56}. But with a 3.2GHz PC (3.2G is about 2^{32}), assuming that each password guess takes just one clock cycle, it would take 2^{24} seconds (which is about a year) to brute-force this space of 2^{56}. Thus, brute-force attacks are not easy *if* passwords are chosen randomly.

Unfortunately, people do not pick passwords randomly. This makes *dictionary attack* possible. In a dictionary attack, an attacker does not try all *possible* character combinations. Instead, he builds a dictionary of *likely* passwords, which many users' passwords fall into, and tries this small set. The size of a typical password dictionary is 10,000, which is about 2^{14}, and it is much smaller than 2^{48} and 2^{56}.

Dictionary attacks can be mounted in an on-line or off-line manner. The former is called *on-line password guessing attack* and the latter is called *off-line* dictionary attack.

In an on-line password guessing attack, an attacker guesses a password (from the password dictionary) and uses it to log into a server (hence online). These steps are repeated until the correct password is found and the attacker successfully logs in. Thus, in an on-line password guessing attack, an attacker repeatedly queries the server.

In an off-line dictionary attack, the attacker steals some password-related data first, through either passive eavesdropping or active operations. It then mounts a dictionary attack in an off-line way without repeatedly querying the server. As a result, compared to on-line password guessing attacks, off-line dictionary attacks are more subtle and harder to detect.

How can on-line password guessing attacks be countered? The server can enforce a three-strike-out policy and lock out an account after three failed login attempts. This *throttle strategy* has two downsides: degraded usability and availability. An honest user with a lapse in memory may end up trying three wrong passwords and get locked out, causing the poor system usability. Secondly, when user account names are publicly available (as is the case of the student account names of many public universities), an attacker can cause all user accounts be locked out by running a computer program to try three logins on each account.

Increasing the number of failed login attempts allowed may improve the usability but also allows an attacker to guess more passwords. Several such countermeasures have been developed to mitigate this lock-out problem.

- Introduce a delay between failed log-ins. If a user gives a wrong password, before he can try another password, he has to wait a certain amount of time. The delay is set at a level acceptable to legitimate users. For an online password guessing, this delay will cause the attack to take longer, making it to have a higher chance of being detected.

- Introduce *Completely Automated Public Turing test to tell Computers and Humans Apart* (*CAPTCHA*) in the authentication (Naor, 1996; von Ahn and Blum, 2003): CAPTCHAs are techniques that can tell whether a remote entity is a computer program or a human being. In a password guessing attack, an attacker usually employs a computer program to automate the password guessing. This is different from a legitimate log-in where a human being types in a password. With a good CAPTCHA, the server can effectively detect a guessing program at the other end and stop the attack. An example CAPTCHA is to send a scrambled image and ask the logging party to type back its content. However, it remains a challenge to design a good CAPTCHA and some existing CAPTCHAs have been found weak (Yan & Ahmad, 2007, 2008; Golle, 2008).

- Additional user-specific knowledge can be used against online password guessing. In addition to PVD, the server can pre-store some questions − such as "What is your dog's name?" − and their answers about a user. When a remote entity wants to login in as that user, one or more these questions are presented. A password guessing program will *not* be able to proceed as it does not know the answer to the question.

Offline dictionary attacks, on the other hand, are more subtle and harder to handle. (The severity of the off-line dictionary attack has been witnessed in (Wu, 1998).) They play a central role in the generation of PVD and the design of password-authenticated key exchange protocols discussed below.

The Generation of Password Verification Data (PVD)

In a password authentication system, to verify the correctness of a given password, the server has to store *password verification data* (PVD). How is this PVD generated?

It is *not* a good idea to have a password itself as the PVD for two reasons. First, the server may be compromised and the attacker will have the password and can simply use it to impersonate the user. Second, the server system administrator, an insider, may misbehave. Since the system administrator can read any files, a bad system administrator can steal passwords and impersonate any users.

It is a standard practice to store the one-way *cryptographic* hash of a password on the server as PVD. A *one-way cryptographic hash function* is a special function: given a password, it is easy to calculate its hash but it is hard to derive the password from its hash value. (The definitions of "easy" and "hard" are computational.) Thus, given a password p, its PVD = $h(p)$. Even when such PVD is stolen, the attacker cannot *easily* find the corresponding password to impersonate that user. A misbehaving system administrator cannot *easily* use the stolen PVD to impersonate either.

However, if an attacker managed to steal this kind of PVD, he could still mount a dictionary attack: he can guess a password p' from the password dictionary, calculate PVD' = $h(p')$, and compare PVD' against the stolen PVD. If a match is found, the attacker has discovered the correct password.

This is one example of *off-line* dictionary attack: in this attack, the attacker does *not* query

the server after the PVD is obtained. As a result, off-line dictionary attacks are harder to detect and thus are worse than on-line password guessing.

Once the PVD is stolen, we cannot completely eliminate off-line dictionary attacks, but we can make them harder with two countermeasures: salting and iteration count.

Salting

Given a password dictionary, an attacker can hash each password inside it and then *reuse* this pre-hashed dictionary for *multiple* off-line dictionary attacks against PVD stolen from different servers.

To disable this type of computational reuse, a server can introduce an individualized value in the generation of PVD. Instead of PVD = $h(p)$, the server calculates PVD = $h(s, p)$, where s is a random value called a *salt*. Each user is assigned his own salt and the salt is stored with that user's PVD. Consequently, an attacker who has successfully stolen PVD will *not* able to reuse the pre-hashed dictionary and have to start from scratch for each off-line dictionary attack.

To make pre-computation infeasible, a salt should have at least 64 bits.

Iteration Count

Another way to increase an attacker's computation cost in an off-line dictionary attack is to use an *iteration count* in PVD generation (RSA Laboratories. (1999)). To verify a given password p' from a legitimate user, the server needs to calculate $h(s, p')$ and then compare the result against the stored PVD. An attacker mounting off-line dictionary attacks needs to do *many* such calculations, one for each guessed password from the password dictionary.

Thus, we can encumber the attacker by increasing the computational cost to hash passwords. Instead of PVD = $h(s, p)$, we have $PVD = \underbrace{h(h(\cdots h(s, p)))}_{n}$. That is, (s, p) is hashed

n times to be used as PVD. Hereafter, we use $h^n(s,p)$ to denote that (s, p) is hashed n times.

To significantly impede an off-line dictionary attacker, n should be at least 1000.

The salting and iteration count mechanisms have been implemented on UNIX to mitigate off-line dictionary attacks. In contrast, the NTLM authentication on previous MS Windows versions did not implement these security-enhancing techniques (Glass, 2006).

Password-Based Challenge/ Response & Password-Authenticated Key Exchange (PAKE)

Password-Based Challenge/Response

In a *remote* password authentication where the client has some computational capability, the client does *not* have to send its password p to the server for verification. To authenticate the client, the server can generate a random challenge c and send it, along with the client's salt s and iteration count i, if it is applicable, to the client. The client will calculate a response value r based on its password p and the challenge c; that is, $r = f(p, s, i, c)$. The response value r is then sent back to the server, which can calculate r' as $r' = g(\text{PVD}, c)$ from the client's PVD and check whether $r' = r$. If they match, the client is authenticated. Otherwise, the client authentication fails. (Both f and g are public functions and their details will come shortly.)

This type of password-based client-side authentication is called *password-based challenge/response authentication*.

In the calculation of f, the client first calculates its PVD$'$ as $PVD' = h^i(s,p)$ (note that $h^i(s, p) = \underbrace{h(h(\cdots h(s, p)))}_{i}$). The client then calculates $r = g(\text{PVD}', c)$, where g is a function agreed upon between the client and the server in advance.

What should g be? It turns out that g can be either a symmetric-key encryption scheme such as AES-128 encryption or a message authentication code (MAC) such as hash-based MAC (HMAC). When AES-128 encryption is used as g, the PVD$'$ is used as the key to encrypt c; the resulting ciphertext is r. If HMAC is used as g, the PVD$'$ is used as the key to generate a MAC on message c; the resulting MAC value is used as r.

The basic idea behind password-based challenge/response is that a client who does not know p will not be able to calculate the correct PVD$'$ or a valid r. To this end, the challenge r should be unique. It does not have to be random. (As we shall see later, this challenge/response paradigm can be extended to be with symmetric keys and private keys.)

The password-based challenge response protocol has been implemented in HTTP digest authentication (Franks et al., 1999) and by Microsoft Windows in LM, NTLM and NTLMv2 authentications (Glass, 2006), where g is implemented as DES and HMAC-MD5 respectively.

How secure is the password-based challenge/response protocol? Even when the challenge value r is never repeated and g is strong, the password-based challenge/response protocol is still vulnerable to *off-line* dictionary attacks. A passive attacker can eavesdrop to obtain one (challenge, response) pair (c, r) and then mount an *off-line* dictionary attack: for each password p' in the password dictionary, the attacker calculates $r' = g(p', c)$; it then checks whether $r' = r$. This process repeats until $r' = r$. The corresponding p' is the correct password. Only one (challenge, response) pair is required to mount this off-line dictionary attack.

A quick fix for the password-based challenge/response protocol is to authenticate the server first and establish a secure channel to the server. It is over this secure channel that (r, c) are transported. In this way, an attacker will not be able to eavesdrop to get a single pair (r, c).

Password-Authenticated Key Exchange

Another password-based authentication paradigm that does not send passwords is the *password-authenticated key exchange* (PAKE) protocol (Bellovin & Merritt, 1992, 1993). Like the password-based challenge/response, PAKE does not send passwords. Unlike the password-based challenge/response, in PAKE, the client authentication is accomplished *implicitly* through the capability of establishing an *authenticated* session key K with the server, which stores the related PVD. This authenticated session key K would *not* be possible if the client does not have the password or the server does not have the related PVD. Thus, PAKE also differs from the password-based challenge/response in that it uses passwords for mutual authentication, not for client authentication alone.

In PAKE, the authenticated session key K is cryptographically strong and can be used to protect subsequent communications after the authentication. As such, a PAKE protocol allows the client and the server to bootstrap, in a mutually authenticated manner, from a weak password to a cryptographically strong secret K. PAKE is a special case of a more general protocol paradigm called *Authenticated Key Exchange* (AKE), which will be discussed further in later sections of this chapter.

A good PAKE protocol is secure against both the eavesdropping-based dictionary attack and any active attacks. PAKE protocols achieve these security goals through the marriage with public key exchange techniques (Diffie & Hellman, 1976). Several PAKE protocols have been proposed, including the *Encrypted Key Exchange* (EKE) (Bellovin & Merritt, 1992, 1993), *Secure Password Exponential Key Exchange* (SPEKE) (Jablon, 1996, 1997), *Simple Remote Password* (SRP) (Wu, 1998), *the PAK protocol* (Boyko, MacKenzie, & Patel, 2000), *the BPR00 protocol* (Bellare, Pointcheval, & Rogaway, 2000), *the SNAPI protocol* (MacKenzie, Patel, & Swami-

nathan, 2000), and *the KOY01 protocol* (Katz, Ostrovsky, & Yung, 2001). The SPEKE, SRP, PAK and KOY01 protocols use the Diffie-Hellman key exchange algorithm (Diffie & Hellman, 1976) while BPR00 and SNAPI use the RSA algorithm (Rivest, Shamir, & Adleman, 1978).

It is worth noting three facts about PAKE: 1) a PAKE user memorizes a password only; 2) the client program used by the user to log into the system has only system-wide public parameters (such as the g and q for Diffie-Hellman and these parameters are public); the client program has no hard-coded secrets (say, a private key). Thus, an attacker cannot compromise PAKE security by obtaining a copy of the client program and examining it; 3) a PAKE protocol does *not* assume pre-existing secure channels between the client and the server; yet, it is still secure against eavesdropping or active attacks.

Below, we use the SRP version 6 (called *SRP-6*) to explain how PAKE works (Wu, 2002). SRP-6 works by integrating passwords into the unauthenticated Diffie-Hellman protocol.

SRP-6 has two public system-wide parameters, g and N, where N is a big prime and g is a generator of the multiplicative group F_N^*. (Since p is already used to denote a password, we use N to denote the big prime here.) The client's reusable password is p and its corresponding password verification data (PVD) is $v = g^x \bmod N$, where s is the salt and $x = h(s, p)$. (s, v) are stored on the server.

Table 1 gives the data flow for a log-in.

In Step 1, the client sends its ID to the server for login. The server uses this login ID as index to look up its salt s and its PVD v. The server then sends s back to the client. The client calculates $x = h(s, p)$. If the client is authentic, it will be able to derive v from x.

In Step 2, the client picks a random number a between 1 and N (denoted as $a \in_R [1, N]$ in Table 1) and calculates A as $A = g^a \bmod N$, which is sent to the server. The server checks whether A

Table 1. SRP-6

	CLIENT (p)		**SERVER** (v, s)
1		$U \Rightarrow$	
2			Look up s, v
		$s \Leftarrow$	
	$x = h(s, p)$		
3	$a \in_R [1, N]\ A = g^a \bmod N$		
		$A \Rightarrow$	
			If $A \equiv 0 \bmod N$, quit
4			$b \in_R [1, N],\ B = 3v + g^b \bmod N$ $u = h(A \parallel B)$
		$\Leftarrow B$	
	If $B \equiv 0 \bmod N$, quit		
5	$S_C = (B - 3g^x)^{a+ux} \bmod N$		$S_S = (Av^u)^x \bmod N$
6	$K = h(S_C)$		$K = h(S_S)$
7	$M_1 = h(A \parallel B \parallel S_C)$		
		$M_1 \Rightarrow$	
			Verify M_1
8			$M_2 = h(A, M_1, K)$
		$\Leftarrow M_2$	
	Verify M_2		

$\equiv 0 \bmod N$. If it is, the server quits. Otherwise, the server continues.

In Step 3, the server picks a random number b between 1 and N and calculates B as $B = (3v + g^b) \bmod N$, which is sent to the client. The client checks whether $B \equiv 0 \bmod N$. If it is, the client quits. Otherwise, the client continues.

In Step 4, the client calculates $S_C = (B - 3g^x)^{a+ux} \bmod N$ and the server calculates $S_S = (Av^u)^x \bmod N$. If both parties are authentic, S_S should have the same value as S_C. In Step 5, both parties calculate K. If both parties are authentic, they should have the same value K.

Step 7 and Step 8 are for two-way explicit key confirmation. In Step 7, the client proves that it has S_C by calculating and sending out M_1, which can be verified by the server. If the server cannot verify M_1, it will quit. Otherwise, in Step 8, the server will prove to the client that it has K by calculating and sending out M_2, which the client verifies. If the client cannot verify M_2, it will quit. Otherwise, both parties will use K to protect subsequent communications between them.

In the above protocol, p is never sent to the server. If the server does not have v, it will not be able to agree on the common value K with the client. If the client does not know p, it will not be able to calculate K.

In SRP-6, a passive eavesdropper can observe (U, s, A, B, M_1, M_2) but these values do *not* allow the attacker to calculate K or recover p. SRP-6 is also secure against active attacks.

SRP-6 has yet to be deployed to protect cyber systems.

CRYPTOGRAPHY KEY-BASED TOKEN AUTHENTICATION AND AUTHENTICATED KEY EXCHANGE

Most memorable passwords are weak secrets in that they only have a small amount of entropy. Consequently, password authentication is fundamentally vulnerable to brute-force attacks. In contrast, long secrets like cryptographic keys contain enough entropy to resist brute-force attacks.

However, human beings are not good at remembering long random secrets. Token authentication overcomes the drawback by storing a strong secret on a *hardware* token (such as a smartcard) and giving it to a user. This secret is then used for authentication. To protect the secret, the token should use the secret onboard and does not allow the secret to leave. A token may also employ some tamper-resistant measures to prevent the secret from being forcibly read from outside.

Since the secret is not allowed to leave the token, token authentication is often achieved through demonstrating the possession of the secret, most likely in a challenge/response protocol for client-side authentication. Unlike the password-based challenge/response protocol, strong secret-based challenge/response protocols are *not* vulnerable to dictionary attacks or brute-force attacks.

The strong secret stored on a token can be either a symmetric key (such as an AES-128 key) or a private key of a public/private key pair (such as a 1024-bit RSA private key), which are discussed below.

Symmetric Key-Based Token Authentication

When a token stores a symmetric key k, a copy of this key is also stored on the server. A remote entity is then authenticated to the server through demonstrating the possession of k in a challenge/response protocol.

To authenticate the client, the server will send a challenge c to the client. The client will use k to generate a response value r, $r = g(k, c)$.

(Since k is stored on a token, the actual calculation is performed by the token and there must be a simple way to feed c to the token and read r from the token; this may pose a usability issue.) r is then sent back to the server, which generates $r' = g(k, c)$ and checks whether $r' = r$. The client is considered authenticated if $r' = r$ holds.

As in password-based challenge/response, g can be either a strong symmetric-key encryption algorithm such as AES-128 or a MAC algorithm such as HMAC. In both cases, k is used as a key and c is used as a message. For the challenge/response protocol to be secure, the challenge c must be unique in each authentication; it does *not* have to be random though.

There is a risk for the client to indiscriminatingly encrypt a given message (or generate MAC value for a given message when g is MAC). An honest client may be used by an attacker as an encryption oracle (or as a MAC generation oracle when g is a MAC), which may have undesirable security effects. For example, an attacker may deviate from the protocol by forging the challenge c as a meaningful message and ask the client to encrypt it. If the client also uses the token secret for encrypting regular messages to Bob, the attacker can now send r to Bob, claiming that it comes from the client.

To avoid this pitfall, we can utilize the fact that c needs to be unique only. As a result, c can be the current time, which is unique, and does *not* need to be sent if the token and the server share synchronized time. The introduction of synchronized time as c also partially solves the usability issue raised above: the token owner does not have to type c into the token; the token owner still needs to read the response r from the token and sends it to the server.

This is how RSA Data Security's SecurID works: the token has a clock that is synchronized with the server's clock and in every minute the token generates a PIN, which can be read by the token owner and sent to the server for client-side authentication.

Private Key-Based Authentication and Authenticated Key Exchange

A token may also store the private key of a public/private key pair and use it for client-side authentication in a challenge/response protocol. Before an authentication, the server will first obtain an authentic copy of the client's public key. Let's use UK_C to denote the client's public key and its corresponding private key is PK_C.

How the authentication happens depends on the type of the public/private key pair. When the public/private key pair can be used for encryption, the server may pick a random number r_1 and encrypt it with the client's public key as $c = E_{UK_C}(r_1)$. The server sends c to the client. If the client is authentic, it should have PK_C and should be able to decrypt c as $r_1' = D_{PK_C}(c)$. To demonstrate that it has PK_C, the client can either send r_1' to the server, which can check whether $r_1' = r_1$, or use r_1' to derive a session key and use it to prove, in an *indirect* manner, that the client knows r_1'. The former is called *explicit authentication* and the latter is called *implicit authentication*. Explicit authentication of this type has the potential drawback that an honest client may be used as a decryption oracle, which has security downsides. (An attacker can eavesdrop to get a ciphertext to the client and then use it as c; after getting r_1', the attacker knows the message behind c.) Implicit authentication, on the other hand, can avoid the pitfall of decryption oracle and falls within the *authenticated key exchange* (AKE) paradigm. (PAKE discussed earlier is one type of authenticated key exchange protocol.)

When the public/private key pair is used for digital signature only, the server can pick a challenge c and send c to the client. If the client is authentic, it should have PK_C and should be able to digitally sign c as $r_s = S_{PK_C}(c)$. To demonstrate that it has PK_C, the client sends r_s back to the server, which can use UK_C to verify the digital signature. For strong authentication, the challenge value c should be unique. There is a risk for the client to indiscriminately digitally sign a given message c, as an honest client might be used as a signing oracle, which has security downsides: an attacker can forge a message m, calculate $c = h(m)$ and send c to the client; after getting r_s from the client, the attacker can use (m, r_s) to claim that the client has digitally sign message m. To prevent this pitfall, the challenge to be digitally signed by a client usually comes from two sources, one from the server and the other from the client itself; what is digitally signed by the client is actually the cryptographic hash of the combined message.

The above idea can be extended to private key-based server-side authentication. When private key-based *mutual* authentication is required, the message exchanges can be integrated to reduce the number of communication rounds. This idea has been used in *Secure Socket Layer* (SSL) / *Transport Layer Security* (TLS) (Frier, Karlton, & Kocher, 1996; Dierks & Allen, 1999), *IP Security* (IPsec) *Internet Key Exchange* (IKE) version 1 (Harkins & Carrrel, 1998) and version 2 (Kaufman, 2005), and *Secure Shell* (SSH) (Ylonen, Kivinen, Saarinen, Rinne, & Lehtinen, 2002).

As an example, we use the RSA-based SSL mutual authentication to explain how private key-based authentication works. In this SSL mode, the server has a RSA public/private key pair UK_S/PK_S and the client has its own RSA public/private key pair UK_C/PK_C. The server's public key UK_S has been reliably distributed to the client and the client's public key UK_C has been reliably distributed to the server. In our following description, we focus on the security data flow and ignore other details.

In Step 1 of Table 2, the client generates a random number r_1 and sends it to the server. In Step 2, the server generates a random number r_2 and sends it to the client.

In Step 3, the client calculates the cryptographic hash of the concatenation of r_1 and r_2 as a and picks a random number r_3. It then digitally signs a with its RSA private key PK_C to get s and

Table 2. Simplified data flow for RSA-based SSL mutual authentication

	CLIENT (PK_C/UK_C; UK_S)		SERVER (PK_S/UK_S; UK_C)
1	$r_1 \in_R$		
		$r_1 \Rightarrow$	
2			$r_2 \in_R$
		$r_2 \Leftarrow$	
3	$a = h(r_1 \| r_2)$ $r_3 \in_R, s = S_{PK_C}(a), c = E_{UK_s}(r_3)$		
		$s, c \Rightarrow$	
			Use UK_C to verify s; Decrypt c to get r_3;
4	$K = h(r_3)$		$K = h(r_3)$
5		Subsequent communications are protected by K	

encrypts r_3 with the server's RSA public key UK_S to get c. (c, s) are then sent to the server.

Upon the receipt of c and s, the server first uses the client's RSA public key UK_C to verify s. If the signature verification fails, the server complains and quits. Otherwise, the server uses its own RSA private key PK_S to decrypt c to get r_3.

At this moment, if both the client and the server are authentic, they will agree on a common secret value r_3 and can derive a symmetric key K from it. This key K is then used to protect the confidentiality and integrity of subsequent communications.

How is the client authenticated in this mode? The client authenticates itself *explicitly* by digitally signing a challenge a. This challenge is collectively generated by the client and the server. The challenge is unique in that r_2 is randomly generated by the server. A malicious attacker cannot use the client as a digital signing oracle, as the client also contributes a random number r_1 to what it digitally signs (what the client digitally signs is a, which is the cryptographic hash of r_1 and r_2); a is unpredictable to an attacker.

If the client is bogus, he will not be able to generate a valid s.

How is the server authenticated in this mode? The server is *implicitly* authenticated through demonstrating the possession of PK_S via decrypting c. This authentication is implicit as the server does not send the decrypted value back to the client. Instead, it uses the decrypted value to derive a symmetric key K to decrypt and verify future communications.

If the server is bogus, it will not be able to recover r_3 and thus will not be able to continue the conversation.

FUZZY EXTRACTORS FOR BIOMETRIC AUTHENTICATION

The early development of biometric authentication is largely independent from cryptography. In recent years, new cryptographic mechanisms have been designed to enhance the security and privacy of biometric authentication by protecting biometric verification data.

Biometric Authentication

Knowledge-based authentication is essentially sharable: the authentication knowledge can be shared among several entities. Token-based authentication is not sharable if the token is hard to clone but it is transferable: entity A may pass its token to entity B, allowing B to be authenticated as A. These two authentications actually authenticate either a password or a cryptographic key.

In contrast, biometric authentication aims to authenticate a *human being user* through either biological characteristics or behavioral characteristics. This property makes it especially appropriate for applications such as custom and nuclear plants, where human being authentication is required.

To be used for biometric authentication, a biometric characteristic needs to have several properties. First, it has to be universal: most human being users should have it. Second, for each human being, this characteristic should be unique. Third, the characteristic should remain persistent for some time. Fourth, such a characteristic should be collectible (for both enrollment and authentication).

Typical biological biometric authentication mechanisms include *fingerprint*, *voice*, *facial*, *hand geometry*, *palm*, *iris*, *retina*, and *DNA* (DeoxyriboNucleic Acid). Typical behavioral biometric authentications include *handwritten signature* and *typing pattern*.

Compared to passwords and cryptographic keys, biometric authentication has two distinguishing characteristics. First, human biological biometrics such as fingerprints do *not* change much over a long period of time, making their revocations and system recovery after compromise very hard. Second, unlike passwords or cryptographic keys, the comparison of two biometric samples is *not* exact. Indeed, two consecutive readings of the *same* biometric are usually close but not exactly the same. Consequently, comparisons of biometric samples are often threshold-based (Maltoni, 2005).

As a result, biometric authentications are affected by two types of errors: *false match* (FM), where two different biometrics are incorrectly considered the same, and *false non-match* (FNM), where two samples of the same biometric are incorrectly deemed different. Different applications tolerate different FMR/FNMR and thus choose different threshold. The bigger the threshold value is, the higher the FNMR will be and the lower the FMR will be.

Let's use fingerprint authentication as an example to give some details. A person's fingerprint consists of many *ridges* (black lines) and *valleys* (the white space between ridges) (Maltoni, 2005). Ridges and valleys form *fingerprint patterns*, such as left loop, right loop, whorl, arch, and tented arch. These patterns can categorize fingerprints but they do not contain enough information for fingerprint authentication. The ridges of a fingerprint may terminate or bifurcate. These terminating and dividing points are called *minutiae*. A minutia point is identified by its coordinates and angle. The minutiae collection of a fingerprint contains enough information for authentication.

The Security/Privacy Issues of Biometric Authentication

Like passwords, biometrics are typically used for client-side authentication only. The client first enrolls his biometric sample (called *reference template*), from which the authentication server generates and stores related *biometric verification data* (BVD). Given a cryptographic hash function h and two close biometric samples A and B, their cryptographic hashes $h(A)$ and $h(B)$ are very different, making $h(A)$ *not* appropriate for BVD. A common practice is to use the reference template A itself as BVD.

However, storing biometric reference templates on a server in cleartext has negative security and privacy implications. If the server were compromised, all biometric templates stored on it would be revealed and it would be hard to recover from this break.

Fuzzy Extractors

To address this BVD security and privacy issue, the concept of *fuzzy extractor* was developed (Juels & Wattenberg, 1999; Dodis, Reyzin, & Smith, 2004). Given a reference template A, a fuzzy extractor generates a value U and a uniformly random secret *s*. U leaks *little* information about A or *s*, and can be made public. For a fresh biometric sample B that is sufficiently *close* to A, one can use U and B to reproduce *s*. Thus, {U, $h(s)$} can be used as capture-resistant BVD: if {U, $h(s)$} were stolen because of a server compromise, the attacker still could *not* recover A or *s*.

Depending on how biometrics are represented, there are different metrics to measure the closeness of biometric samples, including *Hamming distance, set difference, edit distance*, and *set intersection*. These representational differences call for different designs of fuzzy extractor. (Juels & Wattenberg, 1999) gave a fuzzy extractor for the Hamming distance metric. (Dodis, Reyzin, & Smith, 2004; Dodis, Ostrovsky, Reyzin, & Smith, 2008) described several fuzzy extractors based on the set difference metric, where biometric samples are represented as a *set* of points and the difference of two biometric samples A and B is their *symmetric difference* (that is, |(A–B) Ç (B–A)| where || denotes set size and Ç denotes set union). (Socek, Bozovic, & Culibrk, 2007) developed a fuzzy extractor based on the *set intersection* metric, where the similarity of two biometric samples A and B is their intersection.

Building Blocks for Fuzzy Extractors

Several fuzzy extractor schemes, including those based on the set difference metric, the edit distance metric, and the Hamming distance metric, are built upon error-correcting codes such as the Reed-Solomon code (Reed & Solomon, 1960; Berlekamp, 1968; Massey, 1969).

Error-correcting codes (ECC) protect messages from communication errors (by noisy channels) through *encoding* redundant information into the messages. By utilizing this redundant information in the *decoding* of the received message, the receiver can correct certain errors and recover what is sent. A good error-correcting code often requires as least redundant information as possible and has a fast *decoding algorithm*.

A (n, k) *linear block code* encodes a k-symbol message into a n-symbol *codeword* C (n is called the *block length* and there are $(n–k)$ parity check symbols in C). There are 2^k such codewords and they form the code. The minimal Hamming distance of any two codewords is the minimal distance of the code and is often denoted as d. If C is corrupted in the transfer and is received as C', if the number of errors t satisfies $t \leq (d–1)/2$, the decoding algorithm will be able to decode C' back to C.

A *cyclic code* is a special linear block code whose decoding can be made easy. Among the famous cyclic codes are the Bose, Ray-Chaudhuri, and Hocquenghem (BCH) code and the Reed-Solomon (RS) code, which is a special type of BCH code. An error-correcting code that can correct up to t errors is called *t-error-correcting code*. A message symbol is often taken from a finite field GF(q), where q is either 2, a prime p, 2^l (l is an integer), or a prime power ($q = p^l$, p is a prime and l is an integer). When q is 2, the code is called *binary*. In a binary t-error-correcting (n, k) BCH code, the block length can be chosen as $n = 2^m – 1$ for some integer m and the number of parity-check symbols is $(n–k)$, $n – k \leq mt$; the distance of the code is d, $d \geq 2t + 1$. In a non-binary t-correcting (n, k) BCH code, the block length can be chosen as $n = q^m – 1$ for some integer m and the number of parity-check symbols is $(n–k)$, $n – k \leq 2mt$; the distance of the code d, $d \geq 2t + 1$. (Lin & Costello, 2003).

In a non-binary t-error-correcting (n, k) RS code, the block length is $n = q - 1$ and the number of parity-check symbols is $n - k = 2t$; the distance of the code is $d = 2t + 1$ (Lin & Costello, 2003). RS code is especially useful in correcting burst errors.

Fuzzy Extractors for Hamming Distance Metric

(Juels & Wattenberg, 1999) described an elegant fuzzy extractor scheme under the Hamming distance metric, where a biometric sample is represented as a *fixed-size* and *fixed-order* binary string. This scheme, called *JW99* hereafter, is based on error-correcting codes. To generate biometric verification data from a biometric sample x, the server first picks a random codeword C and calculates $v = (x \oplus C)$ and $y = h(C)$, where $\oplus$ denotes bitwise exclusive OR and h is a cryptographic hash function like SHA-192. (v, y) is the biometric verification data and is stored on the server.

To verify a given biometric sample x', the server first calculates $u = v \oplus x'$ and then applies the decoding function of the error-correcting code on u. If x and x' are close enough under the Hamming distance metric, u can be corrected to C, whose correctness can be verified by checking whether $h(u) = y$. (The essence of this and other ECC-based schemes is to use the error-correcting capability of ECC to tolerate small differences between biometric samples.)

In the *JW99* scheme, if the server were compromised and (v, y) were stolen, since C is randomly picked, an attacker would *not* be able to recover x or a close biometric sample. This scheme is also secure against the *multiple-use attack* (called *chosen perturbation attack* in (Boyen, 2004)): a client may use his biometrics in several applications with each server storing a set of (v_i, y_i); compromising multiple such servers to obtain (v_i, y_i) does *not* give the attacker more useful information about the client's biometric x.

Fuzzy Extractors for the Set Difference Metric

Fuzzy extractors based on the set difference metric employ a *difference* threshold t_d. A set B is considered close to A only when their set symmetric difference, $t = |(A–B)Ç(B–A)|$, is *not* greater than t_d.

(Dodis, Ostrovsky, Reyzin, & Smith, 2008) improved a set difference-based fuzzy extractor scheme developed by (Juels & Sudan, 2002, 2006). This fuzzy extractor can tolerate up to t_d symmetric difference.

Given a reference template A = $\{a_1, a_2, …, a_n\}$, the server calculates $f(x)=(x-a_1)(x-a_2)…(x-a_n)$. After expansion, let $f(x)$ be $f(x) = x^n + v_{n-1}x^{n-1} + … + v_1x^n + v_0$. The biometric verification data for A is $\Gamma = (v_{n-1}, v_{n-2}, …, v_{n-t_d})$. (This implicitly requires that $t_d \leq n$.)

When a fresh biometric sample B = $\{b_1, b_2, …, b_n\}$ is presented for authentication, the server uses Γ to create a new polynomial $f_h(x) = x^n + v_{n-1}x^{n-1} + … + v_{n-t}x^{n-t}$. It then evaluates $f_h(b_i)$, $1 \leq i \leq n$, to get n pairs $(b_i, f_h(b_i))$.

With a Reed-Solomon decoding algorithm, the server can find $f_l(x)$ of degree $(n–t_d–1)$ such that $f_l(b_i) = f_h(b_i)$ for at least $(n–t_d/2)$ of the b_i values. If no such $f_l(x)$ can be found, the authentication is considered failed. Otherwise, the client is considered authenticated successfully.

Fuzzy Extractors for the Set Intersection Metric

(Socek, Bozovic, & Culibrk, 2007) proposed a fuzzy extractor (FE) based on set intersection (SI), which is called *FESI* hereafter. *FESI* is based on *threshold* secret sharing schemes (Shamir, 1979), *not* directly on error-correcting codes.

In FESI, for a given reference template A=$\{a_1, a_2, …, a_n\}$, where n is an integer and $t \leq n$, a random secret s is first chosen and its t-out-of-n secret shares $(s_1, s_2, …, s_n)$ are generated (Shamir,

1979). Let h be a cryptographic hash function and $f_A(x)$ be a *discrete* function such that

$$f_A(x) = s_i \text{ if } x = a_i \text{ and } f_A(x) = \tilde{s}_i \text{ otherwise,}$$

where $\tilde{s}_i$ is a random number (thus very likely $s_i \neq \tilde{s}_i$.

$\Gamma = \{H_A, y, f_A(x)\}$ is then stored on the server as A's biometric verification data (BVD), where $H_A = \{h(sa_1), h(sa_2), \ldots, h(sa_n)\}$ and $y = h(s)$.

When a fresh biometric sample $B = \{b_1, b_2, \ldots, b_m\}$ $(t \leq m)$ is presented, the server takes the following steps to verify its authenticity: for each t-subset B_i of B, $1 \leq i \leq \binom{m}{t}$, where $\binom{m}{t}$ denotes the number of t-combinations out of m, the server evaluates $f_A(B_i)$ to get t values $(\tilde{s}_i^1, \tilde{s}_i^2, \cdots, \tilde{s}_i^t)$, which are then used as shares to reconstruct a secret value s_{Bi} (Shamir, 1979). Next, the server checks whether $h(s_{Bi}) = y$. If not, the next B_{i+1} is tried; otherwise, the server calculates $H_{Bi} = \{h(s_{Bi}b_1), h(s_{Bi}b_2), \ldots, h(s_{Bi}b_m)\}$ and $\Theta_{Bi} = H_A \dot{E} H_{Bi}$, where $\dot{E}$ denotes set intersection. If the cardinality of Θ_{Bi} is not smaller than t, B is considered close to A and the client is authenticated. (After a successful authentication, the reconstructed secret s can be used for other security purposes such as being used as an AES key.)

FUTURE RESEARCH DIRECTIONS

Some cryptographic mechanisms covered in this chapter are less mature than others. Especially, the fuzzy extractor schemes are developed in recent years and can be improved in many ways. For instance, the computation and storage of the FESI developed by (Socek, Bozovic, & Culibrk, 2007) have been improved in (Wang, Huff, & Tjaden, 2008). Fuzzy extractors under other metrics remain to be designed.

The PAKE authentication paradigm uses passwords for mutual authentication and thus has the potential to fight phishing attacks. Nonetheless, PAKE has not seen wide deployment yet and its deployment hurdles need to be researched.

CONCLUSION

Cryptography is widely known for providing data confidentiality, data integrity, and non-repudiation. In contrast, its important role in entity authentication is less clear and thus is studied in this chapter. We systematically examined the roles of cryptography in knowledge-based authentication, token authentication, and biometric authentication.

By generating PVD as $PVD = h^n(s, p)$, where h is a cryptographic hash function, s is a salt value, and n is an iteration count, cryptography makes password authentication more resilient against server compromise-based off-line dictionary attacks and malicious server administrators.

Passwords have been integrated with cryptographic authenticated key exchange protocols as password-authenticated key exchange protocols to provide password-based mutual authentication.

In token authentication, cryptographic algorithms have been used for symmetric key-based token authentication and private key-based token authentication. The former is often implemented as a challenge/response authentication protocol while the latter is typically implemented as an authenticated key exchange protocol.

Most recently, a new cryptographic scheme called fuzzy extractor has been developed to protect biometric reference templates. This significantly enhances the security and privacy of biometric authentication and hopefully will speed up the adoption of biometric authentication on the web.

We believe that this chapter will help security practitioners better understand the roles of cryptography in entity authentication and help them apply authentication techniques to protect cyber systems.

REFERENCES

Bellare, M., Pointcheval, D., & Rogaway, P. (2000). Authenticated key exchange secure against dictionary attacks. In B. Preneel (Ed.), *Advances in Cryptology – Eurocrypt 2000* (pp. 139-155). Berlin: Springer-Verlag. (Lecture Notes in Computer Science Volume 1807)

Bellovin, S., & Merritt, M. (1991). Limitations of the Kerberos authentication system. In *Proceedings of the 1991 winter USENIX conference* (pp. 253-267).

Bellovin, S., & Merritt, M. (1992). Encrypted key exchange: password-based protocols secure against dictionary attacks. In *Proceedings of the 1992 IEEE Computer Society Symposium on Research in Security and Privacy* (pp. 72-84).

Bellovin, S. M., & Merritt, M. (1993). Augmented encrypted key exchange: a password-based protocol secure against dictionary attacks and password file compromise. In *Proceedings of the 1st ACM Conference on Computer and Communications security* (pp. 244-250).

Berlekamp, E. R. (1968). *Algebraic coding theory*. New York: McGraw-Hill.

Boyen, X. (2004). Reusable cryptographic fuzzy extractors. In *Proceedings of the 11th ACM conference on Computer and Communications Security (CCS'04)* (p. 82-91).

Boyko, V., MacKenzie, P., & Patel, S. (2000). Provably secure password-authenticated key exchange using Diffie-Hellman. In B. Preneel (Ed.), *Advances in Cryptology – Eurocrypt 2000* (pp. 156-171). Berlin: Springer-Verlag. (Lecture Notes in Computer Science Volume 1807)

Davida, G. I., Frankel, Y., & Matt, B. J. (1998). On enabling secure applications through offline biometric identification. In *Proceedings of the 1998 IEEE Symposium on Security and Privacy* (p. 148-157).

Dierks, T., & Allen, C. (1999, January). *The TLS protocol version 1.0*. Internet RFC 2246.

Diffie, W., & Hellman, M. E. (1976). New directions in cryptography. *IEEE Transactions on Information Theory, 22*(6), 644–654. doi:10.1109/TIT.1976.1055638

Dodis, Y., Ostrovsky, R., Reyzin, L., & Smith, A. (2008). Fuzzy extractors: How to generate strong keys from biometrics and other noisy data. *SIAM Journal on Computing, 38*(1), 97–139. doi:10.1137/060651380

Dodis, Y., Reyzin, L., & Smith, A. (2004). Fuzzy extractors: How to generate strong keys from biometrics and other noisy data. In C. Cachin & J. Camenisch (Eds.), *Advance in Cryptology – Eurocrypt 2004* (pp. 523-540). Berlin: Springer-Verlag. (Lecture Notes in Computer Science Volume 3027)

Franks, J., HallamBaker, P., Hostetler, J., Lawrence, S., Leach, P., Luotonen, A., & Stewart, L. (1999, June). *HTTP authentication: basic and digest access authentication*. Internet RFC 2617.

Frier, A., Karlton, P., & Kocher, P. (1996, November 18). *The SSL 3.0 protocol*. Netscape Communications Corp.

Garman, J. (2003). *Kerberos: The definitive guide*. New York: O'Reilly.

Glass, E. (2006). *The NTLM authentication protocol and security support provider*. Retrieved from http://davenport.sourceforge.net/ntlm.html

Golle, P. (2008). Machine learning attacks against the Asirra CAPTCHA. In *Proceedings of the 15th ACM Conference on Computer and Communications Security* (p. 535-542). Alexandria, VA.

Harkins, D., & Carrel, D. (1998, November). *The Internet Key Exchange (IKE)*. Internet Request For Comments 2409.

Jablon, D. (1997). Extended password key exchange protocols immune to dictionary attack. In *Proceedings of the 6th IEEE Workshops on Enabling Technologies: Infrastructure for collaborative enterprises* (pp. 248-255).

Jablon, D. P. (1996). Strong password-only authenticated key exchange. *ACM SIGCOMM Computer Communication Review, 26*(5), 5–26. doi:10.1145/242896.242897

Jain, A. K., Ross, A., & Prabhakar, S. (2004). An introduction to biometric recognition. *IEEE Trans. on Circuits and Systems for Video Technology, 14*(1), 4–19. doi:10.1109/TCSVT.2003.818349

Juels, A., & Sudan, M. (2002). A fuzzy vault scheme. In *Proceedings of the IEEE International Symposium on Information Theory (ISIT 2002)*. Lausanne, Switzerland.

Juels, A., & Sudan, M. (2006). A fuzzy vault scheme. *Designs, Codes and Cryptography, 38*(2), 237–257. doi:10.1007/s10623-005-6343-z

Juels, A., & Wattenberg, M. (1999). A fuzzy commitment scheme. In *Proceedings of the Sixth ACM Conference on Computer and Communication Security* (p. 28-36).

Katz, J., Ostrovsky, R., & Yung, M. (2001). Efficient password-authenticated key exchange using human-memorable passwords. In B. Pfitzann (Ed.), Advances in Cryptology – Eurocrypt 2001 (pp. 475-494). Berlin: Springer-Verlag. (Lecture Notes in Computer Science Volume 2045)

Kaufman, C. (2005, December). *Internet key exchange (IKEv2) protocol*. IETF Request for Comments: 4306.

Klein, D. (1990). Foiling the cracker: A survey of, and improvements to, password security. In *Proceedings of the UNIX Security Workshop II*.

Klensin, J., Catoe, R., & Krumviede, P. (1997, January). *IMAP/POP AUTHorize extension for simple challenge/response*. Internet RFC 2095.

Kohl, J., & Neuman, C. (1993, September). *The Kerberos network authentication service (V5)*. Internet RFC 1510.

Kohl, J. T., Neuman, B. C., & Ts'o, T. Y. (1991). The evolution of the Kerberos authentication service. In *Proceedings of the Spring 1991 EurOpen Conference*.

Laboratories, R. S. A. (1999). *PKCS #5 v2.0 password-based cryptography standard*. Available from http://www.rsasecurity.com/rsalabs/pkcs/pkcs-5/

Lin, S., & Costello, D. J. (2004). *Error control coding* (SECOND Ed.). Upper Saddle River, NJ: Prentice Hall.

MacKenzie, P., Patel, S., & Swaminathan, R. (2000). Password-authenticated key exchange based on RSA. In T. Okamoto (Ed.), *Asiacrypt 2000* (pp. 599-613). Springer-Verlag. (Lecture Notes in Computer Science Volume 1976)

Maltoni, D. (2005). A tutorial on fingerprint recognition. In *Advanced studies in biometrics*. Berlin: Springer. (Lecture Notes in Computer Science Volume 3161)

Massey, J. (1969). Shift-register synthesis and BCH decoding. *IEEE Transactions on Information Theory, 15*(1), 122–127. doi:10.1109/TIT.1969.1054260

Monrose, F., Reiter, M. K., & Wetzel, S. (2002). Password hardening based on keystroke dynamics. *International Journal of Information Security, 1*(2), 69–83. doi:10.1007/s102070100006

Morris, R., & Thompson, K. (1979). Password security: a case history. *Communications of the ACM, 22*(11), 594–597. doi:10.1145/359168.359172

Naor, M. (1996, Sept. 13th). *Verification of a human in the loop or identification via the Turing test.*

Neuman, B., & Ts'o, T. (1994). Kerberos: an authentication service for computer networks. *IEEE Communications Magazine, 32*(9), 33–38. doi:10.1109/35.312841

Reed, I. S., & Solomon, G. (1960). Polynomial codes over certain finite fields. *SIAM Journal on Applied Mathematics, 8*(2), 300–304. doi:10.1137/0108018

Rivest, R., Shamir, A., & Adleman, L. (1978). A method for obtaining digital signature and public key cryptosystems. *Communications of the ACM, 21*(2), 120–126. doi:10.1145/359340.359342

Shamir, A. (1979). How to share a secret. *Communications of the ACM, 22*(11), 612–613. doi:10.1145/359168.359176

Socek, D., Bozovic, V., & Culibrk, D. (2007). Practical secure biometrics using set intersection as a similarity measure. In *Proceedings of International Conference on Security and Cryptography (SECRYPT 2007)*. Barcelona, Spain: INSTICC.

von Ahn, J. L., & Manuel Blum. (2003). CAPTCHA: Using hard AI problems for security. In E. Biham (Ed.), *Proceedings of Eurocrypt'03* (p. 294-311). Berlin: Springer-Verlag. (Lecture Notes in Computer Science Volume 2656)

Wang, X., Huff, P. D., & Tjaden, B. (2008). Improving the efficiency of capture-resistant biometric authentication based on set intersection. In *Proceedings of the 24th Annual Computer Security Applications Conference* (p. 140-149). Anaheim, CA: IEEE Computer Society.

Wu, T. (1998). The secure remote password protocol. In *Proceedings of the 1998 network and distributed system security symposium* (pp. 97-111).

Wu, T. (1999). A real-world analysis of Kerberos password security. In *Proceedings of the 1999 network and distributed system security symposium.*

Wu, T. (2002, October 29). *SRP-6: Improvements and refinements to the secure remote password protocol.* Retrieved from http://grouper.ieee.org/groups/1363/passwdPK/contributions.html#Wu02

Yan, J., & Ahmad, A. S. E. (2007). Breaking visual CAPTCHAs with naive pattern recognition algorithms. In *Proceedings of the 23rd Annual Computer Security Applications Conference.*

Yan, J., & Ahmad, A. S. E. (2008). A low-cost attack on a Microsoft CAPTCHA. In *Proceedings of the 15th ACM conference on Computer and Communications Security* (p. 543-554). Alexandria, VA.

Ylonen, T., Kivinen, T., Saarinen, M., Rinne, T., & Lehtinen, S. (2002, September 20). (Manuscript submitted for publication). *SSH protocol architecture.* Internet-Draft draft-ietf-secsh-architecture-13.txt. *Working.*

APPENDIX

The cryptographic authentication techniques of this chapter are based on the one-client one-server model. This model can be naturally extended to the case of many clients and one server, where the server stores verification data for each client and each client performs authentication with the server independently.

Some web applications (such as those peer-to-peer applications) may require authentication between clients who do not share authentication credentials. A central server can be employed as an authentication infrastructure component to bridge the authentication between these clients. This central server stores an authentication credential for each client. Kerberos is such an authentication infrastructure based on cryptography and interested readers can read (Garman, J. 2003; Kohl, Neuman, & Ts'o, 1991; Kohl & Neuman, 1993; Neuman & Ts'o, 1994; Bellovin & Merritt, 1991). It is worth noting that Kerberos v5 is still vulnerable to off-line dictionary attacks (Wu, 1999) and this vulnerability can be fixed by PAKE.

For good usability, multiple web applications may share the same authentication and to access these applications, users need to authenticate only once. This is commonly known as single sign-on and several single sign-on solutions have been developed, including Windows Live and the Liberty Alliance.

Section 2
Cryptography in E-Mail and Web Services

Chapter 3
E–Mail, Web Service and Cryptography

Wasim A. Al-Hamdani
Kentucky State University, USA

ABSTRACT

Cryptography is the study and practice of protecting information and has been used since ancient times in many different shapes and forms to protect messages from being intercepted. However, since 1976, when data encryption was selected as an official Federal Information Processing Standard (FIPS) for the United States, cryptography has gained large attention and a great amount of application and use. Furthermore, cryptography started to be part of protected public communication when e-mail became commonly used by the public. There are many electronic services. Some are based on web interaction and others are used as independent servers, called e-mail hosting services, which is an Internet hosting service that runs e-mail servers. Encrypting e-mail messages as they traverse the Internet is not the only reason to understand or use various cryptographic methods. Every time one checks his/her e-mail, the password is being sent over the wire. Many Internet service providers or corporate environments use no encryption on their mail servers and the passwords used to check mail are submitted to the network in clear text (with no encryption). When a password is put into clear text on a wire, it can easily be intercepted. Encrypting email will keep all but the most dedicated hackers from intercepting and reading a private communications. Using a personal email certificate one can digitally sign an email so that recipients can verify that it's really from the sender as well as encrypt the messages so that only the intended recipients can view it. Web service is defined as "a software system designed to support interoperable machine-to-machine interaction over a network" and e-mail is "communicate electronically on the computer". This chapter focus on introduce three topics: E-mail structure and organization, web service types, their organization and cryptography algorithms which integrated in the E-mail and web services to provide high level of security. The main issue in this article is to build the general foundation through Definitions, history, cryptography algorithms symmetric and asymmetric, hash algorithms, digital signature, suite B and general principle to introduce the use of cryptography in the E-mail and web service.

DOI: 10.4018/978-1-61520-783-1.ch003

INTRODUCTION

Cryptography is the science of writing in secret code and is an ancient art; the first documented use of cryptography in writing dates back to circa 1900 B.C. when an Egyptian scribe used non-standard hieroglyphs in an inscription. Some experts argue that cryptography appeared spontaneously sometime after writing was invented, with applications ranging from diplomatic missives to war-time battle plans. It is no surprise, then, that new forms of cryptography came soon after the widespread development of computer communications. In data and telecommunications, cryptography is necessary when communicating over any untrusted medium, which includes just about any network, particularly the Internet.

The Internet is a big place with a lot of people on it. It is very easy for someone who has access to the computers or networks through which someone information is traveling to capture this information and read it; this could cause threat such as: identity theft, message modification, false messages, message replay, unprotected backups and repudiation.

Web service is defined as "a software system designed to support interoperable machine-to-machine interaction over a network" and e-mail is "communicate electronically on the computer".

There are many electronic services. Some are based on web interaction and others are used as independent servers, called e-mail hosting services, which is an Internet hosting service that runs e-mail servers. E-mail hosting services usually offer quality e-mail at a cost as opposed to advertising-supported free e-mail or free webmail. E-mail hosting services thus differ from typical end-user e-mail providers, such as webmail sites. They outfit mostly to demanding e-mail users and small and mid-size businesses, while larger enterprises usually run their own e-mail hosting service. E-mail hosting providers allow for quality e-mail services besides the custom configurations and large number of accounts. Hosting providers manage a user's own domain name, including any e-mail authentication scheme that the domain owner wishes to enforce in order to convey the meaning that using a specific domain name identifies and qualifies e-mail senders.

The chapter starts with a general definition and short history of the two major themes, e-mail and Web service, followed with a cryptography section that discusses an encryption algorithm and the practical application of encryption as a digital signature, general cryptography classifications, and the standard cryptography suites authorized by the National Security Agency (NSA). Next are the short studies on e-mail protocols as a general then a deep look at encryption e-mail protocols such as S/MIME and PGP.

Cryptography is the practice and study of hiding information; the Integration of cryptography in email and web service provides:

- Confidentiality (the information cannot be understood by anyone for whom it was unintended),
- Integrity (the information cannot be altered in storage or transit between sender and intended receiver without the alteration being detected),
- Non-repudiation (the creator/sender of the information cannot deny at a later stage his or her intentions in the creation or transmission of the information) and
- Authentication (the sender and receiver can confirm each other's identity and the origin/destination of the information.

The cryptography section covers: definition, symmetric, asymmetric, stream cipher, hash, digital signature, the suite B standard, authentication, cryptography message syntax an the last section is general introduction to Cryptography standards algorithms.

The article start with definition and history, followed with detail description for the three elements of this article.

The Web service section covers general definitions End to End Quality of Service and Protection, Security techniques for Web services and how Web services security can provides message integrity, confidentiality, and authentication.

The E-mail section covers client base and web base E-mail, E-mail protocols, application-based e-mail and different E-mail protocols

DEFINITION AND HISTORY

In this section, we will look at the definition and a short history for the three major elements of this chapter, which are:

- E-mail
- Web
- Cryptography

E-mail

Electronic mail, often abbreviated to e-mail, email or eMail, is any method of creating, transmitting, or storing primarily text-based human communications with digital communications systems (Wikipedia.org, E-mail, 2009).

E-mail is much older than the Advanced Research Projects Agency Network (ARPANET) of the U.S. Department of Defense or the Internet (Peter, 2003; Crocker, 2009). It was never invented; it evolved from very simple beginnings.

Early e-mail was just as a file directory, it just put a message in another user's directory in a spot where they could see it when they logged in, like leaving a note on someone's desk. Probably the first e-mail system of this type was MAILBOX, used at Massachusetts Institute of Technology from 1965. Another early program to send messages on the same computer was called SNDMSG. E-mail could only be used to send messages to various users of the same computer.

Once computers began to talk to each other over networks, however, the problem became a little more complex. This is why Ray Tomlinson (Wikipedia.org, Ray Tomlinson, 2009) is credited with inventing e-mail in 1972. Tomlinson worked for Bolt, Beranek, and Newman as an ARPANET contractor. He picked the @ symbol from the computer keyboard to denote sending messages from one computer to another. It was simply a matter of recommend name-of-the-user@name-of-the-computer. Internet pioneer Jon Postel (Wikipedia. org, Jon Postel, 2009; Postel.org, 2009) was one of the first users of the new system, and is credited with describing it as a "nice hack".

Despite what the World Wide Web offers, e-mail remains the most important application of the Internet and the most widely used facility it has. Now more than 600 million people internationally use e-mail. Larry Roberts (Pioneers, 2009) invented some e-mail folders for his boss so he could sort his mail, a big advance. In 1975, John Vital (Peter, 2003) developed some software to organize e-mail. By 1976 e-mail had really taken off, and commercial packages began to appear. Within a couple of years, 75% of all ARPANET traffic was e-mail.

The first important e-mail standard was called simple message transfer protocol (SMTP) (Postel, 1982), It was very simple and is still in use – however, as we will hear later in this series, SMTP was a fairly naïve protocol. When Internet standards for e-mail began to mature, the POP (or post office protocol) servers began to appear as a standard.

E-mail servers are probably about the most complicated servers (CrazySquirrel, 2009)to set up because not only is there a huge number of security implications to running your own mail server, but they also tend to be split up into many small parts that all do different, highly specialized, things. At the pointy end of the system is the Mail Transport Agent MTA which does the grunt work of moving e-mail around on the Internet. Probably the most popular MTA is sendmail, but there are plenty of others to choose from, including courier-mta, postfix, and qmail as well as pay for offerings. The MTA probably has the most security issues as it is world facing. There used to be problems (and to some extent there still is) with open relays. These are badly configured MTAs that allow anyone to connect and send e-mail through them. Many modern MTAs make it deliberately quite difficult to configure an open relay.

The next step down is the mail delivery agent (MDA) and its job of delivering the e-mail to the user. Typically, this means placing the e-mail in mbox or maildir. A popular MDA is maildrop, but, as with MTAs, plenty of others exist (for instance, procmail). As well as delivering the mail, the MDA often filters the mail as well. This can be just a simple set of rules for putting certain e-mail in certain folders or it can be as complex as integrating multiple external mail scanners that check to spam and viruses.

Depending on the set up, the next part is optional but almost always present and is either an IMAP or POP server.

An IMAP server means that you will be able to easily check your mail from anywhere in the world. Again, there are loads of IMAP servers, but they vary in quality. The IMAP server essentially owns your mailbox and provides a view of it to the next layer of software, the mail user agent (MUA). The MUA is the bottom step of the ladder. This is the application that one actually read his e-mail with. The reason that the layer above is optional is because there are a few MUAs that can directly read mbox format files.

E-mail represents all the systems and mechanisms by which a message entered into a network-connected device finds its way to a destination device. The way we normally speak about e-mail encompasses the messages themselves, the systems that handle the delivery of the messages, the software that allows users to send and receive the e-mail, the specifications that define how those messages are formatted, addressed, sent, transmitted, and received. You've mastered e-mail if you can understand how those five things — formatting, addressing, sending, transmitting, and receiving — work. Those five

things are what the standards are all about, and what this book is all about. Those things work in specific ways for the Internet.

CRYPTOGRAPHY

The word cryptography means "secret writing". Some define cryptography as the study of mathematical techniques. Cryptography is a function that transfers plaintext (P_t) into ciphertext $(C_t,)$ and decryption is the inverse function that transfers ciphertext into plaintext (Al-Hamdani, 2008).

Cryptographic Goals

The cryptography goals are privacy or confidentiality, data integrity, authentication, and non-repudiation.

Classification

A crypto system could be classified generally as "Unkeyed" (key is not required for encryption and decryption) -based algorithms and "keyed" (key is required for encryption and decryption) based. Unkeyed based are classified further into "hash functions" (a method of turning data into a (relatively) small number that may serve as a digital "fingerprint" of the data) and "pseudorandom generator" (an algorithm generates a sequence of numbers that approximate the properties of random numbers). Keyed based is classified into "symmetric" key ("secret key") (uses identical key for encryption and decryption) and "asymmetric" ("public key") (the key for encryption and decryption are not identical). Symmetric algorithms are classified into "block cipher" (encryption and decryption accomplish on fixed size of plaintext/ciphertext called block of bits), "stream ciphers" (encryption and decryptions are accomplished on sequence of bits one bit at a time), "digital signatures" (an electronic signature that can be used to authenticate the identity of the sender of a message or the signer of a document), hash functions, pseudorandom generator, "identification" (identifying something, map a known entity to unknown entity to make it known), and "authentications" (who or what it claims to be). Asymmetric are classified into digital signatures, identification, and authentications.

The symmetric could be classified as "conventional" or "classical" and "modern" algorithms. The classical are classified into "transposition "and "substitution"; another type of cryptography is called the "hybrid", which combines symmetric and asymmetric to form hybrid ciphers.

Attacks on a crypto system are "passive attacks" (called "traffic analysis" in which the intruder eavesdrops but does not modify the message stream) and "active attack" (intruder modifies (deletes, replays) the message) (Stallings, 2005). There are many different attacks, such as:

- Ciphertext only attack
- known-plaintext attack
- chosen-plaintext attack
- adaptive chosen-plaintext attack
- Chosen ciphertext attack
- adaptive chosen ciphertext attack
- algebraic attack
- man-in-the-middle attack
- exhaustive key search or brute force attack

Cryptography Terminology (Public-Key Cryptosystems, 2008)

Algorithm: is an explicit description of how a particular computation should be performed (or a problem solved). The efficiency of an algorithm can be measured as the number of elementary steps it takes to solve the problem, which can be expressed using the big -O notation. Another definition is or "effective method" (Rosser 1939)

Computational complexity: investigates the problems related to the amounts of resources required for the execution of algorithms (e.g., execution time), A problem is polynomial time or

in P if it can be solved by an algorithm that takes less than $O(n^t)$ steps. If a guessed solution to a problem can be verified in polynomial time, then the problem is said to be in NP (non-deterministic polynomial time). The set of problems that lie in NP is very large and includes the problem of integer factorization.

A problem is NP-hard if there is no other problem in NP that is easier to solve. There is no known polynomial time algorithm for any NP-hard problem, and it is believed that such algorithms in fact do not exist. In public-key cryptography, the attacker is interested in solving particular instances of a problem (factoring some given number), rather than providing a general solution (an algorithm to factor any possible number efficiently). This causes some concern for cryptographers, as some instances of a problem that is NP-hard in general may be easily solvable.

- **Primes**: A prime number is a number that has no divisors except for itself and 1.
- **Factoring**: Every integer can be represented uniquely as a product of prime numbers.
- **Discrete logarithms**: is the problem of finding n given only some y such that $y = g^n$.
- **Knapsacks**: Given a small set of integers, the knapsack problem consists of determining a subset of these integers such that their sum is equal to a given integer.
- **Lattices**: The problem of finding the shortest vector in a lattice (using the usual Euclidean distance).

PRACTICAL CRYPTOSYSTEMS

Symmetric Key Algorithms: DES, AES

- **DES:** Data encryption standard (Federal Register, 2005) was approved as a federal standard in November 1976, and published on 15 January 1977 as FIPS PUB 46, authorized for use on all unclassified data. It was subsequently reaffirmed as the standard in 1983, 1988 (revised as FIPS-46-1), 1993 (FIPS-46-2), and again in 1999 (FIPS-46-3), the latter prescribing "Triple DES" which still used in some application. DES applies a 56-bit key to each 64-bit block of data. The process involves 16 rounds with major two processes – key and plaintext (Simovits, 1995).

- **Triple-DES** (3DES) is a 64-bit block cipher with 168-bit key and 48 rounds, 2^{56} times stronger than DES, and uses three times the resources to perform the encryption/decryption process compared to DES.
  - DES-EEE3 – three different keys
  - DES-EDE3 – three different keys
  - ES-EEE2 – two different keys
  - DES-EDE2 – two different keys
- **DESX** is a strengthened variant of DES supported by RSA Security's toolkits. The difference between DES and DESX is that in DESX, the input plaintext is bitwise XORed with 64 bits of additional key material before encryption with DES and the output is also bitwise XORed with another 64 bits of key material (RSA.com, 2007).
- **Advanced Encryption Standard (AES):** "Rijndael" designed to use simple byte operations, the key size and the block size may be chosen from of 128, 192, or 256 with a variable number of rounds. The numbers of rounds are:
  - Nine if both the block and the key are 128 bits long.
  - 11 if either the block or the key is 192 bits long, and neither of them is longer than that.
  - 13 if either the block or the key is 256 bits long.

The total number of rounds key bits is equal to block length multiplied by the number or rounds

plus 1. In the general process of SAE, the first (r-l) rounds are similar and they consists of four transformation called: ByteSub-Substitution Bytes, ShiftRow- Shift Rows, MixColumn- Multiply Columns and AddRoundKey- XORed by the key. The last round only performs the transformations ByteSub and ShiftRow.

The AES standard (NIST FIPS Pub. 197) was published in 2002. The algorithm is adopted for the Internet community through the use of Request for Comments: 3394. The purpose of this document is to make the algorithm conveniently available to the Internet community.

AES is used for other applications and specified with ISO as ISO 26429-6:2008. This defines the syntax of encrypted digital cinema non-interleaved material exchange format (MXF) frame-wrapped track files and specifies a matching reference decryption model. It uses the advanced encryption standard (AES) cipher algorithm for essence encryption and, optionally, the HMAC-SHA1 algorithm for essence integrity. The digital cinema track file format is designed to carry digital cinema essence for distribution to exhibition sites and is specified in the sound and picture track file specification.

- **International Data Encryption Algorithm (IDEA):** IDEA operates on 64-bit blocks using a 128-bit key, and eight rounds and an output transformation (the half-round). It has been used with PGP.
- **Other Block Cipher Algorithms (Al-Hamdani, 2008):** RC2 (block size: 64, key size: 1..128;), RC5 (block size: 32, 64 and 128; key size: 0..2040; number of rounds: 0..255) RC6 (block size: 128; keysize: 0..2040 (128, 192, and 256)).

Block Cipher Modes of Operation

The block cipher works with a message of block size n bits (for example DES n=64), a message M that exceed the size of n bits must be partitioned into m block, then linking these blocks in a certain mechanism. The method of combining all encrypted blocks is called *mode of operations*. There are four basic modes of operations, which are electronic code book (ECB), cipher block chaining (CBC), K-bit cipher feedback (CFB), and K-bit output feedback (OFB).

First Part: Five Confidentiality MODES (Dworkin 2001)

In Special Publication 800-38A, five confidentiality modes are specified for use with any approved block cipher, such as the AES algorithm. The modes in SP 800-38A are updated versions of the ECB, CBC, CFB, and OFB modes that are specified in FIPS Pub. 81; in addition, SP 800-38A specifies the CTR mode.

The NIST has developed a proposal to extend the domain of the CBC mode with a version of "ciphertext stealing."[1] Eventually, the NIST expects to incorporate into a new edition of SP 800-38A some form ciphertext stealing for CBC mode.

Second Part: An AuthenticationMODE (Dworkin 2005)

The CMAC authentication mode is specified in Special Publication 800-38B for use with any approved block cipher. CMAC stands for cipher-based message authentication code (MAC), analogous to HMAC, the hash-based MAC algorithm.

Third Part: An Authenticated Encryption MODE (Dworkin 2004)

Special Publication 800-38C specifies the CCM mode of the AES algorithm. CCM combines the counter mode for confidentiality with the cipher block chaining technique for authentication. The specification is intended to be compatible with the use of CCM within a draft amendment to the IEEE 802.11 standard for wireless local area networks.

Fourth Part: A High-Throughput Authenticated Encryption Mode (Dworkin 2007)

Special Publication 800-38D specifies the Galois/Counter Mode (GCM) of the AES algorithm. GCM combines the counter mode for confidentiality with an authentication mechanism that is based on a universal hash function. GCM was designed to facilitate high-throughput hardware implementations; software optimizations are also possible, if certain lookup tables can be precomputed from the key and stored in memory.

In the future, the NIST intends to recommend at least one additional mode: the AES Key Wrap (AESKW). AESKW is intended for the authenticated encryption ("wrapping") of specialized data, such as cryptographic keys, without using a nonce for distribution or storage. AESKW invokes the block cipher about 12 times per block of data. The design provides security properties that may be desired for high assurance applications; the tradeoff is relatively inefficient performance compared to other modes.

Asymmetric Algorithms

There are four general practical cryptography systems. These are:

- **public key**, and includes factorization, RSA, and Rabin
  - **RSA** (Rivest-Shamir-Adleman) (Rivest, Shamir, & Adleman, 1983) is the most commonly used public-key algorithm. It can be used both for encryption and for digital signatures. The security of RSA is generally considered equivalent to factoring, although this has not been proved (RSA.com, 2008).
  - **Rabin** is an asymmetric cryptographic technique, whose security, like that of RSA, is related to the difficulty of

factorization, although it has a quite different decoding process.

- **Discrete logs**: Diffie-Hellman, ElGamal, and DSS
  - ○ **Diffie-Hellman** (RSA.com, 2007) is a commonly used protocol for key agreement protocol (also called exponential key agreement) was developed by Diffie and Hellman (Diffie & Hellman, 1976) in 1976 and published in the groundbreaking paper "New Directions in Cryptography." The protocol allows two users to exchange a secret key over an insecure medium without any prior secrets.
  - ○ **ElGamal** is an extension of Diffie/Hellman's original idea on shared secret generation, it generates a shared secret and uses it as a one-time pad to encrypt one block of data. The ElGamal algorithm provides an alternative to the RSA for public key encryption.
    1) Security of the RSA depends on the (presumed) difficulty of factoring large integers.
    2) Security of the ElGamal algorithm depends on the (presumed) difficulty of computing discrete logs in a large prime modulus.

ElGamal has the disadvantage that the ciphertext is twice as long as the plaintext. It has the advantage the same plaintext gives a different ciphertext (with near certainty) each time it is encrypted.

- **DSS** (Digital Signature Standard): Not to be confused with a digital certificate (SearchSecurity.com, 2008) DSS is an electronic signature that can be used to authenticate the identity of the sender of a message or the signer of a document, and possibly to ensure that the original content

of the message or document that has been sent is unchanged. Digital signatures are easily transportable, cannot be imitated by someone else, and can be automatically time-stamped. The ability to ensure that the original signed message arrived means that the sender cannot easily repudiate it later. A signature-only mechanism endorsed by the United States Government. The underlying digital signature algorithm (DSA) is similar to the one used by ElGamal or by the Schnorr signature algorithm. Also it is fairly efficient, although not as efficient as RSA for signature verification. The standard defines DSS to use the SHA-1 hash function exclusively to compute message digests. The main problem with DSS is the fixed subgroup size (the order of the generator element), which limits the security to around only 80 bits. A digital signature can be used with any kind of message, whether it is encrypted or not, simply so that the receiver can be sure of the sender's identity and that the message arrived intact. A digital certificate contains the digital signature of the certificate-issuing authority so that anyone can verify that the certificate is real.

- **Elliptic Curve:** Elliptic curves are mathematical constructions from number theory and algebraic geometry, which in recent years have found numerous applications in cryptography. An elliptic curve can be defined over any field (e.g., real, rational, complex). Elliptic curves can provide versions of public key methods that, in some cases, are faster and use smaller keys, while providing an equivalent level of security. Their advantage comes from using a different kind of mathematical group for public key arithmetic.

- **Elliptic curves over real numbers:** They are named because they are described by cubic equations. In general, cubic equations for elliptic curves take the form $y^2+axy+by=x^3+cx^2+dx+e$ where a,b,c,d and e are real numbers and x and y take on values in the real numbers. It is sufficient to be limited to equations of the form $y^2=x^3+ax+b$(Cubic). Also included in the definition is a single element denoted **O** and called the *point at infinity* or the *zero point,* which to plot such a curve, we need to compute $y=\sqrt{x^3+ax+b}$ for given values of a and b; thus, the plot consists of positive and negative values of y for each value of x.

Stream Cipher

A onetime pad system (*vernam cipher)* is defined as $C_{ti}=Pti\oplus Ki$ for i=1,2,3,4…n where $P_{t1},P_{t2},P_{t3},…P_{tn}$ plaintext bits, $k_1,k_2,k_3…k_n$ key bits, $C_{t1},C_{t2},C_{t3},…C_{tn}$ ciphertext bits, and $\oplus$ is the XOR function. The decryption is defined by $P_{ti}=Cti\oplus Ki$ for i=1,2,3,4.

- **RC4:** RC4 (RSA.com 2007) is a software type of stream cipher based on tables and internal memory. It is based on the use of a random permutation based on numbers 0... 255 represented as an array of length 256 and two indices in this array. RC4 is most commonly used to protect Internet traffic using the secure sockets layer (SSL) protocol and wired equivalent privacy (WEP).

Integrity and Authentication

The mechanism for ensuring that data is not altered when transmitted from source to destination, or when it is stored, is called integrity; this includes the message authentication code (MAC), hash functions, and the keyed-hash message authentication code (HMAC).

- **MAC**: (RSA.com, 2007): A message authentication code (MAC) is an authentica-

tion tag (also called a checksum) derived by applying an authentication scheme, together with a secret key, to a message. Unlike digital signatures, MACs are computed and verified with the same key, so that they can only be verified by the intended recipient. There are four types of MACs: (1) unconditionally secure, (2) hash function based, (3) stream cipher based, or (4) block cipher based.

- **Hash functions** (Mogollon, 2007) are used to prove that transmitted data was not altered. A hash function *H* takes an input message *m* and transforms it to produce a hash value *h* that is a function of the message *h = H (m)*; the input is a variable string and the output is a fixed-size string.

- **The SHA** (Federal Information, 1993; Eastlake & Motorola, 2001) hash functions are a set of cryptographic hash functions designed by the National Security Agency (NSA) and published by the NIST as a U.S. Federal Information Processing Standard. SHA stands for secure hash algorithm. The three SHA algorithms are structured differently and are distinguished as SHA-0, SHA-1, and SHA-2. The SHA-2 family uses an identical algorithm with a variable key size which is distinguished as SHA-224, SHA-256, SHA-384, and SHA-512.SHA-1 is the best established of the existing SHA hash functions, and is employed in several widely used security applications and protocols. In 2005, security flaws were identified in SHA-1, namely that a possible mathematical weakness might exist, indicating that a stronger hash function would be desirable. Although no attacks have yet been reported on the SHA-2 variants, they are algorithmically similar to SHA-1 and so efforts are underway to develop improved alternatives. A new hash function, to be known as SHA-3, is currently under development, to be selected via open competition starting in 2008, and to be made official in 2012.

- **A keyed-hash message authentication code** (Bellare, Canetti, & Hugo, 1996a, b; Kim, Biryukov, Prenee, & Hong, 2006) (HMAC or KHMAC) is a type of message authentication code (MAC) calculated using a specific algorithm involving a cryptographic hash function in combination with a secret key. As with any MAC, it may be used to simultaneously verify both the data integrity and the authenticity of a message. Any iterative cryptographic hash function, such as MD5 or SHA-1, may be used in the calculation of an HMAC; the resulting MAC algorithm is termed HMAC-MD5 or HMAC-SHA-1 accordingly. The cryptographic strength of the HMAC depends upon the cryptographic strength of the underlying hash function, on the size and quality of the key and the size of the hash output length in bits. An iterative hash function breaks up a message into blocks of a fixed size and iterates over them with a compression function. For example, MD5 and SHA-1 operate on 512-bit blocks. The size of the output of HMAC is the same as that of the underlying hash function (128 or 160 bits in the case of MD5 or SHA-1, respectively), although it can be truncated if desired.

Authentication Mechanisms Class

Authentication mechanism fall into two basic categories: password and challenge response.

Password SHA

Password SHA is popular and has some natural limitations. The simplest kind of connection-oriented authentication uses a shared secret in the form of a password, a personal identification number (PIN), or passphrase. The most significant characteristic of password-based systems is that the authentication does not depend on information sent by the side performing the authentication check. HTTP basic authentication is not considered to be a secure method of user authentication, unless used in conjunction with some external secure system such as SSL.

Challenge-Response Authentication

It can be more complex to set up, but it provides a significantly higher level of security the entity performing the authentication check first sends out a challenge. The client system trying to prove the user's identity performs some function on the challenge based on information only available to the user/client and returns the result. If the result is as expected, the user is authenticated.

Kerberos (Mit.edu, 2007)

A computer network authentication protocol, which allows individuals communicating over a non-secure network to prove their identity to one another in a secure manner, is also a client-server model, and it provides mutual authentication — both the user and the server verify each other's identity. Kerberos protocol messages are protected against eavesdropping and replay attacks. Kerberos builds on symmetric key cryptography and requires a trusted third party. Extensions to Kerberos can provide for the use of public-key cryptography during certain phases of authentication.

OTHER ALGORITHMS

Cryptographic Message Syntax (Housley, 1999, 2004)

The CMS describes encapsulation syntax for data protection. It supports digital signatures and encryption. The syntax allows multiple encapsulations; one encapsulation envelope can be nested inside another. Likewise, one party can digitally sign some previously encapsulated data. It also allows arbitrary attributes, such as signing time, to be signed along with the message content, and provides for other attributes such as countersignatures to be associated with a signature. The CMS can support a variety of architectures for certificate-based key management. The CMS values are generated using ASN.1 [X.208-88], using BER-encoding [X.209-88]. Values are typically represented as octet strings. While many systems are capable of transmitting arbitrary octet strings reliably, it is well known that many electronic mail systems are not. This document does not address mechanisms for encoding octet strings for reliable transmission in such environments.

The CMS is derived from PKCS #7 version 1.5, which is documented in RFC 2315 [PKCS#7]. A PKCS #7 version 1.5 was developed outside of the IETF. It was originally published as an RSA Laboratories technical note in November 1993. Since that time, the IETF has taken responsibility for the development and maintenance of the CMS. Advance encryption standard has be enforced with CMS since 2003 (Schaad, 2003).

NSA Suite B Cryptography (Nsa.gov, 2005)

Suite B is a set of cryptographic algorithms promulgated by the National Security Agency as part of its cryptographic modernization program. It is to serve as an interoperable cryptographic base for both unclassified information and most classified information. Suite B was announced on February 16, 2005. A corresponding set of unpublished algorithms, Suite A, is intended for highly sensitive communication and critical authentication systems. Suite B only specifies the cryptographic algorithms to be used. Many other factors need to be addressed in determining whether a particular device implementing a particular set of crypto-

graphic algorithms should be used to satisfy a particular requirement. These include:

1. The quality of the implementation of the cryptographic algorithm in software, firmware or hardware;
2. Operational requirements associated with U.S. government-approved key and key-management activities;
3. The uniqueness of the information to be protected (e.g. special intelligence, nuclear command and control, U.S.-only data);
4. Requirements for interoperability both domestically and internationally.

The process by which these factors are addressed is outside the scope of Suite B. Suite B focuses only on cryptographic technology, a small piece of an overall information assurance system. Another suite of NSA cryptography, Suite A, contains classified algorithms that will not be released. Suite A will be used for the protection of some categories of especially sensitive information (a small percentage of the overall national security related information assurance market).

Suite B includes:

- **Encryption:** Advanced Encryption Standard (AES) - FIPS 197(with keys sizes of 128 and 256 bits)
- **Digital Signature:** Elliptic Curve Digital Signature Algorithm - FIPS 186-2 (using the curves with 256 and 384-bit prime moduli)
- **Key Exchange:** Elliptic Curve Diffie-Hellman Draft NIST Special Publication 800-56 (using the curves with 256 and 384-bit prime moduli)
- **Hashing:** Secure Hash Algorithm - FIPS 180-2 (using SHA-256 and SHA-384)

The Committee on National Security Systems (CNSS) (Cnss.gov, 2003) stated that AES with either 128-or 256-bit keys are sufficient to protect classified information up to the SECRET level. Protecting top secret information would require the use of 256-bit AES keys[1] as well as numerous other controls on manufacture, handling and keying. These same key sizes are suitable for protecting both national security and non-national security related information throughout the USG.

Consistent with CNSSP-15, Elliptic Curve Public Key Cryptography using the 256-bit prime modulus elliptic curve as specified in FIPS-186-2 and SHA-256 are appropriate for protecting classified information up to the SECRET level. Use of the 384-bit prime modulus elliptic curve and SHA-384 are necessary for the protection of TOP SECRET information.

All implementations of Suite B must, at a minimum, include AES with 256-bit keys, the 384-bit prime modulus elliptic curve and SHA-384 as a common mode for widespread interoperability.

Standards

The Suite B Base Certificate and CRL Profile is provided as part of the overarching Cryptographic Interoperability Strategy

Testing, Evaluation and Certification of "Suite B" Products

Creating secure cryptographic equipment involves much more than simply implementing a specific suite of cryptographic algorithms. Within the USG there are various ways to have cryptographic equipment tested or evaluated and certified. These methods include:

1. The Cryptographic Module Verification Program (CMVP)
2. The Common Criteria Evaluation and Validation Scheme (CCEVS)
3. Evaluation by the National Security Agency

Access Authentication

Authentication is essential for two parties to be able to trust in each other's identities. Authentication is based on something you know (a password), on something you have (a token card, a digital certificate), or something that is part of you (fingerprints, voiceprint). A strong authentication requires at least two of these factors. The mechanisms of authentication for example are:

- IEEE 802.1X Access Control Protocol;
- Extensible Authentication Protocol (EAP) and EAP methods;
- traditional passwords;
- Remote Authentication Dial-in Service (RADIUS);
- Kerberos authentication service; and
- X.509 authentication.

Cryptography Algorithms Standards

There are three types of standardization organizations.

- National standardization organizations: National Institute of Standards and Technology (NIST), American National Standards Institute (ANSI), and British Standards Institute (BSI).
- International standardization organizations: International Organization for Standardization (ISO), International Electrotechnical Commission (IEC), and International Telecommunication Union (ITU).
- Industrial standardization organizations: Institute of Electrical and Electronics Engineers (IEEE), Public-Key Cryptography Standards (PKCSs), Internet Engineering Task Force (IETF), Standards for Efficient Cryptography Group (SECG), Third Generation Partnership Project (3GPP) and European Telecommunications Standard Institute (ETSI).

Standard is defined as "a level of quality"; "an accepted example of something against which others are judged or measured"; and "a reference point against which other things can be evaluated".

A cryptography standard is the "level of algorithm quality in which an algorithm that's been proved theoretically and practically is strong and can stand different attacks for years". Some algorithms need special procedures to satisfy the standard and it should be clarified that certain standardized techniques are known to be weak unless used with care and such guidance is also typically present in the standard itself.

Standards are important because they define common practices, methods, and measures/metrics. Therefore, standards increase the reliability and effectiveness of products and ensure that the products are produced with a degree of quality. Standards provide solutions that have been accepted by a wide community and evaluated by experts in relevant areas. By using standards, organizations can reduce costs and protect their investments in technology.

Standards provide the following benefits:

- Interoperability
- Security
- Quality

Many NIST standards and recommendations contain associated conformance tests and specify the conformance requirements. The conformance tests may be administered by NIST-accredited laboratories and provide validation that the NIST standard or recommendation was correctly implemented in the product.

In sum, standards provide a common form of reference and cost savings. In particular, the NIST Special Publication 800-21 provides a Guideline for Implementing Cryptography in the Federal Government.

The Standards for Efficient CryptographyGroup (SECG)

The Standards for Efficient Cryptography Group (SECG), an industry consortium, was founded in 1998 to develop commercial standards that facilitate the adoption of efficient cryptography and interoperability across a wide range of computing platforms. SECG members include leading technology companies and key industry players in the information security industry. The group exists to develop commercial standards for efficient and interoperable cryptography based on elliptic curve cryptography (ECC).

WEB SERVICES

Web service is defined as "a software system designed to support interoperable machine-to-machine interaction over a network" (W3C, 2004). Some defines Web service as a network accessible interface to application functionality, built using standard Internet technologies (Costello, 2009). Web services are frequently just Web APIs that can be accessed over a network, such as the Internet, and executed on a remote system hosting the requested services.

The Web services that we see deployed on the Internet today are HTML Web sites. In these, the application services the mechanisms for publishing, managing, searching, and retrieving content are accessed through the use of standard protocols and data formats: HTTP and HTML. Client applications (Web browsers) that understand these standards can interact with the application services to perform tasks like ordering books, sending greeting cards, or reading news.

The W3C Web service definition encompasses many different systems, but in common usage the term refers to clients and servers that communicate over the HTTP protocol used on the Web. Such services tend to fall into one of two camps: Big Web Services and RESTful Web Services (Wikipedia.org, Web service, 2009). Big Web Services use XML messages that follow the SOAP standard and have been popular with traditional enterprise. In such systems, there is often machine-readable description of the operations offered by the service written in the Web services description language (WSDL). The latter is not a requirement of a SOAP endpoint, but it is a prerequisite for automated client-side code generation in many Java and .NET SOAP frameworks (frameworks such as Spring, Apache Axis2, and Apache CXF being notable exceptions). Some industry organizations, such as the WS-I, mandate both SOAP and WSDL in their definition of a Web service. More recently, RESTful Web services (Costello, 2009) have been regaining popularity, particularly with Internet companies. These also meet the W3C definition, and are often better integrated with HTTP than SOAP-based services. They do not require XML.

Because of the abstraction provided by the standards-based interfaces, it does not matter whether the application services are written in Java and the browser written in C++, or the application services deployed on a Unix box while the browser is deployed on Windows. Web services allow for cross-platform interoperability in a way that makes the platform irrelevant. The Web services architecture is implemented through the layering of five types of technologies, organized into layers that build upon one another: Discovery, Description, Packaging, Transport, and Network. It should come as no surprise that this stack is very similar to the TCP/IP network model used to describe the architecture of Internet-based applications.

There are many ways that a requester entity might use a Web service. In general, the following broad steps are required (W3C, 2004):

(1) The requester and provider entities become known to each other (or at least one becomes know to the other);

(2) The requester and provider entities (somehow) agree on the service description and semantics that will govern the interaction between the requester and provider agents;

(3) The service description and semantics are understand by the requester and provider agents; and

(4) The requester and provider agents exchange messages, thus performing some task on behalf of the requester and provider entities. (I.e., the exchange of messages with the provider agent represents the concrete manifestation of interacting with the provider entity's Web service.) These steps are explained in more detail in 3.4 Web Service Discovery. Some of these steps may be automated, others may be performed manually.

The basic Web services platform is XML + HTTP. The HTTP protocol is the most used Internet protocol. XML provides a language that can be used between different platforms and programming languages and still express complex messages and functions. Web services platform elements:

• SOAP (Simple Object Access Protocol): SOAP is a simple XML-based protocol to let applications exchange information over HTTP. Or simpler, SOAP is an independent platform and protocol for accessing a Web service; SOAP stands for Simple Object Access Protocol; SOAP is a communication protocol via Internet; SOAP is a W3C standard

• UDDI (Universal Description, Discovery and Integration): Universal Description Discovery and Integration (UDDI) is a directory service where businesses can register and search for Web services; for storing information about web services; interfaces described by WSDL, it communicates via SOAP and built into the Microsoft .NET platform

- WSDL (Web Services Description Language): Web Services Description Language WSDL is an XML-based language for describing Web services and how to access them: used to describe Web services; used to locate Web services and a W3C standard

End to End Quality of Service and Protection

Most Web services deployed do not provide guarantees for Quality of Service (QoS) or Quality of Protection (QoP) under the scenario of attacks. QoS is important in defining the expected level of performance a particular Web service will have. The WS-Reliability and WS-Reliable Messaging standards provide some level of QoS. Both standards support guaranteed message delivery and message ordering.

Web Service Modes: there are three operation modes:

- Requester Web Services
- Provider Web Services
- Intermediary Web Services

Security techniques for Web services (Singhal, Winograd, & Scarfone, 2007):

- **Confidentiality of Web service messages using XML Encryption,** from the World Wide Web Consortium (W3C) and it provides a mechanism to encrypt XML documents.
- **Integrity of Web service messages using XML Signature.,** jointly by the W3C and the Internet Engineering Task Force (IETF). The power of XML Signature is to selectively sign XML data.
- **Web service authentication and authorization using XML Signature,** Security Assertion Markup Language (SAML) and eXtensible Access Control Markup

Language (XACML) as proposed by the Organization for Advancement of Structured Information Standards (OASIS) group. SAML and XACML provide mechanisms for authentication and authorization in a Web services environment.

- **Web Services (WS) Security,** by OASIS, defines a set of SOAP header extensions for end-to-end SOAP messaging security. It supports message integrity and confidentiality by allowing communicating partners to exchange signed encrypted messages in a Web services environment.
- **Security for Universal Description, Discovery and Integration (UDDI),** by OASIS, UDDI allows Web services to be easily located and subsequently invoked. Security for UDDI enables publishers, inquirers and subscribers to authenticate themselves and authorize the information published in the directory.

Some specifications have been developed or are currently being developed to extend Web Services capabilities. These specifications are generally referred to as WS-*. Here is a non-exhaustive list of these WS-* specifications.

- **WS-Security:** Defines how to use XML Encryption and XML Signature in SOAP to secure message exchanges? as an alternative or extension to using HTTPS to secure the channel.
- **WS-Reliability:** Standard protocol to handle reliable messages between two Web services.
- **WS-Transaction:** Methods of manage transactions.
- **WS-Addressing:** Standard to insert address in the SOAP header

Web Services Security Provides Message Integrity, Confidentiality, and Authentication (IBM, 2009)

OASIS Web Services Security (WS-Security) is a flexible standard that is designed to secure Web services within a wide variety of security models. SOAP secure messages can be achieved through XML digital signature, confidentiality through XML encryption, and credential propagation through security tokens. Web services implements security using technology that includes transport-level Secure Sockets Layer (SSL).

The Web services security specification defines the core facilities for protecting the integrity and confidentiality of a message and provides mechanisms for associating security-related claims with the message. Message-level security, or securing Web services at the message level, addresses the same security requirements as for traditional Web security. These security requirements include: identity, authentication, authorization, integrity, confidentiality, nonrepudiation, basic message exchange, and so forth. Both traditional Web and message-level security share many of the same mechanisms for handling security, including digital certificates, encryption, and digital signatures. While HTTPS and SSL transport-level technology may be used for securing Web services, some security scenarios are addressed more effectively by message-level security.

Traditional Web security mechanisms, such as HTTPS, might be insufficient to manage the security requirements of all Web service scenarios. For example, when an application sends a document with JAX-RPC using HTTPS, the message is secured only for the HTTPS connection, meaning during the transport of the document between the service requester (the client) and the service. However, the application might require that the document data be secured beyond the HTTPS connection, or even beyond the transport layer. By securing Web services at the message level,

message-level security is capable of meeting these expanded requirements.

Message-level security applies to XML documents that are sent as SOAP messages. Message-level security makes security part of the message itself by embedding all required security information in the SOAP header of a message. In addition, message-level security can apply security mechanisms, such as encryption and digital signature, to the data in the message itself.

With message-level security, the SOAP message itself either contains the information needed to secure the message or it contains information about where to get that information to handle security needs. The SOAP message also contains information relevant to the protocols and procedures for processing the specified message-level security. However, message-level security is not tied to any particular transport mechanism. Because the security information is part of the message, it is independent of a transport protocol, such as HTTPS.

The client adds to the SOAP message header security information that applies to that particular message. When the message is received, the Web service endpoint, using the security information in the header, verifies the secured message and validates it against the policy. For example, the service endpoint might verify the message signature and check that the message has not been tampered with. It is possible to add signature and encryption information to the SOAP message headers, as well as other information such as security tokens for identity (for example, an X.509 certificate) that are bound to the SOAP message content.

E-MAIL SYSTEM

In an e-mail system there are three players, they could be combined in one system or separated;

For example Microsoft outlook server could have the three players set up for an organization. These players are:

Webmail (or Web-Based E-Mail)

The primarily intend is to accessed e-mail via a web browser, as opposed to through an e-mail client, such as Microsoft Outlook, Mozilla's Thunderbird, or Apple Inc.'s Mail. Very popular webmail providers include Gmail, Yahoo! Mail, Hotmail and AOL (Brownlow, 2008). In 1997 Hotmail introduced its service, which became one of the first popular web-based e-mail offerings. Following Hotmail's initial success, Google's introduction of Gmail in 2004 sparked a period of rapid development in webmail, due to Gmail's new features such as JavaScript menus, text-based ads, and bigger storage. This type of e-mail all e-mails are on the server, one can reads a message whenever there is an access to the Internet.

Application-Based E-Mail

The application base is something like Outlook Express, where all your e-mail is downloaded to the user machine. The difference between (PCL cable, 2003) webmail and application based e-mail is in webmail; all your e-mail messages are located on the server, so you can check your e-mail from any computer with an Internet connection. On an application based e-mail, like Outlook Express, all your e-mail messages are downloaded from the server onto your computer, once you make a connection to the server. With this, you can check your e-mail only on the computer where your e-mail account is setup

E-Mail Client

It is an application that runs on a personal computer or workstation and enables a user to send, receive and organize e-mail. It's called a client because e-mail systems are based on client-server architecture. Mail is sent from many clients to a central server, which re-routes the mail to its intended destination.

Message Transfer Agents (MTAs) MTAs have links with other MTAs and are able to forward messages through the network. One might think that the aggregation of all linked MTAs can be viewed as the functional equivalent of a centralized

Mail user agent (MUA) or e-mail reader is an e-mail client it is known. The term e-mail client is also used to refer to any agent acting as a client toward an e-mail server, independently of it being a real MUA, a relaying server, or a human typing directly on a telnet terminal. In addition, a web application providing the relevant functionality is sometimes considered an e-mail client. MUA to permit users to deal with their mail with minimal technical knowledge, some functionality are provided to the end users to for making configuration decisions appropriate to the user's requirements. MUA is only active when a user runs it. Messages arrive on the Mail Transfer Agent (MTA) server. Unless the MUA has access to the server's disk, messages are stored on a remote server and the MUA has to request them on behalf of the user.

The relation between MTA and MUA is shown in Figure 1

E-Mail Protocols

Post Office Protocol (POP) (Myers & Rose, 1996) POP3 has made earlier versions of the protocol, informally called POP1 and POP2, obsolete. In contemporary usage, the less precise term POP almost always means POP3 in the context of e-mail protocols

The design of POP3 and its procedures supports end-users with intermittent connections (such as dial-up connections), allowing these users to retrieve e-mail when connected and then to view and manipulate the retrieved messages without needing to stay connected. Although most clients have an option to leave mail on server, e-mail clients using POP3 generally connect, retrieve all messages, store them on the user's PC as new messages, delete them from the server, and then disconnect

Once the TCP connection has been opened and the POP3 server has sent the greeting, the session enters the AUTHORIZATION state. In this state, the client must identify itself to the POP3 server. Once the client has successfully done this, the server acquires resources associated with the client's maildrop, and the session enters the TRANSACTION state. In this state, the client requests actions on the part of the POP3 server. When the client has issued the QUIT command, the session enters the UPDATE state. In this state, the POP3 server releases any resources acquired during the TRANSACTION state and says good-bye. The TCP connection is then closed.

Internet Message Access Protocol (IMAP) (Crispin, Internet Message Access Protocol-V4rev1, 1996) (Crispin, Internet Message Access Protocol-V4rev1, 2003) It was designed as a superset of POP3 and supports some additional features, for example searching capability through e-mail messages for keywords while the messages are still on mail server. It was designed to enhance both message retrieval and management as well as resolves many of the limitations of POP3 (e.g., password protection). The base IMAP specification is defined in RFC 2060. Version 4rev1 allows a client to access and manipulate electronic mail messages on a server and permits manipulation of mailboxes (remote message folders) in a way that is functionally equivalent to local folders, also provides the capability for an offline client to resynchronize with the server.

IMAP4rev1 includes operations for creating, deleting, and renaming mailboxes, checking for new messages, permanently removing messages, setting and clearing flags, RFC 2822 and RFC 2045 parsing, searching, and selective fetching of message attributes, texts, and portions thereof. Messages in IMAP4rev1 are accessed by the use of numbers. These numbers are either message sequence numbers or unique identifiers. IMAP4rev1 supports a single server. A mechanism for accessing configuration information to support multiple IMAP4rev1 servers is discussed in RFC 2244. IMAP4rev1 does not specify a means of posting mail; this function is handled by a mail transfer protocol such as RFC 2821. All interactions transmitted by client and server are in the form of lines, that is, strings that end with a CRLF. The protocol receiver of an IMAP4rev1 client or server is either reading a line, or is reading a sequence of octets with a known count followed by a line.

Figure 1. The relationships between MTA MUA

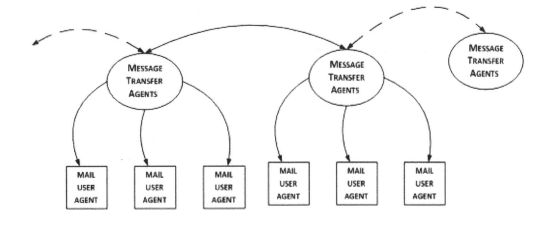

IMAP offered very little functionality beyond that of POP, but since 1988, it has evolved into a robust mailbox access protocol. The current edition of the IMAP standard is RFC 3501: *Internet Message Access Protocol – Version 4, Revision 1* (4rev1). Because IMAP 4rev1 supports many different features, it has a much wider command set than that of POP.

The following lists the associated RFCs for the noted IMAP extensions:

- MAP URL Scheme, RFC:2192
- IMAP/POP AUTHorize Extension for Simple Challenge/Response, RFC:2195
- IMAP4 ID extension, RFC:2971
- IMAP4 IDLE command, RFC:2177
- IMAP4 Login Referrals, RFC:2221
- IMAP4 Mailbox Referrals, RFC:2193
- IMAP4 Multi-Accessed Mailbox Practice, RFC:2180
- IMAP4 Namespace, RFC:2342
- IMAP4 non-synchronizing literals, RFC:2088
- IMAP4 QUOTA extension, RFC:2087
- IMAP4 UIDPLUS extension, RFC:4315

IMAP has been extended with a challenge/response mechanism comparable to APOP, which is called the Challenge-Response Authentication Mechanism (CRAM). CRAM requires the client to make note of the challenge data sent by the server and respond with a string consisting of the user's name, a space, and a digest computed by applying a keyed hash algorithm6 against the timestamp sent with the challenge, using a shared secret as the key(Tracy, Jansen and Bisker 2007).

Simple Mail Transfer Protocol (SMTP) (Bernstein, 2008) (wikipedia.org, Simple Mail Transfer Protocol (SMTP), 2008) The (SMTP) is the most widely used protocol to send messages by Message Transfer Agents (MTA) on the Internet. The protocol is defined in the RFC 821 and RFC 1123, and was designed to transfer mail independently of any specific transmission subsystem. Simple Mail Transport Protocol (SMTP) is the standard transport protocol for sending messages from one MTA to another MTA over the Internet. Using MIME encoding, it enables the transfer of text, video, multimedia, images, and audio attachments.

SMTP is a relatively simple, text-based protocol, in which one or more recipients of a message are specified (and in most cases verified to exist) along with the message text and possibly other encoded objects. The message is then transferred to a remote server using a series of queries and responses between the client and server. Either an end-user's e-mail client, a.k.a. MUA (Mail User Agent), or a relaying server's MTA (Mail Transport Agents) can act as an SMTP client.

A relaying server typically determines which SMTP server to connect to by looking up the MX (Mail eXchange) DNS record for each recipient's domain name. Conformant MTAs (not all) fall back to a simple A record in the case of no MX (relaying servers can also be configured to use a smart host). The SMTP client initiates a TCP connection to server's port 25 (unless overridden by configuration). It is quite easy to test an SMTP server using the netcat program.

SMTP is a "push" protocol that cannot "pull" messages from a remote server on demand. To retrieve messages only on demand, which is the most common requirement on a single-user computer, a mail client must use POP3 or IMAP. Another SMTP server can trigger a delivery in SMTP using ETRN. It is possible to receive mail by running an SMTP server. POP3 became popular when single-user computers connected to the Internet only intermittently; SMTP is more suitable for a machine permanently connected to the Internet.

The RFC document supports SMTP are:

- SMTP Service Extension for Authentication, RFC: 2554
- SMTP Service Extension for Command Pipelining RFC: 2920

- SMTP Service Extension for Delivery Status Notifications (DSNs) RFC: 3461
- SMTP Service Extension for Message Size Declaration, RFC: 1870
- SMTP Service Extension for Message Tracking, RFC: 3885
- SMTP Service Extension for Remote Message Queue Starting, RFC: 1985
- SMTP Service Extension for Returning Enhanced Error Codes, RFC: 2034
- SMTP Service Extension for Secure SMTP over Transport Layer Security, RFC: 3207
- SMTP Service Extensions for Transmission of Large and Binary MIME Messages, RFC: 3030

The Multipurpose Internet Mail Extension (MIME) (Freed, 2008) (Wikipedia.org, Multipurpose Internet Mail Extension, 2009) protocol is an Internet standard that extends the format of e-mail. MIME uses the convention of content-type/subtype pairs to specify the native representation or encoding of, for example:

- Audio: audio or voice data.
- Video: video or moving image data
- Image: picture data.
- Application: application data or binary data.
- Message: encapsulating another mail message.
- Multipart: combine several body parts, possibly of differing types of data, into a single message.
- Text: textual information in a number of characters sets and formatted text description languages in a standardized manner.

MIME's use, however, has grown beyond describing the content of e-mail to describing content type in general. The basic Internet e-mail transmission protocol, SMTP, supports only 7-bit ASCII characters (see also 8BITMIME). This effectively limits Internet e-mail to messages which, when transmitted, include only the characters sufficient for writing a small number of languages, primarily English. Other languages based on the Latin alphabet typically include diacritics not supported in 7-bit ASCII, meaning text in these languages cannot be correctly represented in basic e-mail.

MIME defines mechanisms for sending other kinds of information in e-mail. These include text in languages other than English using character encodings other than ASCII, and 8-bit binary content such as files containing images, sounds, movies, and computer programs. MIME is also a fundamental component of communication protocols such as HTTP, which requires that data be transmitted in the context of e-mail-like messages even though the data might not fit this context. Mapping messages into and out of MIME format is typically done automatically by an e-mail client or by mail servers when sending or receiving Internet (SMTP/MIME) e-mail.

The default protocol for standard text messages is defined in RFC 822, and is widely used on the Internet. These messages are sent via the de facto mail transfer protocol, SMTP, defined in RFC 821. Multi-purpose Internet Mail Extensions (MIME), a SMTP message structure, is the standard specification for the attachment of binary files

CONCLUSION

Cryptography is the science of writing in secret code and is an ancient art; the first documented use of cryptography in writing dates back to circa 1900 B.C. when an Egyptian scribe used non-standard hieroglyphs in an inscription. Some experts argue that cryptography appeared spontaneously sometime after writing was invented, with applications ranging from diplomatic missives to war-time battle plans. It is no surprise, then, that new forms of cryptography came soon after the widespread development of computer communications. In data and telecommunications, cryptography is necessary when communicating over any untrusted medium, which includes just about any network, particularly the Internet.

Cryptography, then, not only protects data from theft or alteration, but can also be used for user authentication. There are, in general, three types of cryptographic schemes typically used to accomplish these goals: secret key (or symmetric) cryptography, public-key (or asymmetric) cryptography, and hash functions, each of which is described below. In all cases, the initial unencrypted data is referred to as plaintext. It is encrypted into ciphertext, which will in turn (usually) be decrypted into usable plaintext.

Cryptography is the art or science of secret writing; it over objective is to provide confidentiality, integrity, Non-repudiation and Authentication. Integration this service within E-mail and web service will provide high level of assurance and security.

This article is general introduction and some history of three parts: E-mail services, Web service with general definitions, history and cryptography algorithm as a tool to secure the two services.

The article focus on introduce and create a background three topics: E-mail structure and organization, web service types and their organization and the other part is cryptography algorithms integrated in the E-mail and web services to provide high level of security.

There are several section to cover general introduction, general definitions of Cryptography, e-mail and web service. This followed by history and Cryptography algorithms details. These details cover symmetric and asymmetric, hash algorithm, digital signature, and suit B cryptography components. The last section is email service and cryptography.

REFERENCES

W3C. (2002). *Decryption transform for XML signature*. Retrieved from http://www.w3.org/TR/xmlenc-decrypt

W3C. (2004). *Web services architecture*. Retrieved from http://www.w3.org/

W3C. (2009). *XML digital signature*. Retrieved from http://www.w3.org/TR/xmldsig-core/

W3C.org. (2003). *How secure is the encryption used by SSL*. W3C.org FAQ. Retrieved from http://www.w3.org/

W3.org. (2002). *XML encryption syntax and processing W3C recommendation*. Retrieved from http://www.w3.org/TR/2002/REC-xmlenc-core-20021210/Overview.html

Adams, C., & Farrell, S. (1999). *Internet X.509 public key infrastructure: Certificate management protocols RFC 2510*. Retrieved from http://www.ietf.org/rfc/rfc2510.txt

Al-Hamdani, A. (2008). Cryptography for information security. In J. N. Gupta & S. K. Sharma (Eds.), Information security and assurance (pp. 122–138). Hershey, PA: Information Science Reference.

Al-Hamdani, A. (2009). *Cryptography for information security (chapter 5)*. Unpublished.

Alvestrand, H. T. (1995). *X.400 FAQ A comprehensive list of resources on x.400 series of standards*. Retrieved from http://www.alvestrand.no/x400/index.html

Ansi.org. (1998). *X9.31-1998, Digital signatures using reversible public key cryptography for the financial services industry (rDSA)*. American National Standards Institute.

Apache.org. (2007). *XML security*. Retrieved from http://xml.apache.org/security/

Balaski, B. (1993, February). *Privacy enhancement for Internet electronic mail: Part IV: Notary, co-issuer, CRL-storing and CRL-retrieving services. RFC 1424*. Retrieved from http://www.ietf.org/rfc/rfc1424.txt

E-Mail, Web Service and Cryptography

Balenson, D. (1993). *Privacy enhancement for Internet electronic mail: Part III: Algorithms, modes, and identifiers. RFC 1423.* Retrieved from http://www.ietf.org/rfc/rfc1423.txt

Bauchle, R., Hazen, F., Lund, J., & Oakley, G. (2008). *Encryption.* Retrieved from http://search-security.techtarget.com/sDefinition/0,sid14_gci212062,00.html

Bellare, M., Canetti, R., & Hugo, K. (1996a). Keying hash functions for message authentication. *CRYPTO, 1996,* 1–15.

Bellare, M., Canetti, R., & Hugo, K. (1996b). The HMAC construction. *CryptoBytes, 2(1).*

Bernstein, D. J. (2008). *Simple mail transfer protocol reference manuals.* Retrieved from http://cr.yp.to/immhf.html

Brownlow, M. (2008). *E-mail and webmail statistics.* Retrieved from http://www.email-marketing-reports.com/metrics/email-statistics.htm

Callas, J., Donnerhacke, L., Finney, H., & Thayer, R. (2007). *OpenPGP message format RFC: 4880.* Retrieved from http://tools.ietf.org/html/rfc4880

Callas, J., Donnerhacke, L., Finney, H., & Thayer, R. (2007). *OpenPGP message format RFC: 4880.* Retrieved from http://www.ietf.org/rfc/rfc2440.txt

Cerami, E. (2002). *Web services essentials (O'Reilly XML).* City, O'Reilly Media, Inc.

Cnss.gov. (2003). *FACT SHEET CNSS Policy No. 15, Fact Sheet No. 1, National policy on the use of the advanced encryption standard (AES) to protect national security systems and national security information.* Retrieved from http://www.cnss.gov/Assets/pdf/cnssp_15_fs.pdf

Corporation, I. B. M. (1999). *XML security suite.* Retrieved from http://www.alphaworks.ibm.com/tech/xmlsecuritysuite

Costello, R. L. (2009). *Building Web services the REST way.* Retrieved from http://www.xfront.com/

CrazySquirrel. (2009). *How does e-mail work?* Retrieved from http://www.crazysquirrel.com/computing/debian/mail.jspx

Crispin, M. (1996). *Internet message access protocol-V4rev1.* ietf.org RFC: 2060.

Crispin, M. (2003). *Internet message access protocol-V4rev1.* ietf.org RFC: 3501.

Crocker, D. (2009). *E-mail history.* Retrieved from http://www.livinginternet.com

Crocker, S., Freed, N., Galvin, J., & Murphy, S. (1995). *MIME object security services RFC 1848.* Retrieved from http://www.ietf.org/rfc/rfc1848.txt?number=1848

David, M. L. (2007). *The history of encryption and ciphers.* Retrieved from http://searchwarp.com/swa148381.htm

Davis, Z. (2008). *An intro to elliptical curve cryptography.* Retrieved from http://www.deviceforge.com/

Dierks, T., & Allen, C. (1999). *The TLS protocol version 1.0: RFC 2246.* Retrieved from http://www.ietf.org/rfc/rfc2246.txt

Dierks, T., & Allen, C. (1999). *The TLS protocol version 1.0. RFC 2246.* Retrieved from http://www.ietf.org/rfc/rfc2246.txt?number=2246

Diffie, W., & Hellman, M. E. (1976). New directions in cryptography. *IEEE Transactions on Information Theory, 22,* 644–654. doi:10.1109/TIT.1976.1055638

Djajadinata, R. (2002). *XML encryption keeps your XML documents safe and secure.* Retrieved from http://www.javaworld.com/javaworld/jw-08-2002/jw-0823-securexml.html

Dournaee, B. (2002). *XML security*. New York: McGraw-Hill Osborne Media.

Drummond, R. (1996). *Brief comparison of e-mail encryption protocols*. Retrieved from http://www.imc.org/ietf-ediint/old-archive/msg00117.html

Dworkin, M. (2001). Recommendation for Block Cipher Modes of Operation NIST Special Publication 800-38A. Retrieved from http://csrc.nist.gov/publications/PubsSPs.html

Dworkin, M. (2004). *Recommendation for Block Cipher Modes of Operation: The CCM Mode for Authentication and Confidentiality*. NIST Special Publication 800-38C Retrieved from http://csrc.nist.gov/publications/PubsSPs.html

Dworkin, M. (2005). *Recommendation for Block Cipher Modes of Operation: The CMAC Mode for Authentication*. NIST Special Publication 800-38B Retrieved from http://csrc.nist.gov/publications/PubsSPs.html

Dworkin, M. (2007). *Recommendation for Block Cipher Modes of Operation: Galois/Counter Mode (GCM) and GMAC*. NIST Special Publication 800-38C Retrieved from http://csrc.nist.gov/publications/PubsSPs.html

Eastlake, D., & Motorola, P. J. (2001). *US secure hash algorithm 1 (SHA1)*. RFC: 3174.

Eastlake, D. E., & Niles, K. (2002). *Secure XML: The new syntax for signatures and encryption*. Pearson Education.

Edge, C., Barker, W., & Smith, Z. (2007). *A brief history of cryptography* (reprint). Retrieved from http://www.318.com/techjournal/?p=5

Eide, K. (2004). *The next generation of mail clients*. Retrieved from http://home.dataparty.no/kristian/reviews/nextgen-mua/

Elkins, M., Torto, D. D., Levien, R., & Roessler, T. (2001). *MIME security with OpenPGP: RFC 3156*. Retrieved from http://www.faqs.org/rfcs/rfc3156.html

Encryptomatic.com. (2008). *HIPAA: The Health Insurance Portability and Accountability Act of 1996*. Retrieved from http://www.encryptomatic.com/about-us/index.html

Federal Information. (1993). *Secure hash standard*. Processing standards publication 180-1 FIPS PUB 180-1 Supersedes FIPS PUB 180.

Federal Information Processing Standards Publication 197 Announcing the *ADVANCED ENCRYPTION STANDARD (AES) November 26, 2001*

Federal Register. (2005, May 19). Announcing approval of the withdrawal of Federal Information. *Federal Register, 70*(96), 28907.

Ferguson, N., & Schneier, B. (2003). *Practical cryptography*. New York: Wiley.

Fernandez, E. B. (2002). *Web services security current status and the future*. Retrieved from http://www.webservicesarchitect.com/content/articles/fernandez01.asp

Fielding, R., Gettys, J., Mogul, J., Frystyk, H., Masinter, L., Leach, P., & Berners-Lee, T. *Hypertext transfer protocol -- HTTP/1.1*. Retrieved from http://www.ietf.org/rfc/rfc2616.txt

Freed, N. (2008). *Name and filename parameters*. Retrieved from http://www.imc.org/ietf-smtp/mail-archive/msg05023.html

Galvin, J., Murphy, G., Crocker, S., & Freed, N. (1995). *Security multiparts for MIME: Multipart/signed and multipart/encrypted: RFC 1847*. Retrieved from http://www.faqs.org/rfcs/rfc1847.html

Gurski, M. A. (1995). *Privacy-enhanced mail (PEM)*. Retrieved from http://www.cs.umbc.edu/~woodcock/cmsc482/proj1/pem.html

Hagens, R., & Hansen, A. (1994). *Operational requirements for X.400 management domains in the GO-MHS community*. Retrieved from http://tools.ietf.org/html/rfc1649

Hartman, B., Flinn, D. J., Beznosov, K., & Kawamoto, S. (2003). *Mastering Web services security.* New York: Wiley Publishing.

Hoffman, P. (1999). *SMTP service extension for secure SMTP over TLS: RFC 2487.* Retrieved from http://www.ietf.org/rfc/rfc2487.txt?number=2487

Housley, R. (1999). *Cryptographic message syntax.* Retrieved from http://www.ietf.org/rfc/rfc2630.txt

Housley, R. (1999). *Cryptographic message syntax RFC: 2630.* Retrieved from http://www.ietf.org/rfc/rfc2630.txt

Housley, R. (2004). *Cryptographic message syntax (CMS): RFC 3852.* Retrieved from http://www.ietf.org/rfc/rfc3852.txt

Housley, R., & Solinas, J. (2007). *Suite B in secure/multipurpose Internet mail extension: RFC5008.* Retrieved from http://www.rfc-editor.org/rfc/rfc5008.txt

Houttuin, J., & Craigie, J. (1994). *Migrating from X.400(84) to X.400(88) RFC1615.* Retrieved from http://www.faqs.org/rfcs/rfc1615.html

IBM. (2009) Application Server - Express for IBM i, Version 7.0 http://publib.boulder.ibm.com

Ibm.com. (2008). *Creating a secure sockets layer configuration.* Retrieved from http://publib.boulder.ibm.com/

Ietf.org. (1988). *X.400(1988) for the academic and research community in Europe RFC1616.* Retrieved from http://www.ietf.org/rfc/rfc1616.txt

Ietf.org. (2008). *Public-key infrastructure.* Retrieved from Retrieved from http://www.ietf.org/html.charters/pkix-charter.html

ITU. (2005). *T-REC-X.509-200508-I information technology - Open systems interconnection - The directory: Authentication framework.* Retrieved from http://www.itu.int/rec/T-REC-X.509-200508-I/en

Kaliski, B. (1993). *Privacy enhancement for Internet electronic mail: Part IV: Key certification and related services RFC 1424.* Retrieved from http://www.ietf.org/rfc/rfc1424.txt

Katz, J., & Lindell, Y. (2007). *Introduction to modern cryptography: Principles and protocols* (Chapman & Hall/CRC cryptography and network security series, 1st ed.). Boca Raton, FL: Chapman & Hall/CRC.

Kelm, S. (2008). *The PKI page.* Retrieved from http://www.pki-page.org/

Kent, S. (1993). *Privacy enhancement for Internet electronic mail: Part II: Certificate-based key management RFC 1422.* Retrieved from http://www.ietf.org/rfc/rfc1422.txt

Kessler, G. C. (2009). *An Overview of Cryptography.* Retrieved from http://www.garykessler.net/library/crypto.html#intro

Khosrow-Pour, M. (Ed.). (2004). *E-Commerce security: Advice from experts (IT solutions series).* New York: Cybertech Publishing.

Kim, J., Biryukov, A., Prenee, B., & Hong, S. (2006). On the security of HMAC and NMAC based on HAVAL, MD4, MD5, SHA-0 and SHA-1. *IACR.org ePrint.*

Levien, R. (1999). *A brief comparison of e-mail encryption protocols.* Retrieved from http://www.imc.org/

Linn, J. (1993). *Message encryption and authentication procedures Part I: Message encryption and authentication procedures. RFC 1421.* Retrieved from http://www.ietf.org/rfc/rfc1421.txt

Loshin, P. (1999). *Essential e-mail standards: RFCs and protocols made practical.* New York: John Wiley & Sons.

Mao, W. (2003). *Modern cryptography: Theory and practice (Hewlett-Packard professional books).* Prentice Hall.

Mel, H. X., & Baker, D. M. (2000). *Cryptographydecrypted* (5th ed.). Reading, MA: Addison-Wesley.

Microsoft Corporation. (2009). *TLS enhancements to SSL*. Retrieved from http://technet.microsoft.com/en-us/library/cc784450.aspx

Microsoft Corporation. (2009). *X.400 transport architecture*. Retrieved from http://technet.microsoft.com/en-us/library/aa997753(EXCHG.65).aspx

Mit.edu. (2007). *Kerberos: The network authentication protocol*. Retrieved from http://mit.edu.

Mogollon, M. (2007). *Cryptography and security services: Mechanisms and applications*. New York: CyberTech Publishing.

Myers, J., & Rose, M. (1996). *Post office protocol - Version 3*. ietf.org, RFC 1939.

Netegrity. (2001). *The standard XML framework for secure information exchange*. Retrieved from http://xml.coverpages.org/Netegrity-SAMLWP.pdf nist.gov. (2000). *FIPS Pub 186-2 digital signature standard (DSS)*. Retrieved from http://csrc.nist.gov/publications/fips/fips186-2/fips186-2-change1.pdf

Nsa.gov. (2005). *Fact sheet NSA suite B cryptography*. Retrieved from http://www.nsa.gov/ia/industry/crypto_suite_b.cfm

O'Neill, M. (2003). *Web services security*. New York: McGraw-Hill Osborne Media.

OASIS. (2009). *Organization for the Advancement of Structured Information Standards*. Retrieved from http://www.oasis-open.org/who/

Openssl.org. (2005). *OpenSSL Project*. Retrieved from http://www.openssl.org/

PCLcable. (2003). *WEBMAIL notes*. Retrieved from http://my.pclnet.net/webmail.html

Peter, I. (2003). *The history of e-mail*. Retrieved from http://www.nethistory.info/

Peterson, J. (2004). *S/MIME advanced encryption standard (AES) requirement: RFC3853*. Retrieved from http://www.faqs.org/rfcs/rfc3853.html

Pioneers, I. (2009, January). *Internet pioneers*. Retrieved from http://www.ibiblio.org/pioneers/roberts.html

Postel, J. B. (1982). *Simple mail transfer protocol RFC: 821 Obsoleted by 2821*. Retrieved from http://tools.ietf.org/html/rfc821

Postel.org. (2009, January). *Postel organization*. Retrieved from http://www.postel.org/postel.html

Ramsdell, B. (Ed.). (1999). *S/MIME version 3 message specification*. Retrieved from http://www.faqs.org/rfcs/rfc2633.html

Ramsdell, B. (Ed.). (2004). *Secure/multipurpose Internet mail extensions (S/MIME) version 3.1 message specification: RFC3851*. Retrieved from http://www.ietf.org/rfc/rfc3851.txt

Rivest, R., Shamir, A., & Adleman, L. M. (1983). *Patent No. 4405829*. U.S.

Rosenberg, J., & Remy, D. (2004). *Securing Web services with WS-security: Demystifying WS-security, WS-policy, SAML, XML signature, and XML encryption*. Sams.

Rosser, J.B. (1939). "An Informal Exposition of Proofs of Godel's Theorem and Church's Theorem". Journal of Symbolic Logic 4

RSA.com. (2007). *What are message authentication codes?* Retrieved from http://www.rsa.com

RSA.com. (2007). *What is DESX?* Retrieved from http://www.rsasecurity.com

RSA.com. (2007). *What is Diffie-Hellman?* Retrieved from http://www.rsa.com/

RSA.com. (2007). *What is RC4?* Retrieved from http://www.rsa.com

RSA.com. (2008). *What is RSA?* Retrieved from http://www.rsa.com/

SAML. (2008). *Security assertion markup language (SAML)*. Retrieved from http://xml.coverpages.org/saml.html

Schaad, J. (2003). *Use of the advanced encryption standard (AES) encryption algorithm in cryptographic message syntax (CMS): RFC 3565*. Retrieved from http://www.ietf.org/rfc/rfc3565.txt

Schneier, B. (1995). *Applied cryptography*. New York: Wiley.

Schneier, B. (1995). *E-mail security: How to keep your electronic messages private*. New York: Wiley.

Schneier, B. (1996). *Applied cryptography: Protocols, algorithms, and source code in C* (2nd ed.). New York: Wiley.

SearchSecurity.com. (2008). *DSS definition*. Retrieved from http://searchsecurity.techtarget.com/sDefinition/

SearchSecurity.com. (2008). *Spotlight article: Domain 3, cryptography*. Retrieved from http://searchsecurity.techtarget.com/generic/0,295582,sid14_gci1328971,00.html

Sharpe, M. (2008). *Getting started with HTTPS*. Retrieved from http://searchsoftwarequality.techtarget.com/sDefinition/0,sid92_gci214006,00.html#

Simovits, M. (1995). *The DES: An extensive document and evaluation*. New York: Agent Park Press.

Singh, S. (2000). *The code book: The science of secrecy from ancient Egypt to quantum cryptography (reprint)*. Anchor.

Singhal, A., Winograd, T., & Scarfone, K. (2007). Guide to Secure Web Services. NIST, SP800-95.

Snell, J., Tidwel, D., & Kulchenko, P. (2001). *Programming Web services with SOAP*. O'Reilly.

SSH Communications Security, Inc. (2008). Public-key cryptosystems. Retrieved from http://www.ssh.com/support/cryptography/

Sun.com. (2002). *Introduction to SSL*. Retrieved from http://docs.sun.com/source/816-6156-10/contents.htm#1041986

SunMicrosystems. (2008). *JSR 106: XML digital encryption APIs*. Retrieved from http://jcp.org/en/jsr/detail?id=106

Thomas, S. A. (2000). *SSL & TLS essentials securing the Web*. John Wiley & Sons.

Tracy, M., Jansen, W., & Bisker, S. (2002). Guidelines on Electronic Mail Security. NIST Special Publication 800-45, Tracy, M., Jansen, W., & Bisker, S. (2007). Guidelines on Electronic Mail Security. NIST Special Publication 800-45, V2

Trappe, W., & Washington, L. C. (2005). *Introduction to cryptography with coding theory* (2nd ed.). Prentice Hall.

Turner, S., & Housley, R. (2008). *Implementing E-mail and security tokens: Current standards, tools, and practices*. Wiley.

Verma, M. (2004). *XML security: The XML key management specification*. Retrieved from http://www.ibm.com/developerworks/xml/library/x-seclay3/

Weekly, D. (2008). *The need For next-generation e-mail*. Retrieved from http://david.weekly.org

Weise, J. (2001). *Public key infrastructure overview*. Retrieved from http://www.sun.com/blueprints/0801/publickey.pdf

Wenbo, M. (2003). *Modern cryptography: Theory and practice*. Upper Saddle River, NJ: Prentice Hall.

Wikipedia.org. (2008). *Simple Mail Transfer Protocol (SMTP)*. Retrieved from wikipedia.org

Wikipedia.org. (2009). *PGP: PRETTY GOOD PRIVACY*. Retrieved from wikipedia.org

Wikipedia.org. (2009). *PKI*. Retrieved from wikipedia.org

Wikipedia.org. (2009). *Privacy Enhanced* Mail. Retrieved from wikipedia.org

Wikipedia.org. (2009). *The Multipurpose Internet Mail Extension (MIME)*. Retrieved from Wikipedia.org

Wikipedia.org. (2009). *WEB OF TRUST*. Retrieved from wikipedia.org

Wikipedia.org. (2009). *SSL*. Retrieved from wikipedia.org

Wikipedia.org. (2009). *HTTP*. Retrieved from wikipedia.org

Wikipedia.org. (2009). *Web Services Security*. Retrieved from wikipedia.org

Wikipedia.org. (2009). *Digital Signature*. Retrieved from wikipedia.org

Wikipedia.org. (2009). *Email*. Retrieved from wikipedia.org

Wikipedia.org. (2009). *Ray Tomlinson*. Retrieved from wikipedia.org

Wikipedia.org. (2009). *Jon Postel*. Retrieved from wikipedia.org

Wikipedia.org. (2009). *Web service*. Retrieved from wikipedia.org

Wikipedia.org. (2009). *Multipurpose Internet Mail Extension*. Retrieved from wikipedia.org

Wikipedia.org. (2009). *Certification Authority*. Retrieved from wikipedia.org

Zimmermann, P. (1995). *PGP source code and internals*. Cambridge, MA: MIT Press.

Zimmermann, P. (1995). *The official PGP user's guide*. Cambridge, MA: MIT Press.

ENDNOTE

[1] In cryptography, ciphertext stealing (CTS) is a general method of using a block cipher mode of operation that allows for processing of messages that are not evenly divisible into blocks without resulting in any expansion of the ciphertext, at the cost of slightly increased complexity.

Chapter 4
Cryptography in E–Mail and Web Services

Wasim A. Al-Hamdani
Kentucky State University, USA

ABSTRACT

Cryptography has been used since ancient times in many different shapes and forms to protect messages from being intercepted. However, since 1976, cryptography started to be part of protected public communication when e-mail became commonly used by the public. Webmail (or Web-based e-mail) is an e-mail service intended to be primarily accessed via a web browser, as opposed to through an e-mail client, such as Microsoft Outlook, Mozilla's Thunderbird Mail. Very popular webmail providers include Gmail, Yahoo! Mail, Hotmail and AOL. Web based email has its advantages, especially for people who travel. Email can be collected by simply visiting a website, negating the need for an email client, or to logon from home. Wherever a public terminal with Internet access exists one can check, sends and receive email quickly and easily. Another advantage of web based email is that it provides an alternate address allowing user to reserve his/her ISP address for personal use. If someone would like to subscribe to a newsletter, enter a drawing, register at a website, participate in chats, or send feedback to a site, a web based email address is the perfect answer. It will keep non-personal mail on a server for you to check when you wish, rather than filling up your private email box. Web service is defined as "a software system designed to support interoperable machine-to-machine interaction over a network". Web services are frequently just Internet application programming interfaces (API) that can be accessed over a network, such as the Internet, and executed on a remote system hosting the requested services. Other approaches with nearly the same functionality as web services are Object Management Group's (OMG) Common Object Request Broker Architecture (CORBA), Microsoft's Distributed Component Object Model (DCOM) or SUN's Java/Remote Method Invocation (RMI). Integrating Encryption with web service could be performing in many ways such as: XML Encryption and XML Signature. In this article we present client and Web-based E-mail, next generation E-mail and secure E-mail, followed by cryptography in web service and the last part is the future of web service security. The article start with the integration of cryptography with E-mail client and web base then the integration of cryptography

DOI: 10.4018/978-1-61520-783-1.ch004

and web service is presented. At the end of the major two sections: e-mail service and web service there is a general prospect vision of encryption future for e-mail service and web service. This section presents our view for the cryptography integration with the second generation of e-mail and web service.

INTRODUCTION

Encryption is the process of transforming information (plaintext) using an algorithm to make it unreadable through using a key. The result of the process is encrypted information (ciphertext). In many contexts, the word encryption also implicitly refers to the reverse process, decryption, to make the encrypted information readable again. The use of encryption/decryption is as old as the art of communication. In wartime, a cipher – often called a "code" – can be employed to keep the enemy from obtaining the contents of transmissions (examples are Morse code and ASCII). Simple ciphers include the substitution of letters for numbers, the rotation of letters in the alphabet, and the "scrambling" of voice signals by inverting the sideband frequencies. More complex ciphers work according to sophisticated computer algorithms that rearrange the data bits in digital signals.

In a Web services world, everyone communicates with everyone else. Many intermediaries could exist between, say, supplier and buyer. What if one of these intermediaries becomes compromised? End-to-end security becomes fundamentally important if someone wants to do something considered more significant operations (such as a money transaction or international e-commerce). For all these reasons and others, this chapter is written to present two subjects: (a) E-mail and web service integrating with encryption algorithms to protect personal, business, and financial information, and (b) authenticating and authorizing a user or business entity.

Web service is defined by the W3C as, "a software system designed to support interoperable machine-to-machine interaction over a network" (Web Services Glossary from W3 organization, 2004) It has an interface described in a machine-processable format (specifically WSDL). Other systems interact with the Web service in a manner prescribed by its description using SOAP messages, typically conveyed using HTTP with an XML serialization in conjunction with other Web-related standards.

WSDL is an XML format for describing network services as a set of endpoints operating on messages containing either document-oriented or procedure-oriented information. The operations and messages are described abstractly, and then bound to a concrete network protocol and message format to define an endpoint. Related concrete endpoints are combined into abstract endpoints (services). WSDL is extensible to allow description of endpoints and their messages, regardless of what message formats or network protocols are used to communicate. However, the only bindings described in this document explain how to use WSDL in conjunction with SOAP 1.1, HTTP GET/POST, and MIME.

XML Encryption, also known as XML-Enc, is a specification governed by a W3C recommendation that defines how to encrypt the contents of an XML element. Although XML Encryption can be used to encrypt any kind of data, it is nonetheless known as "XML Encryption" because an XML element (either an EncryptedData or Encrypted-Key element) contains or refers to the ciphertext, keying information, and algorithms.

In the section which covers Web service and the use of encryption algorithms, we will look at XML security, signature, encryption algorithms, and security requirements for Web service infrastructure. This section is the expected future for encryption with Web services protecting privacy and b2b infrastructure.

The next generation of Cryptography integration with e-mail service and web service is the subject of the last section with cryptography combination with e-mail and web service. And the end of each part there is a section focuses on the future of cryptography algorithms with the two services. These sections discuss the next generation of E-mail service and secure E-mail, and next generation of using cryptography in web service and the future of web service security.

EMAIL ENCRYPTION INTEGRATION

As the e-mail technique used two methods: client and Web-based e-mail; the integration of confidentiality is different depends upon the method is used. Generally the confidentiality with e-mail and the use of encryption are classified into three categories:

- Client base as in Secure/Multipurpose Internet Mail Extensions
- Web base as hotmail
- System base which required infrastructure as PGP

Client Base

Privacy Enhanced Mail (PEM) It is an Internet standard that provides for secure exchange of electronic mail; employs a range of cryptographic techniques to allow for confidentiality, sender authentication, and message integrity. The message integrity aspects allow the user to ensure that a message hasn't been modified during transport from the sender. The sender authentication allows a user to verify that the PEM message that they have received is truly from the person who claims to have sent it. The confidentiality feature allows a message to be kept secret from people to whom the message was not addressed. PEM standardized in Internet RFC 1421 (Linn, 1993), RFC 1422 (Kent, 1993), RFC 423 (Balenson, 1993), and RFC 1424 (Balaski, Feb 1993).

PEM provides a range of security features. They include originator authentication, (optional)

message confidentiality, and data integrity. Each of these will be discussed in turn.

Originator Authentication In RFC 1422 (Kent, 1993)an authentication scheme for PEM is defined. It uses a hierarchical authentication framework compatible X.509, ``The Directory --- Authentication Framework.'' Central to the PEM authentication framework are certificates, which contain items such as the digital signature algorithm used to sign the certificate, the subject's Distinguished Name, the certificate issuer's Distinguished name, a validity period, indicating the starting and ending dates the certificate should be considered valid, the subject's public key along with the accompanying algorithm. This hierarchical authentication framework has four entities.

The first entity is a central authority called the Internet Policy Registration Authority (IPRA), acting as the root of the hierarchy and forming the foundation of all certificate validation in the hierarchy. It is responsible for certifying and reviewing the policies of the entities in the next lower level. These entities are called Policy Certification Authorities (PCAs), which are responsible for certifying the next lower level of authorities. The next lower level consists of Certification Authorities (CAs), responsible for certifying both subordinate CAs and also individual users. Individual users are on the lowest level of the hierarchy.

This hierarchical approach (wikipedia.org, Certification Authority, 2009)to certification allows one to be reasonably sure that certificates coming users, assuming one trust the policies of the intervening CAs and PCAs and the policy of the IPRA itself, actually came from the person whose name is associated with it. This hierarchy also makes it more difficult to spoof a certificate because it is likely that few people will trust or use certificates that have untraceable certification trails, and in order to generate a false certificate one would need to subvert at least a CA, and possibly the certifying PCA and the IPRA itself.

Message Confidentiality (Gurski, 1995) Message confidentiality in PEM is implemented by using standardized cryptographic algorithms. RFC 1423 (Balenson, 1993) defines both symmetric and asymmetric encryption algorithms to be used in PEM key management and message encryption. Currently, the only standardized algorithm for message encryption is the Data Encryption Standard (DES) in Cipher Block Chaining (CBC) mode. Currently, DES in both Electronic Code Book (ECB) mode and Encrypt-Decrypt-Encrypt (EDE) mode, using a pair of 64-bit keys, are standardized for symmetric key management. For asymmetric key management, the RSA algorithm is used.

Data Integrity (Gurski, 1995) In order to provide data integrity, PEM implements a concept known as a message digest. The message digests that PEM uses are known as RSA-MD2 and RSA-MD5 for both symmetric and asymmetric key management modes. Essentially both algorithms take arbitrary-length ``messages,'' which could be any message or file, and produce a 16-octet value. This value is then encrypted with whichever key management technique is currently in use. When the message is received, the recipient can also run the message digest on the message, and if it hasn't been modified in-transit, the recipient can be reasonably assured that the message hasn't been tampered with maliciously. The reason message digests are used is because they're relatively fast to compute, and finding two different meaningful messages that produce the same value is nearly impossible.

Key hierarchy (Linn, 1993) A two-level keying hierarchy is used to support PEM transmission:

1. Data Encrypting Keys (DEKs) are used for encryption of message text and (with certain choices among a set of alternative algorithms) for computation of message integrity check (MIC) quantities. In the asymmetric key management environment, DEKs are also used to encrypt the signed representations of MICs in PEM messages to which has been applied. DEKs are generated individually for each transmitted message; no pre distribution of DEKs is needed to support PEM transmission.

2. Interchange Keys (IKs) are used to encrypt DEKs for transmission within messages. Ordinarily, the same IK will be used for all messages sent from a given originator to a given recipient over a period of time. Each transmitted message includes a representation of the DEK(s) used for message encryption and/or MIC computation, encrypted under an individual IK per named recipient. The representation is

Key Certification (Kaliski, 1993) The key-certification service signs a certificate containing a specified subject name and public key. The service takes a certification request signs a certificate constructed from the request, and returns a certification reply containing the new certificate.

The certification request specifies the requestor's subject name and public key in the form of a self-signed certificate. The certification request contains two signatures, both computed with the requestor's private key:

1. The signature on the self-signed certificate, having the cryptographic purpose of preventing a requestor from requesting a certificate with another party's public key.

2. A signature on some encapsulated text, having the practical purpose of allowing the certification authority to construct an ordinary RFC 1421 privacy-enhanced message as a reply, with user-friendly encapsulated text

Security Considerations (Kaliski, 1993) the self-signed certificate (prevents a requestor from requesting a certificate with another party's public key) such an attack would give the requestor the minor ability to pretend to be the originator of any message signed by the other party. This attack is significant only if the requestor does not know the message being signed, and the signed part of the message does not identify the signer. The requestor would still not be able to decrypt messages

One reason for the lack of deployment was that the PEM protocol depended on prior deployment of a hierarchical public key infrastructure (PKI) with a single root (does not offer cross certifications). Deployment of such a PKI proved operational cost and legal liability of the root and 'policy' CAs became understood.

The main issue with PEM is the use of Certification authority with e-mail infrastructure, in which cause an overhead problem for implementation, In addition to being a problem to deployment the single rooted hierarchy was rejected by some commentators as an unacceptable imposition of central authority. This led Phil Zimmermann to propose the Web of Trust as the PKI infrastructure for PGP.

Since 1993 the PEM received minimal market support; in 1997 (Loshin, 1999), the report of the IAB Security Architecture Workshop (RFC 2316) identified PEM as a "not useful" protocol for security due to its lack of acceptance over time. PEM's failure to catch on may have been due to a number of factors, including a lack of generally available software implementations that could do the encryption and digital signature processing it requires as well as lack of a generalized infrastructure for creating and distributing keys

X. 400 with PEM (Houttuin & Craigie, 1994) M (IETF.org, X.400 1988) for the Academic and Research Community in Europe RFC 1616, 1988) (Alvestrand, 1995) (Hagens & Hansen, 1994)

X. 400 is a suite of ITU-T Recommendations that define standards for Data Communication Networks for Message Handling Systems (MHS). The first X.400 Recommendations were published in 1984 (Red Book), and a substantially revised version was published in 1988 (Blue Book). New

features were added in 1992 (White Book) and subsequent updates. Although X.400 was originally designed to run over the OSI Transport service, an adaptation to allow operation over TCP/IP, RFC 1006 has become the most popular way to run X.400. Developed in cooperation with the ISO, the X.400-series Recommendations specify OSI standard protocols for exchanging and addressing electronic messages. The companion F.400-series of Recommendations define Message Handling Services built on Message Handling Systems (MHS), as well as access to and from the MHS for public services. In the late 1990s the ITU-T consolidated Recommendations F.400 and X.400 and published the ITU-T F.400/X.400 (06/1999) Message handling system and service overview Recommendation.

The main variants of X.400 are:

- X.400/1984 - published only by the CCITT (which is now named ITU-T)
- X.400/1988 - a complete rewrite of the standards, published jointly by ISO and X.400
- A number of updates to the standards, sometimes called X.400/1993, but not published as a joint set.

X.400 is not a single standard, but a number of them, ranging from X.400 to X.440.

The currently relevant X.400 standards are:

- X.400 (1993) Message handling system and service overview (also called F.400) (ISO part 1)
- X.402 (1995) Overall architecture (ISO part 2)
- X.407 (1988) Abstract service definition conventions (ISO part 3) (not listed in the current Web site)
- X.408 (1988) Encoded information type conversion rules (ITU only; irrelevant; possibly replaced by a T-series standard, but I haven't found any trace of it here)

- X.411 (1995) Message transfer system: Abstract service definition and procedures (the definition of the P1 protocol) (ISO part 4)
- X.413 (1995) Message store: Abstract-service definition (ISO part 5)
- X.419 (1995) Protocol specifications (what remains after reading X.411 and X.413) (ISO part 6)
- X.420 (1992) Interpersonal messaging system (ISO part 7)
- X.421 COMFAX use of MHS (1994)
- X.435 (1991) Electronic data interchange messaging system (ISO parts 8 and 9; at DIS stage in Jan 95)
- X.440 (1992) Voice messaging system (Amendment 1 1995)

An X.400 address consists of several elements, including:

- C (Country name)
- ADMD (Administration Management Domain), usually a public mail service provider
- PRMD (Private Management Domain)
- O (Organization name)
- OU (Organizational Unit Names)
- G (Given name)
- I (Initials)
- S (Surname)

X.400 Management model and architecture (MicrosoftCorporation, 2009) Microsoft Exchange Server 2003 uses Simple Mail Transfer Protocol (SMTP) for native message transfer. However, the core components of Exchange Server 2003 include a message transfer agent (MTA) that is also compliant with the X.400. Therefore, an organization can use X.400 connectors to build the messaging backbone of Exchange organization or to connect to an external X.400 messaging system. By choosing to use X.400 connectors, rather than SMTP connectors, it adds an extra layer of security.

This occurs because the X.400 standard requires MTAs to authenticate themselves before the MTAs can transmit messages. Note, however, that X.400 MTAs and X.400 connectors are more difficult to maintain than SMTP connectors. For example, X.400 e-mail addresses are not user-friendly because of their numerous attributes. X.400 is a complex standard that defines the architecture of a message handling system (MHS), based on the following recommendations: X.200, X.217, X.218, X.227, X.228, X.402, X.411, X.413, X.419, X.420, X.435, X.680, X.690, X.880, X.881, and X.882.

RFC 1422 specifies asymmetric, certificate-based key management procedures based on CCITT Recommendation X.509 to support the message processing procedures defined in this document. Support for the key management approach defined in RFC 1422 is strongly recommended. The message processing procedures can also be used with symmetric key management, given prior distribution of suitable symmetric IKs, but no current RFCs specify key distribution procedures for such IKs.

X.509 (Adams & Farrell, 1999) (ITU, 2005) International Standard defines a framework for public-key certificates and attributes certificates. These frameworks may be used by other standards bodies to profile their application to Public Key Infrastructures (PKI) and Privilege Management Infrastructures (PMI) X.509 specifies, amongst other things, standard formats for public key certificates, certificate revocation lists, attribute certificates, and a certification path validation algorithm. X.509 was initially issued on July 3, 1988 and was begun in association with the X.500 standard. It assumes a strict hierarchical system of certificate authorities (CAs) for issuing the certificates. This contrasts with web of trust models, like PGP, where anyone (not just special CAs) may sign and thus attest to the validity of others' key certificates. Version 3 of X.509 includes the flexibility to support other topologies like bridges and meshes (RFC 4158). It can be used in a peer-to-peer, OpenPGP-like web of trust, but was rarely used that way as of 2004. The X.500 system has never been fully implemented, and the IETF's Public-Key Infrastructure (X.509), or PKIX, working group has adapted the standard to the more flexible organization of the Internet. In fact, the term X.509 certificate usually refers to the IETF's PKIX Certificate and CRL Profile of the X.509 v3 certificate standard, as specified in RFC 3280, commonly referred to as PKIX for Public Key Infrastructure (X.509).

Certification: In the X.509 system, a CA issues a certificate binding a public key to a particular Distinguished Name in the X.500 tradition, or to an Alternative Name such as an e-mail address or a DNS-entry.

An organization's trusted root certificates can be distributed to all employees so that they can use the company PKI system. Browsers such as Internet Explorer, Netscape/Mozilla, Opera and Safari come with root certificates pre-installed, so SSL certificates from larger vendors who have paid for the privilege of being pre-installed[citation needed] will work instantly; in effect the browsers' owners determine which CAs are trusted third parties for the browsers' users. Although these root certificates can be removed or disabled, users rarely do so. If pre-installed root certificates are removed on the Microsoft-platform, the operating system re-installs them as soon as a Web site using the certificate is visited [citation needed]. As this mechanism relies on hash-values, pre-installed with the operating system, it is not even possible to determine which certificates are permanently trusted.

X.509 also includes standards for certificate revocation list (CRL) implementations, an often-neglected aspect of PKI systems. The IETF-approved way of checking a certificate's validity is the Online Certificate Status Protocol (OCSP). Firefox 3 enables OCSP checking by default.

Structure of a certificate: The structure of an X.509 v3 digital certificate is as follows: Certificate, Version, Serial Number, Algorithm ID, Issuer, Validity, Not Before, Not After, Subject, Subject Public Key Info, Public Key Algorithm, Subject Public Key, Issuer Unique Identifier (Optional), Subject Unique Identifier (Optional), Extensions (Optional),..., Certificate Signature Algorithm, Certificate Signature

Issuer and subject unique identifiers were introduced in Version 2, Extensions in Version 3.

A public key infrastructure (PKI) is an arrangement that binds public keys with respective user identities by means of a certificate authority (CA). The user identity must be unique for each CA. The binding is established through the registration and issuance process, which, depending on the level of assurance the binding has, may be carried out by software at a CA, or under human supervision. The PKI role that assures this binding is called the Registration Authority (RA). For each user, the user identity, the public key, their binding, validity conditions and other attributes are made un forgeable in public key certificates issued by the CA.

The term trusted third party (TTP) may also be used for certificate authority (CA). The term PKI is sometimes erroneously used to denote public key algorithms, which do not require the use of a CA.

Web of Trust (wikipedia.org, WEB OF TRUST, 2009) (Weise, 2001) (Kelm, 2008) (ietf.org, Public-Key Infrastructure, 2008)

An alternative approach to the problem of public authentication of public key information is the web of trust scheme, which uses self-signed certificates and third party attestations of those certificates. Speaking of the Web of Trust does not imply the existence of a single web of trust, or common point of trust, but any number of potentially disjoint "webs of trust". Examples of implementations of this approach are PGP (Pretty Good Privacy) and GnuPG (an implementation of OpenPGP, the standardized specification of PGP). Because PGP and implementations allow the use of e-mail digital signatures for self-publication of public key information, it is relatively easy to implement one's own Web of Trust. One of the benefits of the Web of Trust, such as in PGP, is that it can interoperate with a PKI CA fully-trusted by all parties in a domain (such as an internal CA in a company) that is willing to guarantee certificates, as a trusted introducer. Only if the "web of trust" is completely trusted, and because of the nature of a web of trust trusting one certificate is granting trust to all the certificates in that web. A PKI is only as valuable as the standards and practices that control the issuance of certificates and including PGP or a personally instituted web of trust would significantly degrade the trust ability of that enterprise or domains implementation of PKI.

PKI Framework: The framework of a PKI consists of security and operational policies, security services, and interoperability protocols supporting the use of public-key cryptography for the management of keys and certificates. The generation, distribution, and management of public keys and associated certificates normally occur through the use of Certification Authorities (CAs), Registration Authorities (RAs), and directory services, which can be used to establish a hierarchy or chain of trust. CA, RA, and directory services allow for the implementation of digital certificates that can be used to identify different entities. The purpose of a PKI framework is to enable and support the secured exchange of data, credentials, and value in various environments that are typically insecure, such as the Internet.

A PKI enables the establishment of a trust hierarchy. This is one of the primary principles of a PKI. In Internet-based e-commerce, formal trust mechanisms must exist to provide risk management controls. The concept of trust, relative to a PKI, can be explained by the role of the CA. In the Internet environment, entities unknown to each other do not have sufficient trust established between them to perform business, contractual, legal, or other types of transactions. The implementation of a PKI using a CA provides this trust.

In short, a CA functions as follows. Entities that are unknown to one another, each individually establish a trust relationship with a CA. The CA performs some level of entity authentication, according to its established rules as noted in its Certificate Practices Statement or CPS, and then issues each individual a digital certificate. That certificate is signed by the CA and thus vouches for the identity of the individuals.

Unknown individuals can now use their certificates to establish trust between them because they trust the CA to have performed an appropriate entity authentication, and the CA's signing of the certificates attests to this fact. A major benefit of a PKI is the establishment of a trust hierarchy because this scales well in heterogeneous network environments.

Trust Models: The implementation of a PKI requires an analysis of business objectives and the trust relationships that exist in their environment. The awareness of these trust relationships leads to the establishment of an overall trust model that the PKI enforces. The following three common examples of trust models are presented for comparison purposes.

Hierarchical: A hierarchical trust model represents the most typical implementation of a PKI. In its most simple instantiation, this trust model allows end entities' certificates to be signed by a single CA. In this trust model, the hierarchy consists of a series of CAs that are arranged based on a predetermined set of rules and conventions. For example, in the financial services world, rather than have a single authority sign all end entities' certificates, there may be one CA at a national level that signs the certificates of particular financial institutions. Then each institution would itself be a CA that signs the certificates of their individual account holders. Within a hierarchical trust model there is a trust point for each certificate issued. In this case, the trust point for the financial institution's certificate is the national or root CA. The trust point for an individual account holder is their institution's CA. This approach allows for an extensible, efficient, and scalable PKI.

There are trade-offs to be considered when determining the placement of trust points for end entities in a PKI. In a tiered hierarchy with multiple CAs, compartmentalization of risk can be established, but each CA multiplies the administrative effort necessary to maintain the entire hierarchy. Conversely, a flat hierarchy with a single CA is much easier to administer; however, a failure of that single CA will corrupt the entire trust model and potentially all certificates signed by it.

Distributed (Web of Trust): A distributed Web of trust is one that does not incorporate a CA. No trusted third party actually vouches for the identity or integrity of any end entity. Pretty Good Privacy (PGP) uses this type of trust model in e-mail environments. This trust model does not scale well into the Internet-based e-commerce world because each end entity is left to its own devices to determine the level of trust that it will accept from other entities.

Direct (Peer to Peer): Direct peer-to-peer trust models are used with secret or symmetric key-based systems. A trusted third party does not exist in a direct trust model. Thus, each end entity in a peer-to-peer relationship establishes trust with every other entity on an individual basis. This of course, is rather labor-intensive and similar to the Web of trust model. This trust model does not scale well into the Internet-based e-commerce world.

Cross Certification: If PKIs are to be implemented in any widespread fashion, cross certification is another important factor to consider. Instead of using a single global CA, cross certification allows end entities to use a CA based on their particular needs. It is possible that end entities under one CA may need to authenticate end entities under another CA; however, cross certification supports this relatively straightforward process. Essentially, what occurs in a cross certification is that one CA certifies another. As with the generation of an end entity's digital certificate, a CA performs various due diligence tests on the CA it will cross certify. These tests are taken in accordance with the published Certificate Policy and Certificate Practices Statement of the certifying CA. When a cross-certificate is issued, it extends the trust relationship of a CA. A relying entity, for example, may desire to validate the public key certificate of an end entity who's signing CA's public key it is not aware of. Assuming that the relying entity trusts its own CA, when it sees a cross-certificate signed by that CA, it will then also trust that other CA, and subsequent certificates signed by it. The net effect of cross certification is to allow many PKI deployments to be both extensible and scalable.

Security Services: The principle business objectives and risk management controls that can be implemented by a PKI are summarized in this section. An organization should only consider the implementation of a PKI if they have an actual business need for one or more of the security services: Confidentiality, Integrity, Authentication and Non-Repudiation.

PKIs of one type or another, and from any of several vendors, have many uses (wikipedia.org, PKI, 2009) including providing public keys and bindings to user identities, which are used for:

- Encryption and/or sender authentication of e-mail messages (e.g., using OpenPGP or S/MIME)
- Encryption and/or authentication of documents (e.g., the XML Signature or XML Encryption standards if documents are encoded as XML)
- Authentication of users to applications (e.g., smart card logon, client authentication with SSL)
- Bootstrapping secure communication protocols, such as Internet key exchange (IKE) and SSL. In both of these, initial set-up of a secure channel (a "security association") uses asymmetric key (a.k.a. public key) methods, whereas actual communica-

tion uses faster secret key (a.k.a. symmetric key) methods.

PGP: Pretty Good Privacy

(AL-Hamdani, PGPAL-Hamdani, PGP: Pretty Good Privacy, 2009) (Schneier, Applied Cryptography, 1995) (Zimmermann, PGP Source Code and Internals, 1995) (wikipedia.org, PGP: PRETTY GOOD PRIVACY, 2009) (Zimmermann, The Official PGP User's Guide, 1995). Phil Zimmermann created the first version of PGP encryption in 1991. Pretty Good Privacy (PGP) is a package of computer programs makes the RSA algorithm available to users. In addition to providing Encryption and decryption, signatures, and authentication, PGP manages sets of public and private keys.

PGP combines some of the best features of both conventional and public key RSA cryptography. PGP is a hybrid cryptosystem. When a user encrypts plaintext with PGP, first compresses the plaintext. Compression reduces these patterns in the plaintext, thereby greatly enhancing resistance to cryptanalysis.

PGP then creates a session key, which is a one-time-only secret key, this key is a random number generated from the random movements of the mouse and the keystrokes. Once the data is encrypted, the session key is then encrypted to the recipient's public key. This public key-encrypted session key is transmitted along with the ciphertext to the recipient. Decryption works in the reverse. A block diagram is shown in Figure 1.

PGPsteps: Encrypt files; create secrete and public keys and manage keys

The Session Key: The session key is randomly generated for every message encrypted with PGP's public key encryption system. PGP's session key is 128-bit IDEA key (no longer used for new versions).

When PGP is used to encrypt a mail message and send it, the following occurs:

(1) Creates a random session key for the message.
(2) Uses the IDEA algorithm to encrypt the message with session key.
(3) Uses the RSA algorithm to encrypt the session key with the recipient's public key.
(4) handles the encrypted message and the encrypted session key together and prepares the message for mailing

Figure 1. PGP

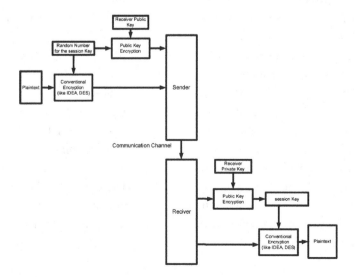

PGP Certificates: PGP keeps each public key in a key certificate. Each certificate contains: The public key itself; One or more user ID for the key's creator (usually that person's name and e-mail address); the date that the key was created and (optional) a list of digital signature on the key, provided by people who attest to the key's veracity.

PGP Rings: PGP keeps all of the public keys for the people (a person) communicate with in a single file called key ring. Most PGP users have at least two PGP ring files, these are:

- *Secring:* PGP use this file to hold all person secret keys.
- *Pubring*: PGP uses this file to hold the public key with whom the person communicate with

Pass Phrases: Each time a user creates a public key/secret key pair, PGP asks the person to create and enter a pass phrase. A PGP pass phrase has several functions; the most important is that it decrypts the secrete key that is stored on a person secrete key ring. It is up to the user to have a separate pass phrase for each secrete key, or all secrete keys have the same pass phrase.

Signature on Key Certificates: One major difficulty with the public key cryptography is the mechanics of distributing the public keys themselves. In order to send person x an encrypted message you must have x public key. Likewise, x must have your public key to verify your signature. Ideally, everyone's public key could be listed (such as phone book) a user could look up a x public key before send x an e-mail. PGP key sever that fulfill this function. PGP does not solve the key distribution problem, but it does make it less problematic by allowing people to sign each other's key certification.

The following steps are signing and encrypting a message with PGP:

- PGP creates a random session key (in some implementations of PGP, users are required to move their mouse at will within a window to generate random data)
- Message is encrypted using the random session key, and a symmetric algorithm (e.g., 3DES, AES)
- Session key is encrypted using the recipient's public key
- SHA algorithm generates a message digest (cryptographic hash); and this hash is "signed" with the sender's private key creating a digital signature
- Encrypted session key is attached to the message
- Message is sent to the recipient.

PGP Encryption System: The cryptographic security of PGP encryption depends on the assumption that the algorithms used are unbreakable by direct cryptanalysis with current equipment and techniques. For instance, in the original version, the RSA algorithm was used to encrypt session keys; likewise, the secret key algorithm used in PGP version 2 was IDEA, which might, at some future time, be found to have a previously unsuspected cryptanalytic flaw. Specific instances of current PGP, or IDEA, insecurities if they exist are not publicly known.

PGP 3 introduced use of the CAST-128 (a.k.a. CAST5) symmetric key algorithm, and the DSA and ElGamal asymmetric key algorithms. For example Version 7 supports the following:

- Data Encryption Standard (DES) in triple DES mode (3DES) for data encryption
- Advanced Encryption Standard (AES) for data encryption
- Digital Signature Algorithm (DSA) for digital signatures
- RSA for digital signatures

- Secure Hash Algorithm (SHA-1) for hashing.

Recommend PGP Cipher Suites (Tracy, Jansen and Bisker 2002)

- **Highest Security:**
  - Encryption: Advanced Encryption Standard (AES) 256-bit encryption
  - Authentication & Digest: Digital Signature Standard (DSS) with a key size of 1024 bits or higher and
  - Secure Hash Algorithim-1 (SHA-1)
- **Security and Performance:**
  - Encryption: AES 128-bit encryption
  - Authentication & Digest: DSS with a key size of 1024 bits or higher and SHA-1
- **Security and Compatibility:**
  - Encryption: Triple Data Encryption Standard (3DES) 168/112-bit encryption (note: 3DES is considerably slower than AES)
  - Authentication & Digest: DSS with a key size of 1024 bits or higher and SHA-1
- **Authentication and Tamper:**
  - Detection Authentication & Digest: DSS with a key size of 1024 bits or higher and SHA-1

OpenPGP

(wikipedia.org, Open PGP, 2009) (Callas, Donnerhacke, Finney, & Thayer, OpenPGP Message Format RFC: 4880, 2007). OpenPGP provides data integrity services for messages and data files by using these core technologies: Digital signatures; encryption; compression and Radix-64 conversion (Many electronic mail systems can only transmit blocks of ASCII text. This can cause a problem when sending encrypted data, since ciphertext blocks might not correspond to ASCII characters,

which can be transmitted. PGP overcomes this problem by using radix-64 conversion.)

In addition, OpenPGP provides key management and certificate service only once, the session key is bound to the message and transmitted with it. To protect the key, it is encrypted with the receiver's public key. The sequence is as follows:

- The sender creates a message.
- The sending OpenPGP generates a random number to be used as a session key for this message only.
- The session key is encrypted using each recipient's public key. These "encrypted session keys" start the message.
- The sending OpenPGP encrypts the message using the session key, which forms the remainder of the message. Note that the message is also usually compressed.
- The receiving OpenPGP decrypts the session key using the recipient's private key.
- The receiving OpenPGP decrypts the message using the session key. If the message was compressed, it will be decompressed

With symmetric-key encryption, an object may be encrypted with a symmetric key derived from a passphrase (or other shared secret), or a two-stage mechanism similar to the public-key method described above in which a session key is itself encrypted with a symmetric algorithm keyed from a shared secret.

Both digital signature and confidentiality services may be applied to the same message. First, a signature is generated for the message and attached to the message. Then, the message plus signature is encrypted using a symmetric session key. Finally, the session key is encrypted using public-key encryption and prefixed to the encrypted block.

OpenPGP is on the Internet Standards Track; the current specification is RFC 4880 (November 2007). OpenPGP is still under active development

Algorithm 1. Public-Key Algorithms

```
ID Algorithm
-- ---------
 1 - RSA (Encrypt or Sign) [HAC]
 2 - RSA Encrypt-Only [HAC]
 3 - RSA Sign-Only [HAC]
16 - ElGamal (Encrypt-Only) [ELGAMAL] [HAC]
17 - DSA (Digital Signature Algorithm) [FIPS186] [HAC]
18 - Reserved for Elliptic Curve
19 - Reserved for ECDSA
20 - Reserved (formerly ElGamal Encrypt or Sign)
21 - Reserved for Diffie-Hellman (X9.42, as defined for IETF-S/MIME)
100 to 110 - Private/Experimental algorithms
```

Implementations MUST implement DSA for signatures and ElGamal for encryption. Implementations SHOULD implement RSA keys (1). RSA Encrypt-Only (2) and RSA Sign-Only are deprecated and SHOULD NOT be generated, but may be interpreted. Elliptic Curve (18), ECDSA (19), ElGamal Encrypt or Sign (20), and X9.42 (21). Implementations MAY implement any other algorithm.

and the successor to RFC 2440, which is RFC 4880, has been made a proposed standard. Many e-mail clients provide OpenPGP-compliant e-mail security as described in RFC 3156.

The Free Software Foundation has developed its own OpenPGP-compliant program called GNU Privacy Guard (abbreviated GnuPG or GPG). GnuPG is freely available together with all source code under the GNU General Public License (GPL) and is maintained separately from

several Graphical User Interfaces (GUIs) that interact with the GnuPG library for encryption, decryption and signing functions (see KGPG, Seahorse, MacGPG). Several other vendors have also developed OpenPGP-compliant software.

The implementation considerations in Open-PGP are *Public-Key Algorithms, Symmetric-Key Algorithms, Compression Algorithms,* and *Hash Algorithms,* shown in Algorithms 1-4.

OpenPGP is highly parameterized, and consequently there are a number of considerations for allocating parameters for extensions.

OpenPGP Messages

OpenPGP provides data integrity services for messages and data files: (Callas, Donnerhacke, Finney, & Thayer, OpenPGP Message Format RFC: 4880, 2007) In addition, OpenPGP provides key management and certificate services, but many of these are beyond the scope of this document. With symmetric-key encryption, an object may be encrypted with a symmetric key derived from a passphrase (or other shared secret)

Both digital signature and confidentiality services may be applied to the same message. First, a signature is generated for the message and attached to the message. Then, the message plus signature is encrypted using a symmetric

Algorithm 2. Symmetric-Key Algorithms

```
ID Algorithm
-- ---------
 0 - Plaintext or unencrypted data
 1 - IDEA [IDEA]
 2 - TripleDES (DES-EDE, [SCHNEIER] [HAC] -
 168-bit key derived from 192)
 3 - CAST5 (128 bit key, as per [RFC2144])
 4 - Blowfish (128 bit key, 16 rounds) [BLOWFISH]
 5 - Reserved
 6 - Reserved
 7 - AES with 128-bit key [AES]
 8 - AES with 192-bit key
 9 - AES with 256-bit key
10 - Twofish with 256-bit key [TWOFISH]
100 to 110 - Private/Experimental algorithms
```

Implementations MUST implement TripleDES. Implementations SHOULD implement AES-128 and CAST5. Implementations that interoperate with PGP 2.6 or earlier need to support IDEA, as that is the only symmetric cipher those versions use. Implementations MAY implement any other algorithm.

Algorithm 3. Compression Algorithms

```
ID Algorithm
-- ---------
 0 - Uncompressed
 1 - ZIP [RFC1951]
 2 - ZLIB [RFC1950]
 3 - BZip2 [BZ2]
 100 to 110 - Private/Experimental algorithms


Implementations MUST implement uncompressed data. Imple-
mentations SHOULD implement ZIP. Implementations MAY
implement any other algorithm.
```

Algorithm 4. Hash Algorithms

```
ID Algorithm Text Name
-- --------- ---------
 1 - MD5 [HAC] "MD5"
 2 - SHA-1 [FIPS180] "SHA1"
 3 - RIPE-MD/160 [HAC] "RIPEMD160"
 4 - Reserved
 5 - Reserved
 6 - Reserved
 7 - Reserved
 8 - SHA256 [FIPS180] "SHA256"
 9 - SHA384 [FIPS180] "SHA384"
 10 - SHA512 [FIPS180] "SHA512"
 11 - SHA224 [FIPS180] "SHA224"
 100 to 110 - Private/Experimental algorithms


Implementations MUST implement SHA-1. Implementations
MAY implement other algorithms. MD5 is deprecated.
```

session key. Finally, the session key is encrypted using public-key encryption and prefixed to the encrypted block.

An OpenPGP message is a packet or sequence of packets that corresponds to the following grammatical rules (comma represents sequential composition, and vertical bar separates alternatives) shown in Algorithm 5.

In addition, decrypting a Symmetrically Encrypted Data packet or a Symmetrically Encrypted Integrity Protected Data packet as well as decompressing a Compressed Data packet must yield a valid OpenPGP Message.

GNU PRIVACY GUARD

The GNU Privacy Guard (GnuPG) is the OpenPGP implementation of the GNU project. GnuPG is fully OpenPGP compliant supports most of the optional features and provides some extra features. GnuPG is used as the standard encryption and signing tool of all GNU/Linux distributions. GnuPG is freely available for GNU/Linux, nearly all other UNIX systems, Microsoft Windows systems and a few other operating systems.

Secure/Multipurpose Internet Mail (S/MIME) (Ramsdell(Ed), 2004) (Ramsdell(Ed), 1999)

S/MIME was originally developed by RSA Data Security Inc. The original specification used the recently developed IETF MIME specification with the de facto industry standard PKCS #7 secure message format. Change control to S/MIME has

Algorithm 5.

```
OpenPGP Message: - Encrypted Message |¹ Signed Message | Compressed Message
                        | Literal Message.
Compressed Message: - Compressed Data Packet.
Literal Message: - Literal Data Packet.
ESK: - Public-Key Encrypted Session Key Packet |Symmetric-Key Encrypted Session Key Packet.
ESK Sequence: - ESK | ESK Sequence, ESK.
Encrypted Data: - Symmetrically Encrypted Data Packet |
Symmetrically Encrypted Integrity Protected Data Packet
Encrypted Message: - Encrypted Data | ESK Sequence, Encrypted Data.
One-Pass Signed Message: - One-Pass Signature Packet, OpenPGP Message, Corresponding
                        Signature Packet.
Signed Message: - Signature Packet, OpenPGP Message | One-Pass Signed Message.
```

since been vested in the IETF and the specification is now layered on Cryptographic Message Syntax, The Cryptographic Message Syntax is derived from PKCS #7 version 1.5 as specified in RFC 2315 [PKCS#7]. Wherever possible, backward compatibility is preserved; however, changes were necessary to accommodate attribute certificate transfer and key agreement techniques for key management. S/MIME provides a consistent way to send and receive secure MIME data. Digital signatures provide authentication, message integrity, and non-repudiation with proof of origin. Encryption provides data confidentiality. Compression can be used to reduce data size. S/MIME Based on the popular Internet MIME standard, S/MIME provides the following cryptographic security services for electronic messaging applications:

* authentication,
* Message integrity
* Non-repudiation of origin (using digital signatures), and
* Data confidentiality (using encryption).

S/MIME is not restricted to mail; it can be used with any transport mechanism that transports MIME data, such as HTTP. S/MIME takes advantage of the object-based features of MIME and allows secure messages to be exchanged in mixed-transport systems. It can be used in automated message transfer agents that use cryptographic security services that do not require any human intervention, such as the signing of software-generated documents and the encryption of FAX messages sent over the Internet.

S/MIME remains firmly grounded in the X.509 certification hierarchy; although the FAQ claims that the guidelines for hierarchies are "more flexible" than in PEM.

One cryptographic weakness of S/MIME is that eavesdroppers can distinguish between encrypted and signed-and-encrypted messages (Levien, 1999). This violates the principle of disclosing a minimum amount of information. PGP, PGP/MIME, and MOSS do not have this problem.

S/MIME version 2 specified by the following informational RFCs:

* S/MIME Version 2 Message Specification (RFC 2311)
* S/MIME Version 2 Certificate Handling (RFC 2312)
* PKCS #1: RSA Encryption Version 1.5 (RFC 2313)
* PKCS #10: Certification Request Syntax Version 1.5 (RFC 2314)
* PKCS #7: Cryptographic Message Syntax Version 1.5 (RFC 2315)
* Description of the RC2 Encryption Algorithm (RFC 2268)

S/MIME version 3 is specified by the following RFCs:

* Cryptographic Message Syntax (RFC 2630)
* S/MIME Version 3 Message Specification (RFC 2633)
* S/MIME Version 3 Certificate Handling (RFC 2632)
* Diffie-Hellman Key Agreement Method (RFC 2631).
* Enhanced Security Services for S/MIME (RFC 2634)

The S/MIME Algorithms

The protocol uses the following algorithms

* The RSA public key algorithm with key wrapping algorithm,
* the Diffie-Hellman
* The AES symmetric encryption algorithm
* The RSA public key algorithm for signature algorithm.
* Header protection through the use of the message/rfc822 MIME

- Compressed Data as a Cryptographic Message Syntax (CMS)
- sha1
- RC2 Algorithm

AES has been enforced with the protocol since 2004 with Session Initiation Protocol (SIP)

(Schaad, 2003) Since SIP is 8-bit clean, all implementations MUST use 8-bit binary Content-Transfer-Encoding for S/MIME in SIP. Implementations MAY also be able to receive base-64 Content-Transfer-Encoding. The migration of the S/MIME requirement from Triple-DES to AES is not known to introduce any new security considerations

Some S/MIME functions

- Signature Algorithm Identifier
- Key Encryption Algorithm Identifier
- General Syntax: Only the Data, Signed Data, Enveloped Data, and Compressed Data content types are Currently used for S/MIME
- The SMIME Capabilities attribute includes signature algorithms (such as "sha1WithR-SAEncryption"), symmetric algorithms (such as "DES-EDE3-CBC"), and key encipherment algorithms (such as "RSA Encryption"). SMIME Capabilities were designed to be flexible and extensible so that, in the future, a means of identifying other capabilities and preferences such as certificates can be added in a way that will not cause current clients to break.
- MIME Capability For the RC2 Algorithm For the RC2 algorithm preference SMIME Capability, the capability ID MUST be set to the value rc2-cbc

Choosing Weak Encryption

Like all algorithms that use 40 bit keys, RC2/40 is considered by many to be weak encryption. A sending agent that is controlled by a human

SHOULD allow a human sender to determine the risks of sending data using RC2/40 or a similarly weak encryption algorithm before sending the data, and possibly allow the human to use a stronger

One cryptographic weakness of S/MIME is that eavesdroppers can distinguish between encrypted and signed-and-encrypted messages. This violates the principle of disclosing a minimum amount of information. PGP, PGP/MIME, and MOSS do not have this problem.

Secure/Multipurpose Internet Mail Extension (Housley & Solinas, Suite B in Secure/Multipurpose Internet Mail Extensio:RFC5008, 2007) The use the United States National Security Agency's Suite B algorithms in Secure/Multipurpose Internet Mail Extensions (S/MIME) as specified in RFC 3851

Suite B Security Levels

Suite B offers two security levels: Level 1 and Level 2. Security Level 2 offers greater cryptographic strength by using longer keys. For S/MIME signed messages, Suite B follows the direction set by RFC 3278, but some additional algorithm identifiers are assigned. Suite B uses these algorithms:

For S/MIME-encrypted messages, Suite B follows the direction set by RFC 3278 and follows the conventions set by RFC 3565 additional algorithm identifiers are assigned. Suite B uses the algorithms shown in Algorithms 6 and 7.

CHOOSING AN APPROPRIATE ENCRYPTION ALGORITHM (TRACY, JANSEN AND BISKER 2002)

Decide on appropriate encryption algorithm depends on several issues that will vary with each organization. It might appear that the strongest encryption should be used for high security, which is not always true. The higher the level of the encryption, the greater impact it will have on the

Algorithm 6.

	Security Level 1	Security Level 2
Message Digest:	SHA-256	SHA-384
Signature:	ECDSA with P-256	ECDSA with P-384

Algorithm 7.

	Security Level 1	Security Level 2
Key Agreement:	ECDH with P-256	ECDH with P-384
Key Derivation:	SHA-256	SHA-384
Key Wrap:	AES-128 Key Wrap	AES-256 Key Wrap
Content Encryption:	AES-128 CBC	AES-256 CBC

mail client resources and communications speed (encryption can increase the size of an email considerably). In addition, a number of countries still maintain restrictions on the export, import, and/or use of encryption. In addition, patents and licensing issues may impact which encryption schemes can be used in a particular country. Finally, the choice of email encryption standard (PGP, S/MIME, etc.) may limit the choice of encryption algorithms. Fortunately, for Federal organizations, the choice is simple and clear – either 3DES or AES.

Common factors that can influence the choice of an encryption algorithm include the following items:

- Required security: value of the data, threat to data, other protective measures
- Required performance encryption
- System resources
- Import, export, or usage restrictions
- Client application and operating system to support the encryption scheme

Key Management (Tracy, Jansen and Bisker 2002)the biggest difference between PGP and S/MIME is the key management model. The default and traditional model that PGP uses key management is "circle of trust," which has no central key issuing or approving authority. The circle of trust relies on users for management and control. While this is suitable for very small organizations, the overhead of such a system is unworkable in medium to large organizations. Conversely, S/MIME and some newer versions of PGP work on a classic, more hierarchical design. Typically, there is a master registration and approving authority, referred to as a Certificate Authority (CA), with subordinate local registration authorities (Tracy, Jansen and Bisker 2002).

PGP or S/MIME

The advantages of PGP are as follows:

- Suitable for small groups or single users
- More secure with support for AES, though S/MIME is not far behind Freeware versions available
- (S/MIME requires an organization to purchase certificates or setup their own certificate authority)
- Does not require (but supports, if required) an external public key infrastructure (PKI)
- Can be used with any mail client application.

The advantages of S/MIME are as follows:

- Suitable for large groups and organizations
- Most widely compatible mail encryption standard
- Support is built into most major email client applications
- More transparent to the end-user

MIME Security with Pretty Good Privacy (PGP) (Elkins, Torto, Levien, & Roessler, 2001)

OpenPGP Message Format can be used to provide privacy and authentication using the Multipurpose Internet Mail Extensions (MIME) security. privacy with OpenPGP: "application/pgp-encrypted", "application/pgp-signature" and "application/pgp-keys".

OpenPGP Data Formats

OpenPGP implementations can generate either ASCII armor (described in or 8-bit binary output when encrypting data, generating a digital signature, or extracting public key data. The ASCII armor output is the REQUIRED method for data transfer. This allows those users who do not have the means to interpret the formats described in this document to be able to extract and use the OpenPGP information in the message. When the amount of data to be transmitted requires that it be sent in many parts, the MIME message/partial mechanism SHOULD be used rather than the multi-part ASCII armor OpenPGP format.

PGP Encrypted Data (Elkins, Torto, Levien, & Roessler, 2001)

Before encryption with PGP, the data should be written in MIME canonical format (body and headers).

PGP encrypted data is denoted by the "multipart/encrypted" (Galvin, Murphy, Crocker, & Freed, 1995), and MUST have a "protocol" parameter value of "application/pgp-encrypted". Note that the value of the parameter MUST be enclosed in quotes. The multipart/encrypted MUST consist of exactly two parts. The first MIME body part must have a content type of "application/pgp- encrypted". This body contains the control information. A message complying with this standard MUST contain a "Version: 1" field in this body. Since the PGP packet format contains all other information necessary for decrypting, no other information is required here.

The second MIME body part MUST contain the actual encrypted data. It must be labeled with a content type of "application/octet- stream".

Use of this protocol has the same security considerations as PGP, and is not known to either increase or decrease the security of messages using it,

MIME Security with OpenPGP (Elkins, Torto, Levien, & Roessler, 2001)

OpenPGP Message Format can used to provide privacy and authentication using the Multipurpose Internet Mail Extensions (MIME). Before OpenPGP encryption, the data is written in MIME canonical format (body and headers).

OpenPGP encrypted data is denoted by the "multipart/encrypted" content type, and MUST have a "protocol" parameter value of "application/pgp-encrypted". Note that the value of the parameter MUST be enclosed in quotes.

The multipart/encrypted MIME body MUST consist of exactly two body parts, the first with content type "application/pgp-encrypted". This body contains the control information. A message complying with this standard MUST contain a "Version: 1" field in this body.

The second MIME body part MUST contain the actual encrypted data. It MUST be labeled with a content type of "application/octet-stream".

The multipart/encrypted MIME body: consist of exactly two body parts, the first with content type "application/pgp-encrypted". This body contains the control information. A message complying with this standard MUST contain a "Version: 1" field in this body. Since the OpenPGP packet format contains all other information necessary for decrypting, no other information is required here. The second MIME body part MUST contain the actual encrypted data. It MUST be labeled with a content type of "application/octet-stream".

The multipart/signed body: consist of exactly two parts. The first part contains the signed data in MIME canonical format, including a set of appropriate content headers describing the data. The second body MUST contain the OpenPGP digital signature. It MUST be labeled with a content type of "application/pgp-signature".

When the OpenPGP digital signature is generated:

- The data to be signed MUST first be converted to its content- type specific canonical form. For text/plain, this means conversion to an appropriate character set and conversion of line endings to the canonical <CR><LF> sequence.
- An appropriate Content-Transfer-Encoding is then applied. In particular, line MUST use the canonical <CR><LF> sequence where appropriate endings in the encoded data(note that the canonical line ending may or may not be present on the last line of encoded data and MUST NOT be included in the signature if absent).
- MIME content headers are then added to the body, each ending with the canonical <CR><LF> sequence.
- Any trailing white space MUST then be removed from the signed material.
- The digital signature MUST be calculated over both the data to be signed and its set of content headers.

- The signature MUST be generated detached from the signed data so that the process does not alter the signed data in any way.

WEB-BASED E-MAIL

The second type of technology for e-mail is the WEB base, Web-based mail, also known as Webmail, is used as a means of email service delivery, because Web browsers that enable access to the client are available on nearly every Internet-enabled device. A user simply runs a Web browser and connects to a Web site that hosts the Web-based mail application. The connection is made using either Hypertext Transfer Protocol (HTTP) or HTTP over Transport Layer Security (TLS), known as HTTPS. HTTPS encrypts the communications, which protects both authentication information and email message content. HTTP does not offer any protection.

Web-based mail applications incorporate much of the mail-handling functionality of traditional mail clients and communicate with their associated mail servers using the same mailbox access protocols SMTP, POP, and IMAP, as well as proprietary protocols. The mailbox access protocols are used between the Web servers and mail servers only; the protocols are not carried between the Web servers and Web browsers(Tracy, Jansen and Bisker 2007)..

Secure Sockets Layer (SSL) (Dierks & Allen, 1999) (Hoffman, 1999) (Thomas, 2000) (sun.com, 2002) (wikipedia.org, SSL,2009)

Secure Sockets Layer technology protects Web site and makes it easy for your Web site visitors to trust the web in three essential ways:

1. An SSL Certificate enables encryption of sensitive information during online transactions.

2. Each SSL Certificate contains unique, authenticated information about the certificate owner.

3. A Certificate Authority verifies the identity of the certificate owner when it is issued

Encryption

SSL uses public-key encryption to exchange a session key between the client and server; this session key is used to encrypt the http transaction (both request and response). Each transaction uses a different session key so that if someone manages to decrypt a transaction, that does not mean that they've found the server's secret key; if they want to decrypt another transaction, they'll need to spend as much time and effort on the second transaction as they did on the first. Netscape servers and browsers do encryption using either a 40-bit secret key or a 128-bit secret key. A 40-bit key is insecure because it's vulnerable to a "brute force" attack. Using a 128-bit key eliminates this problem.

Each SSL uses a certificate consists of a public key and a private key. The public key is used to encrypt information and the private key is used to decipher it. When a Web browser points to a secured domain, a Secure Sockets Layer handshake authenticates the server (Web site) and the client (Web browser). An encryption method is established with a unique session key and secure transmission can begin. True 128-bit SSL Certificates enable every site visitor to experience the strongest SSL encryption available to them.

Authentication

Imagine receiving an envelope with no return address and a form asking for your bank account number.

SSL Certificate is created for a particular server in a specific domain for a verified business entity. When the SSL handshake occurs, the browser requires authentication information from the server. By clicking the closed padlock in the browser window or certain SSL trust marks, the Web site visitor sees the authenticated organization name. In high-security browsers, the authenticated organization name is prominently displayed and the address bar turns green when an Extended Validation SSL Certificate is detected. If the information does not match or the certificate has expired, the browser displays an error message or warning.

Like a driver's license, an SSL Certificate is issued by a trusted source, known as the Certificate Authority (CA). Many CAs simply verify the domain name and issue the certificate. VeriSign verifies the existence of your business, the ownership of your domain name, and your authority to apply for the certificate, a higher standard of authentication.

History

The timeline begins in November 1993, with the release of Mosaic 1.0 by the National Center for Supercomputing Applications (NCSA). Mosaic was the first popular Web browser. Only eight months later, Netscape Communications completed the design for SSL version 1.0; five months after that, Netscape shipped the first product with support for SSL version 2.0—Netscape Navigator. Other milestones in the timeline include the publication of version 1.0 of the Private Communication Technology (pct) specification. Microsoft developed pct as a minor enhancement to SSL version 2.0. It addressed some of the weaknesses of SSL 2.0, and many of its ideas were later incorporated into SSL version 3.0

The Secure Sockets Layer protocol provides effective security for Web transactions, but it is not the only possible approach. The Internet architecture relies on layers of protocols, each building on the services of those below it. Many of these different protocol layers can support security services, though each has its own advantages and disadvantages. As we'll see in this section, the designers of SSL chose to create an entirely new protocol layer for security. It is also possible to include security services in the application protocol or to add them to a core networking protocol. As another alternative, applications can rely on parallel protocols for some security services. All of these options have been considered for securing Web transactions, and actual protocols exist for each alternative.

Using SSL (in comparison) with other secure protocol could be in one of the following categories:

- SSL is a separate protocol layer just for security.
- SSL can add security to applications other than HTTP.
- Security can be added directly within an application protocol
- IPSEC adds security to a core network protocol.
- Kerberos supplements application protocols.

Secure Sockets Layer is simply a communication protocol, and any SSL implementation will rely on other components for many functions, including the cryptographic algorithms.

No SSL implementation can be any stronger than the cryptographic tools on which it is based

SSL Roles

The Secure Sockets Layer protocol defines two different roles for the communicating parties. One system is always a client, while the other is a server. The distinction is very important, because SSL requires the two systems to behave very differently. The client is the system that initiates the secure communications; the server responds to the client's request. In the most common use of SSL, secure Web browsing, the Web browser is the SSL client and the Web site is the SSL server. These same two roles apply to all applications that use SSL, For SSL itself, the most important distinctions between clients and servers are their actions during the negotiation of security parameters.

SSL Messages

When SSL clients and servers communicate, they do so by exchanging SSL messages. Technically, SSL defines different levels of messages, but that topic is best left for Chapter 4. Since this chapter concentrates strictly on functionality, distinguishing between the various SSL levels is not critical. Messages are: Alert, Application Data, Certificate, CertificateRequest, CertificateVerify, ChangeCipherSpec, ClientHello, ClientKeyExchange, Finished, HelloRequest, ServerHello, ServerHelloDone, ServerHelloDone

Establishing Encrypted Communications

The most basic function that an SSL client and server can perform is establishing a channel for encrypted communications. Steps:

- Client sends ClientHello message proposing SSL options.
- Server responds with ServerHello message selecting the SSL options.
- Server sends its public key information in ServerKeyExchange message.
- Server concludes its part of the negotiation with ServerHello-Done message.
- Client sends session key information (encrypted with server's public key) in ClientKeyExchange message.
- Client sends ChangeCipherSpec message to activate the negotiated options for all future messages it will send.

Authenticating the Server's Identity and includes: Certificate, ClientKeyExchange, ClientKeyExchange

Separating Encryption from Authentication and includes: Certificate, ServerKeyExchange, ClientKeyExchange

Authenticating the Client's Identity and includes: CertificateRequest, Certificate, CertificateVerify

Transport Requirements

The Secure Sockets Layer does not exist as a protocol in isolation. Rather, it depends on additional lower-level protocols to transport its messages between peers. The SSL protocol requires that the lower layer be reliable; that is, it must guarantee the successful transmission of SSL messages without errors and in the appropriate order. In all practical implementations, SSL relies on the Transmission Control Protocol (TCP) to meet those requirements.

Record Layer

The Secure Sockets Layer uses its Record Layer protocol to encapsulate all messages, and it provides a common format to frame Alert,

ChangeCipherSpec Protocol

The ChangeCipherSpec protocol is the simplest possible protocol that activates the negotiated security parameters; those parameters will be in effect for the next message that the sender transmits.

Alert Protocol

Systems use the Alert protocol to signal an error or caution condition to the other party in their communication. A component of the SSL protocol that defines the format of Alert messages

Handshake Protocol

Responsible for negotiating security parameters and relies on the Record Layer to encapsulate its messages.

Securing Messages

The Finished message is the first to actually use the security services that SSL negotiates. Once those services are in place, however, all subsequent messages in the session also make use of them—even additional handshake messages, should the parties want to renegotiate new security parameters. The most important messages, though, are application protocol messages. Those messages contain the actual data that the two parties want to exchange; the security requirements of that data are what make SSL necessary.

Cipher Suites

Version 3.0 of the SSL specification defines 31 different cipher suites, representing a varied selection of cryptographic algorithms and parameters. The cipher suite descriptions that follow refer to these algorithms:

- DES. Data Encryption Standard (3 DES used)
- Mostly after 2002 the use of AES start to substitute some of 3DES
- DSA. Digital Signature Algorithm, part of the digital authentication standard used by the U.S. Government.
- IDEA International Data Encryption Algorithm (IDEA) is a block cipher
- KEA. Key Exchange Algorithm, an algorithm used for key exchange by the U.S. Government.
- MD5. Message Digest algorithm developed by Rivest.
- RC2 and RC4. Rivest encryption ciphers developed for RSA Data Security.

- RSA. A public-key algorithm for both encryption and authentication.
- RSA key exchange. A key-exchange algorithm for SSL based on the RSA algorithm.
- SHA-1. Secure Hash Algorithm, a hash function used by the U.S. Government.
- SKIPJACK. A classified symmetric-key algorithm implemented in FORTEZZA-compliant hardware used by the U.S. Government

The 31 different cipher suites are (note that the ExportRestriction means: The sending party indicates that it detected a negotiation parameter not in compliance with applicable U.S. export restrictions; this message is always fatal.) some of these cipher suites are listed below in Table 1.

Key Exchange Algorithms

Key-exchange algorithms like KEA and RSA key exchange govern the way in which the server and client determine the symmetric keys they will both use during an SSL session. The most commonly used SSL cipher suites use RSA key exchange.

The SSL 2.0 and SSL 3.0 protocols support overlapping sets of cipher suites. Administrators can enable or disable any of the supported cipher suites for both clients and servers. When a particular client and server exchange information during the SSL handshake, they identify the strongest enabled cipher suites they have in common and use those for the SSL session.

Decisions about which cipher suites a particular organization decides to enable depend on trade-offs among the sensitivity of the data involved, the speed of the cipher, and the applicability of export rules.

Some organizations may want to disable the weaker ciphers to prevent SSL connections with weaker encryption. However, due to U.S. government restrictions on products that support anything stronger than 40-bit encryption, disabling support for all 40-bit ciphers effectively restricts access to network browsers that are available only in the United States (unless the server involved has a special Global Server ID that permits the international client to "step up" to stronger encryption). For more information about U.S. export restrictions.

To serve the largest possible range of users, its administrators may wish to enable as broad a range of SSL cipher suites as possible. That way, when a domestic client or server is dealing with another domestic server or client, respectively, it will negotiate the use of the strongest ciphers available. And when an domestic client or server is dealing with an international server or client, it will negotiate the use of those ciphers that are permitted under U.S. export regulations.

However, since 40-bit ciphers can be broken relatively quickly, administrators who are concerned about eavesdropping and whose user communities can legally use stronger ciphers should disable the 40-bit ciphers.

Some of key exchange algorithms used are:

Diffie-Hellman with DSS signatures and key size = DH: 512 bits

Table 1. Cipher suites.

SSL_RSA_EXPORT_	WITH_RC4_40_	MD5
SSL_RSA_	WITH_RC4_128_	MD5
SSL_DH_DSS_EXPORT_	WITH_DES40_CBC_	SHA
SSL_DH_DSS_	WITH_3DES_EDE_CBC_	SHA

The fall set can be found in (Thomas, 2000) chapter 4

Diffie-Hellman with RSA signatures and key size = DH: 512 bits

Diffie-Hellman, with key size = DH: 512 bits

Diffie-Hellman with DSS certificates and key size = DH: 512 bits

Diffie-Hellman with RSA certificates and key size = DH: 512 bits

RSA key exchange RSA and key size =: 512 bits

Encryption Algorithms

The SSL protocol supports nine different encryption algorithms, counting variations:

3DES_EDE_CBC, with key size 168 bits ; DES40_CBC, with key size of 40 bits and IDEA_CBC, with key size of 128 bits. (Thomas, 2000)

Hash Algorithms

The final component of an SSL cipher suite is the hash algorithm used for the message authentication code.

MD5, hash size=16 bytes, padding size=48 bytes; SHA with hash size=20 byte and padding size40 bytes

Most SSL implementation after 2002 enforce the use of AES rather than 3 DES, some implementation for SSL could fail in the use of only AES such are configuration of SSL with Vista operating system (ibm.com, 2008)

Cipher suites supported by the SSL protocol that use the RSA key-exchange algorithm:

- **Strongest cipher suite**. Permitted for deployments within the United States only. This cipher suite is appropriate for banks and other institutions that handle highly sensitive data.

   Triple DES or AES which supports 168-bit encryption, with SHA-1 message authentication. There are more possible keys than for any other cipher--approximately $3.7 * 10^{50}$. Both SSL 2.0 and SSL 3.0 support this cipher suite.

- **Strong cipher suites.** Permitted for deployments within the United States only. These cipher suites support encryption that is strong enough for most business or government needs.

   RC4 with 128-bit encryption and MD5 message authentication: Because the RC4 and RC2 ciphers have 128-bit encryption, they are the second strongest next to Triple DES (Data Encryption Standard) or AES, with 168-bit encryption. RC4 and RC2 128-bit encryption permits approximately $3.4 * 10^{38}$ possible keys, making them very difficult to crack. RC4 ciphers are the fastest of the supported ciphers. Both SSL 2.0 and SSL 3.0 support this cipher suite.

   RC2 with 128-bit encryption and MD5 message authentication: Because the RC4 and RC2 ciphers have 128-bit encryption, they are the second strongest next to Triple DES (Data Encryption Standard) or AES,, with 168-bit encryption. RC4 and RC2 128-bit encryption permits approximately $3.4 * 10^{38}$ possible keys, making them very difficult to crack. RC2 ciphers are slower than RC4 ciphers. This cipher suite is supported by SSL 2.0 but not by SSL 3.0.

   DES, which supports 56-bit encryption, with SHA-1 message authentication: DES is stronger than 40-bit encryption, but not as strong as 128-bit encryption. DES 56-bit encryption permits approximately $7.2 * 10^{16}$ possible keys. Both SSL 2.0 and SSL 3.0 support this cipher suite, except that SSL 2.0 uses MD5 rather than SHA-1 for message authentication

- **Exportable cipher suites.** These cipher suites are not as strong as those listed above, but may be exported to most countries (note that France permits them for SSL but not for S/MIME). They provide the strongest encryption available for exportable products

> **RC4 with 40-bit encryption and MD5 message authentication:** RC4 40-bit encryption permits approximately 1.1 $* 10^{12}$ (a trillion) possible keys. RC4 ciphers are the fastest of the supported ciphers. Both SSL 2.0 and SSL 3.0 support this cipher.

> **RC2 with 40-bit encryption and MD5 message authentication:** RC2 40-bit encryption permits approximately $1.1 * 10^{12}$ (a trillion) possible keys. RC2 ciphers are slower than the RC4 ciphers. Both SSL 2.0 and SSL 3.0 support this cipher.

- **Weakest cipher suite:** This cipher suite provides authentication and tamper detection but no encryption. Server administrators must be careful about enabling it, however, because data sent using this cipher suite is not encrypted and may be accessed by eavesdroppers.

> **No encryption, MD5 message authentication only.** This cipher suite uses MD5 message authentication to detect tampering. It is typically supported in case a client and server have none of the other ciphers in common.

This cipher suite is supported by SSL 3.0 but not by SSL 2.0.

SSL Security Check List: A Check List has Been Created for Security Implementation Evaluation

Authentication: Certificate Authority, Certificate Signature, Certificate Validity Times, Certificate Revocation Status, Certificate Subject, Diffie-Hellman Trapdoors, Algorithm Rollback and Dropped ChangeCipherSpec Messages.

Encryption Issues: Encryption Key Size, Traffic Analysis and The Bleichenbacher Attack.

General Issues: RSA Key Size, Version Rollback Attacks, Premature Closure, SessionID Values, Random Number Generation and Random Number Seeding.

For one additional refinement, TLS uses the pseudorandom output procedure to create a pseudorandom function, or PRF. The PRF combines two separate instances of the pseudorandom output procedure; one uses the md5 hash algorithm and the other uses the SHA hash algorithm. The TLS standard specifies a function that uses both algorithms just in case one of the two is ever found to be insecure.

Should that happen, the other algorithm will still protect the data.

FORTEZZA is an encryption system used by U.S. government agencies to manage sensitive but

Table 2. Differences between SSL and TLS

	SSL v3.0	TLS v1.0
Protocol version in messages	3	3.1
Alert protocol message types	12	23
Message authentication	ad hoc	standard
Key material generation	ad hoc	PRF*
CertificateVerify	complex	simple
Finished	ad hoc	PRF
Baseline cipher suites	With Fortezza	no Fortezza

* PRF is abbreviated for pseudorandom function

unclassified information. It provides a hardware implementation of two classified ciphers developed by the federal government: FORTEZZA KEA and SKIPJACK. FORTEZZA ciphers for SSL use the Key Exchange Algorithm (KEA) instead of the RSA key-exchange algorithm mentioned in the preceding section, and use FORTEZZA cards and DSA for client authentication.

Cipher suites supported by Netscape products with FORTEZZA for SSL 3.0.

- Strong FORTEZZA ciphers suites. Permitted for deployments within the United States only. These cipher suites support encryption that is strong enough for most business or government needs.

  RC4 with 128-bit encryption and SHA-1 message authentication: Like RC4 with 128-bit encryption and MD5 message authentication, this cipher is one of the second strongest ciphers after Triple DES. It permits approximately $3.4 * 10^{38}$ possible keys, making it very difficult to crack. This cipher suite is supported by SSL 3.0 but not by SSL 2.0.

  RC4 with SKIPJACK 80-bit encryption and SHA-1 message authentication, The SKIPJACK cipher is a classified symmetric-key cryptographic algorithm implemented in FORTEZZA-compliant hardware. Some SKIPJACK implementations support key escrow using the Law Enforcement Access Field (LEAF). The most recent implementations do not. This cipher suite is supported by SSL 3.0 but not by SSL 2.0.

- **Weakest FORTEZZA cipher suite:** This cipher suite provides authentication and tamper detection but no encryption. Server administrators must be careful about enabling it, however, because data sent using

this cipher suite is not encrypted and may be accessed by eavesdroppers.

No encryption, SHA-1 message authentication only. This cipher uses SHA-1 message authentication to detect tampering. This cipher suite is supported by SSL 3.0 but not by SSL 2.0.

TLS Protocol Version

Perhaps it is unfortunate that the IETF decided to rename SSL to TLS. That decision has certainly introduced some confusion in the version numbers for the TLS protocol. The existing Transport Layer Security standard is named version 1.0. it is the first version of TLS. in order to maintain interoperability with SSL version 3.0 systems, the protocol version reported in the actual protocol messages must be *greater* than 3.0. Because TLS is a modest rather than a drastic improvement over SSL, TLS designers have specified that the protocol version that appears in TLS messages be 3.**1**. Presumably, should TLS ever undergo a major revision itself, the new protocol would be named version 2.0, but would be indicated in the protocol messages as 4.0.

Message Authentication

Another area in which TLS improves on SSL is in the algorithms for message authentication. The way SSL message authentication combines key information and application data is rather ad hoc, created just for the SSL protocol. The TLS protocol, on the other hand, relies on a standard message authentication code known as HMAC (for Hashed Message Authentication Code). The HMAC algorithm is a defined standard, and has been subjected to rigorous cryptographic analysis. The HMAC specification (see the References section) includes a precise description of the approach, as well as sample source code, but HMAC does not specify a particular hash algorithm (such as md5 or SHA); rather, it works effectively with any competent hash algorithm. The TLS message authentication code is a straightforward application of the HMAC standard. The MAC is the result of the HMAC approach, using whatever hash algorithm the negotiated cipher suite requires. The HMAC secret is the MAC write secret derived from the master secret

Data Protected by H-MAC

- Sequence number
- TLS protocol message type
- TLS version (e.g., 3.1)
- Message length
- Message contents

Key Material Generation

Building on the HMAC standard, TLS defines a procedure for using HMAC to create pseudorandom output. This procedure takes a secret value and an initial seed value (which can be quite small), and securely generates random output. The procedure can create as much random output as necessary.

Baseline Cipher Suites

As a baseline, TLS supports nearly the same set of cipher suites as SSL; however, explicit support for Fortezza/dms cipher suites has been removed. The set of defined TLS cipher suites will likely expand as new cipher suites are developed and implemented. Because the ietf has a well-defined process for evaluating these proposals, enhancements will be much easier to add to TLS than they were to SSL. The following table list baseline TLS cipher suites, along with their values in hello messages.

SSL V3 Baseline CipherSuite Values include something like: SSL_RSA_WITH_ NULL_MD5 with value of 0,1; SSL_RSA_ EXPORT_WITH_RC4_40_MD5 with the

value of (03); and SSL_RSA_EXPORT_ WITH_RC2_CBC_40_MD5 with value of (0,6)

TLS Enhancements to SSL (MicrosoftCoparation, 2009) (Dierks & Allen, The TLS Protocol Version 1.0. RFC 2246, 1999)

The keyed-Hashing for Message Authentication Code (HMAC) algorithm replaces the SSL Message Authentication Code (MAC) algorithm. HMAC produces more secure hashes than the MAC algorithm. The HMAC produces an integrity check value as the MAC does, but with a hash function construction that makes the hash much harder to break. In TLS, it is not always necessary to include certificates all the way back to the root CA. TLS specifies padding block values that are used with block cipher algorithms. RC4, which is used by Microsoft, is a streaming cipher, so this modification is not relevant.

Fortezza algorithms are not included in the TLS RFC, because they are not open for public review.

OpenSSL (openssl.org, 2005)

The OpenSSL Project is a collaborative effort to develop a robust, commercial-grade, full-featured, and Open Source toolkit implementing the Secure Sockets Layer (SSL v2/v3) and Transport Layer Security (TLS v1) protocols as well as a full-strength general purpose cryptography library. The project is managed by a worldwide community of volunteers that use the Internet to communicate, plan, and develop the OpenSSL toolkit and its related documentation.

OpenSSL is based on the excellent SSLeay library developed by Eric A. Young and Tim J. Hudson. The OpenSSL toolkit is licensed under an Apache-style license, which basically means that you are free to get and use it for commercial and non-commercial purposes subject to some simple license conditions.

The OPENSSL program is a command line tool for using the various cryptography functions of OpenSSL's **crypto** library from the shell. It can be used for:

- Creation and management of private keys, public keys and parameters
- Public key cryptographic operations
- Creation of X.509 certificates, CSRs and CRLs
- Calculation of Message Digests
- Encryption and Decryption with Ciphers
- SSL/TLS Client and Server Tests
- Handling of S/MIME signed or encrypted mail
- Time Stamp requests, generation and verification

Hypertext Transfer Protocol Secure (HTTPS) (Sharpe, 2008) (wikipedia.org, HTTP,2009)

It is a combination of the Hypertext Transfer Protocol and a network security protocol. Both HTTP and the security protocol operate at the highest layer of the TCP/IP Internet reference model, the Application layer; but the security protocol operates at lower sub layer, encrypting an HTTP message prior to transmission and decrypting a message upon arrival. HTTPS was developed by Netscape, has also been known as "Hypertext Transfer Protocol over Secure Socket Layer", but now HTTPS may be secured by the Transport Layer Security (TLS) instead of Secure Sockets Layer (SSL) protocol.

HTTPS (HTTP over SSL or HTTP Secure) is the use of Secure Socket Layer (SSL) or Transport Layer Security (TLS) as a sub layer under regular HTTP application layering. HTTPS encrypts and decrypts user page requests as well as the pages that are returned by the Web server. The use of HTTPS protects against eavesdropping and man-in-the-middle attacks.

To invoke HTTPS, one replaces "http://" with "https://" in the URI, or Web address. Suppose you visit a Web site to view their online catalog. When you're ready to order, you will be given a Web page order form with a Uniform Resource Locator (URL) that starts with https://. When you click "Send," to send the page back to the catalog retailer, your browser's HTTPS layer will encrypt it. The acknowledgement you receive from the server will also travel in encrypted form, arrive with an https:// URL, and be decrypted for you by your browser's HTTPS sub layer.

HTTPS connections are often used for payment transactions on the Web and for sensitive transactions in corporate information systems.

HTTPS is a separate protocol, but refers to the combination of a normal HTTP interaction over an encrypted Secure Sockets Layer (SSL) or Transport Layer Security (TLS) connection. (TLS is newer.) This ensures reasonable protection from eavesdroppers and man-in-the-middle attacks, provided that adequate cipher suites are used and that the server certificate is verified and trusted.

Limitations

The level of protection depends on the correctness of the implementation by the Web browser and the server software and the actual cryptographic algorithms supported.

Also, HTTPS is insecure when applied on publicly available static content. The entire site can be indexed using a Web crawler, and the URI of the encrypted resource can be inferred by knowing only the intercepted request/response size. This allows an attacker to have access to the plaintext (the publicly-available static content), and the encrypted text (the encrypted version of the static content).

Because SSL operates below HTTP and has no knowledge of higher-level protocols, SSL servers can only strictly present one certificate for a particular IP/port combination.

With the newer Internet Explorer 7 browser, Microsoft has increased the warnings sent when certificates are not registered. Whereas previously only a "security advice" pop-up appeared (which differentiated between name, source, and run time of the certificate), now a warning is displayed across the entire window, which recommends not using the Web site. Therefore, a certificate that is not registered in the browser is not usable for mass applications.

SSL and Hotmail Security

SSL (Secure Sockets Layer) is a communications protocol for transmitting private information over the Internet. SSL works by encrypting data that is transmitted over the SSL connection. Both Netscape Navigator and Internet Explorer support SSL.

When you sign in to MSN Hotmail, your sign-in name and password are encrypted and then sent over the Internet using an SSL connection. No one can read or access the data that is being transmitted.

After you sign in and leave the encrypted connection, MSN Hotmail keeps track of who you are by using a computer-generated key rather than your Hotmail sign-in name. MSN Hotmail regularly refreshes this key to make it difficult for anyone else to pose as you.

Note: If you are using a public or shared computer, such as at a library or cyber café, select the Public/shared computer option on the sign-in page. Also, remember to click .NET Passport sign out at the top center of the Hotmail page when you are finished to prevent others from using your Passport

E-Mail Reputation

E-mail reputation lets you know something about the reputation of the sender of the e-mail message. More and more Internet service providers are digitally signing outgoing e-mail to provide a secure way to allow recipients to verify that this e-mail really did come from the listed sender's domain. Once this is verified, then your address book and lists of known good domains can be used to determine if the sender's domain has a good reputation. In addition, if the sender's domain is found in a list of known bad domains, that can be used to alert the recipient of this situation.

AT&T Webmail will use a green star in the Reputation Information column to indicate that the message (1) had a good digital signature and (2) that the sender was in your address book, or the sender's domain appeared in a list of domains known to send only legitimate e-mail. This e-mail is highly likely to be legitimate. A "Do not enter" sign will be used to indicate a message had a domain that appeared in a list of known bad domains. This e-mail should not be trusted.

No symbol will be used to indicate that the message either (1) had no digital signature, (2) had digital signatures, but none could be verified, or (3) had a good digital signature, but the sender wasn't found in your address book and the sender's domain wasn't found in any domain list.

Moss

It is **MIME Object Security Services** is an attempt at an e-mail encryption protocol in accordance with MIME (Crocker, Freed, Galvin, & Murphy, 1995). It uses the multipart/signed and multipart/encrypted to apply digital signature and encryption services to MIME objects. It use the end-to-end cryptography between an originator and a recipient at the application layer. Public key cryptography is used in support of the digital signature and encryption key management. Secret key cryptography is used in support of the encryption service. The procedures are intended to be compatible with a wide range of public key management approaches, including both ad hoc and certificate-based schemes. There is a reference implementation (TIS/MOSS 7.1) (Drummond, 1996)

HIPAA Secure E-Mail
(encryptomatic.com, 2008)

HIPAA encryption requirements call for 112-bit symmetric encryption and 1024-bit asymmetric encryption. Message lock exceeds this requirement, providing selectable 128-bit or 256-bit AES encryption to protect e-mails.

NEXT GENERATION E-MAIL AND SECURE E-MAIL

We believe that the next generation of e-mail service (in next few years) would provide some of the following capabilities:

- Easy creating personal digital signature
- One encryption key and many decryption keys to open part of the message
- Security (Authentication + Encryption) integrated in an easy fashion
- Easy server-side filtering of mail (weekly, 2008)
- Support for one user -> many mailboxes [many-to-many] (weekly, 2008)
- Support for many users -> one mailbox (weekly, 2008)
- Integrating audio and video within the message
- Integrating e-mail with social networking
- Integration net meeting with e-mail messages
- Integrating metadata with e-mail service (encryptomatic.com, 2008)
- Secures e-mail messages in an AES encrypted zip-compatible envelope
- Adds zip, unzip and decryption to Microsoft Outlook (encryptomatic.com, 2008)
- Widely compatible with Hundreds of Millions of Computers that can already decrypt Zip files
- Easy to Use, One-Click e-mail Encryption

- Easy-to-implement clients for all platforms (weekly, 2008)
- Priority-filtered notifications (e.g., if I'm busy, only tell me about e-mails from my boss or my girlfriend or if they contain the subject "URGENT") (weekly, 2008)
- Efficient, query (searching method) server storage of many messages, some large, for many users. (Pre-decoding & separate storage of attachments might be a wise idea here) (weekly, 2008)
- Anthology and semantic searching method
- Message threading model for export of discussion to Internet/Intranet (integrated web/FTP export mechanism w/digesting capability) (weekly, 2008)
- virtual folders (also known as search folders), faster and more flexible searching, easier creation of filters and lots of small things to make common tasks quicker (Eide, 2004)
- Advanced mail-forwarding & message tracking (multi/random recipient [sales automation] tracking who responded to what) (weekly, 2008)

In all above expectation we believe the next generation of secure e-mail will introduce more use of new infrastructure based of quantum security and quantum computing and generally quantum information security. The resent research in quantum cryptography (Quantum cryptography is best known for key distribution. The most complete paper written on the subject) shows that the use of quantum Cryptography overcome some key problems of public key called key recycling (A symmetric encryption scheme allows for secure key recycling if part of the encryption key can be re-used for the transmission of a new encrypted message.)

In addition of key management we will see more and more use of Elliptic curve application as these type of algorithms are "ECC offers considerably greater security for a given key size.

The smaller key size also makes possible much more compact implementations for a given level of security, which means faster cryptographic operations, running on smaller chips or more compact software. This means less heat production and less power consumption — all of which is of particular advantage in constrained devices, but of some advantage anywhere. There are extremely efficient, compact hardware implementations available for ECC exponentiation operations, offering potential reductions in implementation footprint even beyond those due to the smaller key length alone." (Davis, 2008). We will see in near future more portable secure e-mail devices based on more secure E-mail protocols based on new application of Elliptic curve

CRYPTOGRAPHY IN WEB SERVICES

"Securing Web Services with WS-Security" (Rosenberg & Remy, 2004)will take a Web services securely to the security standards including

- WS-Security, a model that defines how to put security specifications into practice
- XML Encryption to ensure confidentiality
- XML Signature to ensure data integrity
- Security Assertion Markup Language (SAML) to authenticate and authorize users
- WS-Policy to set policies across trust domains

WS-Security (Web Services Security) (wikipedia.org, Web Services Security, 2009) "is a communications protocol providing a means for applying security to Web services". On 2004 the WS-Security 1.0 standard was released by Oasis-Open(OASIS)

Organization for the Advancement of Structured Information Standards is a nonprofit group that drives the development, convergence

and adoption of open standards for the global information society); 2006 they released version 1.1. Originally developed by IBM, Microsoft, and VeriSign, the protocol is now officially called WSS and developed via committee in Oasis-Open.

The protocol covers the enforcement of integrity and confidentiality on Web services messaging. The WSS protocol includes details on the use of SAML (Security Assertion Markup Language: is an XML-based standard for exchanging authentication and authorization data between security domains, that is, between an identity provider (a producer of assertions) and a service provider (a consumer of assertions). SAML is a product of the OASIS Security Services Technical Committee.) The protocols includes: Kerberos, and certificate formats such as X.509.

WS-Security specifies message attachment with digital signatures, encryption headers to SOAP messages, security tokens: including binary security tokens (such as X.509 certificates) and Kerberos tickets. WS-Security incorporates security features in the header of a SOAP message, working in the application layer to ensure end-to-end security. Other than the interface to the service, a Web Services front end can be added to an existing information-processing infrastructure (Hartman, Flinn, Beznosov, & Kawamoto, 2003)

Security Requirements (Hartman, Flinn, Beznosov, & Kawamoto, 2003)

Web Services operations can be complex and can engage many different entities. There is the initiator of the Web Services transaction, who may use a generic browser rather than a Web Services client to start the transaction going. Then, there is the Web Services subscriber, who will be a business or a business unit. There may be intermediaries who handle Web Services messages and may even affect the content of the message. A SOAP intermediary receives a SOAP message and may process SOAP headers addressed to it, but leaves the SOAP body intact.

Elements:

- **WS-Security:** Attach signature and encryption information as well as security tokens to SOAP messages
- **WS-Policy:** Identify the security requirements and capabilities of Web Services nodes
- **WS-Trust:** Establish trust in a Web Services environment, either directly or indirectly using a security token service
- **WS-Privacy:** Specify the privacy policies in place and privacy preferences Additional specifications are:
- **WS-Secure Conversation:** authenticate the subscriber, the provider, or both
- **WS-Federation:** support federation (that is, how to make dissimilar security systems interoperate)
- **WS-Authorization:** manage access control policies

The security services to support end-to-end a security:

- **Cryptography:** protects communications from disclosure or modification by using encryption or digital signatures
- **Authentication:** of principals by means of passwords, tokens, public key certificates, or secret keys
- Authorization of access to resources, including sending/receiving packet transmissions, access to a specified Uniform Resource Locator
- **Security Association:** To establish trust between client and target components
- **Delegation:** Allows a delegated principal to use the identity of an initiating principal so that the delegate may act on behalf of the initiating principal

- **Accountability:** Ensures that principals are accountable for their actions.
- **Security administration:** Defines the security policy maintenance life cycle embodied in user profiles, authentication, authorization, and accountability mechanisms as well as other data relevant to the security framework

Authentication Systems (Hartman, Flinn, Beznosov, & Kawamoto, 2003)

There are several different authentication systems for Web Services that use the security authentication mechanisms we've described. These are:

- **Operating System - Based Authentication:** Web Services are usually requested and delivered via HTTP. Therefore, Web Services systems often have Web servers as front ends. Some Web servers perform authentication by using the facilities of the underlying operating system.
- **Web Server-Based Authentication:** Web servers generally come with a built-in authentication capability to handle the authentication requirements for HTTP, namely HTTP basic authentication (which is password based)
- **Token-Based Authentication:** the user must possess a physical token that plays some part in the authentication process, which makes this approach stronger than passwords by themselves. Tokens provide two factor authentication (physical possession of the token card and knowledge of a PIN).
- **Web Single Sign-On:** The difficulty with HTTP is its statelessness and inability to keep track of a user session. Each request to a Web server is treated as a new request and the user must, theoretically, be authenticated again. A solution to this problem is

to have the Web browser cache authentication information and present it with each request to the Web server.

- **Client/Server Single Sign-On:** Just as Web interactions need SSO capability, client/server systems need SSO. Kerberos is the most common approach for client/server systems, and is used, for example, in Microsoft COM+.
- **Biometrics:** Biometrics includes mechanisms such as retina scanners, voice recognition systems, and palm or fingerprint readers. These provide strong authentication.

Authentication Options

Options for authentication are divided into two grouping: connection oriented and document oriented. Connection-oriented systems identify who or what is at the other end of a connection. Even where the communication protocol does not support a continued connection, some connection-oriented systems maintain the concept of a session by using URL or cookies extensions so that users do not have to authenticate themselves each time they make a request on a server. Document-oriented authentication systems embed an authentication token(s) with a message. Messages and their authentication token(s) may be transported using any number of protocols: SMTP, HTTP, and FTP. Messaging systems such as Message Queue (MQ) may also be used. The significance of the authentication information contained in the token varies and must be negotiated by the sender and the receiver of the message. For instance, authentication information may pertain to the sender or it may pertain to the initiator, the system user, who caused the message to be sent.

Connection-Oriented Authentication

There are two principal types of connection-oriented authentication techniques, password and challenge-response, Getting Started with Web Services Security. Password-based systems send authentication information that does not depend on any data being sent from the side that will do the authentication. With challenge-response authentication systems, the side that is doing the authentication sends data, called a challenge, to the side wishing to be authenticated. This information is transformed and returned as the response

Classes of authentication systems are:

- Operating system-based authentication
- Web server-based authentication
- Token-based authentication
- Web single sign-on (SSO)
- Client/server SSO

Document-Oriented Authentication

Document-oriented authentication systems embed information about an entity in the body of the document. This information allows the receiver to authenticate the creator of the document or a trusted third party vouching for the identity of an entity who is related to the document. The exact relationship of the entity to the document can vary and must be agreed to previously, for example token and digital signature

They are digital signatures and tokens.

Tokens

It is embedding authenticated identity information in a document which is insert a token bound to a subject. One token type is the SAML assertion (which are XML representations defined by the SAML specifications), SAML assertions are specifically defined to carry security-relevant information. An authentication assertion describes when and under what conditions the subject is authenticated. The attribute assertion identifies characteristics of the subject, and the authorization assertion identifies the subject's privileges with respect to a resource and an action. SAML assertions can be embedded in the header of a SOAP message.

A second option is WS-Security which is customized to SOAP and recognizes several token types such as Passport, Kerberos, and X.509.

Digital Signatures

With digital signatures, one or more parties sign the entire message or parts of the message using a digital signature algorithm such as RSA (ansi.org, 1998) or DSA (nist.gov, 2000). The Digital signature been implemented using XML. The other option for signing an XML-based Web Services document is the Cryptographic Message Syntax (CMS) (Housley R., Cryptographic Message Syntax RFC: 2630, 1999). CMS is used with Secure Multipart Internet Message Extension (S/MIME) (Ramsdell(Ed), 1999). CMS and S/MIME were developed by the IETF as ways to secure e-mail. The assumptions were that" the input is text but not XML".

XML Security (Hartman, Flinn, Beznosov, & Kawamoto, 2003)

XML security focuses on message security. Message encryption and digital signatures are the principal techniques used. While e-mail or file-encryption techniques can be used with XML messages, XML-specific techniques are more suitable for the way XML messages and SOAP messages are processed. The W3C leads most of the XML security standardization efforts. A digital signature standard exists in the form of a W3C recommendation. There is also a candidate recommendation for XML encryption. There are three approaches to Xml Encryption:

Encrypt the XML Using Symmetric Encryption: Only one session key is used and it's the same key that encrypts the xml which is used to decrypt it. The key is not stored with the encrypted xml and so the key needs to be loaded during the process and protected when stored.

Encrypt the XML Using a Combination of Asymmetric and Symmetric Encryption: The dual approach requires a symmetric session key to encrypt the data and an asymmetric key to protect the session key. Both the encrypted session key and the encrypted data are stored together in the xml document. The public asymmetric key is used to encrypt the session key while the private asymmetric key is used to decrypt the key.

Encrypt the XML Using a X.509 Certificate: This approach uses a X.509 certificate as the symmetrical key. X.509 certificates are provided by a third party vendor such as VeriSign.

XML Encryption

Can encrypt:

- An XML element
- The content of an XML element
- Arbitrary binary data with a UR

The ciphertext can be stored in an Encrypted-Data element or referenced (through a URI) by an EncryptedData element.

XML Encryption Algorithms

Arbitrary encryption algorithms are supported. Required encryption algorithms include:

- AES with (Cryptographic Message Syntax)CMS key length
- 3DES
- RSA-OAEP used with AES
- RSA-v1.5 used with 3DES

Required key transport algorithms include:

- RSA-OAEP used with AES
- RSA-v1.5 used with 3DES

Required Symmetric Key Wrap algorithms include:

- AES KeyWrap
- CMS-KeyWrap-3DES

Complete Standard Algorithm List (w3.org, 2002)

- **Block Encryption**
  - REQUIRED AES-256
  - OPTIONAL AES-192
  - REQUIRED AES-128
  - REQUIRED TRIPLEDES
- **Key Transport**
  - REQUIRED RSA-v1.5
  - REQUIRED RSA-OAEP
- **Key Agreement**
  - OPTIONAL Diffie-Hellman
- **Symmetric Key Wrap**
  - OPTIONAL AES-192 KeyWrap
  - REQUIRED AES-256 KeyWrap
  - REQUIRED AES-128 KeyWrap
  - REQUIRED TRIPLEDES KeyWrap
- **Message Digest**
  - REQUIRED SHA1
  - RECOMMENDED SHA256
  - OPTIONAL SHA512
  - OPTIONAL RIPEMD-160
- **Message Authentication**
  - RECOMMENDED XML Digital Signature
- **Canonicalization**
  - OPTIONAL Canonical XML with Comments
  - OPTIONAL Canonical XML (omits comments)
- **Encoding**
  - REQUIRED base64

XML Encryption Software

- xss4j, IBM's XML Security Suite: (IBMCopration, 1999)
  - enc.XMLCipher2 reads an XML document and encrypts the part of it specified by an XPath expression using a template file: % java enc. XMLCipher2 -e keyinfo.xml hotcop. xml /SONG/PUBLISHER template1. xml
  - API
- Apache XML Security Suite (apache.org, 2007)
  - org.apache.xml.security.c14n. Canonicalizer
  - I have not been able to build this. No precompiled binaries yet.
- JSR-106: XML Digital Encryption APIs (SunMicrosystems, 2008)

Issues XML Encryption Doesn't Address

- Authentication
- Authorization
- Access Control

XML Signature (W3C, XML Digital Signature, 2009)

Signature Generation

1. Create SignedInfo element with SignatureMethod, CanonicalizationMethod and Reference(s).
2. Canonicalize and then calculate the SignatureValue over SignedInfo based on algorithms specified in SignedInfo.
3. Construct the Signature element that includes SignedInfo, Object(s) (if desired, encoding may be different than that used for signing), KeyInfo (if required), and SignatureValue.

Note, if the Signature includes same-document references, [XML] or [XML-schema] validation of the document might introduce changes that break the signature. Consequently, applications should be careful to consistently process the document or refrain from using external contributions (e.g., defaults and entities

Signature Validation

1. Obtain the keying information from KeyInfo or from an external source.
2. Obtain the canonical form of the Signature Method using the CanonicalizationMethod and use the result (and previously obtained KeyInfo) to confirm the Signature Value over the SignedInfo element.

The DigestMethod Element

DigestMethod is a required element that identifies the digest algorithm to be applied to the signed object. This element uses the general structure here for algorithms specified in Algorithm Identifiers and Implementation Requirements. If the result of the URI dereference and application of Transforms is an XPath node-set (or sufficiently functional replacement implemented by the application) then it must be converted as described in the Reference Processing Model. If the result of URI dereference and application of transforms is an octet stream, then no conversion occurs (comments might be present if the Canonical XML with Comments was specified in the Transforms). The digest algorithm is applied to the data octets of the resulting octet stream.

Digest: Required SHA1 http://www.w3.org/2000/09/xmldsig - sha1**Encoding:** Required base64

MAC: Required HMAC-SHA1

Signature: Required DSAwithSHA1 (DSS), Recommended RSAwithSHA1

Canonicalization: Required Canonical XML 1.0(omits comments), Recommended Canonical XML 1.0 with Comments, Required Canonical XML 1.1 (omits comments), Recommended Canonical XML 1.1 with Comments

Transform: Optional XSLT, Recommended XPath, Required Enveloped Signature

XML Canonicalization (Hartman, Flinn, Beznosov, & Kawamoto, 2003)

The creation of XML Signatures is a bit more complex than the creation of an ordinary digital signature because a given XML Document (an "Infoset," in common usage among XML developers) may have more than one legal serialized representation. For example, white space inside an XML Element is not syntactically significant, so that <Elem > is syntactically identical to <Elem>.

The digital signature is created by using an asymmetric key algorithm (RSA) (wikipedia.org, Digital Signature, 2009) to encrypt the results of running the serialized XML document through a Cryptographic hash function (SHA1), a single-byte difference would cause the digital signature to vary. To avoid this problem and guarantee that logically-identical XML documents give identical digital signatures, an XML canonicalization transform (frequently abbreviated C14n) is nearly always employed when signing XML documents (for signing the SignedInfo, a canonicalization is mandatory). These algorithms guarantee that logically identical documents produce exactly identical serialized representations.

Another complication arises because of the way that the default canonicalization algorithm handles namespace declarations; frequently a signed XML document needs to be embedded in another document; in this case the original canonicalization algorithm will not yield the same result as if the document is treated alone. For this reason, the so-called Exclusive Canonicalization, which serializes XML namespace declarations independently of the surrounding XML, was created.

XML Decryption Transform for Signature (Hartman, Flinn, Beznosov, & Kawamoto, 2003)

When a digital signature is combined with encryption, it is necessary to know whether a signature was applied to encrypted data or to unencrypted data that was subsequently encrypted. In the first case, the encrypted data must be left encrypted for the signature to be verified. In the second case, the encrypted data must be decrypted before the signature is verified. **Decryption Transform for XML Signature** ((W3C, Decryption Transform for XML Signature, 2002)is a W3C candidate recommendation that specifies how the signer of a document can inform the signature verifier which signed portions of a document must be left encrypted so that a signature will be verified. All other portions of the document should be decrypted before the signature verification is attempted. This procedure is not a separate transform. Instead, it is an instruction to the signature verifier that is used during the decrypt transform.

XML Key Management Specification (XKMS) (Verma, 2004)

Objectives: The primary objectives of XKMS are:

*   Create an abstract layer between the application and the PKI solution. This allows the application to plug in different PKI solutions based on the need, without requiring any modification of the application itself.
*   Eliminate the need for the application to understand complex PKI syntax and semantics by providing a simple XML-based protocol for processing key information through the XKMS service.
*   Move complexity from the client application to the infrastructure level, thereby allowing the application to remain simpler and smaller. This allows even small footprint devices to take advantage of PKI.
*   Implement XKMS such that it is platform-, vendor-, and transport protocol-neutral.

Overview: XKMS is implemented as a Web service that allows a client application to access PKI features, thereby reducing the client applica-

tion's complexity. The client application need not be concerned about the syntax of the underlying PKI, which could be any of the following:

*   X.509 (the most widely used)
*   Pretty Good Privacy (PGP)
*   Simple Public Key Infrastructure (SPKI)
*   Public Key Infrastructure X.509 (PKIX)

XKMS specifications are made up of two specs, one that relates to registration of the public keys -- XML Key Registration Service Specification (XKRSS) -- and one that's concerned with the retrieval of information based on key information -- XML Key Information Service Specification (XKISS).

Another specification, X-Bulk, has been released by the Worldwide Web Consortium (W3C); it addresses the issue of registering key pairs in bulk. I will explain X-Bulk after discussing XKRSS.

XML Key Registration Service Specification (XKRSS)

This part of the XKMS deals with the mechanism for registering a key pair with a service provider. You can register keys with an XKMS service in two ways: The client generates a key pair and provides the public key, along with other information, to the service provider for registration. The XKMS service generates a key pair for the client, registers the public key of the pair with itself, and sends the private key of the pair to the client for its use. The client can also tell the XKMS service to keep the private key as well. The private key is kept with the XKMS service in case the client loses its private key.

An XKRSS service specification defines four operations:

*   Register
*   Reissue
*   Revoke

- Recover

An XKMS service implementing XKRSS service specifications may choose to offer some, all, or none of these operations. The XKRSS service specification does not make it mandatory for the XKMS service to implement any of the operations.

Bulk Registration of Key Pairs (X-Bulk)

X-Bulk handles registration of multiple key pairs in one request message, unlike XKRSS which addresses registration of one key pair at a time. the X-Bulk service supports all four operations -- Register, Reissue, Revoke, and Recover. X-Bulk can handle bulk registrations of client- as well as server-generated key pairs.

XML Key Information Service Specification (XKISS)

The client authenticates the encrypted/signed data by passing the corresponding key information to the service provider. The service provider then responds with "true" or "false." The XKISS service specification defines the following two operations:

- **Locate:** Locate resolves a <ds:KeyInfo> element that may be associated with XML encryption or XML signature, but it does not prove the validity of data binding in the <ds:KeyInfo> element.
- **Validate:** This operation does all that locate does, plus more. The locate service finds a key based on the <ds:KeyInfo> element, but does not assure the trustworthiness of the key binding information. The validate operation not only searches the public key corresponding to the <ds:KeyInfo> element, but also assures that the key binding information that it returns is trustworthy.

OASIS (OASIS, 2009)

"OASIS (Organization for the Advancement of Structured Information Standards) is a not-for-profit consortium that drives the development, convergence and adoption of open standards for the global information society. The consortium produces more Web services standards than any other organization along with standards for security, e-business, and standardization efforts in the public sector and for application-specific markets. OASIS Founded in 1993."

Specifications and Standards Addressing Security of SOAs (Singhal, Winograd, & Scarfone, 2007) are:

- Messaging Confidentiality and Integrity WS-Security, SSL/TLS
- Authentication WS-Security Tokens, SSL/TLS X.509 Certificates
- Resource Authorization XACML, XrML, RBAC, ABAC
- Privacy EPAL, XACML
- Negotiation Registries UDDI, ebXML
- Semantic Discovery SWSA, OWL-S
- Business Contracts ebXML
- Trust Establishment XKMS WS-Trust, X.509
- Trust Proxying SAML, WS-Trust
- Federation WS-Federation, Liberty IDFF, Shibboleth
- Security Properties Policy WS-Policy
- Security Policy WS-SecurityPolicy
- Availability WS-Reliable, Messaging, WS-Reliability

SAML

"SAML, developed by the Security Services Technical Committee of OASIS, is an XML-based framework for communicating user authentication, entitlement, and attribute information. As its name suggests, SAML allows business entities to make assertions regarding the identity, attributes, and entitlements of a subject (an entity that is often a human user) to other entities, such as a partner company or another enterprise application. Federation is the dominant movement in identity management today. Federation refers to the establishment of some or all of business agreements, cryptographic trust, and user identifiers or attributes across security and policy domains to enable more seamless cross-domain business interactions. As Web services promise to enable integration between business partners through loose coupling at the application and messaging layer, federation does so at the identity management layer insulating each domain from the details of the others' authentication and authorization infrastructure. Key to this loose coupling at the identity management layer are standardized mechanisms and formats for the communication of identity information between the domains the standard provides the insulating buffer. SAML defines just such a standard" (SAML, 2008).

SAML authentication statements indicate that a subject was authenticated and provide:

- What authentication method was used,
- When the authentication occurred, and
- Who the authenticating entity was.

Different techniques for establishing identity are supported, ranging from use of a password to use of hardware tokens and personal physical attributes (biometrics).

SAML allows assertions to specify any type of authentication mechanism used and provides a vocabulary for a number of commonly used mechanisms (Singhal, Winograd, & Scarfone, 2007).

A SAML authorization decision statement may be used to assert that a request by a subject to access a specified resource has resulted in the specified decision and may optionally include evidence to support the decision.

SAML attribute statements provide information about a particular subject that may be useful or necessary for determining whether or not access should be granted. In a Role Base Access Control (RBAC) environment, a SAML attribute statement can provide information about the subject's roles; similarly, in an ABAC environment, a SAML attribute statement can provide the attributes required by the policy

SAML to Bridge the Gap Between Different Security Models

The heart of the SAML specification is the XML Schema that defines the representation of security data, which can be used as part of a general solution to pass the security context between applications. This representation of security data is an assertion by a trusted third-party security service that the activity of authentication, attribute retrieval, or authorization is correct as represented. For example, the authentication assertion is a representation by a third party that the subject of the assertion, the security principal, has been authenticated. As long as the target trusts this third party, it can accept the assertion as true and can accept the principal named by the authentication assertion as authenticated. The designers of the SAML specification did not intend it to work alone.

There are four 'drivers' behind the creation of the SAML standard

- Limitations of Browser cookies
- SSO Interoperability
- Web Services
- Federation

SAML Delivers the Following Benefits: (Netegrity, 2001)

- **Interoperability** - With SAML, e-marketplaces, service providers, and end-user companies of all sizes can now securely exchange information about users, Web services, and authorization information without requiring partners to change their current security solutions. SAML will become the common language for how different systems communicate data about security.

- **Open Solution** - SAML is designed to work with multiple, industry-standard transport protocols such as HTTP, SMTP, FTP, and others, as well as multiple XML document exchange frameworks such as SOAP, Biztalk, and ebXML.

- **Single Sign-On Across Sites** - SAML will enable Web users to travel across sites with their entitlements so that companies and partners in a trusted relationship can deliver single sign-on across Web sites, together with secure access to shared resources.

SAML Scope and Purpose (Netegrity, 2001)

The basic SAML objects are assertions (Authentication, Attribute). SAML assertions are submitted to, and generated by, trusted authorities using a request / response protocol. SAML assertions are embedded in industry-standard transport and messaging frameworks. SAML defines a data format for: authentication assertions, including descriptions for authentication events, authorization attributes (i.e., the attributes that a service uses to make authorization decisions, such as an identifier, a group or role, or other user profile information). SAML will support Web user sessions (message format to end a session due to logout by an end-user or service), although this feature may be available in a later version of the SAML standard due to time constraints.

SAML defines a message format and protocol for distributing SAML data among trusted partners in a business relationship. SAML's message protocol supports "pushing" data assertions from an authoritative source to a receiver. Likewise, SAML is designed to support "pulling" data assertions from an authoritative source to a receiver, thus

allowing exchange of event notifications between partners in a trusted relationship.

SAML allows assertions to be shared over standard Internet protocols by binding SAML information to the following industry-standard transport and messaging frameworks:

Commercial Web browsers: SAML assertions are communicated by a Web browser through cookies or URL strings.

- **HTTP:** SAML assertions are conveyed from a source Web site to a destination Web site via headers or HTTP POST.
- **MIME:** SAML assertions are packaged into a single MIME security package (combined with the message payload, e.g., a purchase order, a bank's line-of-credit statement, etc.).
- **SOAP:** SAML assertions are bound to the SOAP document's envelope header to secure the payload.
- **ebXML:** Provides a MIME-based envelope structure used to bind SAML assertions to the business payload.

SAML does not define any new cryptographic technology or security models. Instead, the emphasis is on describing industry-standard security technologies using an XML-based syntax in the context of the Internet.

SAML does not provide for negotiation between partnering Web sites. A business agreement must be made as a prerequisite to the use of SAML in a trusted environment.

SAML does not define a data format for expressing authorization policies. This is left to the security system that implements SAML for authentication and authorization services

SAML Overview (Netegrity, 2001)

- End-user submits credentials to Authentication Authority (any security engine or business application that is SAML-aware).

- Authentication Authority asserts user's credentials against user directory and generates an Authentication Assertion together with one or more Attribute Assertions (e.g., role and other user profile information). End-user is now authenticated and identified by SAML assertions assembled in a token.
- End-user attempts to access a protected resource using her SAML token.
- Policy Enforcement Point (PEP) intercepts end-user request to protected resource and submits the end-user's SAML token (Authentication Assertion) to the Attribute Authority (which can also be any SAML-aware security engine or business application).
- Attribute Authority or Policy Decision Point (PDP) makes a decision based on its policies. If it authorizes access to resource, it then generates an Attribute Assertion attached to the user's SAML token. The end-user's SAML token can be presented

SAML Security Goals

- Credentials
- Assertion
- Authorization
- Assertion
- Attribute
- Assertion
- Authentication
- Assertion
- Authorization
- Authority
- Attribute
- Authority
- Authentication

- Authority

Establishing Trust between Services

For SAML or WS-Security to be useful on a large scale, trust relationships need to be established between remote Web services. A signed SAML assertion or WS-Security message is of no use if the receiver of the assertion cannot guarantee that the information asserted is trustworthy.

In the original SAML specification, only direct trust relationships are discussed—these are referred to as pairwise circles of trust. By contrast, SAML v2.0 provides two additional trust models for SAML: brokered trust and community trust (Singhal, Winograd, & Scarfone, 2007).

Security of Infrastructures for Web Services

Middleware technologies are the software foundation of modern enterprise computing systems, which process the requests coming through Web Services gateways. Understanding the middleware security mechanisms that are available is the first step toward achieving end-to-end security for applications exposed as Web Services. This chapter covers the security mechanisms in the mainstream middleware technologies: Common Object Request Broker Architecture (CORBA), Component Object Model (COM+),.NET, and Java 2 Platform, Enterprise Edition (J2EE).

Middleware, which is quickly becoming synonymous with enterprise applications integration (EAI), is software that is invisible to the user. It takes two or more different applications and makes them work seamlessly together. This is accomplished by placing middleware between layers of software to make the layers below and on the sides work with each other.

Middleware, or EAI, products enable information to be shared in a seamless real-time fashion across multiple functional departments, geographies and applications. Benefits include better customer service, accurate planning and forecasting, and reduced manual re-entry and associated data inaccuracies.

Involved in EAI/Middleware:

- Business Process Integration (BPI)
- Application Integration
- Data Integration
- Standards of Integration
- Platform Integration

Middleware accomplishes the above tasks via one of the following forms:

1. Transaction processing (TP) monitors, which provide tools and an environment for developing and deploying distributed applications.
2. Remote Procedure Call (RPCs), which enable the logic of an application to be distributed across the network. Program logic on remote systems can be executed as simply as calling a local routine.
3. Message-Oriented Middleware (MOM), which provides program-to-program data exchange, enabling the creation of distributed applications. MOM is analogous to e-mail in the sense it is asynchronous and requires the recipients of messages to interpret their meaning and to take appropriate action.
4. Object Request Brokers (ORBs), which enable the objects that comprise an application to be distributed and shared across heterogeneous networks.
5. Transaction Flow Manager (TFM) or Intelligent Trade Management (ITM) – emerging technologies - which will act as a radar screen that tracks transactions from launch to landing.

Security and the Client/Server

This includes:

- Access control
- Request authentication
- Response authentication
- Integrity protection
- Confidentiality protection
- Accountability
- Non repudiation

Security and the Object

CORBA, COM+,.NET, and J2EE are all *object-based*. These days, the computing world takes for granted that any modern computational technology—distributed or not—has inherent support for objects.

Object-based security architecture must support large numbers of protected resources. Traditionally, this has been done via resource groupings. Objects are grouped, and policies are defined on those groups. Objects with similar names, or those that reside in the same location, should not be required to belong to the same group, since policies do not necessarily follow your application's topology or naming organization. The same is true for objects to be assigned to the same group; name similarity and co-location should not be required for being governed by similar policies

Of additional security concern is that the methods on objects are no longer limited to just two or three universal "read," "write," and "delete" operations. The methods could be very complex and potentially involve many diverse activities. Consequently, security administrators should not have to understand the semantics of the methods on objects to secure them

Client Application: Makes RPC-like calls to the server. Because of the abstraction provided by the proxy of the server object, the client application does not have to be aware of any layers below the proxy.2

Server Application: Receives RPC calls, serves them, and returns replies.

Application Server: The runtime environment that provides important services to the critical high-performance and high-scale business applications. Its presence in the stack distinguishes CORBA component model (CCM) from plain CORBA, COM+ from COM, and J2EE from Java 2 Platform, Standard Edition (J2SE). If you have ever tried to implement a business application using plain COM, Java, or CORBA, you are familiar with how much you need to do to manage the object life cycle, engage in distributed transactions, and implement load balancing and fault tolerance. The application server layer handles those functions in CCM, COM+, and J2EE. Due to its complexity, the layer is often tightly integrated with the ORB and object adapters (defined below) and therefore comes bundled with them.

Proxy: A local implementation of the remote server object on the client. It isolates the application from all the details and complexities of the RPC implementation by realizing syntactically the same interface as the object on the target. A proxy marshals requests to and un marshals responses from the server, and could perform some other housekeeping work. A client must have a proxy for each interface it uses on the server. Proxies are usually compiled out of the interface descriptions. These are interface definition language (IDL) files in COM(+)

Security Concerns of WS-Security

There are several concerns prevalent in a WS-Security acquiescent Web service. Many of these concerns are not specific to WS-Security and apply to message integrity and confidentiality in general. WS-Security uses timestamps, sequence numbers, and expirations should be sent signed within the WS-Security message to protect against replay attack. The receiving should then check. WS-Security provides support for tokens that can be sent in the WS-Security header of a SOAP message. Without proper safeguards, these security tokens can be substituted. It is important when using WS -Security tokens to sign the appropriate portions of the message. WS-Security headers that are signed by the sender can be used to detect alterations. Credential management may be a concern with WS-Security (Singhal, Winograd, & Scarfone, 2007).

WS-Federation and WS-Trust

WS-Trust is used to exchange trust tokens between Web services. WS-Trust is an extension to WS Security that provides methods for issuing, renewing, and validating security tokens as well as methods for establishing and brokering trust relationships between Web services. If the requester does not supply appropriate claims, it can use the security policy declared by WS-Security Policy to determine the URI of the provider's Security Token Service (STS), who can provide the requester with the appropriate claims. Additionally, WS-Trust supports multi-messaging exchanges, allowing providers to use a challenge response mechanism for authorization. Because WS-Trust builds upon WS-Security, claims can be anything from a digital signature to a X.509 certificate or an XML-based token such as a SAML assertion (Singhal, Winograd, & Scarfone, 2007).

Web Services Policies (WS-Policy)

WSDL describes how to communicate with a Web service by detailing the protocol bindings and message formats the Web service expects. In many cases, knowledge of protocol bindings and message formats is not sufficient for requesters to dynamically bind to the provider. WSDL is limited to describing what needs to be placed in the message itself; it does not specify what type of metadata should be supplied, such as how the message will be authenticated or what portions of the message should be signed. To this end, Microsoft, IBM, BEA and others developed the

Web Services Policy (WS-Policy) Framework, which allows providers to express the capabilities, requirements and characteristics of the Web service (Singhal, Winograd, & Scarfone, 2007). WS-Policy can also be used to describe the parameters necessary when using WS-ReliableMessaging to ensure message delivery.

FUTURE OF WEB SERVICE SECURITY

Promising security products and the basic frameworks for Web Services such as security architecture, security risk assessment, cryptography risk assessment have show great commitment with web service. New architecture base on security assessment and cross web service authentication and authorization will improve new generation of web service. Further, cryptographic measures have solved some of the important security problems, such as authentication, message confidentiality, signatures, and non-repudiation, and all their power can be applied to Web Services as well. The expectation for web service will based on:

- New accepted standardization for security issue based on Security Assertion Markup Language (SAML)
- Possible more security procedures implemented to be integrated with the existing web service
- Possible new standard to solve the problem of cross web service as SAML now for exchanging authentication and authorization data between security domains, that is, between an identity provider
- Integrating more Cryptography standard (as the use of The Elliptic Curve Digital Signature Algorithm (ECDSA))
- And possible Quantum cryptography for key exchange between web service

- High speed cryptography algorithm for: encryption, cross certification, non-reputation, to match the 3G speed web servicing
- One single Authentication box continue: all required authentication parameters encrypted travel with you as you serving the web whenever authentication, authorization needed will present these information to the authorized gentility

CONCLUSION

"Cryptography is the science of Information Security". Cryptography Algorithms are one major segment in computer security Mechanisms. The method of transfer the readable text into is called encryption or the method of hidden clear text. Encrypting plaintext results in unreadable gibberish called ciphertext. The main goals of modern cryptography can be seen as: user authentication, data authentication (data integrity and data origin authentication), non-repudiation of origin, and data confidentiality

This article presents the integration of cryptography algorithms with E-mail service to create secure E-mail and web service to construct secure web service. There are two major parts as: E-mail and covers client and Web-based E-mail, next generation E-mail and secure E-mail; the other part is cryptography in web service and the last part is the future of web service security. This chapter is presenting the encryption integration with web E-mail and web service. In the web service we look at security with XML, such as encryption, Digital signature, then forth we look at other standard such as Security Assertion Markup Language (SAML) which been designed to exchanging authentication and authorization data between security domains, that is, between an identity provider. SSL been studied as part Web based e-mail security suit support e-mail.

At the end of each these two major sections e-mail and Web service we have present the expectation for the next step in integrating Cryptography with these services.

Our vision for the next generation in integrating cryptography is focus on:

- Use of elliptic curve as is faster and more portable than existing Asymmetric algorithms.
- The use of quantum cryptography for key management.
- Moving more to word standardization suits (as suit B from NSA)to control the quality of the implementation of the cryptographic algorithm in e-mail: at different level of security and cross Web authentication
- We will see more suits to implement cross web certification faster

We expected will be something likes (USB secure ID) as authenticate box to be designed on software based travel with someone across web surfing as required to pass authentication information will be passed to authorize web, the box is encrypted and only authorize web can decrypt only part of the box.

REFERENCES

W3C. (2002). *Decryption transform for XML signature*. Retrieved from http://www.w3.org/TR/xmlenc-decrypt

W3C. (2004). *Web services architecture*. Retrieved from http://www.w3.org/

W3C. (2009). *XML digital signature*. Retrieved from http://www.w3.org/TR/xmldsig-core/

W3C.org. (2003). *How secure is the encryption used by SSL*. W3C.org FAQ. Retrieved from http://www.w3.org/

W3.org. (2002). *XML encryption syntax and processing W3C recommendation*. Retrieved from http://www.w3.org/TR/2002/REC-xmlenc-core-20021210/Overview.html

Adams, C., & Farrell, S. (1999). *Internet X.509 public key infrastructure: Certificate management protocols RFC 2510*. Retrieved from http://www.ietf.org/rfc/rfc2510.txt

Al-Hamdani, A. (2008). Cryptography for information security. In Gupta, J. N., & Sharma, S. K. (Eds.), *Information security and assurance* (pp. 122–138). Hershey, PA: Information Science Reference.

Al-Hamdani, A. (2009). *Cryptography for information security (chapter 5)*. Unpublished.

Alvestrand, H. T. (1995). *X.400 FAQ A comprehensive list of resources on x.400 series of standards*. Retrieved from http://www.alvestrand.no/x400/index.html

Ansi.org. (1998). *X9.31-1998, Digital signatures using reversible public key cryptography for the financial services industry (rDSA)*. American National Standards Institute.

Apache.org. (2007). *XML security*. Retrieved from http://xml.apache.org/security/

Balaski, B. (1993, February). *Privacy enhancement for Internet electronic mail: Part IV: Notary, co-issuer, CRL-storing and CRL-retrieving services. RFC 1424*. Retrieved from http://www.ietf.org/rfc/rfc1424.txt

Balenson, D. (1993). *Privacy enhancement for Internet electronic mail: Part III: Algorithms, modes, and identifiers. RFC 1423*. Retrieved from http://www.ietf.org/rfc/rfc1423.txt

Bauchle, R., Hazen, F., Lund, J., & Oakley, G. (2008). *Encryption*. Retrieved from http://search-security.techtarget.com/sDefinition/0,sid14_gci212062,00.html

Bellare, M., Canetti, R., & Hugo, K. (1996a). Keying hash functions for message authentication. *CRYPTO, 1996*, 1–15.

Bellare, M., Canetti, R., & Hugo, K. (1996b). The HMAC construction. *CryptoBytes, 2(1)*.

Bernstein, D. J. (2008). *Simple mail transfer protocol reference manuals*. Retrieved from http://cr.yp.to/immhf.html

Brownlow, M. (2008). *E-mail and webmail statistics*. Retrieved from http://www.email-marketing-reports.com/metrics/email-statistics.htm

Callas, J., Donnerhacke, L., Finney, H., & Thayer, R. (2007). *OpenPGP message format RFC: 4880*. Retrieved from http://tools.ietf.org/html/rfc4880

Callas, J., Donnerhacke, L., Finney, H., & Thayer, R. (2007). *OpenPGP message format RFC: 4880*. Retrieved from http://www.ietf.org/rfc/rfc2440.txt

Cerami, E. (2002). *Web services essentials (O'Reilly XML)*. City, O'Reilly Media, Inc.

Cnss.gov. (2003). *FACT SHEET CNSS Policy No. 15, Fact Sheet No. 1, National policy on the use of the advanced encryption standard (AES) to protect national security systems and national security information*. Retrieved from http://www.cnss.gov/Assets/pdf/cnssp_15_fs.pdf

Corporation, I. B. M. (1999). *XML security suite*. Retrieved from http://www.alphaworks.ibm.com/tech/xmlsecuritysuite

Costello, R. L. (2009). *Building Web services the REST way*. Retrieved from http://www.xfront.com/

CrazySquirrel. (2009). *How does e-mail work?* Retrieved from http://www.crazysquirrel.com/computing/debian/mail.jspx

Crispin, M. (1996). *Internet message access protocol-V4rev1*. ietf.org RFC: 2060.

Crispin, M. (2003). *Internet message access protocol-V4rev1*. ietf.org RFC: 3501.

Crocker, D. (2009). *E-mail history*. Retrieved from http://www.livinginternet.com

Crocker, S., Freed, N., Galvin, J., & Murphy, S. (1995). *MIME object security services RFC1848*. Retrieved from http://www.ietf.org/rfc/rfc1848.txt?number=1848

David, M. L. (2007). *The history of encryption and ciphers*. Retrieved from http://searchwarp.com/swa148381.htm

Davis, Z. (2008). *An intro to elliptical curve cryptography*. Retrieved from http://www.deviceforge.com/

Dierks, T., & Allen, C. (1999). *The TLS protocol version 1.0: RFC 2246*. Retrieved from http://www.ietf.org/rfc/rfc2246.txt

Dierks, T., & Allen, C. (1999). *The TLS protocol version 1.0. RFC 2246*. Retrieved from http://www.ietf.org/rfc/rfc2246.txt?number=2246

Diffie, W., & Hellman, M. E. (1976). New directions in cryptography. *IEEE Transactions on Information Theory, 22*, 644–654. doi:10.1109/TIT.1976.1055638

Djajadinata, R. (2002). *XML encryption keeps your XML documents safe and secure*. Retrieved from http://www.javaworld.com/javaworld/jw-08-2002/jw-0823-securexml.html

Dournaee, B. (2002). *XML security*. New York: McGraw-Hill Osborne Media.

Drummond, R. (1996). *Brief comparison of e-mail encryption protocols*. Retrieved from http://www.imc.org/ietf-ediint/old-archive/msg00117.html

Dworkin, M. (2001). Recommendation for Block Cipher Modes of Operation NIST Special Publication 800-38A. Retrieved from http://csrc.nist.gov/publications/PubsSPs.html

Dworkin, M. (2004). *Recommendation for Block Cipher Modes of Operation: The CCM Mode for Authentication and Confidentiality*. NIST Special Publication 800-38C Retrieved from http://csrc.nist.gov/publications/PubsSPs.html

Dworkin, M. (2005). *Recommendation for Block Cipher Modes of Operation: The CMAC Mode for Authentication.* NIST Special Publication 800-38B Retrieved from http://csrc.nist.gov/publications/PubsSPs.html

Dworkin, M. (2007). *Recommendation for Block Cipher Modes of Operation: Galois/Counter Mode (GCM) and GMAC.* NIST Special Publication 800-38C Retrieved from http://csrc.nist.gov/publications/PubsSPs.html

Eastlake, D., & Motorola, P. J. (2001). *US secure hash algorithm 1 (SHA1).* RFC: 3174.

Eastlake, D. E., & Niles, K. (2002). *Secure XML: The new syntax for signatures and encryption.* Pearson Education.

Edge, C., Barker, W., & Smith, Z. (2007). *A brief history of cryptography* (reprint). Retrieved from http://www.318.com/techjournal/?p=5

Eide, K. (2004). *The next generation of mail clients.* Retrieved from http://home.dataparty.no/kristian/reviews/nextgen-mua/

Elkins, M., Torto, D. D., Levien, R., & Roessler, T. (2001). *MIME security with OpenPGP: RFC 3156.* Retrieved from http://www.faqs.org/rfcs/rfc3156.html

Encryptomatic.com. (2008). *HIPAA: The Health Insurance Portability and Accountability Act of 1996.* Retrieved from http://www.encryptomatic.com/about-us/index.html

Federal Information. (1993). *Secure hash standard.* Processing standards publication 180-1 FIPS PUB 180-1 Supersedes FIPS PUB 180.

Federal Information Processing Standards Publication 197 Announcing the *ADVANCED ENCRYPTION STANDARD (AES) November 26, 2001*

Federal Register. (2005, May 19). Announcing approval of the withdrawal of Federal Information. *Federal Register, 70*(96), 28907.

Ferguson, N., & Schneier, B. (2003). *Practical cryptography.* New York: Wiley.

Fernandez, E. B. (2002). *Web services security current status and the future.* Retrieved from http://www.webservicesarchitect.com/content/articles/fernandez01.asp

Fielding, R., Gettys, J., Mogul, J., Frystyk, H., Masinter, L., Leach, P., & Berners-Lee, T. *Hypertext transfer protocol -- HTTP/1.1.* Retrieved from http://www.ietf.org/rfc/rfc2616.txt

Freed, N. (2008). *Name and filename parameters.* Retrieved from http://www.imc.org/ietf-smtp/mail-archive/msg05023.html

Galvin, J., Murphy, G., Crocker, S., & Freed, N. (1995). *Security multiparts for MIME: Multipart/signed and multipart/encrypted: RFC 1847.* Retrieved from http://www.faqs.org/rfcs/rfc1847.html

Gurski, M. A. (1995). *Privacy-enhanced mail (PEM).* Retrieved from http://www.cs.umbc.edu/~woodcock/cmsc482/proj1/pem.html

Hagens, R., & Hansen, A. (1994). *Operational requirements for X.400 management domains in the GO-MHS community.* Retrieved from http://tools.ietf.org/html/rfc1649

Hartman, B., Flinn, D. J., Beznosov, K., & Kawamoto, S. (2003). *Mastering Web services security.* New York: Wiley Publishing.

Hoffman, P. (1999). *SMTP service extension for secure SMTP over TLS: RFC 2487.* Retrieved from http://www.ietf.org/rfc/rfc2487.txt?number=2487

Housley, R. (1999). *Cryptographic message syntax.* Retrieved from http://www.ietf.org/rfc/rfc2630.txt

Housley, R. (1999). *Cryptographic message syntax RFC: 2630.* Retrieved from http://www.ietf.org/rfc/rfc2630.txt

Housley, R. (2004). *Cryptographic message syntax (CMS): RFC 3852.* Retrieved from http://www. ietf.org/rfc/rfc3852.txt

Housley, R., & Solinas, J. (2007). *Suite B in secure/multipurpose Internet mail extension: RFC5008.* Retrieved from http://www.rfc-editor. org/rfc/rfc5008.txt

Houttuin, J., & Craigie, J. (1994). *Migrating from X.400(84) to X.400(88) RFC1615.* Retrieved from http://www.faqs.org/rfcs/rfc1615.html

IBM. (2009) Application Server - Express for IBM i, Version 7.0 http://publib.boulder.ibm.com

Ibm.com. (2008). *Creating a secure sockets layer configuration.* Retrieved from http://publib.boulder.ibm.com/

Ietf.org. (1988). *X.400(1988) for the academic and research community in Europe RFC1616.* Retrieved from http://www.ietf.org/rfc/rfc1616.txt

Ietf.org. (2008). *Public-key infrastructure.* Retrieved from Retrieved from http://www.ietf.org/html.charters/pkix-charter.html

ITU. (2005). *T-REC-X.509-200508-I information technology - Open systems interconnection - The directory: Authentication framework.* Retrieved from http://www.itu.int/rec/T-REC-X.509-200508-I/en

Kaliski, B. (1993). *Privacy enhancement for Internet electronic mail: Part IV: Key certification and related services RFC 1424.* Retrieved from http://www.ietf.org/rfc/rfc1424.txt

Katz, J., & Lindell, Y. (2007). *Introduction to modern cryptography: Principles and protocols* (Chapman & Hall/CRC cryptography and network security series, 1st ed.). Boca Raton, FL: Chapman & Hall/CRC.

Kelm, S. (2008). *The PKI page.* Retrieved from http://www.pki-page.org/

Kent, S. (1993). *Privacy enhancement for Internet electronic mail: Part II: Certificate-based key management RFC 1422.* Retrieved from http://www.ietf.org/rfc/rfc1422.txt

Kessler, G. C. (2009). *An Overview of Cryptography.* Retrieved from http://www.garykessler. net/library/crypto.html#intro

Khosrow-Pour, M. (Ed.). (2004). *E-Commerce security: Advice from experts (IT solutions series).* New York: Cybertech Publishing.

Kim, J., Biryukov, A., Prenee, B., & Hong, S. (2006). On the security of HMAC and NMAC based on HAVAL, MD4, MD5, SHA-0 and SHA-1. *IACR.org ePrint.*

Levien, R. (1999). *A brief comparison of e-mail encryption protocols.* Retrieved from http://www.imc.org/

Linn, J. (1993). *Message encryption and authentication procedures Part I: Message encryption and authentication procedures. RFC 1421.* Retrieved from http://www.ietf.org/rfc/rfc1421.txt

Loshin, P. (1999). *Essential e-mail standards: RFCs and protocols made practical.* New York: John Wiley & Sons.

Mao, W. (2003). *Modern cryptography: Theory and practice (Hewlett-Packard professional books).* Prentice Hall.

Mel, H. X., & Baker, D. M. (2000). *Cryptography decrypted* (5th ed.). Reading, MA: Addison-Wesley.

Microsoft Corporation. (2009). *TLS enhancements to SSL.* Retrieved from http://technet.microsoft.com/en-us/library/cc784450.aspx

Microsoft Corporation. (2009). *X.400 transport architecture.* Retrieved from http://technet.microsoft.com/en-us/library/aa997753(EXCHG.65).aspx

Mit.edu. (2007). *Kerberos: The network authentication protocol*. Retrieved from http://mit.edu.

Mogollon, M. (2007). *Cryptography and security services: Mechanisms and applications*. New York: CyberTech Publishing.

Myers, J., & Rose, M. (1996). *Post office protocol - Version 3*. ietf.org, RFC 1939.

Netegrity. (2001). *The standard XML framework for secure information exchange*. Retrieved from http://xml.coverpages.org/Netegrity-SAMLWP.pdf nist.gov. (2000). *FIPS Pub 186-2 digital signature standard (DSS)*. Retrieved from http://csrc.nist.gov/publications/fips/fips186-2/fips186-2-change1.pdf

Nsa.gov. (2005). *Fact sheet NSA suite B cryptography*. Retrieved from http://www.nsa.gov/ia/industry/crypto_suite_b.cfm

O'Neill, M. (2003). *Web services security*. New York: McGraw-Hill Osborne Media.

OASIS. (2009). *Organization for the Advancement of Structured Information Standards*. Retrieved from http://www.oasis-open.org/who/

Openssl.org. (2005). *OpenSSL Project*. Retrieved from http://www.openssl.org/

PCLcable. (2003). *WEBMAIL notes*. Retrieved from http://my.pclnet.net/webmail.html

Peter, I. (2003). *The history of e-mail*. Retrieved from http://www.nethistory.info/

Peterson, J. (2004). *S/MIME advanced encryption standard (AES) requirement: RFC3853*. Retrieved from http://www.faqs.org/rfcs/rfc3853.html

Pioneers, I. (2009, January). *Internet pioneers*. Retrieved from http://www.ibiblio.org/pioneers/roberts.html

Postel, J. B. (1982). *Simple mail transfer protocol RFC: 821 Obsoleted by 2821*. Retrieved from http://tools.ietf.org/html/rfc821

Postel.org. (2009, January). *Postel organization*. Retrieved from http://www.postel.org/postel.html

Ramsdell, B. (Ed.). (1999). *S/MIME version 3 message specification*. Retrieved from http://www.faqs.org/rfcs/rfc2633.html

Ramsdell, B. (Ed.). (2004). *Secure/multipurpose Internet mail extensions (S/MIME) version 3.1 message specification: RFC3851*. Retrieved from http://www.ietf.org/rfc/rfc3851.txt

Rivest, R., Shamir, A., & Adleman, L. M. (1983). *Patent No. 4405829*. U.S.

Rosenberg, J., & Remy, D. (2004). *Securing Web services with WS-security: Demystifying WS-security, WS-policy, SAML, XML signature, and XML encryption*. Sams.

Rosser, J.B. (1939). "An Informal Exposition of Proofs of Godel's Theorem and Church's Theorem". Journal of Symbolic Logic 4

RSA.com. (2007). *What are message authentication codes?* Retrieved from http://www.rsa.com

RSA.com. (2007). *What is DESX?* Retrieved from http://www.rsasecurity.com

RSA.com. (2007). *What is Diffie-Hellman?* Retrieved from http://www.rsa.com/

RSA.com. (2007). *What is RC4?* Retrieved from http://www.rsa.com

RSA.com. (2008). *What is RSA?* Retrieved from http://www.rsa.com/

SAML. (2008). *Security assertion markup language (SAML)*. Retrieved from http://xml.coverpages.org/saml.html

Schaad, J. (2003). *Use of the advanced encryption standard (AES) encryption algorithm in cryptographic message syntax (CMS): RFC 3565*. Retrieved from http://www.ietf.org/rfc/rfc3565.txt

Schneier, B. (1995). *Applied cryptography*. New York: Wiley.

Schneier, B. (1995). *E-mail security: How to keep your electronic messages private.* New York: Wiley.

Schneier, B. (1996). *Applied cryptography: Protocols, algorithms, and source code in C* (2nd ed.). New York: Wiley.

SearchSecurity.com. (2008). *DSS definition.* Retrieved from http://searchsecurity.techtarget.com/sDefinition/

SearchSecurity.com. (2008). *Spotlight article: Domain 3, cryptography.* Retrieved from http://searchsecurity.techtarget.com/generic/0,295582,sid14_gci1328971,00.html

Sharpe, M. (2008). *Getting started with HTTPS.* Retrieved from http://searchsoftwarequality.techtarget.com/sDefinition/0,sid92_gci214006,00.html#

Simovits, M. (1995). *The DES: An extensive document and evaluation.* New York: Agent Park Press.

Singh, S. (2000). *The code book: The science of secrecy from ancient Egypt to quantum cryptography (reprint).* Anchor.

Singhal, A., Winograd, T., & Scarfone, K. (2007). Guide to Secure Web Services. NIST, SP800-95.

Snell, J., Tidwel, D., & Kulchenko, P. (2001). *Programming Web services with SOAP.* O'Reilly.

SSH Communications Security, Inc. (2008). Public-key cryptosystems. Retrieved from http://www.ssh.com/support/cryptography/

Sun.com. (2002). *Introduction to SSL.* Retrieved from http://docs.sun.com/source/816-6156-10/contents.htm#1041986

SunMicrosystems. (2008). *JSR 106: XML digital encryption APIs.* Retrieved from http://jcp.org/en/jsr/detail?id=106

Thomas, S. A. (2000). *SSL & TLS essentials securing the Web.* John Wiley & Sons.

Tracy, M., Jansen, W., & Bisker, S. (2002). Guidelines on Electronic Mail Security. NIST Special Publication 800-45, Tracy, M., Jansen, W., & Bisker, S. (2007). Guidelines on Electronic Mail Security. NIST Special Publication 800-45, V2

Trappe, W., & Washington, L. C. (2005). *Introduction to cryptography with coding theory* (2nd ed.). Prentice Hall.

Turner, S., & Housley, R. (2008). *Implementing E-mail and security tokens: Current standards, tools, and practices.* Wiley.

Verma, M. (2004). *XML security: The XML key management specification.* Retrieved from http://www.ibm.com/developerworks/xml/library/x-seclay3/

Weekly, D. (2008). *The need For next-generation e-mail.* Retrieved from http://david.weekly.org

Weise, J. (2001). *Public key infrastructure overview.* Retrieved from http://www.sun.com/blueprints/0801/publickey.pdf

Wenbo, M. (2003). *Modern cryptography: Theory and practice.* Upper Saddle River, NJ: Prentice Hall.

Wikipedia.org. (2008). *Simple Mail Transfer Protocol (SMTP).* Retrieved from wikipedia.org

Wikipedia.org. (2009). *PGP: PRETTY GOOD PRIVACY.* Retrieved from wikipedia.org

Wikipedia.org. (2009). *PKI.* Retrieved from wikipedia.org

Wikipedia.org. (2009). *Privacy Enhanced* Mail. Retrieved from wikipedia.org

Wikipedia.org. (2009). *The Multipurpose Internet Mail Extension (MIME).* Retrieved from Wikipedia.org

Wikipedia.org. (2009). *WEB OF TRUST.* Retrieved from wikipedia.org

Wikipedia.org. (2009). *SSL.* Retrieved from wikipedia.org

Wikipedia.org. (2009). *HTTP*. Retrieved from wikipedia.org

Wikipedia.org. (2009). *Web Services Security*. Retrieved from wikipedia.org

Wikipedia.org. (2009). *Digital Signature*. Retrieved from wikipedia.org

Wikipedia.org. (2009). *Email*. Retrieved from wikipedia.org

Wikipedia.org. (2009). *Ray Tomlinson*. Retrieved from wikipedia.org

Wikipedia.org. (2009). *Jon Postel*. Retrieved from wikipedia.org

Wikipedia.org. (2009). *Web service*. Retrieved from wikipedia.org

Wikipedia.org. (2009). *Multipurpose Internet Mail Extension*. Retrieved from wikipedia.org

Wikipedia.org. (2009). *Certification Authority*. Retrieved from wikipedia.org

Zimmermann, P. (1995). *PGP source code and internals*. Cambridge, MA: MIT Press.

Zimmermann, P. (1995). *The official PGP user's guide*. Cambridge, MA: MIT Press.

ENDNOTE

[1]   I is adopted from regular expression and read as "OR"

Chapter 5
Applied Cryptography in E-Mail Services and Web Services

Lei Chen
Sam Houston State University, USA

Wen-Chen Hu
University of North Dakota, USA

Ming Yang
Jacksonville State University, USA

Lei Zhang
Frostburg State University, USA

ABSTRACT

E-mail services are the method of sending and receiving electronic messages over communication networks. Web services on the other hand provide a channel of accessing interlinked hypermeida via the World Wide Web. As these two methods of network communications turn into the most popular services over the Internet, applied cryptography and secure authentication protocols become indispensable in securing confidential data over public networks. In this chapter, we first review a number of cryptographic ciphers widely used in secure communication protocols. We then discuss and compare the popular trust system Web of Trust, the certificate standard X.509, and the standard for public key systems Public Key Infrastructure (PKI). Two secure e-mail standards, OpenPGP and S/MIME, are examined and compared. The de facto standard cryptographic protocol for e-commerce, Secure Socket Layer (SSL) / Transport Layer Security (TLS), and XML Security Standards for secure web services are also discussed.

INTRODUCTION

In e-mail services, Wiki-E-mail (2009), and Web services, Wiki-Web (2009), various cryptographic algorithms are used to achieve the security goals, Stallings, W. (2006) and Stallings, W. (2007),

of confidentiality, integrity, authentication and non-repudiation. Data confidentiality is commonly provided via encryption. Since symmetric key ciphers, such as DES, Triple-DES and AES, perform faster than public key ciphers, such as RSA, they are preferable in choosing ciphers to protect the secrecy of data.

DOI: 10.4018/978-1-61520-783-1.ch005

Hash functions, such as MD5 and SHA-1, are used to preserve data integrity. The sender hashes the data content using one or multiple hash functions and sends the message digests to the receiver who is capable to verify the message integrity by running the same hash functions on the received message and then comparing the output digests to the received ones.

There are two types of authentication: entity authentication and data-origin authentication both of which make use of cryptographic mechanisms. Entity authentication is based on cryptographic keys, including both symmetric key-based authentication and public key-based authentication. SSL/TLS in web security services uses this type of authentication. Data-origin based authentication is accomplished through Message Authentication Code (MAC), Stallings, W. (2007) and Wiki-MAC (2009), and digital signatures. Secure email services provide data-origin authentication through digital signatures.

Non-repudiation, a security feature which makes a communication party not able to repudiate what has been done, utilizes public key cryptographic ciphers, such as RSA. These public key ciphers allow a party to sign a message using the private key and this signing can later be verified by applying the paired public key to the signed message. Before move on to the discussion of secure e-mail services and Web services, it is preferred to survey the common cryptographic ciphers and security protocols and standards in these services.

COMMONLY USED CRYPTOGRAPHIC CIPHERS AND SECURITY PROTOCOLS

Data Encryption Standard (DES) and Triple-DES

In 1973, National Institute of Standards and Technology (NIST, previously NBS) solicited proposals for a government-wide standard for encryption and decryption. Based on the IBM Lucifer cipher (developed by 1973 Feistel and his colleagues in 1973! and 1974), DES was accepted as an official Federal Information Processing Standard (FIPS) for the U.S. in 1976, later widespread internationally. Many later ciphers, including RC5, Blowfish and CAST5, were designed based on DES. DES is basically an iterative symmetric key algorithm that uses a relatively short key with only 56 binary bits in length. In each of its 16 rounds, DES takes a 64-bit data block and a 48-bit sub-key as the inputs and goes through a series of steps including expansion, Substitution Boxes (S-Boxes) and Permutation Boxes (P-Boxes) resulting 64-bit output. Everything except the S-Boxes in DES is linear. Due to short key length of DES, Triple-DES or 3DES was introduced to increase the key length to 112-bit in EDE mode and 168-bit in EEE mode. DES and 3DES had been the most popular symmetric key block ciphers before the emergence of AES.

DES has eight different S-boxes, each of which maps a 6-bit input to a 4-bit output. The first bit and the last bit of the 6-bit input of an S-box form the binary row indexes and the rest 4-bit of the input forms the column indexes of a single S-box conversion table. The table then has the dimension of 4 (00 to 11) rows by 16 (0000 to 1111) columns and the 64 intersections show the possible values of the 4-bit output. Each possible 4-bit output value has 4 occurrences among the intersections. Therefore, a specific 6-bit input value points to a specific intersection and output value. On the other hand, a unique output value does not help find the input value due to the 4 occurrences.

Advanced Encryption Standard (AES)

AES, also known as Rijndael algorithm, was announced by NIST in 2001 as the new standard symmetric block cipher to replace DES and 3DES. AES was selected from fifteen proposed candidate algorithms and has become the most popular cipher of its kind. AES offers options of 128-bit, 192-bit and 256-bit key sizes depending on the number of rounds that the algorithm goes through in the encryption process. No successful or effective attack on the algorithm has been reported so far. However, Side Channel Attacks can be used to assail the implementation of the AES cipher on system which inadvertently leaks data.

Message-Digest Algorithm 5 (MD5)

MD5 is a 128-bit hash function widely used in security applications to verify the integrity of data. It was designed by Ron Rivest in 1991 to replace MD4. The output hash value is often presented in 32-bit hexadecimal format which is easy to read and compare. One of the design goals of a successful hash function is that it needs to be extremely unlikely that two different inputs will generate the same hash. In 1993, MD5 was found that two different initialization vectors produce same digest. In 2006, an algorithm was published to find collisions in one minute on an average notebook computer. It is now recommended to use more reliable hash functions such as SHA.

Secure Hash Algorithm (SHA)

SHA is a set of cryptographic hash functions designed by the National Security Agency (NSA) and published by the NIST as a U.S. Federal Information Processing Standard (FIPS). The various versions of SHA include SHA-0, SHA-1, SHA-2 and the future SHA-3. SHA-0 and SHA-1 both produce 160-bit digests and SHA-1 has been widely used in security applications and protocols since MD5 faded. In 2005, an attack by Xiaoyun Wang and her colleagues was announced lowering the complexity of finding collisions, Wang, X.Y., Yin, Y.Q., & Yu, H.B. (2005), in SHA-1 to 2^{69}. In 2006, Christophe De Cannière and his fellow researchers were able to reduce the complexity to 2^{35}. Despite of the greatly reduced complexity in theoretical attacks, no practical attack has ever been conducted resulting SHA-1 still the most

widely used hash function. Four SHA-2 functions, each of which has a different key size, were published by NIST in 2002. However, SHA-2 has not received much attention. An open competition was announced in the Federal Register in Nov. 2007 for a new SHA-3 function which is expected to become the new government standard for hash functions in 2012.

RSA

RSA, named after its three authors, is the first algorithm suitable for both signing and encryption. It was publicly described in 1977 by Ron Rivest, Adi Shamir, and Leonard Adleman. Unlike symmetric key ciphers, RSA makes use of factoring, modular and exponential operations in mathematics to generate a pair of keys, namely public key and private key. A private key, which is only known to its owner, is used for signing data, and the paired public key can be known to everyone for verifying the signature. A public key can also be used to encrypt data destined for the party who holds the paired private key. However, due to its relatively high complexity, it is often used to protect data of small size, e.g. using a public key to encrypt and protect a symmetric key.

Diffie-Hellman (D-H) Key Exchange

D-H, Stallings, W. (2006) and Wiki-DH (2009), is a cryptographic protocol that enables two communication parties, without sharing any information, to establish, using modular and exponential operations, a shared secret key over a public communication channel such as the Internet. D-H by itself suffers from the man-in-the-middle attacks where a third party in the middle establishes two distinct D-H key exchanges with the two end communication parties. Nevertheless, the immunity to such attacks can be achieved by allowing the two end parties to authenticate themselves to each other through the use of digital signatures prior to the D-H key exchange.

Message Authentication Code (MAC)

Message Authentication Code, Wiki-MAC (2009), is basically a short piece of information for authenticating a message. A MAC algorithm, basically a keyed hash or cipher function, takes both the shared secret key and the message to be authenticated as inputs and outputs a MAC value, or a tag. The verifiers, who also possess the shared secret key, can apply the same MAC algorithm to test the data integrity and authenticity of the message received. Depending on the type of algorithm used, MAC algorithms can be further categorized into HMAC, HMAC (2002), as in HMAC-MD5 or HMAC-SHA-1 which uses hash functions MD5 or SHA-1, and CMAC, as in AES-CMAC, Song, J.H., Lee, J., & Iwata, T. (2006), which uses symmetric key cryptographic cipher AES.

SECURITY STANDARDS

Web of Trust

In 1992 Phil Zimmermann incorporated the concept of Web of Trust, Wiki-WOT (2009), in the manual of Pretty Good Privacy (PGP) 2.0. The concept of Web of Trust is applied not only to PGP, but also GnuPGP and other systems compatible with OpenPGP standard. The core concept is to bind a public key with its owner through a decentralized trust model as opposed to a centralized trust model in Public Key Infrastructure (PKI) which relies entirely on Certificate Authorities (CA). Zimmermann describes this concept in PGP version 2.0:

As time goes on, you will accumulate keys from other people that you may want to designate as trusted introducers. Everyone else will each choose their own trusted introducers. And everyone will gradually accumulate and distribute with their key a collection of certifying signatures from other people, with the expectation that any-

one receiving it will trust at least one or two of the signatures. This will cause the emergence of a decentralized fault-tolerant Web of confidence for all public keys.

All OpenPGP-compliant systems have two schemes: certificate vetting and vote counting. Certificate vetting refers to the process of digitally signing the OpenPGP identity certificates (binding public keys and their owners) to endorse the association of the public key and the ID in the certificate. This process is termed a web of trust. A user can have the right to trust or reject a certain certificate and the vote counting scheme lets users configure their trusting strategy, e.g. to decide whether in order to accept a signed certificate it will need four partially trusted endorsers or just one fully trusted endorser.

The advantage of Web of Trust is its flexibility which allows users to decide their own trusting parameters, unlike PKIs which normally require certain root certificate authorities, Wiki-RC (2009), that must be trusted. However, this also means that a user needs to be cautious and intelligent enough to manage and supervise his trusting settings. Problems of Web of Trust include losing tracking of a private keys, slow start of building trust, and being unable to find someone to endorse a new certificate, all of which are the direct consequences of the fact Web of Trust being decentralized.

The propagation of trust across the network has been an important and challenging research area over the years. Guha et al developed a framework of trust propagation schemes, Guha, R., Kumar, R., Raghavan, P., & Tomkins, A. (2004), each of which fits in certain circumstances, and the schemes were evaluated over a large trust network of 800K trust scores among 130K users. In their research, they introduced the propagation of both trust and distrust and the algorithm starts with the atomic propagation over a basis set and then the propagation iterates until the whole network is reached. As shown in the evaluation over Epinions website, a small number of expressed trusts per individual allows the system to predict the trust between any two users in the system with high accuracy.

X.509

X.509, Stallings, W. (2006) and Wiki-X.509 (2009), is one of the series of computer networking standards of X.500, Wiki-X.500 (2009), covering electronic directory services. X.509 and the whole set of X.500 were developed by the Telecommunication Standardization Sector of the International Telecommunication Union (ITU-T). The goal of X.509 is to have formal specifications for standard formats for public key certificates, Certificate Revocation Lists (CRLs), attribute certificates, and a certification path validation algorithm in PKI. X.509 requires a strict hierarchical system of Certificate Authorities for issuing certificates. This is in contrast with Web of Trust in which everyone may sign, establish and verify the validity of other's certificates. The flexibility to support peer-to-peer or OpenPGP type Web of Trust was added in version 3 of X.509. However, in practice it is barely used in this way. Nowadays, the name X.509 broadly refers to the PKI certificate and Certificate Revocation List (CRL), Housley, R., Ford, W., Polk, W., & Solo, D. (1999), Profile of

the X.509 Version 3 standard by the Internet Engineering Task Force (IETF). This latest version is often called PKIX in short.

An X.509 Version 3 digital certificate has three main parts, the certificate, the certificate signature algorithm and the certificate signature, as shown in Figure 1. The certificate part contains a number of attributes such as version, serial number, and algorithm ID, etc. Some of the attributes are further detailed. Figure 2 shows in Windows XP an X.509 e-mail certificate issued by Thawte Consulting, a certificate authority offering free personal e-mail certificates.

A root certificate is either an unsigned public key certificate or a self-signed certificate that identifies the Root CA. If a tree is considered a good metaphor of the hierarchy of a certificate system, then the root certificates are located at the root of the tree and hold private keys for signing other certificates. All certificates above the root certificate thus have full trust in the root certificates. Table 1 is a list of trusted root certificates, MS-293781 (2007), required by Win-

Figure 2. An example of X.509 certificate

Figure 1. Structure of X.509 certificates

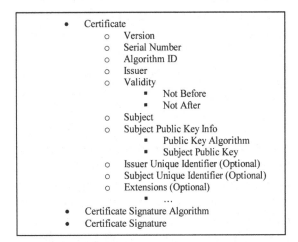

dows XP. Different versions of operating systems may require different root certificates.

PUBLIC KEY INFRASTRUCTURE (PKI)

PKI, Adams, C., & Farrell, S. (1999), is a set of hardware, software, people, policies, and procedures needed to create, manage, store, distribute and revoke digital certificates. PKI binds public keys with their owners by means of a Certificate Authority (CA). It is required that the user's identity must be unique for each CA. As shown in Figure 3, instead of just requiring a Web log-in user name and password, PKI requires a valid certificate for each party of the communication. Alice sends certificate application along with her public key to the Registration Authority (RA) who verifies Alice's identity and forwards the application to the CA when the ID check is successful. For every user, the identity, the public key, their binding, validation conditions (e.g. expiration dates) and other attributes are packed in a certificate which is then signed by the CA with CA's private key. Since no one else, other than the CA, has his own private key, this certificate is unforgeable. At the other end of the communication, the online shop, who received Alice's certificate along with the electronic contract signed with Alice's private key, will verify the certificate by sending it to the Validation Authority (VA) who examines the

validity of the certificate according to the information provided by the CA. Finally the online shop receives the validation result from the VA and decides whether to process the order.

Even though PKI seems to emerge as a promising standard for e-commerce, there have been debates and unsolved issues, Gutmann, P. (2006), with PKI. Carl Ellison and Bruce Schneier have pointed out in their research ten risks, Ellison, C., & Schneier, B. (2000), of using PKI. We should note that some of these risks are not just for PKI. They are listed and briefly discusses as below:

*   Risk 1. "Who do we trust, and for what" – A CA in PKI is often defined as "trusted". However, in cryptographic literature, it only means that a CA handles its own private keys well, and it does not mean that one can necessarily trust a certificate from that CA for a particular purpose: making a micropayment or signing a million-dollar purchase order.
*   Risk 2. "Who is using my key" – Most of the time, a private key is saved on a user's conventional computer and is not well protected. Under some digital signature laws (e.g. Utah and Washington), if a signing key has been certified by an approved CA, the owner is responsible for whatever that private key does.
*   Risk 3. "How secure is the verifying computer?" – The verifying computer needs to

Table 1. Trusted root certificates required by Windows XP

Issued to	Issued by	Intended purposes
Copyright (c) 1997 Microsoft Corp.	Copyright (c) 1997 Microsoft Corp.	Time Stamping
Microsoft Authenticode(tm) Root Authority	Microsoft Authenticode(tm) Root Authority	Secure E-mail, Code Signing
Microsoft Root Authority	Microsoft Root Authority	All
NO LIABILITY ACCEPTED, (c)97 VeriSign, Inc.	NO LIABILITY ACCEPTED, (c)97 VeriSign, Inc.	Time Stamping
VeriSign Commercial Software Publishers CA	VeriSign Commercial Software Publishers CA	Secure E-mail, Code Signing
Thawte Timestamping CA	Thawte Timestamping CA	Time Stamping
Microsoft Root Certificate Authority	Microsoft Root Certificate Authority	All

Figure 3. A general model of Public Key Infrastructure (PKI)

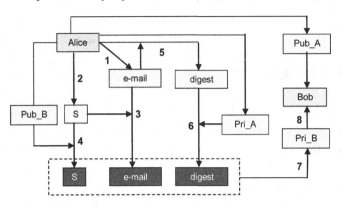

use one or more "root" public keys to verify that the certificate was indeed signed by a CA. If an attacker can add his own public key to that list, then he can issue his own "legitimate" certificates.

- Risk 4. "Which John Robinson is he?" – If you received a certificate from Alice, how do you find out if the particular Alice is your friend Alice? You could have received her public key in person or verified it in person which is allowed by PGP, but more likely you received a certificate in e-mail and are simply trusting that it is the correct Alice.

- Risk 5. "Is the CA an authority?" – CA is not an authority on some of the information in a certificate, for example, none of the Secure Socket Layer CAs listed in the popular browsers is a DNS name authority.

- Risk 6. "Is the user part of the security design?" – The corporate name in the certificate is not compared to anything the user sees in the browser and there are some Web pages whose certificate is for a company that does Web hosting, not for the company whose logo appears on the displayed page.

- Risk 7. "Was it one CA or a CA plus a RA?" – CAs can have two structures: the RA+CA structure where RA is operated by the authority on the content, and the CA only structure. The RA+CA model is less

secure than a system with a CA at the authority's desk and it allows some entity (the CA) to forge a certificate with that content.

- Risk 8. "How did the CA identify the certificate holder?" – There was a credit bureau that thought they would get into the CA business. Credit bureaus are good at business of collecting and selling facts about people, but they do not share any secret with the subjects.

- Risk 9. "How secure are the certificate practices?" – In practice there are many unsolved questions in PKI, for example, the Certificate Revocation Lists (CRLs) are built into some certificate standards, but many implementations avoid them as they are seen as too big and too outdated to be relevant. However, if CRLs are not used, how is revocation handled?

- Risk 10. "Why are we using the CA process, anyway?" – Implementing PKI may require massive change in the underlying system software.

APPLIED CRYPTOGRAPHY IN E-MAIL SERVICES

The way how e-mails are secured, Garfinkel, S.L., Margrave, D., Schiller, J.I., Nordlander, E., & Miller, R.C. (2005), is quite different from how

Figure 4. A general secure e-mail service model

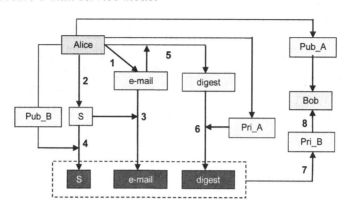

Web communication sessions are protected. In a secure Web communication session (e.g. using Secure Socket Layer, or SSL), a sender and receiver need to exchange multiple messages just to establish cryptographic assurances and parameters before the Web content can be transmitted; whereas in secure e-mail services, a single e-mail is the only message between the sender and receiver. Therefore, this e-mail message must contain all information required to provide authentication, confidentiality, integrity, and non-repudiation of origin.

Authentication in e-mail services is referred to the process of identifying the sender of the e-mail and this is often done by sender signing the e-mail using his private key. Confidentiality is provided through encrypting the message content with a symmetric session key which allows much faster encryption and decryption than public key ciphers. Message digests can be generated using hash functions to verify the integrity (that the e-mail has not been altered) of the e-mail. The sender's private key also provides non-repudiation ensuring that the sender cannot repudiate or refute the fact that he has sent the specific e-mail.

A general model, Mel, H.X., & Backer, D. (2000), providing the above secure e-mail services is shown in Figure 4 and described below:

1. The sender (Alice) composes the e-mail.

2. Alice generates a secret session key (S) which will only be used once in encryption.

3. Alice uses S to encrypt the content of the e-mail. S needs to be protected before passed to the receiver (Bob).

4. Alice uses Bob's public key (Pub_B) to encrypt S. This is a very common way to protect a secret key over the Internet.

5. In order for Bob to verify the integrity of the e-mail, Alice generates a message digest of the e-mail plaintext and the timestamp.

6. For the purpose of providing non-repudiation, Alice signs the digest using her private key (Pri_A).

7. Alice sends the e-mail package (the encrypted e-mail, the encrypted session key, and the signed message digest) to Bob.

8. When Bob receives Alice's e-mail package, he uses his private key Pri_B to decrypt the encrypted session key S, which is then used to decrypt the e-mail message; finally Bob applies the same hash function to the e-mail message and compares the output message digest to the digest he received. If the two digests match, data integrity is verified.

The keys used in this model are summarized in Table 2.

In the above secure e-mail services model, data confidentiality is provided by the secret symmetric key S. Integrity can be verified by compar-

Table 2. Keys used in the general secure e-mail service model

Name	Owner	Type	Function
S	Alice	Symmetric	Used to encrypt e-mail content by Alice and decrypt by Bob
Pub_A	Alice	Public	Used by Bob to "decrypt" the digest signed using Pri_A
Pri_A	Alice	Private	Used by Alice to sign the message digest
Pub_B	Bob	Public	Used by Alice to encrypt session key S
Pri_B	Bob	Private	Used by Bob to decrypt session key S

ing the received message digest to the calculated digest on the received e-mail content. Non-repudiation is also guaranteed as Bob can prove, using Pub_A, that Alice, the only person in the world who possesses Pri_A, has signed the digest. Since Pri_A serves as the identity of Alice and Pri_B as the identity of Bob, authentication of both sides is successful. This model appears to be perfect as far as cryptography is concerned. But is it safe and sound when applied in a real environment? Is there any problem in this model that has been overlooked? We have actually made an assumption without which the above system would be insecure: both Pub_A and Pub_B must be genuine, or in other words, Pub_A and Pub_B must indeed be Alice's and Bob's public keys respectively. The way this can be handled is to use digital certificates and a trusted third party. Different programs provide various ways to retrieve digital certificates. S/MIME uses X.509 digital certificates and PGP uses OpenPGP digital certificates (called keys). More details of this will be covered in the following sections.

PRETTY GOOD PRIVACY (PGP) AND OPENPGP

PGP, Zimmermann, P. (1995), is a program that fulfills all the security goals in e-mail services. PGP was created by Philip Zimmermann in 1991 and now follows the OpenPGP standard, Callas, J., Donnerhacke, L., Finney, H., & Thayer, R. (1998). Following the general model in Figure 4,

PGP, Stallings, W. (2006) and Wiki-PGP (2009), applies public-key cryptography in protecting the session key and providing authentication. The initial version of PGP uses Web of Trust system and in the later versions, the X.509 standard for Public Key Infrastructure (PKI) is also implemented. PGP users are allowed to both verify other users' keys and choose to trust certification statements made by other users.

Even though PGP had been quite popular in some technical communities, without a centrally managed hierarchy, it suffered in trying to work with existing e-mail systems. In 1997, a commercial PGP version was introduced which included all necessary patent licenses and plug-ins in order to work with popular e-mail systems such as Microsoft Outlook and Eudora.

OpenPGP is a non-proprietary protocol for secure e-mail systems. It is based on PGP and defines standard formats for message encryption, signing, as well as certificates for exchanging public keys. The OpenPGP working group was formed in 1997 in the IETF and OpenPGP has become the biggest competitor of S/MIME, IMC-SMIME (2006). The goal of OpenPGP is to bring companies together to promote the same standard and apply the PKI, or more accurately the OpenPGP PKI, to other non-e-mail applications.

An article by Philip Zimmermann, the author of PGP, provided another view angle on OpenPGP and PKI, Zimmermann, P. (2001). He indicated that the term PKI is not a synonym of CA as in X.509 systems. In OpenPGP, PKI is "an emergent property of the sum total of all the keys in the user population, all the signatures on all those keys, the individual opinions of each OpenPGP user as to who they choose as trusted introducers, all the OpenPGP client software which runs the OpenPGP trust model and performs trust calculations for each client user, and the key servers which fluidly disseminate this collective knowledge". The most important thing in OpenPGP PKI is, every user gets to choose who they trust as trusted introducers and he "should only trust honest and sophisticated introducers that understand what it means to sign a key, and will exercise due diligence in ascertaining the identity of the key holder before signing the key in question". In fact, the OpenPGP trust model is a proper superset of the centralized trust model of the X.509 systems.

The question of which to choose between Open-PGP PKI and X.509 PKI actually lies mainly on the issue of trust propagation over the Web which still was an active research topic at the time this book was written.

SECURE/MULTIPURPOSE INTERNET MAIL EXTENSION (S/MIME)

The Multipurpose Internet Mail Extensions (MIME), Stallings, W. (2006) and Wiki-SMIME (2009), is an Internet standard created and published by the Internet Engineering Task Force (IETF). MIME supports text in character sets other than ASCII, non-text attachments, message bodies with multiple parts, header information in non-ASCII character sets. Almost all Internet e-mails are transmitted in MIME format.

The standard for e-mail security encapsulated in MIME is referred to S/MIME, Dusse, S., Hoffman, P., Ramsdell, B., Lundblade, L., & Repka, L. (1998), which utilizes public key encryption and signing of e-mails to provide confidentiality, integrity, authentication and non-repudiation. S/MIME follows the industry standard Public Key Cryptography Standards #7 (PKCS #7) for secure message format. Although both S/MIME and PGP

are described in IETF standards, S/MIME seems to emerge as the industry standard for commercial and organizational use, while PGP will still remain as a choice for personal e-mail security.

The functions provided by S/MIME include:

- Enveloped data – encrypted data along with the corresponding keys for one or more recipients.
- Signed data – the message digest (hash) is signed with the private key of the signer. Both the content and the signature are encoded using base-64 encoding. Singed messages can only be viewed by recipients installed with S/MIME capability.
- Clear-signed data – only the digital signature is encoded using base-64. Therefore all recipients can view the message content, though those without S/MIME capability are not able to verify the signature.
- Signed and enveloped data – signed-only and encrypted-only data are allowed. In this way, encrypted data can be signed and signed data or clear-signed data can be encrypted.

Nowadays support for S/MIME is integrated into quite a number of e-mail clients including Microsoft Outlook and Outlook Express, Netscape Communicator, Lotus Notes, etc. But there are clients, such as Yahoo, Gmail and Hotmail, and many Web-based e-mail systems that do not support S/MIME. In these systems, messages digitally signed using S/MIME will appear as conventional messages with an additional attachment named smime.p7s (Figure 5). E-mails that are encrypted using S/MIME are not decipherable in these systems.

S/MIME V3 VS. OPENPGP

Even though S/MIME v3, Ramsdell, B. (2004), and OpenPGP both provide confidentiality, integrity,

Figure 5. A digitally signed S/MIME e-mail received in Google's Gmail

authentication and non-repudiation, and both use MIME to structure their messages, they are quite different in many ways and are not compatible to each other. Table 3 compares these two protocols.

APPLIED CRYPTOGRAPHY IN WEB SERVICES

The Web services are provided in client/server applications running over the Internet and TCP/

IP protocol stack. Unlike e-mail security services which can be embedded into a single e-mail, Web client and server need a series of messages to establish a secure communication channel. Nevertheless, web secure services still share a number of things with e-mail secure services, e.g. Secure Socket Layer (SSL) and Transport Layer Security (TLS) utilize digital certificate to verify the identity, the validity of the public key and their binding. In the rest of this section, we will discuss the security protocol SSL/TLS which is the de facto security standard for e-commerce. XML security standards for secure web services are also discussed.

SSL/TLS

Both SSL and its successor TLS, Stallings, W. (2006) and Wiki-SSL (2009), encrypt TCP segments in network connections at the end-to-end Transport Layer in the TCP/IP protocol stack. These two cryptographic protocols aim to provide confidentiality, integrity and authentication for communications over public networks.

SSL was originally designed by Netscape in the early 1990s and version 1.0 was never published. Version 2 was released in 1995 but contained a number of security flaws, Bard, G.V. (2004), Brumley, D., & Boneh, D. (2003), and Klima, V., Pokorny, O., & Rosa, T. (2003), which ultimately led to the design of SSL version 3.0, which was

Table 3. Comparison between S/MIME v3 and OpenPGP

Features	S/MIME v3	OpenPGP
message format	binary, based on Cryptographic Message Syntax (CMS, RFC 3852)	binary, based on previous PGP
certificate format	binary, based on X.509 v3	binary, based on previous PGP
symmetric encryption algorithm	Triple-DES	Triple-DES
signature algorithm	RSA or Diffie-Hellman	ElGamal with Digital Signature Standard (DSS)
hash algorithm	SHA-1	SHA-1
MIME encapsulation of signed data	multipart/signed or CMS	multipart/signed with ASCII armor
MIME encapsulation of encrypted data	application/pkcs7-mime	multipart/encrypted

released in 1996 and became the basis for TLS version 1.0. The IETF defined TLS version 1.0 in RFC 2246 in 1999.

Though theoretically SSL/TLS can be used to provide security for all application level protocols, such as HTTP, FTP, SMTP and, it is most commonly used with HTTP as in HTTPS, which in practice becomes the standard security protocol for e-commerce over the Internet. Figure 6 shows that Chase Bank's Web server requires HTTPS and it provides users with a certificate signed by a CA (in this case VeriSign). Instead of port 80 used by HTTP, HTTPS uses TCP port 443.

A user can view the details of the certificate in an operating system as shown in Figure 7. The details of this certificate follow the X.509 certificate structure. This shows that the mechanism of certificate system in both S/MIME and TLS is same.

The following steps describe an SSL/TLS handshake process between a Web client and server:

1. Client browser sends the server:
   ◦ TLS/SSL version number
   ◦ Cryptographic preferences
2. Sever sends the browser:
   ◦ TLS/SSL version number
   ◦ Cryptographic preferences
   ◦ Server's certificate which includes the server's RSA public key and is certified by a CA
3. The client browser has a trusted list of CAs and a public key for each CA on the list. Browser compares the received certificate with the list.
   ◦ If there is no match - user is warned that encrypted and authenticated connection cannot be established.
   ◦ If there is a match, browser uses the CA's public key to validate the certificate and obtains the server's public key.
4. Browser generates a symmetric session key and encrypts it with the server's public key then sends the encrypted session key to the server.
5. Browser sends a message to the server that the session key will be applied to the future communication in the same session. Browser portion of handshake is finished.
6. Server sends a message to the browser to confirm using the session key in the future. Server portion of handshake is finished.
7. Handshake is complete and SSL/TLS communication session begins. The same session key is applied to data on both directions.

Figure 6. Chase Bank's Web site requiring HTTPS

Figure 7. The details of a certificate issued to Chase Bank by VeriSign

There is research on attacking SSL/TLS, such as the chosen plaintext attacks, Bard, G.V. (2004), the remote timing attacks, Brumley, D., & Boneh, D. (2003), attacking RSA-based sessions. Most of these attacks, however, do not aim at the cryptographic algorithms used in SSL/TLS, but rather in their implementation or against the peculiarities of SSL/TLS itself. These attacks can be prevented by applying certain patches to the SSL/TLS software.

XML Security

The Extensible Markup Language (XML) provides XML security standards, Hirsch, F. (2002), to meet security requirements in secure web services. The core XML security standards include:

1. XML Digital Signature for integrity and signatures
2. XML Encryption for confidentiality
3. XML Key Management (XKMS) for key management

4. Security Assertion Markup Language (SAML) for making authentication and authorization assertions
5. XML Access Control Markup Language (XACML) for stating authorization rules

Among the five XML security standards, the first one, XML Digital Signature, is the most important because it establishes the approach and information used in other standards. An example of this, the <Key Info> element in XML, is used by other standards. Each of the five XML security standards is briefly discussed below.

The purposes of XML Digital Signature are to provide persistent content integrity, enabling the user of content to detect unexpected malicious or accidental changes to the content, and to create and verify portable electronic signatures. The <Signature> tag is associated with this standard.

The XML encryption standard serves the purpose of maintaining the confidentiality of information, both while in transit as well as when stored. This is an advantage of XML security over other technologies such as SSL/TLS and virtual private networks (VPNs) which only provide confidentiality while the information is being transmitted. The tags related to this standard include <EncryptedData>, <EncryptedKey>, <CipherData>.

Public Key management services are provided through the protocols defined in XML Key Management Specification (XKMS), which specifies the creation of public and private key pair, the binding of key pair with identity, and the representation of the key pair in various formats.

XML Authentication and Authorization Assertions are provided through Security Assertion Markup Language (SAML). SAML defines the following:

1. a vocabulary for expressing authentication and authorization assertions
2. a request response protocol for carrying SAML assertions

3. unique identifiers for different authentication mechanisms and authorization actions
4. how digital signatures are associated with assertions

The XML Access Control Markup Language (XACML) is needed for expressing the rules for making authorization decisions. XACML defines an XML vocabulary for expressing authorization rules, an XML vocabulary for expressing a variety of conditions to be used in creating rules, how rules are to be combined and evaluated, and a means for creating a collection of rules, also known as policy statements, applicable to a subject.

To summarize XML security, the XML Security Standards define XML vocabularies and processing rules to meet security requirements of privacy, confidentiality, integrity and authentication. A practical, extensible and flexible solution is provided through these XML Security Standards using legacy cryptographic, security and XML technologies. XML security can be applied to both secure web services and Digital Rights Management (DRM).

CONCLUSION

In this chapter, we first reviewed a number of cryptographic ciphers, security protocols and standards used in secure e-mail and Web services. We then discussed a few practical systems and standards supporting the use of public keys and private keys in a real environment. For example, Web of Trust builds a flexible decentralized trust system for PGP under the standard of OpenPGP while X.509 defines a formal format of certificates used in PKI which standardizes a centralized public key and certificate system. The de facto secure e-mail standard S/MIME was introduced and compared to OpenPGP. For Web security services, we reviewed the standards of SSL/TLS which makes use of the certificate systems previously discussed, and XML security.

It is not difficult to see that, in secure email systems, all security goals must be achieved via a single email while a series conversation between the communication parties are required in secure web applications. However, they are in common that the underlining certificate and public key systems are same.

REFERENCES

Adams, C., & Farrell, S. (1999). Internet X.509 Public Key Infrastructure: Certificate Management Protocols. RFC 2510

Bard, G. V. (2004). Vulnerability of SSL to chosen plaintext attack, Cryptology ePrint Archive, Retrieved from http://eprint.iacr.org/

Brumley, D., & Boneh, D. (2003). Remote timing attacks are practical. In Proceedings of the 12th USENIX Security Symposium. Washington, DC.

Callas, J., Donnerhacke, L., Finney, H., & Thayer, R. (1998). OpenPGP Message Format. RFC 2440

Dusse, S., Hoffman, P., Ramsdell, B., Lundblade, L., & Repka, L. (1998). S/MIME version 2 message specification. RFC 2311

Ellison, C., & Schneier, B. (2000). Ten Risks of PKI: What You're not Being Told about Public Key Infrastructure. Computer Security Journal, 16.

Garfinkel, S. L., Margrave, D., Schiller, J. I., Nordlander, E., & Miller, R. C. (2005). How to Make Secure E-mail Easier To Use. CHI 2005, Portland, OR.

Guha, R., Kumar, R., Raghavan, P., & Tomkins, A. (2004). Propagation of Trust and Distrust. In Proceedings of the 13th International Conference on WWW, New York.

Gutmann, P. (2006). "Everything you Never Wanted to Know about PKI but were Forced to Find Out", www.cs.auckland.ac.nz/~pgut001/pubs/pkitutorial.pdf

Hirsch, F. (2002). Getting Started with XML Security. Retrieved from http://www.sitepoint.com/article/getting-started-xml-security/

HMAC. (2002). The Keyed-Hash Message Authentication Code (HMAC). FIPS PUB 198. NIST.

Housley, R., Ford, W., Polk, W., & Solo, D. (1999). Internet X.509 Public Key Infrastructure: Certificate and CRL Profile. RFC 2459

IMC-SMIME. (2006). S/MIME and OpenPGP. Internet Mail Consortium.

Klima, V., Pokorny, O., & Rosa, T. (2003). Attacking RSA-based sessions in SSL/TLS. Cryptology ePrint Archive, Report 2003/052

Mel, H. X., & Backer, D. (2000). Cryptography Decrypted. Reading, MA: Addison-Wesley.

MS-293781 (2007). Trusted root certificates that are required by Windows Server 2008, by Windows Vista, by Windows Server 2003, by Windows XP, and by Windows 2000", Microsoft Help and Support Article ID 293781

Ramsdell, B. (2004). Secure/Multipurpose Internet Mail Extensions (S/MIME) Version 3.1 Message Specification, RFC 3851.

Song, J.H., Lee, J., & Iwata, T. (2006). The AES-CMAC Algorithm. RFC 4493.

Stallings, W. (2006). Cryptography and Network Security (4th ed.). Upper Saddle River, NJ: Prentice Hall.

Stallings, W. (2007). Network Security Essentials (3rd ed.). Upper Saddle River, NJ: Prentice Hall.

Wang, X. Y., Yin, Y. Q., & Yu, H. B. (2005). "Finding Collisions in the Full SHA-1", Proceedings of 25th Annual International Cryptology Conference, Santa Barbara, California, USA

Wiki-DH. (2009). Wiki-DH. Retrieved from http://en.wikipedia.org/wiki/Diffie-Hellman

Wiki-E-mail. (2009). Wiki-E-mail. Retrieved from http://en.wikipedia.org/wiki/E-mail

Wiki-MAC. (2009). Wiki-MAC. Retrieved from http://en.wikipedia.org/wiki/Message_authentication_code

Wiki-PGP. (2009). Wiki-PGP. Retrieved from http://en.wikipedia.org/wiki/Pretty_Good_Privacy

Wiki-RC. (2009). Wiki-RC. Retrieved from http://en.wikipedia.org/wiki/Root_certificate

Wiki-SMIME. (2009). Wiki-SMIME. Retrieved from http://en.wikipedia.org/wiki/S/MIME

Wiki-SSL. (2009). Wiki-SSL. Retrieved from http://en.wikipedia.org/wiki/Secure_Sockets_Layer

Wiki-Web. (2009). Wiki-Web. Retrieved from http://en.wikipedia.org/wiki/World_Wide_Web

Wiki-WOT. (2009). Wiki-WOT. Retrieved from http://en.wikipedia.org/wiki/Web_of_trust

Wiki-X.500 (2009). Wiki-X.500. Retrieved from http://en.wikipedia.org/wiki/X.500

Wiki-X.509 (2009). Wiki-X.509. Retrieved from http://en.wikipedia.org/wiki/X.509

Zimmermann, P. (1995). The Official PGP User's Guide. Cambridge, MA: MIT Press.

Zimmermann, P. (2001). Why OpenPGP's PKI is better than an X.509 PKI. Retrieved from http://www.openpgp.org/technical/whybetter.shtml

Section 3
Cryptography in Wireless Communication

Chapter 6
Applied Cryptography in Wireless Sensor Networks

Dulal C. Kar
Texas A&M University-Corpus Christi, USA

Hung Ngo
Texas A&M University-Corpus Christi, USA

Clifton J. Mulkey
Texas A&M University-Corpus Christi, USA

ABSTRACT

It is challenging to secure a wireless sensor network (WSN) because of its use of inexpensive sensor nodes of very limited processing capability, memory capacity, and battery life that preclude using traditional security solutions. Due to perceived excessive computational and architectural overhead, public key algorithms are altogether avoided for WSNs. Currently security in WSNs is provided using only symmetric key cryptography, but it requires keys to be embedded in sensor nodes before deployment and the entire network has to go through a key establishment phase after deployment. Accordingly, in this chapter, we summarize, discuss, and evaluate recent results reported in literature on sensor network security protocols such as for key establishment, random key pre-distribution, data confidentiality, and broadcast authentication. In addition, we discuss promising research results in public key cryptography for WSNs, particularly related to elliptic curve cryptography and its application for identity based encryption.

INTRODUCTION

A wireless sensor network consists of sensor nodes that communicate wirelessly using multi-hop network. Sensor nodes are typically deployed in an area to collect data as well as monitor and control activities. Specific applications of wireless sensor networks include wildlife monitoring, seismic activity monitoring, volcanic activity monitoring, target tracking, battlefield reconnaissance and surveillance, and emergency rescue operations (Akyildiz, Sankarasubramaniam, & Cayirci, 2002). It is envisioned that wireless sensor networks will be ubiquitous in every day aspects of our life and even be integrated to and accessible from the Internet.

A wireless sensor is a simple data sensing, computing, and communicating device which is

DOI: 10.4018/978-1-61520-783-1.ch006

designed to be powered by battery. As such, it has very limited memory capacity and processing and communicating capabilities. Because of their simple architecture, wireless sensor nodes are inexpensive and can be deployed in large numbers cost-effectively in many situations. As for operation of a simple wireless sensor network, all sensor nodes communicate with their neighbors and a base station. A base station is a relatively powerful computing and communicating node which often acts as a gateway or a storehouse of collected data. Figure 1 shows a typical configuration of a sensor network. However, it is possible to have a complex communicating configuration of a network with multiple base stations and multiple levels of communications among the sensor nodes.

Security of a wireless sensor network is crucial as it is typically deployed in an accessible area where there is no physical security thus making it very vulnerable for easy attacks (Huang, Cukier, Kobayashi, Liu, & Zhang, 2003; Perrig, Szewczyk, Tygar, Wen, & Culler, 2002; Zhu, Setia, & Jajodia, 2006). It is very challenging to secure a wireless sensor network mainly due to its resource-constrained sensor nodes

which cannot run the conventional cryptographic algorithms or protocols that are being used to guarantee security of traditional network communications. *Data aggregation* (ability to aggregate reported values from other nodes) and *passive participation* (ability to not send overhead values) are also the crucial issues for sensor network security. Often implementing security on resource-starved sensor devices imposes extra

computational and communication overhead that can be viewed excessive in some applications. This is due to the fact that a security application has to compete for resources with the main application. As such, a lightweight yet effective security solution is sought for wireless sensor networks. Fortunately, recent research on security of wireless sensor networks has produced many promising results. For example, two symmetric key algorithms, Skipjack and RC5 are found to be very suitable for resource constrained wireless sensor networks. Similarly, elliptic curve based public key cryptosystems (e.g., identity based encryption) are found to be very promising for wireless sensor networks. A good number of security schemes of significant performance using Skipjack, RC5, Elliptic Curve Cryptography (ECC), and Identity Based Encryption (IBE) for sensor network applications have been proposed in literature particularly with some pioneering contributions in the areas of key distribution, key management, and authentication. In this chapter, we discuss the results of these key and pioneering contributions of the contemporary research in applied cryptography for wireless sensor networks and illustrate their operations, scopes, and limitations for wireless sensor networks.

In the following, we describe and analyze security protocols for key establishment, key distribution, confidentiality, authentication, and data freshness in wireless sensor networks. In addition, we describe and evaluate recent development in elliptic curve cryptography for identity

Figure 1. A typical sensor network

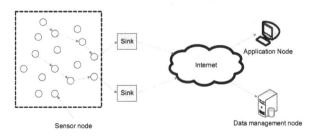

based encryption with applications for security in wireless sensor networks.

KEY MANAGEMENT

Key management is one of the most important and complex issues in every security protocol. The duties of key management are distributing key values and taking care of keys' lifecycle. While public key cryptography is widely used in traditional network applications to exchange keys, it seems to be unsuitable for resource-constrained wireless sensor networks. Some good studies on applying public-key cryptographic schemes on wireless sensor networks are RSA and Diffie-Hellman (Watro et al., 2004) and Elliptic Curve Cryptography (Oliveira et al., 2007). However, experiments show that public-key based schemes with only software implementation incur a delay up-to tens of seconds (Malan, Welsh, & Smith, 2004; Wander, Gura, Eberle,Gupta, & Shantz, 2005). Although the performance can be improved significantly with the support of special hardware, the goal of low-cost sensor networks is not satisfied yet due to high manufacturing cost of such hardware devices. In contrast, key management in symmetric-key based protocols is negligible when compared with that of public key based protocols in terms of computation complexity and power consumption (Huang et al., 2003). Unfortunately, it is more complicated and is subject to attacks by adversaries.

In wireless sensor networks, adversaries can compromise sensor nodes and use them to attack the networks. With the ability of full control on compromised nodes, the attackers can read all data stored in nodes' memory including information of secret keys. They can also change the behavior of captured sensor nodes to inject malicious code into the network. Although special secure memory devices can be used to prevent attackers from reading compromised nodes' memory, this

solution considerably increases the cost of tiny sensor nodes (Karl & Willig, 2005).

SECURITY PROTOCOLS FOR SENSOR NETWORKS (SPINS)

SPINs is one of the first and well-known security protocols developed for wireless sensor network. Perrig et al. proposed two security blocks in SPINs which are Secure Network Encryption Protocol (SNEP) and "micro" Timed Efficient Stream Loss-tolerant Authentication (μTESLA). While SNEP provides data confidentiality, two-party data authentication, and data freshness, μTESLA is developed to provide authenticated broadcast for resource-constrained environments. However, SPINs only deals with three kinds of communication patterns:

- *Node to base station* such as sensor readings
- *Base station to node communication* such as requests from base station to a specific node
- *Base station to all nodes* such as routing beacons or queries on the entire network.

In SPINs, each sensor node shares a pre-distributed master secret key with the base station. All other keys are bootstrapped from the initial master secret key. The derivation procedure F is a pseudo-random function which is implemented as $F_K(x) = MAC(K,x)$. Encryption Protocol SNEP, a sub-protocol of SPINs, derives two keys from the master secret key: K_{encr} and K_{mac} where K_{encr} is used for encryption/decryption and K_{mac} is used to create message authentication code (MAC). To minimize the power requirements, the number generator key K_{rand} is also derived from master secret key K. Figure 2 shows how the master key is used to derive all these three keys.

Broadcast authentication is very important to defend wireless sensor networks from adversaries

Figure 2. Deriving keys from master secret key K

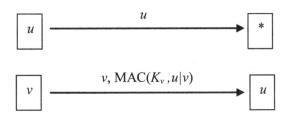

who try to take control of the network. To broadcast authenticated packets, SPINs uses **μTESLA** protocol. In μTESLA, the sender generates one-way key chain by using a one-way function such as MD5. The sender then chooses the last key K_n randomly and generates the other keys in reverse order from K_{n-1} to K_1 as $K_i = F(K_{i+1})$. The receiver can verify received keys by computing and comparing $F(K_{j+1})$ with K_j. A mechanism called *delayed key disclosure* is used in μTESLA to implement the authenticated broadcasting (see section 3.2 for more details on *Authentication*). For node-to-node communications, SPINs uses the base station as a trusted agent to set up keys. Since all sensor nodes share a master secret key with the base station, they can transmit session keys securely through the base station.

LOCALIZED ENCRYPTION AUTHENTICATION PROTOCOL (LEAP)

One of the drawbacks of SPINs is that it does not consider different security requirements for different types of messages, which may reduce lifetime of sensor networks unnecessarily. For example, routing control information may not require confidentiality whereas sensor readings and aggregated reports should be encrypted before they are sent to the base station. Because of this disadvantage, different security mechanisms should be used for different types of messages in wireless sensor networks (Zhu et al., 2006). Since one single key mechanism is not enough to satisfy

different security requirements, LEAP provides four types of keys for wireless sensor network communication:

- **Individual Key:** This is a key shared by the base station and every sensor node in the network. This key is preloaded in each sensor node before deployment and is used to secure the communication between the base station and sensor nodes.
- **Pairwise Shared Key:** This type of key is only shared by two sensor nodes. A newly added sensor node u has to follow four steps to set up a pairwise shared key with each of its neighbors.
  ○ **Key Pre-distribution:** Node u is loaded with an initial key K and derives a master key $K_u = f_K(u)$.
  ○ **Neighbor Discovery:** Node u initializes a timer with a time T_{min} and broadcasts a HELLO message to contact its neighbors where T_{min} is the minimum time necessary for an adversary to compromise a sensor node. In this phase, node u can verify the identity of its neighbors since it can easily compute its neighbors' keys. Figure 3 illustrates how node u discovers one of its neighboring node v. For example, it can compute a key for node v as $K_v = f_K(v)$. A very important assumption in establishing this type of key is that T_{min} has to be greater than T_{est} in which T_{est} is the time to complete the key establishment process.

Figure 3. Neighbor Discovery

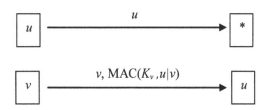

- ○ **Pairwise Key Establishment:** Nodes *u* and *v* compute pairwise shared key $K_{uv} = f_{Kv}(u)$. After that, any subsequent message exchanging between *u* and *v* are authenticated using K_{uv}.
- ○ **Key Erasure:** When the timer T_{min} expires, node *u* erases the initial key *K* and all the master keys of its neighbors but keeps its key K_u.

Later in this chapter, we will discuss the requirements of establishing pairwise shared keys for two sensor nodes that are multi-hops away from each other.

- • **Cluster Key:** This type of key is shared by a node and its neighbors. Unlike group keys (discussed below), a cluster key is used to broadcast messages locally. A cluster key can be easily set up by using pairwise shared keys. A node uses its pairwise keys shared with its neighbors to encrypt the cluster key. Then encrypted messages which contain the cluster key are sent to neighboring nodes.
- • **Group Key:** This type of key is shared by all nodes in the network. A simple and most efficient way to bootstrap a group key is to pre-load it to every sensor node. Another way to establish a group key is by using cluster keys. One important issue with group keys is that when a node is compromised, the network group key must be changed and redistributed to all nodes in a secure, energy- and time-efficient fashion. This process is called *group rekeying*. To revoke a node, LEAP employs μTESLA protocol (proposed in SPINs) to broadcast a revoking message to all sensor nodes in the network. The revoked node's neighbors will authenticate the message, remove their pairwise keys shared with the revoked node, and update a new cluster key.

Assume that sensor nodes in the network are organized into a breadth first spanning tree, the base station can send an encrypted message that contains the new group key by using its children's cluster key. These children then can continue sending the new group key recursively down the spanning tree using their own cluster keys for encryption.

LINK LAYER SECURITY PROTOCOL: TINYSEC

TinySec is a security architecture which operates on the data link layer. Unlike SPINs and LEAP, TinySec is not limited to any keying mechanism (Karlof, Sastry, & Wagner, 2004). TinySec uses a pair of Skipjack keys to encrypt data and compute MACs of packets. Below are three different keying mechanisms that can be used with TinySec to secure sensor network applications. Each mechanism has its own advantages and disadvantages. The tradeoffs among different keying mechanisms should be considered.

- • **Single Network-Wide Key:** This type of keys is shared by all authorized sensor nodes in sensor networks. It is easy to deploy by simply pre-loading shared keys into every node in the networks before deployment. In a sensor network using single network-wide key mechanism, a node will reject all messages sent from unauthorized nodes. Networks using this type of keys support both passive participation and local broadcasting among authorized sensor nodes. The major drawback of network-wide keys is that if any authorized node is compromised, adversaries can eavesdrop or inject malicious codes into the networks.
- • **Per-Link Key:** This key is shared by each pair of sensor nodes only if they need to

communicate with each other. Per-link keys can be used to overcome the problem of network-wide keys because a compromised node can only inject malicious codes into its immediate neighbors and decrypt messages addressed to it. There are some drawbacks when using this keying mechanism. Not only does it limit passive participation capability, a type of in-network processing used to save energy and prolong network lifetime, but it is also not suitable for local broadcast, an important feature allowing sensor nodes cheaply send messages to all their neighbors. Although key distribution become challenging (Karlof et al., 2004), this problem can be solved by Random Key Pre-distribution Schemes (Chan, Perrig, & Song, 2003) or by some different pairwise key distribution mechanisms (Du et al., 2005; Liu, Ning, & Li, 2005).

- **Group Key:** This key is shared by a group of neighboring nodes. When a sensor node is compromised, the extent of damage due to exposure of a group key is confined within the neighboring nodes only. The compromised node can only decrypt messages sent from sensor nodes in its group. It cannot inject malicious codes to and decrypt messages from other groups. Although this key supports passive participation and local broadcast, how to distribute and set up this type of key is still a problem.

TinySec is now fully-implemented and included in TinyOS distribution (Karlof et al., 2004). Hence, users can easily develop a secure wireless sensor network without changing application code except for some special situations. However, one should always consider the trade-off between security and network lifetime.

PATH KEY ESTABLISHMENT

For two sensor nodes that are multi-hop away from each other, Eschenauer and Gligor (2002) proposed a random key predistribution scheme. This scheme has two main phases: initialization phase and key-setup phase. The initialization phase is conducted before a network is deployed in the environment. In this phase, a random pool of keys S is picked from the total possible key space. Each sensor node then randomly selects m keys from S and stores them in its memory. This *m-key* set is called a key ring. The number of keys in S and value of m are chosen in such a way that two random subsets of size m in S will share at least one key with an expected probability p. After deployment, the key-setup phase is automatically performed by sensor nodes. In this phase, a sensor node discovers which neighbors share a common predistributed key with it. The simplest way to do this is to broadcast the list of key identifiers to its neighbors. When recipients receive the list, they compare the sender's list with its own list. If receivers find a common key identifier, they will send a message which contains the shared identifier back to the sender. Another way can be used is to establish a *private discovery*. In this approach, for each key K_i in its key ring, the node broadcasts a set $(\alpha, E_{Ki}(\alpha))$ where α is a challenge. The recipient can verify the challenge α by decrypting $E_{Ki}(\alpha)$ using the proper key. If the verification is successful, the key will be used for the respective link for later communications. A connected graph of secure links is created after the key-setup phase completes. For any communication later, a source can use this graph to reach the destination.

Instead of using a single common key, Chan et al. (2003) proposed q-composite random key predistribution scheme that needs at least q common keys. By increasing the number of shared keys in key-setup phase, the network can increase the resilience against node capture attacks. As a compromised node also stores key ring information containing secret keys for other secure links, it is important to update the communication keys for those links immediately once the compromised node is discovered. For example in Figure 4, if node N_5 which contains shared keys K_{15}, K_{45}, and K_{12} is captured, the keys of the connection N_1-N_2 need to be updated. Node N_1, in this case, cannot use the direct link N_1-N_2 and the key K_{12} to set up a new key since N_5 can use K_{12} to decrypt key-update messages and obtain the new keys. This problem can be solved by using *Multipath Key Reinforcement* scheme which splits a message into many different parts and sends them on disjoint paths to the destination (Chan et al., 2003). Essentially, the new key K' is split into n parts where n is the number of disjoint paths from source to destination:

$$K' = K \oplus v_1 \oplus v_2 \oplus ... \oplus v_n$$

in which $\oplus$ is *XOR* operation.

Then the source sends v_1, v_2, ... v_n on n disjoint paths to a destination so that adversaries cannot reveal the new key K' if they do not have all n split parts. In the above example, N_1 can send two split parts using two disjoint paths N_1-N_2 and N_1-N_4-N_3-N_2.

To produce shorter path lengths, Mehallegue, Bouridane, and Garcia (2008) proposed a novel algorithm which can quickly find common trusted nodes that are closer to both end nodes. An important assumption of this algorithm is that every sensor node has the identifier list of its first neighbors. First neighbors of N_i are defined as

nodes that are one hop away from N_i and share a secret with N_i. Assuming *TIER(N_i, x)* is the set of nodes that are x hops away from node N_i, Figure 5 shows an example for the algorithm proposed by Mehallegue et al. (2008). In the example, node N_1 wants to set up a secure link with node N_2. It initially sends a request to set up a secure link to N_2. After receiving the key identifier list from N_2, N_1 compares its own list with N_2's list (*CMP$_0$*). If there is a common key(s), N_1 and N_2 can set up a direct secure link between them. Otherwise, N_1 requests the list of N_2's first neighbors, then after receiving the list, it continues comparing its first neighbors' list and N_2's list (*CMP$_1$*). If the number of *proxies* is zero or less than *prx* which is the number of common trusted nodes required to send the secret, N_1 will ask *TIER(N_1,1)* for *TIER(N_1,2)* and *TIER(N_2,1)* for *TIER(N_2,2)*. The comparing process becomes more and more complicated as N_1 continues finding proxies. In *CMP$_2$*, N_1 has to compare three pairs: *TIER(N_1,1)* with *TIER(N_2,2)*, *TIER(N_1,2)* with *TIER(N_2,1)*, and *TIER(N_1,2)* with *TIER(N_2,2)*. The proxy discovery process continues until the number of proxies found is equal or greater than *prx*.

Though effective, but the multipath key reinforcement scheme is complex and incurs excessive communication overhead. For a sensor node, typically communication cost is much higher than computation cost in terms of energy consumption and is the main reason of its early failure. Therefore, it is important to have a scheme that can minimize communication overhead as much as possible.

Figure 4. Path key establishment problem

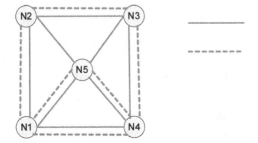

AUTHENTICATION, INTEGRITY, CONFIDENTIALITY AND DATA FRESHNESS

Confidentiality, authentication, integrity, and data freshness are important requirements in every security protocol. While confidentiality is achieved using different symmetric-key algorithms such as

Skipjack and RC5, message authentication codes (MACs) are used for authentication and message integrity. In addition, sensor networks can ensure semantic confidentiality by using different operation modes such as Cipher Block Chaining (CBC) and Output Feedback Mode (OFB).

Confidentiality

Data confidentiality is needed to protect sensitive information from being disclosed to unauthorized parties. Confidentiality plays a very important role in wireless sensor network applications such as military applications (smart uniforms, target tracking, and battlefield monitoring) or healthcare applications (to protect patient information). In wireless sensor networks, encryption is the technique used to achieve data confidentiality. Unfortunately, pure encryption may not be enough to protect data from adversaries since two same plaintexts can have the same ciphertext (Electronic Codebook mode). To overcome this problem, the use of other operation modes such as CBC (Cipher Block Chaining) and OFM (Output Feedback Mode) is necessary.

Due to the limit in storage capacity and energy, public-key cryptography is not suitable for such energy-consuming operations like encryption and decryption. Symmetric-key cryptographic algorithms such as Skipjack or RC5, on the other hand, are proposed in many other protocols such as SPINs, LEAP, and TinySec (Karlof et al., 2004; Law et al., 2006; Perrig et al., 2002; Zhu et al., 2006).

Another security issue that needs to be considered is end-to-end security. Because sensor nodes are energy-constrained devices, the requirement of in-network processing (data aggregation and passive participation) is the most crucial. Unfortunately, to use this mechanism, intermediate nodes need to access, aggregate, and modify information in the packets, which makes end-to-end security more difficult.

SNEP, a building block of SPINs, uses RC5, a block cipher with two counters shared by parties, to achieve confidentiality. Figure 6 illustrates the operation of RC5. To save energy for sensor nodes, the counters are not sent along with the messages. After each block, sensor nodes increase and keep the state of the counters for themselves. SPINs

Figure 5. Process of finding trusted common sensor nodes. (Adapted from Mehallegue et al., 2008).

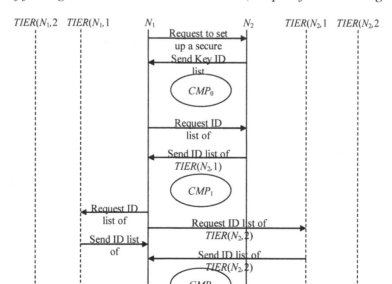

can achieve *semantic security* by using the value of the counters so that even if two plaintexts are the same, the corresponding ciphertexts will be different.

Unlike SNEP which is neither fully specified nor implemented, TinySec is now fully-implemented and included in TinyOS distribution (Karlof et al., 2004). TinySec is a link-layer security protocol which means it is transparent to user. Because the encryption and decryption happen at the link layer automatically, TinySec can support in-network processing. Since RC5 requires 104 extra bytes of RAM per key, Skipjack becomes a better choice for sensor networks (Karlof et al., 2004). In fact, the default block cipher in TinySec is Skipjack. To achieve semantic security, TinySec uses *initialization vector (IV)* with CBC mode. A TinySec-AE packet is partitioned into 7 different fields in which the combination of the first 5 fields is the *IV*. The *IV* is 8 bytes in length including destination address (2 bytes), active message handler type (1 byte), length of the data payload (1 byte), source address (2 bytes), and 16-bit counter (2 bytes).

Authentication and Integrity

Data authentication is essential for many important functions in all sensor network applications.

Controlling nodes' duty cycle and reprogramming a group of nodes or the entire network are two typical examples. Besides data confidentiality, data authentication and data integrity play crucial roles in applications that need a high level of security such as battlefield reconnaissance and surveillance applications. In applications that require data authentication and integrity, receiving nodes need to ensure that commands are sent from trusted sources (authentication) and are not modified or altered (integrity). If the communication takes place between two parties, they can simply use the message authentication code (MAC) of all communicated data to verify whether the messages originated from the trusted source (Perrig et al., 2002). Broadcast communication, on the other hand, is a much more complex situation. If one sender uses MAC and broadcasts messages to other nodes, any node which knows the MAC key can impersonate the sender, create fake messages, and send them to other receivers. Although asymmetric mechanisms achieve very good results in traditional networks, they are not suitable for wireless sensor networks due to high cost in terms of time and energy.

SPINs provides two sub-protocols SNEP and μTESLA to deal with data authentication in two-party and broadcast communication respectively. Authentication in two-party communication is

Figure 6. Counter mode encryption and decryption in SPINs

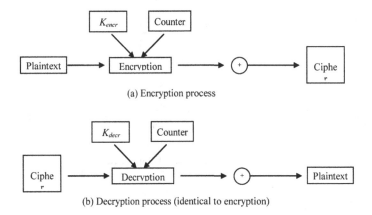

(a) Encryption process

(b) Decryption process (identical to encryption)

simple and based on the MAC of the message while authenticated broadcasting is more complex. μTESLA uses a mechanism called delayed disclosure of symmetric keys to broadcast authenticated messages to all sensor nodes in the network. When the base station wants to broadcast a message, it computes the MAC of the message using a key which is not yet disclosed at that time. When a node in the network receives the message, it first saves the message in its own buffer and waits until receiving the verification key broadcasted from the base station. When the key arrives, the sensor node can authenticate the key before using that key to verify the message saved in the buffer beforehand. However, μTESLA requires the base station and sensor nodes are loosely synchronized. Moreover, each node has to know the upper bound of the maximum synchronization error and the time schedule at which keys are disclosed.

Figure 7 shows an example of source authentication in μTESLA. We can see that each interval has a key bound to it. The disclosure schedule here means the time at which secret keys in the key chain are disclosed. Let us consider that the sender and receiver are loosely time synchronized and the receiver knows K_0 as the commitment to the key chain. At time intervals 1 and 2, P_1, P_2, and K_1 are sent to receiver. P_1 and P_2 contain their own MACs using corresponding keys K_1 and K_2. Assume that packet containing K_1 is lost. In intervals 3 and 4, the recipient receives P_3, P_4, and K_2 successfully. By using K_2, the receiver can authenticate $K_0 = F(F(K_2))$ and compute $K_1 = F(K_2)$. Hence, the receiver can also authenticate packet P_1 using K_1 and P_2 using K_2. The time de-

lay to broadcast authentication key (K_1 and K_2 in this example) varies from system to system. One major drawback of μTESLA is that the scheme works only when the base station (broadcaster) and sensor nodes are loosely synchronized, which may not be guaranteed in all situations in wireless sensor networks.

Like SPINS, LEAP also uses μTESLA for authenticated broadcasting. However, μTESLA is not an appropriate solution for local broadcasting due to latency and limited storage capacity of sensor nodes (Zhu et al., 2006). Therefore, LEAP uses *One-way Key Chain Based Authentication* to broadcast authenticated messages locally. Let us consider a communication among three nodes x, y, and z. Node x sends a packet that contains the content M and the authentication key K. Node y will receive this packet before node z forwards its received packet to y because $|xy| < |xz| + |zy|$. Hence, if node z is an adversary, it cannot reuse the authentication key K to send another message. This approach, however, may suffer when the link between x and y is also attacked by another adversary.

Unlike SPIN which uses 8 bytes for message authentication code (MAC), TinySec uses only 4 bytes in each packet for MAC. While traditional security protocols use 8 or 16 bytes for MACs, 4-byte MACs should be enough for wireless sensor networks. On a 19.2 kb/s channel with 40 forgery attempts per second, adversaries have to spend over 20 months to try 2^{31} possibilities of a 4-byte MAC (Karlof et al., 2004). Furthermore, such attacks can be solved by a very simple heuristic. Sensor nodes should signal the base station

Figure 7. Source authentication using time-released key chain in μTESLA

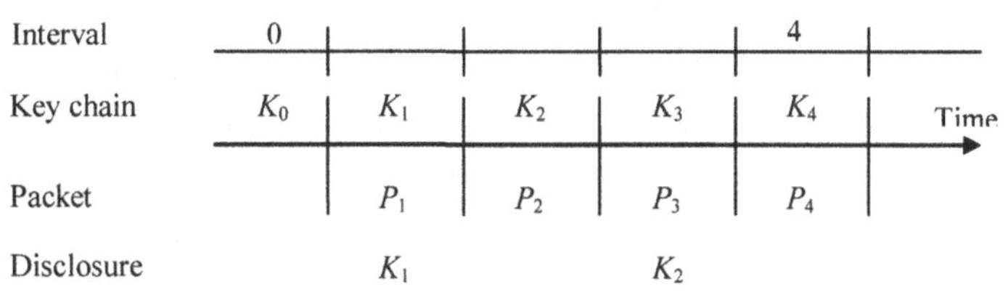

Figure 8. Local Broadcast Authentication in LEAP
$(|xy| < |xz| + |zy|)$

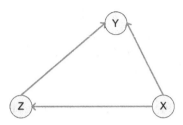

whenever the number of MAC failures exceeds a particular threshold (Karlof et al., 2004).

TinySec has two security options: authentication only (TinySec-Auth) and authentication-encryption (TinySec-AE). With TinySec-Auth option, the maximum size of a data packet is 37 bytes with 4 bytes for MAC. Compared to a TinyOS packet, a TinySec-Auth packet does not have 1 byte of *Group* information and 2 bytes of *Cyclic Redundancy Check (CRC)*. The 4-byte MACs in both TinySec-Auth and TinySec-AE are used for authentication and message integrity. As reported by Karlof et al (2004), TinySec-AE incurs 6% packet overhead and 10% energy overhead.

Non-repudiation is an important issue in traditional networks. It is used to ensure a party cannot refute or repudiate the reception or the sending of a message. In wireless sensor networks, this issue is not yet explicitly studied. The reason may be the lack of requirements for this kind of service. However, non-repudiation may become an interesting subject in future as sensor network applications extend to all aspects of our life.

Data Freshness

The freshness of data means that the data is recent and is not replayed (Perrig et al., 2002). Data freshness is important in emergency situations and real-time applications such as forest fire detection, emergency rescue operations, and target tracking. SPINs defines two types of data freshness – weak freshness and strong freshness:

- Weak freshness: provides partial message ordering and carries no delay information.
- Strong freshness: provides full message ordering and carries delay information.

While weak freshness is useful for measurements (e.g. sensor readings), strong freshness can be used for time synchronization in the network. For both weak and strong freshness, protecting network from replay attacks is a big issue. Common defenses in traditional networks are to either use message timestamps or include an increasing counter to detect replayed message. To achieve weak data freshness in SPINs, the sender simply includes a counter (CTR) in messages before sending them to the receiver. By increasing the CTR value, not only is the weak freshness achieved, but the semantic security is also accomplished. For applications that need strong freshness, the sender can create a random nonce and send it together with the request to the receiver. After receiving the request and the nonce, the receiver can include the nonce in the MAC of the response message. If the MAC of the response is verified successfully, the sender knows that the response message was created after it sent the request message, thus achieving the strong freshness. The drawback for the counter approach is that each recipient has to maintain a list (or a table) of last received counter values from other sensor nodes. This leads to the high cost of using memory resource. Since wireless sensor network applications are usually deployed with hundreds or thousands of nodes and sensor devices are very limited in memory capacity, this approach may not be a good solution.

The apparent infeasibility of public key cryptography for wireless sensor networks has motivated research to develop alternative security techniques using key distribution in sensor nodes before deployment. SPINS, LEAP, and TinySec are prime examples of such development. However, these techniques fall short to address many security issues such as node compromises, revocations, and insertions of nodes which can easily be solved using PKC (public key cryptography). In the following, we discuss very recent results on the use of PKC in sensor network platforms.

PUBLIC KEY CRYPTOGRAPHY FOR WIRELESS SENSOR NETWORKS

Recently it has been shown that PKC in wireless sensor networks is feasible to perform limited PKC operations on current sensor platforms. One notable attempted PKC system for wireless sensor networks is TinyPK proposed by Watro, et al. (2004). However, a comparative study on ECC and RSA on the ATmega128 by Gura et al. (2004) shows that ECC outperforms RSA as a cryptosystem. Particularly, ECC has been found very amenable for wireless sensor networks due to its fast computation, small key size, and small packet overhead. For equivalent security, an ECC based scheme requires only 160-bit key in contrast to 1024-bit RSA key (NIST, 2003). Due to ECC's better computational efficiency and less power requirement compared to RSA, ECC is finding applications for security in hand-held mobile devices. Several software implementations of ECC on sensor network platforms have also been reported in literature. Some progress has been made on hardware implementation of ECC, but such solutions have not been integrated with sensor nodes yet (Batina et al. 2006; Luo et al., 2008). In the following, we describe implementation of ECC based cryptosystems for wireless sensor networks.

Background on Elliptic curve cryptography

Elliptic curve cryptography (ECC) was proposed independently by Neal Koblitz (Koblitz, 1987) and Victor Miller (Miller, 1986) as a public key cryptosystem. Compared to RSA public key cryptography, ECC has been found advantageous in many ways including processing requirement,

memory requirement, and energy requirement for its implementation (Cilardo et al., 2006). According to NIST, for example, a 160-bit ECC key can ensure the similar level of security of a 1024-bit RSA key (NIST, 2003). The security of RSA relies on the problem of difficulty of factoring a large number, which is becoming increasingly easier to perform as researchers are working to accelerate the solution of the factorization problem, resulting to increasing vulnerability of the RSA public key cryptosystem. To cope with this, the key size for the RSA key can be used for short time but at the cost of high processing time for computation, communication, and storage. On the contrary, ECC has been found relatively less problematic and has sustained a prolonged time of scrutiny and attacks as its security relies on the difficulty of the Elliptic Curve Discrete Logarithm problem.

For fast, accurate, and efficient operations for cryptography, ECC is typically defined over two finite fields: prime field F_n and binary field. F_{2^m} Specifically, ECC operations are defined over the elliptic curve:

$$y^2=(x^3+ax+b) \tag{1}$$

where a and b are constants such that $(4a^3+27b^2)\neq0$. A point at infinity is also considered to be on the elliptic curve. Let us consider two distinct points $P = (x_p, y_p)$ and $Q = (x_q, y_q)$ on the elliptic curve defined by equation (1) on affine coordinate system. The point addition operation on the elliptic curve is defined as $R = P + Q$ where R is a point on the elliptic curve with a coordinate (x_r, y_r). If $Q = -P$ meaning $Q = (x_p, -y_p)$ then $R = P + (-P) = O$, where O is the point at infinity. If $Q = P$, then the operation $R = 2P$ is called *point doubling*. The computation of point R is summarized in Table 1 for both fields.

Elliptic Curve Discrete Logarithm Problem (ECDLP) is defined as $R = P + P + ... + P = kP$ where k is a scaler and P and R are two points on an elliptic curve. The corresponding operation is

Table 1. Operations in Elliptic Curve Cryptography

ECC Operations over F_n	ECC Operations over F_{2^m}
A. Point Addition: 1) $R=P+Q$ $x_r = (s^2 - x_p - x_q)\bmod n$ $y_r = -y_p + s(x_p - x_r)\bmod n$ where the slope s is: $s=(y_p\text{-}y_q)/(x_p\text{-}x_q)\bmod n$. 2) If $Q = \text{-}P$ meaning $Q = (x_p, \text{-}y_p)$ then $R = P + (\text{-}P) = O$, where O is the point at infinity. B. Point Doubling 1) $R = 2P$ $x_r = s^2 - 2x_p \bmod n$ $y_r = -y_p + s(x_p - x_r)\bmod n$ where the slope s of the tangent at P is: $s=(3x_p+a)/(2y_p)\bmod n$ 2) If $y_p = 0$ then $R = 2P = O$, where O is the point at infinity.	A. Point Addition: 1) $R=P+Q$ $x_r = s^2 + s + x_p + x_q + a$ $y_r = s(x_p + x_r) + x_r + y_p$ where the slope s is: $s=(y_p+y_q)/(x_p+x_q)$. 2) If $Q = \text{-}P$ meaning $Q = (x_p, x_p+y_p)$ then $R = P + (\text{-}P) = O$, where O is the point at infinity. B. Point Doubling 1) $R = 2P$ $x_r = s^2 + s + a$ $y_r = x_p^2 + (s+1)x_r$ where the slope s of the tangent at P is: $s=x_p+y_p/x_p$ 2) If $x_p = 0$ then $R = O$, where O is the point at infinity.

called point multiplication ($R = kP$) which can be achieved using a sequence of point doubling and point addition operations. Given P and R, it is computationally infeasible to find k for sufficiently large k. The scaler k is termed as the elliptic curve discrete logarithm of R to base P. The scaler k constitutes the private key component of any elliptic curve based cryptography and is kept secret. The security of ECC depends on the difficulty of computing k given P, R, and the elliptic curve parameters a and b. As can be seen from Table 1, ECC operations involve many time-consuming operations such as multiplication, squaring, and division/inversion. To expedite such operations, several hardware and software algorithms have been proposed in literature (Ciet et al. 2006). In addition, to avoid division/inversion altogether, ECC operations have been proposed on projective coordinate system.

ECC IMPLEMENTATION FOR WIRELESS SENSOR NETWORKS

Among all ECC implementations on sensor network platforms, TinyECC proposed by Liu and Peng has several competitive advantages (Liu & Peng, 2008). Essentially TinyECC is a configurable software library for ECC operations for public key cryptography targeted at TinyOS for sensor platforms MICAz, TelosB, Tmote Sky, and Imote2 (Crossbow, Inc.). It allows selection of specific components from its library as needed for optimization of an application on a specific sensor platform. The following describes the optimization features of TinyECC for sensor networks:

• Fast Modular Reduction: TinyECC implements ECC over a prime field F_n and utilizes several existing optimization techniques in its implementation for ECC operations for the sake of increased speed, reduced memory requirement, and reduced energy consumption. For modular reduction, TinyECC uses Barrett Reduction method to achieve faster speed than that can be obtained using simple division. However, Barrett Reduction implementation requires more ROM and increases RAM use in a sensor node due to its separate implementation instead of using existing division operation to carry out modular reduction.

- Fast Modular Inversion: As can be seen from Table 1, two essential operations, point addition and point doubling in affine coordinate system (x, y) for ECC require very expensive modular inversion operations. Using a projective coordinate system, TinyECC replaces the inversion operations with a few modular multiplications and squares achieving faster execution of point addition and point doubling operations. However, the projective coordinate representation (x, y, z) requires a larger code size and more RAM than the affine coordinate system as it requires a point to be represented as (x, y, z) instead of (x, y) in the affine coordinate system.

- Fast Mixed/Hybrid Operations: To reduce execution time and program size, TinyECC uses a *mixed point addition algorithm* to add a point in projective coordinate to a second point in affine coordinate and a *repeated Doubling* algorithm for scalar multiplication (Hankerson, Menezes, & Vanstone, 2004). In addition, TinyECC utilizes a hybrid multiplication algorithm by Gura, Patel, and Wander (2004) and also customizes the same hybrid multiplication algorithm for squaring operations.

- Curve Specific Optimizations: TinyECC can also achieve curve specific optimizations particularly for the elliptic curve recommended by NIST using *pseudo-Mersenne primes* of the form $n = 2^m - c$, where c and m are positive integers such that $c \ll 2^m$.

TinyECC includes all of the above optimization modules for generating energy-efficient, storage-efficient, and time-efficient code for various sensor platforms. It may not be possible to generate code that meets all of the optimization objectives for processing time, storage requirement, and energy consumption simultaneously. Depending on the constraints of the sensor platform and the need of an application, a compromise can be achieved by selecting appropriate modules for generating code for the application. The current version of TinyECC provides support for ECDSA (Elliptic Curve Digital Signature Algorithm) for digital signatures, ECDH (Digital Curve Diffie-Hellman) for pairwise key establishment, and ECIES (Elliptic Curve Integrated Encryption System) for PKC-based encryption (Hankerson, Menezes, & Vanstone, 2004).

IDENTITY BASED ENCRYPTION

To thwart "man-in-the-middle" attacks, public key cryptosystems use a trusted certifying authority of Public Key Infrastructure (PKI) for verification and authentication of a public key and its holder. However, such practice of PKC is not feasible in a wireless sensor network environment simply due to extra overhead on sensor nodes and lack of resources prohibiting deployment of PKI. Recently, it has been shown that it is possible to have public key cryptosystems in this environment by using a technique based on random identities of the sensor nodes. The scheme is known as Identity Based Encryption originally introduced by Shamir a long time ago (Shamir, 1984). This is also called pairing based encryption. Due to recent development in ECC and its relation to discrete logarithm, it is now feasible to have IBE for wireless sensor networks. The mathematical theory behind pairing based cryptography can be summarized as follows (Menezes, Okamoto, & Vanstone, 1993):

Let E be an elliptic curve on a finite field F_n. A pairing e is a computable bilinear mapping for given two points P and Q on E to an integer M $F_{n^q}^*$ over that can be described as:

$$E(P, Q) Þ M \bmod n^q \qquad (2)$$

and has the following properties:

$$e(aP,bQ)=e(P,Q)^{ab}=M^{ab} \bmod n^q \qquad (3)$$

for any a and b, and

$$e(P,P) \neq 1 \qquad (4)$$

The integer q, known as the embedding degree, is the least integer such that (n^q-1) is divisible by r where r is a prime order of the group of points on E over F_n, (i.e., r is a prime factor that divides the number of points on E over F_n). Only a few bilinear mappings or pairings are known for small values of q that include the Weil and Tate pairings (Galbraith, 2005; Boneh & Franklin, 2003). Comparatively, the Tate paring has been found to be more efficient and amenable than the Weil pairing.

An IBE based cryptosystem for sensor networks can be developed based on the properties of such pairings of points on an elliptic curve. Although an IBE based public key system does not require any PKI but it requires a trusted party that is responsible to generate a public key to be used by the entire network system and a secret integer corresponding to the public key. In a sensor network environment, the base station is the obvious choice for such a trusted party. The base station needs to:

1. Choose a point P on the designated elliptic curve and a secret integer s.
2. Compute a point $R = sP$ on the elliptic curve and then publish P and R both. In this case, R is the public key.

It is desirable to load each sensor node with P and R before deployment thus avoiding any further communication from the base station to the sensor nodes for P and R. In the following we describe how points P and R as well as the identity of a receiving node are used for secure communication between two sensor nodes. For the sake of simplicity, we assume that simple exclusive-or operation is used for encryption and decryption.

Encryption steps:

1. The sender computes point $Q_x = \text{Hash1}(\text{ID}_x)$ essentially by converting the identity string ID_x of a receiver X to a point Q_x on the elliptic curve by using some function Hash1.
2. The sender selects a random integer k and computes a point $U = kP$ on the elliptic curve.
3. The sender then computes an encryption key $h = \text{Hash2}(e(kR, Q_x))$ using a designated bilinear mapping function e and some function Hash2.
4. For a given message m, the sender computes point $V = m \oplus h$ and then sends (U, V) to receiver X.

Decryption steps:

1. After receiving (U, V) from the sender, the receiver contacts the base station for the private key corresponding to its identity ID_x.
2. The base station first computes $Q_x = \text{Hash1}(\text{ID}_x)$ and then $d = sQ_x$ where d is the private key for receiver X.
3. Using some secure protocols, the base station sends d to the receiving node X.
4. After receiving d from the base station, the receiver reveals the plaintext m by computing $m = V \oplus \text{Hash2}(e(U,d))$.

It is to be noted that $e(U,d) = e(kP,sQ_x) = e(ksP, Q_x) = e(kR, Q_x)$ due to the properties of the bilinear mapping as mentioned earlier. Thus, $\text{Hash2}(e(U,d)) = \text{Hashe2}(e(kR, Q_x))$.

Although IBE solves the PKI problem for sensor networks, the communication with the base station for a sensor node to obtain its private key each time whenever it needs to decrypt a ciphertext is very expensive in terms of energy usage. In addition, the base station becomes a vulnerable point and bottleneck for the entire network. It is, therefore, logical to adopt IBE based public key cryptography for sensor networks only for those situations that symmetric key cryptography cannot provide a satisfactory solution in terms of security and resource usage. For example, IBE based PKC can be used to overcome the shortcomings of key establishment and key distribution using symmetric key cryptography. In the following we summarize a protocol proposed by Oliveira, et. al. (2007) for pairwise key establishment in a sensor network. We assume that each node in the sensor network is deployed with a unique identity string, a private key, and a common function f to derive an IBE public key from a given identity string of any node. Let us consider two nodes X and Y in a sensor network having identities ID_x and ID_y, IBE private keys S_x and S_y, and IBE public keys P_x and P_y respectively where $P_x = f(ID_x)$ and $P_y = f(ID_y)$. In order to establish a pairwise secret key between node X and node Y, the following steps are followed:

1. Node X broadcasts its identity string ID_x and a nonce N_x.
2. Each neighboring node Y upon receiving ID_x and N_x, derives the public key of X as $P_x = f(ID_x)$.
3. Each neighboring node Y generates a secret key K_{xy} to be shared between X and Y for future message transmission.
4. Each neighboring node Y encrypts the combined message K_{xy} appended with ID_y and N_x using node X's public key P_x and sends the ciphertext to node X.
5. Node X decrypts the message sent by Node Y and recovers K_{xy}.

In order to protect from replay attacks, the value of nonce N_x must indicate message freshness. The above protocol allows a sensor node to establish a pairwise secret key with each of its neighbors. Security of the pairwise key during transmission is achieved by using IBE cryptographic techniques as explained earlier. After establishment of secret keys within a group, all private keys of all nodes can be discarded if needed. However, deletion of the private key of a node does not protect its

shared secret keys from an adversary who can capture the node and reveal all shared secret keys. Another notable weakness of the protocol is that the shared secret key K_{xy} is not chosen by X but by a neighbor Y meaning that any adversarial sensor node that have access to the public key of X or the function f can establish a shared secret key with X.

For the purpose of key establishment in a sensor network, recently Oliveira, et. al. (2007) have proposed TinyTate, an implementation of an IBE system based on elliptic curves and Tate pairing. It makes use of TinyECC library since it provides optimized, efficient code modules for ECC operations for popular sensor platforms. For Tate pairing computation, it uses Miller's algorithm with an embedding degree of 2 and a supersingular curve E over F_n: $y^2 = x^3 + x$ where n is 256-bit prime. It has been reported that computing a pairing by TinyTate over MICAz (8-bit, 7.3828-MHz processor, 4KB SRAM, 128KB flash memory) using TinyOS requires 30.21s on average, 1,831 bytes of RAM, and 18,384 bytes of ROM (flash). Although promising, the computation time for Tate pairing presented by Oliveira, et. al. (2007) for wireless sensor networks is significantly high. In order to establish a pairwise secret key between two nodes, it requires computation of Tate pairing twice, one computation by the sender during encryption and another computation by the receiver during decryption. As a result, establishing a secret key between any two pair of nodes would take over a minute (since 30.21s + 31.28s > 1 minute). In an application with thousands of wireless sensor nodes, it will take exorbitant amount of time for a node to establish pairwise keys with a large group of wireless sensor nodes. Hence with current sensor network technology, an IBE based PKC system has limited applications for security in wireless sensor networks.

To assess the performance of public-key cryptographic schemes, TinyPK implements RSA and Diffie-Hellman algorithms on MICA2 platform to exchange secret keys (Watro et al., 2004). While RSA makes the execution time in tens of minutes, Diffie-Hellman shows an obvious speed improvement. However, both code size and execution time are still too expensive for such energy-constrained environment like wireless sensor networks. Among those above asymmetric-key based protocols, Identity-Based Encryption (IBE) and Elliptic Curve Cryptography (ECC) seem to be the most practical public key cryptographic schemes for wireless sensor networks (Law, Doumen, & Hartel, 2006; Oliveira et al., 2007).

Recent IBE Schemes

As mentioned above, the most costly operation involved with IBE is the pairing calculation. More recent implementations have shown that pairings can be calculated more efficiently using the ηT pairing, which is a reduced version of the traditional Tate pairing (Szczechowiak & Collier, 2009; Xiong, Wong, and Deng, 2010). This type of pairing operates on supersingular curves over F_{n^q} just like the original Tate pairing. This type of pairing has the bilinear property as mentioned above, as well as the commutative property, $e(A,B)=e(B,A)$ (Szczechowiak et al., 2009). This property could be used to develop other types of pairing protocols in the future. In addition to the pairing function, a fairly costly hash-to-point function is needed to implement an IBE scheme. This function provides a one way map from a random value or message to a point on the elliptic curve. One method for implementing this function efficiently is discussed below for TinyPairing.

Another drawback of using pairing based cryptography is that it allows the elliptic curve discrete logarithm problem to be transformed into a traditional discrete logarithm problem on the finite field F_{n^q} (Szczechowiak et al., 2009). This makes the IBE scheme more susceptible to a cryptanalysis attack. As a result, the size of elements in F_{n^q} need to be at least 1024 bits to make such attacks infeasible (Szczechowiak & Collier,

2009). Though these elements are large, they are not prohibitive for WSNs since there are no modular operations performed on the elements. Despite the challenges involved with implementing IBE systems, two recent implementations, TinyPairing and TinyIBE, have shown that pairing based cryptosystems are feasible for wireless sensor networks.

TinyPairing

TinyPairing is an implementation of a complete identity based cryptosystem introduced in early 2010 (Xiong, Wong, and Deng, 2010). The goal of this project was to study not only the costs of the pairing function, but to analyze and optimize the costs of other helper functions that are required in an IBE system. TinyPairing comes with a complete IBE library, including support for the traditional Boneh and Franklin IBE scheme as well as two digital signature schemes. TinyPairing uses the ηT pairing on supersingular elliptic curves. Unlike other projects, the curves used for TinyPairing reside in the ternary field $F_{3^{97}}$. Although each element in the ternary finite field require 2 bits for representation, the amount of space needed for storage is still less than that of a binary field of equivalent security level. Using a point compression technique, TinyPairing further reduces the storage requirement of elliptic curve points by about 23% with a minimal computation overhead.

The TinyPairing hash-to-point function is required to convert a random binary number or message into an elliptic curve point on a ternary finite field. To do this, a message digest is first computed using a traditional hash algorithm like SHA. Then, every two bits of the digest is mapped to a digit of an element x in F_{3^m}. If there are not enough bits in the digest, it is rehashed and the process is repeated until there are enough digits generated for x. Finally, the elliptic curve equation is used to calculate the y value corresponding to *x*, thus producing a point on the elliptic curve. In addition to the pairing calculation and the hash-to-point function, TinyPairing includes optimizations for scalar point multiplication which significantly reduces calculation time.

A performance analysis the TinyPairing library was conducted on a standard 8-bit MicaZ sensor node. Table 2 shows the running times of the various IBE functions in the TinyPairing library.

As can be seen from the table, the calculation of the ηT pairing takes 5.32 seconds. With this calculation time, the Boneh and Franklin IBE scheme requires only about 10.6 seconds for encryption and 5.4 seconds for decryption using the TinyPairing library (Xiong, Wong, and Deng, 2010). These results are much better than the previous results of TinyTate by Oliveira et. al. (2007), and further support the feasibility of IBE for sensor networks.

TinyIBE

TinyIBE is another implementation of IBE for wireless sensor networks that was presented in 2009 by Szczechowiak & Collier. The goal of TinyIBE is to provide a scheme for authenticated key distribution in WSNs. This scheme includes algorithms for IBE functions as well as a novel protocol. The TinyIBE protocol is unique in that it focuses on the the use of Heterogeneous Sensor Networks (HSNs). An HSN is a sensor network

that is based on a hierarchy of high power H-nodes and low power L-nodes (Szczechowiak & Collier, 2009). The nodes in this type of network form in to small groups or clusters when they are deployed. The L-nodes have the job of performing sensory functions. These nodes typically consist of Mica class or Tmote Sky motes that have a relatively slow processor and weak radio transmitter. The H-nodes act as cluster heads. These cluster heads have the job of receiving data from the L-nodes and communicating directly with the base station and other cluster heads. H-nodes may consist of Imote2 motes which have a fast processor and a powerful radio transmitter.

The TinyIBE protocol is based on the assumption that L-nodes need only encrypt and transmit data to the H-node cluster heads. The H-nodes on the other hand need to be able to decrypt messages from the L-nodes, as well as encrypt messages for communicating with the base station and other cluster heads. The overall protocol consists of four main functions: setup, extract, encrypt, and decrypt. The setup function is done by the base station before deployment and includes the establishment of curve and encryption parameters. The extract function is also done by the base station before deployment and consists assigning unique IDs and private keys to each sensor node. The encryption function is the only function that is performed by L-nodes, which involves generating a random secret key and encrypting it using the ID of its cluster head. Decryption is performed by the H-nodes and includes checking the identity of the sending L-node and retrieving the private key using its own private key.

Like TinyPairing, TinyIBE uses the ηT pairing as its bilinear paring algorithm. The pairing for this scheme is implemented on supersingular curves over the binary field. The authors Szczechowiak & Collier choose this field $F_{2^{271}}$ based on its security and computational efficiency shown in their previous work (Szczechowiak et al., 2009). The feature of TinyIBE that makes it different

Table 2. Run times of TinyPairing functions (Xiong, Wong, and Deng, 2010)

	Time (sec)
Hash-to-Point (16 bytes msg)	0.89
Point compression	0.38
Point decompression	0.38
Point scalar mult (original)	7.75
Point scalar mult (optimized)	2.50
Point scalar mult (revised)	2.45
ηT pairing	5.32

from other implementations is that the encryption function does not require a pairing calculation. This offers huge advantages since the L-nodes that usually perform encryption have very limited processing power. Although decryption does require a pairing calculation, it is performed by H-nodes which have processors that can better handle the calculations. Overall, this means that only one pairing has to be calculated for each establishment of a shared key. In addition to the savings in pairing operations, the TinyIBE implementation does not require any hash-to-point function, which further reduces the overall calculation time. The authors of TinyIBE evaluated its performance using the AVR Studio and IAR Embedded Workbench simulators. Table 3 shows the time, storage, and energy usage of encryption on L-nodes and decryption on H-nodes:

As can be seen from the table, the performance times of TinyIBE are impressive when compared to the results from TinyTate or even TinyPairing. If these results hold when tested on the actual hardware, this shows that TinyIBE is viable and perhaps ready to be used for authenticated key distribution in working wireless sensor networks.

FUTURE RESEARCH DIRECTIONS

Although research on ECC based IBE systems shows some promising results, it would be still too time-consuming to establish keys among various entities in a large WSN with massive deployment of thousands of sensor nodes. Further research is needed for improvement of ECC based IBE systems for WSNs. To expedite operations of an ECC based IBE system, hardware implementation of ECC coupled with hardware implementation of IBE can be utilized. Integration of such systems to existing sensor network platforms needs to be studied for their feasibility in terms of cost, space, and power requirements.

Detecting of compromised nodes in a sensor network is very challenging. Current solutions to the problem are merely theoretical and excessively burdensome to resource-starved sensor nodes. More realistic research approach is needed to seek an implementable solution to the problem as well as to resolve many issues related to the problem, particularly regarding revocation of compromised nodes after detection.

Replacing aged sensor nodes with new ones in secure authenticated manner is problematic as well. These newly deployed sensor nodes are to be integrated with the existing network without possible security breach or interruption of ongoing service. One possible solution is to deploy a new WSN in the same area of deployment of the old one and then discontinue using the old WSN altogether once the new network is operational. But the solution can be prohibitively expensive and undesirable for certain applications. Future

Table 3. Resource usage of TinyIBE (Szczechowiak & Collier, 2009)

Platform	Encryption			
	Time	ROM	RAM	Energy
MicaZ (7.38MHz)	3.93s	39.6KB	2.9KB	92.67mJ
Tmote (8.19MHz)	2.62s	30.3KB	3.2KB	27.12mJ
Platform	Decryption			
	Time	ROM	RAM	Energy
Imote2 (13MHz)	462ms	32.87KB	4.12KB	12.12mJ
Imote2 (104MHz)	57.7ms	32.87KB	4.12KB	3.76mJ
Imote2 (416MHz)	14.4ms	32.87KB	4.12KB	N/A

research is needed for handling such replenishment of nodes in an existing WSN.

CONCLUSION

Security of wireless sensor networks is important. In this chapter, we report recent, pioneering results from research in the development of security protocols for wireless sensor network platforms. Particularly, we provide comprehensive details of most referenced security protocols and implementations such as SPINS, μTESLA, LEAP, and TinySec and highlight and compare their usefulness, scopes, limitations, and shortcomings. In addition, we also discuss and highlight the current research for implementation of ECC based public key cryptosystems for wireless sensor networks. An ECC based IBE cryptosystem for WSNs seems promising since it does not require any public key infrastructure except the need for a trusted base station. More research is still needed, perhaps in its hardware implementation, since the existing scheme in literature is found to be prohibitively too time-consuming to be used in a real wireless sensor network. Evidently, any drastic progress in research on IBE cryptosystems for wireless sensor networks will make many current security problems easily solvable and will eliminate many existing security obstacles and concerns for wireless sensor networks.

REFERENCES

Akyildiz, I., Su, W., Sankarasubramaniam, Y., & Cayirci, E. (2002, August). A survey on sensor networks. *IEEE Communications Magazine, 40*(8), 102–114. doi:10.1109/MCOM.2002.1024422

Batina, L., Mentens, N., Sakiyama, K., Preneel, B., & Verbauwhede, I. (2006). Low-cost elliptic curve cryptography for wireless sensor networks. *Security and Privacy in Ad-Hoc and Sensor Networks. Springer-Verlag, 4357*, 6-17.

Boneh, D., & Franklin, M. (2003). Identity-based encryption from the weil pairing. *SIAM Journal on Computing, 32*(3), 586–615. doi:10.1137/S0097539701398521

Chan, H., Perrig, A., & Song, D. (2003). Random key predistribution schemes for sensor networks. In *Proceedings of the 2003 IEEE Symposium on Security and Privacy*, 197-213.

Ciet, M., Joye, M., Lauter, K. & Montgomery, P. L. (2006). Trading inversions for multiplications in elliptic curve cryptography. *Journal of Designs, Codes, and Cryptography. Springer-Verlag, 39*, 189-206.

Cilardo, A., Coppolino, L., Mazzocca, N., & Romano, L. (2006). Elliptic curve engineering. *Proceedings of the IEEE, 94*(2), 395–406. doi:10.1109/JPROC.2005.862438

Crossbow Technology, Inc. (n.d.). *Crossbow product information*. Retrieved from http://www.xbow.com/Products/products.htm

Du, W., Deng, J., Han, Y. S., Varshney, P. K., Katz, J., & Khalili, A. (2005). A pairwise key pre-distribution scheme for wireless sensor networks. [TISSEC]. *ACM Transactions on Information and System Security, 8*(2), 228–258. doi:10.1145/1065545.1065548

Eschenauer, L., & Gligor, V. D. (2002, November). A key-management scheme for distributed sensor networks. In *Proceedings of the 9th ACM conference on Computer and communications*, Washington DC.

Galbraith, S. (2005). Pairings. Blake, Seroussi, & Smart (Eds.), *Advances in elliptic curve cryptography,* London Mathematical Society Lecture Notes, chapter IX, 183–213. Cambridge, UK: Cambridge University Press.

Gura, N., Patel, A., & Wander, A. (2004). Comparing elliptic curve cryptography and RSA on 8-bit CPUs. In *Proceedings of the 2004 Workshop on Cryptographic Hardware and Embedded Systems (CHES 2004)*, 119–132.

Hankerson, D., Menezes, A., & Vanstone, S. (2004). *Guide to Elliptic Curve Cryptography.* Berlin-Heidelberg, Germany: Springer-Verlag.

Huang, Q., Cukier, J., Kobayashi, H., Liu, B., & Zhang, J. (2003, September). *Fast Authenticated Key Establishment Protocols for Self-Organizing Sensor Networks.* Paper presented at the Proceedings of the 2nd ACM international conference on Wireless sensor networks and applications, San Diego.

Karl, H., & Willig, A. (2005). *Protocols and Architecture for Wireless Sensor Networks.* New York: John Wiley & Sons. doi:10.1002/0470095121

Karlof, C., Sastry, N., & Wagner, D. (2004, November). TinySec: a link layer security architecture for wireless sensor networks. Paper presented at the *Proceedings of the 2nd international conference on Embedded networked sensor systems,* Baltimore.

Karlof, C., Sastry, N., & Wagner, D. (2004, June). *TinyOS: User Manual.* Retrieved February 10, 2009, from http://www.tinyos.net/tinyos-1.x/doc/tinysec.pdf.

Koblitz, N. (1987). Elliptic curve cryptosystems. *Mathematics of Computation, 48,* 203–209.

Law, Y. W., Doumen, J., & Hartel, P. (2006). Survey and Benchmark of Block Ciphers for Wireless Sensor Networks. [TOSN]. *ACM Transactions on Sensor Networks, 2*(1), 65–93. doi:10.1145/1138127.1138130

Liu, A., & Peng, N. (2008). TinyECC: a configurable library for elliptic curve cryptography in wireless sensor networks. In *Proceedings of the 7th international conference on Information processing in sensor network,* (pp. 245-256).

Liu, D., Ning, P., & Li, R. (2005). Establishing pairwise keys in distributed sensor networks. [TISSEC]. *ACM Transactions on Information and System Security, 8*(1), 41–77. doi:10.1145/1053283.1053287

Luo, P., Wang, X., Feng, J., & Xu, Y. (2008). Low-power hardware implementation of ECC processor suitable for low-cost RFID tags, *Proceedings of the IEEE 9th International Conference on Solid-State and Integrated-Circuit Technology (ICSICT 2008),* 1681-1684.

Malan, D., Welsh, M., & Smith, M. (2004, October). A public-key infrastructure for key distribution in tinyos based on elliptic curve cryptography. Paper presented at *First IEEE International Conference on Sensor and Ad Hoc Communications and Networks (IEEE SECON 2004),* Santa Clara, CA.

Mehallegue, N., Bouridane, A., & Garcia, E. (2008). Efficient path key establishment for wireless sensor networks. *EURASIP Journal on Wireless Communications and Networking, 8*(3), Article No. 3.

Menezes, A., Okamoto, T., & Vanstone, S. (1993). Reducing elliptic curve logarithms to finite field. *IEEE Transactions on Information Theory, 39*(5), 1639–1646. doi:10.1109/18.259647

Miller, V. (1986). Uses of elliptic curves in cryptography, *Advances in Cryptology, CRYPTO '85. Lecture Notes in Computer Science. Springer-Verlag, 218,* 417–426.

NIST. (2003). *Special publication 800-57: Recommendation for key management. Part1: General guidelines.* NIST.

Oliveira, L., Aranha, D., Morais, E., Felipe, D., Lopez, J., & Dahab, R. (2007). TinyTate: Computing the Tate Pairing in Resource-Constrained Sensor Nodes. NCA 2007. In *Proceedings of the Sixth IEEE International Symposium on Network Computing and Applications,* 318 – 323.

Perrig, A., Szewczyk, R., Tygar, J. D., Wen, V., & Culler, D. E. (2002). SPINS: security protocols for sensor networks. *Wireless Networks, 8*(5), 521–534. doi:10.1023/A:1016598314198

Shamir, A. (1984). *Identity-based cryptosystems and signature* (pp. 47–53). Proceedings of Cryptology, Springer-Verlag.

Szczechowiak, P., & Collier, M. (2009). TinyIBE: Identity-Based Encryption for Heterogeneous Sensor Networks. In *5th International Conference on Intelligent Sensors, Sensor Networks and Information Processing*. 319-354.

Szczechowiak, P., Kargl, A., Scott, M., and Collier. (2009). On the Application of Pairing Based Cryptography to Wireless Sensor Networks. In *WiSec '09, Second ACM conference on Wireless Network Security*. 1-12.

Wander, A., Gura, N., Eberle, H., Gupta, V., & Shantz, S. (2005, March). Energy analysis of public-key cryptography for wireless sensor networks. Paper presented at *Third IEEE International Conference on Pervasive Computing and Communication (PerCom 2005)*, Hawaii, USA.

Watro, R., Kong, D., Cuti, S., Gardiner, C., Lynn, C., & Kruus, P. (2004). Tinypk: securing sensor networks with public key technology. *Second ACM Workshop on Security of ad hoc and Sensor Networks (SASN'04)*, 59–64, Washington, DC.

Xiong, X., Wong, D., & Deng, X. (2010). TinyPairing: A Fast and Lightweight Pairing-based Cryptographic Library for Wireless Sensor Networks. In *IEEE Wireless Communications and Networking Conference (WCNC)*. 1-6.

Zhu, S., Setia, S., & Jajodia, S. (2006). LEAP: Efficient security mechanisms for large-scale distributed sensor networks. [TOSN]. *ACM Transactions on Sensor Networks*, 2(4), 500–528. doi:10.1145/1218556.1218559

Chapter 7
Applied Cryptography in Infrastructure–Free Wireless Networks

Lei Zhang
Frostburg State University, USA

Chih-Cheng Chang
Rutgers University, USA

Danfeng Yao
Rutgers University, USA

ABSTRACT

This chapter presents the technical challenges and solutions in securing wireless networks, in particular infrastructure-less wireless networks such as mobile ad hoc networks and wireless sensor networks. Communications in infrastructure-less wireless networks are challenging, as there are no trusted base stations to coordinate the activities of mobile hosts. Applied cryptographic tools, in particular threshold cryptography, play an important role in the trust establishment, message security, and key management in such networks. We describe several technical approaches that integrate applied cryptography techniques into mobile ad hoc networks and wireless sensor networks. We also outline several research directions in these areas.

INTRODUCTION

Wireless networks can be generally categorized into infrastructure-based and infrastructure-less types according to their communication mechanisms. In either type, cryptographic protocols are needed to ensure the security of message flow within the network. The goal of this chapter

DOI: 10.4018/978-1-61520-783-1.ch007

focuses on the technical challenges and solutions in securing advanced infrastructure-less wireless networks, by surveying some of existing research papers that intersect applied cryptography and mobile ad hoc networks or wireless sensor networks.

Let's first briefly introduce basic cryptographic concepts. There are mainly two cryptographic systems, symmetric and asymmetric. Symmetric system is that both the sender and receiver of a message share a single, common key that is used to encrypt and decrypt the message. Symmetric-system is simple and fast, but its main drawback is that the two parties have to exchange the key in a secure way. Public-key encryption is typically asymmetric, which can avoid the problem above. In asymmetric system, the public key can be distributed in a non-secure way, and the private key is never transmitted.

A public key certificate (or identity certificate) is an electronic document which incorporates a digital signature to bind together a public key with an identity — information. The certificate can be used to verify that a public key belongs to an individual. A certificate authority (CA) is an entity which issues digital certificates for use by other parties. The signatures on a certificate are attestations by the certificate signer that the identity information and the public key belong together. We will describe more about these cryptographic concept in the context of wireless networks later.

The IEEE 802.11 is one of the conventional infrastructure-based wireless networks. Its specification identified several services to provide a secure environment. The security services are currently provided largely by the Wi-Fi Protected Access (WPA) protocol to protect link-level data during wireless transmission between clients and access points [45]. The three basic security services defined by IEEE for the wireless local area networks (WLAN) environment are authentication, confidentiality, and integrity. It is worth mentioning that the previous IEEE 802.11 standard, Wired Equivalent Privacy (WEP), has major security vulnerabilities due to the repetitive use of secret one-time keys [45].

A wireless ad hoc network is the most common kind of wireless networks. It is a decentralized wireless network without any predetermined infrastructure. The network is called ad hoc networks, because each node voluntarily forwards data to other nodes. The determination of which nodes forward data is made dynamically based on the network connectivity. In most cases, nodes in

wireless ad hoc networks are mobile. This special kind of ad hoc network is called Mobile Ad Hoc Networks (MANET).

We call MANET infrastructure-less, because unlike traditional wireless networks, MANET does not have base stations to coordinate the activities of mobile hosts. Each node acts as a router to transmit messages from one node to another and also need to perform all other functions involved in any network. Therefore, this causes the network topology to change frequently and dynamically. These networks are useful in military environments or environments where geographical, terrestrial or time constraints make it difficult to have base stations or access points. MANET has many advantages in situations where a network needs to be configured on an ad hoc basis without the support of any fixed infrastructure.

Besides military applications, MANET has also been used in forming vehicular networks [31, 34] or to give One Laptop Per Child users Internet connections. One Laptop Per Child Association (OLPC) is a U.S. Non-profit organization to oversee the creation of an affordable educational device for use in the developing world. OLPC laptops connect to the Internet through a peer-to-peer fashion by forming a MANET. Figure 1 shows the MANET formed by OLPC laptops in a village. The laptops relay messages for each other. All OLPC laptops are connected to the Internet, as they route messages through a computer that connects to a satellite receiver, which serves as a base station. This base station brings the whole village connected [2].

However, traditional security mechanisms cannot be applied to MANET, because of the wireless nature of communication. The lack of any security infrastructures raises several security problems. The mobility nature of MANET also leads to frequent topology change. Security schemes for MANET generally cannot use symmetric mechanisms. The reason is that in ad hoc network, two parties cannot trust each other and

Figure 1. OPLC laptops connecting to the Internet by forming a MANET

exchange their common key in a secure way. In comparison in an asymmetric system, the public keys can be distributed and shared by a group, and the private key is never transmitted.

One of the key issues of asymmetric key management in MANET is how to distribute trust to ensure robustness. Under the dynamic topology, how to distribute a public key with trust is a challenging problem. If a CA is compromised, the attacker can sign any erroneous certificates with the private key. The simple replication of CA can make the network more vulnerable because compromising a single replica can cause the system failure. Hence, it's more prudent to distribute the trust to a set of nodes by letting these nodes share the key management responsibility. The rest of the chapter will describe the applications of advanced cryptographic schemes in security infrastructure-less wireless networks.

A non-cryptographic approach for dealing with MANET security is trust and reputation management [27], where nodes are evaluated based on their previous performance and recommendations by other peers. We will not cover this topic as it is beyond the scope of applied cryptography, but refer readers to existing literature for more details [3, 9, 15, 21, 39].

CRYPTOGRAPHIC TOOLS

Threshold cryptography (TC) [11, 17] is scheme that allows a secret, to be split into shares, such that for a certain threshold $k<n$, any k components could combine and generate a valid signature; whereas, k-1 or fewer shares are unable to do so. Much research has been done to propose the idea of utilizing threshold cryptography to distribute trust and secrets in MANET networks. The challenges associated with key management services such as issuing, revoking and storing of certificates in ad hoc networks can be resolved by distributing Certification Authority (CA) duties among the network nodes.

Threshold cryptography involves the sharing of a key by multiple individuals engaged in encryption or decryption or splitting of message either before or after encryption. The TC avoids trusting and engaging just one individual node for doing the job. Hence, the primary objective is to share this authority in such a way that each individual node performs computation on the message without revealing any secret information about its partial key or the partial message. Another objective is to have distributed architecture in a hostile environment. A certain number of nodes called threshold t, are required to encrypt and/or decrypt a message. Thus threshold cryptography enhances the security and robustness of a scheme.

Threshold cryptography achieves the security needs such as confidentiality and integrity against malicious nodes. It also provides data integrity and availability in a hostile environment and can also employ verification of the correct data sharing. All this is achieved without revealing the secret key. Thus, taking into consideration these characteristics, implementing TC to secure messages seems a perfect solution in both MANETs and general ad-hoc networks.

Shamir's Secret-Sharing Scheme is one of the commonly used threshold cryptographic schemes in wireless security literature [38], which we explain next in order to give readers a concrete example. We refer readers to the literature for more advanced secret sharing and threshold signature schemes [7, 18, 19, 40, 41]. In a *k*-out-of-*n* secret-sharing scheme, the data owner distributes shares, or parts, of the secret to *n* servers in such a way that any *k* of them can cooperate and recover the entire secret, but any smaller group cannot. Secret sharing schemes [38] have been widely used in constructing fault-tolerant key management schemes [29, 42] or password recovery schemes [12].

Shamir's secret-sharing scheme [38] is based on polynomial interpolation. Suppose there are *m* participants, and any *k* of them should be able to recover the secret *S*. Let *q* be a large prime. The distributor chooses a random *(k-1)*- degree polynomial *P* over the field F_q such that $P(0) = S$. That is, he chooses $a_1, \mathbf{K}, a_{k-1}$ independently and uniformly at random from $[0, q - 1]$, and lets $a_0 = S$, where *S* is interpreted as an element of F_q. The corresponding polynomial will be $P = a_{k-1}x^{k-1} + \mathbf{K} + a_1 x + a_0$.

The share for each participant is a distinct point on *P*, but obviously not *P(0)*. If any *k* participants share their knowledge, they collectively will have *k* distinct points on the curve, from which they can determine *P* using polynomial interpolation, and thus recover the secret $S = P(0)$. If only *k - 1* participants cooperate, however, they will be unable to recover the polynomial. Furthermore, each different value of *S* would yield a different polynomial that agrees with their *k - 1* points, so they have gained no knowledge about the secret *S*.

APPLICATIONS OF THRESHOLD CRYPTOGRAPHY IN MANET

In this section, we survey several cryptographic solutions that aim to realize efficient public key authentication, membership control, and key management in infrastructure-free wireless networks, namely MANET that utilize threshold-based

schemes. These topics are very well studied in the past years, and are central questions to securing MANET.

Public Key Authentication in MANET

In a conventional public-key infrastructure (PKI), a centralized Certification Authority (CA) is indispensable for managing public key certificates used to generate confidence in the legitimacy of public keys. However, it is difficult to deploy such a centralized PKI in MANETs for the lack of infrastructure and other centralized services.

A hierarchical distributed public key infrastructure has been proposed [37]. Logically, it is a functional hierarchy of arbitrary level design. In order to setup the proposed PKI, nodes of all levels need to receive different certificates and shares of certification keys. Nodes on the bottom of the hierarchical structure receive no shares. All other nodes receive a share of the certification key that corresponds with their hierarchical level. All nodes receive a bottom layer certificate. This certificate is needed to be able to setup keys that will be used to send data. According to [37], higher level nodes are allowed to request lower layer shares and certificates. All nodes have a copy of all the certification *public* keys. On the top layer, there is a master certification key, whose job is to issue certificates for the public keys of the nodes on layer 1. Next to this, all nodes on layer1 get a share of the layer 1 certification key. Layer 2 nodes receive a certificate signed by level 1 certification key and a share of the level 2 certification key. This process continues until it reaches the desired number of levels in the hierarchy. In this hierarchical design, the distribution of trust uses threshold cryptography. The certification keys are divided into *n* shares. If a node at one level requires a certificate, it contacts *t+1* partial signatures and combine them to compute the signature for the certificate. The scheme in [37] ensures the robustness in different aspects. With these schemes a correct signature is obtained despite a small number of partial signatures being incorrect.

Although the secret-sharing technique can be employed to distribute the CA's role to a pre-selected set of nodes, termed distributed CAs, resource-constrained ad hoc networks might be still unable to afford the rather complicated certificate management, including revocation, storage and distribution, and the computational costs of certificate verification.

To address that issue, an anonymous and certificateless public-key infrastructure (AC-PKI) for ad hoc networks was proposed by [47]. AC-PKI enables public-key services with certificateless public keys and thus avoids the complicated certificate management inevitable in conventional certificate-based solutions. To satisfy the demand for private keys during network operation, a distributed private key generation scheme is designed by utilizing Shamir's (k, n) secret sharing technique to distribute a system master-key among a set of preselected nodes, called Distributed Public Key Generators (D-PKGs). In addition, D-PKGs were offered anonymity protection to defend against pinpoint attacks, which makes AC-PKI more secure than previous applications of the secret-sharing technique in mobile ad hoc networks [47].

Membership and Key Management in MANET

In wireless ad hoc network, frequent updates in group structures make the membership management a challenge. Based on the threshold cryptography, [16] proposes a secure membership control scheme using a new threshold signature. It is a scheme based on which the verifiability is achieved in a simple manner. It controls the joining of a node in the network to give it a share to make it able to anticipate in accepting other nodes. To manage the admission to a secure group, the general membership model is as follows [16]. First, in the initial phase, each group member obtains his secret share and a group membership

certificate (GMC) from an offline-centralized node or by collaborative computation among initial group members. Second, a prospective member initiates the protocol by sending a join request message to the group. If k members or more approve the admission, they cooperatively generate the GMC of the prospective member. Third, if the new member becomes a legitimate member, he acquires his own share which enables him to participate in future admission protocols.

A novel mechanism proposed by [23] allows the creation of a keying service in the network. This service is efficient, robust, and respects constraints and characteristics of ad-hoc networks. It is a novel combination of two cryptographic techniques: ID-based and threshold cryptography. ID-based cryptography primarily provides efficiency gains, and threshold cryptography provides resilience and robustness. The idea of an identity-based cryptography scheme is that an arbitrary string can serve as a public key. The main advantage of this approach is to largely reduce the need for public key certificates and certificate authorities, because a public key is associated with identity information such as a user's email address. A first scheme for identity-based encryption (BF-IBE) was based on the bilinear Diffie-Hellman assumption by Boneh and Franklin [8]. In IBC schemes private key generator (PKG) is responsible for generating private keys for all users, and therefore is a performance bottleneck for organizations with large number of users. Hierarchical identity-based encryption (HIBE) schemes (e.g., [46]) were proposed to alleviate the workload of a root PKG by delegating private key generation and identity authentication to lower-level PKGs.

The main advantage of [23] is the elimination of the need for users to generate their own public keys. The user's identity acts as their public key, because of the use of ID-based cryptography. However, the authors stressed that their scheme does not completely handles the issue of key distribution in ad-hoc networks [23]. For example, malicious members of the network can provide newly-joining members with a false master public key. The problem is partly due to the key escrow nature of ID-based schemes.

By using proactive share refreshing [20], the shared private key of the Threshold Certificate Authority can be redistributed throughout the MANET network [24, 28]. Every trusted node in the network takes part in the Threshold Certificate Authority service. This approach provides a more distributed service and increases availability. [24, 28] employ a key share dealer to create the original key shares used by the Threshold Certificate Authority. Using shared key generation, the formation of the Threshold Certificate Authority can happen 'in the field' without reliance on prior or external security associations like a trusted dealer.

As mentioned by [5], the distributed shared key generation algorithm requires secure communication channels between the participants during the computation. These secure channels can be set up by employing key exchange techniques such as those described in [6]. Thus, the formation of a scalable key management architecture is not contingent on external authentication or keying information. Just as an ad hoc network may be created 'from scratch', or without prior infrastructure, so too, a Public Key Infrastructure can be created 'from scratch' without the reliance on prior security infrastructure.

Due to the lack of infrastructure, it is hard to have fine-grained membership management in wireless ad hoc network. Saxena et al. implemented three membership control mechanisms based on threshold signatures of discrete-logarithm based, namely threshold Digital Signature Scheme (DSA), threshold Schnorr, and threshold Boneh, Lynn, and Shacham (BLS) signature scheme [36]. In addition, they pointed out the existing threshold RSA signature schemes are not applicable for membership control in wireless ad hoc network. We will not cover the above signature schemes as they are beyond the scope of this chapter. Please refer to [36] for more details.

Topology and Performance Considerations in MANET

Threshold cryptography also can be applied to MANET by improving topology assumptions. Improving topology assumptions is an important problem for secure MANET protocols, as restrictive MANET topologies may be hard to be maintained in practice. For instance, protocols for wired networks, that implicitly assume (and often require) that the network graph is fully connected, cannot be directly deployed into MANET as partial connectivity and mobility features may make this assumption very often invalid.

On the other hand, for certain security goals, such as security against Byzantine adversaries [4], certain topology assumptions are necessary to achieve security. Specially, it directly follows from the results in the distributed computing area that threshold cryptography over MANETs cannot be securely implemented for very sparse ad hoc networks regardless of mobility, which indeed only makes things worse. [10] proposed the idea of designing threshold cryptography protocols in MANET that minimize the topology assumption under which their security can be proved. [10] adapts known techniques such as variable-IP-binding signature schemes, and designs a novel signature collection algorithm. The new threshold signature scheme is secure under significantly improved topology assumptions.

When threshold cryptography is used, it is important to know the value of the threshold. A very high threshold level ensures greater security, but the QoS requirement may not be satisfied. If the threshold level is lowered, it becomes easy for a node to construct its digital certificate within the QoS requirements or specified authentication delay time, but the security aspect may be compromised. The threshold level selection process is influenced by various network factors, such as network density, node moving speed, transmission range, and threshold requirements. [30] modeled the threshold level as an optimization problem for a certain QoS requirement.

One drawback for secret sharing schemes is that they add overhead to routing and increases traffic in the network. Furthermore, attacks such as wormhole and Denial of Service (DoS) can compromise routes through spoofing ARP or IP packets, passively or actively. Due to bandwidth constraints and energy conservation, an efficient implementation of the scheme is critical. Previous work proposed various flooding mechanisms, such as multicasting and to reduce the reply storm. However, simply reducing reply keep entities may result in security issues such as DoS attacks targeting a specific group of nodes. Also, neither threshold schemes nor the routing protocol can prevent DoS attacks from compromising the route to destination authority node. If we fail to access destination authority node, the service request would still fail even after the certificate request succeeds. [4] addressed several advanced Byzantine attacks and proposed survivable routing protocol.

CHALLENGES AND SOLUTIONS IN SECURING WIRELESS SENSOR NETWORKS

Wireless sensor networks (WSN) can be viewed as a special type of MANET where computation resources are limited and thus crytographic operations needs to be efficient. In this section, we survey the existing applied cryptographic solutions developed for wireless sensor networks.

A wireless sensor network is a wireless network consisting of spatially distributed autonomous devices using sensors to cooperatively monitor physical or environmental conditions [1]. As pointed out by Perrig et al., the wireless sensor network has limited computation and power resources, traditional key management protocols are not feasible to it [32]. For instance, it may be expensive to apply public key cryptographic primitives to wireless sensor network, due to system overhead reason. [13] also pointed out RSA-based Threshold Certificate using key shar-

ing is unsuitable in resource constrained MANET because it requires much of computational capacity, bandwidth, power, and storage. They suggested that Elliptic Curve Cryptography can be a very effective to MANET.

Elliptic Curve Cryptography (ECC) can achieve the same level of security with much smaller key length than RSA [25]. This performance advantage makes ECC more suitable for wireless senor networks. Liu and Ning have designed and implemented a configurable library for ECC in wireless sensor networks [26]. This library provides typical operations for ECC-based public-key cryptography with flexible configurations based on the developers' needs. The configurations can be used to further improve the performance for some of the ECC operations or when dealing with large integer operations. Other work has shown Paring Based Cryptography (PBC), the related but more complex primitives that utilizes ECC, is also suitable for wireless sensor networks [43].

Apart from ECC-based public-key cryptography, access control is also very important in wireless sensor networks. Access control is used in wireless sensor networks to give users permission to access the network and data collected by the sensors. Since a wireless sensor network is typically shared by a number of users, access restriction has to be enforced to preserve privacy. Wang et al. provide an ECC-based access control framework for sensor networks [44]. This framework has a key distribution center, which manages the network, generates all security primitives (i.e. random number, hash function, elliptic curve operations), and maintains the access privilege for every user. Since the information stored at each sensor node has multiple access levels, the user with a lower access privilege cannot get the information with higher privilege.

It is worth mentioning that recent research discovers that software-only cryptography is indeed practical with today's sensor technology; hardware support is not needed to achieve acceptable security and performance levels. Karlof et al.

fully implemented link layer security architecture for wireless sensor networks [22], which explores the tradeoffs among different cryptographic primitives and uses the inherent sensor network limitations to the advantage when choosing parameters to achieve an optimal spot for security, packet overhead, and resource requirements.

In wireless sensor network, hundreds or thousands of sensor nodes usually work coordinately to achieve a common goal in either entirely distributed fashion or cluster-based fashion. So the key management techniques need to consider the scalability issue, in addition to the infrastructure-free challenge as in MANET. We refer readers to a good survey article [32] and references therein (e.g. [14, 33, 48]) for details about existing key management solutions in wireless sensor networks.

CONCLUSION

In this chapter, we have described the application of threshold cryptographic techniques in securing wireless networks, including MANET and wireless sensor networks. Without any trust infrastructure, a security solution typically requires the existence of certain number of trusted and honest nodes in the network, which makes threshold cryptographic schemes particular suitable and attractive in this environments.

In the future, we expect to see more research on faster public key cryptography, and more advanced solutions for key-establishment and distribution for large-scale wireless sensor networks. In addition, sensor networks interact closely with the physical environments and people, creating more privacy problems. For example, researchers found that sensors on sneakers may cause serious privacy concerns [35]. Efficient and usable ideas are needed, in particular solutions that are power-conservative and non-intrusive to users. In addition, from a cryptography research perspective, there is much work remaining to be done on the formal security model for ad-hoc networks, and on provably-secure solutions in this model.

REFERENCES

Adams, W. J. Hadjichristofi, G. C., & Davis, N. J. (2005). Calculating a Node's Reputation in a Mobile Ad-Hoc Network. In *Proceedings of the 24th IEEE International Performance Computing and Communications Conference* (IPCCC ZOOS), Phoenix, AZ.

Awerbuch, B., Curtmola, R., Holmer, D., Nita-Rotaru, C., & Rubens, H. (2005, September). On the Survivability of Routing Protocols in Ad Hoc Wireless Networks. In *Proceedings of the IEEE Conference on Security and Privacy for Emerging Areas in Communication Networks* (SecureComm).

Balfanz, D., Smetters, D. K., Stewart, P., & Wong, H. (2002, February). Talking to strangers: Authentication in ad-hoc wireless Networks. In *Proceedings of the NDSS '02*, San Diego, California.

Boneh, D., & Franklin, M. (1997). Efficient generation of shared rsa keys. In *Proceedings of CRYPTO*.

Boneh, D., & Franklin, M. K. (2001). Identity-based encryption from the Weil pairing. In *Advances in Cryptology — Crypto '01*. In *LNCS* (*Vol. 2139*, pp. 213–229). Berlin, Germany: Springer-Verlag.

Buchegger, S., & Boudec, J. (2004, June). A robust reputation system for P2P and mobile ad-hoc networks. In *Proc. Second Workshop the Economics of Peer-to-Peer Systems*, Cambridge, MA.

Crescenzo, G., Ge, R., & Arce, G. R. (2005, November 7). Improved Topology Assumptions for Threshold Cryptography in Mobile Ad Hoc Networks. In *Proceedings of SASN'05*. Alexandria, VA.

Desmedt, Y., & Frankel, Y. (2000, February). Threshold cryptosystems. *Advances in Cryptology – Crypto '89, LNCS vol. 435,* Berlin, Germany: Springer-Verlag.

Ellison, C., Hall, C., Milbert, R., & Schneier, B. (2000, February). Protecting secret keys with personal entropy. *Journal of Future Generation Computer Systems, 16*(4), 311–318. doi:10.1016/S0167-739X(99)00055-2

Ertaul, L., & Chavan, N. (2005). Wireless Networks. *In Proceedings. The third International Conference on Wireless Networks, Communications, and Mobile Computing June 13-16, 2005,* (MobiWac) 2005, Maui, Hawaii.

Eschenauer, L., & Gligor, V. (2002). A key-management scheme for distributed sensor networks. In *Proceedings of the 9th ACM Conference on Computer and Communication Security* (Washington, D.C., Nov.). New York: ACM Press.

Eschenauer, L., Gligor, V., & Baras, J. (2002, April). On trust establishment in mobile ad-hoc networks. In *Proceedings of the Security Protocols Workshop.*

Feng, Y., Liu, Z., & Li, J. (n.d.). Securing Membership Control in Mobile Ad Hoc Networks. In *Proceedings of the 9th International Conference on Information Technology* (ICIT'06), (pp. 160-163).

Gemmel, P. (1997). An introduction to threshold cryptography. In *Proceedings of CryptoBytes, Winter 1997,* 7–12.

Gennaro, R., Jarecki, S., Krawczyk, H., & Rabin, T. (1996). Robust and efficient sharing of RSA functions. In *Proceedings of CRYPTO.*

Gennaro, R., Jarecki, S., Krawczyk, H., & Rabin, T. (1996). Robust threshold DSS signatures. In *Proceedings of EUROCRYPT.*

Herzberg, A., Jarecki, S., Krawczyk, H., & Yung, M. (1995). How to cope with perpetual leakage. In *Proceedings of Crypto'95, LNCS 963* (pp. 339–352). Proactive Secret Sharing or.

Hu, J., & Burmester, M. (2006). LARS: a locally aware reputation system for mobile ad hoc networks. In Ronaldo Menezes, editor, *ACM Southeast Regional Conference,* (pp119–123).

Karlof, C., Sastry, N., & Wagner, D. (2004, November 3-5). TinySec: A Link Layer Security Architecture for Wireless Sensor Networks. In *Proceedings of the 2nd international conference on Embedded networked sensor systems* (SenSys '04), Baltimore.

Khalili, A. Katz, J., & Arbaugh, W. (2003). Toward Secure Key Distribution in Truly Ad-Hoc Networks. In *Proceedings of the 2003 Symposium on Applications and the Internet Workshops* (SAINT-w'03).

Kong, J., Zerfos, P., Luo, H., Lu, S., & Zhang, L. (2001). Providing robust and ubiquitous security support for mobile ad-hoc networks. In *Proceedings of the IEEE ICNP.*

Lauter, K. (2004, February). The advantages of elliptic curve cryptography for wireless security. *Wireless Communications, IEEE, 11*(1), 62–67. doi:10.1109/MWC.2004.1269719

Lehane, B. Doyle, L., & O'Mahony, D. (2003). Shared RSA key generation in an mobile ad hoc network. In *Proceedings of MilCom.* Boston: IEEE.

Liu, A., & Ning, P. (2008, April 22-24). TinyECC: A Configurable Library for Elliptic Curve Cryptography in Wireless Sensor Networks. In *Proceedings of the 7th international conference on Information processing in sensor networks.* (pp.245-256).

Liu, J., & Issarny, V. (2004, March). Enhanced Reputation Mechanism for Mobile Ad Hoc Networks. In *Proceedings of the Second International Conference on Trust Management* (iTrust'2004).

Luo, H., & Lu, S. (2000, October). Ubiquitous and Robust Authentication Services for Ad Hoc Wireless Networks (Technical Report). UCLA-CSD-TR-200030.

Miner More, S., Malkin, M., Staddon, J., & Balfanz, D. (2003, October). Sliding window self-healing key distribution. In *Proceedings of the 2003 ACM workshop on Survivable and self-regenerative systems: in association with 10th ACM Conference on Computer and Communications Security*, (pp. 82–90).

Muppala, P., Thomas, J., & Abraham, A. (n.d.). QoS-Based Authentication Scheme for Ad Hoc Wireless Networks. In *Proceedings of the International Conference on Information Technology: Coding and Computing* (ITCC'05), (pp. 709-714).

OLPC. (n.d.). *SES offers OLPC Global Satellite Bandwidth*. Retrieved from http://www.olpcnews.com/internet/access/ses_offers_olpc_glob_1.html

Pathak, V., Yao, D., & Iftode, L. (2008, September 22-24). Securing Geographic Routing in Mobile Ad-hoc Networks. In *Proceedings of the International Conference on Vehicular Electronics and Safety* (ICVES). Columbus, OH.

Perrig, A., Stankovic, J., & Wagner, D. (2004). Security in wireless sensor networks. *Communications of the ACM, 47*(6), 53–57. doi:10.1145/990680.990707

Perrig, A., Szewczyk, R., Wen, V., Culler, D., & Tygar, J. (2002, September). SPINS: Security protocols for sensor networks. *J. Wireless Nets., 8*(5), 521–534. doi:10.1023/A:1016598314198

Rhee, K., Park, Y., & Tsudik, G. (2004, June). An Architecture for Key Management in Hierarchical Mobile Ad-Hoc Networks. *Journal of Communications and Networks, 6*(2).

Saponas, T. S., Lester, J., Hartung, C., & Kohno, T. (2006, December). *Devices That Tell On You: The Nike+iPod Sport Kit*. (Technical Report). University of Washington

Saxena, N., Tsudik, G., & Yi, J. H. (2007). Threshold Cryptography in P2P and MANETs: the Case of Access Control. *Computer Networks, 51*, 3632–3649. doi:10.1016/j.comnet.2007.03.001

Seys, S., & Preneel, B. (2003). Authenticated and Efficient Key Management for Wireless Ad Hoc Networks. In *Proceedings of the 24th Symposium on Information Theory in the Benelux, Werkgemeenschap voor Informatie - en Communicatietheorie, 2003*, (pp. 195-202).

Shamir, A. (1979, November). How to share a secret. *Communications of the ACM, 22*(11), 612–613. doi:10.1145/359168.359176

Shin, K., Kim, Y., & Kim, Y. (n.d.). An Effective Authentication Scheme in Mobile Ad Hoc Network. Seventh ACIS International Conference on Software Engineering, Artificial Intelligence, Networking, and Parallel/Distributed Computing (SNPD'06), (pp. 249-252).

Shoup, V. (2000. Practical threshold signatures. In *Proceedings of EUROCRYPT*.

Srinivasan, A., Teitelbaum, J., Liang, H., Wu, J., & Cardei, M. (2006). Reputation and Trust based System for Ad Hoc and Sensor Networks. In Boukerche, A. (Ed.), *Algorithms and Protocols for Wireless Ad Hoc and Sensor Networks*. New York: Wiley & Sons.

Staddon, J., Miner, S., Franklin, M., Balfanz, D., Malkin, M., & Dean, D. (2002, May). Self-healing key distribution with revocation. In *Proceedings of the 2002 IEEE Symposium on Security and Privacy*.

Szczechowiak, P., Kargl, A., Scott, M., & Collier, M. (2009, March). On the Application of Pairing Based Cryptography to Wireless Sensor Networks. In *Proceedings of the second ACM conference on Wireless network security.*

Wang, H., Sheng, B., & Li, Q. (2006). Elliptic Curve Cryptography Based Access Control in Sensor Networks. *International Journal of Security and Networks, 1(¾)*127-137.

Wi-Fi Alliance. (2003, April). *Wi-Fi Protected Access: Strong, standards-based, interoperable security for today's Wi-Fi networks.* Austin, TX: Wi-Fi Alliance.

WSN. (n.d.). *Wireless Sensor Network.* Retrieved from http://en.wikipedia.org/wiki/Wireless_Sensor_Networks.

Yao, D., Fazio, N., Dodis, Y., & Lysyanskaya, A. (n.d.). ID-Based Encryption for Complex Hierarchies with Applications to Forward Security and Broadcast Encryption. In *Proceeding of the ACM Conference on Computer and Communications Security* (CCS '04). (pp. 354–363). Washington DC: ACM Press.

Zhang, Y., Liu, W., Lou, W., Fang, Y., & Kwon, Y. (2005, May.). ACPKI: Anonymous and certificateless public-key infrastructure for mobile ad hoc networks. In *Prcoceedings of the ICC 2005 - IEEE International Conference on Communications, no. 1* (pp. 3515– 3519).

Zhou, L., & Haas, Z. J. (1999). (n.d.). Securing ad hoc networks. *IEEE. Network Magazine, 13*(6), 24–30. doi:10.1109/65.806983

Section 4
Cryptography in Electronic Commerce

Chapter 8
Applied Cryptography in Electronic Commerce

Sławomir Grzonkowski
National University of Ireland, Ireland

Brian D. Ensor
National University of Ireland, Ireland

Bill McDaniel
National University of Ireland, Ireland

ABSTRACT

Electronic commerce has grown into a vital segment of the economy of many nations. It is a global phenomenon providing markets and commercialization opportunities world-wide with a significantly reduced barrier to entry as compared to global marketing in the 20th century. Providing protocols to secure such commerce is critical and continues to be an area for both scientific and engineering study. Falsification, fraud, identity theft, and disinformation campaigns or other attacks could damage the credibility and value of electronic commerce if left unchecked. Consequently, cryptographic methods have emerged to combat any such efforts, be they the occasional random attempt at theft or highly organized criminal or political activities. This chapter covers the use of cryptographic methods and emerging standards in this area to provide the necessary protection. That protection, as is common for web-based protocols, evolves over time to deal with more and more sophisticated attacks. At the same time, the provision of security in a manner convenient enough to not deter electronic commerce has driven research efforts to find easier to use and simpler protocols to implement even as the strength of the cryptographic methods has increased. This chapter covers current standards, looking at several facets of the secure commercialization problem from authentication to intrusion detection and identity and reputation management. Vulnerabilities are discussed as well as capabilities.

DOI: 10.4018/978-1-61520-783-1.ch008

INTRODUCTION

Commerce is defined as the exchange between parties of goods and services, typically for money. While the exchange of items or services is seen in some non-human species, mating gifts or chimpanzees exchanging grooming with each other for example, the practice of commerce on a significant scale, and in the manner we understand it today, is an intrinsically human phenomenon.

Ecommerce, at its most basic, is simply commerce as usual but transacted using electronic communication methods such as telephone or internet. Primarily, however, ecommerce is coming to be understood as the transaction of business across the internet or 3G cell networks.

Ecommerce brings challenges with it that are unique in the history of commerce. The physical presence of the two parties or of an intermediary, in traditional commerce has always added a degree of security and trust in commercial activities. The use of physical currency demonstrated the ability to pay and the exchange of currency or promissory notes demonstrated the willingness to complete the transaction. While transactions could occur anonymously and untraceably, there was still a component of verification that a transaction was desired.

Ecommerce, on the other hand, is conducted remotely, without the physical presence of the parties and largely anonymously. Mediated electronically, the transaction converted into nothing more than a stream of bits, ecommerce transactions are, in the initial aspect, completely without security or trust. The necessity of other forms of trust became immediately obvious.

Security and trust in economic transactions falls into the areas of verification and authentication. Verification of the transaction and authentication of the parties is vital to the ecommerce model. However, anonymity is still a desirable trait in many transactions and authentication processes need to take this into account.

Identity theft was a cumbersome and manual process for many years, but the advent of electronic records, communications, and commerce has made identity theft far easier and far more prevalent. Governments were unprepared for the possibilities of widespread internet-based identity theft. The notion of a single, widely available, number used to identify an individual was hopelessly susceptible to attack. The ability of computing systems to correlate and mine seemingly disparate and unconnected information was demonstrated and highlights the problem of security in the near panopticon of the internet's vast databases of personal information.

An aspect of ecommerce that is not as prevalent in traditional transactions is the ability to hijack the transaction. It is far more possible for eavesdroppers to access, copy, redirect, and subvert legitimate transactions and the intents of the parties in electronically mediated transactions.

Consequently, an emerging science and industry have grown up around these security and authentication holes. New methods of encrypting transactions, of authenticating participants, and of protecting the identities of participants have been created and distributed. New understandings of the ethics and consequences of anonymous transactions have been elucidated. New discussions of the rights of privacy and of government and private enterprise scrutiny of individuals and their lives have become commonplace.

Without trustable, verifiable, and simple security processes built into the workflow of ecommerce, the current explosion of commerce onto the web could not have happened. As we move from wired connections to the web, however, new techniques and workflows are needed to ensure that wireless ecommerce transactions, which are easier to intercept and perhaps suborn, are secure and protected.

Without reliable security models which expand over time to meet the attempts to break in and subvert them, ecommerce transactions cannot continue to grow in value and convenience. In addition, user privacy and intellectual property must also be protected during these transactions.

In the remainder of this chapter, we shall examine new frontiers of security and privacy protection on the web.

BACKGROUND

We begin our presentation describing authentication solutions for the web. We specifically focus on SSL/TSL (Dierks & Allen 1999, Rescola 2000) protocols that are widely used for ecommerce. Then, we briefly introduce the most notable Password-based Authentication Key Exchange (PAKE) solutions (Bellovin & Merritt 1992, Jablon 1996, Wu 2000) that aims at secure communication using short and memorable passwords.

We continue our presentation through the main vulnerabilities of authentication protocols. We do not describe replay, interleaving, reflection, forced delay and chosen text attacks since they were well-explained by Menezes et al. (1996) as the main threats for authentication protocols. We, however, demonstrate Man-In-The-Middle (MITM), which is often considered as the main threat for web-generic authentication solutions (Berners-Lee et al. 1996; Franks et al. 1999; Fielding et al. 1999).

We also present a number of weaknesses of PAKE protocols. Their main security threats are the possibilities of dictionary attacks (Florencio & Herley 2007) and lack of resistance to a server compromise. We also describe phishing (Agarwal et al. 2007) that is a specifically password-authentication-related problem.

Then, we lead our presentation to identity management (Madsen, Koga, & Takahashi, 2005), a concept that the scope of the previous section to authorization, trust, and reputation in distributed environments. Identity management is also a crucial part of successful Digital Rights Management solutions that we also recall in our presentation. Identity management doesn't purely rely

on cryptography; as we demonstrate successful implementations also require social components for providing trusted and reputable environments (Kruk et al. 2006). In our presentation we specifically focus on forms of digital identities. We also describe a typical infrastructure composed of identity and service providers.

In section 5 we describe Digital Rights Management (DRM) solutions. We focus on two key technologies: Trusted Computing (Erickson 2003) and Digital Watermarking (Memon and Wong 1998). The former technology has been developed since the last decade. The origins of the latter idea, dates to the late 1970s.

Then, we present iTunes, DRM technology designed by Apple. Since DRM caused many controversial situations, we not only describe how iTunes works, but we also discuss its approach to the fair use doctrine (Felten 2003, Erickson 2003).

Finally, we conclude the chapter and present future research directions in ecommerce security.

AUTHENTICATION ON THE WEB

Logins and passwords are the most common way of authenticating users on the Internet. Therefore, everyday users are asked about their logins and the corresponding passwords. Then, the login and the password are sent directly to servers and the servers respond to the requests. Although this approach is widely applied, it does not ensure any security. If security is needed, the HTTPS protocol is applied.

In this section, we explain how SSL and other solutions work. We present the main threats for online authentication. Then, we introduce password-based protocols that are less popular, although passwords are the most used current way of authentication. Password-based protocols have specific vulnerabilities that we also discuss. We also describe generic protocols design vulnerabilities such as man it the middle and dictionary attacks. Menzes et al. (1996) presented more discussion on this matter focusing on interleaving, reflection, forced delay and chosen text attacks.

SSL/TSL

The Secure Socket Layer (SSL) protocol was created by Netscape to encourage sales on the Internet. The protocol ensured secure transactions between web servers and web browsers.

Such a solution was necessary since solutions offered by HTTP (Berners-Lee et al. 1996, Franks et al. 1999) were prone to sniffing and man-in-the-middle attacks. SSL can be also used for FTP and POP, IMAP, etc. SSL provides authentication of both the client and server through the use of digital certificates and digitally signed challenges. SSL version 1.0 was never publicly released. Version 2.0 appeared in 1994 and was implemented in Netscape Navigator. Due to its security flaws, version 3.0 was released shortly after in 1995. Although SSL 3.0 is considered a valuable contribution, it still has some drawbacks classified as active attacks: change cipher spec-dropping, KeyExchangeAlgorithm-spoofing, and version roll-back (Wagner & Schneier 1996).

In 1996 the Internet Engineering Task Force Transport Layer Security established a working group to create an open stream encryption standard based on SSL. The group published RFC 2246 (Dierks & Allen 1999) in 1999 that defines "TLS Protocol Version 1.0"; and then RFC 2818 (Rescorla 2000) to adjust TLS to HTTP/1.1.

SSL/TSL is located in between the raw TCP/IP and the application layer. To transfer data, SSL/TSL uses TCP. A symmetric key used for encryption is negotiated during the handshake phase at the beginning of the TCP session (*see Figure 1*). The negotiations start with a client's Client Hello message that contains information about the version of the protocol, session id and supported algorithms. Then, the server responds with a Server Hello message, which contains a session number and information about supported algorithms. As a result of this phase, both parties determine the strongest cryptographic protocols they share in common. In the next phase, the server sends its certificate to perform authentication. Then, the client checks three conditions:

1. Did a well-known and trusted Certificate Authority (CA) sign the certificate?
2. Is the certificate still valid?
3. Is the name on the certificate coherent with the domain name of the server?

If at least one of the conditions is not satisfied, the user's browser displays a warning message and the user is asked if the communication should proceed. If the communication is continued, the server can start a similar process to verify the client's identity. Then, both sides generate a master key. This key is used to create session keys, which can be used for encryption, decryption or data integrity checking. In the end, the server and the client inform each other that the initial process has been successfully finished and the data transmission can be started.

After the FINISHED message, the user generates a symmetric key that is encrypted with the server's public key. Therefore, it can be only decrypted using the server's private key, and thus only the server is able to decrypt the symmetric key.

Figure 1. SSL session example

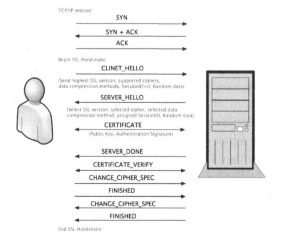

Even if SSL is used, the credentials are still sent through the Internet and servers are able to read them. This is possible although the password is stored in a hashed and salted form. This privacy problem caused the research and development of other solutions.

PAKE Protocols

Password-Authenticated Key Exchange (PAKE) is a family of protocols that affords a reasonable level of security using short memorized passwords for protecting information over insecure channels. Such protocols are also a topic of IEEE P1363[1] standard working group.

Encrypted Key Exchange

In Encrypted Key Exchange (EKE) (Bellovin and Merritt 1992), introduced in 1992, two parties share a secret that is used to obtain a session key. The protocol combines both asymmetric and symmetric cryptography findings. The protocol offers several versions. In the most secure setting, it uses the Diffie-Hellman protocol to establish a shared key. It aims at providing security against man-in-the-middle and other impersonation attacks. Then, the authentication stage is executed. The most valuable property of EKE is that the protocol is resistant against an attacker who records the session and attempts to perform a dictionary attack.

Simplified Password-Authenticated Exponential Key Exchange

EKE was followed by other propositions. Jablon (Jablon 1996) developed simplified Password-authenticated Exponential Key Exchange (SPEKE) protocol for commercial purposes.

In comparison with EKE the main difference was that the password was used to influence the selection of the generator parameter in the session-key generation function.

Zhang (Zhang 2004) showed, however, that an adversary is able to test multiple password candidates using a single impersonation attempt. Whereas in the EKE protocol, an adversary is able to gain information about at most one possible password in each impersonation attempt.

Secure Remote Password

Secure Remote Password (SRP) (Wu 1998, Wu 2000) was developed in 1997. Security of this protocol is dependent on the strength of the applied one-way hash function. The protocol was revised several times, and is currently at revision six. SRP is often applied to telnet and ftp. The protocol is more computationally intensive than EKE. It requires two modulo exponentiations, whereas EKE requires only one. Moreover, the protocol is vulnerable to offline dictionary attacks, if adversary posses session messages.

Social Vulnerabilities of Authentication Protocols

Phishing is a social problem related to authentication. The first problem descriptions date to late 1980s, but its first large-scale successful attempts were noted a decade later. Phishing is an attempt to masquerade a trustworthy entity to obtain customers' credentials, such as usernames, passwords, credit card numbers, etc.

Figure 2 shows an example of how Bank Of Ireland customers were attacked in September 2006. Users were massively sent emails from a hacker acting as a financial institution. This phisihng attack was performed using link manipulation. The aim of the email was to convince them to click on the given link and enter their credentials. Such a link exploits the possibility of displaying information different than the one the link points to. In the given example, the HTML code redirects the user to a website not hosted by the bank:

```
<a href="http://somehacker.
xyz/db/365online.ie/update.
htm">http://www.365online.
ie/secure/update/ssl.cfm</a>
```

Although the user is displayed a link with a website hosted by the bank, the link points to the hacker's site. The hacker hopes that inattentive users will enter their credentials; and thus; they financial details will be compromised. Recent reports (Frost and Sullivan 2008) demonstrate that surprisingly many users become victims of such attacks.

A number of solutions were proposed to stop this problem. However, only a few of them have practical applicability. Public key encryption solves the problem partially. Installing a certificate to a web browser does not exclude phishing possibilities.

Most of the applied anti-phisihing solutions rely on introducing additional elements at the Human-Computer Interaction (HCI) protocol stage. Two most popular of them: Bank of America's SiteKey and Yahoo!'s sign-in seal (Agarwal et al. 2007) display user specific images at the user authentication page. The user must be familiar with such images, such as when the user uploads them during the registration procedure, then, the server displays one of those images at the authentication procedure to prove its identity. This way a mutual authentication is achieved.

Efforts similar to that of Bank of America and Yahoo! in protecting the user from going to fraudulent sites, there are efforts to help the user to better protect their credentials by providing alternative means of authentication such as Multiple Graphic Passwords (Everitt, Bragin, Fogarty & Kohno, 2009). In this type of system a user is presented with multiple graphics in a series and requested to select the correct one (graphic known to them). Their selections are similar to typing in a password, but the objective is to provide the user with an easy means to authenticate while making it difficult for them to divulge it to others easily. An additional benefit is that using this type of password on touch screen phones can make accessing authenticated sites easier. This in turn encourages developers to use user based authentication for its benefits; something that is usually forgone for device based authentication due to ease of implementation and consumer use.

Design Vulnerabilities of Authentication Protocols

The other important group of problems is related to the way the protocols are designed. In this section, we present the most common examples.

Man in the Middle

If an attacker is able to observe and intercept messages exchanged between two potential victims,

Figure 2. A Phishing email example. The boxes display HTML source code of the links

185

the attacker can also easily read, modify and insert content at will. This situation is especially dangerous, if the messages are passed between two parties without either part knowing that the link between them has been compromised. The attack can even work if encryption is used. Nowadays, several solutions to the Man in the Middle attacks have been proposed. They, however, make the communication establishment slightly more complex due to the need of extra steps.

Figure 3 demonstrates a scenario that combines the man-in-the middle-attack with DNS spoofing (changing data records at the DNS server). *Alice* is going to connect with *Bob*, who is for instance her internet bank provider (www.bank. bob.com). In the beginning (step 1) *Carol*, who is the attacker, replaces *Alice's* DNS table. In the DNS table each entry points to a corresponding IP address. In this example www.bank.bob.com points to: *192.168.0.9* and this IP address belongs to *Bob*. If Carol is able to replace this address with one that is under her control (for example *192.168.0.99*), all *Alice's* connections to www. bank.bob.com will be routed through *Carol*.

To establish a connection with *Bob*, *Alice* sends her public key and asks for his (step 2). However, because of the successful DNS attack, *Carol* can modify the address of the sender to get the response from the bank. Then, she modifies it with another for which she has the corresponding private key (step 3). *Carol* forwards the modified request

to *Bob* (step 4) who sends back his own public key, but instead of sending it to *Alice* (step 5) the key is sent directly to the attacker (step 6). *Carol* replaces the *Bob's* key with a key for which she knows the corresponding private key. Then, she sends it to Alice (step 7).

Now, Bob and Alice are convinced that the communication is secure, but in fact it is routed through Carol, who possesses the corresponding private keys. Therefore she is able to read and modify the communication at will.

Dictionary Attacks

Recent research conducted by (Florencio & Herley 2007) has indicated that the users use plenty of passwords every day, but the passwords are low quality and tend to be re-used and forgotten. It has been demonstrated that an attacker equipped with a dictionary of possible users' passwords is able to perform a very efficient attack by checking all the password candidates. There are two kinds of dictionary attacks:

* Off-line attack in which the attacker records a session and then attempts to check the passwords candidates off-line. The difficulty of this attack is that the attacker has to know the hash of the password and also the algorithm used to compute the hash

Figure 3. An example man-in-the-middle attack

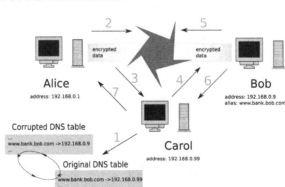

- In on-line attack, the attacker tries to log in using the victims username and password candidates. Usually, the number of unsuccessful login attempts is limited. In most cases, using CAPTCHA (Pinkas & Sander 2002) can stop or significantly slow down this attack.

If users tend to choose low entropy passwords (Narayanan & Shmatikov 2005; Oechslin 2003), dictionary attacks are very effective and were topics of many studies (Gong et al. 1993; MacKenzie et al. 2002). Possible defenses against off-line dictionary attacks are further demonstrated by Halevi and Krawczyk (Halevi & Krawczyk 1999).

Server Compromise

To secure passwords in case of a server compromise, it is necessary to not store them in their plaintext form. Therefore, servers store cryptographic hashes of passwords, computed using functions such as SHA1 or MD5. To introduce additional protection, the protocols designers introduced Salts. A salt is usually a short string that is added as a prefix of the string on which the hash is computed. This way two different users who choose the same passwords, have two different hash values stored in the server database. This small improvement protects from an attacker who poses a dictionary of the all possible password candidates and pre-computed corresponding hashes. Because of the salt, the attacker has to pre-compute the hashes for each user impersonation attempt. Such a protection method is applied in unix-based systems.

In case of password-based solutions, Gentry et al. (Gentry et al. 2006) elaborated on making password-based key exchange resilient to server compromise. Another threat for plain-text stored password is that users tend to reuse the same login-passwords pairs at many services. Thus, a malicious admin would be able to steal their identities.

Replay Attack

Data transferred on the Internet is routed through many peers. It poses a possibility of *replay attack*: a malicious peer is able to read information and is further able to masquerade as the message sender in the service that is the addressee of the message, even if the data was encrypted.

Additionally, Denning-Sacco (Denning and Sacco 1981) demonstrated that the attacker, who intercepts the session, can attempt to compromise the session key and then use it for replay attacks and decrypting the new sessions. Therefore, timestamping services were introduced in many existing protocols.

IDENTITY MANAGEMENT

In this section we introduce identity management (Madsen, Koga, & Takahashi, 2005), a concept that broadens the scope of the previous section to authorization, trust, and reputation in distributed environments. Identity management is a crucial part of successful Digital Rights Management solutions that we demonstrate in the next section. Identity management does not purely rely on cryptography; as we present it also requires social components for providing trusted and reputable environments (Kruk et al. 2006). In our presentation we specifically focus on forms of digital identities. We also describe a typical infrastructure composed of identity and service providers.

Who am I in a digital world? What defines me and what meaning does that have in electronic transactions? Identity management (IdM) is the complete lifecycle of a digital identity from creation to destruction; typically used within a framework that supports the definition (and modifications) of an identity and facilitates the tracking of the identities activities throughout the complete lifecycle. There are different implementations that focus on corporate or closed environments to facilitate defined protections and audit capabilities while others provide for open and public use where such protections are limited, but still of interest. Federated Identity Management (FIM) systems provide a framework by which these digital identities and related information can be used to extend beyond traditional security domains and facilitate identity mobility within those frameworks between participating entities.

While advancements in FIM systems incorporate standards for empowering the owner of the information to choose what to share, there are continued research efforts to help better define these interfaces and interactions. IdM systems are also evolving to provide new methods for individuals to manage their digital identities and their explicit use in digital transactions. The extension of these technologies into ecommerce allows individuals to utilize different identities under their control for different transactions.

Identity management systems are currently being developed by various organizations with standards that are in competition, but the service they are trying to provide is the same. Efforts to establish standards in (FIM) are being led by organizations such as OASIS, Liberty Alliance, Internet2 and Microsoft/IBM/BEA/RSA Security/Verisign with standardization efforts such as SAML, ID-FF, Shibboleth, and WS-Federation. Each recognizes the importance of both developing cohesive policy frameworks and corporate agreements as well as the interoperability of standardization efforts to ensure acceptance. One of the areas of significant growth is the evolution and integration of FIM systems into corporate and ecommerce systems to facilitate rapid automated data exchange and secure transactions with assurances on the credentials of the second party.

Forms of Digital Identities

An entity's identity is made up of a subset of Identifiers related in a common context. This identity may not have any relevance elsewhere as it is context and identifier specific. For example,

how you are known socially (name, nickname, interests, and friends) may not be the same as how you are known in a business transaction (name, education, job title, and employer). Although in both of these situations you are the same person, your identity is different in each (see Figure 4). The identifiers being your name, employer, job title, education, nickname, interests, and friends are all independently non-specific about you, but their correlation in a given context expresses meaning about your identity. Depending on the service accessed, an entity's identity may require various identifiers to establish the necessary level of trust about your identity to provide the service. The key in protecting an entity's identity is to limit the amount of identifiers provided to the smallest number necessary to perform a given task. Being identified at each entry point or when accessing a service is necessary to determine what you are permitted to do, but this requirement may contribute to the unnecessary addition of personal data collection.

Each unique identity can be represented digitally in a number of ways depending on the technology in use and the services being accessed. Based on the anonymity level desired in the transaction, the digital identity can be provided in the form of usernames, smart cards, digital certificates, one-time passwords, digital tokens, public keys, and others. Outside of isolated services, where the digital identity exists only within the service being provided, the digital identity alone is limited without the role of both service providers and identity providers in allowing services to be accessed based on valid and trusted digital identities.

FIDIS (Future of Identity in the Information Society) research demonstrates that there exists a growing requirement for personally managed privacy in an identity centric environment such as an Information Society: "Identity in such environment plays a central role and more and more tools are required to manage identity and deliver suitable services [...] The identity management

Figure 4. Digital Identities & Pseudonyms

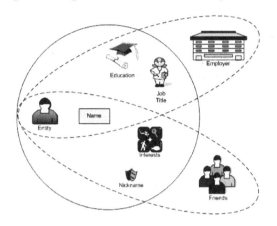

tools will have to respect the user's privacy and security, and they will also have to facilitate the application of laws." (WP2-FIDIS, 2006). The initial solution offerings being developed are mostly relationship focused solutions that rely in an Identity Provider to handle the assertions. Examples of this are Microsoft's Passport (now LiveID), OpenID, and Facebook as well as many others. While there are many benefits associated to using these services, such as the ability to use these services without a client, there are potential risks associated to a provider that participates in all transactions enabling their ability to track and analyze personal activities. Other research and development initiatives work to address credential focused solutions where the credentials are either self-issued or provided by a trusted partner such as is done in secure digital certificate signing. Providers such as SIXIP and Microsoft Live Labs provide such credentials. These systems are more client dependent and help to provide more control to the user, but they still come with their risks as these long-term credentials are susceptible to theft and identity linking.

Identity Providers and Service Providers

While there is potential for risk to be introduced, such as identity theft due to the multitude of connections to various data sources, it has been shown that the proper implementation and use of technologies and standards (Madsen, Koga, & Takahashi, 2005) can result in lower risk. The typical systems involved are the Service Provider (SP) also known as the Relying Party the Identity Provider (IdP) issues trusted identity assertions and the user. Within FIM, it is typical for the personally identifiable information to be stored with the IdP on behalf of the user, but this also may require the user to keep track of multiple IdPs and information released to each. The identity of a user with each IdP is made up of a subset of their complete identity information and are typically related in the context of use for that particular identity; also referred to as pseudonyms (see Figure 5). While each independent identity may not have relevance external to a given context, there is risk when the data release can be aggregated to provide potential opportunity for re-identification. Part of the risk is to know how much is too much information and which identity is the most appropriate to use in the current context.

The collection of data about an entity exists in many locations around the world and is usually done in relation to a service. Governments, health organizations, credit card companies, local stores, online retailers, and many other points of collection exist for private information where they operate in a SP role. In many instances, pieces of data are only important to each independent organization possessing it, but collectively, this information can be correlated to reveal more about an entity than desired. The protection of this data is only one part of the task; prevention of unauthorized use is the other. The ownership and control of the data must reside with the entity to which it represents in order to protect against abuse. Figure 5 shows a simple view of a typical IdP and SP scenario.

One of the solutions provided to address personal identity management is Microsoft Windows CardSpace; a secure store for digital identities on the Microsoft Windows platform (native to Vista and part of a .NET update to XP) which facilitates

Figure 5. Example Personal Identity Management Scenario

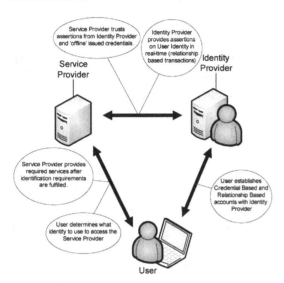

identity selection for use in electronic transactions. Microsoft has published their vision for their Identity Metasystem based on WS-* technologies, although their work aims to support competing standards in future revisions. This will be essential if the personal identity management application is to gain significant growth on this platform as not all services providers will be part of the initial Microsoft Identity Metasystem. The application provides the user with the ability to have multiple identity cards (various pseudonyms) with either personally issued credentials or certified credentials from an IdP. These cards can then be used to access SP sites that support the card technology. While encryption of the transactions is incorporated into the solution and users have control over what identities that the SP will see, there are no current mechanisms to assist enforcing privacy protections such as anonymity, unlinkability, and transaction history. These are only a few of the more critical requirements for delivering a Personal Identity Manager (PIdM).

A PIdM is targeted at resolving the self-management of personal digital identities by individuals of varied technical capabilities. This

challenge comes as the solution needs to deliver effective protections for both the user's identity and privacy. Research on user centric design and privacy protections is incorporated into the building blocks of the design to provide users with informed control over their digital identities (Council, 2002; Hansen, et al., 2004; Hoffmann, 2004; Mont, Pearson, & Bramhall, 2003). With this challenge also arrives significant risk as the information being collected on identities and transactions is stored with the user and now places the responsibility on the user to ensure their critical information is secure. The requirement to store 'History and Context-Based Identity Management' is defined in the design model for a PIdM from the PRIME project (Camenisch, et al., 2005; PRIME-WP14.2, 2007) which is the type of data that would have significant impact on any system component that uses this data to take or recommend particular actions should it be compromised.

Centralized and De-Centralized Identity Management

In a centralized IdM system a singular IdP is used for all services (relationship-focused). Single-signon IdPs such as LiveID and OpenID provide such a role, but when users are accessing each service with the same credentials this limits the capability of users to choose how their identities are seen in each independent service. De-centralized IdM solutions would be more typical in existing isolated services where the user credentials are specific to the service and do not extend beyond their security borders. This approach provides for service specific identities, but introduces other problems with managing a large number of identities and the potential for user to re-use some of their identity attributes (user ids and passwords) across multiple systems increasing their risk of compromise.

Identity management is implemented through various methods to accomplish defined requirements driven by the systems in use and the framework they operate upon. Depending on the purpose of the network, different methods of handling identity can include isolated, federated (FIM), centralized, and personal identity and authentication management systems. Each of these implementations has characteristics which are beneficial in certain contexts, but may present significant challenges in others. One of the key points made in a review of these various models is that "personal identity management is a user centric approach that can be combined with any of the described identity management models, and thereby improve the user experience in those models" (Jøsang, Fabre, Hay, Dalziel, & Pope, 2005). A combination of methods is also necessary at times to provide for flexibility and integration of user centric controlled participation in social and commercial systems.

As a starting point in understanding what user centricity is and its potential benefits and risks, (Bhargav-Spantzel, Camenisch, Gross, & Sommer, 2006) provide a taxonomy for user centricity in FIM and provide insight into potential areas of research in related topics moving forward. The taxonomy focuses on two current systems, credential-focused and relationship-focused, while giving a view towards the evolution of a universal system. While the term universal may insight potential feelings of euphoria, they do highlight the potential pitfalls to such a system if not properly developed for its use -- "a user centric identity management system needs to support user control and consider [user centric] architectural and usability aspects". The relationship-focused system by contrast provides for short term credentials or transaction based identities requiring interaction between the IdP and SP. In either system, or in a universal system, there is a reliance on trust, in conjunction with reputation, in the identities provided and that of the IdP issuing such credentials.

Trust and Reputation

Trust and reputation in commercial transactions are valuable attributes that can adversely impact the relationship should either be viewed negatively. Ecommerce transactions have similar requirements but establishing trust and reputation can be much more complex. In an environment where trust and reputation are compiled into a risk engine for recommendations on entering into an agreement or completing a transaction, the loss of reputation can directly correspond to the loss of revenue. Trust is prevalent in all forms of interactions and has impact on how individuals choose to interact. In many cases there can be a form of blind trust with a SP; for example, if an individual does not have advanced technical or legal knowledge, they may assume interacting with an online store would yield the same protections that they would get from going to a physical store, but this may not truly reflect the circumstances as the online store may be in a location operating under a different set of legislation. Unless the individual is aware of this and informed on how to enforce protections, they are at risk.

In some instances, there are reasons why a customer would wish to remain anonymous, such as having a friend walk into a physical book store to purchase a book with cash in order to remain anonymous which can be supported by selectively provisioning pseudonymity while maintaining accountability (Candebat, Dunne, & Gray, 2005; Seigneur & Jensen, 2004; Taniguchi, Chida, Shionoiri, & Kanai, 2005). The ability to provide such services can increase the trust level in the pseudonymous identity being provided and potentially enhance the service offerings in a personalized way by ensuring non-repudiation and accountability to the SP as an assurance level. The balance between protecting the customer choice to anonymity and ensuring accountability for the SP is necessary for further maturity of ecommerce (Köpsell, Wendolsky, & Federrath, 2006). IdM is an enabling technology for online transactions helping to protect both customer and SP, but the threats associated to such transactions require further research and development to address technical limitations. Until these development become integrated into ecommerce systems, consumer caution and awareness are the best tools to ensure safe computing.

DIGITAL RIGHTS MANAGEMENT

This section briefly introduces the recent advances in Digital Rights Management. Successful DRM implementations take the advantage of the authentication algorithms and identity management solutions presented in the previous sections. In this section we focus on two key technologies: Trusted Computing (Erickson 2003) and Digital Watermarking (Memon and Wong 1998). The former technology has been developed since the last decade. The origins of the latter idea, dates to the late 1970s.

Digital Rights Management (DRM) systems have been in existence since the early 1990s; their initial aim was to control the distribution of consumer media by protecting the content. Since 1998, the controversial Digital Millennium Copyright Act (DMCA) supports all such systems. The act is important for the USA where the creation or distribution of DRM circumvention tools is banned. The same law was also applied in the European Union as European Union Copyright Directive (EUCD). Together with those directives, consumers lost some of their physical world privileges including fair use and first sale.

Fair use (Felten 2003, Erickson 2003) policy permits the legal owners to share the products they bought with their acquaintance; it is based on the assumptions that the owners pass an original product and they cannot use it at the same time. In the digital world, we can hardly apply those assumptions since they are based on a physical availability of an item. Furthermore, digital content

providers want to have control over the distribution of their products.

In various countries, the fair use doctrine may be slightly different and/or have another name, for example copyright exceptions, personal use or fair dealing. For instance, in the USA to determine if a use is fair, a four-factor test must be applied. The test consists of the following questions.

1. The purpose and character of the use, including whether such use is of a commercial nature or is for nonprofit educational purposes;
2. The nature of the copyrighted work;
3. The amount and substantiality of the portion used in relation to the copyrighted work as a whole; and
4. The effect of the use upon the potential market for, or value of, the copyrighted work.

None of these questions is a decision problem; for example, to evaluate question 4, we need to involve human expertise to measure the effect on the market. Furthermore, all of the questions belong to the class of non-algorithmic problems and thus we cannot answer the test questions by means of computers without highly sophisticated intelligence (Felten 2003). Only those policies that can be narrowed to yes/no decision can be automated successfully.

Although there are several approaches to fair use in the virtual world, existing DRM systems do not support fair use at all or provide limited solutions. Both scientists and customers demand more consumer-friendly approach to the problem (Samuelson 2003), claiming that the current restrictive solutions anachronistic and unrealistic.

Trusted Computing

The aim of Trusted Computing Platforms (TCP) is to prevent the use of unlicensed software. The concept of license enforcement was not taken under consideration when the first PC architectures were proposed. Hence, the operating systems are fundamentally not equipped with license enforcement means.

Because access control on customers' computer cannot be solved purely by cryptography, this goal is difficult to achieve in open architectures. This situation changes due to the recent trusted computing initiatives, but it also poses a problem for all the legacy systems that were designed using different principles.

Microsoft Next Generation Secure Computing Base (NGSCB) formerly known as Palladium and Trusted Computing Group (TCG) specification was proposed to address this issue in both software and hardware way. To take the advantage of this technology, the developers would have to rewrite their applications.

Trusted Computing Platform Alliance (TCPA) founded in 1999 by Microsoft, IBM, HP, Compaq, Intel provided a forum for platform vendors. Nowadays, the forum gathers more than 170 companies who aim to produce a Trusted Platform Module (TPM), a tamper resistant chip that is supposed to be included in all future motherboards. The chip supports reporting and measurement of the state of the played digital media. It also provides a number of cryptographic primitives including SHA-1, hashing, encryption, decryption, singing, random number generation, RSA and also private key management.

Because DRM requires users' identities to work effectively, TCP received a lot of criticism regarding user's privacy. Moreover, trusted computations imply security against the owner, and thus the users would not have privileged (root) access to their own computers. Therefore, to make TCP successful still both technical and legislative efforts are still needed.

Digital Watermarking as an Alternative Solution

Memon and Wong (Memon and Wong 1998) defined a digital watermark as a signal added to digital data (audio, video, or still images) that can be detected or extracted later to make an assertion about the data. Digital watermarks do not prevent content from being viewed or played. Preferably, there should be no difference between the original and the watermarked signal.

The Digital Millennium Copyright Act (DMCA) states that any attempts to circumvent any technological measure are illegal, including digital watermarking. This law enforcement effectively protects intellectual properties of digital content owners and producers.

The first group of research papers describing digital watermarking dates to the late 1970s. However, the interest in this technology dramatically grew in the early 1990s due to the need of copyright protection means. Digital watermarks and information embedding systems have been found useful in a number of applications (Podilchuk & Delp 2001):

- Ownership assertion. A digital watermark inserted to a file can be extracted only by the file creator
- Fingerprinting. Distinct information can be inserted to each copy of disseminated content to trace sources of unauthorized duplications
- Authentication and integrity verification. A watermark can be inserted to ensure that sensitive information is not changed
- Usage control. Digital licenses or access rights can be represented by an embedded watermark
- Content protection. Visible watermarks are often inserted to indicate that the obtained content is released with a purpose of preview or demo
- Content labeling. An inserted watermark could give further information about the file, e.g. copyright notice

Digital watermarks are often classified from the perspective of resistance to media manipulation. We distinguish fragile and robust algorithms.

The robust algorithms require that a watermark can be extracted even if the media file containing the watermark was modified, including signal degradation or transformation. When using fragile techniques, watermarks are prone to be lost or damaged as a result of any modifications in the media file.

The watermarking algorithms are content dependent. Algorithms designed for various media formats have completely different design principles, e.g. images, audio and video. For example, watermarks for word documents are usually embedded in specific formatting or layout. When applying watermarks for web-pages, algorithms can be based on mixing upper and lower case characters in the HTML tags.

iTUNES

In this section we present a practical example of how cryptography is used in ecommerce. We present how iTunes works. It is a commercial Digital Rights Management solution developed by Apple for the storage, categorization, and playback of digital media. While early versions of the software focused on music, the ability to manage and play podcasts, television shows and movies, music videos, video games and other plug-in applications, and PDF files (limited function) have been added to its portfolio.

iTunes also has been also popular in supporting mobile access to managed digital media by offering support for both proprietary and non-Apple portable media devices. Some criticism over their DRM enabled digital media, and loss of revenue to competitors, has prompted Apple to recently adjust their strategy with customers and suppliers while remaining competitive in the market.

How it Works

iTunes is a computer based application officially installable on both Macintosh and Windows plat-

forms. In additional to the desktop application being used for playback, Apple developed players (iPod the most popular example) and authorized 3rd party compatible players provide support on other operating systems and handheld devices. iTunes currently supports a number of audio and video formats, including Apple Lossless, AAC audio, WAV, MP3, AIFF, MPEG-4 (including H.264), and MOV. WMA is also supported on Windows, but either has to be converted from WMA or have a specific codec installed; this only applies to unprotected (non-DRM) WMA files. Other conversions can be done, such as MOV files, to allow playback on portable media (iPhone and iPod) devices that require a different format.

iTunes creates and maintains a library of digital media using two files in ITL an XML format as a database to categorise information about the digital media in the library including: artist, genre, comments, ratings, play count, last played date, playlists used by the user, track numbers, location of file, and other media specific details. The ITL file (binary) is used by iTunes for its functionality while the XML file is used by other software that needs the information for operation, such as iPhoto and iDVD. These files are either imported into the iTunes library from existing digital media on the local system or downloaded from portable media and online sources.

The iTunes Store, promoted by Apple as part of their iTunes package, offers downloadable content for free, or at cost, depending on the content. The iTunes Store provides the download of various content (music, videos, applications, audio books, etc), but requires the iTunes application to function. Media can also be streamed from the iTunes Store, but requires the iTunes Music Store streaming protocol (itms) to view. The iTunes application will support others such as MP3 and Quicktime streams. The iTunes application can then be used to stream out content from the digital library to other devices on the local network using its Digital Audio Access Protocol (DAAP) over the Bonjour (previously Rendezvous) network service discovery protocol. Apple had previously included streaming outside of the local network, but this was change in later releases of iTunes. For DRM protected content FairPlay is used and authentication required whether accessing the file locally or through streaming.

Other features have slowly been added to iTunes to provide a more personalized experience, such as using the Genius feature. This is a recommender feature that offers lists of similar songs in the user's library and on iTunes that are similar to the currently selected song, but requires information to be shared with the iTunes Store to build intelligence and accuracy. Personalization in social networking is also targeted through Apple-Script (or iTunes SDK) to allow information about activity in iTunes, such as what is currently being played, to be shared with social networking and instant messaging services and through creating iMix lists on the iTunes Store allowing shared experiences and preferences.

iTunes Approach to Fair Use

Apple approaches fair use by working to integrate capabilities within its FairPlay DRM solution, DAAP enabled streaming, and proprietary player products. An example of this include the ability to stream protected AAC files (requiring authentication), but prevent the storage of that stream on the remote system allowing users to share the music to their preferred device, but limits portability. iTunes also permits the copying of files to an unlimited number of computers or to one of their own devices, but only five connections are permitted simultaneously and the devices must be authorized and running Apple's software. When using one of Apple's devices, such as the iPod, portability is not an issue since it can be stored and played on that device without limit, but these approaches have received significant criticism from competitors claiming Apple's engaging in antitrust activities (Gasser, et al., 2004; Oppenheimer, 2009). Other attempts to address fair use,

which has received similar criticism, includes the permitting of copying music to CDs and DVDs, but these are permitted only with the iTunes Plus Music where DRM is already removed or on special DVDs supporting the iTunes Digital Copy.

The FairPlay DRM uses an MP4 container to hold a protected AAC file with most algorithms applied in the encryption scheme being public (AES, MPEG-4) with the exception of the users key database component (Grzonkowski, et al., 2007), another area of concern since the proprietary protection of FairPlay prevents interoperability. The user key is what is used to decrypt the file and permit playing. The authorisation of a device uses a unique user key in combination with a device identifier to ensure play restrictions are complied with. In synchronizations with Apple devices, such as the iPod, the required keys are copied to enable unlimited distribution to Apple devices. Following a call from Steve Jobs for the music industry to address the requirement for DRM (Jobs, 2007), Apple has just recently announced at the 2009 Macworld Conference & Expo its plan to remove DRM from its iTunes Store (Apple, 2009) by offering all music as iTunes Plus music.

What are the Problems?

While the recent news that Apple will remove DRM from its music, there are still a number of issues to consider. First, for all those who have currently purchased the FairPlay DRM protected versions, they will need to pay per song (or % cost of album) to upgrade their music to a non-DRM iTunes Plus version. While the conversion for the iTunes Store is due to be completed by April 2009, FairPlay will still be used on video as well as the use of Digital Copy (compatible with FairPlay and Windows Media DRM) for DVDs that allow electronic copies.

Apple incorporates FairPlay, built on Quick-Time technology, to enforce constraints on its distributed media. The iPod and iTunes are used to play these files as trusted devices. FairPlay digitally encrypts the open standard AAC file format to produce a media file that prevents unauthorized use and restricts access to personal devices, nominated computers, and CD burning (note that customers do not retain first sale right). The technology used relies on authenticated device relationships to establish rights of use and does not extend to the individual by authentication. This approach severely limits the capability to share among friends, although efforts to crack the hardware restrictions (such as work by Veridisc) have help users to access their protected files on non-authenticated devices.

While FairPlay remains proprietary and the DRM enforcements prevent complete translation of fair use, debate over Apple's willingness to "Play Fair" will continue. Some of the issues to be addressed are interoperability of DRM solutions, support of portability, choice in content provider, support for true archives of owned data, and support for resale and loan (Kim, Howard, Ravindranath, & Park, 2008; Sobel, 2007). The reason for addressing these is that DRM still has a place in protecting intellectual property, but more work is required to digitally model law and better meet user requirements for permitted uses of owned content through better policies and technological interoperability.

Additionally, there is a growing demand to integrate developed Rights Expression Languages (REL), of which many successful DRM developments and implementations contain in some form, with the evolution of identity based rights (Koster, Kamperman, Lenoir & Vrielink, 2006). REL has been developed under competing standards, public and proprietary, with some adopted into commercial DRM solutions. These most notably include Extensible Rights Markup Language (XrML) based on work by ContentGuard (formerly a Xerox technology) and Open Digital Rights Languages (ODRL). XrML version 1.2 was adopted by Microsoft and incorporated into the Windows Rights Management Services and version 2.0 adopted by Moving Picture Experts Group (MPEG) and finalized into and ISO standard (ISO MPEG REL) as part of the MPEG-21 framework on standards for digital media. ODRL was adopted by the Open Mobie Alliance (OMA) to develop OMA REL as part of their DRM v2. The extensibility of these languages allows for the integration of both domain and individual based rights assignment providing an opportunity to integrate with the growing use of IdM infrastructures on the Internet. These languages also support rights expressions that can be enforced based on domain or individual identity allowing for more flexibility in modeling legislation, supporting fair use.

FUTURE TRENDS AND THREATS IN ELECTRONIC COMMERCE

New technologies tend to deliver new means for making online transactions more friendly and convenient. This tendency resulted in creating less restrictive DRM solutions. For instance, less restrictive sharing policies have been introduced in iTunes in the past few years. There is also research on taking into account users' social networks when accessing DRM-protected content (Grzonkowski and McDaniel 2008).

Convenience often causes security problems. The efforts of making the authentication process easier resulted in OpenID[2]. The main objective of OpenID was to provide a Single Sign-On feature for web pages. Therefore, it provided decentralized user identification in a way that users are allowed to use the same logins at many websites. The protocol does not specify the authentication method such as passwords, digital certificates, tokens, etc.

The future of the protocol and its applicability to ecommerce is, however, unsure due to its security and privacy issues such as phishing (Adida 2007).

CONCLUSION

In this chapter we presented technologies that are crucial for performing secure ecommerce. Firstly, we introduced the basic principles of secure authentication. Our presentation included SSL/TSL protocols (Dierks & Allen 1999, Rescola 2000) as well as password-based solutions (Bellovin & Merritt 1992, Jablon 1996, Wu 2000). We also presented vulnerabilities of authentication protocols (Menezes et al. 1996) focusing on the web-related issues (Berners-Lee et al. 1996; Franks et al. 1999; Fielding et al. 1999).

The next part of the chapter extended the initial scope to identity management (Madsen, Koga, & Takahashi, 2005), which covers not only authentication, but also trust, reputation and authorization (Kruk et al. 2006).

Then, we explained the main concepts of Digital Rights Management. We presented both technical and legislative problems (Felten 2003, Erickson 2003). Finally, we described iTunes an applied cryptography solution for ecommerce, which combines all the presented components.

ACKNOWLEDGMENT

The work presented in this paper was supported (in part) by the Lion project supported by Science Foundation Ireland under Grant No. RSF0844 and Enterprise Ireland under Grant No. REI 1005.

REFERENCES

Adida, B. (2007). BeamAuth: two-factor web authentication with a bookmark. In *CCS '07: Proceedings of the 14th ACM conference on Computer and communications security*, pages 48–57, New York: ACM.

Agarwal, N., Renfro, S., & Bejar, A. (2007, May). *Current Anti-Phishing Solutions and Yahoo's Sign-in Seal*. Paper presented at W2SP: Workshop on Web 2.0 Security and Privacy 2007 held in conjunction with the 2007 IEEE Symposium on Security and Privacy.

Apple (2009). *Changes Coming to the iTunes Store*, Retrieved from http://www.apple.com/pr/library/2009/01/06itunes.html

Bellovin, S. M., & Merritt, M. (1992). Encrypted Key Exchange: Password-Based Protocols SecureAgainst Dictionary Attacks. Paper presented at SP'92: In *Proceedings of the 1992 IEEE Symposium on Security and Privacy, page 72,* Washington, DC: IEEE Computer Society.

Berners-Lee, T., Fielding, R., & Frystyk. H. (1996). Hypertext Transfer Protocol. *HTTP/1.0.*

Bhargav-Spantzel, A., Camenisch, J., Gross, T., & Sommer, D. (2006). *User centricity: a taxonomy and open issues*. Paper presented at the Proceedings of the second ACM workshop on Digital identity management.

Camenisch, J., Shelat, A., Sommer, D., Hübner, S. F., Hansen, M., Krasemann, H., et al. (2005). *Privacy and Identity Management for Everyone**. Paper presented at the 2005 Workshop on Digital Identity Management, Fairfax, VA.

Candebat, T., Dunne, C. R., & Gray, D. T. (2005). *Pseudonym management using mediated identity-based cryptography*. Paper presented at the Proceedings of the 2005 workshop on Digital identity management.

Council, T. N. E. C. C. (2002). *Identity Management*. Paper presented at the NECCC Annual Conference. Retrieved December 15, 2007, from http://www.ec3.org/Downloads/2002/id_management.pdf

Denning, D., E., & Sacco, G., M. (1981). Timestamps in key distribution protocols. *Communications of the ACM, 24*(8), 533–536. doi:10.1145/358722.358740

Dierks, T. & Allen, C. (1999). *The TLS Protocol Version 1.0.*

Erickson, J. S. (2003). Fair use, DRM, and trusted computing. *Communications of the ACM, 46*(4), 34–39. doi:10.1145/641205.641228

Everitt, K. M., Bragin, T., Fogarty, J., & Kohno, T. (2009). *A comprehensive study of frequency, interference, and training of multiple graphical passwords*. Paper presented at the Proceedings of the 27th international conference on Human factors in computing systems.

Felten, E., W. (2003). A skeptical view of DRM and fair use. *Communications of the ACM, 46*(4), 56–59. doi:10.1145/641205.641232

Florencio, D., & Herley, C. (2007). *A large-scale study of web password habits*. Paper presented at WWW'07: Proceedings of the 16th international conference on World Wide Web, pages 657-666, New York: ACM Press

Franks, J., Hallam-Baker, P., Hostetler, J., Lawrence, S., Leach, P., Luotonen, A. & Stewart. L. (1999). *HTTP Authentication: Basic and Digest Access Authentication.*

Gasser, U., Bambauer, D., Harlow, J., Hoffmann, C., Hwang, R., Krog, G., et al. (2004). iTunes: *How Copyright, Contract, and Technology Shape the Business of Digital Media – A Case Study. Digital Media Project*, from http://cyber.law.harvard.edu/media/uploads/53/GreenPaperiTunes03.04.pdf

Gentry, C., & MacKenzie, P. D., & Ramzan, Z. (2006). A Method for Making Password-Based Key Exchange Resilient to Server Compromise. Paper presented at CRYPTO2006.

Gong, L., Lomas, M. A., Needham, R. M., & Saltzer, J. H. (1993). Protecting Poorly Chosen Secrets from Guessing Attacks. *IEEE Journal on Selected Areas in Communications, 11*(5).

Grzonkowski, S., Ensor, B., Kruk, S. R., Gzella, A., Decker, S., & McDaniel, B. (2007). *A DRM Solution Based on Social Networks and Enabling the Idea of Fair Use*. Paper presented at the Media in Transition: creativity, ownership and collaboration in the digital age (MiT5).

Grzonkowski, S., & McDaniel, B. *FRM: Towards a Semantic Platform for Fair Content Distribution*. Paper presented at AXMEDIS'08: Proceedings of the Fourth International Conference on Automated Production of Cross Media Content for Multi-Channel Distribution. IEEE Computer Society, November 2008.

Halevi, S., & Krawczyk, H. (1999). Public-Key Cryptography and Password Protocols. *ACM Transactions on Information and System Security, 2*(3).

Hansen, M., Berlich, P., Camenisch, J., Clauß, S., Pfitzmann, A., & Waidner, M. (2004). Privacy-enhancing identity management. *Information Security Technical Report, 9*(1), 35–44. doi:10.1016/S1363-4127(04)00014-7

Hoffmann, M. (2004). *User-centric Identity Management in Open Mobile Environments*. Paper presented at the Workshop on Security and Privacy in Pervasive Computing, Vienna, Austria.

Jablon, D., P. (1996). Strong Password-only Authenticated Key Exchange. *SIGCOMM Comput. Commun. Rev., 26*(5), 5-26.

Jobs, S. (2007). *Thoughts on Music*. Retrieved from http://www.apple.com/hotnews/thoughtsonmusic/

Jøsang, A., Fabre, J., Hay, B., Dalziel, J., & Pope, S. (2005). *Trust requirements in identity management.* Paper presented at the Proceedings of the 2005 Australasian workshop on Grid computing and e-research - Volume 44.

Kim, Y., Howard, J., Ravindranath, S., & Park, J. S. (2008). *Problem Analyses and Recommendations in DRM Security Policies Intelligence and Security Informatics* (*Vol. 5376*, pp. 165–178). Berlin, Germany: Springer.

Köpsell, S., Wendolsky, R., & Federrath, H. (2006). *Revocable Anonymity.* Paper presented at the Emerging Trends in Information and Communication Security; ETRICS 2006, Freiburg, Germany.

Koster, P., Kamperman, F., Lenoir, P., & Vrielink, K. (2006). Identity-Based DRM: Personal Entertainment Domain. *Transactions on Data Hiding and Multimedia Security*, *I*, 104–122. doi:10.1007/11926214_4

Kruk, S. R., Grzonkowski, S., Gzella, A., Woroniecki, T., & Choi, H. C. (2006, September). *D-FOAF: Distributed Identity Management with Access Rights Delegation.* Paper presented at the procedings of Asian Semantic Web Conference 2006.

Madsen, P., Koga, Y., & Takahashi, K. (2005). *Federated identity management for protecting users from ID theft.* Paper presented at the Proceedings of the 2005 workshop on Digital identity management.

Memon, N., & Wong, P., W. (1998). Protecting digital media content. *Communications of the ACM, 41*(7), 35–43. doi:10.1145/278476.278485

Menezes, A. J., Vanstone, S. A., & Van Oorschot, P. C. (1996). *Handbook of applied cryptography.* Boca Raton, FL: CRC Press.

Mont, M. C., Pearson, S., & Bramhall, P. (2003). *Towards Accountable Management of Identity and Privacy: Sticky Policies and Enforceable Tracing Services.*

Narayanan, S., & Shmatikov, V. (2005). Fast dictionary attacks on passwords using time-space tradeoff. Paper presented at CCS05. In *Proceedings of the 12th ACM conference on Computer and communications security, 2005.*

Oechslin, P. (2003). Making a Faster Cryptanalytic Time-Memory Trade-off. In The 23rd Annual International Cryptology Conference. In *Proceedings of CRYPTO03, volume 2729 of Lecture Notes in Computer Science, 2003.*

Oppenheimer, P. (2009). Form 10-Q. *United States Securities and Exchange Commission.* Retrieved January 22, 2009, from http://sec.gov/Archives/edgar/data/320193/000119312509009937/d10q.htm

Pinkas, B., & Sander, T. (2002). Securing passwords against dictionary attacks. Paper presented at CCS02. In Proceedings of the 9th ACM conference on Computer and communications security.

Podilchuk, C., I., & Delp, E., J. (2001, July). Digital watermarking: algorithms and applications. *Signal Processing Magazine, IEEE, 18*(4), 33-46.

PRIME-WP14. 2 (2007). Architecture. In M. Casassa-Mont, S. Crosta, T. Kriegelstein & D. Sommer (Eds.) (Vol. V2, Retrieved from https://www.prime-project.eu/prime_products/reports/arch/

Samuelson, P. (2003). DRM and, or, vs. the law. *Communications of the ACM, 46*(4), 41–45. doi:10.1145/641205.641229

Seigneur, J. M., & Jensen, C. D. (2004, Mar). *Trust Enhanced Ubiquitous Payment without Too Much Privacy Loss.* Paper presented at the Applied computing; SAC 2004, Nicosia.

Sobel, D. (2007). A Bite out of Apple - iTunes, Interoperability, and France's Dadvsi Law. *Berkeley Technology Law Journal, 22*, 26.

Taniguchi, N., Chida, K., Shionoiri, O., & Kanai, A. (2005). *DECIDE: a scheme for decentralized identity escrow*. Paper presented at the Proceedings of the 2005 workshop on Digital identity management.

WP2-FIDIS. (2006). D2.6: Identity in a Networked World. In D.-O. Jaquet-Chiffelle, E. Benoist & B. Anrig (Eds.), *Use Cases and Scenarios*. Retrieved from http://www.fidis.net/fileadmin/fidis/deliverables/fidis-wp2-del2.6_Identity_in_a_Networked_World.pdf

Wagner, D., & Schneier, B. (1996). *Analysis of the SSL 3.0 protocol*. Paper presented at Proceedings of the Second UNIX Workshop on Electronic Commerce, pages 29-40. USENIX Association.

Wu, T. (1998). *The Secure Remote Password Protocol*. In *Proceedings of the 1998 Internet Society Network and Distributed System Security Symposium*, pages 97-111.

Wu, T., *The SRP Authentication and Key Exchange System*, 2000.

Zhang, M. (2004, January). Analysis of the SPEKE password-authenticated key exchange protocol. *Communications Letters, IEEE, 8*(1), 63–65. doi:10.1109/LCOMM.2003.822506

ENDNOTES

[1] IEEE P1363: http://grouper.ieee.org/groups/1363/

[2] OpenID 1.1 spec: http://openid.net/specs/openid-authentication-1_1.html

Chapter 9
An Electronic Contract Signing Protocol Using Fingerprint Biometrics

Harkeerat Bedi
University of Tennessee at Chattanooga, USA

Li Yang
University of Tennessee at Chattanooga, USA

Joseph M. Kizza
University of Tennessee at Chattanooga, USA

ABSTRACT

Fair exchange between a pair of parties can be defined as the fundamental concept of trade where none of the parties involved in the exchange have an unfair advantage over the other once the transaction completes. Fair exchange protocols are a group of protocols that provide means for accomplishing such fair exchanges. In this chapter we analyze one such protocol which offers means for fair contract signing, where two parties exchange their commitments over a pre-negotiated contract. We show that this protocol is not entirely fair and illustrate the possibilities of one party cheating by obtaining the other's commitment and not providing theirs. We also analyze a revised version of this protocol which offers better fairness by handling many of the weaknesses. Both these protocols however fail to handle the possibilities of replay attacks where an intruder replays messages sent earlier from one party to the other. Our proposed protocol improves upon these protocols by addressing to the weaknesses which leads to such replay attacks. We implement a complete working system which provides fair contract signing along with properties like user authentication and efficient password management achieved by using a fingerprint based authentication system and features like confidentiality, data-integrity and non-repudiation accomplished through implementation of cryptographic algorithms based on elliptic curves.

DOI: 10.4018/978-1-61520-783-1.ch009

INTRODUCTION

Commerce has come a long way since the beginning of our civilization. The ability to exchange goods and services for items of equivalent value has been widely exercised. Based on the kind of items exchanged between two parties, it can either be classified as a barter system where goods and services are exchanged for other goods and services, or the act of selling and buying where goods and services are sold or bought between parties in exchange for money.

The notion of *fair exchange* can be expressed as the ability to exchange goods or services for other goods or services in a fair manner where both the parties obtain what they expected. Being a fundamental concept, this can be implemented in various scenarios that may include exchanges based on barter system or buying and selling of goods.

With the advent of computers and the Internet, new means of performing commerce have been invented. E-commerce is one such solution where good and services are bought and sold between interested parties using computers over a network. With the rapid growth of the Internet, the magnitude of commerce performed online has also increased significantly. This increase is primarily because commerce conducted online is convenient and fast when compared to the traditional methods of trade. Even though commerce of this type offers benefits like speed and convenience, without properties like fairness and security, such services become less useful as they significantly increase the risk of failure. E-commerce cannot flourish or even sustain if it is not able to provide fairness and security. Therefore the concept of fair exchange plays a vital role in shaping such forms of commerce. When carried out online using computers and the Internet, such fair exchange is known as *fair electronic exchange*.

FAIR ELECTRONIC EXCHANGE

Fair electronic exchange can be demonstrated as e-commerce that takes place between two parties who are online and where exchange of goods and services is performed such that both parties either obtain what they expected or they obtain nothing at all. After an exchange is performed or aborted prematurely, none of the parties should have an unfair advantage over the other. If cheating takes place, where one party refuses to present their part of the exchange, other means for providing fairness should be available. These may include use of additional entities like a human judge or electronic ones that can comprehend the situation and act accordingly to provide fairness. Protocols that provide such facilities are known as *fair exchange protocols*. Such protocols can be used for the following purposes:

a. *Certified E-Mail* (CEM) where a user named Alice sends a message to a user named Bob and gets a receipt from him in return. Providing the quality of fairness would include Alice getting the receipt only when Bob gets the message or Bob getting the message only when Alice gets the receipt.

b. *Electronic Contract Signing* (ECS) where both Alice and Bob wish to sign a contract that has already been negotiated. This would involve Alice sending her commitment (digital signature) on the contract to Bob and him sending his commitment on the same in return. Providing fairness would involve Alice receiving Bob's commitment only when her commitment is received by Bob and vice versa. This example demonstrates contract signing between two parties. However, various multi-party contract signing protocols also exist and have also been proposed in (Baum-Waidner, 2001; Ferrer-Gomila, Payeras-Capella, Huguet-Rotger, 2001; Garay & MacKenzie, 1999).

c. *Online payment systems* (OPS) where Alice is the seller and Bob is the buyer and payment is given in return of the item of value (Cox, Tygar & Sirbu, 1995).

In the ideal case, where both Alice and Bob are guaranteed to be honest and the communication channel is secure and provides resilience, fair exchange can be achieved trivially without the aid of any external fairness provider. The above described scenarios can thus be carried out as follows:

Fair Certified E-Mail:

Step 1. Alice sends her message to Bob.
Step 2. Bob sends his receipt for the message to Alice. The receipt may be the digital signature of Bob on the message. Being a digital signature, this step ensures non-repudiation.

Fair Electric Contract Signing:

It is assumed that both parties have negotiated the contract before hand.
Step 1. Alice sends her digital signature on the contract to Bob.
Step 2. Bob sends his digital signature on the contract to Alice.

Fair Online Payment System:

Step 1. Alice sells goods or services online by sending it to Bob.
Step 2. Bob buys these good or services by paying Alice online via an e-check or e-money.

However in practice, honesty of the parties like Alice and Bob participating in an exchange can never be guaranteed. The availability of secure communication channels is not always possible and unsecured channels are easily prone to attacks. Following are the types of outcomes that may take place rendering the above mentioned exchanges incomplete.

a. Cheating Bob can always refuse to send his signature on the message to Alice after receiving her signature. In such a case, there is not much that Alice can do to obtain fairness.
b. An intruder can always stop the messages from reaching the other party. In this case the messages signed by Bob may never reach Alice. Alice may think that she has been cheated where as Bob may be unaware of this taking place. This confusion may lead Alice to request for cancellation whereas Bob may not wish for the same.
c. An intruder who is listening to messages sent by Alice or Bob can resend them making the other party believe that they were sent from the original sender. In case of electronic contract signing, if the intruder replays Alice's messages, there is no way for Bob to learn that the messages are not from Alice but an intruder. This is because the signature on the intruder's messages will always be verifiable using Alice's corresponding public key. Honest Bob may sign the message and think that he has signed a new contract with Alice, whereas Alice may never know of this taking place.
d. Bob can sign a fake contract is exchange of Alice's signature on the original contract, thus cheating her by providing his commitment on a contract that does not solve her purpose.

Therefore to prevent such unwanted outcomes, external fairness providers are used to comprehend the situation if cheating is suspected and provide resolution. Such fairness providers are separate entities known as the *trusted third parties*. As the name suggests these entities are trusted by everyone. Considering the above scenarios, Alice can communicate with the external fairness provider and obtain fairness if Bob refuses to sign the contract after receiving Alice's signature. Alice can provide the provider with information relating to the contract along with the messages she sent to Bob. The provider, thus after verifying this information and being sure that Alice is not cheating can then provide fairness to her by regenerating Bob's part of exchange or issuing a certificate that can be used as a substitute for Bob's signature.

Based on their role and the method of providing fairness, either by preventing or handling such unwanted outcomes, these providers are classified into the following types:

One class of protocols depends on gathering evidence during the transaction that can later be used to provide fairness. Two parties during their transaction also send additional information along with their messages which can later be used for resolution if one believes that it has been cheated. The cheated party contacts a human judge which looks at the additional information exchanged (evidence) and provides fairness. Such protocols are classified as *weak fair-exchange protocols* due to their inability to provide fairness during the transaction. This becomes a drawback since resolution is provided only after the transaction has been completed. In case of e-commerce where the location and availability of parties taking part in a transaction are not always fixed or known, such methods of dispute resolution may always not be possible.

To handle drawbacks like these, a second class of protocols has been defined by various researchers that provide means of avoiding disputes and obtaining resolution all within the transaction. Thus fairness can be obtained during the transaction and such protocols are known as *strong-fair exchange protocols* (Ray & Ray, 2002). These protocols too use a trusted third party which can provide fairness in case of a dispute.

Trusted third parties that have to involve in every transaction occurring between two parties are known as *online trusted third parties*. Exchanges using such trusted third parties suffer from the disadvantage that they are required to involve in every transaction occurring on the network and this increases the overhead.

Trusted third parties that are not required to involve in every transaction but only required when a dispute occurs are known as *invisible trusted third parties* or *offline trusted third parties* and the protocols implementing them are known as *optimistic protocols*. Following are the advantages provided by protocols that use an invisible trusted third party:

The invisible third party intervenes only when cheating is suspected. In such a case the invisible third party solves the conflict by providing the complaining party with what it truly deserves. Either party can initiate this procedure if they feel they have been cheated.

An invisible third party generates no congestion or bottlenecks as it intervenes only when cheating occurs; which is usually very rare. Under normal execution, transactions between two parties are carried out directly, bypassing the third party altogether.

An invisible third party generates minimal expense and minimal liabilities as it is liable only for the few messages that is sends, which is only in case of a conflict. Even if a system adds a large number of clients that carry out numerous transactions, the expense generated by such a system is minimal, since the third party intervenes only with cheating occurs and stays dormant rest of the time.

Evolution of Fair Exchange Protocols

Earliest work on exchange protocols that provided fairness was based on a class of fair exchange protocols known as *gradual exchange protocols* (Tedrick, 1983, 1985). Such protocols provided fairness as a measure directly proportional to the number of rounds of messages exchanged between the two participating parties. Thus as the number of messages exchanged increases, so does the probability of fairness. These protocols were complex and made use of advanced cryptographic techniques. They also required the assumption that both parties involved in the exchange are to have equivalent computing power. This assumption was removed by the introduction of an improved set of fair exchange protocols called *probabilistic protocols* (Ben-Or, Goldreich, Micali & Rivest, 1990; Markowitch & Roggeman, 1999). These protocols did not require both parties to have equivalent computing power. However a fairly large number of transmissions between the parties were still required to increase the probability of fairness to acceptable levels. This downside was addressed by the introduction of a new class of protocols that used trusted third parties for providing fairness. This reduced the number of transactions required to be exchange to a smaller number. This began with the use of an *inline trusted third party* (Coffey & Saidha, 1996), where the third party was required to involve in every transaction between the parties participating in the fair exchange protocol. Even though the number of transactions required was reduced, the involvement of third party during the protocol was very high. This made the third party as the bottleneck, since every transaction was required to be passed through the third party. Several improvements were made in this direction of third party implementation, beginning with the introduction of *online trusted third parties* (Zhang & Shi, 1996; Zhou & Gollmann, 1996), where the third party was required to involve only once during an entire instance of the protocol. This was major improvement since the involvement of third party was reduced substantially. Another major breakthrough was the introduction of *offline trusted third parties* (Asokan, Schunter & Waidner, 1997; Micali, 1997), where the third party was required to involve only when cheating was suspected or had occurred. This was again a key improvement since now the third party was required to interfere only in case of a conflict, and therefore did not become a bottleneck during the normal execution of the protocol. Such protocols, as stated previously are known as *optimistic protocols*.

This approach of implementing an offline trusted third party has also been used by researchers in execution of various non-repudiation protocols (Kremer & Markowitch, 2000; Zhou & Gollmann, 1997; Zhou, Deng & Bao, 1999). Non-repudiation with respect to exchange protocols can be defined as the concept of ensuring that a party having involved in an exchange or transmission cannot later deny their involvement. The advent of public key cryptography (Diffie & Hellman, 1976) and the introduction of digital signatures served as the foundation for non-repudiation. A property like non-repudiation is required by fair exchange protocols to provide fairness efficiently. However, the first set of non-repudiation protocols proposed by the International Organization for Standards (1997a, 1997b, 1998) did not support fairness exclusively.

In this chapter we analyze the several optimistic fair exchange protocols and demonstrate their weaknesses. We start by explaining Micali's protocol and analyzing its weaknesses. Micali's protocol is based on the use of an offline trusted third party where it is used to demonstrate an instance of exchange that implements fair contract signing.

We discuss the revisions made by Bao, Wang, Zhou & Zhu (2004) on Micali's protocol and how his protocol handles some of its weaknesses. We then explain our protocol and demonstrate how replay attacks which are not addressed by both these protocols are identified and can be prevented.

MICALI'S ELECTRONIC CONTRACT SIGNING PROTOCOL

In 2003, during the ACM Symposium on Principles of Distributed Computing (PODC) Silvio Micali presented a fair exchange protocol that could perform electronic contract signing (Micali, 2003). The protocol was also filed under US Patent No. 5666420 in 1997. In his protocol, contract signing was achieved in a fair way by using an invisible trusted third party. Fairness in this context means that either both parties are bound to the contract (i.e. obtain each others' signature on the contract) or neither one is.

However, the protocol is not as fair as claimed by the author, since either party is able to cheat the other under certain scenarios. The protocol also does not provide any means to handle or prevent replay attacks that may take place if an intruder replays messages sent earlier by one party to another. Some of these scenarios are also illustrated in the paper by Bao et al. (2004). Following is the actual protocol for contract signing as proposed by Micali.

Protocol

Contract signing can be implemented between two parties say, Alice and Bob through the following steps. Steps 4 and 5 are required only when a dispute occurs.

Pre-Requisites

It is assumed that both parties have negotiated the contract beforehand. Alice begins by selecting the contract file "*C*" that she needs to sign with Bob. She also selects a random value *M* and creates a packet "*Z*".

Packet *Z* contains the following information:

1. Identity of sender: This is a string that represents the sender. Public key of the sender can also be used. In this case the sender is Alice "*A*".
2. Identity of the receiver: A string that represents the receiver. Public key of the receiver can also be used. In this case the receiver is Bob "*B*".
3. Random value *M*: This can also be a number. It is a value known only to Alice and will later be used for completion of the contract signing process.

This information is encrypted using the public key of the third party, which is known to everyone.

Thus *Z* can be represented as $Z = E_{TP}(A, B, M)$, where E_{TP} is performing encryption using the trusted third party's (*TP*) public key.

Due to the practical requirements for the encryption functions to be so secure, Micali also explains the implementation of the encryption function "E^R_{TP}", where *R* emphasizes the use of a unique random value for performing encryption while using the trusted third party's (*TP*) public key.

A, B are the identifiers for Alice and Bob respectively and *M* is the secret random value known only to Alice.

Steps

1. Once the packet *Z* is created, Alice initiates the protocol by sending her signature on the packet *Z* and the contract *C* to Bob.

A1: $A \rightarrow B$: $SIG_A(C, Z)$

2. Upon receiving Alice's message, Bob sends his signature of *(C, Z)* and *Z* to Alice.

B1: $B \rightarrow A$: $SIG_B(C, Z) + SIG_B(Z)$

3. After receiving Bob's message, Alice verifies his signatures on both *(C, Z)* and *Z* and if they are valid, she sends *M* to Bob.

A2: $A \rightarrow B$: M

Dispute Resolution Phase

4. Bob receives the random *M* and uses it to reconstruct *Z*. If the newly created *Z* matches with the one he received in *Step 1*, he halts and the contract signing protocol is complete. Else, Bob sends his signature of *(C, Z)* and *Z* to the trusted third party.

If values of Z do not match:

B2: B → TP: SIG_B (C, Z) + SIG_B (Z)

5.   Third Party verifies the signatures it received from Bob. If they are valid, it decrypts Z using its private key and sends M to Bob and SIG_B (C, Z) + SIG_B (Z) to Alice.

TP1: TP → A: SIG_B (C, Z) + SIG_B (Z)

TP2: TP → B: M

Micali defines the commitments of Alice and Bob on the contract C as following:
Alice's commitment to contract C:

SIG_A (C, Z) and M

Bob's commitment to contract C:

SIG_B (C, Z) + SIG_B (Z)

To illustrate the fairness of the above mentioned contract signing protocol, Micali provided the following argument (Micali, 2003):
Quote:

"Indeed, if Bob never performs Step B1, then he is not committed to C, but neither is Alice, because Bob only has received SIG_A(C, Z), and has no way of learning M. However, if Bob performs Step B1, then he is committed to C, but Alice too will be so committed: either because she will honestly send M to Bob, or because Bob will get M from the invisible TP. Again, if Bob tries to cheat bypassing Step B1 and accessing directly the invisible TP to learn M, then Alice will get SIG_B(C, Z) and SIG_B (Z) from the invisible TP, because the invisible TP will not help Bob at all unless it first receives both signatures, and because once it decrypts Z to find M, it will also discover that Alice is the first signatory, and thus that she is entitled to SIG_B(C, Z) and SIG_B (Z)."

In case of the use of the encryption function "E^R_{TP}" during the generation of Z, Alice would also be required to send R along with M in Step 3.

Analysis

This section discusses the vulnerabilities in Micali's contract signing protocol and how it is unfair in certain scenarios.

Inadequate Commitment Requirements for Both Parties

As per Micali's definition, for Alice to show Bob's commitment on the contract C, she only requires Bob's signatures on *(C, Z)* and Z, which are SIG_B *(C, Z)* and SIG_B *(Z)*. Alice is not required to provide the value M that creates Z. This flaw can be exploited such that Alice can always get Bob's commitment on a contract while Bob gets nothing. Following is the attack:

Dishonest Alice creates a random value of length Z and sends her signature of *(C, Z)* to Bob. Bob verifies Alice's signature and since it holds true, he sends his signatures of *(C, Z)* and Z to her. Alice now quits the protocol as she has received Bob's commitment. Bob on the other hand cannot get resolution form third party as Z is a random value and it cannot find M such that $Z = E_{TP}$ *(A, B, M)*. This leads to Alice obtaining an advantage since she is not required to present a value M that can recreate the packet Z.

Attack 1

Alice creates a random value of length Z.

A1: A → B: SIG_A (C, Z)

B1: B → A: SIG_B (C, Z) + SIG_B (Z)

A2: No response

Bob contacts the third party for resolution:

B2: B → TP: SIG_B (C, Z) + SIG_B (Z)

The third party is not able to provide M to Bob as Z is a random value and it does not contain a value M such that $Z = E_{TP}$ (A, B, M).

TP: Halts, as it is unable to provide the value of M.

The above mentioned attacks are also explained in the paper by Bao et al (2004). They propose a protocol that handles these attacks by changing the requirements of the dispute resolution phase, the commitment parameters for both parties and the contents of Z.

Inadequate Requirements for Resolution of Dispute

The third party only requires Bob's signatures $(SIG_B$ (C, Z) and SIG_B (Z)) during the dispute resolution phase and nothing from Alice's side is required. This can cause the following attack:

After receiving Alice's signature $(SIG_A$ (C, Z)), dishonest Bob prepares a new contract C^I, creates the following signatures $SIG_B (C^I, Z)$ and SIG_B (Z) and sends them both to third party requesting for dispute resolution. Since these two signatures are valid and third party does not require any signatures from Alice, it forwards $SIG_B (C^I, Z)$ and SIG_B (Z) to Alice and M to Bob. This result in Bob having Alice's commitment on contract C and Alice only having Bob's commitment on a contract C^I which is of no use to Alice.

Attack 2

A1: A → B: SIG_A (C, Z)

B1: B → TP: SIG_B (C^1, Z) + SIG_B (Z)

Since Z does not contain any information about the contract C and the signature of Bob on C^I and Z are valid, the third party provides Bob with the

value of M contained in Z and Alice with Bob's signature over the fake contract C^I.

TP1: TP → A: SIG_B (C^1, Z) + SIG_B (Z)

TP2: TP → B: M

Scope for Replay Attacks

Even though the above mentioned attacks are addressed in Bao's revised protocol, both protocols (Micali and Bao) still leave one possible attack. These protocols provide no means of identifying a replay attack that may take place during a contract signing instance. Since both the protocols do not handle this type of attack, one of them namely, Micali's original protocol, is used for the replay attack demonstration and is illustrated as follows:

Attack 3

Consider the normal execution of Micali's protocol:

A1: A → B: SIG_A (C, Z)

B1: B → A: SIG_B (C, Z) + SIG_B (Z)

A2: A → B: M

Let us assume an intruder has access to the transmissions between Alice and Bob and is able to record all the messages sent by Alice. An intruder can thus replay a message that was previously sent by Alice to Bob.

Consider the following execution of the protocol by an intruder:

I1: I → B: SIG_A (C, Z)

B1: B → A: SIG_B (C, Z) + SIG_B (Z)

I2: I → B: M

If the intruder replays the message *A1* as a new request, then there is no way for Bob to indentify the sender. Bob will assume the request as genuine since its signature will still be valid and respond back with his signature of the same. To this, the intruder can then send the message *A2*. This leads to commitment of a new contract between Alice and Bob. Bob assumes that he has signed a new contract with Alice and she on the other hand knows nothing about it. Consider a scenario where Alice periodically purchases selected items from Bob using the above protocol. The contracts then signed between them would also be the same, which is also the case in real world transactions and if it is agreed that all contracts expire immediately upon fulfillment (i.e. Bob gets the order, signs it, and then forgets about it), it would be hard to trace the intruder or even identify the attack. It should also be noted that the intruder does not need to involve the third party to stage this attack thus making it even harder to identify.

BAO'S ELECTRONIC CONTRACT SIGNING PROTOCOL

Micali's protocol suffers from several weaknesses due to the following design issues:

1.   The packet *Z* does not contain any information about the contract the parties negotiated to sign.
2.   The protocol provides no means or mechanisms for handling replay attacks that may take place if an intruder replays messages sent earlier from Alice to Bob.

In 2004, during the *Australasian Conference on Information Security and Privacy (ACISP)*, Bao et al. proposed a contract signing protocol that improved upon Micali's work. Attacks made possible due to the first design issue were identified and addressed. Bao's protocol handles the first two types of attacks (Attack 1 and 2) discussed in the

previous section by changing the requirements of the dispute resolution phase, the commitment parameters for both parties and the structure of the packet *Z*.

Protocol

In this protocol, contract signing between two parties, say Alice and Bob can be achieved through the following prerequisites and steps.

Prerequisites

It is assumed that both parties have negotiated the contract before hand. Alice begins by selecting the contract file "*C*" that she needs to sign with Bob and creates a hash of it *H(C)*. She also selects the random values *M* and *R* and creates a packet "*Z*".

Packet Z contains the following information:

1.   Identity of sender: This is a string that represents the sender. Public key of the sender can also be used. In this case the sender is Alice "*A*".
2.   Identity of the receiver: A string that represents the receiver. Public key of the receiver can also be used. In this case the receiver is Bob "*B*".
3.   Random value *M*: This can also be a number. It is a value known only to Alice and will later be used for completion of the contract signing process.
4.   Hash of the contract *C*.

This information is encrypted using the public key of the third party, which is known to everyone.

Thus packet Z can be represented as $Z = E^R_{TP} (A, B, H(C), M)$

Where E^R_{TP} is performing encryption using the trusted third party's (*TP*) public key using the randomness R. The values *A* and *B* are the identifiers of Alice and Bob respectively. *M* is the random value known only to Alice and *H(C)* is the hash of the contract.

Steps

1. Once the packet Z is created, Alice then initiates the protocol by creating her signature on the packet Z, the contract C, and the identities of her, Bob and the third party, and sending them to Bob.

A1: A $\rightarrow$ B: SIG_A (A, B, TP, C, Z)

2. On receiving Alice's message, Bob verifies her signature and if valid, sends his signature of *(A, B, TP, C, Z)* to Alice. Otherwise he halts.

B1: B $\rightarrow$ A: SIG_B (A, B, TP, C, Z)

3. After receiving Bob's message. Alice verifies his signatures on *(A, B, TP, C, Z)* and if valid, sends M and R to Bob.

A2: A $\rightarrow$ B: M, R

Dispute Resolution Phase

4. Bob receives the values M and R and uses them to reconstruct Z. If the newly created Z matches with the one he received in Step 1, he halts and the contract signing protocol is complete. Else, Bob sends his and Alice's signature of *(A, B, TP, C, Z)* to the trusted third party.

If values of Z do not match

B2: B $\rightarrow$ TP: SIG_B (A, B, TP, C, Z) + SIG_A (A, B, TP, C, Z)

5. Third Party verifies the signatures it received from Bob. If they are valid, it decrypts Z using its private key and sends *(SIG_B (A, B, TP, C, Z), M, R)* to Alice and *(SIG_A (A, B, TP, C, Z), M, R)* to Bob.

If contents of Z are legit and signatures are valid:

TP1: TP $\rightarrow$ A: SIG_B (A, B, TP, C, Z) + M + R

TP2: TP $\rightarrow$ B: SIG_A (A, B, TP, C, Z) + M + R

Else: Halts or sends an error message

Following are the new commitments as revised by Bao:

Alice's commitment to the contract C can be defined as:

SIG_A (A, B, TP, C, Z), M, R where $Z = E^R_{TP}$ (A, B, H(C), M)

Bob's commitment to the contract C can be defined as:

SIG_B (A, B, TP, C, Z), M, R where $Z = E^R_{TP}$ (A, B, H(C), M)

The second design weakness of the unavailability of a mechanism to identify and prevent replay attacks was not addressed by both Micali and Bao. Our protocol provides a mechanism to address these types of attacks and is our unique contribution to the fair exchange protocol.

OUR SYSTEM

We present a complete working system that provides fair electronic exchange along with user authentication. We implement an invisible third party that can be used to provide fairness if cheating is suspected. Our work comprises of three major parts. We begin with a revised protocol that is based on Micali's contract signing protocol. We improve upon Micali's protocol by handling certain types of weaknesses that may lead to attacks where one party can obtain another's commitment to contract without providing theirs. We also handle the possibility of replay attack that may take place if an intruder resends the messages sent earlier from one party to the other.

We implement a fingerprint based authentication technique to provide user authentication and enrollment. The user can scan his finger for fingerprint which is then used for authentication. When authenticated, the user can proceed and use the system to sign contracts with others. Feature of enrollment is also provided if the user is new and wants to use the system for the first time. To provide confidentiality, handle replay attacks and confirm the identity of the other party, cryptography and digital signatures are used. All messages communicated between users participating in the contract signing process are encrypted using a hybrid cryptosystem. This offers better performance by achieving the convenience of asymmetric cryptography with the efficiency of symmetric cryptography. These three parts are explained in detail in the following sections.

This work extends our prior publication (Bedi, Yang and Kizza, 2009) to provide a comprehensive understanding and presentation of the subjects discussed in the paragraph above and includes the demonstration of our working software implementation.

Our Fair Contract Signing Protocol

This section discusses our protocol and describes how it provides fair contract signing. Following is an adaptation of the protocol where the privacy of messages is not essential. It is assumed that both parties are not concerned about the privacy of their messages (or contracts), provided that fairness is guaranteed. This approach is taken for a simpler illustration of the protocol. Privacy of messages can be achieved using cryptography, which is explained in detail in the subsequent topics. Following is the protocol under normal execution when both Alice and Bob are honest and there is no intruder. Contract signing between two parties, say Alice and Bob, can be achieved through following the below prerequisites and steps.

Prerequisites

It is assumed that both parties have negotiated the contract before hand. Alice selects the contract file "*C*" that she needs to sign with Bob. She also selects a secret random value *M* and creates a packet "*Z*". Packet *Z* contains the following information:

1. Identity of sender: This is a string that represents the sender. Public key of the sender can also be used. In our case the sender is Alice "*A*".
2. Identity of the receiver: A string that represents the receiver. Public key of the receiver can also be used. In our case the receiver is Bob "*B*".
3. Random value *M*: This can also be a number. It is a value known only to Alice and will later be used for completion of the contract signing process.
4. Hash of the contract *C*, that is $H(C)$

This information is encrypted using the public key of the third party, which is known to everyone.

Thus *Z* can be represented as: $Z = E^R_{TP} (A, B, H(C), M)$

Where E^R_{TP} is performing encryption using the trusted third party's (*TP*) public key using the randomness *R*. The values *A* and *B* are the identifiers of Alice and Bob respectively. $H(C)$ is the hash of the contract file *C*. *M* is the random value known only to Alice.

Steps:

1. Alice sends a nonce NA_1 to Bob. Nonce is a random number used only once for the prevention of replay attacks.

A1: A → B: NA_1

2. On receiving Alice's nonce, Bob signs it using his private key and sends it back to

her along with his nonce. This step ensures Alice that it was indeed Bob who signed the message as Bob's private key is a secret known only to Bob.

B1: B → A: SIG_B (NA_1) + NB_1

3. After receiving the above package Alice can verify the digital signature of Bob on NA_1 using his public key. If it matches, Alice is sure that it is indeed Bob and there is no replay attack. Alice now signs Bob's nonce using her private key so that he can be sure of the same. Alice also signs Z along with $H(C)$ and sends all of it to Bob.

This step makes Alice partially committed to the contract as she has signed the hash of contract using her private key.

A2: A → B: SIG_A (NB_1) + SIG_A ($H(C)$, Z) + Z + C

4. On receiving Alice's signatures, Bob can now verify them using her public key. If they match, Bob is sure that it is indeed Alice and there is no replay attack. It is now Bob's turn to send his commitment to Alice. Bob does this by signing the hash of contract $H(C)$ along with Z and sending it to Alice.

B2: B → A: SIG_B ($H(C)$, Z)

5. After receiving the message, Alice can verify Bob's signature and if it holds true, she sends him the values M and R signed by her.

A3: A → B: SIG_A (M, R) + M + R

Bob receives this package and learns the values M and R which is then used to reconstruct Z. If the newly created Z matches with the one he received in Step 3, the transaction is complete

and both the parties have successfully signed the contract together.

Following is the protocol under abnormal execution where Alice does not provide Bob with the correct secret values of M and R in the final step.

Dispute Resolution Phase

Upon receiving Alice's signature of Z and $H(C)$, Bob sends his signature of the same to Alice. Alice is then required to send the values of M and R to Bob to provide her complete commitment on the contract. For the purpose of discussion let us assume that Alice cheats Bob by not providing him with the correct secret values of M and R after she receives his signature on the contract. Thus Bob is left with a partial commitment from Alice, where as Alice has Bob's complete commitment. Bob can thus execute the following steps to obtain resolution.

1. Bob sends the packet Z that he initially received from Alice, the contract C that was to be signed, Alice's signature of Z and $H(C)$ and his own signature of Z and $H(C)$ to the third party.

B1: B → TP Z + C + SIG_A ($H(C)$, Z) + SIG_B ($H(C)$, Z)

2. Third party, upon receiving Bob's request performs the following steps:
   a. Computes the value of $H(C)$ from C.
   b. Decrypts the packet Z since it knows its own private key and extracts the secret M.
   c. Verifies the contents of Z to include the identities A for Alice and B for Bob and $H(C)$ for the hash of the contract.
   d. Verifies the signatures of Alice and Bob over $H(C)$ and Z. Third party can do this since it knows the public keys of both Alice and Bob. If the signatures are valid, third party provides Bob with

M it recovered from *Z* and Alice with the signature of Bob over *H(C)* and *C*.

If contents of *Z* are legit and the signatures are valid:

TP1: TP → B: M + R

TP2: TP → A: SIG_B (H(C), Z)

Else: No action.

If secrecy of the contract is required, the cheating party can directly send the hash of the contract instead of the original contract to the third party during the dispute resolution phase. The third party can then skip the step where it is required to compute the hash of the contract, and can proceed directly with the remaining steps. This completes the dispute resolution phase as the third party provides Bob with the correct values of *M* and *R* which gives him complete commitment from Alice on the contract.

Protocol Description

To sign a contract in theory would mean exchange of signatures from both the parties on the same contract. That is if Alice and Bob were to sign a contract with each other, Alice would need to have Bob's signature (commitment) on the contract in the form of $SIG_B(C)$ and Bob would need to have Alice's signature $SIG_A(C)$.

For this to be fair it would require that each party gets the other party's signature only when their signature is received by the other party. Implementation of this exchange may be straightforward under conventional transactions where both the parties are physically available or geographically locatable. However under e-commerce where the transactions take place over the Internet, it becomes reasonably complicated. This is because these transactions transcend geographical boundaries and it is not always possible to contact

the other party for resolution or queries once the transaction is complete.

A party can always refuse to provide their signature once they receive the same from the other party. And since locating someone over the Internet or to know when the other party will be available online again is not always possible, fairness cannot be guaranteed. Therefore to provide fairness, additional information (e.g. packet *Z*) is exchanged along with the contract (or messages) during these fair exchange transactions. This additional information is then examined and used for resolution if a party does not respond appropriately. Thus the commitments for both parties are modified as follows:

For Bob to have Alice's commitment on the contract, he would need:

SIG_A (H(C), Z), M and R where Z = E^R_{TP} (A, B, H(C), M)

For Alice to have Bob's commitment on the contract, she would need:

SIG_B (H(C), Z), M and R where Z = E^R_{TP} (A, B, H(C), M)

To prove the commitments, parties will be required to present not only the signatures but also the contents *M, R, A, B* and *H(C)* that altogether satisfy $Z = E^R_{TP}$ (A, B, H(C), M). Failing to do so shall render the commitments as well as the signed contract as invalid.

The additional information used in our protocol is $Z = E^R_{TP}$ (A, B, H(C), M) and values *R* and *M*.

The packet *Z* is created using the following information,

1. Identities of both the parties: Those are *A* for Alice and *B* for Bob. We use text strings for this purpose. The public keys of parties or any other type of identifiable information can also be used.

2. Hash of the Contract: A Message digest created by using a cryptographic hash function. It is usually of fixed length and is unique to the data hashed. A change in hash generated would represent a change in the data hashed.

3. Random number M: Alice creates this random number that is used as a part of the contract signing process and for contract verification by Bob. Initially, Alice signs the packet Z which includes this random number M along with contract C and sends it to Bob. After receiving her signature, Bob still does not have her complete commitment over the contract as he does not know the value of M that was used to create the packet Z. Bob cannot find this value on his own since the packet Z is encrypted using the third party's public key and the third party's corresponding private key is a secret known only to it. Bob also cannot obtain it from Alice unless he provides his commitment of the same to Alice. Thus the only option available to Bob is to send his commitment to Alice. Alice then verifies his signature and if valid, sends him the values M and R. Upon receiving M and R from Alice, Bob can reconstruct Z using A, B and $H(C)$. Bob does so by encrypting these values using the third party's public key along with the random R. If the newly created Z matches with the one he received earlier, he has Alice's complete commitment on the contract.

4. The value R: It is this randomness that is used by the public-key cryptosystem during encryption to produce the same cipher text for a given data using the same public key. This is usually not the case since most public-key cryptosystems produce different cipher texts for the same data over the same public key if this value is not explicitly specified. In our protocol, during the final step, comparison of cipher texts is performed for contract verification purposes. Thus the production

of same cipher text over the same data and same public key becomes a requirement and can only be achieved if the randomness used for encryption is stored and reused.

Our Contribution

Our contribution in the revised protocol encompasses the following design changes:

Exchange of Random Nonce Prior to Exchange of Commitments

Random nonces are exchanged between both parties prior to exchange of the contract commitments. This step ensures that both parties are certain about the other's identity. It also helps to identify a replay attack that may occur if an intruder tries to replay messages previously sent by Alice. This can be achieved through the following three steps. Let the two parties be Alice and Bob,

1. Alice sends a random nonce to Bob.
2. Bob signs the nonce it received from Alice using his private key and sends his random nonce to her.
3. Alice verifies the signed value using Bob's public key. If valid, she signs his nonce using her private key and sends it to Bob. Bob can verify the same using her public key.

Inclusion of Hash of Contract in Packet Z

Information about the hash of the contract is added in the packet Z. A Hash is basically a fixed length value returned by a cryptographic hash function that takes the contract file data as the input. These hash values are usually unique for a given message (contract) and changes if the message is altered. If one party modifies the contract during the contract signing protocol, the hash generated on the modified contract will not match with the one generated on the original contract. If the hashes on this contract do not match between the parties, it can be concluded that they have different contracts and cheating can be identified. It can be concluded so as it is extremely unlikely to find the same hash on two different contracts. We specifically assume that SIG_A () and SIG_B () are secure signing algorithms that exhibit the following four properties:

a.   It is easy to compute hash for any given data.
b.   It is extremely difficult to recreate the data from its hash.
c.   It is extremely unlikely to find the same hash for two different data.
d.   It is extremely difficult to modify a given data without changing its hash.

Inclusion of Hash of Contract in Signature

Hash of the contract instead of the actual contract is used during the digital signature generation process. This step ensures privacy of the contract between both the parties. On the contrary, if the contract is part of the digital signature, during dispute resolution the cheated party would also have to provide the contract along with the other information to the third party. This is necessary since all information that is part of the signature is required in order to verify it and which includes the contract. If the secrecy of the contract is essential to the cheated party, executing this step would make them lose the same. Protocols by Micali and Bao both use the actual contract instead of its hash during the digital signature generation process.

Reduction of Attacks

This section discusses how the attacks discovered in Micali's protocol are being handled by our protocol.

Inadequate Commitment Requirements for Both Parties

As per Micali's definition, for Bob to be committed to the contract C, Alice only requires Bob's signatures on the contract C and packet Z that are $SIG_B(C, Z)$ and $SIG_B (Z)$. Alice is not required to provide the value M that creates Z. This flaw can be exploited such that Alice can always get Bob's commitment on a contract while Bob gets nothing. Following is the attack:

Dishonest Alice creates a random value of length Z and sends her signature of *(C, Z)* to Bob. Bob verifies Alice's signature and since it holds true, he sends his signatures of *(C, Z)* and Z to her. Alice now quits the protocol as she has received Bob's commitment. Bob on the other hand cannot get resolution form third party as Z is a random value and it cannot find M such that $Z = E^R_{TP}$ (A, B, M). This leads to Alice obtaining an advantage since she is not required to present a value M that can recreate the packet Z.

This attack is handled by our protocol by changing the requirements of contract commitment such that Alice is also required to provide a value of M such that $Z=E^R_{TP}$ (A, B, M).

Inadequate Requirements for Resolution of Dispute

In Micali's protocol, the third party only requires Bob's signatures *(SIG_B(C, Z) and SIG_B (Z))* during the dispute resolution phase. Nothing from Alice's side is required. This can lead to the following attack:

After receiving Alice's signature *(SIG_A (C, Z))* dishonest Bob can prepare a new contract C^1, create the following signatures $SIG_B (C^1, Z)$ and SIG_B *(Z)* and send them to the third party requesting for resolution. Since these two signatures are valid and third party does not require any signatures from Alice or even the contract, it forwards SIG_B *(C^1, Z)* and SIG_B *(Z)* to Alice and *M* to Bob. This result in Bob having Alice's commitment on contract

C and Alice only having Bob's commitment on another contract C^1.

This attack is handled by our protocol since now the third party requires signatures of both parties participating in the contract signing process. Also, since hash of the contract file is now included in the packet *Z*, if Bob signs a fake contract, the hashes will be different and the signature will not be verifiable.

Scope for Replay Attacks

Even though the above mentioned attacks are addressed by Bao's protocol, both protocols (Micali and Bao) still leave one possible attack. These protocols provide no means of identifying a replay attack that may take place during a contract signing instance. Let us assume an intruder has access to the transmissions between Alice and Bob and is able to record all the messages sent by Alice. An intruder can thus always replay a message that was previously sent by Alice. Bob will assume the request as genuine as its signature will still be valid and respond back with his signature of the same. This leads to signature of a new contract between Alice and Bob. Bob assumes that he has signed a new contract with Alice and she on the other hand knows nothing about it.

This attack is handled by our protocol since both parties are required to exchange random nonce between each other before they exchange their commitments. Therefore if an intruder replays a contract signing request sent previously by Alice, Bob would respond with a nonce which has to be signed using Alice's private key. Since Alice's private key is a secret known only to Alice, the intruder will not be able to provide the signature and the contract signing process would halt, preventing the replay attack.

To recognize a replay attack Bob can also recompute *Z* by using previously obtained values of *M* from Alice. If a match occurs Bob can conclude that it is a replay attack. However, only limited values of *M* (or contracts) can be accessible to a

party in practice due to physical limitations on database sizes. Our use of nonce removes this limitation and does not require storage of previous values of *M* or even the contract since the attack can be easily identified if nonce verification fails.

Implementation of Cryptography

In our system, cryptography is being used for two main purposes which include creation and verification of digital signatures and implementation of hybrid cryptography. Following is a brief discussion on both these purposes and their implementation in our system.

Digital Signatures

Digital signatures are derived from asymmetric cryptography where messages signed by a party using their private key can later by verified by anybody using the party's corresponding public key. This provides the property of non-repudiation where the signer cannot refuse to have signed the message since the private key used to sign the message is a secret known only to the signer. Digital signatures can be considered equivalent to traditional handwritten signatures in many aspects and when implemented properly are extremely effective. In a contract signing instance, the initiating party can sign messages using any of the various digital signature algorithms. This way during the transaction it can always be proved that the messages signed and sent by the initiating party indeed belong to them.

We implement a digital signature algorithm based elliptic curves known as Elliptic Curve Digital Signature Algorithm or ECDSA (ANSI X9.63, 1999). The ECDSA API's used by our software were provided by a cryptography provider called *FlexiProvider*. FlexiProvider provides a powerful toolkit available for both Java Cryptography Architecture and Java Cryptography Extension. It provides various cryptographic modules that can be plugged into any application that is built on top of the Java Cryptography Architecture such as ours. Our implementation of ECDSA produces a digital signature of 448 bits (Piotrowski, Langendoerfer & Peter, 2006) on the provided data in byte array format.

Hybrid Cryptography

Our system uses hybrid cryptography for secure communication since it offers better efficiency and properties like data integrity and non-repudiation when compared individually to techniques like asymmetric and symmetric cryptography. Following is a brief discussion on both these forms of cryptography (asymmetric and symmetric) for clear understanding of our implementation and its benefits.

Cryptography basically consists of the following four elements:

1. Plaintext: Information or data that can be understood by everyone, which is required to be encrypted (scrambled) using a secret key so that it cannot be understood by someone who does not possess that secret key.
2. Ciphertext: The resultant encrypted data that is achieved by use of a cryptographic mathematical algorithm function.
3. Cryptographic Function or Cipher: A mathematical function that is used to encrypt or decrypt information by using a secret key.
4. Key: Information that is usually kept as a secret, which is used along with the cryptographic function to encrypt or decrypt data.

Based on the type of key used for encryption and decryption, the process of cryptography can be classified into the following types:

Symmetric Cryptography

This process of cryptography uses the same key for encryption and decryption. The secrecy of the information is dependent on how well this

secret key can be kept private. Compared to its counterpart *asymmetric cryptography* which is explained later, symmetric cryptography is very fast and efficient. For this reason it is used widely for encrypting and decrypting large files. Even though this process is highly efficient, it suffers from the following disadvantages:

• Key Sharing: Since an initial exchange of the secret key is required between the parties before they can begin encrypting and decryption data, safe transmission or sharing of this key becomes a problem.
• Key Management: A key is required to be shared between every two parties who are willing to exchange information securely. Therefore in a large network of users who want to exchange information with others, a unique key is required for every user pair. This storage and management of keys become difficult for each user who wants to participate is such transactions.
• Integrity: Since the receiver cannot verify whether the message has been altered or not before receipt, the integrity of data can be compromised.
• Repudiation: Since the same secret key has to be shared between users, the sender can always repudiate the messages because there is no mechanism for the receiver to make sure that the message has been sent by the claimed sender.

Asymmetric Cryptography

This process of cryptography also known as *public key cryptography* uses different keys for encrypting and decrypting information. These keys together form a key-pair and are known as public and private keys. Public keys are the one that are shared with everyone and private keys on the other hand are kept secret and known only to the individual to whom it belongs. For a party to send information securely to another, they need to encrypt the information using the recipient's public key. The recipient can then decrypt this data and recover the message by using their corresponding private key. Since this private key is a secret known only to the recipient, the information can be communicated securely without the requirement of initial key exchange thus handling the key sharing problem. Key management also becomes convenient since there are no unique keys that are required for each user pair willing to communicate. The user can simply use the recipient's public key and begin secure communication. Non-repudiation and data integrity can be achieved by making a party encrypt or sign the message using their private key. This can be verified by anybody using the signer's corresponding public key. Data can be securely communicated between two parties (sender and receiver) along with data integrity and non-repudiation through the following steps:

1. Sender first encrypts the message to be sent using their private key.

2. Sender then encrypts the resultant ciphertext using the receiver's public key.

The receiver upon receiving the message first decrypts the ciphertext using its private key. This ensures secure communication since the receiver's private key is a secret known only to him. The resultant data is then decrypted again using the sender's public key. This provides non-repudiation and data integrity since the sender's public key is known to everybody and can be used to confirm his identity. Even though asymmetric cryptography offers features like non-repudiation and data integrity, its execution is still far slower than symmetric cryptography making it less favorable for encrypting and decrypting large files.

Hybrid Cryptography

Hybrid cryptography handles the above mentioned disadvantages in symmetric and asymmetric cryptography. It does so by using both these cryptosystems together which provides the convenience of asymmetric cryptography along with the efficiency of symmetric cryptography.

Hybrid cryptography consists of the following two stages:

1. **Data Encapsulation:** The process in which data to be communicated securely is encrypted using symmetric cryptography schemes which are highly efficient.

2. **Key Encapsulation:** The symmetric secret key used to encrypt the data is then encrypted using any of the asymmetric cryptography schemes.

To encrypt a message for Bob, Alice performs the following steps:

1. Creates a random symmetric key and encrypts the message using the data encapsulation scheme.

2. Encrypts the symmetric key using Bob's public key under the key encapsulation scheme.

3. Sends both the encrypted message and the encrypted symmetric key to Bob.

To recover the message sent by Alice, Bob performs the following steps:

1. Use his private key to decrypt the encrypted symmetric key.

2. Use the recovered symmetric key to decrypt and recover the original message.

Since the major portion of the encryption that includes the actual message is encrypted using a symmetric cryptosystem, the efficiency of the system is improved. By encrypting the symmetric key using asymmetric cryptography, properties like key management, data integrity and non-repudiation are also achieved.

We use Elliptic Curve Integrated Encryption Scheme, also known as ECIES for performing asymmetric cryptography operations. The ECIES API's used by our software are provided by the same Java cryptography provider called *Flexi-Provider*. We use Advanced Encryption Standard (AES) for symmetric cryptography. It is the current cryptography standard for symmetric cryptosystems and was announced by the National Institute of Standards and Technology (NIST) under the Federal Information Processing Standards (FIPS, 2001) 197 on November 26, 2001. It is also one of the most popular algorithms used for symmetric cryptography at present.

Elliptic Curve Cryptography Overview

Both Elliptic Curve Integrated Encryption Scheme (ECIES) and Elliptic Curve Digital Signature Algorithm (ECDSA) are part of cryptography that is based on elliptic curves. Also known as Elliptic Curve Cryptography or ECC, it is an approach to public key cryptography that is primarily based on elliptic curves which are defined over a finite field. A field is basically a mathematical group that offers operations for addition, subtraction, multiplication, and division that always construct results within the field. A finite field can be defined as a field that contains only finitely many elements. It is this property of being finite that makes it possible to perform cryptography with these elliptic curves that exists over the fields. The use of elliptic curves for cryptography was proposed independently by Neal Koblitz (1987) at the University of Washington and Victor Miller (1986) at IBM in 1985. Being grown into a mature public key cryptosystem, it is endorsed by the United States government (NIST, 1999).

The security of any cryptographic system is based on a hard mathematical problem that is computationally infeasible to solve. For example, RSA gets its security from the difficulty of factoring large numbers. The public and private keys used in RSA cryptography is a function of a pair of large prime numbers, and recovering the plain text from the cipher text that was created using the public key is believed to be computationally equivalent to finding the factors of the primes used to create the pair of public and private keys. Elliptic Curve Cryptography along with many other cryptographic systems achieves their security from the difficulty of solving the discrete logarithmic problem (DLP). ECC to be specific is based upon the difficulty of solving Elliptic Curve Discrete Logarithm Problem (ECDLP) which offers a better implementation when compared to previous generation techniques as used by RSA. ECDLP can be demonstrated with the help of the equation $Ax = B$. For very large values of x, it gets computationally infeasible to derive its value as no efficient algorithm is available for solving it. The primitive approach of solving this would be to keep adding and/or multiplying the value of A to itself until the result matches B. This approach is used on elliptic curve groups where, a point on the group is selected and multiplied by a scalar value. When the scalar value is very large, it becomes computationally infeasible to solve the problem. The primitive approach then becomes using the addition and doubling operations together until the matching value is observed. For example, *7P* can be expressed as *2* ((2 * P) + P)) + P*. This calculation of a point *nP* is referred to as Scalar Multiplication of a point. ECDLP is based upon the intractability of scalar multiplication products.

Not all curves can provide strong security and that ECDLP for some curves can be resolved efficiently. Therefore NIST offers a set of recommended curves (NIST, 1999) whose security properties are well understood and can be safely used for cryptography. Standardization of elliptic curves also makes it convenient for interoperability and use by external third party cryptographic providers to provide cryptographic solutions that comply with the security standards.

Implementation of Fingerprint Based Biometrics

Properties like user authentication increase the robustness of a system that implements such fair exchange protocols and creates a complete system that can be used for making end-to-end transactions. This section discusses the role biometrics in our system. Biometrics is used for user authentication where something the user has, in our case their finger, is used for their identification. The biometric data required by our system is captured by scanning a finger over the fingerprint scanning device. This model is known as a fingerprint-based authentication system. It is one of the cheapest, fastest and most reliable ways to identify someone. Being one of the oldest is it also the most widely used authentication system. Based on their technique of processing fingerprints and identifying users, fingerprint based authentication systems are classified as graph based or minutiae based. Our system implements the minutiae based technique since it is more efficient.

Once a finger is scanned, it is temporarily stored in raw image format. This capture also known as the *fingerprint* is then used for creating a *template*. A Template is a small file created from the unique characteristics extracted from these fingerprints. These unique characteristics are features in the ridges and furrows of the friction skin observed on the fingerprint image and are known as *minutiae* (Watson et al., 2007). Points on the fingerprint where ridges end or split are known as *ridge endings* or *bifurcations* respectively.

Templates in general only take a fraction of the size of a fingerprint image and usually range from a couple of bytes to a couple of kilobytes at most thus making them very efficient for comparisons and storage. A template usually has around 100 to 200 minutiae. It should be noted that it are these templates that are used for verification and identification purposes and not the actual fingerprint image. Biometric template matching algorithms are used to compare these templates with one an-other which basically look for similarities in their minutiae. During a comparison of two templates, every time similarities in the minutiae are discovered, a scalar count variable is incremented. Once this count crosses a pre-defined threshold value, the templates are considered to be of the same person. A utility like MINDTCT, which is part of the NIST Biometric Image Software package, can generate template files. It is a minutiae detector that automatically locates and records ridge ending and bifurcations (minutiae) in a fingerprint image. The generated template file contains a list of minutiae as discovered from the fingerprint image and a set of corresponding values which represent their location based on X and Y axis coordinates and their proximity to other minutiae in the fingerprint. For detailed information on this utility and the description of the contents of the template file, readers are requested to refer the manual (man) pages of MINDTCT software.

Our software is written in Java and implements a minutia based fingerprint authentication system and the API's used were provided by Griaule Biometrics. Figure 1 is a screenshot of the minutiae that were extracted from the fingerprint image captured using our software by scanning a finger over the fingerprint reader.

Figure 1. Minutiae extracted from a fingerprint using Griaule software API

The large blue colored circles represent the minutiae that were extracted from the fingerprint. The smaller red colored circles are used to represent the angles each minutia make from the horizon. The green lines connecting the blue colored circles show proximity between two discovered minutiae. A combination of the above information is contained in each template which is then stored and used later for user authentication.

Benefits of Minutiae Based Fingerprint Authentication System

Minutiae are widely believed to be the most selective and dependable features of a fingerprint. Following are some advantages of using minutiae based fingerprint authentication system:

Compared to its competitive graph-based technique, the amount of information required to be stored in the database for fingerprint matching and the amount of time required for processing are both less (Gupta, Ravi, Raghunathan & Jha, 2005). This is beneficial as fewer resources are used for storage and processing.

Fingerprints have a property of being unique and immutable, allowing for a rather small False Acceptance Rate (1%) and False Rejection Rate (0.1%).

The extracted minutiae cannot be used to recreate the original fingerprint making it a one way procedure that increases security.

Use of Biometrics for Cryptographic Key Generation

Apart from the use for authentication and identification in our system, biometrics is also being used for the generation of cryptographic keys. These keys are used for signing contracts and verifying digital signatures during the contract signing protocol. Our system stores each user's template and their corresponding cryptographic key pair in a database. During user authentication once a user is identified, their corresponding keys

are retrieved from the database and loaded in the software for contract signing purposes. These keys are generated by a cryptographic key generator that uses the user's template as a *seed*. A seed is a random value used by a pseudorandom number generator or a key generator for creating unique and unpredictable outputs or keys. Selection of a good random seed is very critical for the robustness of any security model. Templates solve this purpose efficiently since each template generated is unique.

ANALYSIS

Our Software Implementation

This section provides a detailed explanation of the software implementation for our research work. Our software is written in Java using NetBeans as the Integrated Development Environment (IDE). Biometrics part of our software was achieved using API's from *Griaule Biometrics*. This provided our software the ability to communicate with external USB fingerprint scanners and other features described later in this section. We use a Microsoft Fingerprint Reader to scan user fingers for fingerprints. Cryptography based on elliptic curves and AES was achieved using the external cryptography provider called *FlexiProvider*. Figure 2 shows the main window of our application followed by the protocol execution and explanation.

Normal Execution

This window is used by each party who wants to sign a contract electronically using our improved fair exchange protocol. The above window is of the client Alice who wants to sign a contract with Bob. When the application is first run, the Microsoft Fingerprint Reader along with the databases which store the templates and cryptographic keys are initialized. The user, which is Alice in this case, is then required to scan her finger over

Figure 2. Contract Signing - Fair Execution

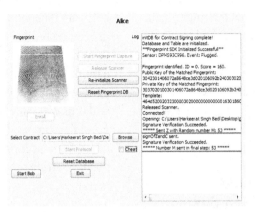

the fingerprint reader. Doing so, an image of her fingerprint scanned is displayed in the fingerprint section of our application window. Once the image is scanned, a new template is created based on the fingerprint and is compared with all the templates in the database to look for matches. The template matching algorithm is run and if a match is found, the user, which in our case is Alice, is successfully identified. In the log window, we can see that the fingerprint was identified with the *ID* of *0* (zero). This *ID* value of zero is an integer that represents the first user enrolled in the database; the second user is represented by 1 and the third by 2 and so on. It also displays a score that shows the number of minutiae similarities identified between the template in question and the template stored in the database. Once identified, the cryptographic keys (both public key and private key) stored along with the matching template are retrieved. These retrieved keys are then used during the contract signing protocol. The log window shows the public and private keys retrieved from the database for quick reference along with the matching template in hexadecimal format.

During the initial user enrollment, users are required to scan their finger over the fingerprint reader. Once scanned, a template is created from the fingerprint image and is used as a *seed* for the cryptographic key generation algorithm. Since templates generated are always unique in nature,

they provide as a good random seed value for such algorithms. The cryptographic keys generated, along with the template are stored in the database under a unique user identification number represented by the variable *ID* as discussed above.

Once the user is identified, the *Start Protocol* button is highlighted. Users can now select the file that they what to sign electronically using the *Browse* button. Once the file is selected, the user can press the *Start Protocol* button and perform contract signing with other users. Note: Both users who want to sign a contract together are required to be authenticated in their own application windows prior to execution of the protocol. Once the *Start Protocol* button is pressed, our fair exchange protocol is executed and messages are exchanged between both the participating parties. All messages exchanged are encrypted using a hybrid cryptosystem which provides efficient encryption and decryption along with properties like non-repudiation and data integrity. In the screenshot above, the two values underlined in red above show the secret value M sent by Alice to Bob during the Steps 3 and 5 of our protocol. For the contract signing to be fair, Alice is required to send the same value of M to Bob in the final Step 5 so that Bob can recreate the information packet Z and obtain complete resolution of Alice over the contract.

222

Abnormal Execution

To demonstrate the functionality of the third party which provides resolution if Alice cheats, a *Cheat* button is provided in our application that forces Alice to cheat by sending the wrong value of M in the final step 5. This way the other party, which is Bob in our case, is not able to recreate the packet Z with the received M and therefore does not have complete commitment of Alice over the contract. Figure 3 is a screenshot that demonstrates Alice cheating Bob and its explanation.

We observe that the *Cheat* button in Figure 3 is enabled. Doing so, forces Alice to cheat by sending the wrong value of M. In our software, Alice is forced to send a value that is one integer higher than the original value. In the example above the original value of M used for creating the packet Z was 10. In the final step Alice sends the value 11 to Bob. Therefore, Bob is not able to recreate the packet Z as he gets 11 and not 10.

Dispute Resolution

In the Figure 4, the first red underline shows the wrong value of $M(11)$ received by Bob from Alice. Our software provides a provision for contacting the third party using the *Contact Third Party* but-ton to obtain resolution. Once the *Contact Third Party* button is pressed, Bob sends his and Alice's signatures on the contract along with the packet Z and the hash of the contract to the third party. On receiving, the third party verifies the signatures of both the parties and if valid, decrypts the packet Z using its private key and extracts the original value $M(10)$. This value of M is then sent to Bob, who on receiving the same tries to recreate the packet Z. Since it is the same value used by Alice, Bob is able recreate the packet Z. The second underline shows the value received from the third party which is 10. Thus, cheated Bob was able to obtain resolution from the third party that provided him with complete commitment from Alice.

Performance Enhancement Using Elliptic Curve Cryptography

Majority of security systems still use first generation public key cryptographic algorithms like RSA and Diffie-Hellman (DH) which were developed in mid-1970. For these systems the current NIST recommended public key parameter size is 1024 bits. NIST states that these systems can be used securely till 2010 after which it is recommended to shift to other systems which provide better security. One alternative can be to keep increasing

Figure 3. Contract Signing - Unfair Execution

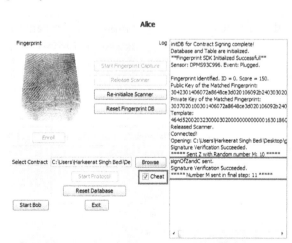

Figure 4. Contract Signing - Dispute Resolution

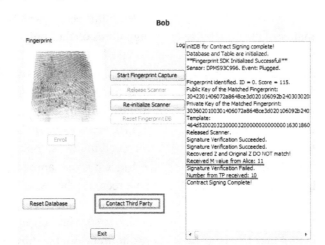

the bit size to higher values so that these systems can be used for some more time. Another option can be to shift to next generation cryptographic systems like elliptic curve cryptography which provide equivalent security for smaller key sizes and are also more efficient. Following is Table 1 that compares ECC with schemes like RSA and Diffie-Hellman in terms of key sizes required for securing symmetric keys for varying length by NSA (2009).

We can see that NIST recommends 1024 bit key sizes for securing 80 bits symmetric keys. The same security can be provided by ECC by using 160 bit key size which makes ECC a better solution. Securing a 256 bit symmetric key would require a RSA key with the bit parameters of size 15,360 which is fifteen times the current size used in Internet today. Comparing to ECC, one would

only require keys of size 521 bits which is far smaller.

ECC is also more computationally efficient when compared to RSA and Diffie-Hellman. Even though ECC has more complex arithmetic than RSA and DH, the security added per bit increase in key size does make for the extra time used to handle such complexity. Following is Table 2 that compares the computation required by ECC and schemes like Diffie-Hellman for varying key sizes by NSA (2009).

We can see that as the security level based on key sizes is increased, the difference in the computation required increases at a higher rate which makes ECC much more efficient than the first generation cryptographic algorithms. To further emphasize the benefits of using ECC, following is a snippet from (Lauter, 2004) that discusses the

Table 1. NIST Recommended Key Sizes

Symmetric Key Size (bits)	RSA and Diffie-Hellman Key Size (bits)	Elliptic Curve Key Size (bits)
80	1024	160
112	2048	224
128	3072	256
192	7680	384
256	15360	521

Table 2. Relative Computation Costs of Diffie-Hellman and Elliptic Curves

Security Level (bits)	Ratio of DH Cost: EC Cost
80	3:1
112	6:1
128	10:1
192	32:1
256	64:1

results obtained by them during their comparison between ECC and RSA:

"At the 163-bit ECC/1024-bit RSA security level, an elliptic curve exponentiation for general curves over arbitrary prime fields is roughly 5 to 15 times as fast as an RSA private key operation, depending on the platform and optimizations. At the 256-bit ECC/3072-bit RSA security level the ratio has already increased to between 20 and 60, depending on optimizations. To secure a 256-bit AES key, ECC-521 can be expected to be on average 400 times faster than 15,360-bit RSA."

Due to the above mentioned reasons which include smaller key sizes, better computational efficiency and greater security, Elliptic Curve Cryptography can be considered as a better solution when compared to first generation techniques like RSA and DH. National Security Agency has also decided to move to Elliptic curve cryptography for protecting both classified and unclassified national security information (NSA, 2009).

CONCLUSION

In this chapter we analyze one fair exchange protocol that offers mechanism for fair contract signing between two parties. We illustrate the various design weaknesses in this protocol and the kinds of attacks possible over the same. We also analyze a revised version of this protocol which provides superior fairness by handling many of the discussed attacks. However both these protocols do not provide protection against replay attacks where an intruder can replay messages sent earlier from one party to the other in the form of new contract signing requests. We propose a contract signing protocol which improves upon these protocols to offer better fairness by addressing this likelihood of replay attacks. We implement a complete working system which provides means for performing fair contract signing between two parties and offers features like strong user authentication and efficient password management using a fingerprint based user authentication scheme. Our system also offers properties like confidentiality, data-integrity and non-repudiation achieved through implementation of hybrid cryptography and digital signatures algorithms based on elliptic curves.

REFERENCES

ANSI X9. 63. (1999). *Elliptic Curve Key Agreement and Key Transport Protocols*. Washington, DC: American Bankers Association.

Asokan, N., Schunter, M., & Waidner, M. (1997). Optimistic protocols for fair exchange. In T. Matsumoto (Ed.), *4th ACM Conference on Computer and Communications Security*. ACM Press, Zurich, Switzerland, 1997, (pp. 6, 8–17).

Bao, F., Wang, G., Zhou, J., & Zhu, H. (2004). Analysis and Improvement of Micali's Fair Contract Signing Protocol. *Information Security and Privacy, 3108*, 176–187.

Baum-Waidner, B. (2001). *Optimistic asynchronous multi-party contract signing with reduced number of rounds. ICALP'01, LNCS 2076* (pp. 898–911). Berlin, Germany: Springer.

Bedi, H., Yang, L., & Kizza, J. (2009). Extended Abstract: Fair Electronic Exchange using Biometrics. *Proceedings of the 5th Annual Workshop on Cyber Security and Information Intelligence Research: Cyber Security and Information Intelligence Challenges and Strategies* (pp. 1-4). Oak Ridge: ACM.

Ben-Or, M., Goldreich, O., Micali, S., & Rivest, R. (1990). A fair protocol for signing contracts. *IEEE Transactions on Information Theory, 36*(1), 40–46. doi:10.1109/18.50372

Coffey, T., & Saidha, P. (1996). Non-repudiation with mandatory proof of receipt, ACMCCR. *Computer Communication Review, 26.*

Cox, B., Tygar, J. D., & Sirbu, M. (1995). NetBill security and transaction protocol. In *Proc. 1st USENIX Workshop on Electronic Commerce, 77–88.*

Diffie, W., & Hellman, M. E. (1976). New directions in cryptography. *IEEE Transactions on Information Theory, 22*(6), 644–654. doi:10.1109/TIT.1976.1055638

Ferrer-Gomila, J. L., Payeras-Capella, M., & Huguet-Rotger, L. (2001). *Efficient optimistic n-party contract signing protocol.* 2001 Information Security Conference, LNCS 2200, pages 394-407, Berlin, Germany: Springer.

FIPS. (2001, November). *Federal Information Processing Standards.* Retrieved from http://csrc.nist.gov/publications/fips/fips197/fips-197.pdf

Garay, J., & MacKenzie, P. (1999). Abuse-free multi-party contract signing. *1999 International Symposium on Distributed Computing, LNCS 1693*, pages 151-165, Berlin, Germany: Springer.

Gupta, P., Ravi, S., Raghunathan, A., & Jha, N. K. (2005, June). Efficient Fingerprint-based User Authentication for Embedded Systems. Annual ACM IEEE Design Automation Conference: In *Proceedings of the 42nd annual conference on Design automation*; 13-17 June 2005.

ISO/IEC 13888-1 (1997a). *Information technology - Security techniques - Non-repudiation - Part 1: General*

ISO/IEC 13888-2 (1998). *Information technology - Security techniques - Non-repudiation - Part 2: Mechanisms using symmetric techniques*

ISO/IEC 13888-3 (1997b). *Information technology - Security techniques - Non-repudiation - Part 3: Mechanisms using asymmetric techniques*

Koblitz, N. (1987). Elliptic curve cryptosystems. *Mathematics of Computation, 48*, 203–209.

Kremer, S., & Markowitch, O. (2000). Optimistic non-repudiable information exchange. In J. Biemond (Ed.), *21st Symp. on Information Theory in the Benelux, Werkgemeenschap Informatie- en Communicatietheorie.* Enschede (NL), Wassenaar (NL), 2000, (pp. 139–146).

Lauter, K. (2004, February). *Microsoft Research.* Washington, DC: IEEE Wireless Communications.

Markowitch, O., & Roggeman, Y. (1999). *Probabilistic non-repudiation without trusted third party.* In Second Conference on Security in Communication Networks'99, Amalfi, Italy.

Micali, S. (1997). *Certified E-mail with invisible post offices.* Presented at the RSA '97 conference (1997).

Micali, S. (2003). Simple and Fast Optimistic Protocols for Fair Electronic Exchange. In *Proceedings of the ACM Symposium on Principles of Distributed Computing,* pages 12-19, 2003.

Miller, V. (1986). *Uses of elliptic curves in cryptography", Lecture Notes in Computer Science 218: Advances in Cryptology - CRYPTO '85* (pp. 417–426). Berlin: Springer-Verlag.

NIST. (1999, July). *Recommended Elliptic Curves for Federal Government Use.* Retrieved from http://csrc.nist.gov/csrc/fedstandards.html

NSA. (2009). *The Case for Elliptic Curve Cryptography*. Retrieved from http://www.nsa.gov/business/programs/elliptic_curve.shtml

Piotrowski, K., Langendoerfer, P., & Peter, S. (2006). How public key cryptography influences wireless sensor node lifetime. In *Proceedings of the fourth ACM workshop on Security of ad hoc and sensor networks*.

Ray, I., & Ray, I. (2002, May). Fair Exchange in E-commerce. *ACM SIGecom Exchange, 3*(2), 9–17. doi:10.1145/844340.844345

Tedrick, T. (1983). How to exchange half a bit. In Chaum, D. (Ed.), *Advances in Cryptology: Proceedings of Crypto 83* (pp. 147–151). New York, London: Plenum Press.

Tedrick, T. (1985). Fair exchange of secrets. In G. R. Blakley, D. C. Chaum (Eds.), *Advances in Cryptology: Proceedings of Crypto 84, Vol. 196 of Lecture Notes in Computer Science*. Berlin, Germany: Springer-Verlag, (pp. 434–438).

Watson, C., Garris, M., Tabassi, E., Wilson, C., McCabe, R., Janet, S., & Ko, K. (2007). *User's Guide to NIST Biometric Image Software*. NIST.

Zhang, N., & Shi, Q. (1996). Achieving non-repudiation of receipt. *The Computer Journal, 39*(10), 844–853. doi:10.1093/comjnl/39.10.844

Zhou, J., Deng, R., & Bao, F. (1999). *Evolution of fair non-repudiation with TTP*. ACISP: Information Security and Privacy: Australasian Conference, Vol. 1587 of Lecture Notes in Computer Science, Springer-Verlag, 1999, (pp. 258–269).

Zhou, J., & Gollmann, D. (1996). A fair non-repudiation protocol. In *IEEE Symposium on Security and Privacy, Research in Security and Privacy*, IEEE Computer Society, Technical Committee on Security and Privacy, IEEE Computer Security Press, Oakland, CA, 1996, (pp. 55–61).

Zhou, J., & Gollmann, D. (1997). An efficient non-repudiation protocol. In *Proceedings of The 10th Computer Security Foundations Workshop*, IEEE Computer Society Press, 1997, (pp. 126–132).

Section 5
Cryptography in Emerging Areas

Chapter 10
Secure and Private Service Discovery in Pervasive Computing Environments

Feng Zhu
University of Alabama in Huntsville, USA

Wei Zhu
Intergraph Co, USA

ABSTRACT

With the convergence of embedded computers and wireless communication, pervasive computing has become the inevitable future of computing. Every year, billions of computing devices are built. They are ubiquitously deployed and are gracefully integrated with people and their environments. Service discovery is an essential step for the devices to properly discover, configure, and communicate with each other. Authentication for pervasive service discovery is difficult. In this chapter, we introduce a user-centric service discovery model, called PrudentExposure, which automates authentication processes. It encodes hundreds of authentication messages in a novel code word form. Perhaps the most serious challenge for pervasive service discovery is the integration of computing devices with people. A critical privacy challenge can be expressed as a "chicken-and-egg problem": both users and service providers want the other parties to expose sensitive information first. We discuss how a progressive and probabilistic model can protect both users' and service providers' privacy.

INTRODUCTION

Every year, billions of computing devices are built and seamlessly integrated into our surroundings and daily lives. In the near future, we will live in pervasive computing environments. In these environments, devices range from traditional PCs, printers, or servers, to devices that people carry, wear, and to the devices that are embedded into commodities and ambient environments. Smart phones, iPods, smartcards, RFID tags, and various sensors are already ubiquitous. New types of devices are emerging rapidly. It is predicted that within a decade one may interact with thousands of computing devices in pervasive computing environments.

Unlike traditional computing environments, pervasive computing poses at least two new chal-

DOI: 10.4018/978-1-61520-783-1.ch010

lenges: a great number of devices and extremely dynamic computing environments. Unattended devices and service or partial failures may cause network services inaccessible. New networks services may be added and old services may be removed.

Service discovery is essential to address the two challenges in pervasive computing environments (Zhu, Mutka & Ni 2005). It enables devices and network services to properly discover, configure, and then communicate with each other via a network protocol. The protocol is called service discovery protocol. In next section, we provide more detailed explanation of service discovery protocols and discuss some representative protocols. These protocols greatly reduce the administrative overhead that users and system administrators have to conduct manually nowadays. Device driver installation and network service configuration are all automated by the protocols. Without service discovery protocols, administrative overhead for thousands of devices in one's vicinity is infeasible even for skilled system administrators in pervasive computing environments.

Moreover, service discovery protocols use soft states and lease-based service access to manage network services in the extremely dynamic pervasive computing environments. Soft state means that a service frequently updates its availability information. Lease-based service access allows a client device to access a service for a predetermined period of time. The client needs to renew the access request to further use the service. Both mechanisms gracefully handle failures of the unattended services and networks as well as service addition and removal.

Coupled with wireless networks, service discovery simplifies communication among devices and services. Without connecting cables and manually setting up devices or services, these devices and services can be discovered and configured automatically. Nevertheless, it creates three new security and privacy challenges.

First, computing environments are different. The boundaries are different. Physical boundaries may be disappeared. For example, at present, a digital camera in a bag is not accessible to others. But, if a digital camera communicates with other devices over wireless networks and runs a service discovery protocol, a stranger sits near the bag on a bus might be able to discover the digital camera and access its photos. As Ross Anderson points out, many security solutions failed because of the environments' change (Ross 2008).

Second, unlike relatively homogeneous computing environments in enterprises, in pervasive computing environments, multiple service providers may co-exist at a place. For instance, in Alice's office, the company provides network services. When Alice and her colleagues carry and wear devices and shares with each other, they become service providers. In addition, services provided by the city might also be accessible from her office. Ideally, secure and private service discovery should determine who has privileges to discover and access services. At the same time, service discovery should prevent unauthorized users to discover and access pervasive services even they are in the vicinity. Without proper protection, privacy may be sacrificed. For example, a malicious attacker may find the presence of a person by querying whether a handheld device is in the vicinity. Attackers may also query the devices and services that one carries or wears to find his or her preferences. If an attacker discovers a medical device that one wears, the patient's health information might be inferred.

Third, as we own more and more devices and become service providers, the relationships among users, devices, services, and service providers become more and more complex. Usability is a serious challenge. It is infeasible to require users to memorize all identities and associated passwords or certificates from various service providers. It is also overwhelming for users to memorize the relationship between services and service providers.

Figure 1. The client-service model

With the new environments and new challenges in pervasive computing environments, the key requirements for service discovery are security, privacy, and good usability. For security, only legitimate users can discover and access devices and services. For privacy, we need to protect service information, users' requests, users' presences information, and identities used to access devices and services. For good usability, service discovery protocols should remove the administrative overhead for owners and users to manually set up devices and services. In addition, users do not need a priori knowledge to discover and access services.

Providing security, privacy, and good usability at the same time is difficult. Usually, when security and privacy increase, usability decreases. In pervasive computing environments, however, all three requirements are necessary. In this chapter, we discuss two approaches to achieve the requirements.

BACKGROUND

We classify service discovery protocols into two models: client-service and client-directory-service models. Figure 1 illustrates the architecture of the client-service model. A client queries all services in the vicinity. The client specifies a list of attributes of a service that it is looking for, for example, a color display, with at least 256 colors, and resolution higher than 1024 by 768. If a service finds itself matches the request, it replies back. Then, the client starts to use the service. If there is more than one service that replies back, the client may

select one service to use. With service discovery software installed, the client does not need to configure server settings. No drivers need to be pre-installed. For example, if a client is looking for printing service, a user does not need to manually install a driver on his device to use a printer. The service discovery protocol installs the driver. Hence, people will be relieved from the burden of upgrading and installing software. In addition, service discovery provides fault tolerance. If one of the services is not available, a client will discover another service to use.

From a service's side, besides answering clients' solicitations, a service may announce its information periodically. Thus, interested clients may learn service information and select a service to use.

Client-directory-service model adds one optional layer, directories, between clients and services. Instead of asking all services directly, a client asks directories first to find related services. Figure 2 shows the architecture of the client-directory-service model.

The directories function as a surrogate for both clients and services. When directories hear a service announcement, they update and record service information. Directories can also ask around for available services. When receiving a query from a client, directories reply to the client. And then the client contacts a service. The client-directory-service model is useful in large-scale computing environments where the overhead of handling unrelated service requests and communication between unrelated clients and services are overwhelming.

Figure 2. The client-directory-service model

Service Discovery Protocols

Research in service discovery attracts much attention in both academia and industry. In this subsection, we briefly discuss nine representative service discovery protocols. Interested readers may refer to a survey paper (Zhu, Mutka & Ni 2005) for detailed taxonomy and comparison of service discovery protocols.

Researchers at MIT designed Intentional Naming System (INS) (Adjie-Winoto, Schwartz, Balakrishnan & Lilley 1999). Unlike other approaches, services in INS are indirectly mapped to fixed service locations. INS resolves a service lookup to a service location at the delivery time. In INS/Twine (Balazinska, Balakrishnan & Karger 2002), service discovery is based on peer-to-peer technology, a more scalable approach to handle millions of services. Service lookups, however, may go through several directories, which may have additional search latency.

Secure Service Discovery Service (SSDS) developed at UC Berkeley puts emphasis on security and supports a huge number of services, known as wide-area support (Czerwinski, Zhao, Hodes, Joseph & Katz 1999). Public key and symmetric key encryptions are used for communication privacy and security. A Message Authentication Code (MAC) is used to ensure message integrity. Authentication and authorization are also addressed. For wide-area support, different hierarchical directory structures are considered. By using Bloom filters, SSDS achieves service information aggregation and filtering when building up the hierarchical directories.

IBM Research has studied and proposed a service discovery protocol for single-hop ad hoc environments, known as DEAPspace (Nidd 2001). In contrast to other service discovery protocols in which services announce their information, DEAPspace's algorithm caches service information at each node. Then, each node broadcasts its knowledge of other services and its own services in turn. The nodes learn from each other. Service lookup is accomplished by searching one's local cache. Furthermore, energy weak devices use idle mode to save power.

Operating system vendors are shipping service discovery protocols in their operating systems. Sun Microsystems' Jini is based on Java technology (Sun Microsystems 2003). One special feature of Jini is the mobile Java codes, which may be moved among clients, services, and directories. The advantage of Jini is its platform independency, but the disadvantage is that all the clients, services, and directories depend on the Java runtime environments directly or indirectly.

Universal Plug and Play (UPnP) is from the UPnP Forum (Miller, Nixon, Tai & Wood 2001). The major player is Microsoft Corporation. UPnP targets unmanaged networking environments, such as home environments. UPnP is a device-oriented service discovery protocol. All the service information and communication are in the XML format, which is platform and programming language independent, and therefore greatly increases interoperability between devices.

Apple Computer's Rendezvous is a DNS-based service discovery protocol (Cheshire 2002). It uses the existing DNS resource record types to name and assist service discovery. Rendezvous is also known as Zero Configuration networking (Zeroconf) (Apple Computer Inc 2003). The advantage of Rendezvous is the utilization of the ubiquity of DNS servers.

Several organizations also proposed service discovery standards. Bluetooth, from the Bluetooth Special Interest Group (SIG), enables nearby devices to communicate with each other at low cost and low power consumption (Bluetooth SIG 2004). Part of the Bluetooth specification is the Bluetooth Service Discovery Protocol, which enables Bluetooth devices to discover each other.

The Salutation Consortium rolled out the Salutation protocol (Salutation Consortium 1999). It is an open source protocol and is royalty-free. Its advantage is that it implements two interfaces. One interface is for applications. The other interface is designed to be independent of the transport layer, so that it is very flexible to use various underlying transport protocols and may be used in more environments. Furthermore, a mapping of Salutation over the Bluetooth Service Discovery Protocol has been specified (Miller 1999).

Service Location Protocol (SLP) Version 2 was posted by IETF as a standard track protocol (Guttman, Perkins, Veizades & Day 1999). As the protocol name states, SLP only defines a way

to locate a service and leaves the interaction between clients and services open. URLs are used for service locations.

Security and Privacy Support in the Service Discovery Protocols

Based on the security and privacy features, service discovery protocols may be classified into three categories. In the first category, no security and privacy features are provided by the service discovery protocol. Figure 3 (a) shows this type of service discovery protocols. For example, DEAPspace and INS fall into this category. These protocols are easy to use because there is no administrative overhead for users to discover and access the services. Easy access, however, becomes the main security and privacy problem, since anyone can discover and access anyone else' devices and services. Without security and privacy protection, devices and services are more likely to be the targets of security and privacy attacks.

In the second category, service discovery protocols directly use existing security and privacy solutions (shown in Figure 3(b)). For example, Jini, Salutation, and Bluetooth SDP fall into this category. These protocols usually require authentication. Therefore, users need to supply proper credentials such as user name and password pairs before and during the initial service discovery process. The protocols may also integrate authorization, and thus only users who have privileges can discover and access services. The

Figure 3. Security, privacy, and usability features provided by the three categories of service discovery protocols (a), (b), and (c) and the PrudentExposure approach (d)

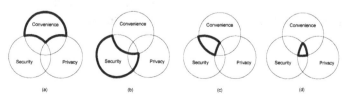

procedure is the same as the traditional network service access. In pervasive computing environments, it is very difficult for users to memorize all the relations among the credentials, services, and services providers. Thus, it dramatically reduces the convenience of the service discovery protocols. In addition, if a user is not aware of a new service, she might not be able to discover the service, and therefore she will miss the opportunity to access it.

SSDS represents the third category, shown in *Figure 3*(c). SSDS applies strong authentication via public key certificates, encryption, and digital signatures. For access control, it uses capabilities. SSDS is a central server design. Suppose there are local directories that are ubiquitously available. Services register their information with local directories. On top of local directories, intermediate directories and the root directory form a hierarchical tree structure. Higher level directories aggregate service information that is available on the lower level directories. To discover and access a service, a user supplies his public key certificate for authentication and authorization. Besides security, SSDS provides convenience as well. Since wherever a user discovers services, his certificate is the only credential needed. The certificate, however, is also a disadvantage for the user. If the certificate is compromised, it affects the user for all service accesses. Privacy is also sacrificed because the server system knows when, where, and what services the user accesses.

PRUDENTEXPOSURE SERVICE DISCOVERY

PrudentExposure service discovery aims to achieve security, privacy, and good usability at the same time as shown in Figure 3(d). However, to achieve convenience, security, and privacy at the same time is challenging. As we have seen in the last section, most existing service discovery

protocols either sacrifice usability to achieve security and privacy or provide good usability but sacrifice security and privacy.

Issues, Controversies, Problems

From a user's side, she may interact with hundreds or thousands of services at different places. She may have hundreds of identities from various service providers. Identity management and proper authentication in such environments have no existing solutions. From a service provider's side, determination of whether a user has the privilege to discover and access a service should be addressed.

We walk through the following scenario first. Throughout this chapter, we base our discussion on this scenario.

1. At home, Bob has various wired and wireless devices, which are shared with his family members.
2. At work, Bob mainly uses his computer to perform job tasks. He shares some of his computing devices such as personal file server and printers with his colleagues. He also brings his personal devices to his office such as cell phone, MP3 player, Bluetooth headphone, etc. He might share some pieces of music on his MP3 player with his colleagues but not the cell phone. He might also access music on his colleagues' MP3 players.
3. On the way that Bob commutes between work and home, he does not want anyone riding the same bus or train to access his digital devices.

A New Service Discovery Architecture

Figure 4 illustrates a new architecture that consists of four components. Besides the components in the client-directory-service model, the PrudentExposure model has a user agent, which aggregates and manages all identities that a user has. A user agent may run on a PDA, a mobile phone, or other device that a user always carries or wears. The user agent acts on behalf of a user and an algorithm will select the proper identities for the authentication. A client and a user agent may establish a secure channel through side channels as discussed in (Stajano & Anderson 1999).

Each service provider has directories. Unlike other service discovery protocols, services only register with directories that belong to the same service provider. For example, Bob may use his cell phone as a directory to manage all his wearable and handheld devices. He may use his home PC as another directory to manger the devices at home. A service and a directory establish a long term control relationship and communicate through an encrypted channel. All service accesses are via the directory and the directory instructs the services which users can access the services.

The client and the user agent may be considered as the user's side. The services and the directory may be considered as the service provider's side. Secure and proper interactions depend on the user agent and the directory. The user agent broadcasts a message to ask for available administrative domains in the vicinity. Then, all directories in the vicinity check whether the user is a valid user. If the directories find the user has privileges, they respond the user agent. Next, the directories and the user agent authenticate each other.

The novelty of PrudentExposure is that the messages exchanged between user agent and service directory are "code words" (Zhu, Mutka & Ni 2006). These code words are in the Bloom filter format. Hundreds of code words can easily fit in one network packet. Without loss of generality, let us assume that Bob access three domains – "Bob", "Office", and "David". David is his colleague next door. When Bob discovers a service in his office, his user agent broadcasts three code words in one network packet for the "Home", "Office", and "David" domains. The "Home" directory is not nearby, so it does not response. The "Office" directory and "David" directory hear the code words. Since the two directories understand their respective code words, they response to Bob's user agent. Another colleague, Alice, may be also in the vicinity. If Bob and Alice do not share a code word, Alice's directory does not understand any code word. And thus, it does not reply.

Generate and Verify Code Words

Figure 5 shows the code word generation. The Bloom filter is an array of bits as shown at the bottom of the figure. A code word is a combination of several bits that are set in a Bloom filter. For example, the two bits in the Bloom filter in

Figure 4. PrudentExpore Model Architecture

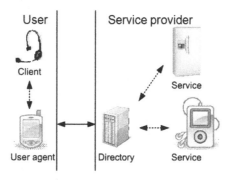

Figure 5. Code word generation

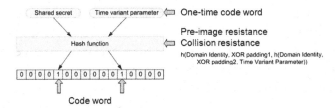

Figure 5 consist of a code word. (All bits are initially set to zero.) We assume that a user and a service provider share a secret before a user can discover services. The shared secret and a time variant parameter are the two inputs to a hash function, specifically, the hash function proposed in (Bellare, Canettiy & Krawczykz 1996). It has the pre-image resistance and collision resistance properties. The hash result is separated into chunks. The chunk length is based on the Bloom filter size. For example, if the Bloom filter is 1024 bits, the chunk length is 10 bits. The chunk is used as an index to set bits in the Bloom filter. If a code word consists of three bits, three chunks of a hash result will be used to set the bits. Readers may find more detailed information about Bloom filter in (Bloom 1970).

Multiple code words can be set in one Bloom filter. The user agent uses the same procedure to generate code words. The same time variant parameter and another shared secret are the two inputs as shown in Figure 6. Another code word

sets two bits in the Bloom filter. If a network packet is 1,500 bytes and an average code word is 5 bits, at least 800 code words can be set in a Bloom filter.

Directories use the same procedure to generate hash results. Instead of setting the bits, directories use the same number of chunks of the hash results to verify whether all the bits of a code word are set in the Bloom filter that it receives. If all bits are set, a directory considers that there is a code word match. However, different chunks of the hash result may set the same bit in the Bloom filter. Similarly, a bit may be set by another code word. This implies that the test of domain match may result in false positive cases. The probability of reporting false positive matches when the user is not a user of this domain is:

$$P(match/nonmember) = \left(\frac{m}{n}\right)^k,$$

Figure 6. Multiple code words in one message

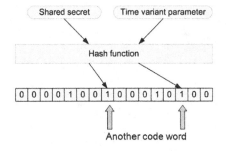

where n is the size of the Bloom filter, m is the number of bits set in the Bloom filter, and k is the number of bits for a domain.

The false positive cases are under user's control. Longer code words or larger Bloom filter size reduces the number of false positive cases. Figure 7 illustrates the change of the false positive rate as the length of the Bloom filter and the number of bits in a Bloom filter change. (Suppose that there are 500 bits set in a Bloom filter (m=500).) As the code word length increases, the false positive rate reduces very quickly. Similarly, as the Bloom filter size increases, the false positive rate decreases quickly.

By using one way hash functions, it is computationally difficult to find the shared secrets from the Bloom filters. More detailed analysis of mathematical properties, the secure service discovery protocol, threat analysis, and formal verification are in the authors' another work (Zhu, Mutka & Ni 2006).

The PrudentExposure approach is efficient. The secure service discovery protocol was implemented on PDAs with 200 MHz CPU, 64 MB RAM, and 2 Mb wireless connections. Experiment results show that generating 100 code words takes less than 16ms, while it takes a directory about 5ms to verify a code word.

In summary, PrudentExposure achieves security via code words, authentication, and encrypted communication. Only users who share secrets with service providers can discover services. Privacy including users' and service providers' identities and their presence information is protected because those who do not know the shared secrets do not understand the communication. PrudentExposure automates the authentication process, and thus users do not need a priori knowledge to discover services and memorize hundreds of identities.

PROGRESSIVE AND PROBABILISTIC EXPOSURE

Let us revisit the example of Bob's cases and think of the following question. If Bob needs to access an electronic book on company's file server, why does David need to know what Bob is looking for? Even if Bob has a credential from David, David doesn't have the service that Bob is looking for at this time. The communication between Bob and David is wasted, until Bob's user agent learns that he cannot get the service from David. Privacy information such as his presence and his service request is unnecessarily exposed to David. If the "need to know" principle is applied, the problem will be solved. If David does not have the electronic book that Bob is looking for, Bob does not query David's directory for services.

Issues, Controversies, Problems

It is difficult in pervasive computing environments to apply the "need to know" principle. The environments are very dynamic. For example, David does not share electronic books with Bob.

Figure 7. False positive rate changes as k and n change

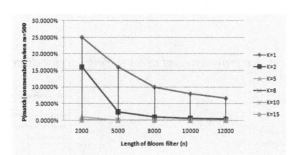

Tomorrow, he may share his books with Bob. It is infeasible for Bob to memorize all service and service provider relationships and to be aware of up-to-date service information.

For service providers, the ideal solution is that a user reveals her request first. If a service provider does not provide the service, she simply doesn't respond. Similarly, for users, the ideal solution is that service providers announce the services provided first. And then, the users can determine which service provider to contact. But who should reveal information first? This is a "chicken-and-egg" problem because both parties want the other party to expose their information first. How should they communicate and establish trust?

Progressively Expose Service Information and Identities

Let's further analyze the PrudentExposure model. A user queries all service providers that she shares a secret with. If the "need to know" principle is applied, a subset of the service providers need to be identified that the user shares secrets with and also provide the requested service as shown in the left side of Figure 8. Similarly, a service provider is interested in identifying a subset of users that she shares secrets with, who request an existing service, and who have privilege to access the service, as shown in the right side of Figure 8.

A novel idea is to expose users' and service providers' identity information, users' service requests, and service providers' service information progressively and in multiple rounds (Zhu, Zhu, Mutka & Ni 2007). In each round, few bits of information are exchanged. Both a user and a

service provider check whether there is any mismatch, as shown in Figure 9. The user checks whether a service provider knows the shared secret and provide the requested service, while the service provider checks whether the user knows the shared secret, has privilege, and requests an existing service. If there is any mismatch, the user and the service provider will quit the service discovery process. Since they exchanged only partial information, neither the user nor the service provider is certain about the sensitive information that she received from the other party.

During the service discovery process, a user and a service provider exchange encrypted information. Like the PrudentExposure approach, they speak code words to verify whether the other party is the party that they want to contact. In addition, they encrypt service information and service requests before they send to the other party by using one-time secret. If the other party knows the shared secret, she can properly decrypt the information.

To generate code words and one-time secrets, a similar method that discussed in Figure 5 may be used. For code word generation, a shared secret and a time variant parameter are the two inputs to a hash function. Instead of setting the bits in a Bloom filter, the bits are directly used. In each round, several bits of the hash result is used and exchanged. Figure 10 shows an example, in which a user and a service provider share a secret and exchange a code word. The user sends the first four bits and the service provider verifies. After the service provider finds that the four bits match her code word, she sends the next two bits. Then, the user verifies. Since the user and the service

Figure 8. Find appropriate service providers and users during service discovery

Figure 9. Progressively expose sensitive information between a service provider and a user

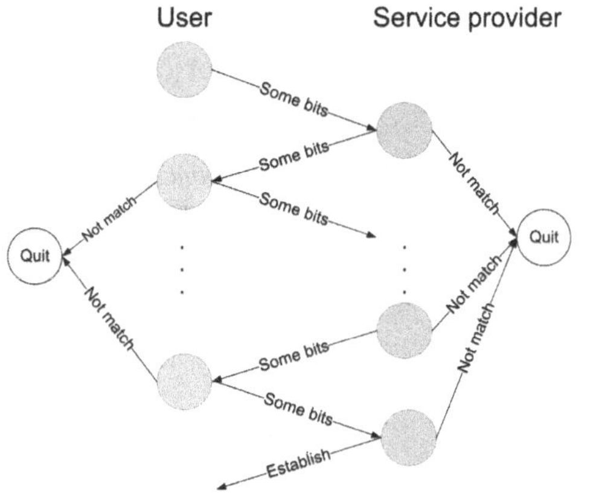

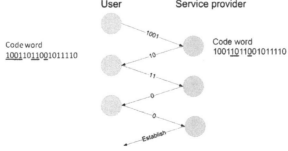

provider share a secret, they keep finding the bits of the code word match. After multiple rounds, both the service provider and the user believe that the other party is extremely likely to understand the code word. Therefore, they establish the connection to provide and use the service. If a user and a service provider do not share a secret, they will find mismatch of some bits, and thus they quit the service discovery process.

Figure 10 shows a simplified version. In the actual service discovery, code words, encrypted service information, and encrypted service requests are exchanged at the same time. The detailed encoding scheme and the strategies to exchange the bits can be found in (Zhu, Zhu, Mutka & Ni 2007).

The Probabilistic Exposures and Strategies

The progressive exposure, shown in Figure 9, may be converted into a Markov chain. Figure 11 illustrates the process. The system starts with a user sending some bits of a code word and some bits of a service request to a service provider. Then, service provider checks. If there is no mismatch, the service provider sends a few bits of the code word and service information for the user to verify. The process repeats. If they should establish a service access session, they will always reach that state. If they should not establish a session, there is a possibility that in each step the bits exchanged are match. These matches are the false positive cases.

The false positive cases can be calculated as shown in (Zhu, Zhu, Mutka & Ni 2007). It is based

Figure 10. An example that a service provider and a user exchange code words

Figure 11. The progressive exposure in the form of a Markov chain

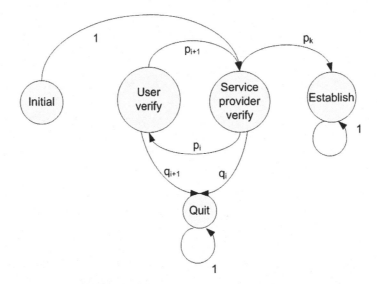

on two factors: how likely a user is a valid user in a certain environment and how many bits are exchanged. By using the properties of the Markov chain, it can be shown that the false positive cases decrease exponentially. Figure 12 shows an example that after few rounds, the number of false positive cases approaches zero. Thus, it is unlikely that a user and a service provider who should not establish a connection will keep finding matches in code words, the service request, and the service information.

Neither users nor service providers need to calculate the probabilities during their interaction. First, they determine the false positive rates for

the code words and the false positive rates for the service information and service requests. Then, they simply conduct table lookups. The tables are pre-calculated with the information about the number of rounds and number of bits that they need to exchange in each round. In general, a user and a service provider exchange one or two bits of a code word, service information, and a service request in a message. Although a user may interact with many service providers in some environments and they exchange few bits of information in a round, the service discovery process always converges as proved in (Zhu, Zhu, Mutka & Ni 2007).

Figure 12. False positive case decreases exponentially

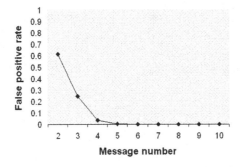

Exchange partial information in multiple rounds minimizes unnecessary privacy exposure. But, the approach does introduce communication overhead between users and service providers. One round of messages becomes multiple rounds. Experiments on a set of similar PDAs (200MHz CPU, 64MB RAM, and 2 Mb wireless connections) have shown that the overhead to generate 100 code words and establish a service access session with a service provider takes 100ms. Each additional service provider involved in a discovery process takes another 30 ms. Therefore, the approach is still efficient in most service discovery cases in pervasive computing environments.

In summary, the progressive exposure approach protects both users' and service providers' privacy. It solves the "chicken-and-egg" problem via a probabilistic approach. Unnecessary exposure is quickly identified and terminated. The approach is designed for service discovery for pervasive computing environments, but it can be used in general for any exposure negotiation when two parties expect the other party to exposure information first.

FUTURE RESEARCH DIRECTIONS

The two approaches that we discussed in this chapter achieve security, privacy, and good usability at the same time in general. Often in different environments or situations, there may be different emphasis on different aspects. One design might give more weight on security, whereas the other may consider usability as the highest priority. As we see in the past that emphasis on only one aspect usually sacrifices other aspects. Thus, new designs need to be properly balanced on all three aspects.

Service discovery in different environments may use different strategies for authentication and information exposure. Ideally, we want to expose appropriate amount of information to the appropriate party at the appropriate time. Nevertheless, there is no one solution fits all situations.

In different situations, one might use completely different strategies for information exposure, for example, discovery of a service for medical emergency and discovery of a toy store location in a shopping mall. There is still lack of approaches to automatically select or help users to select the best strategies.

Users have many identities in pervasive computing environments. For the service providers that they have interacted before, users may have identities that associated with the service providers. Both the PrudentExposure and the progressive exposure approaches address such situations. In many situations, users and service providers are unfamiliar with each other. Users may not have identities to authenticate with the service providers. Service discovery in such environments is still an open problem. For example, one may travel to a country for the first time. It is very likely that service providers and environments are unfamiliar to the user. Although public key infrastructure might be a solution (Zhu, Mutka & Ni 2003), it seems less likely that the name and public key binding provided by the public key infrastructure will solve all problems.

Trust is another critical challenge for service discovery in pervasive computing environments. The more information that a user exchanges with a service provider, the more trust they establish. Nevertheless, trust and privacy may be a conflict, since the more information exchanged the less privacy the user and the service provider may maintain. It might become very difficult for unfamiliar users and service providers to solve the conflict.

CONCLUSION

In pervasive computing environments, service discovery protocols need to provide security, privacy, and good usability at the same time. Unlike traditional computer environments, it is difficult for users to manually handle hundreds of identities and memorize complex relationships among users, services, and service providers. PrudentExposure automates the authentication process by generating and exchanging code words. Via three messages, users and service providers efficiently determine the legitimacy of each other. The approach is scalable to support hundreds of code words in one network packet.

The progressive service discovery approach extended PrudentExposure model. It applies the "need to know" principle in service discovery among users and service providers who have incomplete information about each other. Based on probabilistic and partial exposure, it protects the privacy of both users' and service providers'.

REFERENCES

Adjie-Winoto, W., Schwartz, E., Balakrishnan, H., & Lilley, J. (1999). The design and implementation of an intentional naming system. *17th ACM Symposium on Operating Systems Principles (SOSP '99)*, Kiawah Island, SC.

Apple Computer Inc. (2003). Rendezvous Web Site. Retrieved from http://developer.apple.com/macosx/rendezvous/

Balazinska, M., Balakrishnan, H., & Karger, D. (2002). INS/Twine: A Scalable Peer-to-Peer Architecture for Intentional Resource Discovery. *Pervasive 2002 - International Conference on Pervasive Computing*, Zurich, Switzerland, Springer-Verlag.

Bellare, M., Canettiy, R., & Krawczykz, H. (1996). Keying Hash Functions for Message Authentication. *Advances in Cryptology–CRYPTO '96 (LNCS 1109)*.

Bloom, B. (1970). Space/Time Trade-offs in Hash Coding with Allowable Errors. *Communications of the ACM, 13*(7), 422–426. doi:10.1145/362686.362692

Bluetooth, S. I. G. (2004). *Specification of the Bluetooth System*. Retrieved from http://www.bluetooth.org/

Cheshire, S. (2002). *Discovering Named Instances of Abstract Services using DNS, Apple Computer*. Retrieved from http://files.dns-sd.org/draft-cheshire-dnsext-dns-sd.txt

Czerwinski, S., Zhao, B. Y., Hodes, T., Joseph, A., & Katz, R. (1999). An Architecture for a Secure Service Discovery Service. *Fifth Annual International Conference on Mobile Computing and Networks (MobiCom '99)*, Seattle, WA.

Guttman, E., Perkins, C., Veizades, J., & Day, M. (1999). *Service Location Protocol, Version 2*. Retrieved from http://www.ietf.org/rfc/rfc2608.txt

Miller, B. (1999). *Mapping Salutation Architecture APIs to Bluetooth Service Discovery Layer, Bluetooth SIG*. Retrieved from http://www.salutation.org/whitepaper/btoothmapping.pdf

Miller, B. A., Nixon, T., Tai, C., & Wood, M. D. (2001). Home Networking with Universal Plug and Play. *IEEE Communications Magazine*, (December): 104–109. doi:10.1109/35.968819

Nidd, M. (2001). Service Discovery in DEAPspace. *IEEE Personal Communications* (August): 39-45.

Ross, A. (2008). *Security Engineering: A Guide to Building Dependable Distributed Systems* (2nd ed.). New York: Wiley.

Salutation Consortium. (1999). Salutation Architecture Specification. Retrieved from ftp://ftp.salutation.org/salute/sa20e1a21.ps

Stajano, F., & Anderson, R. (1999). The Resurrecting Duckling: Security Issues for Ad-hoc Wireless Networks. *7th International Workshop on Security protocols*, Cambridge, UK.

Sun Microsystems. (2003). Jini Technology Core Platform Specification, from http://wwws.sun.com/software/jini/specs/

Zhu, F., Mutka, M., & Ni, L. (2003). Splendor: A Secure, Private, and Location-aware Service Discovery Protocol Supporting Mobile Services. *1st IEEE Annual Conference on Pervasive Computing and Communications*, Fort Worth, Texas, IEEE Computer Society Press.

Zhu, F., Mutka, M., & Ni, L. (2005). Service Discovery in Pervasive Computing Environments. *IEEE Pervasive Computing / IEEE Computer Society [and] IEEE Communications Society*, *4*(4), 81–90. doi:10.1109/MPRV.2005.87

Zhu, F., Mutka, M., & Ni, L. (2006). A Private, Secure and User-centric Information Exposure Model for Service Discovery Protocols. *IEEE Transactions on Mobile Computing*, *5*(4), 418–429. doi:10.1109/TMC.2006.1599409

Zhu, F., Zhu, W., Mutka, M., & Ni, L. (2007). Private and Secure Service Discovery via Progressive and Probabilistic Exposure. *IEEE Transactions on Parallel and Distributed Systems*, *18*(11), 1565–1577. doi:10.1109/TPDS.2007.1075

Chapter 11
Multimedia Information Security:
Cryptography and Steganography

Ming Yang
Jacksonville State University, USA

Monica Trifas
Jacksonville State University, USA

Nikolaos Bourbakis
Wright State University, USA

Lei Chen
Sam Houston State University, USA

ABSTRACT

Information security has traditionally been ensured with data encryption techniques. Different generic data encryption standards, such as DES, RSA, AES, have been developed. These encryption standards provide high level of security to the encrypted data. However, they are not very efficient in the encryption of multimedia contents due to the large volume of digital image/video data. In order to address this issue, different image/video encryption methodologies have been developed. These methodologies encrypt only the key parameters of image/video data instead of encrypting it as a bitstream. Joint compression-encryption is a very promising direction for image/video encryption. Nowadays, researchers start to utilize information hiding techniques to enhance the security level of data encryption methodologies. Information hiding conceals not only the content of the secret message, but also its very existence. In terms of the amount of data to be embedded, information hiding methodologies can be classified into low bitrate and high bitrate algorithms. In terms of the domain for embedding, they can be classified into spatial domain and transform domain algorithms. In this chapter, we have reviewed various data encryption standards, image/video encryption algorithms, and joint compression-encryption methodologies. Besides, we have also presented different categories of information hiding methodologies as well as data embedding strategies for digital image/video contents. This chapter is organized as following: in Section-1, we give a brief introduction to data encryption system as well as the state-of-the-art encryption standards; Section-2 presents a review of representative image encryption algorithms; Section-3

DOI: 10.4018/978-1-61520-783-1.ch011

first gives a brief introduction of lossless compression and then moves to joint compression-encryption algorithms; Section-4 presents different video encryption methodologies; Section-5 gives a brief introduction to information hiding techniques; Section-6 presents different categories of low bitrate information algorithms; Section-7 presents different categories of high bitrate information algorithms; Section-8 discusses the embedding strategies within digital video contents; this chapter is summarized in Section-9.

INTRODUCTION

In modern information and communication systems, information security is becoming an increasingly important issue due to the threats from all different types of attacks. Traditionally, information security has been ensured with data encryption. With the development of modern information hiding theory, researchers start to resort to information hiding techniques to enhance the security level of data encryption systems. In this chapter, we will first review different encryption techniques for multimedia data, including digital image and video contents. After that, we will move to the information hiding techniques for digital multimedia contents.

General Model

Encryption is a method to protect information from undesirable attacks by converting it into a form that is non-recognizable by its attackers. Data encryption mainly is the scrambling of the content of data, such as text, image, audio, video, etc. to make the data unreadable, invisible or incomprehensible during transmission. The in-

verse of data encryption is data *decryption*, which recovers the original data. Figure 1 is the general model of a typical encryption/decryption system. The encryption procedure could be described as $C = E\ (P,\ K)$, where P is the plaintext (original message), E is the encryption algorithm, K is the encryption key, and C is the ciphertext (scrambled message). The ciphertext is transmitted through the communication channel, which is subject to attacks. At the receiver end, the decryption procedure could be described as $P = D\ (C,\ K')$, where C is the ciphertext, D is the decryption algorithm, K' is the decryption key (not necessarily the same as the encryption key K), and P is the recovered plaintext.

Claude Shannon pointed out that the fundamental techniques to encrypt a block of symbols are confusion and diffusion. Confusion can obscure the relationship between the plaintext and the ciphertext, and diffusion can spread the change throughout the whole ciphertext. Substitution is the simplest type of confusion, and permutation is the simplest method of diffusion. Substitution replaces a symbol with another one; permutation changes the sequence of the symbols in the block

Figure 1. Data Encryption/Decryption System

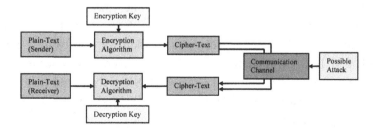

to make them unreadable. These two techniques are the foundations of encryption algorithms.

Secret-Key Versus Public-Key

Kerckhoff claimed that the security of an encryption/decryption system should rely on the secrecy of the key instead of on the algorithm itself. The security level of an encryption algorithm is measured by the length of the key or the size of the key space. Based on the types of encryption/decryption key, the encryption systems can be classified into secret-key systems and public-key systems. The secret-key system is also called the symmetric system because the decryption key is the same as the encryption key. In a secret-key system, the encryption/decryption key has to be transmitted prior to the transmission of the ciphertext, and this requires a separate secure communication channel. The public-key system, which is also called the asymmetric system, has a decryption key that is different from the encryption key. Each person in the group knows the encryption key. This way each member can use the public key to encrypt a message, but only the person who has the decryption key can decrypt the ciphertext. With the public-key encryption system, there is no need for a secure communication channel to transmit the encryption key.

Encryption Standards

Depending on the type of plaintext, data encryption systems can be classified into text encryption, audio encryption, image encryption and video encryption. In order to have a generic cryptosystem that can encrypt different types of data, some encryption standards have been developed. Among them, DES (Data Encryption Standard), RSA (Rivest, Shamir and Adleman), AES (Advanced Encryption Standard) and IDEA (International Data Encryption Algorithm) are widely adopted. In general, these encryption standards consider all forms of multimedia data - such as text, image

and video - as bit stream and encrypt them without any differentiation.

- **DES:** a typical private-key system that was proposed in 1975 by IBM and approved in 1977 as a Federal Information Processing Standard. DES has been adopted in many practical applications, such as electronic funds transfer and civilian satellite communication protection. DES is a 16-round, private-key cipher system. The simplicity of its basic operations makes DES high-speed and low-cost in the hardware/software implementation. The well-known attacks to DES are differential cryptanalysis and linear cryptanalysis. Diffie and Hellman, the inventors of the asymmetric cryptosystem, reported that they had broken a piece of DES-encoded ciphertext with a $20-million parallel machine and exhaustive-search algorithm in around one day. Since 1998, DES is no longer a standard due to its reduced level of security.

- **RSA:** named after its inventors—Rivest, Shamir and Adleman, is basically a public-key, asymmetric cryptosystem for both encryption and authentication. In 1976, Diffie and Hellman proposed the idea for public-key cryptosystems. One year later, Rivest, Shamir and Adleman implemented the first public-key system in the world – RSA. RSA is based on factoring, modular, and exponential operations. It is very easy to implement the encryption function, but it is difficult to implement the reverse of the encryption function unless the decryption key is known. RSA has been used in encryption and authentication applications.

- **AES:** with more powerful computing hardware/software, DES standard has proven to be insecure. As a result, in 1997, NIST (National Institute of Standards and Technology) called for proposals for the next generation of encryption standard.

After three years' work, NIST announced its selection of the AES algorithm. In 2001, AES became the official encryption standard. Rijndael, the algorithm used in the AES standard, was developed by Belgians, Daemen and Rijmen. AES is a block-structured algorithm with variable length keys of 128 bits, 192 bits and 256 bits. The AES algorithm has very good performance in both hardware and software implementations.

- **IDEA:** IDEA (International Data Encryption Algorithm) basically operates on the 64-bit block and 16-bit sub-block with the key length of 128-bit. IDEA operates on a 64-bit plaintext block. The input block is divided into four 16-bit sub-blocks. The basic operations are XOR, addition, and multiplication. The algorithm uses a 128-bit key. Thus, it obtains a higher security level compared to that of DES. IDEA uses an algorithm similar to that of DES. However, IDEA is considered to be superior to DES. For example, it is considered to be immune to differential cryptanalysis from which DES has been suffering.

Comparative Results

A comparison of different encryption standards is illustrated in Table-1.

IMAGE ENCRYPTION

Why Not Naïve Algorithms?

As an important multimedia data type, the digital image and its encryption have attracted a lot of research interests. There are two levels of security for digital image encryption: low-level security encryption and high-level security encryption (Fig. 2). In low-level security encryption, the encrypted image has degraded visual quality compared to that of the original one, but the content of the image is still visible and understandable to the viewers. In high-level security case, the content is completely scrambled and the image just looks like random noise.

If the image data is considered just as a data bitstream, there is no fundamental difference between image encryption and other types of data encryption. We can just input the image data bitstream into the standard encryption system. This type of still image encryption is called a naïve algorithm. However, considering the special properties of digital image/video data contents, more elaborate image/video encryption algorithms are desired for the following reasons:

- Considering the typical size of a digital image compared to that of a text message, the naïve algorithm usually cannot meet the requirements for real-time applications. Thus, we need to avoid encrypting the im-

Table 1. Comparison Table

	Complexity	Speed	Memory Requirement	Key Type	Key Length	Key Space Size	Security Level
DES	Complex	High	N/A	Private-key	56 bits (48 bits Sub-key)	2^{56}	Low
RSA	Simple	High	N/A	Public-key	Variable	Variable	High
IDEA	Simple	High	N/A	Private-key	128 bits	2^{128}	High
AES	Complex	High	Very Low	Private-key	128 bits, 192 bits, 256 bits	$2^{128}, 2^{192}, 2^{256}$	High

Figure 2. Digital Image Encryption

(a) Original Image   (b) Low-Level Encryption   (c) High-Level Encryption

age bit by bit and yet ensure a secure encryption system;

- Naïve algorithms encrypt the image/video contents into a totally un-recognizable format, which may not always be necessary. Sometimes, it is enough to degrade the visual qualities of original image/video contents, and very high levels of encryption (with the standards) is not necessary;

- Digital image/video contents are usually stored and transmitted in compressed formats. It makes sense to integrate the compression and encryption procedures into one single process, which achieves both tasks. Thus, the compression process and the encryption process can enhance each other, share CPU time, and avoid processing delay.

Nowadays, many new algorithms for image/video encryption have been proposed, which exploit the properties inherent to image and video data and thus gain much higher efficiency compared to naïve algorithms. In image encryption, the following properties are always desired:

- The encryption/decryption algorithm has to be fast enough in order to meet the performance requirements of real-time applications;

- The encryption procedure should not decrease the compression ratio or increase the size of the image;

- The encryption algorithms should be robust against the general digital image processing procedures;

- The encryption/decryption procedure should not degrade the quality of the original image.

Affine Transformation Algorithms

Affine transformation basically does a one-to-one mapping between the symbols in the plaintext and the symbols in the ciphertext to protect the data content. Chuang and Lin (1999) proposed a multi-resolution approach for still image encryption. It is basically a symmetric affine cipher system, which has both multi-resolution transmission (a progressive property) and lossless reconstruction functionalities. With multi-resolution transmission, the image can be transmitted progressively with different spatial resolutions. The basic idea of this algorithm is to decompose and encrypt the original image level by level with the proposed E-transform. For each pixel, the algorithm does an affine transformation and converts the grey-level value to another one that still falls into the range of [0, 255]. In the receiver end, the image can be decrypted level by level, and the original image is recovered if the highest level is decrypted. For a 512x512 image, the size of key space is $(256!)^{87366}$. Many image encryption algorithms use similar strategies. However, the drawback of affine transformation is that it is fragile to known/chosen-plaintext attacks. In addition, this type of algorithm has the same drawback as a naïve algorithm: too much computational overhead. It encrypts the whole image pixel by pixel and thus often fails to meet the real-time requirements for many application scenarios.

Chaotic System Based Algorithms

Scharinger (1998) proposed a fast image encryption algorithm with chaotic Kolmogorov flow, which is a class of extraordinary unstable chaotic systems. Basically, this algorithm implements a product cipher, which encrypts large blocks of plaintext by repeating intertwined applications of substitutions and permutations. Scharinger's system combined Kolmogorov flows with a pseudo-random number generator to implement a key-dependent permutation (parameterized permutation), which operates on large data blocks. This is a significant improvement compared to the product ciphers that applies fixed permutation and thus leads to higher level of security. There are three main advantages of Scharinger's algorithm: (1) the integration of a parameterized permutation into the system leads to its robustness against the differential cryptanalysis; (2) the adoption of large data blocks (maybe the whole image) makes the image structure unrecognizable, which leads to higher level of security compared to those encryption systems that operate on small data blocks; (3) this system is faster than some other comparable encryption systems because of its simplicity. However, this algorithm still tries to encrypt the whole image and thus suffers the same problem as a naïve algorithm does. Socek, Li, Magliveras, and Furht (2005) proposed a new methodology to enhance the Chaotic-Key Based Algorithm (CKBA). Their algorithm enhances the CKBA algorithm in three-fold: (1) it changes the 1-D chaotic logistic map to a piecewise linear chaotic map (PWLCM) to improve the balance property; (2) it increases the key size to 128 bits; (3) it adds two more cryptographic primitives and extends the scheme to operate on multiple rounds so that the chosen/known plaintext attacks are

no longer possible. The new cipher proved to be more secure and its performance characteristics remain very good.

Frequency Domain Algorithms

Digital images can be presented in both spatial domain and frequency domain. The term spatial domain refers to the image plane. Frequency domain processing techniques are based on modifying the Fourier transform of an image. The encryption algorithms presented in the previous sections all work in spatial domain. Since many digital image processing/compression techniques operate in the frequency domain, it would be natural to encrypt the digital image in the frequency domain for compatibility issues. Kuo (1993) proposed a novel image encryption technique by randomly changing the phase spectra of the original image. A binary phase spectra of a pseudo-noise image is added to the original phase spectra. This methodology is actually a private-key system, and the reference noise image is the encryption/decryption key. The proposed methodology is suitable for progressive transmission because of its ability to recover the original image to some extent with partial access to the encrypted image. As a result, it is a good candidate for distributed multimedia communication, which sometimes suffers from network congestion and packet loss. However, the proposed methodology has some limitations: (1) the encryption and decryption process requires FFT (Fast Fourier Transform) computation, which is very computationally demanding; (2) it is also vulnerable to known/chosen-plaintext attacks.

Younes and Jantan (2003) proposed a block-based transformation algorithm based on the combination of image transformation and a well-known encryption/decryption algorithm called Blowfish. The original image was divided into blocks, which were rearranged into a transformed image using a transformation algorithm, and then the transformed image was encrypted using the Blowfish algorithm. The results showed that the correlation between image elements was significantly decreased by using the proposed technique. The results also show that increasing the number of blocks by using smaller block sizes resulted in a lower correlation and higher entropy.

Comparative Results

The comparison of the image encryption algorithms discussed in previous sections is in Table 2.

JOINT COMPRESSION-ENCRYPTION METHODOLOGIES

Since digital images are usually transmitted in a compressed format, research is focused on how to encrypt compressed digital images. It is natural to apply naïve algorithm to the compressed image to get the compressed-encrypted image. However, this will cause significant computational overhead, especially for the images with low compression ratio. Thus, research efforts have been focused on integrating lossless compression and encryption algorithms to maximize the overall performance. Basically, compression and encryption can enhance each other and share the computational cost. In this section, we will first review some of the representative lossless compression techniques and then move to joint compression-encryption methodologies.

Lossless Compression Techniques

Lossless image compression can be always modeled as a two-stage procedure: decorrelation and entropy coding. The first stage removes spatial redundancy or inter-pixel redundancy by means of run-length coding, predictive techniques, transform techniques, etc. The second stage, which includes Huffman coding, arithmetic coding, LZW, etc., removes coding redundancy. The techniques employed in lossless image compression are all fundamentally rooted in entropy coding theory and Shannon's noiseless coding theorem, which guarantees that as long as the average number of bits per source symbol at the output of the encoder exceeds the entropy (i.e. average information per symbol) of the data source by an arbitrarily small amount, the data can be decoded without error. Nowadays, the performances of entropy coding techniques are very close to the theoretical bound, and thus more research activities concentrate on decorrelation stage.

Decorrelation Techniques

Correlation between samples, which is present in nearly all kinds of signals, represents redundant information that need not be transmitted if reversible decorrelation techniques are applied. Decorrelation, also known as "whitening", can be accomplished by many techniques.

- **Predictive Techniques:** linear prediction is an effective decorrelation technique that can be completely reversible. Linear prediction is frequently referred to as differential pulse code modulation (DPCM). For each sample, a prediction of its value is formed from a weighted sum of neighbor-

Table 2. Comparative Results (Image Encryption)

	Complexity	Speed	Key Length	Key Space Size (512*512 Image)	Security Level
Affine Transform	Simple	Low	N/A	$(256!)^{87366}$	High
Chaotic Algorithm	Simple	Low	Variable	Variable	High
Frequency Algorithm	Complex	Low	512*512	$2^{512*512}$	High

ing samples. The difference data, or prediction residual, generally has much lower entropy than the original data.

- **Transform Technique:** transform techniques are frequently employed in lossy compression systems. However, most transforms, such as Discrete Cosine Transform (DCT) and DFT, are difficult to be applied in lossless signal coding because their transform coefficients are real-valued or complex-valued and must be quantized for coding. One transform technique that may be directly applied to lossless signal coding is the discrete Walsh-Hadamard transform (WHT). Since the coefficients of the WHT are binary fractions, quantization is not necessary.

- **Multi-resolution Techniques:** a number of multi-resolution techniques including hierarchical interpolation (HINT), Laplacian pyramid, and S-transform have been successfully employed in the decorrelation of image data. These methods all form a hierarchy of data sets which represent the original data with varying resolutions. Therefore, these techniques also support progressive transmission which allows data to be decoded in several stages in increasing resolutions. The basic process of these multi-resolution techniques is to keep sampling the original data and entropy-code the sub-sample until all intermediate samples have been estimated and sampled.

Entropy Coding

Once the data has been decorrelated, more compression can be achieved by applying entropy coding as long as the Probability Mass Function (PMF) of the resulting samples is not uniform. The average bitrate can approach the entropy of the decorrelated data. Most signal compression schemes employ Huffman coding or Arithmetic

coding. In addition, several compression schemes use sub-optimal variable length coders that are specifically designed for speed or ease of implementation.

- **Huffman Coder:** Huffman coder always assigns long codewords to less-frequent symbols and short codewords to frequent symbols. Huffman codes are optimal in the sense that they generate a set of variable length binary codewords of minimum average length, as long as the source alphabet and PMF are available. Huffman codes always produce an average code length within one bit of the entropy bound. Most practical Huffman coders are adaptive and estimate the source PMF from the coded samples.

- **Arithmetic Coding:** In arithmetic coding, codewords are constructed by partitioning the range between zero and one. As each symbol is encoded, the range is decreased by the amount inversely proportional to the probability occurrence of the symbol. When the range is sufficiently narrow, the partitioning is terminated and the codeword is assigned a binary fraction which lies within the final range.

- **LZW Coder:** Lempel-Ziv-Welch (LZW) coder, which was originally developed for text compression, has also been applied to signal compression. LZW is actually a dictionary-based technique. When a sequence of symbols matches a sequence stored in the dictionary, an index is sent rather than the symbol sequence itself. If no match is found, the sequence of symbols is sent without being coded and the dictionary is updated.

- **Adaptive Approaches:** A significant difficulty in employing the above techniques is that alphabets for signal compression tend to be large, leading to implementations that require massive computational resources. To solve this problem, a couple of approaches have been developed. Usually coupled with a simple DPCM predictor, the Rice coder consists of several very simple coders which are nearly optimal over a very narrow range of source entropies. The system adapts to the input data by estimating the source entropy and selecting the appropriate coder.

Joint Compression-Encryption

Image compression can be viewed as a special type of encryption, since it converts the original image into a bitstream that is incomprehensible to human beings. The compression/decompression algorithms can be viewed as the encryption/decryption keys, because there is no way to convert the encoded bitstream back to the original image without the decompression algorithm. However, according to Kerckhoff's principle, an encryption methodology cannot rely on the secrecy of its algorithm to ensure the security of the system. Also, the compression/decompression algorithms for the existing standards are all in the public domain and supposed to be known.

Based on this observation, people start to wonder: is it possible to combine encryption key with the compression algorithms to achieve compression and encryption at the same time? The answer is "yes" and this leads to the development of joint compression-encryption algorithms. In a system that combines compression and encryption, it is better to use the parameter instead of the algorithm itself as the encryption/decryption key. In this type of systems, secret keys have been applied in the compression, and thus the compression algorithm is parameterized and becomes the joint compression-encryption algorithm. Without the private key, it is impossible to decode/decrypt the encoded bitstream and restore the original image/video contents.

Another way to implement a joint compression-encryption system is to compress the image first and then encrypt it. Different from naïve algorithm, which encrypts the whole compressed image, this type of joint compression-encryption algorithms encrypt only some of the key parameters of the encoded image. Since the key parameters of the compressed image are encrypted, the original image cannot be reconstructed even if the other parts of the compressed image are known. Thus, image data security is ensured. This type of algorithms avoids encrypting the image merely as a bitstream and thus has a reduced computational overhead compared to that of naïve algorithm.

Base-Switching Algorithms

Chuang and Lin (1999) proposed a joint compression-encryption methodology for still images. The basic idea is to first decompose the original image, then use a base-switching (BS) algorithm to compress the image in a lossless manner. Finally, the base values of the compressed image will be encrypted with the affine transformation. Thus, the original image cannot be reconstructed even if the other parts of the compressed image remain unencrypted.

Many available encryption algorithms could be applied to the encryption of the base value. With the proposed algorithm, theoretically there are $(128!)*t$ possible ways to encrypt a gray-scaled image and $(128!)*3t$ ways to encrypt a color image (t is the number of layers in the image decomposition procedure). The proposed algorithm provides very high level of security and considerable compression ratio. This methodology can be combined with other encryption methods such as the SCAN language to further improve its security level. The drawback of the algorithm is that it is vulnerable to known/chosen-plaintext attacks.

Entropy Coding Algorithms

Wu and Moo (1999) proposed a joint image/video compression-encryption scheme via a high-order conditional entropy coding of wavelet coefficients. They demonstrated that wavelet image compression and conditional arithmetic coding of wavelet coefficients could be used as a framework for image encryption. Firstly, the image is transformed with the wavelet transformation. Then the wavelet coefficients are quantized and encoded with ECECOW (Embedded Conditional Entropy Coding Of Wavelet coefficients). After that, different kinds of encryption algorithms can be applied to encrypt a very small portion of the bit stream output by ECECOW. As we know, the compressed bit stream will show a certain level of randomness. This can enhance the ability to ensure a certain level of security. Encrypting only a small portion of the bit stream ensures the high-speed performance.

SCAN Language Based Algorithms

Bourbakis and Dollas (2003) proposed a joint compression-encryption-hiding system based on the SCAN language. The name "SCAN" reflects the different ways of scanning the data of a 2D array, such as an image. The SCAN language is a formal language based on a two-dimensional spatial-accessing methodology that can represent and generate a great variety of $\{n \times n\}$! scanning paths from a small set of primitive ones. The SCAN method compresses a given image by specifying a scanning path of the image in an encoded form. The core is the algorithm that determines a near-optimal or a good scanning path which minimizes the total number of bits needed to represent the encoded scanning path and the encoded bit se-

quence along the scanning path. After the image is compressed, the bits of the compressed image are rearranged to obtain the encrypted image (Fig. 3). The rearrangement is done using a set of scanning paths that are kept secret. This set of scanning paths is actually the encryption key. The decryption/decompression procedure is the reverse of the encryption-compression procedure. An additional feature of the SCAN methodology is the confusion function. The major functionality of the confusion function is to make the image histogram flat and look like random noise, and thus the attacks through histogram analysis will be completely disabled. The proposed methodology achieves a higher compression ratio than that achieved by a JPEG encoder (quality=100). The security level is very high and it is computationally infeasible to break the system using an exhaustive search with currently available computing power.

Comparison

A comparison of the joint compression-encryption algorithms is presented in Table 3.

VIDEO ENCRYPTION

In digital video transmission, encryption methodologies that can protect digital video from attacks during transmission become very important. Due to the huge size of digital video contents, they are usually transmitted in compressed formats such as MPEG-x, H.26x, Motion-JPEG, and Motion-

Figure 3. SCAN Language based Joint Encryption-Compression

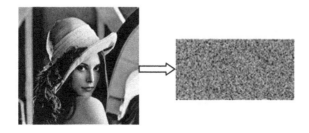

Table 3. Comparative Results (Image Compression-Encryption)

	Complexity	Speed	Key Space Size (512*512 Image)	Security Level	Compression Ratio	Compression Type
Base Switching	High	Slow	$(128!)^t$ (Gray) $(128!)^{3t}$ (Color)	High	Medium	Lossless
Entropy Coding	Low	Fast	N/A	Low	High	Lossy
SCAN * Algorithm	High	Medium	$(512*512)!$	High	High	Lossless

* SCAN offers not only an iterative scrambling with 10^{76000} pairs of keys for a 512x512 digital form of the encrypted information, here an image, where a supercomputer using brutal force requires 10^{75000} years with a slim probability to decrypt the original digital information, but also a confusion function that converts always flat the digital information histogram making the overall encryption process impossible. SCAN has also been efficiently used in video compression-encryption.

JPEG2000. Thus, the encryption algorithms for digital video are usually working in the compressed domain. Again, the most straightforward method to encrypt digital video data is naïve algorithm. However, the performance issues will arise. DES and RSA are obviously not fast enough to meet the real-time requirements of digital video applications such as video-on-demand and video retrieval.

Selective Encryption Algorithms

According to the Group-Of-Pictures (GOP) structure (Figure 4), the reconstruction of the B-frames and the P-frames are dependent on the availability of the preceding I-frame since they need the I-frame as reference frame. With the I-frame being encrypted, the attackers cannot reconstruct the I-frame so they will not be able to reconstruct the B-frame and the P-frame even if these frames are transmitted without being encrypted. Based on this consideration, it is natural to encrypt only the

I-frames to protect the video content. Encryption of only the I-frames will lead to much less computational overhead compared to a naïve algorithm. However, Agi and Gong (1996) have shown that the basic idea behind this method is not correct. A large portion of the encrypted video is still visible, mainly because of unencrypted I-blocks in the P and B frames and partially because of inter-frame correlation. Moreover, this methodology still adds significant computational overhead to the encoding and decoding processes.

Some approaches have been proposed to enhance the low security level caused by the I-blocks in the P- and B-frames: (1) force the MPEG encoder not to generate I-blocks inside P- and B-frames; (2) encrypt all the I-blocks inside P- and B-frames. To improve the security level of the selective algorithm, Spanos and Maples (1995) have proposed to not only encrypt the I-frames in the video stream, but also to encrypt the header information of the MPEG video and make

Figure 4. The GOP (Group of Pictures) with I-, B-, and P- Frames

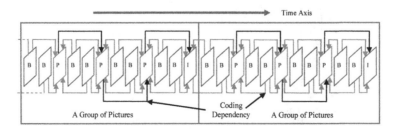

the video stream unrecognizable to the decoder. This modification slightly increases the security level of the system. Agi and Gong (1996) found that increasing the number of I-frames and encrypting the I-frames in the selective algorithm will increase the security level, but at the price of a lower compression ratio. Encrypting the I-blocks inside the B- and the P-frames will not decrease the compression ratio but has the potential to increase security level.

When the selective algorithm is applied to MPEG video encryption, we need to take into account many factors such as computational overhead, security requirements, the sensitivity of the video data, and real-time requirements. Based on these considerations, we can choose the most suitable algorithm for the targeting application scenarios, which is actually a tradeoff between computational complexity and level of security.

Tang's Algorithm

Tang (1996) proposed a methodology in an attempt to incorporate the compression and the encryption of MPEG video streams. In the proposed system, he combines cryptographic techniques such as random permutation and probabilistic encryption with the compression/decompression algorithms. The proposed algorithm does not add much computational overhead to the encoding/decoding of the digital video but can achieve a considerable level of security for the data being processed. As we know, in the MPEG video compression algorithm, zig-zag scanning is applied to map the DCT coefficients in the 8x8 block to a 1-D vector (with 64 elements). In the encryption system proposed by Tang, a random permutation list is used. This list is actually the encryption key to implement the mapping and, thus, scramble the order of the DCT coefficients. Since mapping with the permutation list is not more computationally demanding than mapping with the zig-zag scanning, the proposed system does not add computational overhead. This makes

it a good candidate for real-time digital video applications. This algorithm has some drawbacks:

(1) Scanning the 8x8 DCT block with a random permutation list (rather than zig-zag scanning) will decrease the performance of the subsequent run-length coding and Huffman coding and reduce the compression ratio;

(2) The proposed methodology will be vulnerable to known-plaintext attack, which makes use of partial knowledge of the well-known MPEG codec structure and the distribution property of the DCT coefficients.

To fix this problem, Tang has proposed some additional options. However, they increase the computational complexity and key length without significantly increasing the system's security level. Thus, the proposed methodology is not suitable to protect the highly sensitive digital video data.

Video Encryption Algorithm (VEA)

The VEA algorithm, proposed by Shi and Bhargava (1998a) is based on the modification of DCT coefficients. It uses a randomly-generated bit-stream, which is actually the encryption/decryption key, to change the sign of the AC coefficients of the DCT transformation. Since the only operation in the encryption procedure is XOR, very limited computational overhead is added. Even the software implementation of the system is fast enough for many real-time video applications. This algorithm has some drawbacks. For example, after the encryption procedure, some AC coefficients have changed their sign while others have not. Thus, the video sequence is still comprehensible or understandable to some extent. Because of the well-known MPEG-x structure and the distribution property of the DCT coefficients, attackers may be able to break the system with a partial key. The algorithm is also vulnerable to known-plaintext attack. Thus, the encryption algorithm is not suitable for protecting highly sensitive video data. However, it is still suitable for protecting the commercial digital video data, since the expense to break the encryption system will be much higher than that to buy the video in this case.

To increase the security level of the algorithm, Shi and Bhargava (1998b) proposed a new version of the VEA system. In the proposed system, they change the sign bits of the DC coefficients and the motion vector instead of the AC coefficients. With this modification, they obtain a higher security level while reducing the computational overhead. Since the attackers may make use of the AC coefficients to derive the DC coefficients, they suggested encrypting AC coefficients as well if a higher level of security is desired.

Qiao-Nahrstedt Algorithm

Qiao and Nahrstedt (1997) have proposed a video encryption algorithm based on the statistical analysis of the MPEG video stream. Considering the MPEG stream as a sequence of bytes, they observed that a video stream has a more uniform distribution of byte values. They analyzed the distribution of the byte value, the pair of two adjacent bytes, and the pair of two bytes with a fixed distance in between. Based on the experimental results, they concluded that there is no repeated byte pattern within any 1/16 chunk of an I-frame.

The proposed algorithm first divides a chunk of the MPEG video stream into two byte lists: an odd list and an even list. Then it performs the XOR operation to encrypt the odd list, and uses another encryption function to encrypt the even list to get the ciphertext. Since this chunk of data is a non-repeated pattern, it is considered to be perfectly secure. Some key selection approaches, which are procedures to generate random bit sequences as the keys, have been adopted to increase the security. This methodology is 47% faster than DES. Experimental results show that the encryption/decryption time for each frame is slightly less than the frame rate time of 0.33ms. As a result, this methodology is suitable for real-time applications. Also, the security level is high enough for some sensitive video-on-demand ap-

plications. This algorithm has some drawbacks: (1) it still needs to go through all the I-frames, which is kind of computationally expensive; (2) the basic idea of this algorithm is similar to that of a selective algorithm and thus may lead to the same security issues.

Hierarchical Algorithms

Hierarchical algorithms offer different levels of security by encrypting different portions of the video data, at the price of different levels of computational cost. Li, Chen, Tan, and Campbell (1996) proposed a MPEG video stream encryption algorithm, which has three layers. The first layer encrypts only the I-frames of the MPEG video stream with the standard encryption algorithm PGP (Pretty Good Privacy). The second layer provides higher security level by encrypting the I-frames and P-frames. The third level offers the highest security level by encrypting all of the frames.

Meyer and Gadegast (1995) have proposed a new MPEG-like video encryption algorithm called SECMPEG. This methodology incorporates selective algorithms and additional header information to enhance its level of security. It has a high-speed software implementation. SECMPEG can be combined with both DES and RSA encryption standards. SECMPEG has four levels of implementations. The algorithm for the higher level is always the superset to the algorithm immediately under it. With the increase of the layer number, the security level is increased and so is the computational overhead. In the first level, the algorithm encrypts only the header information. In the second level, the algorithm encrypts parts of the I-blocks in addition to the implementation in the first level. In the third level, I-frames and all of the I-blocks (within P-frames and B-frames) are encrypted. In the fourth level, the algorithm is the same as the naïve algorithm.

SECMPEG provides a hierarchical encryption system for digital MPEG video. We can choose different combinations of security levels and computational overhead to meet the requirements of various application scenarios. However, SECMPEG is not compatible with the standard MPEG because the header information of the video stream is changed. Thus, a special encoder/ decoder would be required for the playback of unencrypted SECMPEG streams.

Comparison

The video encryption algorithms are always a tradeoff between the computational complexity and the security level. Highly secure algorithms always have to pay the price of high computational overhead; on the other hand, the fast algorithms always provide relatively low level of security. To develop efficient MPEG video encryption algorithms, we need to investigate the MPEG codec structure, search for key parameters, and try to encrypt as few as possible bits while obtaining a certain level of security according to the different applications' requirements. Comparative result among these methods is in Table-4.

INTRODUCTION TO IMAGE/VIDEO INFORMATION HIDING

General Model

With the advancements in computing power, an encryption system may be broken more easily than before. For this reason, researchers have

started to use information hiding techniques to enhance encryption and increase the level of security. Information hiding conceals not only the content and location of the protected data, but also its very existence. Information hiding techniques can be used to protect the copyright of the content, track the user of the media data, and convey side information. The following example illustrates an application of information hiding in secure communication:

- Apparently neutral's protest is thoroughly discounted and ignored. Isman hard hit. Blockade issue affects pretext for embargo on by-products, ejecting suets and vegetable oils.

This paragraph is a message sent by a spy during World War II. The content of the message is nothing secret and attracted very little or even no suspicion. However, if we extract the second letter from each word of the original message, we will be able to obtain the secret message "Pershing sails from NY June 1."

The generic model of an information embedding-extracting system is illustrated in Fig. 5 (Yang & Bourbakis, 2005). Given a cover object I, a message M, the embedding algorithm E, and an optional key K, the embedding process can be defined as a mapping of the form: $I \times K \times M \times E \to I'$, where I' is the stego-object. The information extraction procedure is: $I' \times K \times E' \to M'$, where I'

Table 4. Comparative Results (Video)

	Complexity	Speed	Computation Overhead	Security Level	Compression Ratio
Selective Algorithm	Low	Fast	High	Low	Unchanged
Tang	Low	Fast	Low	Low	Reduced
VEA	Low	Fast	Low	Low	Unchanged
Qiao-Nahrstedt	High	Fast	High	High	Unchanged
SECMPEG	Low-High	High	Four levels	Four levels	N/A

Figure 5. A Typical Information Hiding and Retrieval System

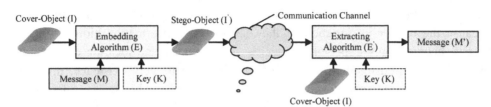

is the stego-object, *K* is the key, *E'* is the extracting algorithm, and *M'* is the extracted message, which could be different from the original message *M*.

Digital image is one of the most popular digital multimedia data types. Thus, information hiding techniques using digital images as the host signal have attracted significant research interests. According to modern information hiding theory, the embedding capability of the host image/video frames provides an additional communication channel with a certain capacity, which could be used to transmit secure data. Compared to digital video, digital images provide less channel capacity for information embedding.

Digital Image/Video Information Hiding

With information hiding techniques, it is possible to hide secret messages within digital image/video content without degrading its visual quality. There are lots of properties inherent to digital images and human visual system that can be utilized for information hiding. Human eyes have different levels of sensitivity to contrast in relation to spatial frequency and masking effect of edges. Moreover, human eyes are more sensitive to low-frequency components than to high-frequency components. Similarly, human eyes perceive brightness components better than chromatic information. In Figure 6, we have successfully embedded a secret image within four larger images, and as can be seen, visually there is no difference between the original and stego images.

Different types of attacks aim to remove or disable the embedded information. In order to develop robust and efficient information hiding algorithms, it is beneficial to identify different kinds of attacks. Basically, attacks can be classified into the following categories:

- Removal attack: it generally tries to reduce the effective channel capacity of the information hiding scheme;

Figure 6. Image Information Hiding with SCAN based Methodologies

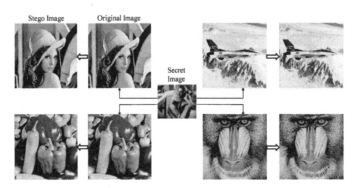

- Geometrical attack: it tries to degrade or cut part of the host signal and indirectly remove the embedded information;
- Cryptographic attack: it is named so because of its similarity to the encryption systems attack, which tries to remove the embedded information by cryptanalysis such as exhaustive search of the key space;
- Protocol attack: a high-level attack which analyzes the embedding methodology on the system level and finds the weak points of the methodology.

For information hiding systems, the definition of robustness and efficiency are always application-dependent. For example, the general information hiding schemes require robustness to all possible modifications. However, in a fragile watermarking system, the embedded information is supposed to be sensitive to any kind of modification, no matter how slight it is. In the system design procedure, it is important to take into account the applications of the system and the possible attacks for the time being.

LOW BITRATE INFORMATION HIDING ALGORITHMS

In information hiding techniques, bitrate refers to the amount of data embedded in the host signal. In terms of the amount of data to be embedded, information hiding systems can be classified as high bitrate and low bitrate algorithms. In low bitrate information hiding, relatively small amount of data is embedded in the host image to indicate some important ownership information. In high bitrate information hiding, relatively large amount of information is embedded in the host signal for covert communication, side information delivery, etc.

The most representative low bitrate information hiding application is digital watermarking, which embeds a few bits for ownership verification. Watermarking is defined (Cox, Miller, & Bloom 2002) as being the practice of imperceptibly altering a piece of data to embed information. A watermarking system should have two modules: one module that embeds the information in the host data and another module that detects and extracts the watermark. Depending on the type, quantity, and properties of the embedded information, watermarking can serve a multitude of applications, such as:

- **Owner Identification and Proof of Ownership**: the embedded data can carry information about the legal owner or distributor or any rights holder of a digital item and be used to warn the user that the item is copyrighted, track illegal copies, and prove the ownership of the item;
- **Broadcast Monitoring**: the embedded information is utilized for various functions related to digital media (audio, video) broadcasting in order to verify whether the actual broadcasting of commercials took place as scheduled;
- **Transaction Tracking**: each copy of a digital item that is distributed as part of a transaction has a different watermark. The purpose of this watermark is not only to carry information about the legal owner/distributor of the digital item but also to mark the specific transaction copy;
- **Usage Control**: the watermarking plays an active protection role by controlling the terms of use of the digital content. The embedded information can be used to prohibit unauthorized recording of a digital item or playback of unauthorized copies;
- **Authentication and Tamper-Proofing**: the role of the watermark is to verify the authenticity and integrity of a digital item for the benefit of either the owner/distributor or the user;

- **Enhancement of Legacy Systems**: data embedded through watermarking can be used to enhance the information or functionalities provided by legacy systems while ensuring backwards compatibility.

Spatial Domain Algorithms for Low Bitrate Hiding

In terms of the embedding domain, information hiding systems can be classified as spatial domain and frequency domain algorithms. Spatial domain information hiding algorithms embed information within digital image/video contents by directly modifying the grey values of the data samples. The most straightforward spatial-domain image information hiding algorithm embeds information by modifying the least-significant-bit (LSB) of pixels. However, this algorithm is sensitive to lossy compression and the watermark can be easily removed. Duplication is a possible approach to enhance the security level of LSB algorithm.

Koch and Zhao (1995) proposed a copyright labeling methodology called Randomly Sequenced Pulse Position Modulated Code (RSPPMC). The proposed method splits the problem into two components. The first component produces the actual copyright code and a random sequence of locations for embedding the code in the image. The second component actually embeds the code at the specified locations. It was demonstrated that a copyright label code could be embedded in several images, using pulses with sufficient noise margins to survive common processing such as lossy compression, color space conversion, and low-pass filtering.

The patchwork method was proposed by Bender, Gruhl, Morimoto, and Lu (1996), which basically embeds the message in a host image by increasing the grey level of certain pixels and decreasing the grey level of other pixels by the same amount. The pixels are chosen in pairs and thus the overall average brightness of the host image is not modified. Several modifications have

been made to the original algorithm in order to improve the performance and robustness. This methodology is suitable for low bit-rate applications such as digital watermarking. Texture block coding was proposed by Bender, Gruhl, Morimoto, and Lu (1996). In this algorithm, the message is embedded within the continuous random texture pattern of a digital image. A region from a random texture pattern found in a picture is copied to an area that has similar texture. The embedded message could be extracted easily by autocorrelation, shifting, and thresholding. This methodology is robust against filtering, compression, and rotation. Possible improvements to this methodology include automatic detection and automatic texture region selection.

Bas, Chassery, and Davoine (1998) proposed a self-similarity based image watermarking scheme. Their approach is based on a fractal compression method. In the proposed methodology, the first step is to build a fractal code for the image. Therefore, each image corresponds to a fractal code, which is called "collage map". The fractal code can also be expressed in the DCT domain and is used in image compression. Image watermark is then embedded by altering the collage map. It is statistically rare to find a block equal to another one in an ordinary image. This algorithm basically adds artificial and invisible local similarities to the image in order to control the collage map.

Allen and Davidson (1998) proposed an information hiding technique, which used an image transform called Minimax Eigenvalue Decomposition (MED) to decompose an image into layered images. MED transform does not have to deal with the computational and roundoff penalties encountered in typical linear transforms. The MED transform combines message data and a subset of the layer images to create an image that is close to the original one. This technique differs from existing methodologies in that the embedded message is not the only piece of information needed for authentication. Thus, even if the message is corrupted, authentication could still be achieved.

Another technique for watermark embedding is to exploit the correlation properties of additive pseudo-random noise patterns as applied to an image (Langelaar, Setyawan & Lagendijk, 2000). To retrieve the watermark, the same pseudo-random noise generator algorithm is seeded with the same key, and the correlation between the noise pattern and possibly watermarked image is computed. If the correlation exceeds a certain threshold T, the watermark is detected. This method can be easily extended to a multiple-bit watermark by dividing the image into blocks and performing the above procedure independently on each block.

Transform Domain Algorithms for Low Bitrate Hiding

Transform-domain algorithms embed information in the frequency domain of the host image/video. Transform domain algorithms are increasingly common, because they can enhance the robustness against transform based compression, filtering, and noise. Actually, it is observed that the use of a particular transform is usually robust against compression algorithms based on the same transform. One of most popular transformations for image processing is Discrete-Cosine-Transform (DCT). The DCT allows an image to be transformed into different frequency bands.

Koch and Zhao (1995) proposed an approach to watermarking images based on the JPEG image compression algorithms. Their approach divides the image into individual 8x8 blocks. In each 8x8 block, only eight coefficients in particular positions of DCT coefficients can be marked. These comprise the low frequency components of the image block, but exclude the mean value coefficient at coordinate $(0, 0)$ as well as the low frequencies at coordinates $(0, 1)$ and $(1, 0)$. Three of these coefficients are selected using a pseudo-random number generator to convey embedded information.

Cox, Kilian, Leighton, and Shamoon (1996) applied the spread spectrum theory in communication and proposed a digital watermarking system for image, audio, and video. They proposed to embed information in the perceptually significant region in order to be robust against certain procedures such as lossy compression, signal processing, and other kinds of attacks. In a digital watermarking system, the host media could be viewed as a broadband channel and as such the embedded watermark could be viewed as a signal to be transmitted through the channel. The watermark could be spread over many frequency components so that it becomes imperceptible in any certain frequency component. Thus, the visual distortion would not be noticeable. However, the presence of original cover data is needed to extract the embedded information. This problem could be fixed by a more elaborate design of an embedding/extracting algorithm.

With the standardization process of JPEG 2000 and the shift from DCT to wavelet-based image compression methods, watermarking schemes that work in the wavelet transform domain have become more interesting. The wavelet transform has a number of advantages that can be exploited for both image compression and watermarking applications.

Xia, Boncelet, and Arce (1997) proposed a multi-resolution watermarking method for digital images. Before that, most of the frequency-domain watermarking schemes were based on discrete cosine transform (DCT), where pseudo-random sequences were added to the DCT coefficients at the middle frequencies as signatures. Since wavelet image/video coding has been included in the image/video compression standard such as JPEG2000 and Motion-JPEG2000, this method works in wavelet transform domain. They added pseudo-random codes to the coefficients at the high and middle frequency bands of the discrete wavelet transform of an image. This watermarking method has multi-resolution characteristics and is hierarchical. Adding watermarking to the large coefficients in high and middle frequency bands (which correspond to the edge and texture of the image) is difficult for the human eyes to perceive. It has been shown that the proposed methodology is very robust to wavelet transform based image compression and common image distortions such as additive noise and half-toning.

Based on the multi-resolution technique introduced by Xia, Boncelet, and Arce (1997), Kim and Moon (1999) utilized Discrete Wavelet Transform (DWT) coefficients of all subbands (including the approximation image) to equally embed a random Gaussian distributed watermark sequence in the whole image. Perceptually significant coefficients have been selected by level-adaptive thresholding to achieve a high level of robustness.

Pereir, Voloshynovskiy and Pun (2000) described a method based on a one-level decomposition of non-overlapping 16x16 image blocks using Haar wavelet filters. The proposed watermarking algorithm uses linear programming to optimize watermark robustness. For each bit to be embedded, a 2x2 block of neighboring coefficient is selected from a LL subband of size 8x8. Cheng and Huang (2001) presented an additive approach to achieve transform domain information hiding for images and video. The watermark embedding method is designed to satisfy the perceptual constraints and improve the detectability. They proposed information hiding schemes in three transform domains: Digital Cosine Transform (DCT) domain, Digital Wavelet Transform (DWT) domain, and Pyramid Transform Domain. The embedding of the watermark into the host signal is usually either multiplicative or additive. Their proposed system provides both good transparency and precise control of detection error.

HIGH BITRATE INFORMATION HIDING ALGORITHMS

High bitrate information hiding, unlike digital watermarking, tries to hide relatively large amounts of secure information within the host image/ video contents. High bitrate information hiding techniques could be elaborately designed to cause unnoticeable visual degradation to the host signal in spite of its large data capacity. The main applications of high bitrate information hiding are secure communication, captioning, speech-in-video, video-in-video, etc. In high bitrate information hiding, four performance metrics are of interest:

(1) Transparency: the embedding of protected data should not interfere with the visual fidelity of host video (Zhang, Cheung & Chen, 2005);

(2) Channel capacity: how many bits can be effectively embedded within the host video (Cvejic & Seppanen, 2004; Kundur, 2000; Lin & Chang, 2001; Briffa & Das, 2002; Moulin & Mihcak, 2002);

(3) The impact of embedded information on the performance of image/video compression (Chang, Chen, & Lin, 2004);

(4) Robustness against lossy compression: how much hidden information can survive the lossy video codec (Gunsel, Uludag, & Tekalp, 2002; Fei, Kundur, & Kwong, 2001; Ni, Shi, Ansari, Su, Sun, & Lin, 2004).

Like low bitrate algorithms, high bitrate information hiding algorithms can be classified into spatial-domain and transform-domain algorithms.

Spatial Domain Algorithms for High Bitrate Hiding

The most commonly used spatial domain algorithm for high bitrate information hiding is the LSB algorithm. Again, it is very sensitive to lossy compression and can be removed easily. Wu and Tsai (1998) proposed a methodology where data is embedded in each pixel of a cover image by changing its grey value without exceeding a certain threshold. A multiple-based number system is proposed to convert the information in the message into values to be embedded in certain pixels of the cover image. Pseudo-random mechanisms may be used to enhance the level of security. It has been found from the experiments that the signal-to-noise ratio of the stego-images is larger than those observed in compressed images. This proves that the visual distortion caused by the data embedded is less than that caused by image compression. The proposed method can be easily applied to embed data in a color image. Maniccam and Bourbakis (2004) proposed a spatial-domain algorithm based on the texture analysis of each 3x3 neighborhood within the image. The proposed algorithm obtains higher robustness against JPEG because the modifications of non-LSB bits are more robust to lossy compression.

Chang, Chen, and Lin (2004) proposed a steganography scheme based on the search-order coding (SOC) compression method of vector quantization (VQ) indices. Their goal is to embed secret data into the compression codes of the host image such that the interceptors will not notice the existence of the secret data. In the proposed scheme, the embedding process induces no extra coding distortion and adjusts the bit rate according to the size of secret data. The receiver can efficiently receive both the compressed image and the embedded data almost at the same time. According to the experimental results, the proposed scheme yields a good and acceptable compression ratio of the image.

A novel LSB embedding algorithm for hiding encrypted messages in non-adjacent and random pixel locations in edges of images was proposed in (Singh, Singh, & Singh, 2007). It first encrypts the secret message and detects edges in the cover image. Message bits are then embedded in the least significant bits and random locations of the edge pixels. The proposed algorithm does not require the original cover-image for the extraction of the secret message. It has been shown that the blind LSB detection technique like the gradient energy method could not estimate the length of the secret message bits accurately for the proposed algo-

rithm. A new improved version of Least Significant Bit (LSB) method was presented in (Kekre, Athawale, & Halarnkar, 2008). This approach is simple in implementation but still achieves a high level of embedding capacity and imperceptibility. The proposed method can also be applied to 24-bit color images and achieve embedding capacity much higher than PVD.

Transform Domain Algorithms for High Bitrate Hiding

Spatial domain hiding is easier to implement but it is not as robust as transform domain hiding. Transform domain hiding is more robust but the detection of hidden data is more complex. Various DCT-domain algorithms embed the information by modifying the DCT coefficients. The high bitrate frequency-domain algorithms have proven to be more robust to lossy compression compared to spatial-domain algorithms. Swanson, Zhu, and Tewfik (1997) proposed a vector projection based high bitrate information hiding algorithm, which embeds data by the projection of the DCT coefficients vector. Chae and Manjunath (1999) made use of lattice structure to code and embed information in the mid-frequency region of the DCT block. Alturki and Mersereau (2001) proposed data embedding through whitening the image and quantizing each DCT coefficient. Their algorithm significantly improved the security level and data capacity.

Yang and Bourbakis (2005) proposed a novel information hiding based methodology to deliver secure information with the transmission of digital video contents. In the proposed algorithm the original host frame is first transformed into DCT domain. After that, each 4x4 DCT block is divided into sub-blocks, and then the DCT coefficients within low-frequency sub-blocks will be modified to hide the message by means of zig-zag scanning and vector quantization. Information is hidden within DCT domain in order to make the algorithm compatible to DCT-based H.264/AVC compression and obtain robustness against lossy compression. Since vector quantization is more robust to noise (including inverse DCT transform round-off noise and quantization noise) than scalar quantization, the coefficient vectors (rather than the coefficient scalars) are chosen for information hiding. Their algorithm has achieved a good balance between channel capacity and robustness against lossy compression.

Yang and Deng (2006) proposed a novel steganography method to hide a small-size gray image in a large-size gray image. Discrete Wavelet Transformation (DWT) was performed on both the cover image and the secret image. The coefficients of the wavelet decomposition of the secret image were quantized and coded into bit streams. Then, the approximation subband of secret image was embedded into the approximation subband of the cover image using an improved version of the LSB algorithm. Original image is not required for the extraction of embedded information.

A novel Discrete Wavelet Transform (DWT) domain high bitrate information hiding algorithm was proposed in (Yang, Trifas, Truitt, & Xiong, 2008). In the proposed algorithm, the coefficients within the approximation subband of the one-level wavelet decomposition have been grouped into vectors to embed information bits. Low-frequency cocfficients have been chosen for information hiding due to their relatively large amplitudes and the corresponding smaller step size in JPEG2000 quantization. A mathematical model has been proposed to predict the Bit-Error-Rate (BER) of the algorithm under JPEG2000 compression.

Naoe and Takefuji (2008) proposed a new information hiding technique by using neural network trained on frequency domain. Proposed method can detect a hidden bit codes from the content by processing the selected feature sub-blocks into the trained neural network. Hidden codes can be retrieved from the neural network only if the proper extraction key is provided. The extraction keys are the coordinates of the selected feature subblocks, and the link weights are generated by supervised learning of a neural network. The supervised learning uses the coefficients of the selected feature subblocks as set of input values. The hidden bit patterns are used to train the neural network. The information hiding scheme can be combined with other algorithms to enhance the level of security.

EMBEDDING STRATEGIES FOR DIGITAL VIDEOS

Digital video is essentially a sequence of still images. Thus, it is natural to extend the digital image information hiding algorithms to corresponding approaches within digital video contents. The simplest way to implement video information hiding is to apply a still image information hiding algorithm to each frame of the video content. Figure 7 is an example of video information hiding. However, due to the inherent properties of digital video contents and the different video codec structures, information hiding within digital video also has its own characteristics. In this section, the

Figure 7. Comparison between Original and Stego-Frames: "foreman_qcif.yuv"

(a) Original Frames – "foreman_qcif.yuv"

(b) Stego Frames – "stego_foreman_qcif.yuv"

Figure 8. Temporal Location of Hidden Information

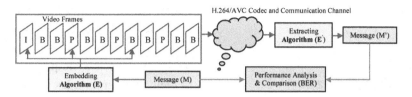

strategies of data embedding within digital video contents will be discussed.

Temporal Locations of Hidden Information

A generic video information hiding system is illustrated in Fig. 8. As can be seen, a message is embedded within the host video content, resulting in a stego-video which will go through H.264/AVC codec and the communication channel. The packet loss of Internet transmission is not under consideration for the time being, and thus the only procedure that may cause hidden information loss is H.264/AVC coding.

In H.264/AVC, with the Group-Of-Pictures (GOP) structures, there are three different types of frames: I-frame, P-frame, and B-frame, each of which is compressed with different algorithms. I-frame is intra-coded and has the lowest compression ratio; P-frame is inter-coded uni-directionally and has the medium compression ratio; B-frame is inter-coded bi-directionally and has the highest compression ratio. Due to the different compression algorithms, it is expected that I-frames have the highest channel capacity for in-

formation hiding, while B-frames have the lowest channel capacity. Accordingly, information within I-frames has the best chance to survive, and information within B-frames has the least chance to survive. Usually, we use I-frames for information embedding. If higher channel capacity is desired, P- and B- frames will also be used for information embedding.

Spatial Locations of Hidden Information in YUV Domain

In video compression, the source picture and the decoded picture are both comprised of three sample arrays: one luminance (luma) array and two chrominance (chroma) arrays. Since human vision system is more sensitive to luminance than to chrominance, the luma array is kept as it is and the chroma arrays are down-sampled (Figure 9). With the down-sampling of chroma arrays, the data rate of the video content is largely reduced.

In order not to cause any color distortion, usually only the luma sample array is chosen as the host for information hiding. The luma array will be modified as a gray-level image to hide information. In case that higher channel capacity is

Figure 9. YUV Sampling of Video Contents

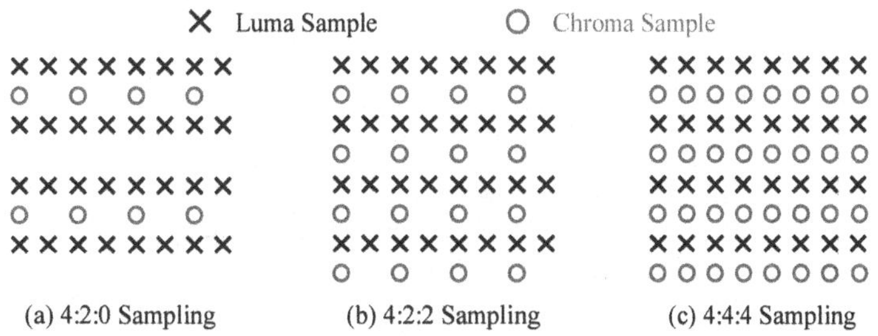

X Luma Sample   O Chroma Sample

(a) 4:2:0 Sampling   (b) 4:2:2 Sampling   (c) 4:4:4 Sampling desired, chroma samples will also be used for information hiding, at the price of slight color distortion.

Locations of Hidden Information in DCT Domain

As mentioned before, information embedded within the spatial-domain can be easily removed by a transformation based image/video codec. In order to gain robustness against lossy video codecs, it is better to embed information within the transformation domain. Two transformation domains have been investigated: Discrete Wavelet Transform (DWT) and Discrete Cosine Transform (DCT) in the research of Yang, Trifas, Truitt, and Xiong (2008). It is believed that information hiding and compression being in the same domain will make performance analysis and prediction easier. DWT based information hiding has been investigated and proven to be robust to JPEG 2000 image codec and Motion JPEG 2000 video codec.

In several studies (Yang & Bourbakis, 2005; Yang, Trifas, Truit, & Xiong, 2008), H.264/AVC was used as the video codec. Thus, the information embedding algorithm will work in DCT domain for the following reasons: (1) H.264/AVC uses 4x4 integer transformations for decorrelation; (2) DCT is a close approximation of integer transformation. Some existing embedding algorithms proposed to embed information by modifying the whole DCT block. However, this algorithm has two drawbacks: (1) too much visual distortion due to the modification of every coefficient within the block; (2) the modification of high-frequency coefficients will degrade the performance of run-length coding.

In order to fix the problem, current research efforts suggest to hide information within low-frequency coefficients. Preliminary experimental results also show that the proposed algorithm works best at low-frequency coefficients due to their high amplitudes. As such, the choice of the sub-block for information hiding is biased to low-frequency DCT coefficients (Figure 10). The reasons to choose low-frequency coefficients are:

(1) Low-frequency coefficients have relatively larger amplitudes compared to high-frequency ones, and thus have more room for information embedding;
(2) The quantization step sizes for low-frequency coefficients in lossy codec are relatively small, and the hidden information on low-frequency coefficients will have a better chance to survive;
(3) High-frequency DCT coefficients will be easily removed by lossy compression because of their relatively low energy;

High-frequency coefficients are left unchanged and the number of non-zero coefficients in high-frequency region will not be increased. Thus, the performance of run-length coding in the video codec will not be degraded.

CONCLUSION

Data Encryption is the backbone of information security and steganography works as the complement to data encryption. The most promising direction for the research of digital image/video encryption

Figure 10. Sub-blocking Strategies of 4x4 Block

(a)   (b)   (c)

is to analyze the unique properties of digital image and video, make full use of the properties, and search for highly-secure algorithms that cause minimal computational overhead. Joint encryption/compression is a very promising direction. Since compression can be viewed as a special type of encryption, it can be combined with encryption to reduce the overall computational cost. The same principle applies to video encryption, too.

Information hiding techniques have attracted more and more research interests. It can be used as an enhancement to data encryption to further increase the level of security. For example, Bourbakis, Rwabutaza, Yang, and Skondras (2009) have proposed a novel methodology to protect patient information during the electronic transmission of medical images. In the proposed methodology, they first adaptively identify locations to embed the patient information. After that, the locations of patient information are converted to two 2-D arrays. The 2-D arrays are compressed and encrypted using SCAN based encryption techniques. Finally, the encrypted location information is embedded with the medical images through LSB techniques. This is a very typical example of combining cryptography and steganography techniques to enhance the security of sensitive information.

The future challenges for information hiding include the following:

(1) How to minimize visual distortion: the information embedding procedure should not interfere with the visual quality of the host image/video contents;

(2) How to make the hiding algorithms robust to lossy compression: lossy image/video compression could possibly remove the embedded information. Existing research efforts work on how to improve the robustness of the embedded information against the lossy compression procedures;

(3) How to achieve higher level of channel capacity: there is always a tradeoff between channel capacity and the robustness again

lossy compression. The more information to embed, the less level of robustness can be expected. Right now, the research challenge is: how to embed a significant amount of information while making it robust against loss compression;

(4) Look for more practical applications for information hiding techniques: so far, many different information hiding techniques have been developed, and some of them are very mature in terms of the different performance metrics. Right now, the task is about how to find practical application scenarios and commercialization potentials for these research efforts.

Overall, the future trend on the development of information security techniques will be the combination of encryption, information hiding, and lossless compression. These techniques will enhance each other and increase the security level of modern information security systems.

REFERENCES

Agi, I., & Gong, L. (1996). An empirical study of secure MPEG video transmissions. In *Proceedings of the Internet Society symposium on network and distributed system security*, 137-144.

Allen, C. A., & Davidson, J. L. (1998). Steganography using the Minimax Eigenvalue Decomposition. In *Proceedings of the conference on mathematics of data/image coding, compression, and encryption, 3456*, 13-24.

Alturki, F., & Mersereau, R. (2001). A novel approach for increasing security and data embedding capacity in images for data hiding applications. *Proceedings of the international conference on information technology: Coding and computing*, 228–233.

Bas, P., Chassery, J., & Davoine, F. (1998). Self-similarity based image watermarking. In *Proceedings of the 9ᵗʰ European signal processing conference (EUSIPCO)*, 2277-2280.

Bender, W., Gruhl, D., Morimoto, N., & Lu, A. (1996). Techniques for data hiding. *IBM Systems Journal, 35*(3&4), 313–336. doi:10.1147/sj.353.0313

Bourbakis, N., & Dollas, A. (2003). SCAN based multimedia-on-demand. *IEEE multimedia magazine*, 79-87.

Bourbakis, N., Rwabutaza, A., Yang, M., & Skondras, T. (2009). A synthetic stegano-crypto scheme for securing multimedia medical records. In Proceedings of the *2009 IEEE Digital signal processing and signal processing education workshop*.

Briffa, J. A., & Das, M. (2002). Channel models for high-capacity information hiding in images. In *Proceedings of the SPIE, 4793*.

Chae, J. J., & Manjunath, B. S. (1999). Data hiding in video. In *Proceedings of the 6th IEEE international conference on image processing (ICIP'99), 1*, 311-315.

Chang, C., Chen, G., & Lin, M. (2004). Information hiding based on search-order coding for VQ indices. *Pattern Recognition Letters, 25*, 1253–1261. doi:10.1016/j.patrec.2004.04.003

Cheng, Q., & Huang, T. S. (2001). An additive approach to transform-domain information hiding andoptimum detection structure. *IEEE Transactions on Multimedia, 3*(3), 273–284. doi:10.1109/6046.944472

Chuang, T. J., & Lin, J. C. (1999). A new multi-resolution approach to still image encryption. *Pattern recognition and image analysis, 9*(3), 431-436.

Cox, I., Miller, M., & Bloom, J. (2002). *Digital watermarking*. San Francisco: Morgan Kaufmann Publishers.

Cox, I. J., Kilian, J., Leighton, T., & Shamoon, T. (1996). A secure, robust watermark for multimedia. In *Proceedings of the first international workshop on information hiding*, 185-206.

Cvejic, N., & Seppanen, T. (2004). Channel capacity of high bit rate audio data hiding algorithms in diverse transform domains. In *Proceedings of the international symposium on communications and information technologies (ISCIT 2004)*.

Fei, C., Kundur, D., & Kwong, R. (2001). The choice of watermark domain in the presence of compression. In *Proceedings of international conference on information technology: Coding and computing*, 79-84.

Gunsel, B., Uludag, U., & Tekalp, A. M. (2002). Robust watermarking of fingerprint images. *Journal of pattern recognition, 35*(12), 2739-2747.

Kekre, H. B., Athawale, A., & Halarnkar, P. N. (2008). Increased capacity of information hiding in LSB's method for text and image. *International journal of electrical, computer, and systems engineering*.

Kim, J., & Moon, Y. (1999). A robust wavelet-based digital watermark using level-adaptive thresholding. In *Proceedings of the IEEE international conference on image processing (ICIP'99)*.

Koch, E., & Zhao, J. (1995). Toward robust and hidden image copyright labeling. In *Proceedings of IEEE workshop on nonlinear signal and image processing*, 452-455.

Kundur, D. (2000). Implications for high capacity data hiding in the presence of lossy compression. In *Proceedings of the international conference on information technology: Coding and computing*, 16-21.

Kuo, C. J. (1993). Novel image encryption technique and its application in progressive transmission. *Journal of Electronic Imaging, 2*(4), 345–351. doi:10.1117/12.148572

Langelaar, G. C., Setyawan, I., & Lagendijk, R. L. (2000). Watermarking digital image and video data: a state-of-the-art overview. *IEEE Signal Processing Magazine, 17*(5), 20–46. doi:10.1109/79.879337

Li, Y., Chen, Z., Tan, S. M., & Campbell, R. H. (1996). Security enhanced MPEG player. In *Proceedings of the international workshop on multimedia software development,* 169-175.

Lin, C. Y., & Chang, S. F. (2001). Watermarking capacity of digital images based on domain-specific masking effects. In *Proceedings of the international conference on information technology: Coding and computing (ITCC '01).*

Maniccam S. S., & Bourbakis, N. (2004). Lossless compression and information hiding in images. *Pattern recognition journal, 36,* 2004.

Meyer, J., & Gadegast, F. (1995). Security mechanisms for multimedia-data with the example MPEG-I Video. In *Proceedings (IEEE) of the international conference on multimedia computing and systems.*

Moulin, P., & Mihcak, M. K. (2002). A framework for evaluating the data-hiding capacity of image sources. *IEEE Transactions on Image Processing, 11*(9), 1029–1042. doi:10.1109/TIP.2002.802512

Naoe, K., & Takefuji, Y. (2008). Damageless information hiding using neural network on YCbCr domain. *International journal of computer science and network security, 8*(9).

Ni, Z., Shi, Y., Ansari, N., Su, W., Sun, Q., & Lin, X. (2004). Robust lossless image data hiding. *International conference on multimedia & expo (ICME), 3,* 2199-2202.

Pereira, S., Voloshynovskiy, S., & Pun, T. (2000). Optimized wavelet domain watermark embedding strategy using linear programming. In Szu, H. (Ed.), *SPIE Aerosense 2000: Wavelet Applications VII.*

Qiao, L., & Nahrstedt, K. (1997). A new algorithm for MPEG video encryption. In *Proceedings of CISST'97 international conference,* 21-29.

Scharinger, J. (1998). Fast encryption of image data using chaotic Kolmogorov flows. *Journal of Electronic Imaging, 7*(2), 318–325. doi:10.1117/1.482647

Shi, C., & Bhargava, B. (1998a). A fast MPEG video encryption algorithm. *ACM Multimedia, 98,* 81–88.

Shi, C., & Bhargava, B. B. (1998b). An efficient MPEG video encryption algorithm. In *Proceedings of the symposium on reliable distributed systems,* 381-386.

Singh, K. M., Singh, S. B., & Singh, S. S. (2007). Hiding encrypted message in the features of images. *International journal of computer science and network security (IJCSNS), 7*(4).

Socek, D., Li, S., Magliveras, S. S., & Furht, B. (2005). Short paper: enhanced 1-d chaotic key-based algorithm for image encryption. *First international conference on security and privacy for emerging areas in communications networks.*

Spanos, G. A., & Maples, T. B. (1995). Performance study of a selective encryption scheme for the security of networked, real-time video. *Proceedings of the 4th IEEE international conference on computer communications and networks (ICCCN '95),* 2-10.

Swanson, M. D., Zhu, B., & Tewfik, A. H. (1997). Data hiding for video-in-video. In *Proceedings of the 1997 international conference on image processing (ICIP '97), 2,* 676-679.

Tang, L. (1996). Methods for encrypting and decrypting MPEG video data efficiently. *ACM Multimedia, 96*, 219–229.

Wu, D. C., & Tsai, W. H. (1998). Data hiding in images via multiple-based number conversion and lossy compression. *IEEE Transactions on Consumer Electronics, 44*(4), 1406–1412. doi:10.1109/30.735844

Wu, X., & Moo, P. W. (1999). Joint image/video compression and encryption via high-order conditional entropy coding of wavelet coefficients. *Proceedings (IEEE) of the international conference on multimedia computing and systems (ICMCS'99), 2*, 908-912.

Xia, X. G., Boncelet, C. G., & Arce, G. R. (1997). A multi-resolution watermark for digital images. In *Proceedings of IEEE international conference on image processing, 1*, 548-551.

Yang, B., & Deng, B. (2006). Steganography in gray images using wavelet. In *Proceedings of the second international symposium on communication, control and signal processing (ISCCSP)*.

Yang, M., & Bourbakis, N. (2005). A high bitrate multimedia information hiding algorithm in DCT domain. In *Proceedings of the 8th world conference on integrated design and process technology (IDPT 2005)*.

Yang, M., & Bourbakis, N. (2005). A high bitrate information hiding algorithm for digital video content under H.264/AVC compression. In *Proceedings of the IEEE international midwest symposium on circuits and systems (MWSCAS 2005)*.

Yang, M., Trifas, M., Truitt, C., & Xiong, G. (2008). Wavelet domain video information embedding. *Proceedings of the 12th world multi-conference on systemics, cybernetics and informatics*.

Younes, M. A., & Jantan, A. (2003). Image encryption using block-based transformation algorithm, *IAENG International Journal of Computer Science, 35*(1).

Zhang, W., Cheung, S., & Chen, M. (2005). Hiding privacy information in video surveillance system. In *Proceedings of the international conference on image processing (ICIP'2005), 3*, II- 868-71.

Chapter 12
Secure Electronic Voting with Cryptography

Xunhua Wang
James Madison University, USA

Ralph Grove
James Madison University, USA

M. Hossain Heydari
James Madison University, USA

ABSTRACT

In recent years, computer and network-based voting technologies have been gradually adopted for various elections. However, due to the fragile nature of electronic ballots and voting software, computer voting has posed serious security challenges. This chapter studies the security of computer voting and focuses on a cryptographic solution based on mix-nets. Like traditional voting systems, mix-net-based computer voting provides voter privacy and prevents vote selling/buying and vote coercion. Unlike traditional voting systems, mix-net-based computer voting has several additional advantages: 1) it offers vote verifiability, allowing individual voters to directly verify whether their votes have been counted and counted correctly; 2) it allows voters to check the behavior of potentially malicious computer voting machines and thus does not require voters to blindly trust computer voting machines. In this chapter, we give the full details of the building blocks for the mix-net-based computer voting scheme, including semantically secure encryption, threshold decryption, mix-net, and robust mix-net. Future research directions on secure electronic voting are also discussed.

INTRODUCTION

"Those who vote determine nothing; those who count the votes determine everything."—Joseph Stalin

Fair elections are the foundation of democracy. The integrity of an election depends heavily on the voting technologies used. In human history, several voting technologies have been used in various elections, including *stones*, *colored balls or beans*, *paper ballots*, *mechanical lever machines*, *punched cards*, *optical scanners*, and most recently, *computers*. Computer voting is

DOI: 10.4018/978-1-61520-783-1.ch012

also called *electronic voting* and computer voting machines are often called *Direct Recording Electronics* (DRE).

Just as in many other applications, computers have the potential to make ballot casting, vote tallying, and vote recounting much easier and faster. On the other hand, computer voting also poses a big security challenge as it uses *electronic* ballots, not the traditional *paper* ballots.

Unlike paper ballots, electronic ballots can be easily modified, forged, and discarded without a trace. Such modification, forgery, and removal of electronic ballots can happen in all stages of electronic voting, including the *casting* (e.g., by faulty or malicious voting software), *storage*, *transferring*, and *tallying* of electronic ballots. The following examples of computer voting glitches happened in the November 4th, 2004 election.

- Carteret county, North Carolina, used an electronic voting system with a storage unit that has capacity of 3005 votes. The voting system allowed 7535 electronic ballots to be cast without reporting any errors. As a result, more than 4500 votes were lost (USA Today, 2004).
- One precinct in Franklin county, Ohio, used computer voting and reported 4258 votes for Bush. But records showed that only 638 voters cast their ballots in that precinct (McCarthy, 2004).
- Broward county, Florida, used computer voting equipment with faulty software that could not handle more than 32,000 votes in a precinct. When more than 32,000 votes were counted, the tallying software started counting backward. As a result, the outcome of Amendment 4 in the ballot was erroneously reported (Internet Broadcasting Systems, 2004).
- Sarpy county, Nebraska, used computer voting equipment and a computer problem caused double votes in half the county's precincts, leading to about 3000 phantom votes (WOWT.COM, 2004).

Because of the fragility of electronic ballots and voting and tallying software, it is desirable to have a paper trail for each electronic vote (for example, let each voter bring home a *paper receipt*). In case of a dispute, this paper receipt can be used at a later time for tracing the vote and for vote recounting.

However, this idea of a paper receipt may jeopardize several other properties of the voting system. First, the voter can use a plain paper receipt to prove to a candidate how the vote is cast, thus making vote selling possible: the candidate may pay a fee to the voter upon proof that the vote is actually for the candidate. Second, paper receipts also make vote coercion possible: a rogue candidate may seek revenge if a paper receipt shows that the vote is not for him. Thus, introducing plain paper receipts into electronic voting may improve accountability but will negatively impact the integrity of an election.

To overcome these difficulties, (Benaloh, 1988; Benaloh & Tuinstra, 1994; Chaum, 2004a, 2004b) developed the concept of *secret-ballot receipt*, which is an *encrypted* ballot. The resulting computer voting solution is essentially a *cryptography-based voting scheme* and is sometimes called *secret-ballot voting* or *receipt-free voting*. For this cryptographic solution, several issues need to be resolved: what cryptographic key and encryption algorithm are used? How are the encrypted ballots tallied? How is the integrity of the encrypted ballots guaranteed?

The introduction of *encrypted* paper receipts into computer voting may bring several additional desirable properties that do *not* exist in non-electronic traditional voting systems. First, in traditional voting systems, there is no direct method for a voter to verify that his/her vote is actually counted or counted correctly. A voter has to place his/her trust in the voting system for counting votes. As we shall see in this chapter, vote verifiability is achievable in cryptography-based computer voting systems.

Second, cryptography-based computer voting also allows individual voters to check the behavior of computer voting machines and the integrity of the voting system. Voters do *not* have to blindly trust the system.

The remainder of this chapter is organized as follows. We shall first give the data flow of general voting and summarize its security properties. Next, we shall describe, in detail, the building blocks of the cryptographic computer voting system, including the semantically secure ElGamal encryption, threshold ElGamal decryption, re-encryption mix-net, and robust mix-net. We shall then present the details of cryptography-based computer voting and analyze its security. Future research direction and concluding remarks are given toward the end of this chapter. This chapter also suggests some additional reading materials.

BACKGROUND

Traditional Voting Process

Figure 1 depicts a traditional voting process. A voter, Alice, first registers to vote with the voter registration authority, which verifies Alice's eligibility to vote. Alice will get a notification for the voter registration, along with other details about the election, such as her poll location (usually in the precinct close to her home). Before election day, the registration authority will transfer the voter roster to poll workers at Alice's voting precinct.

To cast her ballot, Alice needs to show up in person on the election day at the polling place. She will cast her vote in a private *voting booth*, which allows only one voter at a time. Alice's ballot, along with other ballots cast in the same precinct, is stored in a *ballot box*. When the poll is closed, all ballot boxes are shipped to a tally place, where votes are tallied. The election result is certified by the election officials in the end.

Computer Voting

The computerization of a voting system has three aspects: *the digitalization of ballots, the transfer of electronic ballots through computer networks or storage devices*, and *the automatic tallying of electronic ballots by computers*. In computer voting, voters cast their ballots on a touch screen and the ballots are stored, transferred and tallied in a digital manner. This makes vote counting and recounting automatic and faster.

SECURITY PROPERTIES OF COMPUTER VOTING: ISSUES AND CHALLENGES

The voting application has several security properties, namely, *voter privacy* (also called *ballot secrecy*) and *election integrity*. The latter includes no *vote buying/selling*, no vote coercion, ballot

Figure 1. Voting data flow

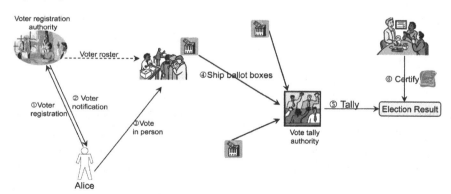

integrity (i.e., no unauthorized modification or dropping of ballots, no phantom ballots), and the accuracy of vote counting and recounting. Some of these properties are related to each other and thus deserve more elaboration.

- Voter privacy (ballot secrecy) is a property such that the ballot of an *honest* voter who follows all procedures should be kept secret. This is usually achieved through a private voting booth, where no camera is allowed and only one voter is allowed each time. The voter privacy property allows a voter to vote her own choice and thus it is the foundation of democracy.
  - ○ In addition to private voting booths, voter privacy also depends on how a ballot is cast and the number of ballots in a ballot box when it is opened. In many states, voters are *not* allowed to put down their name initials or other identity-leaking marks on a ballot, since these marks may compromise voter privacy.
  - ○ It is less obvious that voter privacy also depends on the number of votes in a ballot box when it is opened. As an extreme example, if a precinct has only one voter and the ballot box is opened with a single vote for tallying, then a private voting booth does not help voter privacy as one can always infer how the single voter voted at tally time. This is less of a problem when a precinct has many (say 1000) voters.
- Vote buying/selling: a *dishonest* voter may sell his vote for a fee if he can prove to a candidate how he has voted. Vote selling compromises the integrity of an election. Through a private voting booth and not allowing a voter to bring home any receipts, vote buying/selling can be effectively prevented.

- Vote coercion: a rogue election candidate may intimidate a voter to vote one way or another. This practice should be prevented in a technical manner. Private voting booths and the absence of voting receipts can effectively prevent vote coercion, as a voter may vote one way but tell the candidate later otherwise.
- Ballot integrity: the integrity of an election also depends on the integrity of ballots over their whole lifetimes, including their *creation* at polling places, the *storage* of ballots at the polling places, the *transportation* of ballots from polling places to a tally place, and the *storage* of ballots at the tally place before they are counted.
  - ○ In this whole life cycle, ballot integrity can be compromised in several ways: ballots may be created incorrectly by malicious voting machines at the polling place when voters cast their votes; ballots may be modified without authorization while in storage or during transportation; they may be deleted; phantom ballots may be forged and introduced.
  - ○ These security threats pose several questions for computer voting: do voters have to blindly trust the computer voting machines? Do voters have to trust the channel, which might be a computer network, to transport ballots from the polling place to the tally place? Do voters have to blindly trust the tallying software?
- Vote verifiability: a voting system is *vote verifiable* if any voter can verify, in a direct manner, that her vote is counted and counted as intended. Thus, a vote-verifiable voting system is not blindly trusted and its behaviors can be checked.
  - ○ If the ballot integrity property is guaranteed at all stages of an election, a voter can be sure, in an *indirect*

manner, that her vote is counted and counted as intended. But this assurance depends on the blind trust in the voting system. In contrast, vote verifiability is more direct in that each voter can verify her vote by herself or through a third party and the voter does not have to blindly trust the voting system. Vote verifiability is very desirable.

○ It is worth noting that in the traditional paper-ballot voting system, a voter has to depend on the ballot integrity of the voting system and the integrity of the tally authority for counting accuracy.

• Voting system availability: since elections are particularly time sensitive, the availability of a voting system is crucial for election integrity. An election system cannot be called fair if the whole or part of the system is not available in time.

The status quo of computer voting: As of this writing, most of the computer voting machines on the market are just digitalized versions of the traditional paper ballot-based voting system. They do *not* offer direct vote verifiability and voters have to blindly trust the computer voting machines for ballot creation and the whole voting system for ballot integrity and vote counting. However, since electronic ballots are much more fragile than paper ballots and software can be hacked, these computer voting and tallying machines may be manipulated/hacked to compromise election integrity (Kohno, Stubblefield, Rubin, & Wallach, 2004).

The cryptography-based computer voting system reviewed in this chapter, which has yet to be implemented and deployed for real-world elections, achieves all these properties through *secret-ballot receipts*. Since a secret-ballot receipt is encrypted, a voter cannot prove to a third party how she voted, thus avoiding the problems of vote

selling/buying and vote coercion. On the other hand, the secret-ballot receipt can be used later by the voter for vote verifiability. This verification capability still does *not* enable the voter to prove to a third party how she voted.

The remainder of this chapter explains how these properties are achieved.

BUILDING BLOCKS

In this section, we shall give the details of the cryptographic building blocks of secure electronic voting, including *semantically secure ElGamal encryption*, *threshold ElGamal decryption*, *mix-nets*, and *robust mix-nets*.

Semantically Secure ElGamal Encryption

A secret-ballot receipt is an encrypted ballot and it must leak *no* knowledge about the ballot. This no-leaking requirement effectively prevents vote selling/buying and vote coercion. Such an encryption is called *semantically secure*. Several public-key encryption schemes (including the raw RSA and standard ElGamal) are not semantically secure in their original forms. The following variant of ElGamal encryption (ElGamal, 1985) is semantically secure and can be used to encrypt Alice's plaintext ballot m.

Let p be a large prime such that $p=2q+1$ and q is also a prime. p is called a *safe prime*. Let g be an element of finite field F_p with order q. The set $\{g, g^2 \bmod p, g^3 \bmod p, ..., g^q \bmod p\}$ forms a subgroup of F_p and it is denoted as $<g>$. We assume that m is also in $<g>$, denoted as $m \in <g>$. (If the encoding of a candidate's name happens to be not in $<g>$, we will encode that candidate as $-m$, which is guaranteed to be in $<g>$.)

(p, q, g) are public system-wide parameters.

To generate a public/private key pair for ballot encryption, the election authority chooses a random number s such that $1 \leq s \leq q$ as private key and calculates $Y = g^s \bmod p$. Y is the public key used for encrypting a ballot m and is distributed to all voting machines.

To encrypt Alice's plaintext ballot $m \in <g>$, the voting machine chooses a random value r, $1 \leq r \leq q$, and encrypts m into $c = (c_1 = g^r \bmod p, c_2 = Y^r \times m \bmod p)$.

To decrypt c with the private key s, one applies the private key s to c_1 to calculate $\mu_1 = c_1^s \bmod p$. Note that $\mu_1 = (g^r)^s \bmod p = (g^s)^r \bmod p = Y^r \bmod p$. One then calculates $\mu_2 = \mu_1^{-1} \bmod p$ and $m' = \mu_2 \times c_2 \bmod p$. Since μ_2 is the inverse of $Y^r \bmod p$, we have $m' = m$, which is Alice's plaintext ballot.

It is worth noting that this public key encryption scheme is different from the standard ElGamal encryption in two respects: first, g is an element of order q and g is not a generator of F_p; second, the message to be encrypted must be in $<g>$. These two changes make the scheme semantically secure.

Threshold ElGamal Decryption

In the above ElGamal encryption scheme, the private key s exists as a whole and it is used for ballot decryption. However, for critical applications like secure electronic voting, it is too risky to let a single entity have s and decrypt ballots, as it may lead to power abuse: the single entity may decrypt encrypted ballots without authorization to compromise voter privacy; she may also refuse to decrypt to make the election system unavailable.

To avoid such a pitfall, private key s can be shared among a group of n election authorities ($n > 1$), each getting a *share*, such that any t or more of these authorities can collectively decrypt *without* reconstructing s. The non-reconstruction requirement is important as reconstruction may create a single point of attack. This sharing and collective use of s can effectively prevent the aforementioned power abuse.

With Shamir secret sharing (Shamir, 1979), s can be shared by a trusted third party (called *the dealer*) as follows. The dealer picks $(t-1)$ random

numbers, $a_1, a_2, ..., a_{t-1}$, where $0 \leq a_i \leq q-1$. Let $f(x) = s + a_1 x + a_2 x^2 + ... + a_{t-1} x^{t-1} \bmod q$. (For convenience, we define $a_0 = s$ and use a_0 and s interchangeably.) The dealer calculates shares as $s_i = f(i)$, $1 \leq i \leq n$.

The dealer then sends $<i, s_i>$ to authority i in a secure manner.

To collectively decrypt an encrypted ballot c, where $c = (c_1 = g^r \bmod p, c_2 = Y^r \times m \bmod p)$, t such election authorities, $\{i_1, i_2, ..., i_t\}$, where $1 \leq i_j \leq n$, for $1 \leq j \leq t$, perform the following calculations (Desmedt & Frankel, 1990):

- Each entity uses its share s_{i_j} to calculate

  $\alpha_{i_j} = c_1^{s_{i_j}} \bmod p$ and broadcasts it.

- Each entity calculates

  $c_{i_j} = \prod_{1 \leq k \leq t, k \neq j} \dfrac{i_k}{i_k - i_j} \bmod q$ and

  $\mu_1 = \prod_{j=1}^{t} \alpha_{i_j}^{c_{i_j}} \bmod p$. Note that

  $\mu_1 = c_1^s \bmod p$.

- Each entity calculates $\mu_2 = \mu_1 - 1 \bmod p$ and $m' = \mu_2 \times c_2 \bmod p$, where m' is the recovered ballot.

In the above steps, s is never reconstructed.

Mix, Mix-Nets, and Re-Encryption Mix-Nets

A *mix* is a computer that receives l input messages, transforms and shuffles them, and outputs l messages in such a way that from any output message, an outsider cannot tell which input messages it comes from (Chaum, 1981). This unlinkability property is called *privacy* of the mix. Since a passive attacker may link an output message to an input message through message *size*, message *content*, and message arriving/leaving *times*, a mix needs to *pad* all output messages to the same size, *scramble* message contents to prevent content-based linking, and *buffer* input messages to prevent timing-based linking. To this end, a mix's transforming operation and shuffling operation (usually denoted as a permutation π; see Figure 2) should also be kept secret.

Multiple mixes are often cascaded together to form a mix sequence called a *mix-net*, where one mix's output is fed into the next mix. Figure 2 gives an example mix-net, which has four mixes, S_1, S_2, S_3, and S_4. Before being sent to a mix-net, the messages to be mixed are first *pre-processed*. The exact details of the pre-processing step depend on the type of the mix-net. The pre-processed messages (α_1, α_2, α_3, …, α_8 of Figure 2) go through the mix one by one and the output of the last mix (τ_1, τ_2, τ_3, …, τ_8 of Figure 2) is the final output of the mix-net.

Compared to a single mix, a mix-net is more reliable: if some of these mixes are compromised and their transforming and shuffling operations are revealed, as long as one mix remains secure, an attacker still can't link a specific output message τ_i to a specific input message α_j.

Mix-nets can be used for anonymity. If a mix-net removes the source address from an input message, after the mix-net processes the message, the ultimate message receiver will not be able to tell who has sent the message.

The first mix-net was designed by David Chaum (Chaum, 1981) and thus is often called the *Chaumian mix-net*. A Chaumian mix-net is *decryption mix-net*, where each mix has a private/ public key pair and each mix decrypts its input messages. For this type of mix-net, in the pre-processing step, the input messages to be mixed are encrypted multiple times, successively by each of the mix's public key, in the reverse order of the mixes in the mix-net. For example, in Figure 2, the message is first encrypted by mix 4's public key, then by mix 3's public key, then by mix 2's public key, and lastly by mix 1's public key. As shown in Figure 2, upon receiving the messages, each mix decrypts the messages (denoted as "D" in Figure 2), shuffles them with a private permutation (denoted as π_i in Figure 2), and then outputs them.

For the electronic voting application discussed in this chapter, the *re-encryption mix-net* is used (Park, Itoh, & Kurosawa, 1993). As shown in Figure 3, a re-encryption mix-net consists of two stages: the mix cascade and a threshold decryption. A mix in a re-encryption mix-net does not decrypt. Instead, it performs a "re-encryption" operation, denoted as RE in Figure 3.

Let's use the semantically secure ElGamal encryption described earlier to explain how a re-encryption mix-net works. (g, q, p) are public parameters described earlier and Y is a public key whose corresponding private key s is shared among a group of entities.

Each mix in the re-encryption mix-net is configured with system parameters (g, q, p, Y). Before sent to the re-encryption mix-net, all messages to be mixed, m_i, are first pre-processed through an encryption by Y as $\alpha_i = (c_{i1} = g^r \bmod p, c_{i2} = Y^r \times m_i$

Figure 2. Chaumian/Decryption mix-net

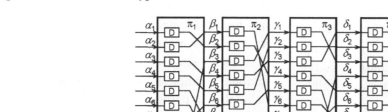

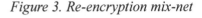

Figure 3. Re-encryption mix-net

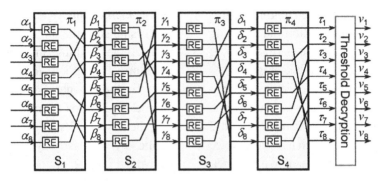

mod p). α_i, $1 \leq i \leq 8$, are then sent to the first mix S_1. For each α_i, $1 \leq i \leq 8$, mix S_1 will pick a random number r_{i1}, $1 \leq r_{i1} \leq q - 1$, and transform α_i into α_i' as $\alpha_i' = (c_{i1} \times g^{r_{i1}} \bmod p, c_{i2} \times Y^{r_{i1}} \bmod p)$. α_i' is called the *re-encryption* of α_i. Note that this re-encryption operation is *not* a regular elgamal encryption, but a transformation of α_i. It is not hard to see that both α_i and α_i' are a valid encryption of the same message m_i under Y.

As shown in Figure 3, mix S_1 then generates a random permutation π_1 and uses it to shuffle $(\alpha_1', \alpha_2', \alpha_3', \alpha_4', \alpha_5', \alpha_6', \alpha_7', \alpha_8')$ into $(\beta_1, \beta_2, \beta_3, \beta_4, \beta_5, \beta_6, \beta_7, \beta_8)$, which are sent to mix S_2.

Mix S_2 and other mixes behave in a similar way and the mix cascade outputs $(\tau_1, \tau_2, \tau_3, \tau_4, \tau_5, \tau_6, \tau_7, \tau_8)$.

In the second stage of the re-encryption mix-net, a group of entities sharing the private key s collectively decrypt τ_i into v_i, which should be m_j in an unknown order. There are two reasons to use threshold decryption in this stage. First, threshold decryption can improve the mix-net's availability: the mix-net will be unavailable if the private key s is assigned to a single entity and this entity refuses to decrypt. Second, the privacy of the mix-net depends on the secrecy of s and sharing s among a group of entities improves its confidentiality: even after an attacker has compromised smaller than a threshold number of such entities, the mix-net's privacy is still guaranteed.

As long as one of these mixes keeps its re-encryption operation and its random permutation secret, an attacker cannot link any τ_i, $1 \leq i \leq 8$, to a specific α_j, $1 \leq j \leq 8$.

Robust Privacy, Verifiability, Availability, and Robust Mix-Nets

Robust Privacy

The mix-net of Figure 3 uses to cascade topology, in which a mix's next is pre-set. As a result, one honest and secure mix can guarantee the privacy of the whole mix-net.

A mix-net can also be in the free-routing topology (Sampigethaya & Poovendran, 2006), where a mix can dynamically choose its next mix. Within such a mix-net, an adversary who has compromised and controlled multiple mixes may manage to recover the messages being mixed through manipulating the routing.

The privacy of a mix-net may also depend on the pre-processing step. For example, the aforementioned re-encryption mix-net based on ElGamal implicitly assumes that the input messages are valid ElGamal ciphertexts and are generated from the messages to be mixed. However, this implicit assumption may be exploited for various malicious purposes (Pfitzmann & Pfitzmann, 1989; Pfitzmann, 1995), including compromising the privacy of a mix-net. A well-designed mix-net should be able to resist such privacy attacks.

A mix-net is said to have *robust privacy* if privacy is still achieved in the presence of these attacks.

Universal and Local Verifiability

In the re-encryption mix-net of figure 3, we implicitly assume that each mix will perform its operations honestly. That is, it will only transform (and shuffle) the messages as prescribed and will *not* drop, replace, or change their content. However, in transforming α_i to α_i', a *malicious* mix S_1 (compromised and controlled by an attacker) may modify the message content by introducing an additional value ζ_i as

$$\alpha_i' = \left(c_{i1} \times g^{r_{i1}} \bmod p, c_{i2} \times Y^{r_{i1}} \times \zeta_i \bmod p\right).$$

The resulting α_i' will *not* be the encryption of m_i but the encryption of $m_i \times \zeta_i$, which may be advantageous to the attacker.

A mix is called *verifiable* if it provides *proof* or *evidence* to show the correctness of its operations. For example, in Figure 3, a verifiable mix S_1 should provide proof/evidence that $(\beta_1, \beta_2, \beta_3, \beta_4, \beta_5, \beta_6, \beta_7, \beta_8)$ is indeed the re-encryption of $(\alpha_1, \alpha_2, \alpha_3, \alpha_4, \alpha_5, \alpha_6, \alpha_7, \alpha_8)$ without revealing r_{i1}, $1 \le i \le 8$, and π_1. This may sound a little self-contradictory but as shown in (Goldreich, Micali, & Wigderson, 1987, 1991; Ben-Or et al., 1989), any NP statement can be proved in a zero-knowledge manner.

If the proof/evidence can be verified by any outsider, then it is called *universally* (or *publically*) *verifiable* (Sako & Kilian, 1995). If the correctness of a mix can be verified only by an insider (such as the next mix in the mix sequence), it is called *locally verifiable* (Jakobsson, 1998).

When the correctness of a mix in a verifiable mix-net cannot be verified, it may have to be removed or replaced. It is very desirable that a mix-net can replace/remove a failed mix and can continue to operate, as such a mix-net enjoys high-level availability.

Robust Mixing & Availability

In a mix-net, a certain number of *malicious* mixes may be compromised and then controlled by an attacker; these mixes may collaborate in a malicious manner to prevent the mix-net from producing the correct result. A mix-net that tolerates such attacks (i.e., operates correctly despite the compromise) is said to achieve *robust* mixing

Robust Mix-Nets

A mix-net is *robust* if it achieves robust privacy, the operations of all mixes are verifiable, and it can continue to operate in the presence of any failed mix (through replacing the failed mixes). For the application of electronic voting, universal verifiability and high availability are very desirable as the former allows the public to verify the integrity of the election and the latter makes the voting system highly available. As we shall show later, robust privacy is a smaller problem for electronic voting.

Several techniques have been developed to achieve universal verifiability for a robust mix-net, including *zero-knowledge proof* and *cut-and-choose* (Sako & Kilian, 1995; Ogata, Kurosawa, Sako, & Takatani, 1997), *pairwise permutations* based on verifiable discrete logarithm computations (Abe, 1999; Jakobsson & Juels, 1999), the *matrix representative* approach (Furukawa & Sako, 2001), the *polynomial scheme* (through verifiable secret exponent) (Neff, 2001, 2004), *randomized partial checking* (RPC) (Jakobsson, Juels, & Rivest, 2002), the *optimistic mixing scheme* (Golle, Zhong, Boneh, Jakobsson, & Juels, 2002), and the *proof-of-subproduct* approach (Boneh & Golle, 2002). These techniques vary in the computational efficiency of generating and verifying a proof/evidence (in terms of the number of modular exponentiations), the size of the proof/evidence, the level of the mix-net's privacy, and the level of the mix-net's computational correctness.

Randomized Partial Checking

Due to its conceptual simplicity, we shall use the randomized partial checking (rpc) approach (jakobsson, juels, & rivest, 2002) to explain how a robust mix-net works. In rpc, mixes of a mix-net are organized in pairs and a private permutation π_i is viewed as a set of (input, output correspondences. For example, in figure 4, mixes S_1 and S_2 form a pair; mixes S_3 and S_4 form another pair. Mix S_1's private permutation π_1 is represented in a set of (input, output) correspondences $(i, \pi_1(i))$, $1 \le i \le 8$, where $\pi_1(i)$ denotes output $\beta_{\pi_1(i)}$ is generated from input α_i. In figure 4, $\pi_1(1) = 2$, $\pi_1(2) = 4$; $(\pi_1(1), \pi_1(2), \ldots, \pi_1(8)) = (2, 4, 1, 3, 6, 8, 7, 5)$ and $(\pi_2(1), \pi_2(2), \ldots, \pi_2(8)) = (8, 4, 2, 3, 1, 5, 7, 6)$.

In RPC, when each mix S_i produces and publishes its output messages, it also publishes a commitment on its private permutation π_i. (This commitment alone does *not* leak π_i and its details are described below.) After all mixes finish their operations, for each mix pair, the first mix will be asked to *randomly* reveal half of its (input, output) correspondences and show how these inputs are mapped to the outputs. The second mix will be asked to reveal the *complement* (input, output) correspondences. Due to the randomness of its revelation, if one mix cheats on one (input, output) correspondence – by either replacing the

message or changing its content, this misbehavior will be detected with a chance of 50%. A change of multiple messages will lead to a very high probability of being detected.

Under this pairing and complement revelation strategy, when a pair of mixes is honest, any output message from the pair cannot be linked to a specific message to the pair. As a result, as long as one pair of mixes is honest, the privacy of the message being mixed by the mix-net is still guaranteed.

Let's use an example to explain how RPC works. In Figure 4, at the mixing stage, mix S_1 produces its output messages β_i and it also generates a commitment of π_1 as a *list* of values. The commitment is computed as follows: S_1 picks a random long string w, computes and publishes commitment values $\theta_j = h(w \,\|\, \pi_1(j))$ for $1 \le j \le 8$, where $\|$ denotes string concatenation and h is a cryptographic hash function.

After all mixes have finished their operations and published their commitments, value k is calculated in a public manner as $k = h(\alpha_1 \| \alpha_2 \| \ldots \| \alpha_8 \| \beta_1 \| \beta_2 \| \ldots \| \beta_8 \| \gamma_1 \| \gamma_2 \| \ldots \| \gamma_8 \| \delta_1 \| \delta_2 \| \ldots \| \delta_8 \| \tau_1 \| \tau_2 \| \ldots \| \tau_8 \| v_1 \| v_2 \| \ldots \| v_8)$ and some secondary values k_i are calculated as $k_i =$ HMAC-SHA1(k, i), $1 \le i \le 8$, where HMAC-SHA1 is the SHA-1 based message authentication code (MAC).

Next, each mix is asked to reveal *half* of its π_i (that is, half of the input/output correspondences)

Figure 4. Robust mix-net through randomized partial checking

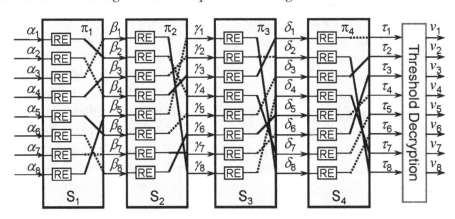

and k_i is used to decide which part of π_i should be revealed. Note that k_i is unpredictable for S_i.

In Figure 4, let's assume that after all mixes have finished their operations, k_1 is calculated as $\{2, 3, 6, 7, \ldots\}$. Thus mix S_1 is asked to reveal π_1 for the following (input, output) correspondences $\{\{(\alpha_2, \beta_{\pi_1(2)}), (\alpha_3, \beta_{\pi_1(3)}), (\alpha_6, \beta_{\pi_1(6)}), (\alpha_7, \beta_{\pi_1(7)})\}$. This revelation consists of two steps.

First, mix S_1 should reveal both a string w', which is supposed to be w, and $\{\pi_1(2), \pi_1(3), \pi_1(6), \pi_1(7)\}$. Mix S_1's this revelation can be verified by the public by checking whether $\theta_j = h(w' \| \pi_1(j))$, $j \in \{2, 3, 6, 7\}$. If any of these does not hold, S_1 will be caught cheating and will be removed from the mix-net. (Note that h is a cryptographic hash function and it is second preimage-resistant; if mix S_1 lied in the earlier calculations of $(\theta_2, \theta_3, \theta_6, \theta_7)$, it would *not* be able to reveal a set of values w', $\pi_1(2)$, $\pi_1(3)$, $\pi_1(6)$, $\pi_1(7)$, to make all these four hold.)

Second, if the verification in step 1 succeeds, mix s_1 will be asked to reveal links $\{(\alpha_2, \beta_{\pi_1(2)}), (\alpha_3, \beta_{\pi_1(3)}), (\alpha_6, \beta_{\pi_1(6)}), (\alpha_7, \beta_{\pi_1(7)})\}$, which in figure 4 are links $\{(\alpha_2, \beta_4), (\alpha_3, \beta_1), (\alpha_6, \beta_8), (\alpha_7, \beta_7)\}$, marked as dashed lines. For each of these links, mix S_1 has to reveal the corresponding $r_{j1}, j = 2, 3, 6, 7$, and the public can check whether

$$\beta_4 = (c_{21} \times g^{r_{21}} \bmod p, c_{22} \times Y^{r_{21}} \bmod p),$$

$$\beta_1 = (c_{31} \times g^{r_{31}} \bmod p, c_{32} \times Y^{r_{31}} \bmod p),$$

$$\beta_8 = (c_{61} \times g^{r_{61}} \bmod p, c_{62} \times Y^{r_{61}} \bmod p), \text{ and}$$

$$\beta_7 = (c_{71} \times g^{r_{71}} \bmod p, c_{72} \times Y^{r_{71}} \bmod p).$$ If any of these does not hold, S_1 will be caught cheating.

If mix S_1 cheats in the links of $\{(\alpha_2, \beta_4), (\alpha_3, \beta_1), (\alpha_6, \beta_8), (\alpha_7, \beta_7)\}$, it will be detected. These are half of S_1's links. Since the links to be opened are determined by k_1 and are unpredictable to S_1 beforehand, if S_1 cheats on any link, it will be caught with a probability of 50%.

As the pair to S_1, S_2 is asked to open the complement of the links revealed by mix S_1, which in

Figure 4 are $(\beta_2, \gamma_4), (\beta_3, \gamma_2), (\beta_5, \gamma_1), (\beta_6, \gamma_5)$. (These links are marked as dashed lines.) S_2's revelation is verified in a similar manner. If mix S_2 cheats in these links, this cheating will be detected. Since the links to be opened by S_2 are determined by k_1 and are unpredictable to S_2 beforehand, if S_2 cheats on any link, it will be caught with a probability of 50%.

If mix S_1 cheats on one of its eight links, it will get caught with a probability of 50%. If it cheats on two links, it will get caught with a probability of $(1 - \frac{1}{4})$. If it cheats on n links, it will get caught with probability of $(1 - 1/2^n)$, which is close to 1 when n is large. Thus, when S_1 cheats on multiple links, it will be caught with a very high probability. (In a similar way, when S_2 cheats on multiple links, it will be caught with a very high probability.)

Revealing part of a mix's input/output correspondences may harm the privacy of a single mix. However, through careful pairing of revelation, the privacy of the whole mix-net can still be guaranteed as a *global* property. In Figure 4, S_1 is asked to reveal links $\{ (\alpha_2, \beta_4), (\alpha_3, \beta_1), (\alpha_6, \beta_8), (\alpha_7, \beta_7)\}$ and S_2 is asked to reveal links $\{(\beta_2, \gamma_4), (\beta_3, \gamma_2), (\beta_5, \gamma_1), (\beta_6, \gamma_5)\}$. From these exposed links, one can still *not* tell which α_i is mapped to γ_1. This is also true for the other γ_j, $2 \leq j \leq 8$. As a result, as long as one pair of mixes is secure, the privacy of the mix-net is guaranteed.

In summary, each mix's computations are publically verifiable and the mix-net's privacy is achieved.

It is worth noting that in an implementation of the above robust mix-net, the mixes do *not* have to be in the same location and they can be geographically distributed and connected by a computer network such as the Internet. For this distributed implementation, the only requirement is that there is an *append-only public bulletin board*, from which every mix can read and to which every mix can append messages. Before processing any input messages from its preceding mix, each mix checks the public bulletin board to make sure that the input messages are indeed outputted by the preceding mix.

CRYPTOGRAPHY-BASED EVOTING SCHEME

There are two different lines of cryptography-based computer voting schemes. Earlier work tried to use homomorphic encryption schemes to tally encrypted votes *without* decrypting them (Cohen & Fischer, 1985; Benaloh, 1986; Benaloh, 1988; Benaloh & Tuinstra, 1994; Cramer, Franklin, Schoenmakers, & Yung, 1996; Cramer, Gennaro, & Schoenmakers, 1997). These schemes achieve voter privacy and voter verifiability but place some restrictions on the types of ballots supported.

The other line of research does not have this restriction on the ballot type and tries to decrypt ballots before tallying them. For voter privacy, decrypting ballots requires the support of either an *anonymous channel* or a *mix-net* (Park, Itoh, & Kurosawa, 1993; Abe, 1998). Much work has been done along this line on the privacy and robustness properties of a mix-net. Figure 5 gives the data flow of this type of solution. It consists of two parts: the voting booth where voters cast their ballots on computer voting machines and a **robust** re-encryption mix-net, which has been discussed earlier in this chapter.

As shown in Figure 5, on election day voter Alice walks into a voting booth to cast her vote.

After Alice picks her candidate (the full details of this vote casting procedure are described below), the voting machine encrypts her choice, sends the encrypted ballot α_1 to a robust mix-net, and also posts α_1 to the *public bulletin board*, which is an append-only storage device. The voting machine generates a receipt for the vote, which Alice can take home.

After receiving all input messages (α_1, α_2, α_3, α_4, α_5, α_6, α_7, α_8), the robust mix-net posts them to the append-only public bulletin board. Next, the robust mix-net processes messages as described earlier and each mix posts its input/output messages, along with its operation verifiability proof/evidence, to the public bulletin board. In the second stage of the robust mix-net, the messages are collectively decrypted as (v_1, v_2, v_3, v_4, v_5, v_6, v_7, v_8), which are also posted to the public bulletin board. (v_1, v_2, v_3, v_4, v_5, v_6, v_7, v_8) are supposed to be the plaintext ballots and they are tallied afterward. The tally result is posted to the public bulletin board.

Next, let's examine the computing voting system against the properties given at the beginning of this chapter.

Detecting Cheating Voting Machines

In Figure 5, an honest voting machine should use the semantically secure ElGamal encryption scheme to encrypt Alice's ballot m into $\alpha_1 = (c_{11}, c_{12})$.

Figure 5. Secure computer voting with cryptography

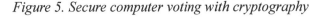

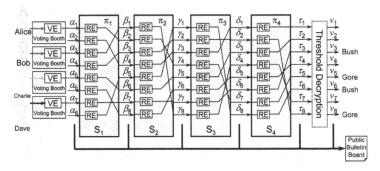

However, a *cheating* voting machine may display "Bush" to Alice but secretly encrypt "Gore" into α_1. The cheating voting machine then prints α_1 on Alice's secret-ballot receipt and also sends α_1 to the robust mix-net. Since the encryption is semantically secure, from α_1, Alice has *no* way to tell whether α_1 is the encryption of "Bush" or "Gore."

In Figure 5, the encryption operation of the voting machine is denoted as "VE", which stands for verifiable encryption. This special encryption allows Alice to check the voting machine's computations and if it is cheating, it will be detected with a non-negligible probability by Alice (Rivest, 2004a).

We shall now describe the full details of this vote casting procedure. Let's assume that Alice's choice is m (which is "Bush") and $m \in \langle g \rangle$. The actual encryption of m into α_1 goes as follows: the voting machine generates two random numbers r_1 and r_2, $1 \leq r_1, r_2 \leq q$, and then calculates $c_1 = (c_{11}, c_{12}) = (g^{r_1} \bmod p, (Y^{r_1} \times m) \bmod p)$. Next, the voting machine calculates $c_2 = (c_{21}, c_{22}) = (c_{11} \times g^{r_2} \bmod p, c_{12} \times Y^{r_2} \bmod p)$.

α_1 is $c_2 = (c_{21}, c_{22})$. There are two facts about α_1:

- $c_{21} = g^{r_1 + r_2} \bmod p, c_{22} = (Y^{r_1 + r_2} \times m) \bmod p$ Thus, α_1 is actually the ElGamal encryption of m under public key Y (with random number $r_1 + r_2$). c_1 is also the ElGamal encryption of m under public key Y (but with random number r_1).

- Values $[m; r_1, c_1; r_2, c_2]$ form a chain: c_1 is the encryption of m with r_1; c_2 is then calculated from c_1 with r_2. This chain is written as $m \xrightarrow{r_1} c_1 \xrightarrow{r_2} c_2$ and it has two links: the first link is $m \xrightarrow{r_1} c_1$ and the second link is $c_1 \xrightarrow{r_2} c_2$.

Next, the voting machine prepares two sets of values, $\{c_1, c_2; r_1\}$ and $\{c_1, c_2; r_2\}$, and asks Alice to pick one. Before making her choice, Alice checks to make sure that these two sets of values have common values $\{c_1, c_2\}$. If not, Alice will complain that the voting machine is cheating. Alice's choice i will be a random and it is either 1 or 2. Alice also remembers $\{c_1, c_2\}$ (or their fingerprints).

If Alice's choice is 1, the voting machine prints out the receipt ω as $\omega = \{c_1, c_2; r_1\}$. If Alice's choice is 2, the voting machine will print out ω as $\omega = \{c_1, c_2; r_2\}$. That is, $\omega = \{c_1, c_2; r_i\}$, where i is Alice's choice.

After getting her receipt ω and before walking out of the voting booth, Alice checks that (c_1, c_2) on her receipt are actually what she saw on the voting computer screen. If not, Alice will complain that the voting machine is cheating.

How can Alice detect a cheating voting machine? Alice can perform the following verification at home (using a simple public program):

1) If Alice's choice is $i = 1$, what she has is $(c_1, c_2; r_1)$, where $c_1 = (c_{11}, c_{12})$. Alice can calculate
   $c_1' = (g^{r_1} \bmod p, Y^{r_1} \times m \bmod p)$ and checks whether $c_1' = c_1$. This check is about the first link of the chain.

2) If her choice is $i = 2$, what she has is (c_1, c_2, r_2). Alice can calculate
   $c_2' = (c_{11} \times g^{r_2} \bmod p, c_{12} \times Y^{r_2} \bmod p)$ and checks whether $c_2 = c_2'$. This check is about the second link of the chain.

When the voting machine is cheating, c_2 will *not* be the encryption of m under public key Y, breaking the chain $m \xrightarrow{r_1} c_1 \xrightarrow{r_2} c_2$. That is, either the first link or the second link (or both) is broken. By picking a random i, Alice randomly chooses a link to check and this chain break can be detected with a probability of 50%. Consequently, Alice has a one out of two chance to detect when the voting machine is cheating.

This 50% probability is for a single vote. The chance of a voting machine cheating on 100 votes successfully (without being detected) is $\left(\frac{1}{2}\right)^{100}$, which is close to zero.

Thus, a cheating voting machine has significant chance to be detected and voters do not have to blindly trust voting machines.

Readers interested in further details of this voting procedure can find more materials in the additional reading section.

Voter Privacy

In the above voting procedure, Alice brings home her receipt $\omega = (c_1, c_2; r_i)$ and her encrypted ballot to be tallied is c_2. Since the encryption scheme is semantically secure and only one of (r_1, r_2) is revealed, c_2 leaks no useful information about Alice's vote m and one cannot tell whether c_2 is the encryption of "Bush" or "Gore."

Voter Buying/Selling and Vote Coercion

Can Alice go malicious and sell her vote?

Alice's vote is $m =$ "Bush" and Alice's encrypted ballot to be tallied by the system is c_2. To sell her vote, Alice has to convince a third party that c_2 is indeed the encryption of m. To prove this, Alice needs the whole chain $m \rightarrow_{r_1} c_1 \rightarrow_{r_2} c_2$. That is, she needs both r_1 and r_2. However, the receipt has only r_i, where i is Alice's choice and it is either 1 or 2. Thus, Alice will ***not*** be able to prove to any third party how she voted.

Let's have a further discussion about the cases of $i = 1$ and $i = 2$.

When $i = 1$, $\omega = (c_1, c_2; r_1)$. Can Alice prove to a third party how she voted? Let's assume that $m =$ "Bush" — Alice actually voted Bush. Since r_2 is not known to Alice, Alice has no way to prove that $\alpha_1 (= c_2)$ is the encryption of m. But with r_1

on the receipt, Alice can prove that c_1 is the encryption of m. However, since it is c_2, not c_1, that is finally posted to the public bulletin board and tallied, proving c_1 does not really allow Alice to convince others how she voted.

This can be explained from another perspective. At home, for $m' =$ "Gore", Alice can pick a random number $\tilde{r}_1$, calculate $\tilde{c}_1 = (g^{\tilde{r}_1} \bmod p, Y^{\tilde{r}_1} \times m' \bmod p)$ and construct $\overline{\omega} = (\tilde{c}_1, c_2; \tilde{r}_1)$ (for this step, Alice simply copies c_2 from ω). Thus, Alice has both $\omega = (c_1, c_2; r_1)$ and $\overline{\omega} = (\tilde{c}_1, c_2; \tilde{r}_1)$: the former is generated from a vote for Bush and the latter is forged from a value for Gore. Consequently, in theory, having ω does not allow Alice to prove how she voted, as she can prove the opposite in the same manner.

When $i = 2$, $\omega = (c_1, c_2; r_2)$ and this case is even more straightforward: Alice does not have the link between m and c_1 and thus cannot prove anything about m.

Ballot Integrity

The above voting procedure forces all voting machines to be honest. This guarantees the ballot integrity in the ballot creation stage of Figure 5. The robustness of the mix-net allows one to check that the mix-net has maintained the ballot integrity. Thus, the ballot integrity of the voting system is guaranteed.

Vote Verifiability

How can Alice verify that her vote is counted and is counted correctly?

Note that Alice's receipt is $\omega = (c_1, c_2; r_i)$, which contains $\alpha_1 = c_2$.

From the public bulletin board, Alice first checks whether her encrypted vote, α_1, actually appears in the input to the mix-net. If not, Alice should file a vote-missing report.

Next, Alice checks the proof/evidence that each mix posts to the bulletin board to make sure that they do perform their operations honestly. In this way, Alice can be sure that her vote is indeed transformed correctly: it has not been dropped or modified.

Last, Alice can check the correctness of the threshold decryption to make sure that her vote is decrypted correctly. From all these checks, Alice can be sure that her vote is indeed counted and counted correctly.

Voting System Availability

The voting system of Figure 5 also enjoys high availability. If one mix misbehaves, it will be detected and removed from the system. If certain entities who share the decryption key s refuses to decrypt $(\tau_1, \tau_2, \tau_3, \tau_4, \tau_5, \tau_6, \tau_7, \tau_8)$, due to the threshold property of the decryption, the other entities will still be able to collectively decrypt them. As a result the overall system has high availability.

FUTURE RESEARCH DIRECTIONS

Several issues in the mix-net-based voting scheme need improvement. First, in the voting steps to detect cheating voting machines, a voter is asked to check two given choices to make sure that they share the same values (c_1, c_2). A voter is also asked to remember parts of (c_1, c_2) to check that what she sees on the screen is what is printed on her receipt. This significantly degrades the system's usability. (Chaum, 2004a, 2004) proposed using visual cryptography techniques to improve this usability but the scheme is still daunting. Designing a good user voting interface that retains the desirable security properties remains a challenge.

Second, there have been extensive studies on designing robust mix-nets and several schemes have been developed. These schemes are often computation-intensive and are hard to understand.

Designing computationally efficient and simple robust mix-nets is another challenge.

Third, ballot design has been an important issue in traditional voting systems. It poses a critical issue for computer voting too. With a bad ballot design, an election can go terribly wrong even when its underlying technologies are sound. In the 2006 election, Florida's district 13 used computer voting and a poor ballot design caused a serious undervote (Ash & Lamperti, 2008). The principles for good computer ballot design remain to be researched.

CONCLUSION

In this chapter, we studied the security problems of computer voting and examined the full details of the mix-net-based computer voting scheme, including semantically secure ElGamal encryption, threshold ElGamal decryption, and robust mix-nets. The mix-net-based computer voting scheme provides voter privacy, voter verifiability, ballot integrity, and mechanisms to detect cheating voting machines. It is a very promising toolkit for the next generation of computer and network-based voting.

ACKNOWLEDGMENT

The authors wish to thank Christopher Fox for reviewing the earlier version of this manuscript and for his many constructive comments.

REFERENCES

Abe, M. (1998). Universally verifiable mix-net with verification work independent of the number of mix-servers. In K. Nyberg (Ed.), *Eurocrypt '98* (pp. 437-47). Berlin, Germany: Springer-Verlag. (Lecture Notes in Computer Science Volume 1403)

Abe, M. (1999). Mix-networks on permutation networks. In Lam, K.-Y., Okamoto, E., & Xing, C. (Eds.), *Asiacrypt '99* (*Vol. 1716*, pp. 258–273). Berlin, Germany: Springer-Verlag.

Ash, A., & Lamperti, J. (2008). Florida 2006: Can statistics tell us who won congressional district13? *Chance, 21*(2), 1824. doi:10.1007/s00144-008-0015-5

Ben-Or, M., Goldreich, O., Goldwasser, S., Hastad, J., Kilian, J., Micali, S., & Rogaway, P. (1989). Everything provable is provable in zero-knowledge. In S. Goldwasser (Ed.), *Advances in Cryptology - Crypto '88* (pp. 37-56). Berlin, Germany: Springer-Verlag. (Lecture Notes in Computer Science Volume 403)

Benaloh, J., & Tuinstra, D. (1994). Receipt-free secret-ballot elections. In *Proceedings of the 26th ACM Symposium on Theory of Computing* (pp. 544-553). Montreal, PQ.

Benaloh, J. D. C. (1988). *Verifiable secret-ballot elections*. (Unpublished doctoral dissertation), Yale University.

Boneh, D., & Golle, P. (2002). Almost entirely correct mixing with applications to voting. In V. Atlury (Ed.), *Proceedings of the 9th ACM Conferences on Computer and Communication Security (CCS-02)* (p. 68-77). Alexandria, VA.

Canetti, R., & Rivest, R. L. (2004). *6.897 selected topics in cryptography*. Retrieved from http://courses.csail.mit.edu/6.897/spring04/.

Chaum, D. (1981). Untraceable electronic mail, return addresses, and digital pseudonyms. *Communications of the ACM, 24*(2), 84–88. doi:10.1145/358549.358563

Chaum, D. (2004a). Secret ballot receipts: True voter-verifiable elections. *CryptoBytes, 7*(2), 13–26.

Chaum, D. (2004b). Secret-ballot receipts: True voter-verifiable elections. *IEEE Security & Privacy, 2*(1), 38–47. doi:10.1109/MSECP.2004.1264852

Cohen, J., & Fischer, M. (1985). A robust and verifiable cryptographically secure election scheme. In *Proceedings of the 26th IEEE Symposium on Foundations of Computer Science* (p. 372-382).

Cohen Benaloh, J. (1986). Secret sharing homomorphisms: keeping shares of a secret secret. In A. M. Odlyzko (Ed.), *Advances in Cryptology - Crypto '86* (pp. 251-260). Berlin, Germany: Springer-Verlag. (Lecture Notes in Computer Science Volume 263)

Cramer, R., Franklin, M. K., Schoenmakers, B., & Yung, M. (1996). Multi-authority secret-ballot elections with linear work. In U. Maurer (Ed.), *Advances in Cryptology - Eurocrypt '96* (pp. 72-83). Berlin, Germany: Springer-Verlag. (Lecture Notes in Computer Science Volume 1070)

Cramer, R., Gennaro, R., & Schoenmakers, B. (1997). A secure and optimally efficient multi-authority election scheme. In W. Fumy (Ed.), *Advances in Cryptology - Eurocrypt '97* (pp. 103-118). Berlin, Germany: Springer-Verlag. (Lecture Notes in Computer Science Volume 1233)

Desmedt, Y., & Frankel, Y. (1990). Threshold cryptosystems. In Brassard, G. (Ed.), *Advances in Cryptology - Crypto '89* (pp. 307–315). Berlin, Germany: Springer-Verlag. doi:10.1007/0-387-34805-0_28

Desmedt, Y., & Kurosawa, K. (2000). How to break a practical MIX and design a new one. In B. Preneel (Ed.), *Advance in Cryptology - Eurocrypt 2000* (pp. 557-572). Berlin, Germany: Springer-Verlag. (Lecture Notes in Computer Science Volume 1807)

El Gamal, T. (1985). A public key cryptosystem and a signature scheme based on discrete logarithms. *IEEE Transactions on Information Theory*, *31*, 469–472. doi:10.1109/TIT.1985.1057074

Furukawa, J., & Sako, K. (2001). An efficient scheme for proving a shuffle. In Kilian, J. (Ed.), *Crypto 01* (*Vol. 2139*, pp. 368–387). Berlin, Germany: Springer-Verlag.

Goldreich, O., Micali, S., & Wigderson, A. (1987). Proof that yield nothing but their validity and a methodology of cryptographic protocol design. In *Proc. 27th IEEE Symposium on Foundations of Computer Science*.

Goldreich, O., Micali, S., & Wigderson, A. (1991). Proofs that yield nothing but their validity or all languages in NP have zero-knowledge proof systems. *Journal of the ACM*, *38*(3), 691–729. doi:10.1145/116825.116852

Golle, P., Zhong, S., Boneh, D., Jakobsson, M., & Juels, A. (2002). Optimistic mixing for exit-polls. In Zheng, Y. (Ed.), *Asiacrypt 2002* (*Vol. 2501*, pp. 451–465). Berlin, Germany: Springer-Verlag. doi:10.1007/3-540-36178-2_28

Internet Broadcasting Systems. (2004, November 4). *Broward vote-counting blunder changes amendment result*. Published at News4Jax.com, Retrieved from http://www.news4jax.com/politics/3890292/detail.html

Jakobsson, M. (1998). A practical mix. In K. Nyberg (Ed.), *Eurocrypt '98* (pp. 448-461). Berlin, Germany: Springer-Verlag. (Lecture Notes in Computer Science Volume 1403)

Jakobsson, M. (1999). Flash mixing. In *Proceedings of the Eighteenth Annual ACM Symposium on Principles of Distributed Computing (PODC 99)* (pp. 83-89).

Jakobsson, M., & Juels, A. (1999). *Millimix: Mixing in small batches* (Tech. Rep. No. 99-33). DIMACS.

Jakobsson, M., & Juels, A. (2001). An optimally robust hybrid mix network. In *Proceedings of the Twentieth Annual ACM Symposium on Principles of Distributed Computing (PODC 01)*.

Jakobsson, M., Juels, A., & Rivest, R. L. (2002). Making mix nets robust for electronic voting by randomized partial checking. In D. Boneh (Ed.), In *Proceedings of the USENIX Security '02* (p. 339-353). San Francisco.

Kohno, T., Stubblefield, A., Rubin, A., & Wallach, D. (2004). Analysis of an electronic voting system. In *Proceedings of the 2004 IEEE Symposium on Security and Privacy* (p. 2740).

McCarthy, J. (2004, November). *Machine error gives Bush 3,893 extra votes in Ohio*. Associated Press. Available at http://www.usatoday.com/tech/news/techpolicy/evoting/2004-11-06-ohio-evote-trouble_x.htm

Mitomo, M., & Kurosawa, K. (2000). Attack for flash MIX. In T. Okamoto (Ed.), *Asiacrypt '00* (pp. 192-204). Berlin, Germany: Springer-Verlag. (Lecture Notes in Computer Science Volume 1976)

Molnar, D., Kohno, T., Sastry, N., & Wagner, D. (2006). Tamperevident, historyindependent, subliminalfree data structures on prom storage or how to store ballots on a voting machine (extended abstract). In *Proceedings of the 2006 IEEE Symposium on Security and Privacy* (p. 365370).

Neff, A. (2001). A verifiable secret shuffle and its application to e-voting. In Samarati, P. (Ed.), *ACM CCS '01* (pp. 116–125). Philadelphia.

Neff, C. A. (2004, April 21). Verifiable mixing (shuffling) of ElGamal pairs. Retrieved from http://people.csail.mit.edu/rivest/voting/papers/Neff-2004-04-21-ElGamalShuffles.pdf

Ogata, W., Kurosawa, K., Sako, K., & Takatani, K. (1997). Fault tolerant anonymous channel. In *Proceedings of the First International Conference on Information and Communications Security (ICICS '97)* (pp. 440-444). Berlin, Germany: Springer-Verlag. (Lecture Notes in Computer Science Volume 1334)

Park, C., Itoh, K., & Kurosawa, K. (1993). Efficient anonymous channel and all/nothing election scheme. In T. Helleseth (Ed.), *Advances in Cryptology - Eurocrypt '93* (pp. 248-259). Berlin: Springer-Verlag. (Lecture Notes in Computer Science Volume 765)

Pfitzmann, B. (1995). Breaking an efficient anonymous channel. In A. De Santis (Ed.), *Advances in Cryptology - Eurocrypt '94* (pp. 332-340). Berlin, Germany: Springer-Verlag. (Lecture Notes in Computer Science Volume 950)

Pfitzmann, B., & Pfitzmann, A. (1989). How to break the direct RSA-implementation of MIXes. In J.-J. Quisquater & J. Vandewalle (Eds.), *Advances in Cryptology - Eurocrypt '89* (pp. 373-381). Berlin, Germany: Springer-Verlag. (Lecture Notes in Computer Science Volume 434)

Rivest, R. L. (2004, June 3). *Electronic voting*. (Talk given at NSA) Retrieved from http://theory.csail.mit.edu/~rivest/2004-06-03%20NSA%20talk%20electronic%20voting.ppt

Rivest, R. L. (2004, June 1). *Remarks on electronic voting*. (Text of remarks at the Harvard Kennedy School of Government Digital Voting Symposium). Retrieved from http://people.csail.mit.edu/rivest/2004-06-01%20Harvard%20KSG%20Symposium%20Evoting%20remarks.txt

Rivest, R. L. (2004c, May 26). *Some thoughts on electronic voting*. (Talk given at DIMACS Workshop on Electronic Voting). Retrieved from http://people.csail.mit.edu/rivest/2004-05-26%20DIMACS%20voting%20talk.ppt

Rivest, R. L. Voting resources page. Available at http://people.csail.mit.edu/rivest/voting/.

Sako, K., & Kilian, J. (1995). Receipt-free mix-type voting scheme – a practical solution to the implementation of a voting booth-. In L. C. Guillou & J.-J. Quisquater (Eds.), *Advance in Cryptology – Eurocrypt '95* (pp. 393-403). Berlin: Springer-Verlag. (Lecture Notes in Computer Science Volume 921)

Sampigethaya, K., & Poovendran, R. (2006). A survey on mix networks and their secure applications. *Proceedings of the IEEE, 94*(12), 2142–2181. doi:10.1109/JPROC.2006.889687

Shamir, A. (1979). How to share a secret. *Communications of the ACM, 22*(11), 612–613. doi:10.1145/359168.359176

Today, U. S. A. (2004, November 5th). *More than 4,500 North Carolina votes lost because of mistake in voting machine capacity*. Retrieved from http://www.usatoday.com/news/politicselections/vote2004/2004-11-04-votes-lost_x.htm.

WOWT.COM. (2004, November 5th). *3,000 phantom votes detected*. Retrieved from http://www.wowt.com/news/headlines/1164496.html

ADDITIONAL READING

A good survey on mix-net can be found at (Sampigethaya & Poovendran, 2006).

Additional reading materials about the mix-net-based voting scheme can be found at (Canetti & Rivest, 2004) and (Rivest).

Chapter 13
Biometric Security in the E-World

Kunal Sharma
DOEACC Centre, India

A.J. Singh
H.P. University, India

ABSTRACT

The rising number of networked computers and the evolution of the WWW have witnessed the emergence of an E-World where the users are often referred to as e-people. In the new e-world, the evolution of WWW and Internet applications has become a focal point to the question of sustainable competitive advantage (Brennan & Johnson, 2001). The increase in information access terminals along with the growing use of information sensitive applications such as e-commerce, e-learning, e-banking and e-healthcare have generated a real requirement of reliable, easy to use, and generally acceptable control methods for confidential and vital information. On the other hand, the necessity for privacy must be balanced with security requirements for the advantage of the general public. Current global events have shown the significance to provide the police, airport area, and other exposed area, new reliable component security tools such as biometrics. Access to systems that need security from unauthorized access is generally restricted by requesting the user to confirm her identity and to authenticate. Payment systems are undergoing radical changes stirred largely by technical advancement such as distributed network technology, real-time processing and online consumers' inclination to use e-banking interfaces making the study of biometrics even more important in this new E-World.

INTRODUCTION

There are many tools and techniques that can sustain the management of information security and systems based on biometrics that have developed to support some attributes of information security. Identity authentication and verification practices such as keys, cards, passwords, and PIN are commonly employed security applications. Still, passwords or keys may frequently be forgotten, divulged, altered, or stolen. Biometrics is an identity authentication technique which is being

DOI: 10.4018/978-1-61520-783-1.ch013

used currently and is more dependable, contrasted to conventional techniques. The phrase biometrics originated from the Greek words *"bios"* viz. life and *"metrikos"* viz. measure, ie. it is "the measurement of life". Sir Francis Galton, author of the book *Fingerprints* (Stigler, 1995) was an English scientist well acknowledged for his theories on improving the human race through eugenics which is the application of the principles of genetics to the development of humankind and can be considered as the father of biometrics. Exactly speaking, biometrics means a science encompassing the statistical analysis of biological features (Zhang, 2000). A good quality of biometric characteristics is that they are founded on something you are or something you do, so you do not necessitate to memorize anything neither to hold any token.

Biometrics is accordingly defined as the automated way of identifying or authenticating the identity of a living individual, based on physiological or behavioral features. The phrase "biometrics" is used to elucidate two diverse facets of the technology: attributes and procedures. Biometrics as "attributes" refers to quantifiable organic (anatomical and physiological) or behavioral characteristics of the individual that can be employed for automated recognition. Biometrics as "procedures" refers to automated techniques of identifying an individual bascd on quantifiablc biological (anatomical and physiological) and behavioral distinctiveness.

Physiological features used in biometrics include features such as face, fingerprint, and iris. Behavioral traits comprise signature, gait, and voice. This technique of identity verification is favoured over conventional passwords and PIN-based methods for different grounds, such as (Jain *et. al.*, 1999; Jain *et. al.*, 2004):

- The individual to be identified is required to be physically present for the identity authentication.

- Identification based on biometric procedures averts the need to remember a password or carry a token.
- It cannot be misplaced or forgotten.

SECURITY CHALLENGES IN THE E-WORLD

Potentially there are numerous reasons for the growth in security attacks; but one trend that is undeniable is the growth in the number and sophistication of cracking tools (Adams, 2003). Thus, security becomes one of the biggest issues we face today. Crackers have been utilizing the recent technological advances, freely accessible over the WWW, to access important information resources from anyplace in the world. The two most sophisticated tools to crack passwords are L0phtcrack and Pwdump3. With the growing reliance of business organizations on information networks, the security aspects of such networks is becoming necessary, particularly with the surfacing of E-Commerce over Intranets, Extranets, and the Internet. Security challenges to these networks have different unwanted business impacts on organizations, such as: business embarrassment, financial loss, degradation of competitiveness, and lcgal problcms (Rolf, 2002; Rao, 2004).

Security is an important issue. The penetration of personal computers, local area networks and distributed computing has radically changed the way we administer and control information resources. Internal controls that were efficient in the centralized, batch-oriented mainframe environment of yesteryears are insufficient in the distributed computing environment of today. Protection of distributed computing environment is of great importance in any enterprise information system (Caelli, 1994). Attacks on computer systems are on the rise and the sophistication of these attacks continues to rise to startling levels. Throughout much of the academic and practitioner literature, trust, privacy of information and systems security are important reoccurring themes factors in customer retention for a firm that engages in E-Commerce making security important.

Users on the Internet increasingly manage their routine interactions by accessing various Web applications that mandate them to provide private information such as credit card and bank account numbers. An essential condition on such sites is the protection of all information that might be considered as private to the users. Majority of the users don't have an idea if any of their private information that adds up to their identity is dispersed to parties other than the sites they have directly visited. Small businesses carry the burden of malicious attacks because they do not have the resources to immediately rectify security breaches, resulting in extended down-time, limited access to company and customer information, and the cost of cleaning up damaged data and hardware.

Security will remain an issue for all commerce activities, large or small, and lack of it has the greatest potential to paralyze small businesses due to the high financial impact of losing commercially sensitive information, loss of productivity and the cost of fixing security breaches

Therefore security needs to be emphasized, so that such challenges and their undesired consequences can be avoided.

ICT, TRUST, PRIVACY& SECURITY

The general public is rapidly implementing more information and communication technologies (ICT) in services and commerce. Consequently, confidential information is at growing risk and security and reliability problems become common. Undeniably, today citizens are becoming more and more apprehensive about the rising complexity of information and communication systems and the abundance of privacy-invasive information gathering sources and techniques. In their online daily transactions, the people frequently find themselves confronted with high-profile losses

of their personal information and with viruses, spam, phishing and other offenses of growing severity and complexity.

Therefore, in general English practice, trust is what one places his assurance in or expects to be honest. Before we investigate too deeply into the nature of trust, we first require forming a coherent idea of just what trust is. Literature is unsuccessful to take this step and frequently ends up resulting in added misunderstanding and argument amongst researchers rather than adding to the knowledge base. Trust has conventionally been hard to define and measure since it is a social phenomenon that has different definitions depending on the context (McKnight et al., 2002). Rousseau, *et al*. (1998) too concur that trust has been described in different manners, frequently depending on the context in which it appears. The deficiency of a commonly acknowledged definition has been highlighted by several researchers (Belanger *et al.*, 2002; Bigley *et al.*, 1998; Lee & Turban, 2001; Lewis & Weigert, 1985; Yoon, 2002), but most clearly in Hosmer (1995,p.380), where it was quoted that "there appears to be widespread agreement on the importance of trust ...., but unfortunately there also appears to be equally widespread lack of agreement on a suitable definition of the concept". However, there are three dimensions of trust:a) *integrity:* the faith that an enterprise is fair and just b) *dependability:* the faith that an enterprise will do what it says it will do … and, c) *competence:* the confidence that an enterprise has the capability to do what it says it will do(Watson,2004). Nevertheless, Gefen *et. al*. (2005) have put forward the definition of trust in E-Commerce as being contingent on one member's belief about another member's intention to behave in a socially acceptable manner.

Online customers often confuse between confidence, trust, predictability, and decision accuracy.Distinguishing between confidence, trust, predictability, and decision accuracy, Muir (1987) says, predictability is a foundation for trust (and confidence), which on the other hand, is the foundation for an end-user/decision maker to forecast about the potential behaviour of a referent. The precision of that forecast may be evaluated by comparing it with the real behavioural outcome. Additionally, a person who makes a prediction may correlate a specific level of confidence with the prediction. Consequently, confidence is a qualifier which is connected with a specific prediction; it is not the same as trust.

Das & Teng (1998) argued that trust and control are the two fundamental sources of confidence in the cooperative behavior of business partners in strategic alliances particularly in E-Commerce. Fogg and Tseng indicate that trust signifies a positive belief about the perceived reliability of, dependability of, and assurance in an individual, object, or procedure Shneiderman (2000) in the E-World. Trust is imperative for consumer acceptance and consumer decision to enter into a business deal with e-commerce vendors (Geffen, Karahanna, & Straub, 2003). The consumer's perception of the various presentation flaws viz. poor style, incompleteness and error influence their perception of quality of services in the E-World. This perceived quality in turn influences the consumer's level of trust in the E-World which in turn influences the users' plan to transact in the E-World. Trust fluctuates with diversity- online customers have a inclination to extend trust more willingly to people they recognize as similar to themselves—what Zucker (1986) described characteristic-based trust. The concept of trust is intimately related to the idea of sense of security as well. People using a computer system or service are usually incurring some financial or privacy risk.

The figure below illustrates online consumer's intention to transact in the E-World, for e-services.

Trust and Security in ICT is a subject that alters day by day, along with the extensive operation of digital technologies, and their diffusion in all feature of human activity. The initiation of ubiquitous computing and communications which smoothen log on and the development of data in network infrastructures in any place at any time are the main grounds of today's increasing cyber crime phenomena. Crime on the WWW is hindering the proposed management and implementation of digitized information and systems.

Biometrics and Trust

The trustworthiness of this digital data is a vital issue that biometric specialists must consider while developing solutions to theft protection of biometric data. Many vendors provide technology solutions to extract this digital data and once the extraction of the digital data has been accomplished, protecting the digital integrity becomes of supreme concern. The end user hopes that biometric data acquisition equipment will

Figure 1. Consumers' intention to transact in the E-World using a model of trust

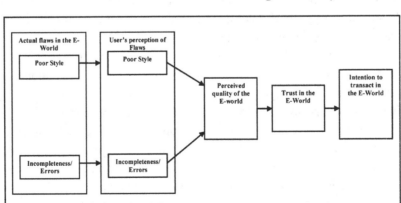

be trustworthy, accurately extract, transform and transmit the live data presented by an individual. The user will suppose that the biometric system may not accept duplicate data provided by a fraud person. Attack scenarios that can have a bearing on such trust have been explained by many authors. In specific, self-service state of affairs present room for fake manipulations of the data acquisition procedure. The common denominator of such state of affairs is that the attacker is in ownership of a duplicate copy or some equivalent data set describing in ample detail and correspondence the original biometric features of an unauthorized user and is consequently able to trick the data acquisition equipment.

End-users are generally more or less inexperienced. Training the end-user to the same level as the particular specialists is just not a sound idea in introducing automation. Nonetheless, a biometric system must be trusted so as to be up to standard. The trust building process is entirely different for specialists and naïve users. Whereas specialists may alone analyze facts and appraise consequences on theoretical basis and in advance, the vital factors for end-user trust building is lack of negative news over a specific timeframe, personal experience, and evidence by trusted sources. With regard to news and evidence of trusted sources biometrics has to counter an unfortunately negative score. With regard to personal experience we can state that there is practically none in the public realm. Factors to be considered in end user bio-

metric training to make it trustworthy are size of user group, place of deployment and the nature of deployment (viz. requirements for mobility), ease of deployment and user training required, error occurrence due to age, surroundings and health, security and precision desired, user acceptance level, privacy and anonymity, long-lasting stability consisting of technology maturity, standards, interoperability and technical support.

Privacy

Privacy is the condition of being free from unauthorized intrusion. With the escalation of the number of computers on the WWW and the reliance of the commercial world on electronic and digital media, privacy is in jeopardy. Many studies state that a lack of privacy is a real concern in ubiquitous computing environments (e.g., Al-Muhtadi *et. al.*, 2002; Soppera *et. al.*, 2004). Most of the networks belonging to diverse organizations utilize policies that protect the privacy of their recruits. The privacy guidelines and practices implemented by a company necessitate support by technologies that execute these policies. The figure below depicts the privacy disclosures as per the Federal Trade Commission for the years 1998-2000 in the electronic marketplace

Studies conducted have shown that majority online customers are apprehensive concerning their privacy (Kim & Montalto, 2002; Kuanchin & Rea, 2004; Sheehan, 2002) in the E-World.

Figure 2. Frequency of privacy disclosures from '98-2000

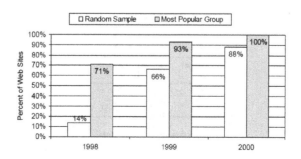

They consider that in spite of the strict privacy policies published on the WWW by organizations, they have no control over the use of their personal data once gathered by a virtual organization.

In order to back the claim laid out by the companies, Privacy-enhancement Technologies (PeTs) are utilized. PeTs comprise data encryption, anonymous services, or anonymous Web browsing (Olivier, 2004).

Privacy, security, and confidentiality are thus natural concerns for businesses and general public (Layne & Lee, 2001) in the E-World. Furthermore, the design of electronic-systems may also discourage some people from using the electronic medium, favouring the expertise of conventional physical interactions (Jupp & Shine, 2001). These issues require the building of trust between people and providers to guarantee successful levels of adoption of Internet-based services (Bellamy & Taylor, 1998).

Security

The internet security glossary [RFC 2828] delineates security from privacy as an event where "a security relevant system event in which the system's security policy is disobeyed or otherwise breached". The growth of ICT security is contingent on the one hand by technological advancement (miniaturization of computers, developments in optics) and the resultant rising vulnerabilities, and on the other hand by the augmentation in applications, the better uptake of digital technology in all sectors of the economy and our routine lives and their subsequent threats and malfunctions. The delineation between physical space and cyberspace will gradually decline with time. The accessibility of ample computing and networking resources, spread of vital data over these resources, and better trust of organizations and the citizens on ICT will catch the attention of more attackers as their incentive increases. To get better consistency of these edifices, new abstractions must be developed so as to devise efficient paradigms; it is also crucial to propose a new trust and security model, production means using innovative programming languages, and protocols with modeling, simulation and verification procedures. The figure below illustrates the model for ICT, trust, security and environmental links.

This model is based on the security architecture of a system, which on the other hand is contingent on a trusted infrastructure. This assurance model is, consequently, at the center of security and privacy, in fact defines its existence, the level and features of the protection it offers, and determines the need and relevance of the deployment of specific security mechanisms. In turn it supports the protection and integrity of the digital world, and hence its soundness.

It is likely to distinguish the trust offering assurance model and the security architecture,

Figure 3. Model for ICT, Trust and Security and environmental links

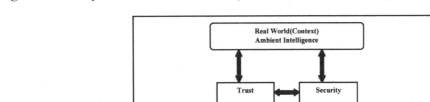

into two separated distributed units (instrumentations, protocols, architectures, management). This would permit to automate and enhance the trusted and security infrastructure, whilst the authorizations, exceptions, and security management on an entire basis, are accomplished through their interaction. Policies are very crucial and provide a superior structure to a system. To have a lucid view of Information Security there is a picture how security policy has such grave repercussions for an organization.

There are a several issues that add up to the successful management of trust relationships in virtual communications, including encouraging the simplicity of the shopping experience and building levels of trust for the consumer about the legitimacy of the vendor and efficiency of e-payment mechanisms (Torkzadeh & Dhillon, 2002) thereby making the study of user authentication techniques as biometrics central theme of this chapter.

USER AUTHENTICATION METHODS

Authentication relates to assurance of identity of person or originator of data. Reliable customer authentication is imperative for institutions engaging in any form of electronic banking or commerce. Strong customer authentication practices are nec-

essary to enforce anti-money laundering measures and help financial institutions detect and reduce identity theft. Customer interaction with institutions is migrating from physical recognition and paper-based documentation to remote electronic access and transaction initiation.

With the rapid growth of networked systems and applications such as e-commerce, the demand for effective computer security is increasing. Most computer systems are protected through a process of user identification and authentication. While identification is usually non-private information provided by users to identify them and can be known by system administrators and other system users, authentication provides secret, private user information which can authenticate their identity. The risks of doing business with unauthorized or masquerading individuals in an electronic environment could be devastating, which can result in financial loss and intangible losses like reputation damage, disclosure of confidential information, corruption of data, or unenforceable agreements. There is a gamut of authentication tools and methodologies that organizations use to authenticate customers. These include the use of passwords and personal identification numbers (PINs), digital certificates using a public key infrastructure (PKI), physical devices such as smart cards or other types of tokens, database comparisons, and biometric identifiers. The level

Figure 4. The Wheel of Security

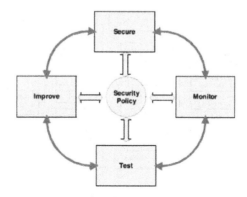

Table 1. Probable combinations for 6 and 8 character passwords

Probable combinations for 6 and 8 character passwords		
Type of password 6 character length 8 character length		
Alphabetic	308915776	208827064576
Upper/lowercase alpha	19770609664	53459728531456
Numeric	1000000	100000000
Upper/lowercase alpha & Numeric	56800235584	218340105584896
Extended	1073741824	1099511627776
Upper/lowercase alpha, Numeric & Extended	689869781056	6095689385410816

of risk protection afforded by each of these tools varies and is evolving as technology changes. Multi-factor authentication methods are more difficult to compromise than single factor systems. Properly designed and implemented multifactor authentication methods are more reliable indicators of authentication and stronger fraud deterrents. Broadly, the authentication methodologies can be classified, based on what a user knows (passwords, PINs), what a user has (smart card, magnetic card), and what a user is (fingerprint, retina, voiceprint, signature).There are various authentication approaches and techniques, from passwords to public keys(Smith,2002).

The most commonly used type of authentication is knowledge based authentication. Examples of knowledge-based authentication include passwords, pass phrases, or pass sentences (Spector & Ginzberg, 1994), graphical passwords, pass faces and personal identification numbers (PINs). Table 1 epitomizes the probable combinations of 6-8 character passwords:

Token-based authentication is based on what the user has. It makes use mainly of physical objects that a user possesses, like tokens. Aside from the fact that presentation of a valid token does not prove ownership, as it may have been stolen or duplicated by some sophisticated fraudulent means(Svigals,1994),there are prob-

Figure 5. Taxonomy of user authentication methods

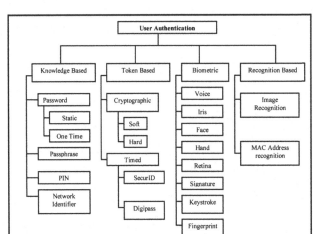

lems of administration and of the inconvenience to users of having to carry them. Pullkis *et. al.*(2006) present an overview of different user authentication methods.

Finally, we have biometric based authentication which is imperative in this E-World. A good characteristic of biometric security systems is that security level is roughly equivalent for all users in a system. This is not true for other security technologies. For instance, in an access control based on password, a malicious hacker just needs to break only one password amidst those of all employees to gain access. In this case, a weak password compromises the overall security of every system that user has access to. Thus, the entire system's security is only as superior as the weakest password (Prabhakar, Pankanti & Jain, 2003). This is particularly significant because good passwords are nonsense groupings of characters and letters, which are hard to memorize (for instance, "7BH8JD6y"). Unluckily, some users still use passwords such as "password", or their own name. Faundez-Zanuy (2004) has carried out a comparison of the advantages and downsides of various authentication methods which is in Table 2.

Gorman(2003) recapitulates the potential attacks on authentication systems as well as defence measures which is according to Tables 3 and 4.

BIOMETRICS: CLARIFYING ENROLLMENT, VERIFICATION AND IDENTIFICATION

Biometrics is fundamentally a multi-disciplinary area of research, which encompasses subjects like pattern recognition or deciphering patterns, digital image processing, computer vision, soft computing, and artificial intelligence. For instance, face image is acquired by a digital camera, which is preprocessed using image enhancement algorithms, and then facial information is extracted and matched. Soldek *et. al.* (1997) have described the various pattern recognition algorithms which are applicable to various biometric techniques which are illustrated in Figure 6.

Throughout this procedure, image processing methods are used to develop the face image and pattern recognition, and soft computing techniques are used to extract and match facial features. A biometric system can serve as an identification system or a verification (authentication) system.

Table 2. Benefits and drawbacks of different authentication methods

Authentication Method	Benefits	Downsides
Handheld tokens(card, ID, passport etc.)	• A new one can be issued • It is quite standard, although moving to a different country, facility etc.	• It can be stolen • A fake one can be issued • It can be shared • One person can be registered with different identities
Knowledge based (password, PIN etc.)	• Simple and an economical method • Problems exist but if this is the case they can be replaced by a new quite easily	• It can be guessed or cracked • Good passwords are difficult remember • It can be shared • One person can be registered with different identities
Biometrics	• It cannot be lost, forgotten, guessed, stolen, shared etc. • It is quite easy to check if one person has several identities • Provides a greater degree of security	• In some cases it can be faked. • It is neither replaceable nor secret • If a person's biometric data is stolen it is not possible to replace it.

Table 3. Potential attacks on authentication systems and suggested defence measures

Attack	Authentication Method	Instances	Typical Defences
Client Attack	Password	Guessing, Exhaustive Search	Large entropy, limited attempts
	Token	Exhaustive Search	Large entropy, limited attempts, theft of object, requires presence
	Biometric	False match	Large entropy, limited attempts
Host Attack	Password	Plaintext theft, dictionary/exhaustive search	Hashing, large entropy, protection by admin password or encryption
	Token	Passcode theft	1-time passcode per session
	Biometric	Template theft	Capture device authentication
Eavesdropping, theft and copying	Password	"Shoulder Surfing"	Use diligence to keep secret; admin diligence to quickly revoke compromised passwords; Multi-factor authentication
	Token	Theft, counterfeiting hardware	Multi-factor authentication; tamper resistant/ evident hardware token
	Biometric	Copying(spoofing) biometric	Copy-detection at capture device and capture-device authentication
Replay	Password	Replay stolen passcode response	Challenge-response protocol
	Token	Replay stolen passcode response	Challenge-response protocol, 1-time passcode per session
	Biometric	Replay stolen biometric template response	Copy-detection at capture device and capture device authentication via challenge response protocol
Trojan Horse	Password/Token/Biometric	Installation of rouge client or capture device	Authentication of client or capture device ; client or capture device within trusted security perimeter
Denial of Service	Password/Token/Biometric	Lockout by multiple failed authentication	Multifactor with token

Biometric jargon such as "verification" and "identification," are used interchangeably in some books. This erroneous overlap creates misunderstanding as each term has a specific definition. A concise description of these important terms is provided here.

Enrollment

During the enrollment stage, the biometric traits of a person are originally scanned by a biometric reader to generate a raw digital version of the attributes. A quality check is normally carried

Table 4. Other security issues according to Gorman(2003) may be as follows:

Security Concerns	Authenticators	Instances	Typical defences
Non-repudiation	Password,token	Claim lost or stolen authenticator	Personal liability,two factor with biometric
	Biometric	Claimed copied biometric	Capture device authentication
Compromise Detection	Password,biometric	Stolen password or copied biometric	"Last login" displayed to user to detect anamoly
	Token	Lost or stolen token	User notes physical absence
Administrative and Policy –Registration/Enrollment	Password	Initial password registration	Delivery to pre-established e-mail address
	Token	New token registration	Delivery to pre-established physical address
	Biometric	Biometric enrollment	In-person with picture ID
Administrative and Policy –Reset and Recovery	Password	Forgotten Password	Secondary authenticator
	Token	Lost Token	Delivery to pre-established physical address
	Biometric	Compromised biometric	Not much option but to revert to password

out to guarantee that the collected sample can be reliably processed by successive phases. So as to assist in matching, the raw digital representation is generally additionally processed by a feature extractor to produce a compact but expressive representation, entitled a template. Depending on the application, the template might be placed in the central repository of the biometric system or be recorded on a magnetic card or smartcard given to the person.

Verification

Biometric systems perform verification by contrasting a new biometric to one or more biometrics earlier enrolled in the system. Classically, this process encompasses gathering a sample, converting that sample into a template and matching that template to other templates that were previously collected.

Verification is used to substantiate whether a person is who he or she asserts he or she is. This kind of transaction is usually associated to a

Figure 6. Techniques & algorithms of pattern recognition applied to biometrics

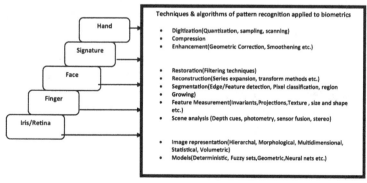

process governing physical and/or logical access to an organization's resources.

There are two principal measurements of the effectiveness of verification:

Verification Rate: The rate at which genuine end users are properly verified.
False Acceptance Rate: The percentage of times a system generates a "false accept" (Vacca, 2007). A false accept takes place when an individual is erroneously matched to another person's existing biometric.

For planning and supervision purposes, it is imperative to appreciate the exact sense of the phrase "whether an individual is who he or she claims to be." The person has an identity outside the system. The system does not conclude who the person is in the global, absolute sense. The system makes a very exact, very narrow decision as to the likelihood of a match between the new biometric template and an existing biometric template that was collected beforehand. If there is a definite statistical similarity the system ends up with a conclusion that the person who originally enrolled is the same person who is now facing the system.

Identification

Biometrics systems make use of "identification" when they try to decide the identity of a person. The procedure of identification encompasses collecting a biometric, creating a biometric template and matching the template to a whole collection of existing biometric templates.

Identification is employed to conclude whether or not an individual is "known." This can be helpful information, principally in circumstances where an organization cannot or for various grounds chooses not to ask the individual to identify him or herself. There are two most important kinds of identification: Open set and closed set (Rose, 2002).

Open-Set

In "open-set" identification (occasionally also called to as a "watchlist") there is no assurance that a record of the individual's biometrics is contained in the existing set of biometric within the organization's data collection. So as to identify the fresh biometric, the system must look for a match across the whole data collected.

There precision of open-set identification systems can be measured using two variables:

False Alarm Rate: The rate at which the system erroneously states a similarity when, actuality, the person's biometrics are not in the data collection or when the system erroneously states a similarity when the biometrics do match but the individual is not, in fact, the same individual referenced in the existing biometric record.
Detection/Identification Rate: The rate at which the system rightly states a match between the person's biometrics and those biometric records previously collected.

Closed-Set

Identification is "closed-set" if the person's biometrics already exist in the database. The key method of evaluating the precision of a closed-set identification system is the "Identification Rate," the rate at which a person in a database is correctly identified.

Identification and verification are delineated as (Jain et al., 1999, 2004; Ross, Nandakumar, & Jain, 2006)-Identification is a one to many process while verification in a one to one process.

The block diagrams of enrollment, identification and verification described by Jain *et. al.* (2004) are as shown Figure 7.

Figure 7. Illustration of the enrollment, identification and verification process

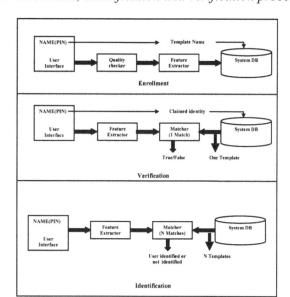

STAGES IN THE FUNCTIONING OF A BIOMETRIC SYSTEM

Biometric authentication is carried out by matching the biometric characteristics of an enrolled individual with the features of the query subject. Several phases of a biometric system are: capture, enhancement, feature extraction, and matching. Throughout capture, raw biometric data is acquired by an appropriate device, such as a fingerprint scanner or a camera. Enhancement encompasses developing the raw data to enhance the quality of the data for exact feature extraction. Enhancement is particularly necessary when the quality of the raw data is not good—for instance, if the face image is unclear or contains noise. The raw data includes plenty of superfluous information which is not helpful for recognition. Feature extraction encompasses extracting invariant characteristics from the raw data and generating biometric template which is distinctive for every individual and can be employed for recognition.

Finally, the matching stage encompasses matching two features or templates. The template

Figure 8. Functioning of a standard biometric system

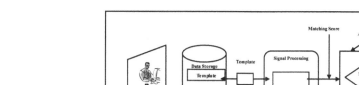

Figure 9. Classification of biometrics by different characteristics in the state of art

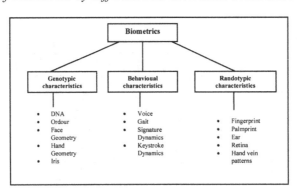

accumulated in the database is matched with the query template. This is illustrated in Figure 8 as described by Gamassi *et. al.* (2005).

TYPES OF BIOMETRIC SYSTEMS

All biometric systems are founded on one of three special types of individual's characteristics. Genotypic characteristics are those that are describes by the genetic makeup of the human being. Instances of genotypic characteristics are face geometry, hand geometry, and DNA patterns. It is significant to note that genotypic characteristics found between the same twins or clones are very alike and often hard to use as a distinctive characteristic to tell the two apart. Genotype means a genetic structure, or a group sharing it, and phenotype is a related term meaning the actual appearance of a feature through the interaction of genotype, growth, and environment. Genetic penetrance explains the heritability of reasons or the degree

to which the features expressed are genetically determined.

Randotypic characteristics are those features that are created during infancy such as the growth of the embryo. Many of the body characteristics that individuals have take on specific patterns throughout this stage of growth, and those patterns are distributed randomly all over the whole population. This makes replication highly impossible and, in some cases, unfeasible. Instances of such characteristics are fingerprints, palmprints, retina patterns, and hand-vein patterns.

Behavioral characteristics are those aspects of a human being that are developed through training or repetitive learning. As individuals grow, they are trained in specific modes of behavior that they practice throughout their lives. Such characteristics are the sole kind of biometric characteristics that can be changed by a human being using retraining or behavior modification through negative or positive reinforcement. Instances of such

Figure 10. Examples of randotypic characterstics in biometrics. Adapted from Cui, J., Wang, Y., Huang, J., Tan, T., & Sun, Z. (2004)

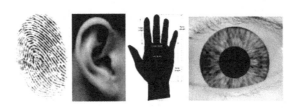

characteristics comprise of signature dynamics and keystroke dynamics. This is depicted in Figure 9.

There are two kinds of biometric systems: unimodal and multimodal. Unimodal biometric systems use merely one characteristic for recognition, viz. face recognition, fingerprint recognition, and iris recognition. Multimodal biometric systems typically use multiple information acquired from one biometric modality—for instance, pores acquired from a single fingerprint image, or information acquired from more than one biometric modality, such as fusing information from face and fingerprint.

Unimodal Biometrics

Fingerprint Recognition

Fingerprints are graphical shapes which are present on an individual's fingers. Their pattern is contingent on the initial circumstances of the embryonic growth and they are supposed to be distinctive to each individual (and each finger). Fingerprints are one of the most established biometric methods used globally for criminal investigation and consequently, have a disgrace of criminality coupled with them. Characteristically, a fingerprint image is acquired using either of two techniques: (i) acquiring an inked impression of a finger using a scanner or (ii) by means of a live-scan fingerprint scanner

A typical scanner digitizes the fingerprint impression at 500 dots per inch (dpi) with 256 gray levels per pixel (Ratha, Connell, &Bolle, 2001).

Key representation of the finger is founded on the whole image, finger ridges, or significant features resulting from the ridges. Four fundamental advances to identification founded on fingerprint are widespread: (i) the invariant characteristics of the gray scale sketch of the fingerprint image or a part thereof; (ii) global ridge patterns, also well-known as fingerprint classes; (iii) the ridge patterns of the fingerprints; (iv) fingerprint minutiae – the skin texture ensuing chiefly from ridge endings and bifurcations.

The benefits of fingerprint recognition encompass invariance and uniqueness of the fingerprints, and its wide acceptance by the public and law enforcement communities as a reliable means of human recognition. Shortcomings encompass of the need for physical contact with the scanner, probability of poor quality images because of deposits on the finger, such as filth and body oils (which can assemble on the glass plate), and damaged fingerprints from scrapes, years of heavy work, or damage.

Reliably matching fingerprint images is an extremely complicated problem, predominantly due to the large inconsistency in various impressions of the same finger (i.e., large intra-class deviations). The key reasons responsible for the intra-class deviations are: displacement, rotation, partial overlap, non-linear distortion, inconsistent pressure, varying skin condition, noise, and

Figure 11. Fingerprint captured from (a) inked image of finger and (b) a live-scan fingerprint. Adapted from Jain, A. K., Hong, L., Pankanti, S., & Bolle, R. (1997)

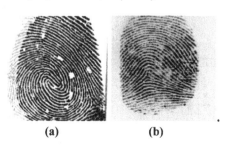

(a)　　　　　(b)

Figure 12. Fingerprint images a) and b) look to be different but in fact are impressions of same person's finger. Adapted from Jain, A. K., Hong, L., Pankanti, S., & Bolle, R.(1997)

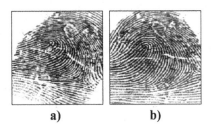

a)   **b)**

feature extraction inaccuracies. Consequently, fingerprints from the same finger may occasionally look relatively different, see Figure 12.

When conventional fingerprint recognition is jointly used with the proven efficacy of the AFIS latent search capability, the new technology has the probability to recognize criminals (U.S. Department of Justice, 2001a, pp. 43-44, U.S. De-

Figure 13. Formation of a template matrix for a fingerprint. Source: RAND Corporation

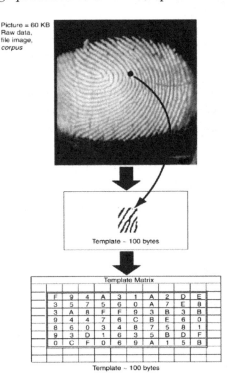

partment of Justice, 2001b, pp. 61-63).Automated Fingerprint Identification Systems (AFIS) match a specific fingerprint against a repository of fingerprints. This can be valuable for law enforcement or civilian purposes. For law enforcement, prints are assembled from crime scenes, often well-known as latent prints, or are acquired from criminal suspects when they are under arrest. For civilian rationales, viz. large scale national identity proposals, prints may be acquired by placing a finger on a scanner or by electronically scanning inked prints on paper. An AFIS can scan and acquire fingerprint data from paper-based prints and then match the acquired data against a database. This technique of acquiring data, presenting an inked or latent print to the system is not about authenticating identity, where an individual's attributes are acquired and matched by some kind of a human/machine interaction. AFIS is concerned with a one-to-many match rather than a one-to-one match (checking to see if a sample is held on file as opposed to verifying that one sample matches with another. The data from a fingerprint sample is captured and extracted. This is then compared against the database of samples to determine if there is a match.

The most preferred form fingerprint identification authentication system is the three-factor authentication system. It encompasses inserting the smart card into the reader, entering the user PIN to unlock the fingerprint template stored, positioning the finger on the authentication device to generate a live-scan fingerprint and matching it. If the template matches, the fingerprint information is transferred in form a number and combined with the smart card PIN and then utilized as a symmetric cryptographic key to decrypt the private key. A random number is generated and transmitted to the smart card. The private key on the smart card is used to encrypt the data and transmit it to the server, which uses a certified public key to decrypt the encrypted message. If the same data that was initially passed to card is revealed, the connection is established. Figure 14 describes the working three factor authentication system using fingerprint identification.

Facial Recognition

Face is one of the most suitable biometric techniques since it is one of the most universal techniques of identification which individuals utilize in their visual communication and interaction. Moreover, the technique of capturing face images is non-intrusive. Two main methods to the identification founded on face recognition are the as follows: (i) Transform approach (Turk & Penland, 1991; Swets & Weng, 1996) the universe of face image domain is represented using a set of orthonormal basis vectors. Presently, the most accepted basis vectors are eigenfaces: every eigenface is a derivative from the covariance analysis of the face image population; two faces are deemed to be alike if they are satisfactorily "close" in the eigenface feature space. Numerous variants of such a technique exist. (ii) Attribute-based approach (Atick,Griffin & Redlich,1996)

in which facial attributes like nose, eyes, etc. are extracted from the face image and the invariance of geometric properties among the face landmark features is used for recognizing features.

Face recognition is a non-intrusive technique where the person's face is photographed, and the resulting image is transformed to a digital code (Li & Jain, 2005; Zhao, Chellappa, Rosenfeld, & Philips, 2000). Face recognition algorithms use special facial appearances for recognition, such as geometry and texture patterns. The performance of face recognition algorithms have a negative experience due to reasons such as uncooperative conduct of the user, lighting, and other environmental variables. One of the major benefits of facial recognition over other biometric methods is that it is practically non-intrusive. Facial recognition does not demand customers to supply fingerprints, talk into phones, nor have their eyes scanned. As contrasted with hand based methods, such as fingerprint scanners, climate and cleanliness do not strongly influence the outcome of facial

Figure 14. Three Factor authentication using fingerprint identification

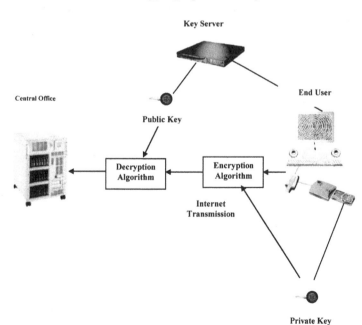

scans, making facial recognition uncomplicated to execute.

Facial recognition systems in fact encompass some noteworthy stages, viz. face detection for locating human faces, face tracking for following moving subjects, face modeling for representing human faces, face coding/compression for efficiently archiving and transmitting faces, and face matching for comparing represented faces and identifying a query subject. Face detection is generally an essential first stage. Distinguishing faces can be considered as a two-class (face versus non-face) classification problem, whilst identifying faces can be viewed as a multiple-class (multiple subjects) classification problem in the face class. Face detection encompasses certain phases of face recognition process, while face recognition makes use of the outcomes of face detection.

We can view face detection and recognition as the first and the second phases in a sequential classification system. The fundamental concern here is to determine a suitable feature space to correspond to a human face in such a categorization system. A flawless combination of face detection, face modeling, and recognition algorithms has the possibility of accomplishing high performance for face identification applications.

Face recognition systems consist of three key components: (a) face detection and feature extraction, (b) face modeling, and (c) face recognition. The face detection or location and feature extraction component is able to locate faces in video sequences. The most significant section of this component is a feature extraction sub-component that extracts geometrical facial appearances (viz. face boundary, eyes, eyebrows, nose, and mouth), and texture/colour facial appearances (estimation of the head pose and illumination). The face modeling component utilizes these extracted features for altering the generic 3D face model in the learning and recognition phases. The recognition/identification component utilizes facial features extracted from an input image and the learned 3 dimensional models to authenticate the face present in an image in the recognition/identification phase.

Zhao(*et. al.*,2000) have described the stages in face recognition which are as shown in Figure 15.

Facial masquerading is of concern in unattended authentication applications. It is very taxing to design face recognition techniques which can accept the consequences of aging, facial expressions, slight disparities in the imaging environment and deviations in the pose of face w.r.t. camera (2 dimensional and 3 dimensional rota-

Figure 15. Stages in Facial recognition

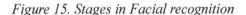

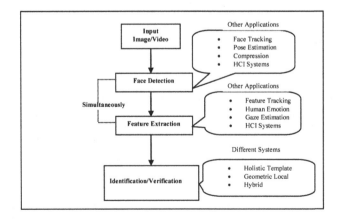

Figure 16. Working of a face recognition system

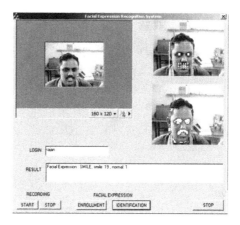

tions). Figure 16 illustrates the working of a face recognition system.

In a review of face recognition techniques, how viewers perceive luminance variations in an image (viz. pigmentation, as shading, as shadows, and so on) has been found to have a profound affect in their ability to identify faces This is illustrated in Figure 17.

When pigmentation is there, variations in image luminance are due to a blending of shading and pigmentation. By comparison, if an object has a surface that consistently reflects light at all points, differences in image luminance are only because of shading,viz. how the objects shape interacts with the light source and the viewers' perspective (Vuong *et. al.*,2005).

Iris Scan

Visual texture of the human iris is established by the chaotic morphogenetic developments during embryonic growth and is posited to be distinctive for each person and each eye (Daughman,1993). An iris image is characteristically acquired using a non-contact imaging method.The image is acquired by means of an common CCD camera with a resolution of 512 dpi. Capturing an iris image encompasses assistance from the user, both to record the image of iris in the central imaging area and to guarantee that the iris is at a fixed distance from the focal plane of the imaging device. A position-invariant stable length byte vector feature results from an annular part of the iris image depending on its texture. The identification error rate using iris technology is supposed to be very

Figure 17.Comparison of pigmented and uniform faces with a positive and negative contrast

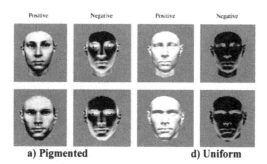

Figure 18. A sample iris code with segmented iris at top left corner

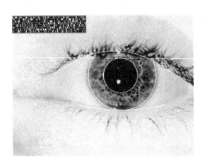

Figure 19. An iris scanning system

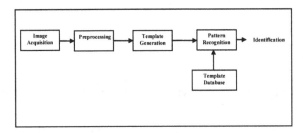

small and the constant length position invariant code allows a tremendously fast technique of iris recognition. Figure 18 shows a sample segmented iris with iris code at the top left corner.

Iris recognition determines the iris pattern in the coloured part of the eye (Daugman, 1993). Iris patterns are created at random, and are distinctive for every human being. Iris patterns in the left and right eyes are dissimilar, and so are the iris patterns of identical clones/twins. The short-comings of iris recognition comprise low user acceptance and expensive imaging technologies. Figure 19 presents the working of an iris scanning system.

The iris scanning system can be deceived if the person uses artificial measures such as contact lens.

Identification using iris scanning has a draw-back that it can be captured by a camcorder.

Figure 20. User Interface of iris recognition system. Adapted from Sirvan, O., Karlik, B. & Ugur, A. (2005)

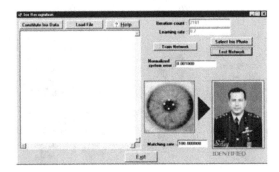

Retina Scanning

Retina scanning has long been acknowledged as an extremely precise and hard to fake biometric, but has not achieved extensive acceptance outside of a rather limited application area requiring very high assurance such as in government and defence environments (Jain, Flynn & Ross, 2007). The appropriateness of the retina vascular pattern for identification use was proposed by Simon and Goldstein in 1935-36, while later studies by Tower recognized experimentally that even identical twins show signs of differing retina vascular patterns (Simon & Goldstein, 1935). Whilst technical solutions for acquiring retina images and their application in biometrics was previously developed in the 1970s (Woodward *et. al.*,2003), it has not seen well-known adoption, which may in part be due to the reason that the data acquisition is regarded as fairly intrusive.

A retina scanner must illuminate an annular region of the retina through the pupil (usually by means of infrared light, even if visible light is also feasible). The annular area centered on the fovea is around 10 degrees off the visual axis of the eye. For the recognition procedure, the reflected contrast information is recorded, which acquires the pattern of blood vessels on the retina itself, and adjacent contrast information.

To guarantee successful signal acquisition, cautious alignment and fixation is necessary. This is normally achieved by a head or chin rest placing the eye close to an aperture, which is illuminated by a guide light on which the person whose retina image is to be captured should focus.

Retina scanning encompasses electronic scanning of retina—ie. innermost layer of wall of the eyeball (Vacca,2007). By emanating a ray of incandescent light that recoils off the person's retina and is acquired by a scanner, a retina scanning system promptly plots the eye's blood vessel blueprint and records it into a readily recoverable digitized repository (Jain et al., 1999). The pros of retina scanning are its reliance on the distinctive characteristics of each person's retina, as well as the fact that the retina usually remains stable throughout life. Nonetheless, some diseases can alter retina vascular structure. Drawbacks of retina scanning involve the necessity for rather close physical contact with the scanning device.

Voice/Speaker Recognition

Voice recognition uses auditory information instead of images. Each human being has a special set of voice characteristics that are hard to impersonate. Individual speech fluctuates based on physiological features such as the size and shape of a person's lips, nasal cavity, vocal chords, and mouth (Hong *et al.*, 2000). Voice recognition has a benefit over other biometrics techniques in that voice data can be broadcasted over phone lines, a characteristic that lends to its pervasive use in areas as defense, fraud prevention, and monitoring (Markowitz, 2000). Voice recognition has revealed very high success as compared to other biometric techniques and much of this success can be elucidated by the way a voice is analyzed when sample speech is requested for validation. The figure below represents the voice patterns of

Figure 21. Retina patterns of twins. Adapted from Kong, A., Zhang, D. & Lu, G.(2005)

three different persons saying "Hello" which is apparently different from others.

Voice biometrics use three types of speaker authentication: text dependent, text prompted, and text independent. Text-dependent authentication contrasts a prompted expression, such as a vocal name, to a prerecorded copy of that expression stored in a database. This form of authentication is often used in such applications as voice-activated dialing in cell phones and bank transactions carried out over a phone system.

Text-prompted authentication offers the best alternative for high-risk systems. In this case, a system requests numerous random expressions from a user to diminish the possibility of tape-recorded fraud. The key obstacle of this authentication process is the total time and space essential to generate a new user on the system (Markowitz, 2000). This practice is regularly used to scrutinize criminals who are under home surveillance or in community-release programs. Text-independent authentication is the most intricate of the three types of voice recognition given that nothing is asked of the user. Everything spoken by the user can be used to corroborate authenticity, a process which can make the authentication process virtually undetectable to the user.

One downside of voice recognition method is that it is gradually more complicated to manage feedback and other forms of interference when authenticating a voice. Voices are made up entirely of sound waves. When broadcasted over analog phone lines these waves tend to become fuzzy. Current technologies can lessen noise and feedback, but these difficulties cannot be totally eradicated. Voice-recognition products are also constrained to somewhat extent in their capability to construe wide variations of voice patterns. Frequently, something used for purposes of verification must be spoken at a balanced pace without much accent or hiatus. Yet individual speech fluctuate so to a great degree among persons that it is a challenge to devise a system that will describe variations in speed of speech as well as in enunciation. Phipps *et. al.*(n.d) have proposed speaker recognition at a remote site which as illustrated in Figure 23.

Recently, there is rising attention in utilizing visual information for automated lipreading (Kaynak, Zhi, Cheok, Sengupta, Jian, & Chung, 2004) and visual speaker authentication(Mok, Lau, Leung, Wang, & Yan, 2004). It has been demonstrated that visual cues, such as lip contours and lip movement, would significantly enhance the performance of these systems. Different methods have been put forward in the past to extract important speech/speaker information from lip image sequences. One such technique is to extract the lip contours from lip image sequences. An instance of lip contour extraction

Figure 22. Voice patterns of 3 different male individuals saying "Hello". Adapted from Rose, P. (2002)

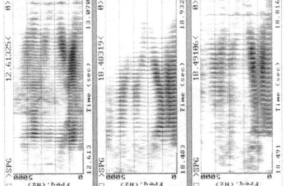

Figure 23. Speech recognition at a remote site

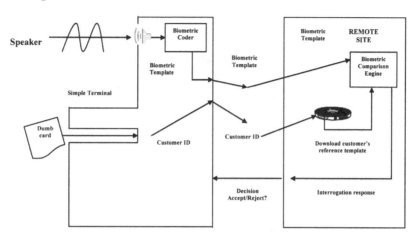

procedure by parametric model fitting for speaker recognition is depicted as per Figure 24.

If the voice patterns of monozygotic twins are very similar, this could be the consequence of not merely their collective physical (e.g. vocal tract morphology) characteristics, but also their shared genes, and shared environments (Plomin & Kosslyn, 2001) which may be a problem in voice recognition as a technique in biometrics.

The main downside in voice recognition is that the voice can be pre-recorded and it is easy to playback it.

Signature Verification

Signature recognition makes use of signatures of the person for recognition. This is being used for numerous security applications where the signatures are matched physically by humans.

For automatic signature recognition, a signature can be acquired using two methods, offline and online. Offline signature verification encompasses signing on a paper and then scanning it to acquire the digital signature image for recognition.

Online signature acquisition makes use of a device entitled signature pad which provides the signature pattern along with numerous other characteristics such as rate, direction, and pressure of writing; the overall time required to make the signature and where the stylus is raised from and lowered onto the "paper." These dynamic features cannot be obtained in offline signature verification.

The key of signature recognition is to discriminate between the elements of signature that are habitual and those that vary with approximately every signature. Weaknesses comprise problems of long-standing reliability and deficiency of accuracy. Offline recognition calls for greater

Figure 24. Lip contour extraction procedure for speaker recognition by parametric model fitting. Adapted from Cetingul, H.E., Yemez, Y, Erzin, E. & Tekalp, A.M. (2005)

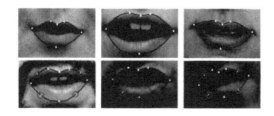

Figure 25. Online signature verification procedure

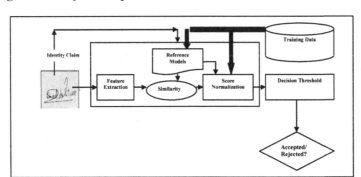

amount of time for processing. Fierrez-Aguilar *et. al.* (2005) have described a procedure of on-line signature verification which is as illustrated in Figure 25.

Hand/Finger Geometry

Hand geometry, along with finger geometry, takes a 3-D image of the hand and gauges the shape and length of fingers and knuckles. It is one of the industry's torch-bearers and has been utilized for many years principally for access control applications. Hand or finger geometry is an automatic measurement of the hand and fingers along various dimensions. None of these methods take real prints of palm or fingers. Only the spatial geometry is observed as the user puts his hand on the sensor's surface (Woodward *et. al.,* 2001). Finger geometry generally examines two or three fingers, and thus necessitates small amount of computational and

storage space. The difficulties with this method are that it has little discriminative power, size of the requisite hardware limits its use in some applications and hand geometry-based systems can be easily circumvented (Jain et al., 1999). Measurement of hand geometry using a biometric system is depicted in Figure 26.

The advantages and drawbacks of hand/finger geometry are as listed below:

Advantages

○ Simplicity - the submission of the biometric is simple, and with appropriate training can be done with little misplacement. The only may be elderly customers or those with sore hands, who may be unable to easily stretch their fingers and place their hand on the unit's surface. The unit also works quite well with filthy hands.

Figure 26. Measurement of hand geometry using a biometric system

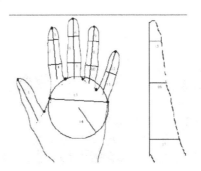

- Resistant to deception - short of casting a model of a registered person's hand and fingers, it would be complicated and time consuming to submit a phony sample. Since a large amount of the value of hand scan is as a restraint in time and attendance scenarios, it would seldom be worth the effort to attempt a bogus submission.
- User opinion - as opposed to facial scan or retina/iris-based technologies, which can encounter some opposition, the use of hand geometry is simplistic for the vast bulk of users. It requires minimal effort as compared to other verification and authentication methods.

Disadvantages
- Static design - as contrasted to other methods, which can take benefit of technological advancements like silicon development or camera quality, hand scan has remained largely unaffected for years. Its size prevents it from being used in most logical access circumstances, where compact design may be a precondition.
- Cost - hand scan readers cost roughly 1338.90 $ to 1912.71 $, placing them toward the high end of the physical security range. Finger scan readers, whatsoever strengths and weaknesses they may have, can be much less costly, in the 765.09 $ -1147.63 $ spectrum.
- Physiological injuries - as with all biometrics, physiological alterations can result in users to be rejected falsely. Injuries are fairly widespread, and would make use of systems unfeasible.
- Precision and Accuracy- although usually more dependable than behav-

ioral biometrics such as voice or signature, hand geometry, in its current manifestation, cannot carry out 1-to-many searches, but as an alternative is restricted to 1-to-1 authentication.

Gait

Gait can be defined as the synchronized, cyclical combination of movements that result in human locomotion. The movements are harmonized in the sense that they must take place with a definite temporal pattern for the gait to happen. The activities in a gait recur as a walker cycles between steps with alternating feet. It is both the harmonized and cyclic nature of the motion that makes gait a unique occurrence. Gait is in fact a not new biometric (Nixon *et. al*, 2005; Nixon & Carter,2006). There was a team of workers in the mid 1990s who demonstrated autonomously and on small databases that gait could be used to recognize people, by the manner they walk. The present state-of-the-art systems have established recognition potential on much bigger databases where persons were walking inside in controlled lighting, and outside where the lighting is uncontrolled, and where other biometrics are at too low a resolution or are masked.

Gait analysis is a behavioral biometrics in which a individual is identified by the style in which he/she walks (Lee & Grimson, 2002; Nixon, Carter, Cunado, Huang, & Stevenage, 1999). This biometric characteristic presents the opportunity to identify people at a distance, even without any interface. Gafurov *et. al.*(2007) describe the gait pattern of a person which is used as biometric which is illustrated in Figure 27 and it is unique for every person.

There exist several gait variables (viz. basic stride-phase variables, joint angles, ground reaction forces etc.) that show aging effects (Princea et al., 1997) making this a limitation of gait in biometric authentication.

Figure 27. Gait pattern of person which is used as biometric. Adapted from Gafurov, D., Snekkenes, E. & Bours, P. (2007)

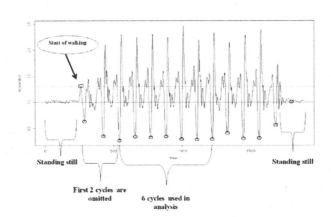

Palmprint Scanning

Palmprint verification is a biometric technique which differentiates an individual depending on his/her palmprint pattern. Palmprint is a dependable individual identifier because the print patterns are not replicated in other human beings, even in twins. More significantly, the information of these ridges is stable. The ridge structures are created at about 13th weeks of the human embryonic growth and are finished by about 18th week. The formation stays unaffected from that time on right through life apart from for size. After death, decay of the skin is last to take place in the region of the palm print.

Palmprint verification is a somewhat modified form of the fingerprint technology. Palmprint scanning makes use of an optical reader that is very akin to that used for fingerprint scanning; yet, its size is much bigger, which is a limiting issue for the use in workstations or mobile devices.

Fingerprint scanning makes use of sophisticated devices to acquire information about a person's fingerprint, which information is used to authenticate the person at a later on. Each finger consists of distinctive patterns of lines. Fingerprint scanners do not capture whole fingerprints; rather, they acquire small particulars about fingerprints, called minutiae (Hong *et al.*, 2000). For instance,

a scanner will select a point on a fingerprint and capture information about what the ridge at that point looks like, which direction the ridge is heading, and so on (Jain, Pankanti, & Prabhakar, 2002). By picking sufficient points, the scanner can be very precise.

Though minutiae recognition is not the only appropriate thing for fingerprint comparison, it is the key aspect used by fingerprint systems. A biometrics system can distinguish a fingerprint from its ridge-flow blueprint; ridge frequency; location and arrangement of singular points; type, direction, and location of key points; ridge counts; and location of pores (Jain et al.,2002). Given their ease and multiple uses, fingerprint scanning is the most expansively used biometrics application.

One fundamental point is that vulnerabilities abound all through the whole process of fingerprint authentication. These vulnerabilities differ from the real scan of the finger to the transmission of the authentication request to the storing of the fingerprint data. Through reasonably effortless means, an illicit person can gain right to use a fingerprint-scanning system (Thalheim, Krissler, & Ziegler, 2002): the scanners may be misled by merely blowing on the scanner surface, rolling a bag of warm water over it, or using artificial wax fingers. Another imperfection with some fingerprint scanners is the storage and broadcast

Figure 28. Sample Palmprint images of different people

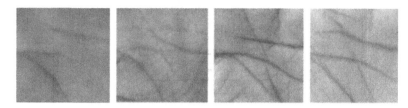

of the fingerprint information. The fingerprint data must be sent to the server, and the method may not be safe. Likewise, the fingerprint templates on a server must be sheltered by firewalls, encryption, and other basic network security procedures to keep the templates secure.

When evaluated with the other physical biometric techniques, palmprint scanning has numerous benefits: low-resolution imaging, low-intrusiveness, steady line features, and low-cost capturing device. Palmprints as a biometric for identification can also be distinguished without any problem (Kong *et. al.*,2005).

Keystroke Dynamics

Psychologists have proved that a person's actions are can be forecasted in the performance of recurring, and everyday acts (Umphress.&Williams, 1985). Deterministic algorithms have been used in keystroke dynamics from the time of the late '70s. In 1980, Gaines *et al.* (1980) presented a report on the study of the typing patterns of seven trained typists. Studies have proved that typing patterns are unique for every individual. (Leggett *et al.*,1991). Keystroke dynamics is an automatic technique

of investigating an individual's keystrokes on a keyboard (Fabian & Rubin, 2000). Keystroke patterns are types of indirectly-acquired biometric that are attained by analyzing the rate of typing of a typist on a keyboard. Different people have distinctive patterns of typing of different words which may present some evidence of user identity.

Keystroke patterns have been employed to "harden" password entry (Monrose, Reiter & Wetzel, 2001). When the user is asked to enter their password, the system not only verifies the password matches the one stored on file, it verifies the rate at which it was entered with a summary of pre-recorded typing patterns for that user. This efficiently develops a challenge-response protocol using a biometric.

This technology scrutinizes dynamics such as typing pace and pressure, the total time of typing a particular password, and the time that a user takes between hitting keys, dwell time (the length of time one holds down each key), as well as flight time (the time it takes to move between keys). Taken over the course of different login sessions, these two metrics generate a measurement of pace which is distinctive to each user. The flowchart

Figure 29. Sample palmprints of twins. Adapted from Kong, A., Zhang, D. & Lu, G.(2005)

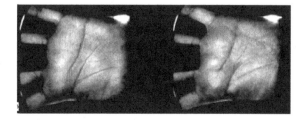

Figure 30. Flowchart for authentication based on keystroke dynamics

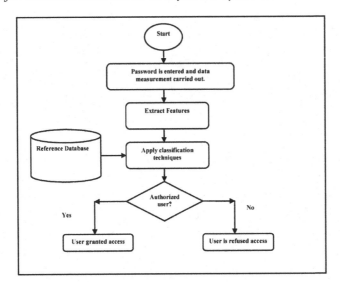

for authentication based on keystroke dynamics as per Jain *et. al.* (1999) is as shown in Figure 30.

Keystroke dynamics can be used to distinguish and detect unauthorized login attempts by imposters using keystroke latency which is defined as the time interval between successive keystrokes. Gagbla(2005) exemplifies how keystroke latency can be used to distinguish between legitimate users and imposters.

Vein Patterns

With the advancement and development of society, how to recognize individual identity and protect

Figure 31. Keystroke dynamics to distinguish between legitimate users and imposters. Adapted from Gagbla (2005)

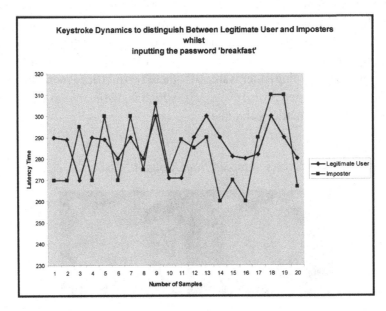

Figure 32. Block diagram of a vein authentication/recognition system

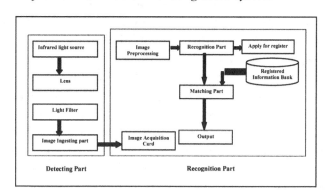

information security is a common trouble that must be resolved in contemporary information age. Therefore, according to the structure features of person's finger vein image, from the secure and practical angle, the uniqueness authentication system on finger vein has been devised. Its misrecognition ratio is 1 percent and its precision rate is 99 percent Zhang *et. al.*(2008).

Vein geometry is founded on the fact that the vein pattern is different for various individuals. Vein measurement usually focuses on blood vessels on the back of the hand. The veins under the skin membrane take in infrared light, and thus have a darker pattern on the image of the hand. An infrared light combined with a special camera maps an image of the blood vessels in the shape of tree patterns. This image is then converted into data and stored in a template. Vein patterns have several advantages:

There are several benefits of this technique of identification. The vein images of most persons can't alter at all with growing age. First of all,

different individuals have specific vein images. Secondly, the vein is in body. Thirdly, finger vein recognition is non-contact recognition. So it doesn't influence body health and is non-invasive. Lastly vein characteristics are hard to be faked and altered by surgery.

However, the method has not yet won full mainstream acceptance. The major disadvantage of vein measurement is the lack of proven reliability (Jain et al., 1999, 2004; Wayman et al., 2005). Zhang *et. al.*(2008) describe stages in recognition of finger veins which is as exhibited in Figure 32.

Figure 33 illustrates the vein patterns produced as a result of exposure to infrared light source.

DNA

Dr. Alec Jeffreys made use of DNA in biometrics for identifying criminals by introducing 'DNA fingerprinting' or DNA typing (profiling) as it is now acknowledged, a technique which he described in mid-1980s(President's DNA Initiative,n.d.).DNA

Figure 33. Infrared Imaging producing vein patterns of the (a) palm, (b) wrist, (c) back of the hand and (d) back of the hand with hair. Adapted from Lingyu, W. & Leedham, G. (2006)

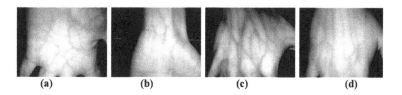

(a)   (b)   (c)   (d)

sampling is rather intrusive at present, and requires a form of tissue, blood, or other body sample (Jain *et al.*, 2004). DNA recognition does not involve enhancement or feature extraction stages; DNA patterns extracted from bodily sample are directly used for matching. DNA of every individual is unique, except for twins who have the same genotype but different phenotypes. The DNA of every person is the same throughout life. Despite all these benefits, the recognition technology still has to be refined. So far, the DNA analysis has not been sufficiently automatic to get ranked as a biometric technology. If the DNA can be matched automatically in real time, it may become more significant.

DNA fingerprinting works by taking a sample of genetic material from individual and comparing short segments that are known to vary significantly between individuals. DNA profiling provides a reliable way to exclude an individual (i.e., to reject a match between an unknown sample and that provided by an individual). However, it only provides a probability measure that two samples match. Hence there is an extremely low false acceptance rate, but an uncertain false rejection rate.

DNA is, however, presently used frequently forensic applications for criminal recognition. Three concerns limit the value of this biometric technique for other applications: 1) contagion and sensitivity: it is simple to steal a DNA sample from an naive subject that can be afterwards misused for criminal purposes; 2) real-time recognition concerns: the current technology for DNA matching necessitates tiresome chemical techniques (wet processes) comprising an expert's proficiency and is not geared for on-line non intrusive identification; and 3) apprehensions such as information about vulnerabilities of an individual due to certain illnesses could be achieved from the DNA blueprint and there is a anxiety that the unintentional misuse of genetic code information may cause discrimination. However, monozygotic twins have the same DNA(Javed, Ostrowski, & McNally,2003) and DNA recognition in biometrics may become a problem but dizygotic twins may be distinguished. Figure 34 illustrates the application of DNA recognition for criminal purposes.

Barcodes are also being used in identification using DNA barcode readers. The process of identification using 2D DNA barcode readers takes place as shown in Figure 35.

Figure 36 represents the DNA pattern of a person similar to the barcode of a bottle on the right.

Ear

The potential of the human ear for human recognition was identified and proposed as long back as 1890 by the French criminologist Alphonse Bertillon who wrote "The ear, thanks to these multiple small valleys and hills which furrow across it, is the most significant factor from the point of view of identification. Immutable in its form since birth, resistant to the influences of environment and education, this organ remains, during the entire life, like the intangible legacy of heredity and of the intra-uterine life" (Hurley, Arbab-Zavar &

Figure 34. Process of DNA recognition for criminal purposes

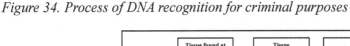

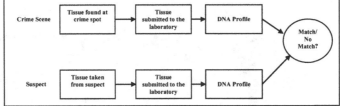

Nixon,n.d.).Conventional and manual techniques for description of ear characteristics and ear identification have been devised for more than ten years (Iannarelli, 1989). In crime scene investigation, ear marks are frequently used for recognition in the absence of (authorized) fingerprints. Similar to fingerprints, the long-held history of the utilization of ear shapes/marks advocates its use for automated person identification.

The ear is the most useful anatomical part for human identification owing to its stability over the lifetime (Choras, 2008) because there are no changes unlike with gait and face with age. Recognizing persons by the ear shape is employed in law enforcement applications where ear markings are found at crime scenes (Burge & Burger, 2000). Recognition tools generally use ear shape for identification. Yet, it is not a regularly used biometric characteristic, because ears are often

covered by hair, and capturing data about them is complicated.

A significant finding is that bimodal identification by means of together the ear and face results presents statistically significant advances over either biometric, for instance, 90.9 percent in one experiment (Pun & Moon, 2004). Figure 37 depicts an ear database for identification.

The phases in generating an ear biometric model are portrayed in Figure 38

A comparison of different biometric methods used for authentication which is as depicted in Tables 5, 6, and 7.

Multimodal Biometrics

Drawbacks of unimodal biometric techniques can be overcome by make the most of multimodal biometric systems(Hong *et. al.*,1999).Unimodal

Figure 35. Identification process using DNA barcode readers

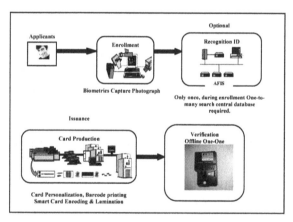

Figure 36.(a) DNA pattern of a person similar to (b) a barcode of a bottle on the right

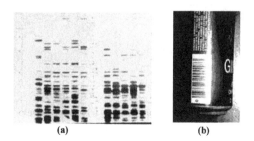

Figure 37. An ear database user for identification purposes. Adapted from Choras, M. (2008)

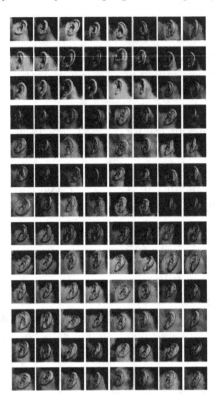

biometric systems face the challenges such as a multiplicity of problems such as noisy data, intra-class deviations, limited degrees of freedom, non-universality, spoof attacks, and undesirable error rates. Some of these disadvantages can be solved by using multimodal biometric systems that incorporate the facts provided by numerous sources of information.

Ross & Jain (2007) discuss the various problems of multimodal biometric systems. These systems have to face a multiplicity of problems viz: (1) Noise in acquired data: A fingerprint image with a wound or a voice sample changed by cold is an instance of noisy data. Noisy data may possibly also result from imperfect or inaccurately maintain sensors (viz., amassing of filth on a fingerprint sensor) or adverse ambient environment (viz., poor lighting of a person's face in a face recognition system). (2) Intra-class deviations: These deviations are usually caused

Figure 38. Phases in generating an ear biometric model. Adapted from Pun & Moon (2004)

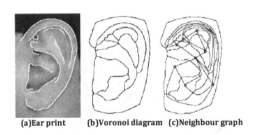

(a)Ear print   (b)Voronoi diagram (c)Neighbour graph

Table 5. Biometric techniques along with the acquisition devices used, sample taken and feature extracted.

Biometric Technique	Acquisition Device	Sample	Feature Extracted
Iris scanning	Infrared-enabled video camera, PC camera	Black and white iris image	Furrows and striations of iris
Fingerprint recognition	Desktop peripheral, PC card, mouse chip or reader embedded in keyboard	Fingerprint image (optical, silicon, ultrasound or touch-less)	Location and direction of ridge endings and bifurcations on fingerprint, minutiae
Voice recognition	Microphone, telephone	Voice Recording	Frequency, cadence and duration of vocal pattern
Dynamic Signature	Signature Tablet, Motion-sensitive stylus	Image of Signature and record of related dynamics measurement	Speed, stroke order, pressure and appearance of signature
Face Recognition	Video Camera, PC camera, single-image camera	Facial image (optical or thermal)	Relative position and shape of nose, position of cheekbones
Hand Geometry	Proprietary Wall-mounted unit	3-D image of top and sides of hand	Height and width of bones and joints in hands and fingers
Retina Scanning	Proprietary desktop or wall mountable unit	Retina Image	Blood vessel patterns and retina

by a person who is erroneously interacting with the sensor (viz., incorrect facial pose), or when the characteristics of a sensor are modified during authentication (viz., optical vs. solid-state fingerprint sensors). (3) Inter-class similarities: In a biometric system consisting of a numerous users, there may perhaps overlap in the feature space of several users. Golfarelli *et al.* (1997) say that the number of distinguishable patterns in two of the most generally used representations of hand geometry and face are only of the order of 105 and 103, respectively. (4) Non-universality: The biometric system might not be able to acquire significant biometric data from a category of individuals. A fingerprint biometric system, for instance, may capture inaccurate fingerprint features of certain persons, due to the bad quality of the ridges. (5) Spoof attacks: This kind of attack is particularly pertinent when behavioural features such as signature or voice are used. Nevertheless, physical features such as fingerprints are also vulnerable to spoof attacks (Ross,Jain &Nandakumar,2006).

Table 6. Comparison of Unimodal biometrics vis-à-vis reliability, error rate and errors

Biometric	Reliability	Error Rate	Errors
Fingerprint	High	1 in 500+	Dryness,age,dirt
Facial Recognition	Medium	No data	Lighting,age,glasses,hair
Hand Geometry	Medium	1 in 500	Hand injury, age
Speaker Recognition	Low	1 in 50	Noise,weather,colds
Iris Scan	High	1 in 131,000	Poor lighting
Retina Scan	High	1 in 10,000,000	Glasses
Signature Recognition	Low	1 in 50	Changing signature
Keystroke Recognition	Low	No data	Hand injury, tiredness
DNA	High	No data	None

Table 7. Comparison of unimodal biometrics vis-à-vis universality, uniqueness, permanence, collectability, performance, acceptability and circumvention

Biometric	Universality	Uniqueness	Permanence	Collectability	Performance	Acceptability	Circumvention
Face	H	L	M	H	L	H	L
Fingerprint	M	H	H	M	H	M	M
Hand Geometry	M	M	M	H	M	M	M
Keystroke Dynamics	L	L	L	M	L	M	M
Hand Vein	M	M	M	M	M	M	H
Iris	H	H	H	M	H	L	H
Retina	H	H	M	L	H	L	H
Signature	L	L	L	H	L	H	L
Voice	M	L	L	M	L	H	L
DNA	H	H	H	L	H	L	L

*H=High, M=Medium and L=Low.

Several researchers have shown that fusion of multiple biometric evidences enhances the recognition performance (Ross et al., 2006). Fusion in multimodal biometric systems can take place at four levels: - (a) Data or feature level fusion: Either the data itself or the feature sets derived from multiple sensors/sources are fused. (b) Match score level fusion wherein: The scores generate by various classifiers regarding diverse modalities are combined. (c) Decision level fusion: The ultimate output of multiple classifiers is consolidated via methods viz.majority voting. Biometric systems that integrate information at an early phase of processing are assumed to be more effectual than those systems which carry out integration at a later on. In view of the fact that the feature set includes better information about the input biometric data than the matching score or the output decision of a matcher, fusion at the feature level is estimated to offer superior recognition results. Finally, rank level fusion involves combining identification ranks obtained from

Figure 39.Fusion of speech recognition and face recognition using mutimodal biometrics

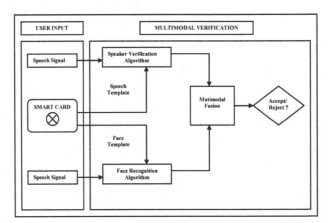

multiple unimodal systems for authentication. Rank level fusion is only applicable to identification systems. Figure 39 illustrates the fusion of speech recognition and face recognition using mutimodal biometrics.

ADVANTAGES AND DRAWBACKS OF BIOMETRIC TECHNIQUES

No biometric technique will be 100% secure, but when contrasted to a PIN or a password, biometrics may offer a superior security. Biometrics in general holds a set of benefits and shortcomings, as Table 8 summarizes.

The advantages are more important than the drawbacks primarily because of the first reason, biometrics provides positive identification. The fundamental objective is to be able to attain positive identification without having any uncertainties. Since one can't misplace, forget, or share their biometric information, then it is known positively that the important information cannot be falsified. While it is very complicated to fabricate a biometric characteristic of an authorized user, biometrics (e.g. a face or fingerprint) are not essentially kept a secret.

For instance, our fingerprints are left in a wide range of places in a given day such as at our house and in the workplace (our fingerprints are all over our computer keyboards, mice, and coffee mugs).

Once an individual has their biological data put into a template for identification or verification afterwards, it is acknowledged that the template is distinctive to that one individual. Depending on the biometric technique employed, identification or authentication can occur in a matter of no time. This time also depends on the kind of system that the administrator is currently using. Though the initiative of digital identification is reasonably new, there is a great deal of competition today with related products, which drives these businesses to lower the cost in general.

Public acceptance is the most significant concern when putting into operation a new system or methods by which one abides. If the community does not acknowledge the notion of biometrics, it would be hard to implement fruitfully because it would not be used. There is a lengthy list of legal concerns that biometrics imposes. Legal concerns are out of scope for this study.

Incorporating a biometric system into a situation where authentication is essential is easy if new systems were incorporated to just do that. There may possibly also be present systems that the integrator may wish to upgrade. Hardware costs will certainly increase and that may become a disadvantage for an organization or enterprise to use biometrics as a tool for identification or authentication. The cost of innovative technology will always become a concern.

Storage allocation of biometric templates will also swell and may pose a difficulty with those who may not comprise ample amount of storage at the present time.

Table 8 lists the advantages and disadvantages of biometrics and Table 9 recapitulates the advan-

Table 8. Advantages and drawbacks of biometrics

Advantages	Drawbacks
Positive Identification	Public Acceptance
One cannot lose, forget, or share his/her biometric information	Legal Issues
A biometric template is specific to a person for whom it is created	Probable increase in hardware costs to current systems
Costs are normally decreasing	Privacy Concerns
Quick identification/authentication	Mandates storage space in large amount

Table 9. Advantages and Drawbacks of various biometric techniques

Biometric Technique	Advantage	Drawback
Fingerprint Scanning	Economical Very secure	Physical contact to a scanning machine may spread germs
Hand geometry	May result in better technology (measurements of the vein structure in a hand)	Not as unique as fingerprint scanning
Retina scanning	Accuracy is guaranteed as the retina remains relatively stable throughout life	Very costly to implement
Iris scanning	Very hard to fool	Costly Precise
Face recognition	Process can be invisible	Costly and its accuracy
Voice authentication	Popularly known to work even over the telephone. Cost is minimal. Able to measure stress	Background noise or sickness viz. soar throat may cause interference. Voice can be altered
Signature Verification	Popularly accepted	Accuracy is difficult to guarantee

tages and drawbacks of various existing biometric techniques on an individual basis.

As the table indicates, the advantages of fingerprint scanning evidently overshadow the drawbacks. Fingerprint scanning provides a very secure means of identification in an economical way. The lone drawback is that there is contact with a scanning device that might spread germs. Merely presenting antiseptic cleansing solution prior to and after the person scans his/her finger may lessen this difficulty. An individual may furthermore use fingerprint recognition as a tool to spot and identify criminals even though the kind of fingerprint recognition carried out in this case is by digital devices rather than conventional ink and paper. Even though hand geometry scanning is not as distinctive as fingerprints, this process may impose a superior means of identification such as vein structure, which is just as distinctive as a fingerprint. Both retina and iris based scanning techniques are very precise and hard to trick. Given that fact that the retina remains comparatively constant throughout a lifetime, accuracy can be accomplished with little thought about environmental issues.

Retina scanning is categorized an extraordinarily accurate and invulnerable biometric tech-

nology and is recognized as a valuable solution for very high security environments. Retina scanning may not be generally accepted because the person has to come into close contact with the scanning device and some people may feel uneasy with having a laser scanning their eyes.

Persons are common with signature and voice verification techniques as a means of identification/verification on a daily basis. The accurateness of signature verification cannot be guaranteed. A signature might alter depending of different reasons such as diseases such as arthritis, or as a matter of fact the temperature of the hand etc. This is identical for voice authentication for the reason that any sort of background noise or sickness such as soar throat may influence accuracy. Both of these techniques are popularly used but do not offer the type of security essential in high security circumstances. Table 10 lists the applications of biometrics in the private sector.

PERFORMANCE MEASUREMENT IN BIOMETRICS

Performance evaluation in general—and technology evaluations specifically—have been influen-

Table 10. Biometric applications in the private sector

Financial Services Industry Applications	
Function	**Biometric Technique**
Account Access over telephone	Voice recognition
ATM Access	Iris Recognition
ATM Access	Finger Imaging
Cash Room & Vault Access	Hand Geometry
Credit Card Access	Finger Imaging
E-Commerce	Signature Verification
Facilities & Personnel Control Applications	
Function	**Biometric Technique**
Computer Access & Encryption	Finger Imaging
Customer Access	Finger Geometry
Customer Access	Hand Geometry
Day Care Services	Hand Geometry
Hospital Records Security	Finger Imaging
Personnel Security	Finger Imaging
Telephone Access	Voice Verification
Telephone Access	Voice Verification
Time & Attendance	Hand Geometry
Time & Attendance	Finger Imaging
VIP Security	Hand Geometry

(Based on Woodward, 1997)

tial in advancing biometric technology. Grothe (*et. al.*, 2007) advocate the use of quality detection algorithms in biometrics and propose detection of error trade-off and error versus reject characteristics as measures for the relative assessment of sample quality measurement algorithms. Regardless of the pain taken by international biometric community, the measurement of the precision of a biometric system is far from being completely explored and, ultimately, standardized (Gamassi *et. al.*,2005).

The result of all these discrepancies in measurement (which is minute in the majority of cases) is that each time a template is created from a live biometric characteristic, the consequence is slightly different. Consequently, the

result generator is required to make available a matching service to try to establish if the live template belongs to the same human being as the presently chosen master template. The false accept rate (FAR) and false reject rate (FRR) are used to measure if the biometric system is reliable (Ratha,Connell,&Bolle,2001).

In order to assess the success of the biometric system at accurately identifying a person a number of error measures have been developed. These measures are frequently used throughout the literature. The definitions are given below:-

- False Accept Rate (FAR) - the likelihood that a biometric system will erroneously identify a person or will fail to reject an unauthorized person. The FAR of a biometric system increases as the corresponding confidence is lowered. This is because the security level has been reduced, which results in a greater probability that a person will be erroneously identified, or authenticated, and consequently accepted.

- False Reject Rate (FRR) - the likelihood that a system will be unsuccessful to identify an authorized person, or authenticate the legitimate claimed identity of an authorized person. The FRR is moreover bound to the corresponding confidence. When the confidence is increased, the requisite score for a match is more complicated to obtain due to the inconsistency of biometric characteristics and the capture process. Consequently, rejections are more probable to take place, even for authorized individuals.
- Equal Error Rate (EER) - when the confidence of a system is set so that the percentage of false rejections will be roughly equivalent to the percentage of false acceptances. The performance measurement metrics in biometrics are as illustrated in the figure below:-

While the EER (also known as the cross-over) has no real importance in the operational precision of a biometric system, it is generally utilized as a description of the overall accuracy of the system, for use as a relative measure against other biometric systems.

Within every biometric system there are statistical error rates that influence the overall accurateness of the system. The False Reject Rate (FRR) is the rate at which valid system users are rejected and regarded as illegitimate and invalid users. False reject rate is also denoted as a Type I error or a false negative error. The common formula for calculating the error rates for performance measurement are as follows:

- False Reject Rate = NFR/NEIA (in case of identification biometric systems)
- False Accept Rate = NFR/NEVA (in case of authentication biometric systems) wherein:
- NFR = No. of times false rejections are made by a biometric system.
- NEIA = No. of times enrollee identification attempts occur.
- NEVA = No. of times enrollee verification attempts occur.

The False Accept Rate (FAR) is the rate at which unauthorized users are acknowledged by the system as valid and classified as genuine users. False accept rate is also famous as a type II Error or a False Positive.

The universal formula for estimating the False Accept Rate is: False Accept Rate = NFR/NEVA (for authentication biometric systems) or

- False Reject Rate = NFA/NIVA (for authentication biometric systems) wherein:
- NFA = No. of times false acceptances that occur in a biometric system.
- NEIA = No. of times imposter identification attempts occur.
- NEVA = Number of times imposter verification attempts occur.

The last error that must be known regarding any biometric system is the Crossover Error Rate (CER), also called as the Equal Error Rate (EER). This is the position where the False Reject Rate and the False Accept Rate are equivalent over the size of the population. Figure 40 illustrates the cross over rate which attempts to combine the two measures of biometric accuracy, viz. the false reject rate and false accept rate.

USABILITY AND ACCESSIBILITY CONCERNS ABOUT BIOMETRICS

The usability, practicality and acceptability, hence the effectiveness of a biometric system incorporating an authentication method is contingent on not only on theoretical and technological concerns, but also on user interaction with and practical execution of the system by an organization (Maple & Norrington, 2006).

Biometrics is getting a lot of focus for the reason that the potential to enhance the precision and dependability of identification and authentication purposes. Many studies have been conducted to evaluate the efficiency of biometric systems, with an importance on false acceptances and rejections. Very little research has been carried out on the acceptability of biometric security systems. Several issues are increasing the usability of biometric devices. The sensors are getting small

in size, economical, more reliable, and devised with superior ergonomic features. The biometric algorithms are also being improved, and various systems consist of characteristics to prepare the users as to how to use the system and provide comments during use. Moreover, biometric devices are being incorporated into allied security systems, such as access control and encryption services, to provide a flawless environment.

Yet there are a several usability issues, however. The precision of several biometric systems is still not good enough for a number of applications (i.e., matching against a big database). Also, there is frequently a negative link between the precision of a biometric system and the ease for use, with the most precise systems (viz.., DNA, Iris, Retina) being the most uncomfortable to use. Biometric devices also have continuing difficulties handling people with exceptional physical features, such as faded fingerprints, resulting in high "failure

Figure 40. The crossover rate combining the two measures of biometric accuracy

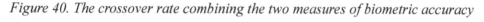
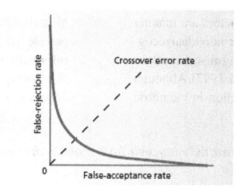

Table 11. Comparative performance evaluation of various biometric techniques

Biometric Technique	EER	FAR	FRR
Face	N.A.	1%	10%
Fingerprint	2%	2%	2%
Hand geometry	1%	2%	0.1%
Iris	< 1%	0.94%	0.99%
Keystrokes	1.8%	7%	0.1%
Voice	6%	2%	10%

to enroll" ratio. Regarding the acceptance of biometric security systems, issues that are making the systems more up to standard comprise of technical interest, apprehensions about identity theft, and border-control initiatives of the government, and the prospects to lessen memory demands by substituting memorized passwords. Research has revealed, nevertheless, that users are still suspicious of accepting biometrics since the advantages are not always apparent, and the chances for abuse and privacy attacks are large and not understood. Table 12 presents the usability of different biometric techniques.

While making the choice of a biometric system certain variables have to be kept into mind viz. the security level, template size, accuracy, user friendliness, speed of processing etc. Table 13 presents a comparison chart of common biometric techniques.

PUBLIC MISCONCEPTIONS ABOUT BIOMETRICS

Both the public and private sectors are making widespread use of biometrics for individual recognition regardless of the prevailing misconceptions about the discipline (Woodward, 1997). Although there has been a drastic reduction in biometric

capturing devices they have not been adopted on a grand scale for civilian applications (Faundez-Zanuy, 2005). As this technology becomes more reasonably viable and theoretically perfected, and thus more routine, the field of biometrics will trigger legal and policy concerns but it is important to clear some misconceptions about biometrics.

There are a number of privacy concerns raised about the use of biometrics. A sound trade-off between security and privacy may be necessary; collective accountability/acceptability standards can only be enforced through common legislation (Jain *et. al.*, 2004).

Following is a sample of some of the more popular misunderstandings regarding the technology. In reviewing this list, it is important to note that the concerns are real and should be addressed particularly in any explanation of a specific biometric technology, if only because members of the public may bring these apprehensions to the privacy discussion. They are as follows:

1. **Biometric systems collect too much private information.** The apprehension is that biometric systems gather a lot of distinctive private information and use the personal information to make small conclusions (a full fingerprint is used to open a door). This apprehension goes to the feeling of a balance

Table 12. Comparison of biometric techniques vis-à-vis usability dimensions viz. robustness, distinctiveness and intrusiveness

Biometric Technique	Identification vs. Verification	Robustness	Distinctiveness	Intrusiveness
Fingerprint	Either	Moderate	High	Touching
Hand/Finger Geometry	Verification	Moderate	Low	Touching
Facial Recognition	Either	Moderate	Moderate	12+ inches
Voice Recognition	Verification	Moderate	Low	Remote
Iris Scan	Either	High	High	12+ inches
Retina Scan	Either	High	High	1-2 inches
Signature Verification	Verification	Low	Moderate	Touching
Keystroke Dynamics	Verification	Low	Low	Touching

in exchange: Does the person consider he or she is giving and getting items of equal value? A meticulous privacy evaluation should provide an answer to this apprehension by indicating a close relationship between the facts gathered and the use of those facts in the biometric system.

2. **Biometrics will be gathered and distributed without agreement of the subject being tracked or adequate justification.** The apprehension is that the person has no power over the choice to use private information and, eventually, to participate in decisions based upon that personal information. A thorough privacy evaluation should provide an answer to this fear by indicating the context and limits of the use of the specific individual biometric information and the role, if any, of the individual in controlling other uses of the information.

3. **Biometrics can be utilized to track people.** The alarm is that biometric systems are proficient in surveillance of individuals, distinguishing each individual based on publicly apparent physical characteristics, and merging that data with information about the time and place of the surveillance. A systematic privacy review should provide an answer to this anxiety by signifying the rationale of the particular biometric system – with a clarification of the system's limits, and elucidating the nature and use of the system to those individuals affected, earlier to the initial collection.

4. **Biometrics discloses sensitive information such as medical status.** The fear among the public is that a biometric system would be used to gather personal biometric data for one use (recognition) and then be extended to collect more personal information (extracting medical information from the biometric) without the subject's consent. A comprehensive privacy evaluation should present an answer to this worry by indicating the biometric system's controlled use of gathered biometric information and the

Table 13. Comparison chart of various variables while choosing a particular biometric method

Comparative chart of various variables while selecting a particular biometric technique							
VARIABLE	**HAND**	**FINGER**	**FACE**	**RETINA**	**IRIS**	**VOICE**	**SIGNATURE**
Security Level	Medium	High	Medium	Excellent	High	Low	Low
Unique identifiers	96	30-90	~128	~192	266-400	6 frequencies	~10 variables
Template Size(bytes)	9	100-1000	84-1300	96	512	2000-10000	....
Accuracy/Precision	High	High	High	Excellent	High	Medium	Medium
User friendliness	High	High	Medium	Low	Medium	High	High
Ease in enrollment	High	Medium	Medium	Low	Low	High	High
Ease in Integration	High	High	High	High	High	High	Excellent
Speed	Excellent	High	Medium	High	High	High	High
Human Factor Limitations/Drawbacks	Missing Fingers, Small or big hand	Worn Fingers	Beards Cosmetic ,Skin toners	None	Blind	Emotional state	Emotional state
Mature Technology	Yes	Yes	Yes	Yes	Yes	No	No
User acceptability	Medium	Medium	Medium	Low	Medium	High	Medium
Stability	Medium	High	Medium	High	High	Medium	Medium

verification of that limit through system audits.

5. **Biometric technology can harm the person.** The fear is that the physical biometric gathering procedure could injure the individual. A detailed privacy review should present an answer to this fear by presenting a comprehensive elucidation of the actual collection mechanism (e.g., iris scanning uses a camera to photograph the eye, not a laser).

FUTURE DIRECTIONS IN BIOMETRIC SECURITY

Biometric systems are being developed which are founded on novel digital image processing technologies and pattern recognition that would be used to distinguish between individuals. There are many well recognized methods of human recognition (face, iris, retina, etc.) which are being employed since years, but yet novel and pioneering solutions are also being proposed. A few of the ground-breaking biometrics techniques are: human scent identification, EEG biometrics, lip biometrics, fingertips tissue identification, heart sound proposed by Phua *et. al.*(2008) as well as tongue-print put forward as a biometric by Zhang *et. al.*(2007)

These promising techniques, emanating from manual criminal and forensic purposes, may be used in automatic computer vision human recognition systems. In view of the fact that most of the techniques have some disadvantages, the proposal of building multimodal (hybrid) biometrics systems is getting lot of interest in the biometric circles. Due to its benefits over conventional techniques, ear, lip, heart sound and palmprint biometrics may support well known techniques such as iris, fingerprint or face identification.

CONCLUSION

Reliable personal recognition is important to many business processes. The traditional techniques do not in fact offer helpful personal identification since they depend on surrogate representations of the individual's identity such as knowledge or possession. It is therefore evident that any system providing trustworthy personal recognition must essentially involve a biometric component. This is not, though, to affirm that biometrics alone can provide reliable personal recognition.

Although it is correct to say that in several applications, biometric data is not secret, in numerous other applications for privacy and trust reasons biometric data is sensitive and we may require protecting it. Biometric systems also have some drawbacks that may have undesirable repercussions for the security of a system. While a few of the drawbacks of biometrics can be overcome with the developments in biometric technology and a cautious system design, it is significant to appreciate that infallible personal recognition systems merely do not exist and possibly, never will. Security is a risk management policy that authenticates, controls, eradicates, or diminishes uncertain events that may negatively affect system resources and information assets. However, well implemented biometric systems are effective deterrents to unauthorized people like crackers, and crooks in the virtual world.

This is a promising but research topic with a bright future. Biometrics will not provide a substitute technology, but it will work as an enhancement tool. Layered with present access control systems, it may make available an incomparable level of security for both the public and private sectors overcoming impediments to online customers' trust in the E-World. By deploying techniques such as biometrics, businesses in the E-World will be adept in achieving online customers' trust.

REFERENCES

Adams, J. (2003). *The Secure Online Business: E-commerce, IT Functionality & Business Continuity*. London: Kogan Page.

Al-Muhtadi, J., Campbell, R., Kapadia, A., Mickunas, M. D., & Seung, Yi. (2002). Routing through the mist: Privacy preserving communication in ubiquitous computing environments. In *Proceedings of the International Conference of Distributed Computing Systems* (pp. 65-74).

Atick, J. J., Griffin, P. A., & Redlich, A. N. (1996). Statistical approach to shape from shading: Reconstruction of 3-dimensional face surfaces from single 2-dimensional images. *Neural Computation, 8,* 1321–1340. doi:10.1162/neco.1996.8.6.1321

Beaver, K. (2003). *Healthcare Information Systems*. Boca Raton, FL: CRC Press.

Belanger, F., Hiller, J., & Smith, W. (2002). Trustworthiness in electronic commerce: the role of privacy, security, and site attributes. *The Journal of Strategic Information Systems, 11,* 245–270. doi:10.1016/S0963-8687(02)00018-5

Bellamy, C., & Taylor, J. A. (1998). *Governing in the Information Age*. Buckingham, UK: Open University Press.

Bigley, G., & Pearce, J. (1998). Straining for Shared Meaning in Organization Science: Problems of Trust and Distrust. *Academy of Management Review, 23*(3), 405–421. doi:10.2307/259286

Brennan, L. L., & Johnson, V. E. (2001). A brave new e-world: technology management for corporate social responsibility. *In International Conference on Management of Engineering and Technology, 1,*1.

Bruce, V., & Langton, S. (1994). The use of pigmentation and shading information in recognising the sex and identities of faces. *Perception, 23,* 803–822. doi:10.1068/p230803

Burge, M., & Burger, W. (2000). Ear biometrics for machine vision. In *Proceedings of ICPR* (pp. 826-830).

Caelli, J. W. (1994). Security in Open and Distributed Systems. *Information Management & Computer Security, 2*(1). doi:10.1108/09685229410058759

Campbell, J. (1997). Speaker recognition: A tutorial. *Proceedings of the IEEE, 85*(9), 1437–1462. doi:10.1109/5.628714

Castelfranchi, C., & Tan, Y.-H. (Eds.). (2001). *Trust and deception in virtual societies*. Boston: Kluwer Academic Publishers.

Cetingul, H. E., Yemez, Y., Erzin, E., & Tekalp, A. M. (2005, March 18-23). Robust Lip-Motion Features For Speaker Identification. In *Proceedings of IEEE International Conference on Acoustics, Speech, and Signal Processing,* (pp. 509-512).

Chirillo, J., & Scott, B. (2003). *Implementing Biometric Security*. Indianapolis, IN: Wiley Publishing Inc.

Choras, M. (2008). Perspective methods of human identification: ear biometrics. *Opto-Electronics Review, 16*(1), 85–96. doi:10.2478/s11772-007-0033-5

Cui, J., Wang, Y., Huang, J., Tan, T., & Sun, Z. (2004). An iris image synthesis method based on PCA and super-resolution. In *Proceedings of the 17th International Conference on Pattern Recognition(ICPR),* (pp. 471-474).

Das, T. K., & Teng, B.-S. (1998). Between trust and control: Developing confidence in partner cooperation in alliances. *Academy of Management Review, 23*(3), 491–512. doi:10.2307/259291

Daugman, J. G. (1993). High confidence visual recognition of persons by a test of statistical independence. *IEEE Pattern Analysis and Machine Intelligence, 15*(11).

Doney, P. M., & Cannon, J. P. (1997). An examination of the nature of trust in buyer-seller relationships. *Journal of Marketing*, *61*(4), 35–51. doi:10.2307/1251829

Fabian, M., & Rubin, A. D. (2000). Keystroke dynamics as a biometric for authentication. *FGCS Journal: Security on the Web*, *16*(4), 351–359.

Fàbregas, J., & Faundez-Zanuy, M. (2008). Biometric dispersion matcher. *Pattern Recognition*, *41*(11), 3412–3426. doi:10.1016/j.patcog.2008.04.020

Faundez-Zanuy, M. (2004). On the vulnerability of biometric security systems. *IEEE Aerospace and Electronic Systems Magazine*, *19*(6), 3–8. doi:10.1109/MAES.2004.1308819

Faundez-Zanuy, M. (2005). Biometric recognition: why not massively adopted yet? *IEEE Aerospace and Electronic Systems Magazine Part 1*, *20*(8), 25-28.

Faundez-Zanuy, M., & Monte-Moreno, E. (2005). State-of-the-art in speaker recognition. *IEEE Aerospace and Electronic Systems Magazine*, *20*(5), 7–12. doi:10.1109/MAES.2005.1432568

Federal Trade Commission. (2000). *Privacy online: fair information practices in the electronic marketplace.* Retrieved October 28, 2008 from http://www.ftc.gov/reports/privacy2000/privacy2000.pdf

Fierrez-Aguilar, J., Ortega-Garcia, J., & Gonzalez-Rodriguez, J. (2005, August). Target dependent score normalization techniques and their application to signature verification. *IEEE Transactions on Systems, Man and Cybernetics. Part C, Applications and Reviews*, *35*(3), 418–425. doi:10.1109/TSMCC.2005.848181

Fukuyama, F. (1995). *Trust: The social virtues and the creation of prosperity.* New York: The Free Press.

Gafurov, D. Snekkenes, E. & Bours, P. (2007, 7-8 June). Gait Authentication and Identification Using Wearable Accelerometer Sensor. In *IEEE Workshop on Automatic Identification Advanced Technologies*, (pp. 220-225).

Gagbla, G. K. (2005). *Applying Keystroke Dynamics for Personal Authentication*, Retrieved October 31, 2008, from http://www.bth.se/fou/cuppsats.nsf/all/0b5c15287d33f3efc1257013007025a3/$file/thesis_report.pdf

Gaines, R. S., Lisowski, W., Press, S. J., & Shapiro, N. (1980). Authentication by Keystroke Timing: Some Preliminary Results. Retrieved September 6, 2008, from http://www.rand.org/pubs/reports/R2526/

Gamassi, M., Lazzaroni, M., Misino, M., Piuri, V., Sana, D., & Scotti, F. (2005, August). Quality assessment of biometric systems: a comprehensive perspective based on accuracy and performance measurement. *IEEE Transactions on Instrumentation and Measurement*, *54*(4), 1489–1496. doi:10.1109/TIM.2005.851087

Garbarino, E., & Johnson, M. S. (1999). The different roles of satisfaction, trust, and commitment in customer relationships. *Journal of Marketing*, *63*(2), 70–87. doi:10.2307/1251946

Gefen, D., Rose, G., Warkentin, M., & Pavlou, P. (2005). Cultural diversity and trust in IT adoption: A comparison of potential e-Voters in the USA and South Africa. *Journal of Global Information Management*, *13*(1), 54–79.

Geffen, D., Karahanna, E., & Straub, D. (2003, March). Trust and TAM in Online Shopping: An Integrated Model. *Management Information Systems Quarterly*, *27*(1), 51–90.

Ghosh, A. K. (1998). *E-Commerce Security: Weak Links, Best Defenses.* New York: John Wiley & Sons, Inc.

Golfarelli, M., Maio, D., & Maltoni, D. (1997). On the error-reject trade-off in biometric verification systems. *IEEE Pattern Analysis and Machine Intelligence, 19*(7), 786–796. doi:10.1109/34.598237

Gorman, L. O. (2003). Comparing passwords, tokens, and biometrics for user authentication. *Proceedings of the IEEE, 91*(12), 2019–2040. doi:10.1109/JPROC.2003.819605

Grothe, P., & Tabassi, E. (2007, April). Performance of Biometric Quality Measures. *IEEE Transactions on Pattern Analysis and Machine Intelligence, 29*(4), 531–543. doi:10.1109/TPAMI.2007.1019

Harris, A. J., & Yen, D. C. (2002). Biometric authentication: assuring access to information. *Information Management & Computer Security, 10*(1), 12. doi:10.1108/09685220210417463

Hoffman, D. L., Novak, T. P., & Peralta, M. (1999). Building Consumer Trust Online. *Communications of the ACM, 42*(4), 80–85. doi:10.1145/299157.299175

Hong, L., Jain, A. K., & Pankanti, S. (1999, October). Can multibiometrics improve performance? In Proceedings of AutoID'99 (pp. 59–64). NJ: Summit.

Hong, L., Pankanti, S., & Prabhakar, S. (2000). Filterbank-based fingerprint matching. *IEEE Transactions on Image Processing, 9*(5), 846–859. doi:10.1109/83.841531

Hosmer, L. (1995). Trust: The Connecting Link Between Organizational Theory and Philosophical Ethics. *Academy of Management Review, 20*(2), 379–403. doi:10.2307/258851

Hurley, D. J., Arbab-Zavar, B., & Nixon, M. S. (nd.). *The Ear as a Biometric.* Retreived 14 Octobor, 2008, from http://eprints.ecs.soton.ac.uk/15725/1/hurleyzavarandnixon.pdf

Iannarelli, A. (1989). *Ear Identification. Forensic Identification Series.* Texas: Paramount Publishing Company.

International Biometric Group. (2006). *Comparative Biometric Testing.* Retrieved August 18, 2008, from http://www.biometricgroup.com/reports/public/reports/CBT6_report.htm

International Biometric Group. (2007). *Biometrics Market and Industry Report 2007-2012.* Retrieved August 28, 2008, from http://www.biometricgroup.com/reports/public/market_report.html

International Biometric Group. (n.d.). *Which is the Best Biometric Technology?* Retrieved September 18, 2008, from http://www.biometricgroup.com/reports/public/reports/best_biometric.html

Jain, A., Pankanti, S., & Prabhakar, S. (2002). On the individuality of fingerprints. *IEEE Transactions on Pattern Analysis and Machine Intelligence, 24*(8), 1010–1025. doi:10.1109/TPAMI.2002.1023799

Jain, A. K., Bolle, R., & Pankanti, S. (Eds.). (1999). *BIOMETRICS: Personal identification in networked society.* London: Kluwer Academic Publishers.

Jain, A. K., Flynn, P. J., & Ross, A. (2007). *Handbook of Biometrics.* New York: Springer-Verlag.

Jain, A. K., Hong, L., Pankanti, S., & Bolle, R. (1997). An identity authentication system using fingerprints. *Proceedings of the IEEE, 85*(9), 1365–1388. doi:10.1109/5.628674

Jain, A. K., Ross, A., & Prabhakar, S. (2004). An introduction to biometric recognition. *IEEE Transactions on Circuits and Systems for Video Technology, 14*(1), 4–20. doi:10.1109/TCSVT.2003.818349

Javed, A., Ostrowski, R. S., & McNally, L. C. (2003). *Twins.* Retrieved October 18, 2008, from http://education.uncc.edu/cmste/Document%20Hold-OLD/Twins2003.doc

Jupp, V., & Shine, S. (2001). Government portals: The next generation of government online. In *Proceedings of the 1st European Conference on E-Government* (pp. 217-223).

Kaynak, M. N., Zhi, Q., Cheok, A. D., Sengupta, K., Jian, Z., & Chung, K. C. (2004). Analysis of lip geometric features for audio-visual speech recognition. *IEEE Transactions on Systems, Man and Cybernetics. Part A, 34*(4), 564–570.

Kemp, R., Pike, G., White, P., & Musselman, A. (1996). Perception and recognition of normal and negative faces: the role of shape from-shading and pigmentation cues. *Perception, 25*, 37–52. doi:10.1068/p250037

Kim, S., & Montalto, C. P. (2002). Perceived risk of privacy invasion and the use of online technology by consumers. *Consumer Interests Annual, 48*, 1–9.

Kiruba, M. (n.d.). *Biometrics*. Retrieved September 09, 2008, from http://ezinearticles.com/?Biometrics&id=16097

Kong, A., Zhang, D., & Lu, G. (2005). *A Study of Identical Twins' Palmprints for Personal Authentication.Advances in Biometrics*. Berlin, Germany: Springer.

Kuanchin, C., & Rea, A. L. Jr. (2004). Protecting personal information online privacy concerns and control techniques. *Journal of Computer Information Systems, 44*(4), 85–92.

Layne, K., & Lee, J. (2001). Developing fully functional egoverment: A four stage model. *Government Information Quarterly, 18*(2), 122. doi:10.1016/S0740-624X(01)00066-1

Lee, L., & Grimson, W. (2002). Gait analysis for recognition and classification. In *Proceedings of the International Conference on Automatic Face and Gesture Recognition* (pp. 148-155).

Lee, M., & Turban, E. (2001). A Trust Model for Consumer Internet Shopping. *International Journal of Electronic Commerce, 6*(1), 75–91.

Leggett, J., Williams, G., Usnick, M., & Longnecker, M. (1991). Dynamic identity verification via keystroke characteristics. *International Journal of Man-Machine Studies, 35*(6), 859–870. doi:10.1016/S0020-7373(05)80165-8

Lewis, D., & Weigert, A. (1985). Trust as a Social Reality. *Social Forces, 63*(4), 967–985. doi:10.2307/2578601

Li, S. Z., & Jain, A. K. (Eds.). (2005). *Handbook of face recognition*. New York: Springer-Verlag.

Lingyu, W., & Leedham, G. (2006,November). Near- and Far- Infrared Imaging for Vein Pattern Biometrics. In *IEEE International Conference on Video and Signal Based Surveillance*.

Liu, C. H., Collin, C. A., Burton, A. M., & Chaudhuri, A. (1999). Lighting direction affects recognition of untextured faces in photographic positive and negative. *Vision Research, 39*, 4003–4009. doi:10.1016/S0042-6989(99)00109-1

Maltoni, D., Maio, D., Jain, A. K., & Prabahakar, S. (2003). *Handbook of fingerprint recognition*. New York: Springer.

Maple, C., & Norrington, P. (2006). The usability and practicality of biometric authentication in the workplace. In *The First International Conference on Availability, Reliability and Security, (ARES'06)*, 1-7.

Markowitz, J. (2000). Voice biometrics. [CACM]. *Communications of the ACM, 43*(9), 66–73. doi:10.1145/348941.348995

McKnight, D., Choudhury, V., & Kacmar, C. (2002). Developing and validating trust measures for e-Commerce: An integrative typology. *Information Systems Research, 13*(3), 334–359. doi:10.1287/isre.13.3.334.81

Mok, L. L., Lau, W. H., Leung, S. H., Wang, S. L., & Yan, H. (2004). Lip features selection with application to person authentication. In. *Proceedings of IEEE ICASSP, 3*, 397–400.

Monrose, F., Reiter, M. K., & Wetzel, S. (2001). *Password hardening based on keystroke dynamics.* Retrieved September 23, 2008, from http://cs.unc.edu/~fabian/papers/acm.ccs6.pdf

Muir, B. M. (1987). Trust Between Humans and Machines, and the Design of Decision Aids. *International Journal of Man-Machine Systems, 27*(5), 527–539. doi:10.1016/S0020-7373(87)80013-5

Nixon, M. S., & Carter, J. N. (2006). Human ID based on Gait. *Proceedings of the IEEE, 94*(11), 2013–2024. doi:10.1109/JPROC.2006.886018

Nixon, M. S., Carter, J. N., Cunado, D., Huang, P. S., & Stevenage, S. V. (1999). Automatic gait recognition. In *Biometrics: Personal Identification in Networked Society* (pp. 231–249). New York: Kluwer.

Nixon, M. S., Tan, T. N., & Chellappa, R. (2005). Human Identification based on Gait. In Jain, A. K., & Zhang, D. (Eds.), *International Series on Biometrics*. New York: Springer.

Olivier, M. (2004). FLOCKS: Distributed proxies for browsing privacy. In *Proceedings of SAICSIT* (pp. 79-88). Stellenbosch, South Africa.

Phipps, T. C., & King, R. A. (n.d.). *A Speaker Verification Biometric In 40 Bytes*. Retrieved October 24, 2008 from http://www.dsp.sun.ac.za/~dupreez/downloads/papers/tespar/cardtech.pdf

Phua, K., Chen, J., Dat, T. H., & Shue, L. (2008). Heart sound as a biometric. *Pattern Recognition, 41*(3), 906–919. doi:10.1016/j.patcog.2007.07.018

Plomin, R., & Kosslyn, S. M. (2001). Genes, brain and cognition. *Nature Neuroscience, 4*(12), 1153–1155. doi:10.1038/nn1201-1153

Prabhakar, S., Pankanti, S., & Jain, A. K. (2003, March/April). Biometric recognition: security and privacy concerns. *IEEE Security and Privacy*, (pp. 33-42).

President's DNA Iniative. (n.d.). *History of Forensic DNA Analysis*. Retrieved October 21, 2008, from http://www.dna.gov/basics/analysishistory/

Princea, F., Corriveaua, H., Héberta, R., & Winter, D. A. (1997). Gait in the elderly. *Gait & Posture, 5*, 128–135. doi:10.1016/S0966-6362(97)01118-1

Pullkis, G., Grahn, J. K., & Karisson, J. (2006). Taxonomies of User Authentication Methods in Computer Networks. In Warkentin, M. (Ed.), *Enterprise Information Systems Assurance and Systems Security*. Hershey, PA: IGI Global.

Pun, K. H., & Moon, Y. S. (2004, May). Recent advances in ear biometrics. In *Proceedings of Sixth International Conference on Automatic Face and Gesture Recognition*, (pp. 164-169).

Rao, G. S. V. R. (2004). Threats and security of Web services – a theoretical short study. In. *Proceedings of IEEE International Symposium Communications and Information Technology, 2*, 783–786.

Ratha, N. K., Connell, J. H., & Bolle, R. M. (2001). Enhancing security and privacy in biometrics based authentication systems. *IBM System Journal, 40*(3). Retrieved August 8, 2008, from http://www.research.ibm.com/journal/sj/403/ratha.html

Rolf, O. (2002). *Security Technologies for the World Wide Web*. Boston, MA: Artech House.

Rose, P. (2002). *Forensic Speaker identification*. Boca Raton, FL: CRC Press.

Ross, A., & Jain, A. K. (2007). Fusion Techniques in Mutibiometric systems. In *Face Biometrics for Personal Identification*. Berlin, Germany: Springer. doi:10.1007/978-3-540-49346-4_12

Ross, A., Nandakumar, K., & Jain, A. K. (2006). *Handbook of multibiometrics*. Berlin, Germany: Springer-Verlag.

Rousseau, D. M., Sitkin, S. B., Burt, R. S., & Camerer, C. (1998). Not so different after all: A cross-discipline view of trust. *Academy of Management Review, 23*(3), 393–404.

Sheehan, K. B. (2002). Toward a typology of Internet users and online privacy concerns. *The Information Society, 18*(1), 21–32. doi:10.1080/01972240252818207

Shneiderman, B. (2000, December). Designing Trust into Online Experiences. *Communications of the ACM, 43*(12), 57–59. doi:10.1145/355112.355124

Simon, C., & Goldstein, I. (1935). A New Scientific Method of Identification. *New York State Journal of Medicine, 35*(18), 901–906.

Sirvan, O., Karlik, B., & Ugur, A. (2005). *An Efficient Iris Recognition for Security Purposes*. Retrieved November 1, 2008 from http://www.icgst.com/GVIP05/papers/P1150549103.pdf

Smith, R. E. (2002). *Authentication: From passwords to public keys*. Reading, MA: Addison-Wesley.

Soldek, J., Shmerko, V., Phillips, P., Kukharev, G., Rogers, W., & Yanushkevich, S. (1997). *Image analysis and pattern recognition in biometric technologies*. Retrieved October 25, 2008 from ">http://enel.ucalgary.ca/People/yanush/publications/lasveg97.pdf

Soppera, A., & Burbridge, T. (2004). Maintaining privacy in pervasive computing—Enabling acceptance of sensor-based services. *BT Technology Journal, 22*(3), 106–118. doi:10.1023/B:BTTJ.0000047125.97546.4a

Spector, Y., & Ginzberg, J. (1994). Pass-sentence: A new approach to computer code. approach to computer code. *Computers & Security, 13*(2), 145–160. doi:10.1016/0167-4048(94)90064-7

Stigler, S. M. (1995). GALTON and Identification by Fingerprints. In Crow, J. F., & Dove, W. F. (Ed.), *Anecdotal, Historical and Critical Commentaries on Genetics*, Retrieved October 23, 2008, from http://www.genetics.org/cgi/reprint/140/3/857.pdf

Svigals, J. (1994). Smartcards: A security assessment. *Computers & Security, 13*(2), 107–114. doi:10.1016/0167-4048(94)90056-6

Swets, D., & Weng, J. J. (1996). Using discriminant eigenfeatures for image retrieval. *IEEE Transactions on Pattern Analysis and Machine Intelligence, 18*, 831–836. doi:10.1109/34.531802

Thalheim, L., Krissler, J., & Ziegler, P.-M. (2002). *Body check: Biometrics defeated*. Retrieved May 04, 2008, from http://www.extremetech.com/article2/0%2C1558%2C13919%2C00.asp

Torkzadeh, G., & Dhillon, G. (2002, June). Measuring Factors that Influence the Success of Internet Commerce. *Information Systems Research, 13*(1), 187–204. doi:10.1287/isre.13.2.187.87

Turk, M., & Pentland, A. (1991). Eigenfaces for recognition. *Journal of Cognitive Neuroscience, 3*(1), 71–86. doi:10.1162/jocn.1991.3.1.71

Umphress, D., & Williams, G. (1985). Identity Verification Through keyboard Characteristics. [London: Academic Press]. *International Journal of Man-Machine Studies, 23*, 263–273. doi:10.1016/S0020-7373(85)80036-5

U.S. Department of Justice. (2001a). *Report of the National Task Force on privacy, technology, and criminal justice information* (NCJ187669). Washington, DC.

U.S. Department of Justice. (2001b). *Use and management of criminal history record information: A comprehensive report, 2001 update* (NCJ187670). Washington, DC.

Vacca, R. J. (2007). *Biometric Technologies and Verification Systems*. Amsterdam: Butterworth-Heinemann.

Vuong, Q. C., Pessig, J. J., Harrison, M. C., & Tarr, M. J. (2005). The role of surface pigmentation for recognition revealed by contrast reversal in faces and Greebles. *Vision Research, 45,* 1213–1223. doi:10.1016/j.visres.2004.11.015

Watson, M. L. (2004). *Can There Be Just One Trust?* Retrieved Octobober 31, 2008 from http://www.instituteforpr.org/files/uploads/2004_Watson.pdf

Wayman, J., Jain, A. K., Maltoni, D., & Maio, D. (2005). *Biometric systems: Technology, design and performance evaluation.* London: Springer-Verlag.

Wayman, J. L. (2008). Biometrics in Identity Management Systems. *IEEE Security & Privacy, 6*(2), 30–37. doi:10.1109/MSP.2008.28

Wilson, O. (n.d.). *Privacy & Identity - Security and Usability: The viability of Passwords & Biometrics.* Retrieved October 13, 2008, from http://facweb.cs.depaul.edu/research/vc/ciplit2004/ppt/Orville_Wilson.ppt

Woodward, D. J. (1997, September). Biometrics: privacy's foe or privacy's friend? *Proceedings of the IEEE, 85*(9), 1480–1492. doi:10.1109/5.628723

Woodward, D. J., Katherine, W. W., Newton, M. E., Bradley, M., Rubenson, D., Lilly, J., & Larson, K. (2001). *Army Biometric Applications: Identifying and Addressing Sociocultural Concerns,* Rand Corporation. Retrieved August 4, 2008, from http://www.rand.org/pubs/monograph_reports/MR1237/index.html

Woodward, D. J., & Orlans, M. N., & Higgins, T. P. (2003). *Biometrics: Identity Assurance in the Information Age.* Berkley, CA: Osborne McGraw Hill.

Yoon, S. (2002). The Antecedents and Consequences of Trust in Online-Purchase Decisions. *Journal of Interactive Marketing, 16*(2), 47–63. doi:10.1002/dir.10008

Yun, Y. W. (2002). *The '123' of Biometric Technology.* Retrieved November 21, 2008, from http://www.cp.su.ac.th/~rawitat/teaching/forensicit06/coursefiles/files/biometric.pdf

Zhang, D. (2000). *Automated Biometrics: Technologies and Systems.* Berlin: Springer-Verlag.

Zhang, D., Liu, Z., Yan, J., & Shi, P. (2007). Tongue-Print: A Novel Biometrics Pattern. In *Advances in Biometrics.* Berlin, Germany: Springer. doi:10.1007/978-3-540-74549-5_122

Zhang, L., Zhang, R., & Chengbo, Y. (2008, May). Study on the Identity Authentication System on Finger Vein. In *Proceedings of IEEE 2nd International Conference on Bioinformatics and Biomedical Engineering,* (pp. 1905-1907).

Zhao, W., Chellappa, R., Rosenfeld, A., & Philips, P. J. (2000). Face recognition: A literature survey. *ACM Computing Surveys, 35*(4), 399–458. doi:10.1145/954339.954342

Zucker, L. G. (1986). Production of Trust: Institutional Sources of Economic Sources. *Research in Organizational Behavior, 8,* 3–111.

Compilation of References

Abe, M. (1998). Universally verifiable mix-net with verification work independent of the number of mix-servers. In K. Nyberg (Ed.), *Eurocrypt '98* (pp. 437-47). Berlin, Germany: Springer-Verlag. (Lecture Notes in Computer Science Volume 1403).

Abe, M. (1999). Mix-networks on permutation networks. In Lam, K.-Y., Okamoto, E., & Xing, C. (Eds.), *Asiacrypt '99* (Vol. 1716, pp. 258–273). Berlin, Germany: Springer-Verlag.

Adams, C., & Farrell, S. (1999). *Internet X.509 public key infrastructure: Certificate management protocols RFC 2510*. Retrieved from http://www.ietf.org/rfc/rfc2510.txt.

Adams, C., & Farrell, S. (1999). *Internet X.509 public key infrastructure: Certificate management protocols RFC 2510*. Retrieved from http://www.ietf.org/rfc/rfc2510.txt.

Adams, J. (2003). *The Secure Online Business: E-commerce, IT Functionality & Business Continuity*. London: Kogan Page.

Adams, W. J. Hadjichristofi, G. C., & Davis, N. J. (2005). Calculating a Node's Reputation in a Mobile Ad-Hoc Network. *In Proceedings of the 24th IEEE International Performance Computing and Communications Conference (IPCCC ZOOS)*, Phoenix, AZ.

Adjie-Winoto, W., Schwartz, E., Balakrishnan, H., & Lilley, J. (1999). The design and implementation of an intentional naming system. *17th ACM Symposium on Operating Systems Principles (SOSP '99)*, Kiawah Island, SC.

Agarwal, N., Renfro, S., & Bejar, A. (2007, May). *Current Anti-Phishing Solutions and Yahoo's Sign-in Seal*. Paper presented at W2SP: Workshop on Web 2.0 Security and Privacy 2007 held in conjunction with the 2007 IEEE Symposium on Security and Privacy.

Agi, I., & Gong, L. (1996). An empirical study of secure MPEG video transmissions. *In Proceedings of the Internet Society symposium on network and distributed system security*, 137-144.

Akyildiz, I., Su, W., Sankarasubramaniam, Y., & Cayirci, E. (2002, August). A survey on sensor networks. IEEE Communications Magazine, 40(8), 102–114. doi:10.1109/MCOM.2002.1024422.

Al-Hamdani, A. (2008). *Cryptography for information security*. In Gupta, J. N., & Sharma, S. K. (Eds.), Information security and assurance (pp. 122–138). Hershey, PA: Information Science Reference.

Al-Hamdani, A. (2009). *Cryptography for information security (chapter 5)*. Unpublished.

Allen, C. A., & Davidson, J. L. (1998). Steganography using the Minimax Eigenvalue Decomposition. *In Proceedings of the conference on mathematics of data/image coding, compression, and encryption*, 3456, 13-24.

Al-Muhtadi, J., Campbell, R., Kapadia, A., Mickunas, M. D., & Seung, Yi. (2002). Routing through the mist: Privacy preserving communication in ubiquitous computing environments. *In Proceedings of the International Conference of Distributed Computing Systems* (pp. 65-74).

Alturki, F., & Mersereau, R. (2001). A novel approach for increasing security and data embedding capacity in images for data hiding applications. *Proceedings of the* international conference on information technology: Coding and computing, 228–233.

Alvestrand, H. T. (1995). X.400 FAQ *A comprehensive list of resources on x.400 series of standards.* Retrieved from http://www.alvestrand.no/x400/index.html

ANSI X9. 63. (1999). *Elliptic Curve Key Agreement and Key Transport Protocols.* Washington, DC: American Bankers Association.

Ansi.org. (1998). X9.31-1998, *Digital signatures using reversible public key cryptography for the financial services industry (rDSA).* American National Standards Institute.

Apache.org. (2007). XML security. Retrieved from http://xml.apache.org/security/

Apple (2009). *Changes Coming to the iTunes Store,* Retrieved from http://www.apple.com/pr/library/2009/01/06itunes.html

Apple Computer Inc. (2003). Rendezvous Web Site. Retrieved from http://developer.apple.com/macosx/rendezvous/

Ash, A., & Lamperti, J. (2008). Florida 2006: Can statistics tell us who won congressional district13? *Chance, 21(2),* 1824. doi:10.1007/s00144-008-0015-5

Asokan, N., Schunter, M., & Waidner, M. (1997). Optimistic protocols for fair exchange. In T. Matsumoto (Ed.), *4th ACM Conference on Computer and Communications Security.* ACM Press, Zurich, Switzerland, 1997, (pp. 6, 8–17).

Atick, J. J., Griffin, P. A., & Redlich, A. N. (1996). Statistical approach to shape from shading: Reconstruction of 3-dimensional face surfaces from single 2-dimensional images. *Neural Computation,* 8, 1321–1340. doi:10.1162/neco.1996.8.6.1321

authentication with a bookmark. In CCS '07: *Proceedings of the 14th ACM conference on Computer and communications security,* pages 48–57, New York: ACM.

Awerbuch, B., Curtmola, R., Holmer, D., Nita-Rotaru, C., & Rubens, H. (2005, September). On the Survivability

of Routing Protocols in Ad Hoc Wireless Networks. *In Proceedings of the IEEE Conference on Security and Privacy for Emerging Areas in Communication Networks* (SecureComm).

Bahn, W. L., Baird, L. C., III, & Collins, M. D. (2008). Jam resistant communications without shared secrets. In *Proceedings of the 3rd International Conference on Information Warfare and Security,* 37-44, Omaha, Nebraska, 2008.

Baird III, L. C., & Bahn, W. L. (2008). *Security Analysis of BBC Coding* (Technical Report). U. S. Air Force Academy, Academy Center for Cyberspace Research, USAFA-TR-2008-ACCR-01, Dec 8

Baird III, L. C., Bahn, W. L., & Collins, M. D. (2007). *Jam-Resistant Communication Without Shared Secrets Through the Use of Concurrent Codes* (Technical Report). U. S. Air Force Academy, USAFA-TR-2007-01, Feb 14.

Balaski, B. (1993, February). *Privacy enhancement for Internet electronic mail: Part IV: Notary, co-issuer, CRL-storing and CRL-retrieving services. RFC 1424.* Retrieved from http://www.ietf.org/rfc/rfc1424.txt

Balazinska, M., Balakrishnan, H., & Karger, D. (2002). INS/Twine: A Scalable Peer-to-Peer Architecture for Intentional Resource Discovery. *Pervasive 2002 - International Conference on Pervasive Computing,* Zurich, Switzerland, Springer-Verlag.

Balenson, D. (1993). *Privacy enhancement for Internet electronic mail: Part III: Algorithms, modes, and identifiers. RFC 1423.* Retrieved from http://www.ietf.org/rfc/rfc1423.txt

Balenson, D. (1993). *Privacy enhancement for Internet electronic mail: Part III: Algorithms, modes, and identifiers. RFC 1423.* Retrieved from http://www.ietf.org/rfc/rfc1423.txt

Balfanz, D., Smetters, D. K., Stewart, P., & Wong, H. (2002, February). Talking to strangers: Authentication in ad-hoc wireless Networks. In Proceedings of the NDSS '02, San Diego, California.

Bao, F., Wang, G., Zhou, J., & Zhu, H. (2004). Analysis and Improvement of Micali's Fair Contract Signing Protocol. *Information Security and Privacy*, 3108, 176–187.

Bard, G. V. (2004). Vulnerability of SSL to chosen plaintext attack, Cryptology ePrint Archive, Retrieved from http://eprint.iacr.org/

Bas, P., Chassery, J., & Davoine, F. (1998). Self-similarity based image watermarking. *In Proceedings of the 9th European signal processing conference* (EUSIPCO), 2277-2280.

Batina, L., Mentens, N., Sakiyama, K., Preneel, B., & Verbauwhede, I. (2006). *Low-cost elliptic curve cryptography for wireless sensor networks. Security and Privacy in Ad-Hoc and Sensor Networks*. Springer-Verlag, 4357, 6-17.

Bauchle, R., Hazen, F., Lund, J., & Oakley, G. (2008). *Encryption*. Retrieved from http://searchsecurity.techtarget.com/sDefinition/0,sid14_gci212062,00.html

Baum-Waidner, B. (2001). *Optimistic asynchronous multi-party contract signing with reduced number of rounds. ICALP'01, LNCS 2076* (pp. 898–911). Berlin, Germany: Springer.

Beaver, K. (2003). *Healthcare Information Systems*. Boca Raton, FL: CRC Press.

Bedi, H., Yang, L., & Kizza, J. (2009). Extended Abstract: Fair Electronic Exchange using Biometrics. *Proceedings of the 5th Annual Workshop on Cyber Security and Information Intelligence Research: Cyber Security and Information Intelligence Challenges and Strategies* (pp. 1-4). Oak Ridge: ACM.

Belanger, F., Hiller, J., & Smith, W. (2002). Trustworthiness in electronic commerce: the role of privacy, security, and site attributes. *The Journal of Strategic Information Systems*, 11, 245–270. doi:10.1016/S0963-8687(02)00018-5

Bellamy, C., & Taylor, J. A. (1998). *Governing in the Information Age*. Buckingham, UK: Open University Press.

Bellare, M., Canetti, R., & Hugo, K. (1996a). Keying hash functions for message authentication. *CRYPTO*, 1996, 1–15.

Bellare, M., Canetti, R., & Hugo, K. (1996b). The HMAC construction. *CryptoBytes*, 2(1).

Bellare, M., Canettiy, R., & Krawczykz, H. (1996). Keying Hash Functions for Message Authentication. *Advances in Cryptology–CRYPTO '96 (LNCS 1109)*.

Bellare, M., Pointcheval, D., & Rogaway, P. (2000). Authenticated key exchange secure against dictionary attacks. In B. Preneel (Ed.), *Advances in Cryptology – Eurocrypt 2000* (pp. 139-155). Berlin: Springer-Verlag. (Lecture Notes in Computer Science Volume 1807)

Bellovin, S. M., & Merritt, M. (1992). Encrypted Key Exchange: Password-Based Protocols Secure Against Dictionary Attacks. Paper presented at SP'92: *In Proceedings of the 1992 IEEE Symposium on Security and Privacy*, page 72, Washington, DC: IEEE Computer Society.

Bellovin, S. M., & Merritt, M. (1993). Augmented encrypted key exchange: a password-based protocol secure against dictionary attacks and password file compromise. *In Proceedings of the 1st ACM Conference on Computer and Communications security* (pp. 244-250).

Bellovin, S., & Merritt, M. (1991). Limitations of the Kerberos authentication system. *In Proceedings of the 1991 winter USENIX conference* (pp. 253-267).

Bellovin, S., & Merritt, M. (1992). Encrypted key exchange: password-based protocols secure against dictionary attacks. I*n Proceedings of the 1992 IEEE Computer Society Symposium on Research in Security and Privacy* (pp. 72-84).

Benaloh, J. D. C. (1988). *Verifiable secret-ballot elections*. (Unpublished doctoral dissertation), Yale University.

Benaloh, J., & Tuinstra, D. (1994). Receipt-free secret-ballot elections. *In Proceedings of the 26th ACM Symposium on Theory of Computing* (pp. 544-553). Montreal, PQ.

Bender, W., Gruhl, D., Morimoto, N., & Lu, A. (1996). Techniques for data hiding. *IBM Systems Journal*, 35(3&4), 313–336. doi:10.1147/sj.353.0313

Ben-Or, M., Goldreich, O., Goldwasser, S., Hastad, J., Kilian, J., Micali, S., & Rogaway, P. (1989). Everything provable is provable in zero-knowledge. In S. Goldwasser

(Ed.), *Advances in Cryptology - Crypto '88 (pp. 37-56)*. Berlin, Germany: Springer-Verlag. (Lecture Notes in Computer Science Volume 403)

Ben-Or, M., Goldreich, O., Micali, S., & Rivest, R. (1990). A fair protocol for signing contracts. IEEE *Transactions on Information Theory, 36(1), 40–46.* doi:10.1109/18.50372

Berlekamp, E. R. (1968). *Algebraic coding theory*. New York: McGraw-Hill.

Berners-Lee, T., Fielding, R., & Frystyk. H. (1996). Hypertext Transfer Protocol. HTTP/1.0.

Bernstein, D. J. (2008). *Simple mail transfer protocol reference manuals*. Retrieved from http://cr.yp.to/immhf.html

Bhargav-Spantzel, A., Camenisch, J., Gross, T., & Sommer, D. (2006). *User centricity: a taxonomy and open issues.* Paper presented at the Proceedings of the second ACM workshop on Digital identity management.

Bigley, G., & Pearce, J. (1998). Straining for Shared Meaning in Organization Science: Problems of Trust and Distrust. *Academy of Management Review, 23(3), 405–421.* doi:10.2307/259286

Bloom, B. (1970). Space/Time Trade-offs in Hash Coding with Allowable Errors. *Communications of the ACM, 13(7), 422–426.* doi:10.1145/362686.362692

Bluetooth, S. I. G. (2004). Specification of the Bluetooth System. Retrieved from http://www.bluetooth.org/

Boneh, D., & Franklin, M. (1997). Efficient generation of shared rsa keys. *In Proceedings of CRYPTO.*

Boneh, D., & Franklin, M. (2003). Identity-based encryption from the weil pairing. *SIAM Journal on Computing, 32(3), 586–615.* doi:10.1137/S0097539701398521

Boneh, D., & Franklin, M. K. (2001). Identity-based encryption from the Weil pairing. In *Advances in Cryptology — Crypto '01.* In LNCS (Vol. 2139, pp. 213–229). Berlin, Germany: Springer-Verlag.

Boneh, D., & Golle, P. (2002). Almost entirely correct mixing with applications to voting. In V. Atlury (Ed.),

Proceedings of the 9th ACM Conferences on Computer and Communication Security (CCS-02) (p. 68-77). Alexandria, VA.

Bourbakis, N., & Dollas, A. (2003). SCAN based multimedia-on-demand. I*EEE multimedia magazine, 79-87.*

Bourbakis, N., Rwabutaza, A., Yang, M., & Skondras, T. (2009). A synthetic stegano-crypto scheme for securing multimedia medical records. In Proceedings of the *2009 IEEE Digital signal processing and signal processing education workshop.*

Boyen, X. (2004). Reusable cryptographic fuzzy extractors. In Proceedings of the 11th ACM conference on *Computer and Communications Security (CCS'04) (p. 82-91).*

Boyko, V., MacKenzie, P., & Patel, S. (2000). Provably secure password-authenticated key exchange using Diffie-Hellman. In B. Preneel (Ed.), *Advances in Cryptology – Eurocrypt 2000 (pp. 156-171).* Berlin: Springer-Verlag. (Lecture Notes in Computer Science Volume 1807)

Brennan, L. L., & Johnson, V. E. (2001). A brave new e-world: technology management for corporate social responsibility. *In International Conference on Management of Engineering and Technology, 1,1.*

Briffa, J. A., & Das, M. (2002). Channel models for high-capacity information hiding in images. *In Proceedings of the SPIE, 4793.*

Brownlow, M. (2008). *E-mail and webmail statistics.* Retrieved from http://www.email-marketing-reports.com/metrics/email-statistics.htm

Bruce, V., & Langton, S. (1994). The use of pigmentation and shading information in recognising the sex and identities of faces. Perception, 23, 803–822. doi:10.1068/p230803

Brumley, D., & Boneh, D. (2003). Remote timing attacks are practical. *In Proceedings of the 12th USENIX Security Symposium.* Washington, DC.

Buchegger, S., & Boudec, J. (2004, June). A robust reputation system for P2P and mobile ad-hoc networks. *In*

Proc. Second Workshop the Economics of Peer-to-Peer Systems, Cambridge, MA.

Burge, M., & Burger, W. (2000). Ear biometrics for machine vision. *In Proceedings of ICPR (pp. 826-830).*

Caelli, J. W. (1994). Security in Open and Distributed Systems. *Information Management & Computer Security, 2(1).* doi:10.1108/09685229410058759

Callas, J., Donnerhacke, L., Finney, H., & Thayer, R. (1998). *OpenPGP Message Format.* RFC 2440

Camenisch, J., Shelat, A., Sommer, D., Hübner, S. F., Hansen, M., Krasemann, H., et al. (2005). *Privacy and Identity Management for Everyone*.* Paper presented at the 2005 Workshop on Digital Identity Management, Fairfax, VA.

Campbell, J. (1997). Speaker recognition: A tutorial. *Proceedings of the IEEE, 85(9), 1437–1462.* doi:10.1109/5.628714

Candebat, T., Dunne, C. R., & Gray, D. T. (2005). *Pseudonym management using mediated identity-based cryptography.* Paper presented at the Proceedings of the 2005 workshop on Digital identity management.

Canetti, R., & Rivest, R. L. (2004). 6.897 *selected topics in cryptography.* Retrieved from http://courses.csail.mit.edu/6.897/spring04/.

Castelfranchi, C., & Tan, Y.-H. (Eds.). (2001). *Trust and deception in virtual societies.* Boston: Kluwer Academic Publishers.

CCV. (2009). *Certificate chain verification.* Retrieved March 15, 2009, from http://publib.boulder.ibm.com/infocenter/tpfhelp/current/index.jsp?topic=/com.ibm.ztpf-ztpfdf.doc_put.cur/gtps5/s5vctch.html

Cerami, E. (2002). *Web services essentials* (O'Reilly XML). City, O'Reilly Media, Inc.

Cetingul, H. E., Yemez, Y., Erzin, E., & Tekalp, A. M. (2005, March 18-23). Robust Lip-Motion Features For Speaker Identification. *In Proceedings of IEEE International Conference on Acoustics, Speech, and Signal Processing, (pp. 509-512).*

Chae, J. J., & Manjunath, B. S. (1999). Data hiding in video. *In Proceedings of the 6th IEEE international conference on image processing (ICIP'99), 1, 311-315.*

Chan, H., Perrig, A., & Song, D. (2003). Random key predistribution schemes for sensor networks. *In Proceedings of the 2003 IEEE Symposium on Security and Privacy, 197-213.*

Chang, C., Chen, G., & Lin, M. (2004). Information hiding based on search-order coding for VQ indices. *Pattern Recognition Letters, 25,* 1253–1261. doi:10.1016/j.patrec.2004.04.003

Chaum, D. (1981). Untraceable electronic mail, return addresses, and digital pseudonyms. *Communications of the ACM, 24(2), 84–88.* doi:10.1145/358549.358563

Chaum, D. (2004a). Secret ballot receipts: True voter-verifiable elections. *CryptoBytes, 7(2), 13–26.*

Chaum, D. (2004b). Secret-ballot receipts: True voter-verifiable elections. *IEEE Security & Privacy, 2(1), 38–47.* doi:10.1109/MSECP.2004.1264852

Cheng, Q., & Huang, T. S. (2001). An additive approach to transform-domain information hiding andoptimum detection structure. *IEEE Transactions on Multimedia, 3(3), 273–284.* doi:10.1109/6046.944472

Cheshire, S. (2002). *Discovering Named Instances of Abstract Services using DNS, Apple Computer.* Retrieved from http://files.dns-sd.org/draft-cheshire-dnsext-dns-sd.txt

Chirillo, J., & Scott, B. (2003). *Implementing Biometric Security.* Indianapolis, IN: Wiley Publishing Inc.

Choras, M. (2008). Perspective methods of human identification: ear biometrics. *Opto-Electronics Review, 16(1), 85–96.* doi:10.2478/s11772-007-0033-5

Chuang, T. J., & Lin, J. C. (1999). A new multi-resolution approach to still image encryption. *Pattern recognition and image analysis, 9(3), 431-436.*

Ciet, M., Joye, M., Lauter, K. & Montgomery, P. L. (2006). Trading inversions for multiplications in elliptic curve cryptography. *Journal of Designs, Codes, and Cryptography. Springer-Verlag, 39, 189-206.*

Cilardo, A., Coppolino, L., Mazzocca, N., & Romano, L. (2006). Elliptic curve engineering. *Proceedings of the IEEE, 94(2),* 395–406. doi:10.1109/JPROC.2005.862438

Cnss.gov. (2003). *FACT SHEET CNSS Policy No. 15, Fact Sheet No. 1, National policy on the use of the advanced encryption standard (AES) to protect national security systems and national security information.* Retrieved from http://www.cnss.gov/Assets/pdf/cnssp_15_fs.pdf

Coffey, T., & Saidha, P. (1996). Non-repudiation with mandatory proof of receipt, ACMCCR. *Computer Communication Review, 26.*

Cohen Benaloh, J. (1986). Secret sharing homomorphisms: keeping shares of a secret secret. In A. M. Odlyzko (Ed.), *Advances in Cryptology - Crypto '86 (pp. 251-260).* Berlin, Germany: Springer-Verlag. (Lecture Notes in Computer Science Volume 263)

Cohen, J., & Fischer, M. (1985). A robust and verifiable cryptographically secure election scheme. *In Proceedings of the 26th IEEE Symposium on Foundations of Computer Science (p. 372-382).*

Cooper, D., Santesson, S., Farrell, S., Boeyen, S., Housley, R., & Polk, W. (2008). *Internet X.509 Public Key Infrastructure Certificate and Certificate Revocation List (CRL) Profile, RFC 5280,* at http://tools.ietf.org/html/rfc5280

Corporation, I. B. M. (1999). *XML security suite.* Retrieved from http://www.alphaworks.ibm.com/tech/xmlsecuritysuite

Costello, R. L. (2009). *Building Web services the REST way.* Retrieved from http://www.xfront.com/

Council, T. N. E. C. C. (2002). *Identity Management. Paper presented at the NECCC Annual Conference.* Retrieved December 15, 2007, from http://www.ec3.org/Downloads/2002/id_management.pdf

Cox, B., Tygar, J. D., & Sirbu, M. (1995). NetBill security and transaction protocol. In Proc. 1st USENIX *Workshop on Electronic Commerce, 77–88.*

Cox, I. J., Kilian, J., Leighton, T., & Shamoon, T. (1996). A secure, robust watermark for multimedia. *In Proceedings of the first international workshop on information hiding, 185-206.*

Cox, I., Miller, M., & Bloom, J. (2002). *Digital watermarking.* San Francisco: Morgan Kaufmann Publishers.

Cramer, R., Franklin, M. K., Schoenmakers, B., & Yung, M. (1996). Multi-authority secret-ballot elections with linear work. In U. Maurer (Ed.), *Advances in Cryptology - Eurocrypt '96 (pp. 72-83).* Berlin, Germany: Springer-Verlag. (Lecture Notes in Computer Science Volume 1070)

Cramer, R., Gennaro, R., & Schoenmakers, B. (1997). A secure and optimally efficient multi-authority election scheme. In W. Fumy (Ed.), *Advances in Cryptology - Eurocrypt '97 (pp. 103-118).* Berlin, Germany: Springer-Verlag. (Lecture Notes in Computer Science Volume 1233)

Crazy Squirrel. (2009). *How does e-mail work?* Retrieved from http://www.crazysquirrel.com/computing/debian/mail.jspx

Crescenzo, G., Ge, R., & Arce, G. R. (2005, November 7). Improved Topology Assumptions for Threshold Cryptography in Mobile Ad Hoc Networks. *In Proceedings of SASN'05.* Alexandria, VA.

Crispin, M. (1996). *Internet message access protocol-V4rev1. ietf.org* RFC: 2060.

Crispin, M. (2003). *Internet message access protocol-V4rev1. ietf.org* RFC: 3501.

Crocker, D. (2009). *E-mail history.* Retrieved from http://www.livinginternet.com

Crocker, S., Freed, N., Galvin, J., & Murphy, S. (1995). *MIME object security services RFC1848.* Retrieved from http://www.ietf.org/rfc/rfc1848.txt?number=1848

Crossbow Technology, Inc. (n.d.). *Crossbow product information.* Retrieved from http://www.xbow.com/Products/products.htm

Cui, J., Wang, Y., Huang, J., Tan, T., & Sun, Z. (2004). An iris image synthesis method based on PCA and super-resolution. *In Proceedings of the 17th International Conference on Pattern Recognition(ICPR), (pp. 471-474).*

Cvejic, N., & Seppanen, T. (2004). Channel capacity of high bit rate audio data hiding algorithms in diverse transform domains. *In Proceedings of the international symposium on communications and information technologies (ISCIT 2004).*

Czerwinski, S., Zhao, B. Y., Hodes, T., Joseph, A., & Katz, R. (1999). An Architecture for a Secure Service Discovery Service. *Fifth Annual International Conference on Mobile Computing and Networks (MobiCom '99)*, Seattle, WA.

Daemen, J., & Rijmen, V. (2002). *The Design of Rijndael: AES-The Advanced Encryption Standard.* Berlin-Heidelberg, Germany: Springer-Verlag.

Das, T. K., & Teng, B.-S. (1998). Between trust and control: Developing confidence in partner cooperation in alliances. *Academy of Management Review, 23(3), 491–512.* doi:10.2307/259291

Data Encryption Standard (DES). (1999). *Federal Information Processing Standards Publication.* Retrieved May 29, 2009, from http://csrc.nist.gov/publications/fips/fips46-3/fips46-3.pdf

Daugman, J. G. (1993). High confidence visual recognition of persons by a test of statistical independence. *IEEE Pattern Analysis and Machine Intelligence, 15(11).*

David, M. L. (2007). *The history of encryption and ciphers.* Retrieved from http://searchwarp.com/swa148381.htm

Davida, G. I., Frankel, Y., & Matt, B. J. (1998). On enabling secure applications through offline biometric identification. *In Proceedings of the 1998 IEEE Symposium on Security and Privacy (p. 148-157).*

Davis, Z. (2008). *An intro to elliptical curve cryptography.* Retrieved from http://www.deviceforge.com/

Denning, D., E., & Sacco, G., M. (1981). Timestamps in key distribution protocols. *Communications of the ACM, 24(8), 533–536.* doi:10.1145/358722.358740

Desmedt, Y., & Frankel, Y. (1990). Threshold cryptosystems. In Brassard, G. (Ed.), *Advances in Cryptology - Crypto '89 (pp. 307–315).* Berlin, Germany: Springer-Verlag. doi:10.1007/0-387-34805-0_28

Desmedt, Y., & Frankel, Y. (2000, February). Threshold cryptosystems. *Advances in Cryptology – Crypto '89, LNCS vol. 435*, Berlin, Germany: Springer-Verlag.

Desmedt, Y., & Kurosawa, K. (2000). How to break a practical MIX and design a new one. In B. Preneel (Ed.), *Advance in Cryptology - Eurocrypt 2000 (pp. 557-572).* Berlin, Germany: Springer-Verlag. (Lecture Notes in Computer Science Volume 1807)

Dierks, T., & Allen, C. (1999). T*he TLS protocol version 1.0. RFC 2246.* Retrieved from http://www.ietf.org/rfc/rfc2246.txt?number=2246

Diffie, W., & Hellman, M. E. (1976). New Directions in Cryptography. *IEEE Transactions on Information Theory, IT-22(6), 644–654.* doi:10.1109/TIT.1976.1055638

Diffie, W., & Hellman, M. E. (2009). *Diffie-Hellman key exchange.* Retrieved March 15, 2009, from http://en.wikipedia.org/wiki/Diffie-Hellman

Dingledine, R., Mathewson, N., & Syverson, P. (2004). Tor: The second-generation onion router. *In Proceedings of the 13th USENIX Security Symposium, 303–320.*

Djajadinata, R. (2002). *XML encryption keeps your XML documents safe and secure.* Retrieved from http://www.javaworld.com/javaworld/jw-08-2002/jw-0823-securexml.html

Dodis, Y., Ostrovsky, R., Reyzin, L., & Smith, A. (2008). Fuzzy extractors: How to generate strong keys from biometrics and other noisy data. *SIAM Journal on Computing, 38(1), 97–139.* doi:10.1137/060651380

Dodis, Y., Reyzin, L., & Smith, A. (2004). Fuzzy extractors: How to generate strong keys from biometrics and other noisy data. In C. Cachin & J. Camenisch (Eds.), *Advance in Cryptology – Eurocrypt 2004 (pp. 523-540).* Berlin: Springer-Verlag. (Lecture Notes in Computer Science Volume 3027)

Dolev, D., & Yao, A. C. (1981). On the security of public key protocols. *In Proceedings of the IEEE 22nd An-*

nual Symposium on Foundations of Computer Science, *350-357.*

Doney, P. M., & Cannon, J. P. (1997). An examination of the nature of trust in buyer-seller relationships. *Journal of Marketing, 61(4), 35–51.* doi:10.2307/1251829

Dournaee, B. (2002). *XML security.* New York: McGraw-Hill Osborne Media.

Drummond, R. (1996). *Brief comparison of e-mail encryption protocols.* Retrieved from http://www.imc.org/ietf-ediint/old-archive/msg00117.html

Du, W., Deng, J., Han, Y. S., Varshney, P. K., Katz, J., & Khalili, A. (2005). A pairwise key pre-distribution scheme for wireless sensor networks. [TISSEC]. *ACM Transactions on Information and System Security, 8(2), 228–258.* doi:10.1145/1065545.1065548

Dusse, S., Hoffman, P., Ramsdell, B., Lundblade, L., & Repka, L. (1998). *S/MIME version 2 message specification. RFC 2311*

Dworkin, M. (2001). Recommendation for Block Cipher Modes of Operation *NIST Special Publication 800-38A.* Retrieved from http://csrc.nist.gov/publications/PubsSPs.html

Dworkin, M. (2004). Recommendation for Block Cipher Modes of Operation: The CCM Mode for Authentication and Confidentiality. *NIST Special Publication 800-38C* Retrieved from http://csrc.nist.gov/publications/PubsSPs.html

Dworkin, M. (2005). Recommendation for Block Cipher Modes of Operation: The CMAC Mode for Authentication. *NIST Special Publication 800-38B* Retrieved from http://csrc.nist.gov/publications/PubsSPs.html

Dworkin, M. (2007). Recommendation for Block Cipher Modes of Operation: Galois/Counter Mode (GCM) and GMAC. *NIST Special Publication 800-38C* Retrieved from http://csrc.nist.gov/publications/PubsSPs.html

Eastlake, D. E., & Niles, K. (2002). *Secure XML: The new syntax for signatures and encryption.* Pearson Education.

Eastlake, D., & Motorola, P. J. (2001). *US secure hash algorithm 1 (SHA1).* RFC: 3174.

Eddy, W. (2007). TCP SYN *Flooding Attacks and Common Mitigations,* RFC 4987, at http://www.ietf.org/rfc/rfc4987.txt

Edge, C., Barker, W., & Smith, Z. (2007). *A brief history of cryptography (reprint).* Retrieved from http://www.318.com/techjournal/?p=5

Eide, K. (2004). *The next generation of mail clients.* Retrieved from http://home.dataparty.no/kristian/reviews/nextgen-mua/

ElGamal, T. (1985). A Public-Key Cryptosystem and a Signature Scheme Based on Discrete Logarithms. *IEEE Transactions on Information Theory, IT-31(4), 469–472.* doi:10.1109/TIT.1985.1057074

Elkins, M., Torto, D. D., Levien, R., & Roessler, T. (2001). *MIME security with OpenPGP: RFC 3156.* Retrieved from http://www.faqs.org/rfcs/rfc3156.html

Ellison, C., & Schneier, B. (2000). Ten Risks of PKI: What You're not Being Told about Public Key Infrastructure. *Computer Security Journal, 16.*

Ellison, C., Hall, C., Milbert, R., & Schneier, B. (2000, February). Protecting secret keys with personal entropy. *Journal of Future Generation Computer Systems, 16(4), 311–318.* doi:10.1016/S0167-739X(99)00055-2

Encryptomatic.com. (2008). *HIPAA: The Health Insurance Portability and Accountability Act of 1996.* Retrieved from http://www.encryptomatic.com/about-us/index.html

Erickson, J. S. (2003). Fair use, DRM, and trusted computing. *Communications of the ACM, 46(4), 34–39.* doi:10.1145/641205.641228

Ertaul, L., & Chavan, N. (2005). Wireless Networks. *In Proceedings. The third International Conference on Wireless Networks, Communications, and Mobile Computing June 13-16, 2005,* (MobiWac) 2005, Maui, Hawaii.

Eschenauer, L., & Gligor, V. (2002). A key-management scheme for distributed sensor networks. *In Proceedings of the 9th ACM Conference on Computer and Communication Security* (Washington, D.C., Nov.). New York: ACM Press.

Eschenauer, L., & Gligor, V. D. (2002, November). A key-management scheme for distributed sensor networks. *In Proceedings of the 9th ACM conference on Computer and communications,* Washington DC.

Eschenauer, L., Gligor, V., & Baras, J. (2002, April). On trust establishment in mobile ad-hoc networks. *In Proceedings of the Security Protocols Workshop.*

Evans, N. S., Dingledine, R., & Grothoff, C. (2009). *A Practical Congestion Attack on Tor Using Long Paths.* To be presented at the 18th USENIX Security Symposium, Montreal, Canada.

Everitt, K. M., Bragin, T., Fogarty, J., & Kohno, T. (2009). A comprehensive study of frequency, interference, and training of multiple graphical passwords. *Paper presented at the Proceedings of the 27th international conference on Human factors in computing systems.*

Fabian, M., & Rubin, A. D. (2000). Keystroke dynamics as a biometric for authentication. *FGCS Journal: Security on the Web, 16(4), 351–359.*

Fàbregas, J., & Faundez-Zanuy, M. (2008). Biometric dispersion matcher. *Pattern Recognition, 41(11), 3412–3426.* doi:10.1016/j.patcog.2008.04.020

Faundez-Zanuy, M. (2004). On the vulnerability of biometric security systems. *IEEE Aerospace and Electronic Systems Magazine, 19(6), 3–8.* doi:10.1109/MAES.2004.1308819

Faundez-Zanuy, M. (2005). Biometric recognition: why not massively adopted yet? *IEEE Aerospace and Electronic Systems Magazine Part 1, 20(8), 25-28.*

Federal Information Processing Standards Publication 197 *Announcing the ADVANCED ENCRYPTION STANDARD (AES)* November 26, 2001

Federal Information. (1993). *Secure hash standard.* Processing standards publication 180-1 FIPS PUB 180-1 Supersedes FIPS PUB 180.

Federal Register. (2005, May 19). Announcing approval of the withdrawal of Federal Information. *Federal Register, 70(96),* 28907.

Fei, C., Kundur, D., & Kwong, R. (2001). The choice of watermark domain in the presence of compression. In Proceedings of international conference on information technology: *Coding and computing, 79-84.*

Felten, E., W. (2003). A skeptical view of DRM and fair use. *Communications of the ACM, 46(4), 56–59.* doi:10.1145/641205.641232

Feng, Y., Liu, Z., & Li, J. (n.d.). Securing Membership Control in Mobile Ad Hoc Networks. *In Proceedings of the 9th International Conference on Information Technology (ICIT'06), (pp. 160-163).*

Ferguson, N., & Schneier, B. (2003). *Practical cryptography.* New York: Wiley.

Fernandez, E. B. (2002). *Web services security current status and the future.* Retrieved from http://www.web-servicesarchitect.com/content/articles/fernandez01.asp

Ferrer-Gomila, J. L., Payeras-Capella, M., & Huguet-Rotger, L. (2001). Efficient optimistic n-party contract signing protocol. *2001 Information Security Conference, LNCS 2200, pages 394-407,* Berlin, Germany: Springer.

Fielding, R., Gettys, J., Mogul, J., Frystyk, H., Masinter, L., Leach, P., & Berners-Lee, T. *Hypertext transfer protocol -- HTTP/1.1.* Retrieved from http://www.ietf.org/rfc/rfc2616.txt

Fierrez-Aguilar, J., Ortega-Garcia, J., & Gonzalez-Rodriguez, J. (2005, August). Target dependent score normalization techniques and their application to signature verification. *IEEE Transactions on Systems, Man and Cybernetics. Part C, Applications and Reviews, 35(3), 418–425.* doi:10.1109/TSMCC.2005.848181

FIPS. (2001, November). *Federal Information Processing Standards.* Retrieved from http://csrc.nist.gov/publications/fips/fips197/fips-197.pdf

Florencio, D., & Herley, C. (2007). A large-scale study of web password habits. Paper presented at WWW'07:

Proceedings of the 16th international conference on World Wide Web, pages 657-666, New York: ACM Press

Franks, J., HallamBaker, P., Hostetler, J., Lawrence, S., Leach, P., Luotonen, A., & Stewart, L. (1999, June). *HTTP authentication: basic and digest access authentication. Internet RFC 2617.*

Franks, J., Hallam-Baker, P., Hostetler, J., Lawrence, S., Leach, P., Luotonen, A. & Stewart. L. (1999). *HTTP Authentication: Basic and Digest Access Authentication.*

Freed, N. (2008). *Name and filename parameters.* Retrieved from http://www.imc.org/ietf-smtp/mail-archive/msg05023.html

Frier, A., Karlton, P., & Kocher, P. (1996, November 18). *The SSL 3.0 protocol.* Netscape Communications Corp.

Fukuyama, F. (1995). T*rust: The social virtues and the creation of prosperity.* New York: The Free Press.

Furukawa, J., & Sako, K. (2001). An efficient scheme for proving a shuffle. In Kilian, J. (Ed.), *Crypto 01 (Vol. 2139, pp. 368–387).* Berlin, Germany: Springer-Verlag.

Gafurov, D. Snekkenes, E. & Bours, P. (2007, 7-8 June). Gait Authentication and Identification Using Wearable Accelerometer Sensor. *In IEEE Workshop on Automatic Identification Advanced Technologies, (pp. 220-225).*

Gagbla, G. K. (2005). *Applying Keystroke Dynamics for Personal Authentication,* Retrieved October 31, 2008, from http://www.bth.se/fou/cuppsats.nsf/all/0b5c15287d33f3efc1257013007025a3/$file/thesis_report.pdf

Gaines, R. S., Lisowski, W., Press, S. J., & Shapiro, N. (1980). *Authentication by Keystroke Timing: Some Preliminary Results.* Retrieved September 6, 2008, from http://www.rand.org/pubs/reports/R2526/

Galbraith, S. (2005). Pairings. Blake, Seroussi, & Smart (Eds.), *Advances in elliptic curve cryptography,* London Mathematical Society Lecture Notes, chapter IX, 183–213. Cambridge, UK: Cambridge University Press.

Galvin, J., Murphy, G., Crocker, S., & Freed, N. (1995). S*ecurity multiparts for MIME: Multipart/signed and multipart/encrypted*: RFC 1847. Retrieved from http://www.faqs.org/rfcs/rfc1847.html

Gamassi, M., Lazzaroni, M., Misino, M., Piuri, V., Sana, D., & Scotti, F. (2005, August). Quality assessment of biometric systems: a comprehensive perspective based on accuracy and performance measurement. *IEEE Transactions on Instrumentation and Measurement, 54(4), 1489–1496.* doi:10.1109/TIM.2005.851087

Garay, J., & MacKenzie, P. (1999). *Abuse-free multiparty contract signing.* 1999 International Symposium on Distributed Computing, LNCS 1693, pages 151-165, Berlin, Germany: Springer.

Garbarino, E., & Johnson, M. S. (1999). The different roles of satisfaction, trust, and commitment in customer relationships. *Journal of Marketing, 63(2), 70–87.* doi:10.2307/1251946

Garfinkel, S. L., Margrave, D., Schiller, J. I., Nordlander, E., & Miller, R. C. (2005). *How to Make Secure E-mail Easier To Use. CHI 2005,* Portland, OR.

Garman, J. (2003). *Kerberos: The definitive guide.* New York: O'Reilly.

Gasser, U., Bambauer, D., Harlow, J., Hoffmann, C., Hwang, R., Krog, G., et al. (2004). *iTunes: How Copyright, Contract, and Technology Shape the Business of Digital Media – A Case Study. Digital Media Project,* from http://cyber.law.harvard.edu/media/uploads/53/GreenPaperiTunes03.04.pdf

Gefen, D., Rose, G., Warkentin, M., & Pavlou, P. (2005). Cultural diversity and trust in IT adoption: A comparison of potential e-Voters in the USA and South Africa. *Journal of Global Information Management, 13(1), 54–79.*

Geffen, D., Karahanna, E., & Straub, D. (2003, March). Trust and TAM in Online Shopping: An Integrated Model. *Management Information Systems Quarterly, 27(1), 51–90.*

Gemmel, P. (1997). An introduction to threshold cryptography. *In Proceedings of CryptoBytes, Winter 1997, 7–12.*

Gennaro, R., Jarecki, S., Krawczyk, H., & Rabin, T. (1996). Robust and efficient sharing of RSA functions. *In Proceedings of CRYPTO.*

Gennaro, R., Jarecki, S., Krawczyk, H., & Rabin, T. (1996). Robust threshold DSS signatures. *In Proceedings of EUROCRYPT.*

Gentry, C., & MacKenzie, P. D., & Ramzan, Z. (2006). A Method for Making Password-Based Key Exchange Resilient to Server Compromise. Paper presented at *CRYPTO2006.*

Ghosh, A. K. (1998). *E-Commerce Security: Weak Links, Best Defenses.* New York: John Wiley & Sons, Inc.

Glass, E. (2006). *The NTLM authentication protocol and security support provider.* Retrieved from http://davenport.sourceforge.net/ntlm.html

Goldreich, O., Micali, S., & Wigderson, A. (1987). Proof that yield nothing but their validity and a methodology of cryptographic protocol design. *In Proc. 27th IEEE Symposium on Foundations of Computer Science.*

Goldreich, O., Micali, S., & Wigderson, A. (1991). Proofs that yield nothing but their validity or all languages in NP have zero-knowledge proof systems. *Journal of the ACM, 38(3),* 691–729. doi:10.1145/116825.116852

Goldschlag, D. M., Reed, M. G., & Syverson, P. F. (1999). Onion routing. *Communications of the ACM, 42(2),* 39–41. doi:10.1145/293411.293443

Golfarelli, M., Maio, D., & Maltoni, D. (1997). On the error-reject trade-off in biometric verification systems. *IEEE Pattern Analysis and Machine Intelligence, 19(7),* 786–796. doi:10.1109/34.598237

Golle, P. (2008). Machine learning attacks against the Asirra CAPTCHA. *In Proceedings of the 15th ACM Conference on Computer and Communications Security (p. 535-542).* Alexandria, VA.

Golle, P., Zhong, S., Boneh, D., Jakobsson, M., & Juels, A. (2002). Optimistic mixing for exit-polls. In Zheng, Y. (Ed.), *Asiacrypt 2002 (Vol. 2501, pp. 451–465).* Berlin, Germany: Springer-Verlag. doi:10.1007/3-540-36178-2_28

Gong, L., Lomas, M. A., Needham, R. M., & Saltzer, J. H. Protecting Poorly Chosen Secrets from Guessing Attacks. *IEEE Journal on Selected Areas in Communications, 11(5).*

Gorman, L. O. (2003). Comparing passwords, tokens, and biometrics for user authentication. *Proceedings of the IEEE, 91(12),* 2019–2040. doi:10.1109/JPROC.2003.819605

Grothe, P., & Tabassi, E. (2007, April). Performance of Biometric Quality Measures. *IEEE Transactions on Pattern Analysis and Machine Intelligence, 29(4),* 531–543. doi:10.1109/TPAMI.2007.1019

Grzonkowski, S., & McDaniel, B. FRM: Towards a Semantic Platform for Fair Content Distribution. Paper presented at AXMEDIS'08: Proceedings of the Fourth International Conference on Automated Production of Cross Media Content for Multi-Channel Distribution. *IEEE Computer Society, November 2008.*

Grzonkowski, S., Ensor, B., Kruk, S. R., Gzella, A., Decker, S., & McDaniel, B. (2007). *A DRM Solution Based on Social Networks and Enabling the Idea of Fair Use.* Paper presented at the Media in Transition: creativity, ownership and collaboration in the digital age (MiT5).

Guha, R., Kumar, R., Raghavan, P., & Tomkins, A. (2004). Propagation of Trust and Distrust. *In Proceedings of the 13th International Conference on WWW, New York.*

Gunsel, B., Uludag, U., & Tekalp, A. M. (2002). Robust watermarking of fingerprint images. *Journal of pattern recognition, 35(12),* 2739-2747.

Gupta, P., Ravi, S., Raghunathan, A., & Jha, N. K. (2005, June). Efficient Fingerprint-based User Authentication for Embedded Systems. Annual ACM IEEE Design Automation Conference: *In Proceedings of the 42nd annual conference on Design automation; 13-17 June 2005.*

Gura, N., Patel, A., & Wander, A. (2004). Comparing elliptic curve cryptography and RSA on 8-bit CPUs. *In Proceedings of the 2004 Workshop on Cryptographic Hardware and Embedded Systems (CHES 2004),* 119–132.

Gurski, M. A. (1995). *Privacy-enhanced mail (PEM).* Retrieved from http://www.cs.umbc.edu/~woodcock/cmsc482/proj1/pem.html

Gutmann, P. (2006). *"Everything you Never Wanted to Know about PKI but were Forced to Find Out"*, www.cs.auckland.ac.nz/~pgut001/pubs/pkitutorial.pdf

Guttman, E., Perkins, C., Veizades, J., & Day, M. (1999). *Service Location Protocol, Version 2*. Retrieved from http://www.ietf.org/rfc/rfc2608.txt

Hagens, R., & Hansen, A. (1994). Operational requirements for X.400 management domains in the GO-MHS community. Retrieved from http://tools.ietf.org/html/rfc1649

Hagens, R., & Hansen, A. (1994). *Operational requirements for X.400 management domains in the GO-MHS community*. Retrieved from http://tools.ietf.org/html/rfc1649

Halevi, S., & Krawczyk, H. Public-Key Cryptography and Password Protocols. *ACM Transactions on Information and System Security, 2(3)*.

Hankerson, D., Menezes, A., & Vanstone, S. (2004). *Guide to Elliptic Curve Cryptography*. Berlin-Heidelberg, Germany: Springer-Verlag.

Hansen, M., Berlich, P., Camenisch, J., Clauß, S., Pfitzmann, A., & Waidner, M. (2004). Privacy-enhancing identity management. *Information Security Technical Report, 9(1)*, 35–44. doi:10.1016/S1363-4127(04)00014-7

Harkins, D., & Carrel, D. (1998, November). *The Internet Key Exchange (IKE)*. Internet Request For Comments 2409.

Harris, A. J., & Yen, D. C. (2002). Biometric authentication: assuring access to information. Information *Management & Computer Security, 10(1), 12*. doi:10.1108/09685220210417463

Hartman, B., Flinn, D. J., Beznosov, K., & Kawamoto, S. (2003). *Mastering Web services security*. New York: Wiley Publishing.

Herzberg, A., Jarecki, S., Krawczyk, H., & Yung, M. (1995). How to cope with perpetual leakage. *In Proceedings of Crypto'95, LNCS 963 (pp. 339–352)*. Proactive Secret Sharing or.

Hirsch, F. (2002). *Getting Started with XML Security*. Retrieved from http://www.sitepoint.com/article/getting-started-xml-security/

HMAC. (2002). T*he Keyed-Hash Message Authentication Code (HMAC)*. FIPS PUB 198. NIST.

Hoffman, D. L., Novak, T. P., & Peralta, M. (1999). Building Consumer Trust Online. *Communications of the ACM, 42(4)*, 80–85. doi:10.1145/299157.299175

Hoffman, P. (1999). *SMTP service extension for secure SMTP over TLS: RFC 2487*. Retrieved from http://www.ietf.org/rfc/rfc2487.txt?number=2487

Hoffmann, M. (2004). *User-centric Identity Management in Open Mobile Environments*. Paper presented at the Workshop on Security and Privacy in Pervasive Computing, Vienna, Austria.

Hong, L., Jain, A. K., & Pankanti, S. (1999, October). Can multibiometrics improve performance? *In Proceedings of AutoID'99 (pp. 59–64)*. NJ: Summit.

Hong, L., Pankanti, S., & Prabhakar, S. (2000). Filterbank-based fingerprint matching. *IEEE Transactions on Image Processing, 9(5), 846–859*. doi:10.1109/83.841531

Hosmer, L. (1995). Trust: The Connecting Link Between Organizational Theory and Philosophical Ethics. *Academy of Management Review, 20(2), 379–403*. doi:10.2307/258851

Housley, R. (1999). *Cryptographic message syntax RFC: 2630*. Retrieved from http://www.ietf.org/rfc/rfc2630.txt

Housley, R. (2004). *Cryptographic message syntax (CMS): RFC 3852*. Retrieved from http://www.ietf.org/rfc/rfc3852.txt

Housley, R., & Solinas, J. (2007). *Suite B in secure/multipurpose Internet mail extension: RFC5008*. Retrieved from http://www.rfc-editor.org/rfc/rfc5008.txt

Housley, R., Ford, W., Polk, W., & Solo, D. (1999). *Internet X.509 Public Key Infrastructure: Certificate and CRL Profile. RFC 2459*

Houttuin, J., & Craigie, J. (1994). *Migrating from X.400(84) to X.400(88) RFC1615*. Retrieved from http://www.faqs.org/rfcs/rfc1615.html

Hu, J., & Burmester, M. (2006). LARS: a locally aware reputation system for mobile ad hoc networks. In Ronaldo Menezes, editor, *ACM Southeast Regional Conference, (pp119–123).*

Huang, Q., Cukier, J., Kobayashi, H., Liu, B., & Zhang, J. (2003, September). *Fast Authenticated Key Establishment Protocols for Self-Organizing Sensor Networks.* Paper presented at the Proceedings of the 2nd ACM international conference on Wireless sensor networks and applications, San Diego.

Hurley, D. J., Arbab-Zavar, B., & Nixon, M. S. (nd.). *The Ear as a Biometric.* Retrieved 14 Octobor, 2008, from http://eprints.ecs.soton.ac.uk/15725/1/hurleyzavarandnixon.pdf

Iannarelli, A. (1989). *Ear Identification. Forensic Identification Series.* Texas: Paramount Publishing Company.

IBM. (2009) *Application Server - Express for IBM i,* Version 7.0 http://publib.boulder.ibm.com

Ibm.com. (2008). Creating a secure sockets layer configuration. Retrieved from http://publib.boulder.ibm.com/

Ietf.org. (1988). X.400(1988) *for the academic and research community in Europe RFC1616.* Retrieved from http://www.ietf.org/rfc/rfc1616.txt

Ietf.org. (2008). *Public-key infrastructure.* Retrieved from Retrieved from http://www.ietf.org/html.charters/pkix-charter.html

IMC-SMIME. (2006). *S/MIME and OpenPGP.* Internet Mail Consortium.

International Biometric Group. (2006). *Comparative Biometric Testing.* Retrieved August 18, 2008, from http://www.biometricgroup.com/reports/public/reports/CBT6_report.htm

International Biometric Group. (2007). *Biometrics Market and Industry Report 2007-2012.* Retrieved August 28, 2008, from http://www.biometricgroup.com/reports/public/market_report.html

International Biometric Group. (n.d.). *Which is the Best Biometric Technology?* Retrieved September 18, 2008, from http://www.biometricgroup.com/reports/public/reports/best_biometric.html

Internet Broadcasting Systems. (2004, November 4). *Broward vote-counting blunder changes amendment result.* Published at News4Jax.com, Retrieved from http://www.news4jax.com/politics/3890292/detail.html

ISO/IEC 13888-1 (1997a). *Information technology - Security techniques - Non-repudiation - Part 1: General*

ISO/IEC 13888-2 (1998). *Information technology - Security techniques - Non-repudiation - Part 2: Mechanisms using symmetric techniques*

ISO/IEC 13888-3 (1997b). *Information technology - Security techniques - Non-repudiation - Part 3: Mechanisms using asymmetric techniques*

ITU. (2005). T-REC-X.509-200508-I *information technology - Open systems interconnection - The directory: Authenticationframework.* Retrieved from http://www.itu.int/rec/T-REC-X.509-200508-I/en

Jablon, D. (1997). Extended password key exchange protocols immune to dictionary attack. *In Proceedings of the 6th IEEE Workshops on Enabling Technologies: Infrastructure for collaborative enterprises (pp. 248-255).*

Jablon, D. P. (1996). Strong password-only authenticated key exchange. *ACM SIGCOMM Computer Communication Review, 26(5), 5–26.* doi:10.1145/242896.242897

Jain, A. K., Bolle, R., & Pankanti, S. (Eds.). (1999). *BIOMETRICS: Personal identification in networked society.* London: Kluwer Academic Publishers.

Jain, A. K., Flynn, P. J., & Ross, A. (2007). *Handbook of Biometrics.* New York: Springer-Verlag.

Jain, A. K., Hong, L., Pankanti, S., & Bolle, R. (1997). An identity authentication system using fingerprints. *Proceedings of the IEEE, 85(9), 1365–1388.* doi:10.1109/5.628674

Jain, A. K., Ross, A., & Prabhakar, S. (2004). An introduction to biometric recognition. *IEEE Trans. on Circuits and Systems for Video Technology, 14(1), 4–19.* doi:10.1109/TCSVT.2003.818349

Jain, A., Pankanti, S., & Prabhakar, S. (2002). On the individuality of fingerprints. *IEEE Transactions on Pattern Analysis and Machine Intelligence, 24(8), 1010–1025.* doi:10.1109/TPAMI.2002.1023799

Jakobsson, M. (1998). A practical mix. In K. Nyberg (Ed.), *Eurocrypt '98 (pp. 448-461)*. Berlin, Germany: Springer-Verlag. (Lecture Notes in Computer Science Volume 1403)

Jakobsson, M. (1999). Flash mixing. *In Proceedings of the Eighteenth Annual ACM Symposium on Principles of Distributed Computing (PODC 99) (pp. 83-89).*

Jakobsson, M., & Juels, A. (1999). *Millimix: Mixing in small batches* (Tech. Rep. No. 99-33). DIMACS.

Jakobsson, M., & Juels, A. (2001). An optimally robust hybrid mix network. *In Proceedings of the Twentieth Annual ACM Symposium on Principles of Distributed Computing (PODC 01).*

Jakobsson, M., Juels, A., & Rivest, R. L. (2002). Making mix nets robust for electronic voting by randomized partial checking. In D. Boneh (Ed.), *In Proceedings of the USENIX Security '02 (p. 339-353)*. San Francisco.

Javed, A., Ostrowski, R. S., & McNally, L. C. (2003). *Twins.* Retrieved October 18, 2008, from http://education.uncc.edu/cmste/Document%20Hold-OLD/Twins2003.doc

Jobs, S. (2007). *Thoughts on Music.* Retrieved from http://www.apple.com/hotnews/thoughtsonmusic/

Jøsang, A., Fabre, J., Hay, B., Dalziel, J., & Pope, S. (2005). *Trust requirements in identity management.* Paper presented at the Proceedings of the 2005 Australasian workshop on Grid computing and e-research - Volume 44.

Juels, A., & Sudan, M. (2002). A fuzzy vault scheme. *In Proceedings of the IEEE International Symposium on Information Theory (ISIT 2002)*. Lausanne, Switzerland.

Juels, A., & Sudan, M. (2006). A fuzzy vault scheme. *Designs, Codes and Cryptography, 38(2), 237–257.* doi:10.1007/s10623-005-6343-z

Juels, A., & Wattenberg, M. (1999). A fuzzy commitment scheme. *In Proceedings of the Sixth ACM Conference on Computer and Communication Security (p. 28-36).*

Jupp, V., & Shine, S. (2001). Government portals: The next generation of government online. *In Proceedings of the 1st European Conference on E-Government (pp. 217-223).*

Kahn, D. (1996). *The Code-Breakers: The Comprehensive History of Secret Communication from Ancient Times to the Internet.* New York: Scribner.

Kaliski, B. (1993). *Privacy enhancement for Internet electronic mail: Part IV: Key certification and related services RFC 1424.* Retrieved from http://www.ietf.org/rfc/rfc1424.txt

Karl, H., & Willig, A. (2005). *Protocols and Architecture for Wireless Sensor Networks.* New York: John Wiley & Sons. doi:10.1002/0470095121

Karlof, C., Sastry, N., & Wagner, D. (2004, June). *TinyOS: User Manual.* Retrieved February 10, 2009, from http://www.tinyos.net/tinyos-1.x/doc/tinysec.pdf.

Karlof, C., Sastry, N., & Wagner, D. (2004, November 3-5). TinySec: A Link Layer Security Architecture for Wireless Sensor Networks. *In Proceedings of the 2nd international conference on Embedded networked sensor systems (SenSys '04)*, Baltimore.

Katz, J., & Lindell, Y. (2007). Introduction to modern cryptography: Principles and protocols (Chapman & Hall/CRC *cryptography and network security series, 1st ed.*). Boca Raton, FL: Chapman & Hall/CRC.

Katz, J., Ostrovsky, R., & Yung, M. (2001). Efficient password-authenticated key exchange using human-memorable passwords. In B. Pfitzann (Ed.), *Advances in Cryptology – Eurocrypt 2001 (pp. 475-494)*. Berlin: Springer-Verlag. (Lecture Notes in Computer Science Volume 2045)

Kaufman, C. (2005, December). *Internet key exchange (IKEv2) protocol.* IETF Request for Comments: 4306.

Kaynak, M. N., Zhi, Q., Cheok, A. D., Sengupta, K., Jian, Z., & Chung, K. C. (2004). Analysis of lip geometric features for audio-visual speech recognition. *IEEE Transactions on Systems, Man and Cybernetics. Part A, 34(4), 564–570.*

Kekre, H. B., Athawale, A., & Halarnkar, P. N. (2008). Increased capacity of information hiding in LSB's method for text and image. *International journal of electrical, computer, and systems engineering.*

Kelm, S. (2008). *The PKI page.* Retrieved from http://www.pki-page.org/

Kemp, R., Pike, G., White, P., & Musselman, A. (1996). Perception and recognition of normal and negative faces: the role of shape from-shading and pigmentation cues. *Perception, 25, 37–52.* doi:10.1068/p250037

Kent, S. (1993). *Privacy enhancement for Internet electronic mail: Part II: Certificate-based key management RFC 1422.* Retrieved from http://www.ietf.org/rfc/rfc1422.txt

Kessler, G. C. (2009). *An Overview of Cryptography.* Retrieved from http://www.garykessler.net/library/crypto.html#intro

Khalili, A. Katz, J., & Arbaugh, W. (2003). Toward Secure Key Distribution in Truly Ad-Hoc Networks. *In Proceedings of the 2003 Symposium on Applications and the Internet Workshops* (SAINT-w'03).

Khosrow-Pour, M. (Ed.). (2004). *E-Commerce security: Advice from experts (IT solutions series).* New York: Cybertech Publishing.

Kim, J., & Moon, Y. (1999). A robust wavelet-based digital watermark using level-adaptive thresholding. *In Proceedings of the IEEE international conference on image processing* (ICIP '99).

Kim, S., & Montalto, C. P. (2002). Perceived risk of privacy invasion and the use of online technology by consumers. *Consumer Interests Annual, 48, 1–9.*

Kim, Y., Howard, J., Ravindranath, S., & Park, J. S. (2008). *Problem Analyses and Recommendations in DRM Security Policies Intelligence and Security Informatics (Vol. 5376, pp. 165–178).* Berlin, Germany: Springer.

Kiruba, M. (n.d.). *Biometrics.* Retrieved September 09, 2008, from http://ezinearticles.com/?Biometrics&id=16097

Klein, D. (1990). Foiling the cracker: A survey of, and improvements to, password security. *In Proceedings of the UNIX Security Workshop II.*

Klima, V., Pokorny, O., & Rosa, T. (2003). *Attacking RSA-based sessions in SSL/TLS.* Cryptology ePrint Archive, Report 2003/052

Koblitz, N. (1987). Elliptic curve cryptosystems. *Mathematics of Computation, 48, 203–209.*

Koch, E., & Zhao, J. (1995). Toward robust and hidden image copyright labeling. *In Proceedings of IEEE workshop on nonlinear signal and image processing, 452-455.*

Kohl, J. T., Neuman, B. C., & Ts'o, T. Y. (1991). The evolution of the Kerberos authentication service. *In Proceedings of the Spring 1991* EurOpen Conference.

Kohl, J., & Neuman, C. (1993, September). *The Kerberos network authentication service (V5).* Internet RFC 1510.

Kohno, T., Stubblefield, A., Rubin, A., & Wallach, D. (2004). Analysis of an electronic voting system. *In Proceedings of the 2004 IEEE Symposium on Security and Privacy (p. 2740).*

Kong, A., Zhang, D., & Lu, G. (2005). *A Study of Identical Twins' Palmprints for Personal Authentication. Advances in Biometrics.* Berlin, Germany: Springer.

Kong, J., Zerfos, P., Luo, H., Lu, S., & Zhang, L. (2001). Providing robust and ubiquitous security support for mobile ad-hoc networks. *In Proceedings of the IEEE ICNP.*

Köpsell, S., Wendolsky, R., & Federrath, H. (2006). *Revocable Anonymity.* Paper presented at the Emerging Trends in Information and Communication Security; ETRICS 2006, Freiburg, Germany.

Koster, P., Kamperman, F., Lenoir, P., & Vrielink, K. (2006). Identity-Based DRM: Personal Entertainment Domain. *Transactions on Data Hiding and Multimedia Security, I, 104–122.* doi:10.1007/11926214_4

Kremer, S., & Markowitch, O. (2000). *Optimistic non-repudiable information exchange*. In J. Biemond (Ed.), 21st Symp. on Information Theory in the Benelux, Werkgemeenschap Informatie- en Communicatietheorie. Enschede (NL), Wassenaar (NL), 2000, (pp. 139–146).

Kruk, S. R., Grzonkowski, S., Gzella, A., Woroniecki, T., & Choi, H. C. (2006, September). D-FOAF: *Distributed Identity Management with Access Rights Delegation*. Paper presented at the procedings of Asian Semantic Web Conference 2006.

Kuanchin, C., & Rea, A. L. Jr. (2004). Protecting personal information online privacy concerns and control techniques. *Journal of Computer Information Systems, 44(4), 85–92*.

Kundur, D. (2000). Implications for high capacity data hiding in the presence of lossy compression. *In Proceedings of the international conference on information technology: Coding and computing, 16-21*.

Kuo, C. J. (1993). Novel image encryption technique and its application in progressive transmission. *Journal of Electronic Imaging, 2(4), 345–351*. doi:10.1117/12.148572

Laboratories, R. S. A. (1999). *PKCS #5 v2.0 password-based cryptography standard*. Available from http://www.rsasecurity.com/rsalabs/pkcs/pkcs-5/

Langelaar, G. C., Setyawan, I., & Lagendijk, R. L. (2000). Watermarking digital image and video data: a state-of-the-art overview. *IEEE Signal Processing Magazine, 17(5), 20–46*. doi:10.1109/79.879337

Lauter, K. (2004, February). The advantages of elliptic curve cryptography for wireless security. *Wireless Communications, IEEE, 11(1), 62–67*. doi:10.1109/MWC.2004.1269719

Law, Y. W., Doumen, J., & Hartel, P. (2006). Survey and Benchmark of Block Ciphers for Wireless Sensor Networks. [TOSN]. *ACM Transactions on Sensor Networks, 2(1), 65–93*. doi:10.1145/1138127.1138130

Layne, K., & Lee, J. (2001). Developing fully functional egovernment: A four stage model. *Government Information Quarterly, 18(2), 122*. doi:10.1016/S0740-624X(01)00066-1

Lee, L., & Grimson, W. (2002). Gait analysis for recognition and classification. *In Proceedings of the International Conference on Automatic Face and Gesture Recognition (pp. 148-155)*.

Lee, M., & Turban, E. (2001). A Trust Model for Consumer Internet Shopping. *International Journal of Electronic Commerce, 6(1), 75–91*.

Leggett, J., Williams, G., Usnick, M., & Longnecker, M. (1991). Dynamic identity verification via keystroke characteristics. *International Journal of Man-Machine Studies, 35(6), 859–870*. doi:10.1016/S0020-7373(05)80165-8

Lehane, B. Doyle, L., & O'Mahony, D. (2003). Shared RSA key generation in an mobile ad hoc network. *In Proceedings of MilCom. Boston: IEEE*.

Levien, R. (1999). *A brief comparison of e-mail encryption protocols*. Retrieved from http://www.imc.org/

Lewis, D., & Weigert, A. (1985). Trust as a Social Reality. *Social Forces, 63(4), 967–985*. doi:10.2307/2578601

Li, S. Z., & Jain, A. K. (Eds.). (2005). *Handbook of face recognition*. New York: Springer-Verlag.

Li, Y., Chen, Z., Tan, S. M., & Campbell, R. H. (1996). Security enhanced MPEG player. *In Proceedings of the international workshop on multimedia software development, 169-175*.

Lin, C. Y., & Chang, S. F. (2001). Watermarking capacity of digital images based on domain-specific masking effects. *In Proceedings of the international conference on information technology: Coding and computing (ITCC '01)*.

Lin, S., & Costello, D. J. (2004). *Error control coding* (SECOND Ed.). Upper Saddle River, NJ: Prentice Hall.

Lingyu, W., & Leedham, G. (2006,November). Near- and Far- Infrared Imaging for Vein Pattern Biometrics. *In IEEE International Conference on Video and Signal Based Surveillance*.

Linn, J. (1993). *Message encryption and authentication procedures Part I: Message encryption and authentication procedures*. RFC 1421. Retrieved from http://www.ietf.org/rfc/rfc1421.txt

Liu, A., & Ning, P. (2008, April 22-24). TinyECC: A Configurable Library for Elliptic Curve Cryptography in Wireless Sensor Networks. *In Proceedings of the 7th international conference on Information processing in sensor networks. (pp.245-256).*

Liu, C. H., Collin, C. A., Burton, A. M., & Chaudhuri, A. (1999). Lighting direction affects recognition of untextured faces in photographic positive and negative. *Vision Research, 39, 4003–4009.* doi:10.1016/S0042-6989(99)00109-1

Liu, D., Ning, P., & Li, R. (2005). Establishing pairwise keys in distributed sensor networks. [TISSEC]. *ACM Transactions on Information and System Security, 8(1), 41–77.* doi:10.1145/1053283.1053287

Liu, J., & Issarny, V. (2004, March). Enhanced Reputation Mechanism for Mobile Ad Hoc Networks. *In Proceedings of the Second International Conference on Trust Management* (iTrust'2004).

Loshin, P. (1999). *Essential e-mail standards: RFCs and protocols made practical.* New York: John Wiley & Sons.

Luo, H., & Lu, S. (2000, October). *Ubiquitous and Robust Authentication Services for Ad Hoc Wireless Networks (Technical Report).* UCLA-CSD-TR-200030.

Luo, P., Wang, X., Feng, J., & Xu, Y. (2008). Low-power hardware implementation of ECC processor suitable for low-cost RFID tags, *Proceedings of the IEEE 9th International Conference on Solid-State and Integrated-Circuit Technology (ICSICT 2008), 1681-1684.*

MacKenzie, P., Patel, S., & Swaminathan, R. (2000). Password-authenticated key exchange based on RSA. In T. Okamoto (Ed.), *Asiacrypt 2000 (pp. 599-613).* Springer-Verlag. (Lecture Notes in Computer Science Volume 1976)

Madsen, P., Koga, Y., & Takahashi, K. (2005). *Federated identity management for protecting users from ID theft.* Paper presented at the Proceedings of the 2005 workshop on Digital identity management.

Malan, D., Welsh, M., & Smith, M. (2004, October). A public-key infrastructure for key distribution in tinyos based on elliptic curve cryptography. Paper presented at *First IEEE International Conference on Sensor and Ad Hoc Communications and Networks (IEEE SECON 2004),* Santa Clara, CA.

Maltoni, D. (2005). *A tutorial on fingerprint recognition. In Advanced studies in biometrics.* Berlin: Springer. (Lecture Notes in Computer Science Volume 3161)

Maltoni, D., Maio, D., Jain, A. K., & Prabahakar, S. (2003). *Handbook of fingerprint recognition.* New York: Springer.

Maniccam S. S., & Bourbakis, N. (2004). Lossless compression and information hiding in images. *Pattern recognition journal, 36, 2004.*

Mao, W. (2003). *Modern cryptography: Theory and practice* (Hewlett-Packard professional books). Prentice Hall.

Maple, C., & Norrington, P. (2006). The usability and practicality of biometric authentication in the workplace. *In The First International Conference on Availability, Reliability and Security, (ARES'06), 1-7.*

Markowitch, O., & Roggeman, Y. (1999). *Probabilistic non-repudiation without trusted third party.* In Second Conference on Security in Communication Networks'99, Amalfi, Italy.

Markowitz, J. (2000). Voice biometrics. [CACM]. *Communications of the ACM, 43(9), 66–73.* doi:10.1145/348941.348995

Marlinspike, M. (2009). *New Techniques for Defeating SSL/TLS.* Presented at Black Hat DC Briefings 2009, Crystal City, USA, Feb 16-19, 2009. Slides are at http://www.blackhat.com/presentations/bh-dc-09/Marlinspike/BlackHat-DC-09-Marlinspike-DefeatingSSL.pdf

Massey, J. (1969). Shift-register synthesis and BCH decoding. *IEEE Transactions on Information Theory, 15(1), 122–127.* doi:10.1109/TIT.1969.1054260

McCarthy, J. (2004, November). *Machine error gives Bush 3,893 extra votes in Ohio.* Associated Press. Available at http://www.usatoday.com/tech/news/techpolicy/evoting/2004-11-06-ohio-evote-trouble_x.htm

McKnight, D., Choudhury, V., & Kacmar, C. (2002). Developing and validating trust measures for e-Commerce: An integrative typology. *Information Systems Research, 13(3)*, 334–359. doi:10.1287/isre.13.3.334.81

Mehallegue, N., Bouridane, A., & Garcia, E. (2008). Efficient path key establishment for wireless sensor networks. *EURASIP Journal on Wireless Communications and Networking, 8(3), Article No. 3.*

Mel, H. X., & Baker, D. M. (2000). *Cryptography decrypted* (5th ed.). Reading, MA: Addison-Wesley.

Menezes, A., Okamoto, T., & Vanstone, S. (1993). Reducing elliptic curve logarithms to finite field. *IEEE Transactions on Information Theory, 39(5), 1639*–1646. doi:10.1109/18.259647

Meyer, J., & Gadegast, F. (1995). Security mechanisms for multimedia-data with the example MPEG-I Video. *In Proceedings (IEEE) of the international conference on multimedia computing and systems.*

Micali, S. (1997). *Certified E-mail with invisible post offices.* Presented at the RSA '97 conference (1997).

Micali, S. (2003). Simple and Fast Optimistic Protocols for Fair Electronic Exchange. *In Proceedings of the ACM Symposium on Principles of Distributed Computing, pages 12-19, 2003.*

Microsoft Corporation. (2009). *TLS enhancements to SSL.* Retrieved from http://technet.microsoft.com/en-us/library/cc784450.aspx

Miller, B. (1999). *Mapping Salutation Architecture APIs to Bluetooth Service Discovery Layer, Bluetooth SIG.* Retrieved from http://www.salutation.org/whitepaper/btoothmapping.pdf

Miller, B. A., Nixon, T., Tai, C., & Wood, M. D. (2001). Home Networking with Universal Plug and Play. *IEEE Communications Magazine, (December): 104–109.* doi:10.1109/35.968819

Miller, V. (1986). Uses of elliptic curves in cryptography, Advances in Cryptology, *CRYPTO'85.* Lecture Notes in Computer Science. Springer-Verlag, 218, 417–426.

Miner More, S., Malkin, M., Staddon, J., & Balfanz, D. (2003, October). Sliding window self-healing key distribution. *In Proceedings of the 2003 ACM workshop on Survivable and self-regenerative systems: in association with 10th ACM Conference on Computer and Communications Security, (pp. 82–90).*

Mit.edu. (2007). *Kerberos: The network authentication protocol.* Retrieved from http://mit.edu.

Mitomo, M., & Kurosawa, K. (2000). Attack for flash MIX. In T. Okamoto (Ed.), *Asiacrypt '00* (pp. 192-204). Berlin, Germany: Springer-Verlag. (Lecture Notes in Computer Science Volume 1976)

Mogollon, M. (2007). *Cryptography and security services: Mechanisms and applications.* New York: CyberTech Publishing.

Mogollon, M. (2007). *Cryptography and security services: Mechanisms and applications.* New York: CyberTech Publishing.

Mok, L. L., Lau, W. H., Leung, S. H., Wang, S. L., & Yan, H. (2004). Lip features selection with application to person authentication. *In Proceedings of IEEE ICASSP, 3, 397–400.*

Molnar, D., Kohno, T., Sastry, N., & Wagner, D. (2006). Tamper evident, history independent, subliminal free data structures on prom storage or how to store ballots on a voting machine (extended abstract). *In Proceedings of the 2006 IEEE Symposium on Security and Privacy (p. 365370).*

Monrose, F., Reiter, M. K., & Wetzel, S. (2001). *Password hardening based on keystroke dynamics.* Retrieved September 23, 2008, from http://cs.unc.edu/~fabian/papers/acm.ccs6.pdf

Mont, M. C., Pearson, S., & Bramhall, P. (2003). *Towards Accountable Management of Identity and Privacy: Sticky Policies and Enforceable Tracing Services.*

Morris, R., & Thompson, K. (1979). Password security: a case history. *Communications of the ACM, 22(11), 594–597.* doi:10.1145/359168.359172

Moulin, P., & Mihcak, M. K. (2002). A framework for evaluating the data-hiding capacity of image sources. *IEEE Transactions on Image Processing, 11(9), 1029–1042*. doi:10.1109/TIP.2002.802512

MS-293781 (2007). *Trusted root certificates that are required by Windows Server 2008*, by Windows Vista, by Windows Server 2003, by Windows XP, and by Windows 2000", Microsoft Help and Support Article ID 293781

Muppala, P., Thomas, J., & Abraham, A. (n.d.). QoS-Based Authentication Scheme for Ad Hoc Wireless Networks. *In Proceedings of the International Conference on Information Technology: Coding and Computing (ITCC'05), (pp. 709-714)*.

Murdoch, S. J., & Danezis, G. (2005). Low-Cost Traffic Analysis of Tor. I*n Proceedings of the 2005 IEEE Symposium on Security and Privacy, 183-195, Washington DC*.

Naor, M. (1996, Sept. 13th). *Verification of a human in the loop or identification via the Turing test*.

Narayanan, S., & Shmatikov, V. (2005). Fast dictionary attacks on passwords using time-space tradeoff. Paper presented at CCS05. *In Proceedings of the 12th ACM conference on Computer and communications security, 2005*.

Neff, A. (2001). A verifiable secret shuffle and its application to e-voting. In Samarati, P. (Ed.), *ACM CCS '01 (pp. 116–125)*. Philadelphia.

Neff, C. A. (2004, April 21). *Verifiable mixing (shuffling) of ElGamal pairs*. Retrieved from http://people.csail.mit.edu/rivest/voting/papers/Neff-2004-04-21-ElGamalShuffles.pdf

Netegrity. (2001). *The standard XML framework for secure information exchange*. Retrieved from http://xml.coverpages.org/Netegrity-SAMLWP.pdf nist.gov. (2000). FIPS Pub 186-2 digital signature standard (DSS). Retrieved from http://csrc.nist.gov/publications/fips/fips186-2/fips186-2-change1.pdf

Neuman, B., & Ts'o, T. (1994). Kerberos: an authentication service for computer networks. *IEEE Communications Magazine, 32(9), 33–38*. doi:10.1109/35.312841

Ni, Z., Shi, Y., Ansari, N., Su, W., Sun, Q., & Lin, X. (2004). *Robust lossless image data hiding*. International conference on multimedia & expo (ICME), 3, 2199-2202.

NIST. (1999, July). *Recommended Elliptic Curves for Federal Government Use*. Retrieved from http://csrc.nist.gov/csrc/fedstandards.html

NIST. (2003). Special publication 800-57: *Recommendation for key management. Part1: General guidelines*. NIST.

Nixon, M. S., & Carter, J. N. (2006). Human ID based on Gait. *Proceedings of the IEEE, 94(11), 2013–2024*. doi:10.1109/JPROC.2006.886018

Nixon, M. S., Carter, J. N., Cunado, D., Huang, P. S., & Stevenage, S. V. (1999). *Automatic gait recognition. In Biometrics: Personal Identification in Networked Society (pp. 231–249)*. New York: Kluwer.

Nixon, M. S., Tan, T. N., & Chellappa, R. (2005). *Human Identification based on Gait*. In Jain, A. K., & Zhang, D. (Eds.), International Series on Biometrics. New York: Springer.

NSA. (2009). *The Case for Elliptic Curve Cryptography*. Retrieved from http://www.nsa.gov/business/programs/elliptic_curve.shtml

O'Neill, M. (2003). *Web services security*. New York: McGraw-Hill Osborne Media.

OASIS. (2009). *Organization for the Advancement of Structured Information Standards*. Retrieved from http://www.oasis-open.org/who/

Oechslin, P. (2003). Making a Faster Cryptanalytic Time-Memory Trade-off. In The 23rd Annual International Cryptology Conference. *In Proceedings of CRYPTO03, volume 2729 of Lecture Notes in Computer Science, 2003*.

Ogata, W., Kurosawa, K., Sako, K., & Takatani, K. (1997). Fault tolerant anonymous channel. I*n Proceedings of the First International Conference on Information and Communications Security (ICICS '97) (pp. 440-444). Berlin, Germany: Springer-Verlag. (Lecture Notes in Computer Science Volume 1334)*

Oliveira, L., Aranha, D., Morais, E., Felipe, D., Lopez, J., & Dahab, R. (2007). TinyTate: Computing the Tate Pairing in Resource-Constrained Sensor Nodes. NCA 2007. *In Proceedings of the Sixth IEEE International Symposium on Network Computing and Applications, 318 – 323.*

Olivier, M. (2004). FLOCKS: Distributed proxies for browsing privacy. *In Proceedings of SAICSIT (pp. 79-88).* Stellenbosch, South Africa.

OLPC. (n.d.). *SES offers OLPC Global Satellite Band-width.* Retrieved from http://www.olpcnews.com/internet/access/ses_offers_olpc_glob_1.html

Openssl.org. (2005). *OpenSSL Project.* Retrieved from http://www.openssl.org/

Oppenheimer, P. (2009). *Form 10-Q. United States Securities and Exchange Commission.* Retrieved January 22, 2009, from http://sec.gov/Archives/edgar/data/320193/000119312509009937/d10q.htm

Park, C., Itoh, K., & Kurosawa, K. (1993). Efficient anonymous channel and all/nothing election scheme. In T. Helleseth (Ed.), *Advances in Cryptology - Eurocrypt '93 (pp. 248-259).* Berlin: Springer-Verlag. (Lecture Notes in Computer Science Volume 765)

Pathak, V., Yao, D., & Iftode, L. (2008, September 22-24). Securing Geographic Routing in Mobile Ad-hoc Networks. *In Proceedings of the International Conference on Vehicular Electronics and Safety (ICVES).* Columbus, OH.

PCLcable. (2003). *WEBMAIL notes.* Retrieved from http://my.pclnet.net/webmail.html

Pereira, S., Voloshynovskiy, S., & Pun, T. (2000). *Optimized wavelet domain watermark embedding strategy using linear programming.* In Szu, H. (Ed.), SPIE Aerosense 2000: Wavelet Applications VII.

Perrig, A., Stankovic, J., & Wagner, D. (2004). Security in wireless sensor networks. *Communications of the ACM, 47(6),* 53–57. doi:10.1145/990680.990707

Perrig, A., Szewczyk, R., Tygar, J. D., Wen, V., & Culler, D. E. (2002). SPINS: security protocols for sensor networks. *Wireless Networks, 8(5), 521–534.* doi:10.1023/A:1016598314198

Perrig, A., Szewczyk, R., Wen, V., Culler, D., & Tygar, J. (2002, September). SPINS: Security protocols for sensor networks. J. *Wireless Nets., 8(5), 521–534.* doi:10.1023/A:1016598314198

Peter, I. (2003). *The history of e-mail.* Retrieved from http://www.nethistory.info/

Peterson, J. (2004). S/MIME *advanced encryption standard (AES) requirement: RFC3853.* Retrieved from http://www.faqs.org/rfcs/rfc3853.html

Pfitzmann, B. (1995). Breaking an efficient anonymous channel. In A. De Santis (Ed.), *Advances in Cryptology - Eurocrypt '94 (pp. 332-340).* Berlin, Germany: Springer-Verlag. (Lecture Notes in Computer Science Volume 950)

Pfitzmann, B., & Pfitzmann, A. (1989). How to break the direct RSA-implementation of MIXes. In J.-J. Quisquater & J. Vandewalle (Eds.), *Advances in Cryptology - Eurocrypt '89 (pp. 373-381).* Berlin, Germany: Springer-Verlag. (Lecture Notes in Computer Science Volume 434)

Phipps, T. C., & King, R. A. (n.d.). *A Speaker Verification Biometric In 40 Bytes.* Retrieved October 24, 2008 from http://www.dsp.sun.ac.za/~dupreez/downloads/papers/tespar/cardtech.pdf

Phua, K., Chen, J., Dat, T. H., & Shue, L. (2008). *Heart sound as a biometric.* Pattern Recognition, 41(3), 906–919. doi:10.1016/j.patcog.2007.07.018

Pinkas, B., & Sander, T. (2002). Securing passwords against dictionary attacks. Paper presented at CCS02. *In Proceedings of the 9th ACM conference on Computer and communications security.*

Pioneers, I. (2009, January). *Internet pioneers.* Retrieved from http://www.ibiblio.org/pioneers/roberts.html

Plomin, R., & Kosslyn, S. M. (2001). Genes, brain and cognition. *Nature Neuroscience, 4(12), 1153–1155.* doi:10.1038/nn1201-1153

Podilchuk, C., I., & Delp, E., J. (2001, July). Digital watermarking: algorithms and applications. *Signal Processing Magazine, IEEE, 18(4), 33-46.*

Postel, J. B. (1982). *Simple mail transfer protocol RFC: 821 Obsoleted by 2821.* Retrieved from http://tools.ietf. org/html/rfc821

Postel.org. (2009, January). *Postel organization.* Retrieved from http://www.postel.org/postel.html

Prabhakar, S., Pankanti, S., & Jain, A. K. (2003, March/ April). Biometric recognition: security and privacy concerns. *IEEE Security and Privacy, (pp. 33-42).*

President's DNA Iniative. (n.d.). *History of Forensic DNA Analysis.* Retrieved October 21, 2008, from http://www. dna.gov/basics/analysishistory/

Princea, F., Corriveaua, H., Héberta, R., & Winter, D. A. (1997). Gait in the elderly. *Gait & Posture, 5, 128–135.* doi:10.1016/S0966-6362(97)01118-1

Pullkis, G., Grahn, J. K., & Karisson, J. (2006). *Taxonomies of User Authentication Methods in Computer Networks.* In Warkentin, M. (Ed.), Enterprise Information Systems Assurance and Systems Security. Hershey, PA: IGI Global.

Pun, K. H., & Moon, Y. S. (2004, May). Recent advances in ear biometrics. *In Proceedings of Sixth International Conference on Automatic Face and Gesture Recognition, (pp. 164-169).*

Qiao, L., & Nahrstedt, K. (1997). A new algorithm for MPEG video encryption. *In Proceedings of CISST'97 international conference, 21-29.*

Ramsdell, B. (2004). *Secure/Multipurpose Internet Mail Extensions (S/MIME) Version 3.1 Message Specification, RFC 3851.*

Ramsdell, B. (Ed.). (1999). *S/MIME version 3 message specification.* Retrieved from http://www.faqs.org/rfcs/ rfc2633.html

Rao, G. S. V. R. (2004). Threats and security of Web services – a theoretical short study. *In Proceedings of IEEE International Symposium Communications and Information Technology, 2, 783–786.*

Ratha, N. K., Connell, J. H., & Bolle, R. M. (2001). Enhancing security and privacy in biometrics based authentication systems. *IBM System Journal, 40(3).* Retrieved August 8, 2008, from http://www.research. ibm.com/journal/sj/403/ratha.html

Ray, I., & Ray, I. (2002, May). Fair Exchange in E-commerce. *ACM SIGecom Exchange, 3(2), 9–17.* doi:10.1145/844340.844345

Reed, I. S., & Solomon, G. (1960). Polynomial codes over certain finite fields. *SIAM Journal on Applied Mathematics, 8(2), 300–304.* doi:10.1137/0108018

Rhee, K., Park, Y., & Tsudik, G. (2004, June). An Architecture for Key Management in Hierarchical Mobile Ad-Hoc Networks. *Journal of Communications and Networks, 6(2).*

Rivest, R. L. (2004, June 1). *Remarks on electronic voting. (Text of remarks at the Harvard Kennedy School of Government Digital Voting Symposium).* Retrieved from http://people.csail.mit.edu/rivest/2004-06-01%20 Harvard%20KSG%20Symposium%20Evoting%20 remarks.txt

Rivest, R. L. (2004, June 3). *Electronic voting.* (Talk given at NSA) Retrieved from http://theory.csail.mit. edu/~rivest/2004-06-03%20NSA%20talk%20electronic%20voting.ppt

Rivest, R. L. (2004c, May 26). *Some thoughts on electronic voting. (Talk given at DIMACS Workshop on Electronic Voting).* Retrieved from http://people.csail.mit.edu/ rivest/2004-05-26%20DIMACS%20voting%20talk.ppt

Rivest, R. L. *Voting resources page.* Available at http:// people.csail.mit.edu/rivest/voting/.

Rivest, R., Shamir, A., & Adleman, L. (1978). A Method for Obtaining Digital Signatures and Public-Key Cryptosystems. *Communications of the ACM, 21(2), 120–126.* doi:10.1145/359340.359342

Rolf, O. (2002). *Security Technologies for the World Wide Web.* Boston, MA: Artech House.

Rose, P. (2002). *Forensic Speaker identification.* Boca Raton, FL: CRC Press.

Rosenberg, J., & Remy, D. (2004). *Securing Web services with WS-security: Demystifying WS-security, WS-policy, SAML, XML signature, and XML encryption. Sams.*

Ross, A. (2008). *Security Engineering: A Guide to Building Dependable Distributed Systems (2nd ed.).* New York: Wiley.

Ross, A., & Jain, A. K. (2007). *Fusion Techniques in Mutibiometric systems. In Face Biometrics for Personal Identification.* Berlin, Germany: Springer. doi:10.1007/978-3-540-49346-4_12

Ross, A., Nandakumar, K., & Jain, A. K. (2006). *Handbook of multibiometrics.* Berlin, Germany: Springer-Verlag.

Rosser, J.B. (1939). "An Informal Exposition of Proofs of Godel's Theorem and Church's Theorem". *Journal of Symbolic Logic 4*

Rousseau, D. M., Sitkin, S. B., Burt, R. S., & Camerer, C. (1998). Not so different after all: A cross-discipline view of trust. *Academy of Management Review, 23(3),* 393–404.

RSA.com. (2007). *What is DESX?* Retrieved from http://www.rsasecurity.com

RSA.com. (2007). *What is Diffie-Hellman?* Retrieved from http://www.rsa.com/

RSA.com. (2007). *What is RC4?* Retrieved from http://www.rsa.com

RSA.com. (2008). *What is RSA?* Retrieved from http://www.rsa.com/

Sako, K., & Kilian, J. (1995). Receipt-free mix-type voting scheme – a practical solution to the implementation of a voting booth-. In L. C. Guillou & J.-J. Quisquater (Eds.), *Advance in Cryptology – Eurocrypt '95 (pp. 393-403).* Berlin: Springer-Verlag. (Lecture Notes in Computer Science Volume 921)

Salutation Consortium. (1999). *Salutation Architecture Specification.* Retrieved from ftp://ftp.salutation.org/salute/sa20e1a21.ps

SAML. (2008). *Security assertion markup language (SAML).* Retrieved from http://xml.coverpages.org/saml.html

Sampigethaya, K., & Poovendran, R. (2006). A survey on mix networks and their secure applications. *Proceedings of the IEEE, 94(12), 2142–2181.* doi:10.1109/JPROC.2006.889687

Samuelson, P. (2003). *DRM and, or, vs. the law. Communications of the ACM, 46(4), 41–45.* doi:10.1145/641205.641229

Saponas, T. S., Lester, J., Hartung, C., & Kohno, T. (2006, December). *Devices That Tell On You: The Nike+iPod Sport Kit. (Technical Report).* University of Washington

Saxena, N., Tsudik, G., & Yi, J. H. (2007). Threshold Cryptography in P2P and MANETs: the Case of Access Control. *Computer Networks, 51, 3632–3649.* doi:10.1016/j.comnet.2007.03.001

Schaad, J. (2003). *Use of the advanced encryption standard (AES) encryption algorithm in cryptographic message syntax (CMS): RFC 3565.* Retrieved from http://www.ietf.org/rfc/rfc3565.txt

Scharinger, J. (1998). Fast encryption of image data using chaotic Kolmogorov flows. *Journal of Electronic Imaging, 7(2), 318–325.* doi:10.1117/1.482647

Schneier, B. (1995). *Applied cryptography.* New York: Wiley.

Schneier, B. (1995). *E-mail security: How to keep your electronic messages private.* New York: Wiley.

SearchSecurity.com. (2008). *DSS definition.* Retrieved from http://searchsecurity.techtarget.com/sDefinition/

SearchSecurity.com. (2008). *Spotlight article: Domain 3, cryptography.* Retrieved from http://searchsecurity.techtarget.com/generic/0,295582,sid14_gci1328971,00.html

Seigneur, J. M., & Jensen, C. D. (2004, Mar). *Trust Enhanced Ubiquitous Payment without Too Much Privacy Loss.* Paper presented at the Applied computing; SAC 2004, Nicosia.

Seys, S., & Preneel, B. (2003). Authenticated and Efficient Key Management for Wireless Ad Hoc Networks. *In Pro-*

ceedings of the 24th Symposium on Information Theory in the Benelux, Werkgemeenschap voor Informatie - en Communicatietheorie, 2003, (pp. 195-202).

Shamir, A. (1979). How to share a secret. *Communications of the ACM, 22(11),* 612–613. doi:10.1145/359168.359176

Shamir, A. (1984). *Identity-based cryptosystems and signature (pp. 47–53).* Proceedings of Cryptology, Springer-Verlag.

Sharpe, M. (2008). *Getting started with HTTPS.* Retrieved from http://searchsoftwarequality.techtarget.com/sDefinition/0,sid92_gci214006,00.html#

Sheehan, K. B. (2002). Toward a typology of Internet users and online privacy concerns. *The Information Society, 18(1),* 21–32. doi:10.1080/01972240252818207

Shi, C., & Bhargava, B. (1998a). A fast MPEG video encryption algorithm. *ACM Multimedia, 98,* 81–88.

Shi, C., & Bhargava, B. B. (1998b). An efficient MPEG video encryption algorithm. *In Proceedings of the symposium on reliable distributed systems, 381-386.*

Shin, K., Kim, Y., & Kim, Y. (n.d.). *An Effective Authentication Scheme in Mobile Ad Hoc Network.* Seventh ACIS International Conference on Software Engineering, Artificial Intelligence, Networking, and Parallel/Distributed Computing (SNPD'06), (pp. 249-252).

Shneiderman, B. (2000, December). Designing Trust into Online Experiences. *Communications of the ACM, 43(12),* 57–59. doi:10.1145/355112.355124

Shoup, V. (2000. Practical threshold signatures. *In Proceedings of EUROCRYPT.*

Simon, C., & Goldstein, I. (1935). A New Scientific Method of Identification. *New York State Journal of Medicine, 35(18),* 901–906.

Simovits, M. (1995). *The DES: An extensive document and evaluation.* New York: Agent Park Press.

Singh, K. M., Singh, S. B., & Singh, S. S. (2007). Hiding encrypted message in the features of images. *International journal of computer science and network security (IJCSNS), 7(4).*

Singh, S. (2000). *The code book: The science of secrecy from ancient Egypt to quantum cryptography (reprint).* Anchor.

Singhal, A., Winograd, T., & Scarfone, K. (2007). Guide to Secure Web Services. *NIST, SP800-95.*

Sirvan, O., Karlik, B., & Ugur, A. (2005). *An Efficient Iris Recognition for Security Purposes.* Retrieved November 1, 2008 from http://www.icgst.com/GVIP05/papers/P1150549103.pdf

Smith, R. E. (2002). *Authentication: From passwords to public keys.* Reading, MA: Addison-Wesley.

Snell, J., Tidwel, D., & Kulchenko, P. (2001). *Programming Web services with SOAP.* O'Reilly.

Sobel, D. (2007). A Bite out of Apple - iTunes, Interoperability, and France's Dadvsi Law. *Berkeley Technology Law Journal, 22,* 26.

Socek, D., Bozovic, V., & Culibrk, D. (2007). Practical secure biometrics using set intersection as a similarity measure. *In Proceedings of International Conference on Security and Cryptography (SECRYPT 2007). Barcelona, Spain: INSTICC.*

Socek, D., Li, S., Magliveras, S. S., & Furht, B. (2005). *Short paper: enhanced 1-d chaotic key-based algorithm for image encryption.* First international conference on security and privacy for emerging areas in communications networks.

Soldek, J., Shmerko, V., Phillips, P., Kukharev, G., Rogers, W., & Yanushkevich, S. (1997). *Image analysis and pattern recognition in biometric technologies.* Retrieved October 25, 2008 from ">http://enel.ucalgary.ca/People/yanush/publications/lasveg97.pdf

Song, J.H., Lee, J., & Iwata, T. (2006). The AES-CMAC Algorithm. RFC 4493.

Soppera, A., & Burbridge, T. (2004). Maintaining privacy in pervasive computing—Enabling acceptance of sensor-based services. BT Technology Journal, 22(3), 106–118. doi:10.1023/B:BTTJ.0000047125.97546.4a

Spanos, G. A., & Maples, T. B. (1995). Performance study of a selective encryption scheme for the security of networked, real-time video. *Proceedings of the 4thIEEE international conference on computer communications and networks (ICCCN '95), 2-10.*

Spector, Y., & Ginzberg, J. (1994). Pass-sentence: A new approach to computer code. approach to computer code. *Computers & Security, 13(2), 145–160.* doi:10.1016/0167-4048(94)90064-7

SSH Communications Security, Inc. (2008). *Public-key cryptosystems.* Retrieved from http://www.ssh.com/support/cryptography/

SSL. (n.d.). *The SSL Handshake,* Retrieved March 15, 2009, from http://publib.boulder.ibm.com/infocenter/tivihelp/v2r1/index.jsp?topic=/com.ibm.itame2.doc_5.1/ss7aumst18.htm

Staddon, J., Miner, S., Franklin, M., Balfanz, D., Malkin, M., & Dean, D. (2002, May). Self-healing key distribution with revocation. *In Proceedings of the 2002 IEEE Symposium on Security and Privacy.*

Stajano, F., & Anderson, R. (1999). *The Resurrecting Duckling: Security Issues for Ad-hoc Wireless Networks.* 7th International Workshop on Security protocols, Cambridge, UK.

Stallings, W. (2006). *Cryptography and Network Security (4th ed.).* Upper Saddle River, NJ: Prentice Hall.

Stallings, W. (2007). *Network Security Essentials (3rd ed.).* Upper Saddle River, NJ: Prentice Hall.

Stamp, M. (2006). I*nformation Security: Principles and Practice.* Hoboken, NJ: John Wiley & Sons.

Stigler, S. M. (1995). *GALTON and Identification by Fingerprints.* In Crow, J. F., & Dove, W. F. (Ed.), *Anecdotal, Historical and Critical Commentaries on Genetics,* Retrieved October 23, 2008, from http://www.genetics.org/cgi/reprint/140/3/857.pdf

Sun Microsystems. (2003). *Jini Technology Core Platform Specification,* from http://wwws.sun.com/software/jini/specs/

Sun.com. (2002). *Introduction to SSL.* Retrieved from http://docs.sun.com/source/816-6156-10/contents.htm#1041986

SunMicrosystems. (2008). *JSR 106: XML digital encryption APIs.* Retrieved from http://jcp.org/en/jsr/detail?id=106

Svigals, J. (1994). Smartcards: A security assessment. *Computers & Security, 13(2), 107–114.* doi:10.1016/0167-4048(94)90056-6

Swanson, M. D., Zhu, B., & Tewfik, A. H. (1997). Data hiding for video-in-video. *In Proceedings of the 1997 international conference on image processing (ICIP '97), 2, 676-679.*

Swets, D., & Weng, J. J. (1996). Using discriminant eigenfeatures for image retrieval. *IEEE Transactions on Pattern Analysis and Machine Intelligence, 18, 831–836.* doi:10.1109/34.531802

Syverson, P., Goldschlag, D., & Reed, M. (1997). Anonymous Connections and Onion Routing. *In Proceedings of the IEEE Symposium on Security and Privacy, 44-54.*

Szczechowiak, P., & Collier, M. (2009). *TinyIBE: Identity-Based Encryption for Heterogeneous Sensor Networks.* In 5th International Conference on Intelligent Sensors, Sensor Networks and Information Processing. 319-354.

Szczechowiak, P., Kargl, A., Scott, M., & Collier, M. (2009, March). On the Application of Pairing Based Cryptography to Wireless Sensor Networks. *In Proceedings of the second ACM conference on Wireless network security.*

Tang, L. (1996). Methods for encrypting and decrypting MPEG video data efficiently. *ACM Multimedia, 96, 219–229.*

Tedrick, T. (1983). How to exchange half a bit. In Chaum, D. (Ed.), Advances in Cryptology: *Proceedings of Crypto 83 (pp. 147–151).* New York, London: Plenum Press.

Tedrick, T. (1985). Fair exchange of secrets. In G. R. Blakley, D. C. Chaum (Eds.), *Advances in Cryptology: Proceedings of Crypto 84,* Vol. 196 of Lecture Notes in

Computer Science. Berlin, Germany: Springer-Verlag, (pp. 434–438).

Thalheim, L., Krissler, J., & Ziegler, P.-M. (2002). Body check: *Biometrics defeated*. Retrieved May 04, 2008, from http://www.extremetech.com/article2/0%2C1558%2C13919%2C00.asp

Thomas, S. A. (2000). *SSL & TLS essentials securing the Web*. John Wiley & Sons.

Today, U. S. A. (2004, November 5th). *More than 4,500 North Carolina votes lost because of mistake in voting machine capacity*. Retrieved from http://www.usatoday.com/news/politicselections/vote2004/2004-11-04-votes-lost_x.htm.

Tor (n.d.). *Tor: Overview*. Retrieved March 16, 2009, from http://www.torproject.org/overview.html.en

Torkzadeh, G., & Dhillon, G. (2002, June). Measuring Factors that Influence the Success of Internet Commerce. *Information Systems Research, 13(1)*, 187–204. doi:10.1287/isre.13.2.187.87

Tracy, M., Jansen, W., & Bisker, S. (2002). Guidelines on Electronic Mail Security. NIST Special Publication 800-45, Tracy, M., Jansen, W., & Bisker, S. (2007). Guidelines on Electronic Mail Security. *NIST Special Publication 800-45, V2*

Trappe, W., & Washington, L. C. (2005). *Introduction to cryptography with coding theory (2nd ed.)*. Prentice Hall.

Treinen, J. J., & Thurimella, R. (2006). A Framework for the Application of Association Rule Mining in Large Intrusion Detection Infrastructures. *In Proceedings of Recent Advances in Intrusion Detection (pp. 1–18)*. RAID. doi:10.1007/11856214_1

Turk, M., & Pentland, A. (1991). Eigenfaces for recognition. *Journal of Cognitive Neuroscience, 3(1)*, 71–86. doi:10.1162/jocn.1991.3.1.71

Turner, S., & Housley, R. (2008). *Implementing E-mail and security tokens: Current standards, tools, and practices*. Wiley.

U.S. Department of Justice. (2001a). *Report of the National Task Force on privacy, technology, and criminal justice information (NCJ187669)*. Washington, DC.

U.S. Department of Justice. (2001b). *Use and management of criminal history record information: A comprehensive report, 2001 update (NCJ187670)*. Washington, DC.

Umphress, D., & Williams, G. (1985). Identity Verification Through keyboard Characteristics. [London: Academic Press]. *International Journal of Man-Machine Studies, 23, 263–273*. doi:10.1016/S0020-7373(85)80036-5

Vacca, R. J. (2007). *Biometric Technologies and Verification Systems*. Amsterdam: Butterworth-Heinemann.

Verma, M. (2004). *XML security: The XML key management specification*. Retrieved from http://www.ibm.com/developerworks/xml/library/x-seclay3/

von Ahn, J. L., & Manuel Blum. (2003). CAPTCHA: Using hard AI problems for security. In E. Biham (Ed.), *Proceedings of Eurocrypt'03 (p. 294-311)*. Berlin: Springer-Verlag. (Lecture Notes in Computer Science Volume 2656)

Vuong, Q. C., Pessig, J. J., Harrison, M. C., & Tarr, M. J. (2005). The role of surface pigmentation for recognition revealed by contrast reversal in faces and Greebles. *Vision Research, 45, 1213–1223*. doi:10.1016/j.visres.2004.11.015

W3.org. (2002). *XML encryption syntax and processing W3C recommendation*. Retrieved from http://www.w3.org/TR/2002/REC-xmlenc-core-20021210/Overview.html

W3C. (2002). *Decryption transform for XML signature*. Retrieved from http://www.w3.org/TR/xmlenc-decrypt

W3C. (2004). *Web services architecture*. Retrieved from http://www.w3.org/

W3C. (2009). *XML digital signature*. Retrieved from http://www.w3.org/TR/xmldsig-core/

W3C.org. (2003). *How secure is the encryption used by SSL. W3C.org FAQ*. Retrieved from http://www.w3.org/

Wagner, D., & Schneier, B. (1996). *Analysis of the SSL 3.0 protocol*. Paper presented at Proceedings of the Second

UNIX Workshop on Electronic Commerce, pages 29-40. USENIX Association.

Wagner, R. (2001). *Address Resolution Protocol Spoofing and Man-in-the-Middle Attacks*. Retrieved from http://www.sans.org/rr/whitepapers/threats/474.php

Wander, A., Gura, N., Eberle, H., Gupta, V., & Shantz, S. (2005, March). *Energy analysis of public-key cryptography for wireless sensor networks*. Paper presented at Third IEEE International Conference on Pervasive Computing and Communication (PerCom 2005), Hawaii, USA.

Wang, H., Sheng, B., & Li, Q. (2006). Elliptic Curve Cryptography Based Access Control in Sensor Networks. *International Journal of Security and Networks, 1(¾)127-137.*

Wang, X. Y., Yin, Y. Q., & Yu, H. B. (2005). *"Finding Collisions in the Full SHA-1"*, Proceedings of 25th Annual International Cryptology Conference, Santa Barbara, California, USA

Wang, X., Huff, P. D., & Tjaden, B. (2008). Improving the efficiency of capture-resistant biometric authentication based on set intersection. In Proceedings of the 24th Annual Computer Security Applications Conference (p. 140-149). Anaheim, CA: *IEEE Computer Society.*

Watro, R., Kong, D., Cuti, S., Gardiner, C., Lynn, C., & Kruus, P. (2004). *Tinypk: securing sensor networks with public key technology. Second ACM*

Workshop on Security of ad hoc and Sensor Networks (SASN'04), 59–64, Washington, DC.

Watson, C., Garris, M., Tabassi, E., Wilson, C., McCabe, R., Janet, S., & Ko, K. (2007). *User's Guide to NIST Biometric Image Software*. NIST.

Watson, M. L. (2004). *Can There Be Just One Trust?* Retrieved Octobober 31, 2008 from http://www.instituteforpr.org/files/uploads/2004_Watson.pdf

Wayman, J. L. (2008). Biometrics in Identity Management Systems. *IEEE Security & Privacy, 6(2), 30–37.* doi:10.1109/MSP.2008.28

Wayman, J., Jain, A. K., Maltoni, D., & Maio, D. (2005). *Biometric systems: Technology, design and performance evaluation*. London: Springer-Verlag.

Weekly, D. (2008). T*he need For next-generation e-mail*. Retrieved from http://david.weekly.org

Weise, J. (2001). *Public key infrastructure overview*. Retrieved from http://www.sun.com/blueprints/0801/publickey.pdf

Wenbo, M. (2003). *Modern cryptography: Theory and practice*. Upper Saddle River, NJ: Prentice Hall.

Wi-Fi Alliance. (2003, April). *Wi-Fi Protected Access: Strong, standards-based, interoperable security for today's Wi-Fi networks*. Austin, TX: Wi-Fi Alliance.

Wiki-DH. (2009). *Wiki-DH*. Retrieved from http://en.wikipedia.org/wiki/Diffie-Hellman

Wiki-E-mail. (2009). *Wiki-E-mail*. Retrieved from http://en.wikipedia.org/wiki/E-mail

Wiki-MAC. (2009). *Wiki-MAC*. Retrieved from http://en.wikipedia.org/wiki/Message_authentication_code

Wikipedia.org. (2008). *Simple Mail Transfer Protocol (SMTP)*. Retrieved from wikipedia.org

Wikipedia.org. (2009). *Certification Authority*. Retrieved from wikipedia.org

Wikipedia.org. (2009). *Digital Signature*. Retrieved from wikipedia.org

Wikipedia.org. (2009). *Email*. Retrieved from wikipedia.org

Wikipedia.org. (2009). *HTTP*. Retrieved from wikipedia.org

Wikipedia.org. (2009). *Jon Postel*. Retrieved from wikipedia.org

Wikipedia.org. (2009). *Multipurpose Internet Mail Extension*. Retrieved from wikipedia.org

Wikipedia.org. (2009). *PGP: PRETTY GOOD PRIVACY*. Retrieved from wikipedia.org

Wikipedia.org. (2009). *PKI*. Retrieved from wikipedia.org

Wikipedia.org. (2009). *Privacy Enhanced Mail.* Retrieved from wikipedia.org

Wikipedia.org. (2009). *Ray Tomlinson.* Retrieved from wikipedia.org

Wikipedia.org. (2009). *SSL.* Retrieved from wikipedia. org

Wikipedia.org. (2009). *The Multipurpose Internet Mail Extension (MIME).* Retrieved from Wikipedia.org

Wikipedia.org. (2009). *WEB OF TRUST.* Retrieved from wikipedia.org

Wikipedia.org. (2009). *Web service.* Retrieved from wikipedia.org

Wikipedia.org. (2009). *Web Services Security.* Retrieved from wikipedia.org

Wiki-PGP. (2009). *Wiki-PGP.* Retrieved from http://en.wikipedia.org/wiki/Pretty_Good_Privacy

Wiki-RC. (2009). *Wiki-RC.* Retrieved from http://en.wikipedia.org/wiki/Root_certificate

Wiki-SMIME. (2009). *Wiki-SMIME.* Retrieved from http://en.wikipedia.org/wiki/S/MIME

Wiki-Web. (2009). *Wiki-Web.* Retrieved from http://en.wikipedia.org/wiki/World_Wide_Web

Wiki-WOT. (2009). *Wiki-WOT.* Retrieved from http://en.wikipedia.org/wiki/Web_of_trust

Wiki-X.500 (2009). *Wiki-X.500.* Retrieved from http://en.wikipedia.org/wiki/X.500

Wiki-SSL. (2009). *Wiki-SSL.* Retrieved from http://en.wikipedia.org/wiki/Secure_Sockets_Layer

Wilson, O. (n.d.). *Privacy & Identity - Security and Usability: The viability of Passwords & Biometrics.* Retrieved October 13, 2008, from http://facweb.cs.depaul.edu/research/vc/ciplit2004/ppt/Orville_Wilson.ppt

Woodward, D. J. (1997, September). *Biometrics: privacy's foe or privacy's friend?* Proceedings of the IEEE, 85(9), 1480–1492. doi:10.1109/5.628723

Woodward, D. J., & Orlans, M. N., & Higgins, T. P. (2003). *Biometrics: Identity Assurance in the Information Age.* Berkley, CA: Osborne McGraw Hill.

Woodward, D. J., Katherine, W. W., Newton, M. E., Bradley, M., Rubenson, D., Lilly, J., & Larson, K. (2001). *Army Biometric Applications: Identifying and Addressing Sociocultural Concerns, Rand Corporation.* Retrieved August 4, 2008, from http://www.rand.org/pubs/monograph_reports/MR1237/index.html

WOWT.COM. (2004, November 5th). 3,000 phantom votes detected. Retrieved from http://www.wowt.com/news/headlines/1164496.html

Wu, D. C., & Tsai, W. H. (1998). Data hiding in images via multiple-based number conversion and lossy compression. *IEEE Transactions on Consumer Electronics, 44(4),* 1406–1412. doi:10.1109/30.735844

Wu, T. (1998). The secure remote password protocol. *In Proceedings of the 1998 network and distributed system security symposium (pp. 97-111).*

Wu, T. (1999). A real-world analysis of Kerberos password security. *In Proceedings of the 1999 network and distributed system security symposium.*

Wu, T. (2002, October 29). *SRP-6: Improvements and refinements to the secure remote password protocol.* Retrieved from http://grouper.ieee.org/groups/1363/passwdPK/contributions.html#Wu02

Wu, T., *The SRP Authentication and Key Exchange System, 2000.*

Wu, X., & Moo, P. W. (1999). Joint image/video compression and encryption via high-order conditional entropy coding of wavelet coefficients. *Proceedings (IEEE) of the international conference on multimedia computing and systems (ICMCS'99), 2,* 908-912.

Xia, X. G., Boncelet, C. G., & Arce, G. R. (1997). A multi-resolution watermark for digital images. *In Proceedings of IEEE international conference on image processing, 1,* 548-551.

Xiong, X., Wong, D., & Deng, X. (2010). TinyPairing: A Fast and Lightweight Pairing-based Cryptographic

Library for Wireless Sensor Networks. *In IEEE Wireless Communications and Networking Conference (WCNC). 1-6.*

Yan, J., & Ahmad, A. S. E. (2007). Breaking visual CAPTCHAs with naive pattern recognition algorithms. *In Proceedings of the 23rd Annual Computer Security Applications Conference.*

Yan, J., & Ahmad, A. S. E. (2008). A low-cost attack on a Microsoft CAPTCHA. *In Proceedings of the 15th ACM conference on Computer and Communications Security (p. 543-554).* Alexandria, VA.

Yang, B., & Deng, B. (2006). Steganography in gray images using wavelet. *In Proceedings of the second international symposium on communication, control and signal processing (ISCCSP).*

Yang, M., & Bourbakis, N. (2005). A high bitrate information hiding algorithm for digital video content under H.264/AVC compression. *In Proceedings of the IEEE international midwest symposium on circuits and systems (MWSCAS 2005).*

Yang, M., Trifas, M., Truitt, C., & Xiong, G. (2008). Wavelet domain video information embedding. *Proceedings of the 12th world multi-conference on systemics, cybernetics and informatics.*

Yao, D., Fazio, N., Dodis, Y., & Lysyanskaya, A. (n.d.). ID-Based Encryption for Complex Hierarchies with Applications to Forward Security and Broadcast Encryption. *In Proceeding of the ACM Conference on Computer and Communications Security (CCS '04). (pp. 354–363).* Washington DC: ACM Press.

Yoon, S. (2002). The Antecedents and Consequences of Trust in Online-Purchase Decisions. *Journal of Interactive Marketing, 16(2),* 47–63. doi:10.1002/dir.10008

Younes, M. A., & Jantan, A. (2003). Image encryption using block-based transformation algorithm, *IAENG International Journal of Computer Science, 35(1).*

Yun, Y. W. (2002). *The '123' of Biometric Technology.* Retrieved November 21, 2008, from http://www.cp.su.ac.th/~rawitat/teaching/forensicit06/coursefiles/files/biometric.pdf

Zetter, K. (n.d.). *Rogue Nodes Turn Tor Anonymizer into Eavesdropper's Paradise,* http://www.wired.com/politics/security/news/2007/09/embassy_hacks

Zhang, D. (2000). *Automated Biometrics: Technologies and Systems.* Berlin: Springer-Verlag.

Zhang, D., Liu, Z., Yan, J., & Shi, P. (2007). *Tongue-Print: A Novel Biometrics Pattern. In Advances in Biometrics.* Berlin, Germany: Springer. doi:10.1007/978-3-540-74549-5_122

Zhang, L., Zhang, R., & Chengbo, Y. (2008, May). Study on the Identity Authentication System on Finger Vein. *In Proceedings of IEEE 2nd International Conference on Bioinformatics and Biomedical Engineering, (pp. 1905-1907).*

Zhang, M. (2004, January). Analysis of the SPEKE password-authenticated key exchange protocol. Communications Letters, *IEEE, 8(1),* 63–65. doi:10.1109/LCOMM.2003.822506

Zhang, N., & Shi, Q. (1996). Achieving non-repudiation of receipt. *The Computer Journal, 39(10),* 844–853. doi:10.1093/comjnl/39.10.844

Zhang, W., Cheung, S., & Chen, M. (2005). Hiding privacy information in video surveillance system. *In Proceedings of the international conference on image processing (ICIP'2005), 3, II- 868-71.*

Zhang, Y., Liu, W., Lou, W., Fang, Y., & Kwon, Y. (2005, May.). ACPKI: Anonymous and certificateless public-key infrastructure for mobile ad hoc networks. In Prcoceedings of the ICC 2005 - *IEEE International Conference on Communications, no. 1 (pp. 3515– 3519).*

Zhao, W., Chellappa, R., Rosenfeld, A., & Philips, P. J. (2000). Face recognition: A literature survey. *ACM Computing Surveys, 35(4),* 399–458. doi:10.1145/954339.954342

Zhou, J., & Gollmann, D. (1996). A fair non-repudiation protocol. In IEEE Symposium on Security and Privacy, Research in Security and Privacy, IEEE Computer Society, Technical Committee on Security and Privacy, *IEEE Computer Security Press, Oakland, CA, 1996, (pp. 55–61).*

Zhou, J., & Gollmann, D. (1997). An efficient non-repudiation protocol. In Proceedings of The 10th Computer Security Foundations Workshop, *IEEE Computer Society Press, 1997, (pp. 126–132).*

Zhou, L., & Haas, Z. J. (1999). (n.d.). Securing ad hoc networks. IEEE. *Network Magazine, 13(6), 24–30.* doi:10.1109/65.806983

Zhu, F., Mutka, M., & Ni, L. (2003). Splendor: A Secure, Private, and Location-aware Service Discovery Protocol Supporting Mobile Services. 1st IEEE Annual Conference on Pervasive Computing and Communications, Fort Worth, Texas, *IEEE Computer Society Press.*

Zhu, F., Mutka, M., & Ni, L. (2005). Service Discovery in Pervasive Computing Environments. *IEEE Pervasive Computing / IEEE Computer Society [and] IEEE Communications Society, 4(4), 81–90.* doi:10.1109/MPRV.2005.87

Zhu, F., Mutka, M., & Ni, L. (2006). A Private, Secure and User-centric Information Exposure Model for Service Discovery Protocols. *IEEE Transactions on Mobile Computing, 5(4), 418–429.* doi:10.1109/TMC.2006.1599409

Zhu, F., Zhu, W., Mutka, M., & Ni, L. (2007). Private and Secure Service Discovery via Progressive and Probabilistic Exposure. *IEEE Transactions on Parallel and Distributed Systems, 18(11), 1565–1577.* doi:10.1109/TPDS.2007.1075

Zhu, S., Setia, S., & Jajodia, S. (2006). LEAP: Efficient security mechanisms for large-scale distributed sensor networks. [TOSN]. *ACM Transactions on Sensor Networks, 2(4), 500–528.* doi:10.1145/1218556.1218559

Zimmermann, H. (1980). OSI Reference Model—The ISO Model of Architecture for Open Systems Interconnection. *IEEE Transactions on Communications, 28(4), 425–432.* doi:10.1109/TCOM.1980.1094702

Zimmermann, P. (1995). *PGP source code and internals.* Cambridge, MA: MIT Press.

Zimmermann, P. (2001). *Why OpenPGP's PKI is better than an X.509 PKI.* Retrieved from http://www.openpgp.org/technical/whybetter.shtml

Zucker, L. G. (1986). Production of Trust: Institutional Sources of Economic Sources. *Research in Organizational Behavior, 8, 3–111.*

About the Contributors

Hamid Nemati is an Associate Professor of Information Systems at the Information Systems and Operations Management Department of The University of North Carolina at Greensboro. He holds a doctorate from the University of Georgia and a Master of Business Administration from The University of Massachusetts. Before coming to UNCG, he was on the faculty of J. Mack Robinson College of Business Administration at Georgia State University. He also has extensive professional experience as a consultant with a number of major corporations. Dr. Nemati is the Editor-in-Chief of International Journal of Information Security and Privacy and the Advances in Information Security and Privacy (AISP) Book Series. His research specialization is in the areas of decision support systems, data warehousing and mining, and information security and privacy. His research articles have appeared in a number of premier journals. He has presented numerous research and scholarly papers nationally and internationally.

Li Yang is an Associate Professor in the Department of Computer Science and Engineering at the University of Tennessee at Chattanooga. She received her Ph.D. Florida International University and joined University of Tennessee at Chattanooga in 2005. Her research interests include network and information security, databases, and engineering techniques for complex software system design. She actively involves students into her research. She authored papers on these areas in refereed journal, conferences and symposiums. She received research awards from College of Engineering in the University of Tennessee at Chattanooga in 2007. She is a member of the ACM and IEEE. Currently she concentrates her teaching in Information Security, database security, and Computer Networks.

* * *

Wasim Al-Hamdani is Associated Professor at Kentucky State University, Department of Computer science Dr. Al-Hamdani, was working at university of Technology (Baghdad 1985-1999) then he taught in many universities , He was Professor of Cryptography at University of Technology, Baghdad; Jordanian University of Zaytoonah, Jordan; Ajman University of Science and Technology, UEA; Etisalat college of Engineering; Emirates Telecommunications Corporation Sharjah, UEA. He supervises the establishing of MSC and PhD programs at deferent universes; He supervises many M.Sc. and PhD projects. He published six text (in Arabic) concerning computer science and Cryptography. His major work for last 19 year is Cryptography algorithms and information security.

Leemon Baird is a Professor of Computer Science and the Director of Research for the Department of Computer Science at the United States Air Force Academy. He is also a researcher in the Academy

Center for Cyberspace Research. His PhD in computer science is from Carnegie Mellon University. His research interests include jam resistant coding, computer security, and machine learning.

Harkeerat Singh Bedi is a graduate student pursuing his Master in Computer Science at the University of Tennessee at Chattanooga. His work includes research on Fair Electronic Exchange where he, with guidance from his advisors Dr. Li Yang and Dr. Joseph Kizza aims to improve an existing fair exchange protocol by handling several possible attacks and creating software that facilitates the same. The software implementation includes use of biometric fingerprint scanners for user authentication and generation of cryptographic keys that are used for fair exchange. His research paper on *Fair Electronic Exchange Using Biometrics* published in *Cyber Security and Information Intelligence Research Workshop* in 2009 provides a brief overview on this research work.

Nikolaos Bourbakis (IEEE Fellow-96) received his Ph.D. in Computer Engineering & Informatics, University of Patras, Greece. He currently is the Associate Dean for Research, the OBR Distinguished Professor of IT and the Director of the Assistive Technologies Research Center (ATRC) at Wright State University, OH. His' industrial experience includes IBM, CA, Soft Sight, NY and AIIS, OH. He pursues research in Applied AI, Machine Vision, Bioinformatics & Bioengineering, Assistive Technology, Information Security/Processors, and Parallel/Distributed Processing funded by USA and European government and industry. He has published extensively in refereed International Journals, book-chapters and Conference Proceedings. His research work has been recognized with several prestigious IBM, IEEE awards, like IEEE Technical Achievement Award 1998.

Chih-Cheng Chang is a Ph.D. student in the Department of Computer Science at Rutgers University, New Brunswick. He received his undergraduate B.S. degree in Computer Science from Rutgers University in 2007. His research interests are in web, network, and information security, in particular browser security, malware detection and data privacy. He is working under the direction of Prof. Danfeng Yao.

Lei Chen received his B.Eng. degree in Computer Science from Nanjing University of Technology, China, in 2000, and Ph.D. degree in Computer Science from Auburn University, USA, in Aug. 2007. He has been with Sam Houston State University as an Assistant Professor in Computer Science since 2007. Dr. Chen has been actively working in research in computer networks, network security, and wireless and multimedia networking. He also serves in the editorial advisory/review board and the technical program committee of a number of books, journals and conferences.

Brian D. Ensor is a Ph.D. student in the Graduate School of Computer and Information Sciences at Nova Southeastern University and Head of Architecture for the National University of Ireland, Galway. He previously worked at the Digital Enterprise Research Institute as the Head of Technical Services and received his Master of Science in Information Assurance from Norwich University, Vermont. He heads a team of forward-thinking IT professionals focused on systems and technical architecture, business process integration, and identity and access management innovations. His current research interests include privacy enhancement and user centric control within identity management.

Ralph F. Grove: Ralph F. Grove is a professor in the Computer Science Department at James Madison University, and coordinator of the Secure Software Engineering program at JMU. He earned his Ph.D.

in Computer Science and Engineering from the University of Louisville. Prior to entering academia he worked for 15 years in the information technology industry as a software developer, IT manager, and IT trainer. His research interests include Web development, artificial intelligence, and software engineering.

Slawomir Grzonkowski is a researcher at DERI, National University of Ireland, Galway. He is the leading person of the DRM lab within the eLearning Cluster in Digital Enterprise Research Institute (DERI Galway). He is the creator and the main developer of SeDiCi and FRM. His research interests and scientific publications are related to semantic web, security, digital rights and trust in social networks. Slawomir also served as a reviewer, PC member and a workshop organizer at many international scientific initiatives related to his research interests. His work on security and digital identity resulted in over 20 scientific articles at international journals, conferences and workshops.

Hossain Heydari is a professor in the Computer Science Department, Coordinator of the Information Security program, and Associate Director for Information Assurance (Institute for Infrastructure and Information Assurance) at James Madison University. He earned his Ph.D. in Computer Science from the University of Texas at Dallas. His research interests include Information Security, Interconnection Networks and Parallel Architectures, Telecommunication Networks, E-Commerce, VLSI Layout and Routing. He is a member of IEEE, ACM, and ISSA.

Wen-Chen Hu received a BE, an ME, an MS, and a PhD, all in Computer Science, from the Tamkang University, Taiwan, the National Central University, Taiwan, the University of Iowa, Iowa City, and the University of Florida,Gainesville, in 1984, 1986, 1993, and 1998, respectively. Currently, he is an associate professor in the Department of Computer Science of the University of North Dakota, Grand Forks. He is the Editor-in-Chief of the International Journal of Handheld Computing Research (IJHCR), and has been over 20 editors and editorial advisory/review board members of international journals/books and more than 10 track/session chairs and program committee members of international conferences. Dr. Hu has published over 70 articles in refereed journals, conference proceedings, books, and encyclopedias, edited three books, and solely authored a book entitled "Internet-enabled handheld devices, computing, and programming: mobile commerce and personal data applications." His current research interests include handheld computing, electronic and mobile commerce systems, Web technologies, and databases.

Dulal C. Kar received the B.Sc.Engg. and the M.Sc.Engg. degrees from Bangladesh University of Engineering and Technology, Dhaka, Bangladesh and the MS and the Ph.D. degrees from North Dakota State University, Fargo, North Dakota. Currently he is working as an Associate Professor in the Department of Computing Sciences at Texas A&M University - Corpus Christi, Texas. Previously, he was a faculty in the Department of Computer Science at Virginia Polytechnic Institute and State University, Virginia; Mountain State University, West Virginia; and Bangladesh University of Engineering and Technology, Bangladesh. He is an associate editor of the International Journal of Distance Education Technologies, a publication of IGI Global. His research interests include wireless sensor networks, *signal and image processing algorithms, network architecture and performance measurement, network and information security, information retrieval, and educational technology.*

Joseph M. Kizza received his Ph.D. from the University of Nebraska-Lincoln in 1989 with a concentration in Combinatorics and Analysis and Design of Algorithms. He joined the Department of Computer Science at the University of Tennessee at Chattanooga in 1989 and he is currently a professor. He is an internationally known speaker on social computing and information security and assurance. He has published extensively in journals and conference proceedings and authored seven books on computer ethics, network security and cyberethics. Some of these books have been translated into several languages. He is a member of ACM and IEEE and a UNESCO expert in Information Technology.

Hua Lin is a senior software engineer at the School of Nursing, University of Virginia. She has over a decade's experience in software engineering, web development, and information security. Hua received her M. S. degree in Software Engineering from George Mason University and is a certified database administrator.

Bill McDaniel is an eLearning cluster leader at the Digital Enterprise Research Institute. Bill brings over 33 years experience as a software entrepreneur and researcher. He has started and sold two software development companies and been CTO of three others. He also opened the first internet café in North Texas. Before joining DERI he spent two and a half years at Adobe Systems as a Senior Scientist in the Advanced Technology Lab researching semantic technology applications in the areas of document search and knowledge discovery. His current research interests are in human computer interaction, eLearning, artificial intelligence, and ubiquitous and pervasive computing. He has co-authored 6 books on the impact of emerging technology on business and society, including Critical Mass: a Primer for Living with the Future. His latest is Semantic Digital Libraries, available from Springer.

Clifton J. Mulkey graduated from Eastern New Mexico University in 2009 with a double major Bachelor's degree in Computer Science and Mathematics. He is currently pursuing a Master's degree in Computer Science at Texas A&M University – Corpus Christi. His current research interests include Identity Based Encryption as well as Quantum Key Distribution. He is also active in information assurance, cyber defense, and system administration.

Hung Ngo received his B.S. in Computer Science from University of Natural Sciences, Vietnam in August 2006. He worked in industry for two years before going back to school to pursue his M.S. in Computer Science. He is now a graduate student in the Department of Computing Sciences at Texas A&M University – Corpus Christi. His current research interests include Wireless Sensor Networks, Wireless Security, and Digital Signal Processing.

Kunal Sharma has been teaching in the Department of Management Studies, now rechristened as Institute of Management Studies as a faculty since 2001. He is employed with DOEACC Society, Chandigarh, Ministry of IT, Govt. of India as Sr. Systems Analyst. He has done his B.Tech (CSE) from NIT, Hamirpur and he is a MBA(IT) from Institute of Management Studies. He is pursuing thesis dissertation from the H.P. University entitled Strategic Architecture for E-Learning-A Case Study of H.P. University. His areas of interest include E-Commerce and E-learning.

A. J. Singh has been teaching in Department of Computer Science, Himachal Pradesh University Shimla, India, since 1992. At present he is designated as Associate Professor. He has done Bachelor of

Engineering in Computer Science from NIT Bhopal (1991), M. Sc. in Distributed Information Systems from University of East London (1996) and Ph. D. from Himachal Pradesh University (2005). His areas of interest are E-Governance, Distributed Information Systems, ICT for Development and Impact of ICT on Society.

Ramakrishna Thurimella received his Ph.D. in Computer Science from the University of Texas at Austin. He is currently the Director of Colorado Research Institute for Security and Privacy, an NSA designated Center for Academic Excellence in Information Assurance Education, at the University of Denver. He is also an associate professor of Computer Science at the University of Denver where he regularly teaches courses on information security and forensics. His research interests include network security, intrusion detection, and mathematical foundations of information security. He has made fundamental contributions to algorithmic graph connectivity, and other areas in theoretical computer science. His current focus is on applying some of the existing theory from graph connectivity to identify weaknesses in the Internet infrastructure. He is a member of ACM and IEEE.

Monica Trifas received her B.S. and M.S. in Computer Science degrees from University of Bucharest, Bucharest, Romania in 1996. She joined JSU in Fall 2005, after she completed the Ph.D. in Computer Science at Louisiana State University. Her dissertation, "Medical Image Enhancement", focused on contrast enhancement for medical images. Dr. Trifas' research interests include Digital Image/Video Processing, Medical Imaging, Human Computer Interaction, Bioinformatics, Artificial Intelligence, Data Mining, and Visualization. She is the author of over fifteen publications on medical image enhancement methods, visualization, data security, video coding in leading computer science journals and conference proceedings. She is the reviewer of various international journals and conferences. Currently, Dr. Trifas is serving as Director of the Center for Information Security and Assurance at JSU. Dr. Trifas' complete background information can be found in http://mcis.jsu.edu/faculty/atrifas/

Xunhua Wang is an Assistant Professor of computer science at James Madison University (JMU) in Virginia, USA, and teaches cryptography and information security courses there. He received his Ph.D. from George Mason University in 2002. Dr. Wang's research interests include applied cryptography, network security, and software engineering. He has published a dozen of refereed papers in information security and his work was sponsored by Cisco. He is a member of IEEE.

Ming Yang received his B.S. and M.S. degrees in Electrical Engineering from Tianjin University, China, in 1997 and 2000, respectively, and Ph.D. degree in Computer Science and Engineering from Wright State University, Dayton, Ohio, USA in 2006. He has been with Jacksonville State University as an Assistant Professor in Computer Science since 2006. His research interests include Digital Image/Video Coding, Multimedia Communication & Networking, and Information Security. He has actively participated in and significantly contributed to various large-scaled research projects funded by different agencies. He is the author/co-author of over twenty publications in leading computer science journals and conference proceedings. He also serves as reviewer of numerous international journals and conferences. He is currently leading a group in Jacksonville State University to conduct research on medical image security and privacy, H.264/AVC video coding, and video streaming over wireless networks.

Danfeng Yao is an Assistant Professor in the Department of Computer Science at Rutgers University, New Brunswick. She received her Computer Science Ph.D. degree from Brown University. Her research interests are in network and information security, in particular user-centric security and privacy, social- and human-behavior pattern recognition, insider threats, secure information sharing, data privacy, and applied cryptography. Danfeng has more than 25 publications on various topics of security and privacy. She won the Best Student Paper Award in ICICS 2006, and the Award for Technological Innovation from Brown in 2006, both for her privacy-preserving identity management work. Danfeng has one provisional patent filed for her recent bot detection techniques. She is a member of DIMACS and DHS DyDAn Centers.

Lei Zhang is an Assistant Professor of computer science, Frostburg State University, University System of Maryland. She received M.S. and Ph.D. from Auburn University in 2005 and 2008. Before she pursued her graduate study in the U.S, she worked as an instructor at school of Electrical Engineering & Automation, Tianjin University, China. Her current research interests include Wireless Networks Protocols Design and Applications, Distributed Algorithm, Information Security, Data Mining and Human Computer Interaction. She is a member of IEEE/ACM. She has been a technical reviewer for numerous international journals and conferences.

Feng Zhu received the B.S. degree in computer science from East China Normal University in 1994, the M.S. degree in computer science and engineering from Michigan State University in 2001, the M.S. degree in statistics from Michigan State University in 2005, and the Ph.D. degree from Michigan State University in 2006. He is an Assistant Professor at The University of Alabama in Huntsville. He was a program manager at Microsoft from 2006 to 2008, and a software engineer at Intel from 1997 to 1999. His current research interests include pervasive computing, security and privacy, computer networks, and statistical system analysis and design.

Wei Zhu received the Ph.D. degree in computer science and engineering from Michigan State University in 2006, the M.S. degree in statistics from Michigan State University in 2004, the M.S. degree in computer science and engineering from Michigan State University in 2001, and the B.S. degree in computer science from East China Normal University in 1994. Her research interests include human-computer interaction, pervasive computing, computer graphics, augmented reality, and multimedia systems. She is currently a software consultant at Intergraph Corporation. She was a software design engineer at Microsoft Corporation from 2006 to 2008.

Index

Symbols

A

B